Textbook on Civil Liberties and Human Rights

Textbook on
Civil Liberties and Human Rights

....

Tenth edition

Richard Stone
University of Lincoln, Lincoln

OXFORD
UNIVERSITY PRESS

OXFORD

UNIVERSITY PRESS

Great Clarendon Street, Oxford, OX2 6DP,
United Kingdom

Oxford University Press is a department of the University of Oxford.
It furthers the University's objective of excellence in research, scholarship,
and education by publishing worldwide. Oxford is a registered trade mark of
Oxford University Press in the UK and in certain other countries

Seventh edition 2008
Eighth edition 2010
Ninth edition 2012

Impression: 1

Published in the United States of America by Oxford University Press
198 Madison Avenue, New York, NY 10016, United States of America

British Library Cataloguing in Publication Data

Data available

Library of Congress Control Number: 2013954307

ISBN 978-0-19-870155-2

Printed and bound by
Ashford Colour Press Ltd, Gosport, Hampshire

PREFACE

This is a law book, not a book on political or moral philosophy. Its aim is to provide an introduction to the legal rules which, in England and Wales, relate to the area of civil liberties and human rights. It seems to me that the right starting point for the *law* student is to learn what the current legal rules are, to provide the context for discussion of the broader issues of policy, morality, and politics. It is all very well to have strong views on, for example, the rights and wrongs of press intrusions on privacy; for the lawyer it is important to know what the law actually does, and to appreciate the problems of turning policy into practice. This does not mean, of course, that the wider implications should be ignored. Chapter 1, in particular, tries to place the subject in a broader framework, and attempts are made throughout to indicate the political context, and the directions in which policy debates might proceed. The main focus, however, is on the law itself.

The approach in a book such as this is inevitably selective. Some may be surprised at some of the matters which are included or omitted. My original aim, however, was to cover a range of topics which would illustrate the variety of approaches which are taken within the English legal system to the protection and restriction of civil liberties. That is still a main purpose. The Human Rights Act 1998 (HRA 1998), however, now provides a particular and unavoidable framework for discussion. It seems as though this Act will remain with us for a few more years at least, despite the clear wishes of a significant number of members of the Conservative section of the coalition government to get rid of it. The Commission set up by the government to consider reform and/or replacement of the Act reported at the end of 2012, but without unaniminity (see chapter 2 (2.6.3)), and it is now clear that no changes will be initiated in advance of the next general election (due in May 2015).

The reaction to the structural changes introduced in the last edition, and designed to reflect the fact that discussion of issues in the areas covered by the text are now inevitably related to the relevant articles of the European Convention on Human Rights (ECHR), was largely positive, and so it has been retained. The section covering disclosure of journalistic sources (i.e. dealing with section 10 of the Contempt of Court Act 1981) has been restored, and will be found at the end of chapter 5.

In terms of legal developments this edition takes account of, for example, the Strasbourg decisions in *Austin* v *United Kingdom* on 'kettling' and the deprivation of liberty, *von Hannover* v *Germany (No 2)* and *Springer* v *Germany* on privacy, *Othman (Abu Qatada)* v *United Kingdom* on asylum and fair trial rights, and *O'Donoghue and ors* v *United Kingdom* on the right to marry. At the domestic level, important decisions include the Supreme Court's views in *R* v *Gul* on the definition of terrorism, and the Court of Appeal's rulings in *Hall* v *Bull* and *Black* v *Wilkinson* on discrimination on grounds of sexual orientation where this conflicts with religious beliefs. The High Court has handed down significant decisions on contempt and the internet (*Attorney-General* v *Davey*), the interpretation of sections 15 (*R (Bhatti)* v *Croydon Magistrates Court*) and 17 (*Syed* v *DPP*) of the Police and Criminal Evidence Act (PACE) 1984, child pornography (*R* v *Dodd*), and aggravated trespass in the context of demonstrations (*Bauer* v *DPP*). The Anti-Social Behaviour and Policing Act, which is expected to be in force at some point during 2014, will replace ASBOs with Injunctions to Prevent Nuisance and Disorder (IPNA). The impact of the Leveson

Report on the Press (noted in chapter 5), following the phone-hacking scandal, is still uncertain at the time of writing. It is hoped that, as with the earlier editions, this book will be of use to the law undergraduate studying civil liberties and human rights as part of public law, or as a course in its own right. This is the audience to whom it is primarily directed. I also hope that it may be of interest to anyone who seeks to discover the law that lies behind the headlines on such matters as police powers, terrorism, public order, and privacy.

I must take this opportunity to express my thanks to my former student, Ebilyana Mulenga, who carried out valuable research in relation to various chapters, alerting me to new case law and legislative changes. Dr Helen O'Nions of Nottingham Trent University has again revised the sections of chapter 11 dealing with deportation and asylum. I am very grateful to Helen for taking this task off me, and performing it so skilfully. Any errors or omissions are, of course, my responsibility.

I would also like to express my thanks to the staff at OUP for their assistance in the production of this edition, and to my wife Maggie, for her continuing support and patience.

The law is in general stated as it stood at the beginning of November 2013, though notes of some subsequent developments have been included at proof stage.

Richard Stone
Elston, Newark
November 2013

NEW TO THIS EDITION

This edition takes account of the Strasbourg decisions in:

- *Austin* v *United Kingdom* on 'kettling' and the deprivation of liberty.
- *von Hannover* v *Germany (No 2)* and *Springer* v *Germany* on privacy.
- *Othman (Abu Qatada)* v *United Kingdom* on asylum and fair trial rights.
- *O'Donoghue and Others* v *United Kingdom* on the right to marry.

At the domestic level, important new cases and legislation discussed include:

- The Supreme Court's views in *R* v *Gul* on the definition of terrorism.
- The Court of Appeal's rulings in *Hall* v *Bull* and *Black* v *Wilkinson* on discrimination on grounds of sexual orientation where this conflicts with religious beliefs.
- *Attorney-General* v *Davey* on contempt and the internet.
- The Anti-Social Behaviour and Policing Act, which will replace ASBOs with Injunctions to Prevent Nuisance and Disorder (IPNA).

This edition also considers the proposals for reform, or replacement, of the Human Rights Act 1998 and the 'Leveson Report' on the Press.

CONTENTS

TABLE OF CASES

TABLES OF LEGISLATION

Codes

European Legislation

Directives

1

Introduction

1.1 **The political context**

The subject matter of this book is the extent to which civil liberties and human rights are protected under the law of England and Wales. Later in this chapter it will be necessary to look at what is meant by the phrases 'civil liberties' and 'human rights'. Before embarking upon that, however, the political context in which the discussion of the law is to take place must be considered.

As indicated in the Preface, this is a book about law, and legal rules, and not about political philosophy. All writing about law, however, involves the writer in making some assumptions about the political, economic, and social context in which the law operates. Often these assumptions are implicit, as it is taken that the reader will share roughly the same viewpoint on such matters as the writer. In the context of a book on civil liberties and human rights, however, it is very important that these assumptions should as far as possible become explicit. The borderline between law and politics in this area is so narrow that the influence of one on the other cannot be ignored, and it is particularly important that the reader should know where the writer stands, and from which political viewpoint the subject is being approached.

Let me start, then, by placing my cards on the table. I write as a white, Anglo-Saxon male, brought up in the Christian tradition, but currently espousing no religious belief. What many would regard as some of the most influential years in the development of a person's ideas, those between the ages of 15 to 21, were for me largely spent in the 1960s, a time when in many parts of the Western world there was particularly strong youthful rebellion against authority, and advocacy of individual freedom. No doubt aspects of that background will subconsciously affect my approach to some of the issues discussed in the following chapters. On the conscious level, my political adherence is to the broad framework of the modern Western liberal democracy, under which the people are ruled by an elected government, and laws are applied by independent courts. On the economic front, central government needs to exercise overall control, but private enterprise should generally be regarded as a beneficial aspect of society. The 'mixed' economy is the desirable model, though the most appropriate balance between the various elements in the mixture may be hard to determine.

Turning specifically to the issue of 'rights and liberties', my starting point is the value of the individual human being, and the diversity between individuals. This leads to the demand that any interference with any aspect of an individual's life requires the strongest justification. To use the terminology of the legal process, the burden of proof lies on those who would restrict the freedom of the individual to show that such restriction is necessary. On this issue, and indeed on many other issues relating to this area, I make no apology for the fact that, despite all that has been written on these topics over the past 100 years, I still find that many of my own feelings find their clearest expression in John Stuart Mill's essay 'On Liberty' (1859). In particular, the following much-quoted passage is my starting point on a wide range of issues:

> [T]he only purpose for which power can be rightfully exercised over any member of a civilised community against his will, is to prevent harm to others. His own good, either physical or moral, is not a sufficient warrant. He cannot rightfully be compelled to do or forbear because it will be better for him to do so, because it will make him happier, because, in the opinions of others to do so would be wise, or even right. These are good reasons for remonstrating with him, or reasoning with him, or persuading him, or entreating him, but not for compelling him, or visiting him with evil in case he do otherwise.

This focus on the individual, and individual freedom, means that, in my view, the benefits to society which might flow from restricting an individual's behaviour must be clear and strong to justify restriction. It also means that I do not feel particularly sympathetic towards what for many people is an increasingly important area of debate, that is, the issue of 'group rights' or 'collective rights'. Those who espouse this idea take the view that in some situations the need to promote the interests of a particular group which has suffered in the past in some way, means that the rights of the individual must be subordinated to the needs of the group. A particularly clear example of the difficulties that this can cause for those concerned with the protection of civil liberties arose from an inquiry by the National Council for Civil Liberties (NCCL) into the policing of the miners' strike of 1984. The conflict which this caused within the NCCL, and its place in the debate about collective and individual rights, is well summarized by Gostin in 'Towards Resolving the Conflict' (L. Gostin (ed.), *Civil Liberties in Conflict* (London: Routledge, 1988), ch. 1). The inquiry was established primarily to investigate the 'civil liberties implications of the role of the police' in relation to the strike. The interim report of the inquiry ('NCCL Independent Inquiry into the Policing of the Miners' Strike' (Interim Report), National Council for Civil Liberties, 1984), however, made comments on such issues as whether:

> In the absence of policing, would mass pickets have physically prevented miners from going to work rather than peacefully trying to dissuade them? What were the nature and extent of violence or threats in mining communities? Does picketing of the private home of a working miner infringe upon the civil liberties of his family? (*Civil Liberties in Conflict*, pp. 15–16).

This led to the inquiry being criticized by both the NCCL Executive Committee and an NCCL Annual General Meeting (AGM), for exceeding its terms of reference, and because the recognition of an individual's right not to take part in an industrial dispute 'undermines the collective rights of others, and cannot be supported as a fundamental freedom'.

In this dispute my sympathies lie entirely with the members of the inquiry rather than the executive and AGM of the NCCL. The freedom of the individual is for me the highest good, and the tyranny of the majority is still tyranny even if exercised by a trade union rather than the organs of the State. It is not surprising, therefore, that the closest that this book comes to discussing 'group rights' is in chapter 12 which deals with discrimination on the basis of race, sex, disability, and various other illegitimate grounds. Even here, however, it is the individual's right to equal treatment which is for me the fundamental issue, rather than the rights of women, members of ethnic or religious groups, disabled people, etc., *as a group* to challenge oppression.

The emphasis on individual freedoms does not, of course, mean that they can never be challenged, nor that the needs of 'society' as a whole have to be ignored. When the behaviour of one individual causes harmful effects, and in particular, harmful effects to another individual, restraints on freedom may well be justified. The issue then becomes that of identifying precisely what kinds of harm will justify intervention. In chapters 3 and 4 there is a discussion of the ways in which police powers to restrict individual freedom are justified on the basis of the need to apprehend those involved with criminal activities (which society has by definition designated 'harmful'). The main problems here relate to the *extent* to which freedom should be able to be limited in relation to those who have not been convicted of any offence, and the *safeguards* which should be put in place to prevent abuse of the powers. This issue becomes particularly sensitive, and difficult to resolve, in the context of threats from terrorism, as is explored in chapter 10. The question of 'balance' is also a central one in chapter 5, in relation to the discussion of actions which may prejudice a fair trial, and in chapter 6 on the extent to which an individual's right to privacy should be protected. In chapter 7, however, which is concerned with publications which may harm the 'State', and chapter 8, which is concerned with the control of obscene publications and related issues, the question of what exactly is 'harmful' in this context is a much more central matter of debate.

As will be seen, a range of harms is accepted by English law as justifying interference with freedoms in different contexts. Part of the issue under consideration in this book is the extent to which the definitions of 'harm' which are used are defensible, and acceptable, from a civil libertarian perspective.

1.2 **Human rights and civil liberties**

The title of this book refers to both 'civil liberties' and 'human rights'. The latter phrase is commonly used in the international context, for example in documents such as the United Nations' Universal Declaration of Human Rights 1948 (Universal Declaration) and the European Convention on Human Rights (ECHR). On the municipal level the discussion is more often framed in terms of civil liberties. We now have, however, a Human Rights Act 1998 (HRA 1998) which, as can be seen (see 1.4.3), brings the ECHR into the domestic context. Does it matter? In other words, are 'civil liberties' and 'human rights' interchangeable concepts?

Or do the two phrases have differences in meaning which it may be important to identify?

There is no doubt that there is a large area of overlap. Several chapters of this book, for example, are concerned with issues related to freedom of expression, which is recognized as a 'human right' by both the Universal Declaration (Art. 19) and the ECHR (Art. 10). Freedom of speech, however, can also be described as a 'civil liberty' in that it is an important part of a citizen's rights as a participant in the political process (see, e.g. C. Gearty and K. Ewing, *The Struggle for Civil Liberties* (Oxford: Oxford University Press, 2000), ch. 1). There are, however, two ways in which it may be important to distinguish between the two concepts. First, there is the question of the difference between a 'right' and a 'liberty'. This is discussed at 1.3. Second, it might be argued that 'human rights' provide the overall framework of freedoms within which more specific 'civil liberties' can operate. In that sense, human rights become more fundamental than civil liberties. Take, for example, the right to a fair trial, as guaranteed by Art. 6 of the ECHR. This is a human right. There are various ways in which such a right can be guaranteed. Article 6 itself suggests some, such as the presumption of innocence and the right to legal representation. It cannot be said, however, that any of these are in all circumstances *essential* to the guarantee of a fair trial. The right to legal representation might, for example, be replaced by providing for independent supervision of police questioning and redefining the role of the 'judge' so as to act more in the role of protector of the defendant's rights. It is not suggested that these changes would be desirable. The point is that the overall objective of protecting the right to a fair trial may be achieved by a variety of methods. When particular methods are chosen by a domestic legal system, or indeed are provided for by an international document such as the ECHR, then these become part of the civil liberties of the citizens within that jurisdiction. On this basis, therefore, civil liberties are subsidiary to human rights, and may legitimately be changed, provided that the human rights objectives which the particular liberties are intended to further are protected in some other way. Another possible distinction is that 'civil liberties' might be limited to those freedoms which relate specifically to a person's position as a 'citizen' within a democratic society—i.e. their 'political' rights and freedoms, such as the right to vote, freedom of speech, freedom of association, etc., as argued by Gearty and Ewing (*The Struggle for Civil Liberties*, ch. 1). The distinctions cannot, however, be said to operate neatly and cleanly in all situations. The line between human rights and civil liberties, if indeed there is one, is blurred and there is probably no particular benefit in spending much time in trying to make it more distinct.

1.3 Meaning of rights

An issue which was raised at 1.2 was the distinction, if any, between 'rights' and 'liberties'. It is important to consider the issue of what is meant by a 'right' for several reasons. First, because the concept of a 'right' is a strong one, it is at times used to give rhetorical force to an argument where its use may be questionable. For example in statements such as 'everyone has a *right* to a house, or a job, or a decent standard of living', it is necessary to be careful to analyse what exactly is meant by a 'right'. Does it mean the same thing as when we assert a '*right* to life', or a '*right* to enforce a contract'? The distinction between positive and natural law approaches to rights should also be noted. This concerns the issue of the derivation of rights: are they purely creatures of a legal system of some kind, and therefore only exist when created by human beings (the positivist viewpoint), or can they be said to be based on some external source, such as a deity, or the nature of being human (the natural law approach)? Some argue, like the eighteenth/nineteenth century political philosopher, Jeremy Bentham, that the only proper use of the word 'rights' is in relation to legal rights. In his 'Anarchical Fallacies' (reproduced in J. Waldron (ed.), *Nonsense upon Stilts* (London: Methuen, 1987)), discussing Art. 2 of the *Declaration of the Rights of Man* of 1789, he commented scathingly (p. 53):

> Natural rights is simple nonsense: natural and imprescriptable rights, rhetorical non-sense—nonsense upon stilts.

Others suggest that natural rights can be identified outside the confines of a positive legal system. For example, it might be argued that some rights are given to us by a deity, with the possible consequence that if human laws are in conflict with such rights, it is legitimate to disobey them. A belief in natural rights is not dependent on religious belief, however. J. M. Finnis, in *Natural Law and Natural Rights*, 2nd edn (Oxford: Clarendon Press, 2011), provides an argument for natural rights which is not based on religion. This is based around a concept which he labels 'practical reasonableness'—the 'good' of 'being able to bring one's own intelligence to bear effectively...on the problems of choosing one's own actions and lifestyle and shaping one's own character' (p. 88). These requirements are worked through in detail in Chapter V of his book, but there is not space to do full justice to this analysis here.

Although this debate is an interesting one, the focus in this book is entirely on rights which have been given recognition within municipal or international legal systems. As a matter of practice, therefore, we are dealing with positive rights, and need not for the most part concern ourselves with whether they have any other provenance. Where there is conflict it will often arise from dysfunctionality between two legal systems—e.g. the domestic and the international—and the question will be as to which system should prevail in a given situation.

The definition of 'rights' may also be important, if it helps us to resolve other difficult issues. If, for example, we decide that a 'right' is stronger than a 'liberty', then we may be able to resolve some situations where the interests of two individuals appear to be in conflict. If one individual has a 'right' and the other simply a 'liberty', then we can say that the right-holder should win, and the other party will have to accept a restriction of liberty.

The following sections look at some suggested analyses of the concepts of rights and liberties, starting with that of W. N. Hohfeld, who in his article 'Some Fundamental Legal Conceptions as Applied in Judicial Reasoning' (1913) 23 *Yale Law Journal* 16, made explicit the variety of meanings which lawyers (and others) often attempt to convey by use of the single word 'right'. Before looking at this, however, it is worth noting, as a final introductory point, that although there is a tendency to talk about a right as if it were a 'thing' (and indeed in some situations 'rights' can be bought and sold in the same way as corporeal property), it is perhaps better regarded as a description of a *relationship* between two people, or perhaps between a person and property.

1.3.1 The Hohfeldian analysis of rights

Hohfeld argued that the relationships generally referred to when we are discussing legal rights can be analysed into eight distinct concepts. The four main ones, any of which might be meant when a person talks generally of 'rights', are 'right', 'privilege', 'power', and 'immunity'. There are four other concepts which are 'correlatives' to these, namely, and respectively, 'duty', 'no-right', 'liability', and 'disability'. What are the characteristics of these concepts?

1.3.1.1 Right or claim

The characteristic of the 'right' or 'claim' is that it places a duty on others. Hohfeld's example relates to the ownership of land, and the right to exclude others:

> [I]f X has a right against Y that he shall stay off the former's land, the correlative (and equivalent) is that Y is under a duty toward X to stay off the place.

It could also apply to a contractual right, such as, for example, the right of a buyer in a sale of goods contract to demand delivery, or the seller to demand payment. In both situations the other party is under a duty to comply, and it is this which identifies the relationship as one of 'rights' in the strict sense. Hohfeld regarded the use of the word right in relation to such situations as its only 'proper' use.

1.3.1.2 Privilege

Again, in defining a privilege Hohfeld uses an example taken from the ownership of land. The owner of a piece of land has the privilege of entering on the land. We might well say that he has a 'right' to do so but, as Hohfeld points out, this is not a 'right' in the sense used above, because there is no correlative duty imposed on anyone. It is therefore better regarded as a privilege, to which the correlative is an absence of a right in anyone else to stop the person from entering. This absence he labels (for want of a better existing word) as a 'no-right'. As Hohfeld himself puts it, in trying to explain the distinction between the right properly so called and a privilege:

> ...the correlative of X's [the landowner's] right that Y shall not enter on the land is Y's duty not to enter; but the correlative of X's privilege of entering himself is manifestly Y's 'no-right' that X shall not enter.

A privilege has a lot of similarities to, and may even be a synonym for, what we should more usually call a freedom, or liberty. Thus, freedom of speech is almost certainly a Hohfeldian 'privilege' rather than a 'claim-right'. There is no correlative duty to the freedom, simply no right in others to stop its exercise. As regards personal freedom, however, an individual has a right not to be interfered with (just as a landowner has a right to prevent trespass) and others are under a duty not to breach that right by assaults, etc.

1.3.1.3 **Powers**

An example of a 'power' is the 'right' of the owner of goods to sell them. This is not a claim-right, because it involves no correlative duty. It is not a privilege either however, because it has the effect of creating liabilities in others, such as, for example, the person to whom the goods are sold. The correlative of a power is thus the existence of a liability on the part of another. In the contractual situation of an offer which has not been accepted we might speak of the offeree having a 'right' to accept. In Hohfeldian terms the offeree has a 'power' (that is, to create a contract by accepting the offer) which will create a liability on the part of the offeror.

1.3.1.4 **Immunity**

Hohfeld's example of an immunity is again drawn from land ownership. The owner of a piece of land has immunity from the exercise of powers by others over the land, and those others are consequently under a correlative 'disability'. Another example might be the power of a bailiff to seize goods in order to satisfy a debt. Under English law certain goods, such as the essentials of life or the tools of the debtor's trade, may not be seized. Here we might say that the debtor has a right that the articles should not be seized. In Hohfeldian terms the debtor has an immunity in relation to the exempted articles, and that the bailiff is likewise under a disability.

1.3.1.5 **Conclusions on Hohfeld**

The analysis outlined above should not be taken as being by any means the last word on legal 'rights'. It has been the subject of criticism, particularly in relation to the concept of duty, which is not analysed (see, e.g. J. Waldron (ed.), *Theories of Rights* (Oxford: Oxford University Press, 1984), p. 8). The most helpful aspects of the approach for our purposes are that, first, it reminds us to be careful in the use of the terminology of 'rights', to be sure that we know exactly what type of relationship we are discussing, and if we find that 'rights' appear to be in conflict, to make sure that we are comparing like with like. Second, the distinction between a 'claim-right' and a 'privilege' may well be helpful in the analysis of civil liberties, many of which may appear to be better categorized as privileges, or freedoms, rather than rights. Although the HRA 1998 means that the courts are required to approach certain civil liberties issues from the basis that there is a 'right' to a particular freedom (e.g. of speech, privacy or assembly) the fact that the ECHR allows, as can be seen below, some of these rights to be qualified significantly, may lead them to be treated in Hohfeldian terms as 'privileges' rather than 'claim-rights', and so be less well protected than they perhaps should be.

1.3.2 **Other analyses of rights**

There have been many other attempts to analyse the nature of rights and liberties. In the area of moral philosophy discussion of the concept of the 'right' has developed an extensive literature. (For an introduction to a range of different approaches see, e.g. Waldron, *Theories of Rights*.) It is beyond the scope of this book to venture very far into this debate. One writer, Ronald Dworkin, will be briefly considered, however, because he has centred his discussion of rights very much in the legal context. Like Hohfeld, Dworkin emphasizes the need to take care in using the word 'right' and to be clear about what is meant by it. In 'Taking Rights Seriously' (*Taking Rights Seriously* (London: Duckworth, 1978), ch. 7) he points out (p. 188) that the word 'right' has a different force in different contexts:

> In most cases when we say that someone has a 'right' to do something, we imply that it would be wrong to interfere with his doing it, or at least that some special grounds are needed for justifying any interference.

This use of the word 'right' (which Dworkin refers to as the 'strong' sense) must be distinguished from the situation where it is said that a particular course of action is the 'right' thing for a person to do, or at least that the person would do no 'wrong' in pursuing it. As Dworkin points out (pp. 188–9):

> Someone may have the right to do something that is the wrong thing for him to do, as might be the case with gambling. Conversely, something may be the right thing for him to do and yet he may have no right to do it ... If our army captures an enemy soldier, we might say that the right thing for him to do is to try to escape, but it would not follow that it was wrong for us to try to stop him.

Applying this distinction to the civil liberties context, the claim that there is a right to freedom of speech, for example, is, Dworkin contends, using 'right' in the strong sense. As a result, governments may be criticized as doing wrong if they restrict this freedom, at least on something other than clearly defined, and exceptional grounds. It is inconsistent with the claim of a 'right' of free speech that a government could be justified in overriding it 'on the minimal grounds that would be sufficient if no such right existed' (pp. 191–2).

Perhaps more importantly for our purposes, Dworkin aims to show, by his analysis of individual rights in the strong sense, the way in which they may be used to challenge utilitarian arguments (promoting the welfare of the majority) which would restrict individual freedom. See, for example, *Taking Rights Seriously* (p. xi):

> Individual rights are political trumps held by individuals. Individuals have rights when, for some reason, a collective goal is not a sufficient justification for denying them what they wish, as individuals, to have or to do, or not a sufficient justification for imposing some loss or injury upon them.

This approach is very much in line with the view of individual rights which is taken in this book.

1.3.3 Categories of rights

Finally, it is worth drawing attention to the distinctions that it is possible to draw between 'political' rights, 'social' or 'economic' rights, and 'collective' rights. Political rights include such things as the right to life, freedom of the person, freedom of speech, freedom from discrimination. These are to be found in all documents purporting to set out human rights. Both the United States Bill of Rights and the ECHR (ignoring the subsequent protocols) are almost exclusively concerned with political rights. Rights of this type are also referred to as 'first-generation rights'. Economic and social rights (or 'second-generation rights') are concerned with such things as the right to work, housing, education, etc. A distinction may be drawn on the basis that political rights do not in general call for any resources to be provided for people to be able to enjoy them. Economic and social rights, on the other hand, will generally require some allocation or redistribution of resources. For this reason, although in practical terms they may contribute far more directly than political rights to the welfare and happiness of individuals, there may well be a reluctance to enshrine them in a constitutional document. Governments may be happy enough to allow people to say what they want, but much less happy at a commitment to providing them with the means to earn a living. This differ-ence may well encourage attempts to argue that economic and social rights are *essentially* different from political rights, and that political rights may be regarded as superior. This may lead on to the argument that it matters less if economic and social rights are infringed. Traditionally the West has given higher status to political rights, whereas the East, particularly in States espousing Communism, has supported social and economic rights. The Universal Declaration, agreed by the United Nations, which is not a legally binding document in international law, included both first- and second-generation rights, reflecting the views of both East and West. When the Universal Declaration was translated into legally binding obligations, this was done by two separate treaties, the International Covenant on Civil and Political Rights (ICCPR), and the International Covenant on Economic, Social, and Cultural Rights (ICESCR). Both treaties were agreed in 1966 but did not come into force until 1976. The first of these contains much more developed enforcement mechanisms than the second, reflecting the view that first-gener-ation rights are easier to guarantee than second-generation rights.

'Collective' or 'third-generation' rights are those attaching to groups rather than individuals, such as the right to self-determination. The recognition of these at international and national level is much less developed than first- and second-generation rights, though they are to be found to some extent in the ICCPR and ICESCR—both of which recognize the right to self-determination—and the African Charter of Human and Peoples' Rights, which as its name suggests treats this type of right as of importance. Generally, however, collective rights are not protected to the same level as political, social, or economic rights. This is certainly true of the protection of rights within the UK.

The debate about the status and importance of different types of right leads into difficult political and philosophical waters, and detailed argument is beyond the scope of this book; but it is nevertheless important to be aware of such distinctions and to look carefully at attempts to categorize rights. What are the motives of the person doing the categorization? Are the distinctions which are drawn valid? Are 'rights' which are given a lesser classification in fact any less important to the indi-vidual than those which are given the higher status?

From these broad issues, we now move to a consideration of the specific ways in which civil liberties and human rights are currently protected within the UK Constitution.

1.4 **Protection of rights and liberties within the UK Constitution**

There is no one constitutional document which provides the rules for the operation of the UK Constitution, and the relationship between its various elements (sovereign, government, Parliament, courts, etc.). Whether this means that the UK Constitution is 'unwritten', or simply 'uncodified' (see, e.g. Neil Parpworth, *Constitutional and Administrative Law*, 7th edn (Oxford: Oxford University Press, 2012), pp. 3–13) need not concern us. What is certainly true is that, prior to the HRA 1998, we had no equivalent to the United States Bill of Rights, or the Canadian Charter of Rights: that is, a document which sets out a range of fundamental freedoms and to which the government, legislature, and courts, must have regard in deciding what laws to enact and enforce, or how such laws should be interpreted. The enactment of the HRA 1998 changed the position significantly and this will be discussed. Previously, although we had a number of important constitutional documents, such as the Magna Carta (1215) and the Bill of Rights 1688, which dealt with such matters as the limits of power of the monarch and Parliament, they did not tell us what are the freedoms of the individual citizen of England or Wales. As regards freedom of speech, for example, the Bill of Rights 1688 simply stated:

> That the freedome of speech and debates or proceedings in Parlyament ought not to be impeached or questioned in any court or place out of Parlyament.

Members of Parliament (MPs) must be allowed to speak their minds, but this says nothing about any more general freedom of expression.

Protection of civil liberties in England and Wales therefore largely rested in the hands of Parliament and the courts. Parliament was expected to ensure that legislation was not passed which would unduly impinge on individual freedom; the courts were expected to interpret the law so as to allow the greatest freedom possible, consonant with the clear dictates of the common law, or the wishes of Parliament expressed through legislation. Before we consider the way in which the HRA 1998 radically changed that position, 1.4.1 and 1.4.2 consider briefly why the previous situation provided inadequate protection for civil liberties and human rights.

1.4.1 **The role of Parliament**

There is no doubt that a government which tried to introduce legislation to remove all political rights from people who are left-handed would not succeed in getting it through Parliament. Such a blatant and arbitrary attack on personal freedom would not be accepted. To that extent, Parliament can act as a guardian of civil liberties. There are, however, several important limitations to the extent to which Parliament can fulfil this role.

First, there is the danger of incremental infringement. Parliament may accept that one type of control is necessary. Its existence in one area may then justify its application to another, in a way that may in fact involve a more significant infringement of liberty. An example might be taken from the powers of the police to obtain access to confidential material. The Police and Criminal Evidence Act 1984 (PACE) gave the police powers in certain situations to obtain a court order compelling people who hold personal or confidential information which is relevant evidence in relation to a serious criminal offence to hand it over. Subsequently, similar powers were included in the Drug Trafficking Offences Act 1986 (now in the Proceeds of Crime Act 2002), and the Prevention of Terrorism (Temporary Provisions) Act 1989 (now in the Terrorism Act 2000). In both cases the powers given looked at first sight to be the same as those contained in PACE. In fact, however, there were significant differences. In neither case under the later Acts did the material have to be 'evidence' which would be admissible in court; it had simply to be likely to be useful to police investigations. Moreover, whereas the procedure under PACE involved an *inter partes* hearing, where the person from whom the information is sought could challenge the application by the police, in relation to both the other powers the hearing was *ex parte*. Thus, the later powers involved a clear further encroachment on civil liberties, but one that was probably made easier by the fact that the first step in that direction had already been taken in PACE. A further example of 'incremental infringement' might be the extended power to detain before charge in relation to those suspected of involvement in terrorism. This started with a period of seven days. This was doubled to 14 days in 2003 (without much discussion). In the Terrorism Act 2006 the period was doubled again to 28 days (though the government wanted 90 days). It was clearly easier for the government to extend the power in small steps, rather than moving directly to a lengthy period of pre-charge detention. The current government has reverted to a 14-day period—see chapter 10, (10.4.3.2)—which is a relatively rare example of a curb on civil liberties being relaxed rather than tightened.

Another limitation on Parliament's control is the fact that it may easily be 'panicked' into reacting with undue disregard for individual liberty by a situation of perceived emergency. The Official Secrets Act 1911, which contained the notorious s. 2, making it an offence to reveal any information concerned with any government department, however innocuous, passed all its Parliamentary stages in a day. Section 2 was not debated at all. The speed was justified on the basis of alleged dangers from German espionage activity. Whatever the justification for that fear, the fact remains that Parliament played no role as a guardian of civil liberties and allowed the enactment of a provision which acted as a serious restraint on freedom of expression for nearly 80 years (for further discussion of this area, see chapter 7).

This limitation does not arise solely from the situation where a government has a large majority and by and large therefore can legislate as it pleases. In the mid-1980s a Private Members' Bill was introduced to establish a comprehensive scheme of pre-censorship for video-cassettes. Because of fears raised by some very dubious research which purported to show massive viewing of so-called 'video-nasties', and subsequent fanning of the flames by sensational press reporting, the civil liberties implications of the Bill received little or no attention. To suggest that it might be unnecessary, or too restrictive, would have been to be labelled as being in favour of polluting the minds of young people with sex and violence. MPs with an eye on the reaction of their constituency if they were identified with the opposition to this Bill, were unlikely to speak against it. It was much safer to support it, and turn a blind eye to the fact that it was introducing the most restrictive control over the home viewing of videos to be applied anywhere in Europe (this case is discussed further in chapter 8 (8.6.2)).

A similar problem arises with any attempt to raise civil liberties issues in relation to measures designed to attack terrorist activities. The problem is not so much that it is decided that the rights of the individual must give way to the desire to prevent moral pollution, or to control terrorists, but that there is a danger this issue is never even raised. An example of this might be found in the passage of the Anti-terrorism, Crime and Security Act 2001, enacted in response to the terrorist attack of 9/11, and containing some exceptional powers to infringe an individual's freedom (particularly in relation to detention without trial). This area is considered further in chapter 10.

For all the above reasons it has been impossible to take Parliament seriously as an effective guardian of individual liberty, other than at the most general level. The extent to which that assessment of the situation should change in the light of the HRA 1998, and the fact that Parliament is now required to pay attention when legislating to the standards set out in the ECHR, is discussed at 1.4.3.

1.4.2 The role of the courts

If Parliament has not been able to fulfil this role effectively, have the courts done so? There is no doubt that our judges have at times taken seriously the need to protect individual freedom. There have been two limitations on their effectiveness, however, one constitutional and one practical. The constitutional limitation is that the courts are subordinate to Parliament, and cannot decide to ignore the clear provisions of legislation which has been properly passed (*British Railways Board* v *Pickin* [1974] AC 765) unless, perhaps, it is in conflict with the UK's legal obligations under EU law (*Factortame Ltd* v *Secretary of State for Transport* [1990] 2 AC 85). That position has been changed to a limited extent by the HRA 1998, in that more flexible interpretation of statutory provisions is possible, and in certain circumstances the courts are able to certify that a provision is in breach of the standards of the ECHR. In the end, however, the courts remain subservient to Parliament and will have to apply a clear and unambiguous provision, even if they feel that it improperly infringes an individual's civil liberties. The practical limitation has been that, even where there is ambiguous statute law, or none at all, the judges have had no guidelines as to the weight to be given to arguments of individual liberty, and how these are to be measured against the needs or demands of society as a whole. We see, for example, in chapter 9 that Lord Denning in one case expressed strong support for the individual's freedom to participate in public protest on matters of concern, but made this subject to there being no 'disruption to the traffic'. This might be thought to be giving undue weight to the maintenance of uninterrupted progress on the highway, as opposed to the right to demonstrate public support for a cause, but there was no easy way for a judge to draw the line between such issues. That position has now changed, in that the courts, by virtue of the HRA 1998, do have a clearer set of standards to apply, and as a result of which (although there may still be difficult issues of 'balancing' to be addressed) they do have guidance as to those rights and freedoms which should be given priority.

A good example of the courts' approach to civil liberties issues prior to the HRA 1998 is to be found in two cases concerned with the privilege against self-incrimination. In *Lam Chi Ming* v *R* [1991] 3 All ER 172, the Privy Council was considering an appeal from Hong Kong as to the admissibility of certain video recordings as evidence against the accused in a murder trial. The recordings, which were produced by the police and showed the accused indicating where the murder weapon had been disposed of, were admitted by the judge although he refused to admit confessions which the accused had made prior to the recordings on the basis that these had been extracted by police brutality and were not voluntary. In holding that the video evidence should not have been admitted Lord Griffiths, giving the opinion of the Privy Council, said (p. 179):

> The privilege against self-incrimination is deep rooted in English law, and it would make a grave inroad upon it if the police were to believe that if they improperly extracted admissions from the accused which were subsequently shown to be true they could use those admissions against the accused for the purpose of obtaining a conviction.

Applying this approach to the video recordings, he felt that:

> ...it is surely just as reprehensible to use improper means to force a man to give information that will reveal he has knowledge that will ensure his conviction as it is to force him to make a full confession.

Thus, in this case, the court not only recognized the strength of the individual's privilege against self-incrimination, but allowed it to be applied in a broad way to achieve its overall purpose, even where it was concerned with incriminating actions (that is, the indication of the whereabouts of the murder weapon) as opposed to statements. This approach may then be contrasted with that of Lord Mustill, speaking on behalf of a unanimous House of Lords, in *Smith* v *Director of Serious Fraud Office* [1992] 3 All ER 456. The House was considering whether the power to question a person under investigation, given to the Serious Fraud Office by s. 2 of the Criminal Justice Act 1987, was limited by the general prohibition on questioning after charge, revealed by the caution required to be administered on charging with an offence (that is, at that time, 'You do not have to say anything unless you wish to do so, but what you say may be given in evidence'; see chapter 4 (4.5.1) for the current version of the caution). The matter was further complicated in that s. 2 of the Criminal Justice Act 1987, where applicable, *required* the person under investigation to answer questions. Lord Mustill referred (p. 471) to the opinion of Lord Griffiths in *Lam Chi Ming* v *R* regarding the importance of the privilege against self-incrimination, and confirmed that he himself would not wish 'to minimise its importance in any way'. He then went on to note, however, that there had been many occasions where there had been statutory interference with the privilege. After a careful analysis of the nature of the privilege, and the general reasons for the prohibition on questioning after charge, he came to the conclusion (p. 474) that the provisions of s. 2 must take precedence:

> ...the principle of common sense, expressed in the maxim *generalia specialibus non derogant*, entails that the general provisions of Code C yield to the particular provisions

> of the 1987 Act in cases to which that Act applies; and that neither history nor logic demands that any qualification of what Parliament has so clearly enacted ought to be implied.

In other words, the courts were bound to apply the clear words of a particular statute, even where this appeared to conflict with generally accepted civil libertarian principles. The criticism here is not that the judges failed to take civil liberties issues seriously: Lord Griffiths' approach in *Lam Chi Ming*, and Lord Mustill's thorough analysis in *Smith*, both indicate otherwise. Whereas, however, in a situation governed primarily by common law (as in *Lam Chi Ming*), those liberties could be given full effect, once Parliament had intervened (as in *Smith*), the court was not willing to use their powers of interpretation to allow the language of a statute to be limited by general principles. For these reasons it cannot be said that the courts provided a mechanism for more than a partial protection of our liberties.

This is not to deny that the *mechanisms* for control of the executive branch of government have not been developed. The remedies available by means of the application for judicial review are referred to at numerous points during the rest of the book and in *M v Home Office* [1993] 3 All ER 537 the House of Lords confirmed that even Ministers of the Crown are bound to obey court orders (in this case not to deport an individual pending a further hearing of his case). The problem is that these mechanisms can only be effective where Parliament allows them to be so. If the executive can prevail upon Parliament to enact laws in specific and unambiguous terms which allow government Ministers, or others, to act in ways which impinge on civil liberties, the courts may not be able to intervene. At the time of writing, for example, the government is proposing reforms to the civil justice system which would significantly reduce the availability of judicial review (see, e.g. 'Reform of Judicial Review: the Government Response', Cm 8611, Ministry of Justice, April 2013).

This is a result in part of the impact of the HRA 1998 on the use of judicial review, which is discussed at 1.4.3 and in chapter 2.

1.4.3 The Human Rights Act 1998

The HRA 1998 brought about a major change in the way in which the law relating to civil liberties operates in the United Kingdom. It is sometimes said that the HRA 1998 has the effect of 'incorporating' the ECHR into English law. As we shall see, however, that is not a wholly accurate description (as was made clear by the Lord Chancellor during the Report Stage in the House of Lords: *Hansard*, HL, 29 January 1998, col. 421). The Act certainly requires that existing rights and obligations, including statutory rights and obligations, should be interpreted so as to be consistent with the ECHR. Full incorporation, however, would enable Convention rights to be used to create *new* rights and obligations under English law. There is some evidence of the courts starting to do this in some limited areas (e.g. the right of privacy, discussed in chapter 6), but the process is slow, and it is not yet clear how far the courts will be prepared to go in using the HRA 1998 in this way.

Full discussion of the HRA 1998 is left to chapter 2. At this point it is sufficient to note the main features of the Act as a contribution to the constitutional protection of individual rights and freedoms. What the Act principally does is to require 'public authorities' (including courts), in taking decisions and carrying out their activities, to respect the rights of an individual as set out in the ECHR. The focus on public authorities means that the main objective is the protection of the individual vis-à-vis the State, rather than against other individuals. 'Public authority' does extend beyond the organs of government, however, and has been held to include, for example, certain actions of housing associations or a private hospital (but not those of a church parish council). Moreover, in some situations the fact that a court is required to act compatibly with the ECHR means that it may interpret the law in a way which incorporates Convention issues into a dispute between individuals. This is particularly so in the areas where privacy and freedom of expression come into conflict, as is discussed in chapter 6.

What of Parliament itself? Parliament is required to give attention to whether its legislation is compatible with the ECHR, and is required to state on the face of each Act whether this is or is not the case. It is not, however, obliged to comply with the ECHR. Parliamentary sovereignty is retained, and Parliament is free to enact laws which infringe an individual's rights if it so chooses. The courts are obliged to enforce such laws—though they have the power to interpret them wherever possible so as to make them compliant. If this is not possible, then a declaration of incompatibility may be made. This does not, however, impose any obligation on Parliament to amend the law (though if it does choose to do so, there is a 'fast-track' procedure to achieve this).

In strict legal terms, therefore, the impact of the HRA 1998 is limited—particularly in relation to its effect on Parliament. Its enactment has had a significant political impact, however, and the volume of litigation which it has produced, as outlined in the rest of this text and in chapter 2 in particular, shows that it is right to regard it as an important constitutional development.

The fact that an individual will not necessarily have a remedy under the HRA 1998 for an alleged breach of a Convention right, means that there is still scope for cases to be taken to the European Court of Human Rights (ECtHR) at Strasbourg. The scope of the ECHR and the process under which the Strasbourg Court receives and considers cases, is dealt with at 1.6.

1.5 **The international context**

As noted in the discussion of 'rights' (see 1.3.2), human rights are recognized in international law. There are both global and regional systems of protection. The Universal Declaration was an important commitment by the international community to the concept of such rights, and provided a list of those rights which ought to be protected. It was not intended to be legally binding on States, and the more practically important documents are the two treaties agreed in 1966—the ICCPR and the ICESCR. Both of these came into force in 1976, when they had been ratified by the required number of States. There are, at the time of writing, 167 State parties to the ICCPR and 160 to the ICESCR, so they have very wide, but not universal, acceptance in the international community (there are 193 members of the United Nations). The UK is a party to both treaties.

The treaties place obligations on States to ensure the protection of the rights listed in them. The primary method of enforcement is through the requirement of reports by States and the carrying out of investigations. The procedures are more developed in relation to the ICCPR and are the responsibility of the Human Rights Committee, which is provided for in the Covenant itself. There is an optional protocol to the ICCPR which allows for petitions by individuals alleging human rights abuses, but the UK has not signed up to this. The enforcement of the ICESCR is the responsibility of the Committee on Economic, Social, and Cultural Rights set up by the Economic and Social Council of the United Nations in 1985.

There is also a more general responsibility for the monitoring of human rights placed on the Human Rights Council (HRC) (http://www.ohchr.org/EN/HRBodies/HRC/Pages/HRCIndex.aspx), established by the General Assembly of the United Nations in 2006 to replace the previous Commission on Human Rights and Sub-Commission on Human Rights, which it had been agreed were rather ineffective. The new HRC reports directly to the General Assembly, and will meet more frequently, but it is too early to judge whether it will have a significant impact on the international protection of human rights. It has already been the subject of criticism that it is too reluctant to criticize human rights' abuses by governments, for example in relation to the Sudan and the Democratic Republic of the Congo.

As well as these global mechanisms, international protection of human rights also operates at a regional level, for example under the African Charter of Human and Peoples' Rights (http://www.africa-union.org/root/au/Documents/Treaties/Text/Banjul%20Charter.pdf), and the American Convention on Human Rights (http://www.oas.org/juridico/english/treaties/b-32.html). These treaties provide scope for individual complaints and do have courts to support them, unlike the UN systems, but they are still rather undeveloped. The most successful system of regional protection is to be found in the ECHR, and this merits consideration in more detail, not least because it is integral to the operation of the UK HRA 1998.

1.6 The European Convention on Human Rights

The ECHR provides the framework of rights to be used by Parliament and courts in operating the HRA 1998. It remains the case, however, that an individual who is dissatisfied with the outcome of his case in the English courts may apply to the ECtHR for redress. This may well happen, for example, where Parliament has enacted legislation which the courts think is in contravention of the ECHR, but are still bound to apply (while possibly issuing a certificate of incompatibility). Even if the law is subsequently changed, this will not assist the individual whose case has already been decided, and an application to the European Court may be the best possibility of forcing the government into providing some redress. An 'appeal to Europe' may also be appropriate if the courts, while purporting to apply the HRA 1998, adopt an interpretation of an area of law which is seen as being unduly restrictive.

This is very likely to occur if the English court's decision appears to run counter to the jurisprudence of the ECHR (for, as we shall see, although English courts are obliged to pay attention to the decisions of the European Court it is arguable that they are not obliged to follow them—see chapter 2 (2.4.1)). Before looking at the detail of the procedure by which this may be done, however, it is desirable first to consider briefly the background to the ECHR, since this provides some explanation for its style and content.

1.6.1 Background

The ECHR was signed in Rome on 4 November 1950, and came into force on 3 September 1953. Its immediate background was the Second World War (1939–45) and the subsequent Nuremberg Trials, which had involved the investigation of many atrocities and abuses of human rights. It was produced by the Council of Europe, which was then a group of ten (currently 47) European nations formed in May 1949 with a view to promoting international action and collaboration to protect human rights. The ECHR was inevitably to some extent a compromise, as regards both content and procedures, given that it was the result of negotiation between countries with varied histories and constitutional systems. This needs to be kept in mind when looking at the provisions of the ECHR, and its appropriateness as a framework for rights in the UK in the twenty-first century.

The other point which it is important to remember, as it is often a source of confusion, is that there is no direct connection (though there is a considerable overlap of membership) between the Council of Europe and the European Union. Both the ECHR and the European Union have had a Commission and a Court (although the ECHR no longer has a Commission), but they are entirely separate pairs of institutions. The ECHR institutions, including its court, are based in Strasbourg, whereas the EU Commission is in Brussels, and the Court of Justice of the European Union (CJEU) sits in Luxembourg. The European Union has now given formal recognition to the ECHR by virtue of Art. 6(2) of the Treaty on European Union, and the European Court of Justice does look to it as a source of fundamental rights. The process of the EU formally acceding to the ECHR (which would mean that the CJEU would be obliged to take account of ECtHR decisions) is underway, but not yet completed. The European Union has also produced its own Charter of Fundamental Rights which, under the Lisbon Treaty, has binding effect on Member States. The UK has negotiated an 'opt-out' from this aspect of the Lisbon Treaty.

1.6.2 Procedure

Prior to November 1998 the ECHR provided for both a Commission and a Court of Human Rights. The Commission, consisting of one member for each State party to the ECHR, dealt with the admissibility of applications, tried to reach a 'friendly settlement' where possible, carried out investigations, and issued an initial ruling on a claim. The case could then be referred to the Court by a State party (but not by an individual applicant). Under new procedures, introduced by Protocol 11 to the ECHR, the Commission was abolished. Protocol 11 was designed to streamline procedures, but proved only partially effective, and has now been superseded by Protocol 14, which came into force in June 2010. As a result, cases on admissibility in 'clear-cut' cases can be heard by a single judge (supported by the newly created 'rapporteurs'), and cases in areas in which the case law of the ECHR is 'well-established' can be heard by a committee of three judges, in a combined admissibility/merits hearing. Decisions on other claims that are admissible are dealt with generally by a Chamber of the Court (seven judges) which will issue judgment. This will be final, unless there is a reference to the Grand Chamber (17 judges).

The total number of judges eligible to sit on the Court is equal to the number of Member States of the Council of Europe. The judges are elected by the Parliamentary Assembly of the Council from candidates nominated by Member States (Art. 22). Judges are usually, but not necessarily, nationals of the State which nominates them, but they sit in an individual rather than a representative capacity (Art. 21(2)).

The reforms contained in Protocols 11 and 14 were designed to deal with the situation where the number of State parties to the ECHR had increased significantly, as had the number of applications per year; a unitary Commission and Court were no longer capable of coping with the level of work; and the backlog of cases was rising steadily. Moreover, with approaching 40 States as parties to the ECHR, bodies consisting of a representative from each State were becoming too unwieldy. It remains to be seen how effective the reforms will be in speeding up the process of dealing with cases. Protocols 11 and 14 resulted in some changes to the numbering of the ECHR Articles concerned with procedure. The new numbering is used here, but care needs to be taken in looking at earlier cases where the original numbering is used.

There are two ways in which the provisions of the ECHR can be enforced. First, there is a procedure under Art. 33 whereby any *State* which is a party to the ECHR can bring an application alleging breach of its provisions against another State which is a party. There has been relatively little use of this procedure, though one notable case, which involved the UK, was *Ireland v United Kingdom* (1979–80) 2 EHRR 25. This resulted in a finding by the Court that certain interrogation practices used by the British Army in Northern Ireland amounted to 'inhuman and degrading treatment' contrary to Art. 3 of the ECHR.

Second, Art. 34 provides for applications by individuals, groups of individuals, or non-governmental organizations. In each case the applicant must be an alleged victim of a violation by one of the State parties to the ECHR. Prior to Protocol 11 this was not an automatic right: it only arose where it had been accepted by the State against which the complaint had been lodged. The UK accepted such claims from 1966 onwards. Under Protocol 11, the right of individual application became mandatory. Most of the claims against the UK have been the result of applications by individuals. It will be noted that in relation to both types of claim, the proceedings must be taken against a State. The ECHR is not concerned with infringements of human rights which are the responsibility of other individuals, or non-governmental organizations. It would not be possible to use Art. 8, for example (which recognizes a right of privacy) directly against a newspaper responsible for intrusions. A challenge may, however, be possible on the basis that the State has failed in its duty under Art. 1 to 'secure to everyone within [its] jurisdiction the rights and freedoms defined' in the ECHR. The Court accepted this approach in *Young, James and Webster* (1982) 4 EHRR 38 (which was concerned with trade union exclusive membership agreements, commonly known as the 'closed shop'), holding (para. 49) that:

> …if a violation of one of those rights and freedoms is the result of a non-observance of the obligation in the enactment of domestic legislation, the responsibility of the State is engaged.
>
> A State can therefore be held to account for failing to enact legislation which prevents one citizen infringing the human rights of another.

A claim under either Art. 33 or Art. 34 is initially considered by a Committee or Chamber of the Court, to determine admissibility.

1.6.2.1 Admissibility

When an application is received from an individual it will be referred to a single judge, to consider admissibility. If the single judge decides that the case is clearly inadmissible then that decision is final (Art. 27). If the single judge is unable to determine the application it will be referred to a Committee. A Committee may, by unanimous vote, either reject the application, or declare it admissible and at the same time give a judgment on the merits (Art. 28). Applications from States, or individual applications which are not determined by a single judge or Committee, will be considered by a Chamber of the Court (Art. 29).

The criteria for admissibility are set out in Art. 35. This requires that all 'domestic remedies' have been exhausted before a claim will be considered. The ECHR does not, therefore, operate as a parallel jurisdiction to the domestic one, but as a system of 'last resort'. This does not necessarily mean, however, that only those cases which in the UK have been heard by the Supreme Court can result in an admissible application. Where an appeal would undoubtedly be rejected, because there is, for example, clear binding authority which goes against the applicant, the application may be accepted. On the other hand, it appears that if there are *administrative* as opposed to legal remedies which might be pursued, it will nevertheless be expected that these should be pursued before petitioning the Commission (see *Golder* v *United Kingdom* (A/18) (1979–80) 1 EHRR 524: appeal to the Home Secretary by a prisoner). Article 35 also requires that the claim must be made within six months of the final decision in relation to the domestic remedies.

Under Art. 35(2) and (3) there are several additional grounds for declaring an individual application inadmissible. First, the Court may not deal with a claim which is anonymous, or which is substantially the same as one which has already been examined by the Court or been submitted to 'another procedure of international investigation or settlement' (e.g. in connection with the United Nations' human rights activities) (Art. 35(2)(a) and (b)). Second, any application which the Court considers 'incompatible with the provisions' of the ECHR (that is, not within its scope), or 'manifestly ill-founded' (within its scope, but showing no prima facie case of a breach), or 'an abuse of the right of application', will be ruled inadmissible (Art. 35(3)(a)). As a result of a change introduced by Protocol 14, the Court may also declare the application inadmissible if the applicant has not suffered a significant disadvantage, unless 'respect for human rights…requires an examination of the application on the merits' or the case 'has not been duly considered by a domestic tribunal' (Art. 35(3)(b)). The Court may decide that an application is inadmissible at any stage of the proceedings (Art. 35(4)).

Only a small percentage of applications are declared admissible. In 2012, 87,879 cases were dealt with, of which 86,201 cases were struck out or declared inadmissible, whereas 1,678 were disposed of by judgment (http://www.echr.coe.int/Documents/Stats_analysis_2012_ENG.pdf). This may well suggest that there is a considerable unfulfilled need in relation to human rights grievances.

1.6.2.2 Investigation and decision

Once the Court has found an application admissible, it will investigate it (Art. 38). This will involve ascertaining the facts through representations (including oral representations) by the parties. The Court may conduct its own investigation, if necessary. The object at this stage is to try to secure a 'friendly settlement' of the dispute. For example, in one case involving the United Kingdom, challenging an aspect of English contempt law, a settlement was reached on the basis of an agreement that the law would be amended, and the costs of the applicant paid by the government (*Harman* v *United Kingdom*, 15 May 1986, 46 DR 57). As we shall see, in two corporal punishment cases against the UK, the settlement took the form of the payment of compensation, plus costs (see 1.7.1).

If a friendly settlement is not possible, the Chamber of the Court, having heard the arguments of the parties, will proceed to give judgment on the application, unless it decides, with the agreement of both parties, that the case should be relinquished to the Grand Chamber (Art. 30). This it may do if the case:

> ...raises a serious question affecting the interpretation of the Convention or the protocols thereto or where the resolution of a question before it might have a result inconsistent with a judgment previously delivered by the Court.

If the Chamber proceeds to hear the case and issues judgment, its decision will become final if neither party has within three months requested that it be referred to the Grand Chamber (Art. 44(2)(b)). It may become final earlier if both parties have declared that they do not intend to request such a reference (Art. 44(2)(1)). If a reference is requested, which should only be 'in exceptional cases', the request will be heard by a panel of five judges who will accept the case if it (Art. 43(3)):

> ...raises a serious question affecting the interpretation or application of the Convention or the protocols thereto, or a serious issue of general importance.

If the panel refuses to accept the reference, the decision of the Chamber will immediately become final (Art. 44(2)(c)).

In cases where the Chamber has relinquished jurisdiction or the Grand Chamber has accepted a reference, there will be a further hearing before the Grand Chamber. Its judgment will then be final, with no further route of appeal or reconsideration.

There is no requirement in the Chamber or the Grand Chamber that the decision should be unanimous and dissenting opinions are common.

The issue of a judgment finding that a State's laws are in breach of the ECHR, will impose an obligation under international law on that State to bring itself into line.

The decision of the Court in *Sunday Times* v *United Kingdom* (1979) 2 EHRR 245 (see 5.4.5), for example, led to amendments in the English law of contempt of court (Contempt of Court Act 1981: see 5.4.6). The Court also has the power to order an infringing State to make 'just satisfaction' to an injured party. This may take the form of financial compensation, as for example in *Young, James, and Webster* (1982) 4 EHRR 38, where it related to loss of earnings and injury to feelings. It may also simply amount to a contribution towards the applicant's costs, as in the *Spycatcher* cases (*Observer and Guardian* v *United Kingdom* (1992) 14 EHRR 153; *Sunday Times* v *United Kingdom* (1992) 14 EHRR 229: see 7.7.2).

The sanction on a State which fails to comply with a judgment of the Court must primarily be one of international pressure, with the threat of expulsion from the Council of Europe as the ultimate penalty. In 1970, Greece temporarily withdrew from the Council of Europe in the face of a finding (by the Committee of Ministers) that it had committed breaches of various Articles of the ECHR, including torture under Art. 3.

1.6.2.3 Committee of Ministers

Under the pre-Protocol 11 procedures, the Committee of Ministers, consisting of the Foreign Ministers of the Member States, had a role in dealing with certain cases which had not been referred to the Court by the Commission. This procedure was rarely used, and under Protocol 11 this role disappeared. The Committee of Ministers therefore no longer has any part in determining whether there have been breaches of the ECHR by Member States. It continues to have a role, however, in supervising whether governments which have been found in breach have brought their law in line with the requirements of the ECtHR's decision, so as to become compatible with the Convention.

1.6.3 Content of the European Convention on Human Rights

Article 1 sets out the basic obligation on States under the ECHR, by requiring the signatories to it to secure to everyone within their jurisdiction the rights defined in it. The only right directly related to the democratic process is Art. 3 of the First Protocol, under which the contracting parties 'undertake to hold free elections at reasonable intervals by secret ballot, under conditions which will ensure the free expression of the opinion of the people in the choice of the legislature'. This does not appear on the face of it to give any individual a right to vote. The Grand Chamber of the ECtHR, however, has held that this Article does in fact provide such a right: *Hirst* v *United Kingdom* (2006) 42 EHRR 41. The case concerned the United Kingdom's blanket disenfranchisement of convicted prisoners while serving their sentence, by virtue of s. 3 of the Representation of the People Act 1983. The Court held that this blanket ban was disproportionate. This led to the Scottish Registration Appeal Court issuing a declaration of incompatibility under the HRA 1998 (*Smith* v *Scott* [2007] CSIH 9; 2007 SLT 137). The decision in *Hirst* v *United Kingdom* has led to a long dispute with the UK government, which has so far refused to implement any change in the law, notwithstanding the fact that a further decision of the Court, dealing with a case emanating from Scotland (*Greens and MT* v *United Kingdom* [2010] ECHR 1826), affirmed its earlier decision, and warned the government as to the risks of having to pay substantial compensation if it did not change the law. The Prime Minister has indicated that the thought of changing this law (*Hansard*, HC, 3 November 2010, col. 921) makes him 'physically ill', and on 11 February 2011 the House of Commons, on a free vote, voted 234 to 22 against any change. A further referral to the Grand Chamber in a similar Italian case (*Scoppola* v *Italy (No. 3)* (2013) 56 EHRR 19), which the UK government hope might lead to a modification of the ECtHR's stance, reaffirmed that a blanket ban on prisoner voting is unacceptable, while at the same time approving the restrictions on such voting operating in Italy (i.e. restrictions only apply to those sentenced to a term of imprisonment of at least three years). The UK government has now put forward (in November 2012) a range of proposals for consideration by Parliament (Voting Eligibility (Prisoners) Draft Bill), and at the time of writing these are being reviewed by a joint parliamentary committee. It is not clear when these are likely to be voted on, or that any relaxation of the current position is likely to be approved. A continued 'stand-off' between the UK government and the ECtHR on this issue seems likely. In the meantime, the Supreme Court has held in *R (Chester)* v *Secretary of State for Justice* [2013] UKSC 63 that while the view of the Strasbourg Court in relation to blanket bans on prisoners' voting rights should be respected, this did not provide any remedy for a prisoner serving a life sentence (who would be unlikely to benefit from any relaxation of the law in any case).

1.6.3.1 Personal freedom

A number of the Articles of the ECHR deal with basic personal freedoms:

(a) Article 2 protects the right to life. Article 2 is discussed in detail below (see 1.7.1).

(b) Article 3 simply states that 'no one shall be subjected to torture or inhuman or degrading treatment'. The Article is unqualified. It is discussed further below (see 1.7.2).

(c) Article 4 contains prohibitions on slavery or forced labour. This has been of little practical consequence and is unlikely to be the subject of actions under the HRA 1998.

(d) Article 5 deals with the right to personal liberty and security. A number of exceptions are recognized to deal with detention after conviction, arrest, and detention for non-compliance with a court order, or for the purpose of criminal investigations, detention of a minor for educational purposes or to be brought before a 'competent legal authority'. There are also several 'process' rights attached to this Article, such as the right to be informed of the reason for any arrest, the right to be brought promptly before a judicial authority, the right to a trial within a reasonable time (or release on bail), and the right to bring proceedings to challenge the lawfulness of any detention. Article 5 issues are considered further in chapters 3 and 4.

(e) Article 12 recognizes the right to marry and have children. It applies to those of 'marriageable age' and operates 'according to the national laws governing the exercise of the right'.

(f) The First Protocol, Art. 1, recognizes the right to 'peaceful enjoyment of possessions'. There is an entitlement not to be deprived of property other than 'in the public interest' and in accordance with law. This is subject to the right of the State to control the use of property in the general interest, and to level taxes, impose penalties, etc.

1.6.3.2 Legal process

There are two Articles of the ECHR dealing specifically with the right to fair treatment within the legal process:

(a) Article 6 guarantees the right to a fair trial, in both criminal and civil matters, and has proved to be one of the most widely used of the Articles. It establishes that, in general, trials should be in public, and before an impartial tribunal. It also contains some specific rules relating to those charged with criminal offences, such as the presumption of innocence, the right to clear information on the charges, the right to adequate facilities to prepare a defence, the right to legal assistance, and the right to examine witnesses. Article 6 is considered in detail in chapter 5.

(b) Article 7 prohibits the creation of retrospective criminal offences, or the imposition of heavier punishments than were applicable when an offence was committed. The only exception relates to offences which, when committed, were 'criminal according to the general principles of law recognised by civilised nations', such as genocide, or other crimes against humanity.

1.6.3.3 Privacy

There is one Article of the ECHR concerned with 'privacy'. Article 8 states that everyone has the right to 'respect for his private and family life, his home and his correspondence'. This right is qualified, however, in that restrictions on it imposed by a public authority are permissible if they are in accordance with law and 'necessary in a democratic society in the interests of national security, public safety or the economic well-being of the country, for the prevention of disorder or crime, for the protection of health or morals, or for the protection of the rights and freedoms of others'. This Article is discussed in detail in chapter 6.

1.6.3.4 Ideas and opinions

There are three Articles of the ECHR concerned with the right to hold and express ideas and opinions:

(a) Article 9 guarantees the right to freedom of thought, conscience, and religion. The right to manifest one's religion or beliefs, however, is subject to qualification on a similar basis to Art. 8 (see 1.6.3.3). The only difference is that the list of permitted grounds does not include 'national security' or 'economic well being'.

(b) Article 10 states that 'everyone has the right to freedom of expression'. This includes the right to receive information. The qualifications permitted by Art. 10 include those involved in the licensing of broadcasting, television, or cinemas. Article 10(2) then recognizes that the exercise of this freedom carries with it duties and responsibilities. It lists qualifications of the same kind as apply to Article 8, but here there are additional grounds for restriction, namely 'territorial integrity', the protection of the reputation of others (as well as their rights), the prevention of the disclosure of confidential information, and to maintain 'the authority and impartiality of the judiciary'. Economic well-being, and the freedoms of others are, however, excluded from the list. This Article is discussed in chapters 7, 8, and 9.

(c) Article 11 deals with freedom of peaceful assembly and freedom of association. This includes the right to join a trade union. As with Arts 8–10, Art. 11 is subject to limitations. Here, in comparison to Art. 8, the only difference is that 'economic well being' is not included in the list. Article 11(2) also states, however, that the exercise of the rights may be restricted in relation to members of the armed forces, of the police, or 'of the administration of the State'. This Article is discussed further in chapter 9.

1.6.3.5 Discrimination

Discrimination is dealt with by Article 14. This provides that the rights and freedoms guaranteed by the ECHR are to be secured without discrimination 'on any ground such as sex, race, colour, language, religion, political or other opinion, national or social origin, association with a national minority, property, birth or other status'. Chapter 12 contains further discussion of this Article.

1.6.3.6 Derogation

Article 15 deals with the power to derogate from the rights guaranteed by the ECHR. It gives States the power to derogate 'in time of war or other public emergency threatening the life of the nation' from any Article, other than 2, 3, 4(1), or 7, 'to the extent strictly required by the exigencies of the situation'. When a derogation is made, it is to be lodged with the Secretary General of the Council of Europe. This enables the Council to supervise the legitimacy of any derogations.

1.6.3.7 Limitations

There are also three Articles concerned with the restrictions on the availability of the Convention rights, and possible abuse of its provisions:

(a) Article 16 provides that nothing in Arts 10, 11, or 14 shall be regarded as preventing the imposition of restrictions on the political activity of aliens.

(b) Article 17 provides that the Convention is not to be interpreted as permitting any State, individual, or group to do anything which is aimed at the destruction of any of the rights guaranteed, or limiting them to a greater extent than is permitted by the Convention itself. This suggests that those who attempt to change society in anti-democratic ways will not be able to find protection within the Convention.

(c) Article 18 provides that the restrictions permitted by the Convention are not to be 'applied for any purpose other than those for which they have been prescribed'. This is a discouragement to States from using the qualifications contained, for example, in Arts 8–11 for illegitimate purposes.

1.6.3.8 **Conclusions**

Two points may be made about this list. First, despite the fact that the preamble recognizes the importance of 'effective political democracy', none of the original rights given relates specifically to this. Thus, there was no right to elect a government, or otherwise to participate in the institutions of democracy. This may well be a reflection of the diverse constitutional backgrounds of the original contracting parties. The addition of Art. 3 of the First Protocol fills this gap to some extent, but as noted, it is on the face of it directed more towards the general democratic process than the rights of individuals within that process. Second, there is the issue of the qualification of rights. As is noted, Arts 5, 8, 9, 10, and 11 are all subject to significant limitations that may be considered 'necessary in a democratic society'. A striking contrast may be drawn, for example, between the First Amendment to the United States Constitution, which states, without qualification, 'Congress shall make no law...abridging the freedom of speech, or of the press'. Article 10 of the ECHR starts equally strongly: 'Everyone has the right to freedom of expression'. Even before the end of the first paragraph, however, the limitations start: 'This Article shall not prevent States from requiring the licensing of broadcasting, television or cinema enterprises'. Then, in Art. 10(2), further restrictions are permitted (on the basis that freedom of expression carries with it duties and responsibilities), in the interests of:

> ...national security, territorial integrity or public safety, for the prevention of disorder or crime, for the protection of health or morals, for the protection of the reputation or rights of others, for preventing the disclosure of information received in confidence, or for maintaining the authority and impartiality of the judiciary.

This lengthy list of exceptions detracts considerably from the force of the opening statement of the right. It is perhaps another reflection of the origins of the ECHR in a political compromise between a group of nations, and is indicative of a rather pragmatic, rather than evangelistic, approach to the promotion of human rights and civil liberties.

The ECHR, perhaps for similar reasons, does not venture into 'social rights', relating to housing, employment, etc. The closest that it comes to this is in Art. 2 of the First Protocol to the ECHR (Cmd 9221, 1952), which states that 'no person shall be denied the right to education'. It continues:

> In the exercise of any functions which it assumes in relation to education and to teaching, the State shall respect the right of parents to ensure such education and teaching in conformity with their own religious and philosophical convictions.

Although the UK government is a party to the Protocol, it has made a reservation (preserved by s. 15 and Pt. II of Sch. 3 to the HRA 1998) that it accepts the principle as to parents' rights only insofar as 'it is compatible with the provision of efficient instruction and training, and the avoidance of unreasonable public expenditure'. Social rights are always liable to face difficulties in relation to resources, and it is not perhaps surprising to find the UK government avoiding what might be, particularly in an increasingly multi-cultural, and multi-religious, society, a very expensive commitment.

1.7 The European Convention on Human Rights in practice

At various points in the rest of this book the specific provisions of the ECHR relevant to a particular area are considered, and any case law discussed. The opportunity is taken here, however, to discuss two important Articles which are not discussed in detail elsewhere in the book, but which may be used as examples of the way in which the ECHR operates in practice. These Articles are Art. 2 on the right to life and Art. 3 on the prohibition of torture and inhuman or degrading treatment.

1.7.1 Article 2

Article 2 states:

> Everyone's right to life shall be protected by law. No one shall be deprived of his life intentionally save in the execution of a sentence of a court following his conviction of a crime for which this penalty is provided by law.

As will be seen, the Article contains an exception to allow for the imposition of the death penalty, but this must be read alongside the Thirteenth Protocol, to which the UK has subscribed and which is, therefore, included in Schedule 1 to the HRA 1998. The Protocol prohibits all use of the death penalty. It appears to be a generally accepted European standard that the death penalty should not be used, which is emphasized by the fact that States which wish to join the European Union must not use capital punishment. In *Al-Saadoon* v *United Kingdom* (2010) 51 EHRR 9 the ECtHR has gone so far as to hold that the imposition of the death penalty can now, because of the its widespread rejection by European States, be regarded as inhuman punishment within Art. 3.

Article 2(2) also contains exceptions in relation to 'absolutely necessary' force used in self-defence, to effect an arrest, or to quell a 'riot or insurrection'.

The application of this exception to Art. 2 was considered by the ECtHR in *McCann* v *United Kingdom* (1995) 21 EHRR 97. This case arose out of a military operation in Gibraltar, in relation to a suspected bomb plot being carried out by members of the Irish Republican Army (IRA). Three suspects who were thought to be about to set off a bomb, were killed by British soldiers, operating under cover. It transpired that none of the three was carrying a bomb, or any device for setting-off a bomb, though they were all part of an IRA active service unit, which was involved with plans for planting of car bombs. Their families took action against the UK government, alleging a breach of Art. 2. The ECtHR held that the soldiers who had actually fired the shots had not acted in breach of Art. 2. They had acted on the basis of information which suggested that the suspects were about to set off a bomb by remote control. The use of lethal force to prevent their doing so was justified, even though it turned out that in the event the information was inaccurate. The Court did, however, find that there was a breach of Art. 2 as a result of actions higher up the chain of command. The suspects had been under surveillance for a period, and it would have been possible to intervene to neutralize any threat without the need to resort to killing them. There were also deficiencies in the intelligence assessments, and the training given to the soldiers. Overall, the killings did not constitute the use of force which was no more than absolutely necessary in defence of persons from unlawful violence (para. 213).

A similar approach to that taken in *McCann* in relation to the actions of State agents who kill was taken in *Andronicou and Constantinou* v *Cyprus* (1998) 25 EHRR 491. This case involved a police action to terminate a siege involving a hostage. The Court ruled that it should not (para. 192):

> ...with detached reflection substitute its own assessment of the situation for that of the officers who were required to act in the heat of the moment in what was for them a unique and unprecedented operation to save life. The officers were entitled to open fire for this purpose and to take all measures which they honestly and reasonably believed were necessary to eliminate any risk either to the young woman's life or their own lives.

The Court thus recognizes the difficulties for those put in a situation involving very quick decisions, but nevertheless requires that their assessment of the situation must be reasonable. Similarly in *Gül* v *Turkey* (2002) 34 EHRR 28, which concerned an operation against a suspected terrorist, the Court found that 'the firing of at least 50–55 shots at the door was not justified by any reasonable belief of the officers that their lives were at risk' (para. 82). Once again, the test is stated objectively, in terms of 'reasonableness'. In this the test is stricter than that which applies in domestic English law, in that a police officer who uses lethal force will have a defence even if his or her mistake as to the need for force to be used was unreasonable, as long as it was honestly held. In other words, the individual's right to life is protected more strongly by the ECHR than by English criminal law.

There are three other issues relating to Art. 2 which should be noted:

- As well as the negative obligation not to take life, the Article also imposes a positive obligation on a State to protect individuals from lethal attack from other citizens.
- The State has an obligation to ensure that any deaths that have occurred as the possible result of the actions of State agents should be independently investigated.
- The extent to which Art. 2 implies a 'right to die' is a matter of continuing debate.

These issues are outlined in 1.7.1.1 and 1.7.1.2.

1.7.1.1 The positive obligations

As well as the negative duty not to take life, Art. 2 requires States to protect its citizens from lethal attack by other individuals. The most obvious way in which this duty is met is by criminalizing homicide. The duty goes beyond this, however. In *Osman* v *United Kingdom* [1988] EHRR 245 a teacher had become obsessed with a pupil, and engaged in a course of disturbing behaviour, including some violence towards property, though not people. The police were aware of this. The teacher then killed the boy's father, and the headmaster's son. He was convicted of manslaughter on grounds of diminished responsibility. The family of the boy's father sought unsuccessfully to sue the police for negligence. The case was taken to the ECtHR which defined a State's obligation in this situation as arising where the relevant authorities 'knew or ought to have known...of the existence of a real and immediate risk to the life of an individual or individuals from the criminal acts of a third party' (para. 116). Where such knowledge exists or ought to have existed, the State is required to take reasonable steps to avoid the risk (para. 116). On the facts of this case the Court found that there was no knowledge of a real and immediate risk to life, and so no breach of the duty. In *van Colle* v *United Kingdom* (2013) 56 EHRR 23 the court confirmed that the *Osman* standard did not need to be modified where the deceased was a witness in a criminal trial. This did not of itself impose any greater duty on the state; it was still necessary to show that the state knew, or ought to have known, of a real and immediate risk to life.

In a number of cases the court has found States to be in breach of this duty. Examples include *Kilic* v *Turkey* (2001) 33 EHRR 58, where a journalist working for a newspaper which supported the minority Kurdish population had previously complained to the police that he had been threatened, and there was evidence that others involved with the newspaper had been attacked and killed. After he was killed, his brother took the case to the ECtHR. It was held that there had been a real and immediate risk to the journalist's life, and that the Turkish authorities had failed in their duty to take reasonable steps to protect him. In *Edwards* v *United Kingdom* (2002) 35 EHRR 19 the deceased, Edwards, who was suffering from mental illness, and had been arrested for a public order offence, was placed in a cell with another prisoner, Linford, who was suffering from schizophrenia. Linford killed Edwards in a violent attack. It was found by the ECtHR that there had been a failure to pass on information relating to Linford's health and background to the prison authorities, and that they in turn had failed to conduct an adequate assessment of him on his arrival at the prison. The authorities should have been aware that there was a real and immediate risk to the life of Edwards from Linford, and the failure to protect Edwards constituted a breach of Art. 2.

The second aspect of the positive duty under Art. 2 is to conduct a proper, independent investigation wherever there is a suggestion that a public authority may carry some responsibility for a death. This will always be the case where it appears that a person has died as a result of force used by a State agent (e.g. a police officer or soldier). Thus in *Kelly* v *United Kingdom*, App. No. 30054/96, 4 May 2001, nine people had been killed by SAS soldiers during an ambush in Northern Ireland, directed at terrorist attack on an RUC police station. One of the deceased had no connection with the IRA and at least two others were unarmed. Although there had been an investigation and an inquest, the investigation had been carried out entirely by RUC officers; at the inquest the families of the deceased had been denied access to information, and the soldiers involved in the operation could not be called to give evidence. In the light of these and other defects, the ECtHR held that there had been a breach of the obligation to carry out a proper investigation of the deaths.

The obligation will also arise where a death occurs in police custody, in prison, or in any other situation where the State is exercising control over an individual, even if there is no suggestion of the involvement of State agents directly in the death. A breach of this obligation was found, for example, in *Edwards* v *United Kingdom* (see also *R (Amin)* v *Secretary of State for the Home Department* [2003] UKHL 51, discussed in chapter 2 (2.5). Wherever there is an obligation to respond to a 'real and immediate' risk to life, there will also be an obligation to carry out an independent investigation. This was an additional basis on which there was found to be a breach of Art. 2 in *Kilic* v *Turkey*.

1.7.1.2 **A right to die?**

Does the right to life under Art. 2 include the right to take one's own life, or to decide when one's life should be taken by someone else? These issues were raised with the ECtHR in the case of *Pretty* v *United Kingdom* (2002) 35 EHRR 1. The applicant, who was suffering from a progressive, incurable, degenerative illness sought a ruling that the Director of Public Prosecutions (DPP) to the effect that, if the applicant's husband assisted her to commit suicide, the husband would not be prosecuted for this offence under the Suicide Act 1961. This was rejected by the English courts: see *R (on the Application of Pretty)* v *DPP* [2001] UKHL 61, [2002] 1 All ER 1. The House of Lords held that Art. 2 of the ECHR, dealing with the right to life, did not require this. The applicant then took her claim to the ECtHR which heard it under an expedited procedure. In this case, the ECtHR upheld the view of the English court. It found that Art. 2, which guarantees the right to life, could not, 'without a distortion of language, be interpreted as conferring the diametrically opposite right, namely a right to die; nor can it create a right to self-determination in the sense of conferring on an individual the entitlement to choose death rather than life' (para. 39). The applicant's right to 'private life' under Art. 8 had been infringed, but only in a way which was justifiable under Art. 8(2). As far as English law is concerned the position on this issue has now changed in the light of the House of Lords' decision in *R (Purdy)* v *DPP* [2009] UKHL 45, [2009] 3 WLR 403. The House of Lords ruled that the DPP should produce guidelines indicating the issues that would be taken into account in relation to decisions to prosecute for assisting suicide. Such guidelines were published by the DPP in February 2010. Cases still continue to be taken to Strasbourg, however, from other countries.

At the other end of life, the ECtHR has refused to rule as to when life begins, holding that this is a matter better left to the discretion of individual States and their particular traditions, customs, religious allegiances, etc.: see *Vo* v *France* (2005) 40 EHRR 12. Thus a State is not required to hold that the protections of Art. 2 apply to a foetus, but nor would it be in conflict with that Article for it to do so. Issues relating to abortion, or the rights over embryos created by *in vitro* fertilization, are likely to be dealt with under Art. 8 rather than Art. 2 (see, e.g. *Tysiac* v *Poland* (2007) 45 EHRR 947 and *Evans* v *United Kingdom* (2008) 46 EHRR 728).

1.7.2 **Article 3**

Article 3, in its entirety, states, 'No one shall be subjected to torture or to inhuman or degrading treatment or punishment.' The obligation placed on States is absolute—there are no exceptions. There is also a positive obligation, similar to that under Art. 2, for States to take reasonable steps to ensure that individuals are protected from actions falling within Art. 3 which come from other individuals (not being agents of the State).

One of the leading cases on Art. 3 is one of the few cases in which one State took action against another—*Ireland* v *United Kingdom* (1978) 2 EHRR 25. This concerned interrogation techniques used by the British Army in Northern Ireland in relation to suspected terrorists. The main issue concerned the so-called 'five techniques' of sensory deprivation, that is:

(a) wall-standing: forcing detainees to remain in a 'stress position', spread-eagled against a wall, standing on toes with the bodyweight mainly on the fingers;

(b) hooding: keeping detainees hooded at all times, except when actually under interrogation;

(c) subjection to noise: holding detainees in room in which there was a continuous loud hissing noise;

(d) deprivation of sleep;

(e) deprivation of food and drink: subjecting detainees to a reduced diet.

In deciding whether this treatment fell within the scope of Art. 3, the Court needed to consider the differences between the three concepts of 'torture', 'inhuman treatment', and 'degrading treatment'. As regards 'torture' the Court was of the view that the distinction between this and the other two concepts lies in the 'difference in the intensity of the suffering inflicted' (para. 167). It referred with approval to a resolution of the United Nations General Assembly (Resolution 3452 (XXX), 9 December 1975) which states that, 'Torture constitutes an aggravated and deliberate form of cruel, inhuman or degrading treatment or punishment'. It concluded that the five techniques did not 'occasion suffering of the particular intensity and cruelty implied by the word torture' (para. 167). They did, however, constitute both inhuman and degrading treatment:

> The five techniques were applied in combination, with premeditation and for hours at a stretch; they caused, if not actual bodily injury, at least intense physical and mental suffering to the persons subjected thereto and also led to acute psychiatric disturbances during interrogation. They accordingly fell into the category of inhuman treatment within the meaning of Article 3. The techniques were also degrading since they were such as to arouse in their victims feelings of fear, anguish and inferiority capable of humiliating and debasing them and possibly breaking their physical or moral resistance.

In *Aksoy* v *Turkey* (1997) 23 EHRR 553 the ECtHR for the first time reached a finding that torture had been used. The applicant, while in police custody, had been subjected to 'Palestinian hanging', which involved him being stripped, his arms tied behind his back, and then being suspended by his arms. The Court considered that this treatment, which must have been planned, would have required preparation, was intended to extract information, and caused lasting physical systems, was 'of such a serious and cruel nature that it can only be described as torture' (para. 64).

For a breach of Art. 3 on the basis of inhuman or degrading treatment or punishment, the treatment must reach a level of seriousness which is not very clearly defined by the European Court. In *Jalloh* v *Germany* (2007) 44 EHRR 667, the ECtHR restated its approach in this way (para. 67):

> [I]ll treatment must attain a minimum level of severity if it is to fall within the scope of Article 3. The assessment of this minimum level of severity is relative; it depends on all the circumstances of the case, such as the duration of the treatment, its physical and mental effects and, in some cases, the sex, age and state of health of the victim.

Prolonged physical ill-treatment or sensory deprivation will almost certainly fall within its scope. Unpleasant conditions of detention, or merely verbal abuse and intimidation, are unlikely to do so. In *Costello-Roberts* v *United Kingdom* (1994) 19 EHRR 112 the slippering of a seven-year-old schoolboy by a teacher was held not to reach the level of degrading treatment within Art. 3, even though in general, as will be seen, the ECtHR has found corporal punishment to be in breach of Art. 3.

In *Selmouni* v *France* (1999) 29 EHRR 403 the European Court indicated that the ECHR is a 'living instrument which must be interpreted in the light of present-day conditions'. This meant that standards could change over time. The Court noted that acts which in the past had been categorized as 'inhuman and degrading' might now be regarded as 'torture'. In the case before it the applicant had been the subject of systematic physical and mental abuse by the police with the intention of making him confess to the offence of which he was suspected. The abuse had continued over a number of days. Although the worst allegation (anal rape with a police truncheon) had not been proved, the Court nevertheless felt that in this case the police behaviour did reach the level of severity which took it into the category of 'torture'. The implication of this decision is that behaviour which in the past has fallen below the minimum level of severity for it to be considered 'inhuman or degrading' might now constitute an infringement of Art. 3. The fact that the definitions can develop is also reflected in the decision in *Al-Saadoon* v *United Kingdom* (2010) 51 EHRR 9 that the imposition of the death penalty can now be treated as inhuman treatment, even though it was specifically permitted by Art. 2 of the Convention as originally drafted.

In two cases involving the UK the ECtHR has considered Art. 3 in relation to conditions of detention in prison. These illustrate that it is not necessary for there to be *deliberate* mistreatment for there to be a breach of Art. 3. First, in *Price* v *United Kingdom* (2002) 34 EHRR 53 it was held that there was a breach of Art. 3 in relation to a severely disabled person in prison for contempt. The Court held that (para. 30):

> ...to detain a severely disabled person in conditions where she is dangerously cold, risks developing sores because her bed is too hard or unreachable, and is unable to go to the toilet or keep clean without the greatest of difficulty, constitutes degrading treatment contrary to Article 3.

Similarly in *McGlinchey* v *United Kingdom* (2003) 37 EHRR 41 the Court held that failure to provide proper medical treatment (in this case for an asthmatic heroin addict) for a prisoner involved ill-treatment within the scope of Art. 3.

Another group of cases which illustrate the way in which Art. 3 operates are those concerned with corporal punishment. The first case to come before the Court was *Tyrer* v *United Kingdom* (1978) 2 EHRR 1. The applicant, when 15, had been convicted of an assault occasioning actual bodily harm, and had been sentenced by a juvenile court in the Isle of Man to three strokes of the birch. Sentence was passed on 7 March 1972. Following an unsuccessful appeal, it was carried out on 28 April 1972. The applicant was examined by a doctor, and then (2 EHRR 4):

> ...[h]e was made to take down his trousers and underpants and bend over a table; two policemen held him while a third administered the punishment...The applicant's skin was raised but not cut and he was sore for about a week and a half afterwards.

The Court (with the UK judge dissenting) held that there had been a breach of Art. 3. The suffering that the applicant underwent was not sufficient to reach the level of 'torture' or 'inhuman treatment'. The birching did, however, constitute 'degrading punishment'. The view of the local population was not relevant to this issue, nor was the fact that birching might there be regarded as deterring crime (para. 31):

> [A] punishment does not lose its degrading character just because it is believed to be, or actually is, an effective deterrent or aid to crime control.

The factors which were relevant to the finding that it was degrading were that it constituted institutionalized violence, carried out by total strangers; that it constituted an assault on 'precisely what it is one of the main purposes of Art. 3 to protect, namely a person's dignity and physical integrity'; and that there was a considerable delay between the passing of sentence and its being carried out, which meant that the applicant 'was subjected to the mental anguish of anticipating the violence he was to have inflicted on him' (para. 33).

Campbell and Cosans v *United Kingdom* (1982) 4 EHRR 293 was again concerned with corporal punishment, but the context was rather different, this being concerned with the use of corporal punishment in state schools. The action was brought by the mothers of two schoolboys. Both of the boys attended schools in Scotland where corporal punishment, in the form of the tawse administered across the pupil's hand, was in use. In Mrs Campbell's case her ground for complaint was that the local authority which was responsible for the school refused to guarantee that her son would not be punished in this way. Mrs Cosan's son was ordered to receive corporal punishment but refused. He was suspended from the school, until he was willing to receive the punishment. After some months, the school agreed to reinstate him, the length of the suspension being regarded as sufficient punishment. His parents, however, refused to send him back to school unless it guaranteed that their son would not be subject to corporal punishment while he remained at the school.

The Court referred to the criteria which it had established in the *Tyrer* case concerning the notion of 'degrading punishment'. Neither of the boys had actually received the tawse, so the Court did not have to consider whether its application would have fallen foul of Art. 3. It accepted, however, that in certain circumstances the threat of conduct prohibited by Art. 3 might in itself conflict with that provision (para. 26). In applying this approach to the case before it, the Court noted that corporal punishment was traditional in Scottish schools, and appeared 'to be favoured by a large majority of parents' (para. 28). This in itself did not, as had been established in *Tyrer*, prevent its being degrading. However, in this case the Court took the view (para. 29), that in the light of the circumstances obtaining in Scotland, it had not been established:

> ... that pupils at a school where such punishment is used are, solely by reason of the risk of being subjected thereto, humiliated or debased in the eyes of others to the requisite degree at all.

Nor was there any evidence that either of the boys had been humiliated or debased in their own eyes. Cosans might well have felt apprehensive when ordered to be punished, but this was not the same as degrading treatment. Still less could Campbell, who had never been directly threatened, be said to have suffered in this way.

The conclusion was that the Court, without actually deciding whether the *use* of the tawse would contravene Art. 3, held that the *threat* of its use did not do so.

In contrast, in *X* v *United Kingdom*, App. No. 7907/77, (1981) 24 YB 402, *The Times*, 27 February 1982 the applicant was the mother of a schoolgirl, who, when 14, had been caned by her headmistress. The caning was found to have produced weals (one over a foot long) on the girl's buttocks and hand. She was 'in discomfort for several days and traces of the caning remained for a considerably longer period' (para. 5). The Commission declared the application admissible. In this case, however, rather than proceeding to a hearing of the merits, the 'friendly settlement' procedure produced a result. The settlement proposed by the Commission, and accepted by the parties, was for:

(a) an *ex gratia* payment to the applicant of £1,200;

(b) a contribution of £1,016.19 towards the applicant's legal costs; and

(c) the dispatch of a circular letter by the government to local education authorities stating that the use of corporal punishment may in certain circumstances amount to treatment contrary to Art. 3 of the ECHR.

The fact that the UK settled this case on these terms indicated a move away from the use of corporal punishment in schools. Subsequent adverse decisions continued this trend. For example, in *Maxine and Karen Warwick* v *United Kingdom* (1986) Commission's Decisions and Reports 60, a 16-year-old girl had received one stroke of the cane across her hand, administered by her headmaster in the presence of the deputy headmaster and another girl. In *Y* v *United Kingdom* (1992) (Series A, No. 247-A) a 15-year-old schoolboy had received four strokes of the cane across his clothed buttocks from his headmaster. In both cases the Commission found that the treatment fell within Art. 3, though in *Warwick* the Committee of Ministers disagreed, and in *Y*, a friendly settlement was reached before the case reached the Court.

Corporal punishment is now banned from all schools in England, Wales, and Scotland, including independent schools. The ban does not infringe the rights of those who might believe as part of their religious convictions that the corporal punishment of children is appropriate. Although the right to freedom of religion in Art. 9 is engaged, the ban is justifiable under Art. 9(2): *R (Williamson)* v *Secretary of State for Education and Employment* [2005] UKHL 15, [2005] 2 All ER 1.

1.7.2.1 Deportation and Article 3

A State can breach Art. 3 by extraditing or deporting a citizen to a country where he or she may face torture or inhuman or degrading treatment or punishment. In *Soering* v *United Kingdom* (1989) 11 EHRR 439 it was held that it would constitute inhuman or degrading treatment to extradite a person suspected of murder to the US where, if convicted, that person might be sentenced to capital punishment. This was primarily because of the so-called 'death-row phenomenon' whereby people sentenced to death could spend many years on death row awaiting execution, and the mental anguish that that would involve.

In *Chahal* v *United Kingdom* (1996) 23 EHRR 413 the same approach was applied to deportation of an alien. In this case the applicant was a Sikh who had been actively involved in the Sikh separatist movement in India. There was evidence that members of this movement were subject to killings and mistreatment at the hands of Indian security forces. On this basis, the ECtHR held that it would be a breach of Art. 3 to deport Mr Chahal to India (for further discussion of the human rights restrictions on deportation, see chapter 11 (11.1.1)).

1.7.2.2 Positive duties

As with Art. 2, Art. 3 imposes positive duties on a State, as well as negative obligations. First, there is a duty to protect individuals from behaviour by other private individuals (as opposed to State agents) which might fall within Art. 3. Criminal offences and tortious remedies will generally satisfy this requirement. An example where English law has been found to be lacking can again be found in the area of the application of corporal punishment to children.

In *A* v *United Kingdom* (1999) 27 EHRR 611 the applicant was a boy who had been beaten regularly by his stepfather with a garden cane causing considerable bruising. When the boy was nine his stepfather was prosecuted for assault occasioning actual bodily harm in relation to these beatings. The stepfather's defence was that the beatings only amounted to reasonable and necessary force in the chastisement of a difficult child (which is not unlawful under English law). The jury acquitted. The boy then applied to the European Commission, alleging that the State had failed to protect him from ill treatment by his stepfather, amounting to, *inter alia*, violation of his rights under Art. 3 of the ECHR. The Commission found in favour of the applicant and the case was referred to the Court. The Court held that the treatment which the boy had suffered at the hands of his stepfather reached the level of severity prohibited by Art. 3. It ruled that the law relating to 'reasonable chastisement' did not provide adequate protection against treatment or punishment contrary to Art. 3. The UK was, therefore, held to be in breach of the ECHR, and the applicant was awarded £10,000 in compensation. As a result of this ruling, the UK government undertook to amend the law relating to parental chastisement of children. It seemed initially, however, that reform might be left to the courts. The directions to be given to a jury in relation to the defence of 'reasonable chastisement' were reviewed by the Court of Appeal in *R* v *H* [2002] 1 Cr App R 7, in the light of the ECtHR's decision in *A* v *United Kingdom*. The Court indicated that the direction to the jury should instruct them that (para. 31):

...when they are considering the reasonableness or otherwise of the chastisement, they must consider the nature and context of the defendant's behaviour, its duration, its physical and mental consequences in relation to the child, the age and personal characteristics of the child and the reasons given by the defendant for administering punishment.

There was some feeling that this might be sufficient to meet the requirement of the ECHR. Subsequently, however, the government decided to legislate. It did not ban smacking by parents, but provided, by s. 58 of the Children Act 2004, that 'reasonable chastisement' can no longer be used as a defence in criminal or civil proceedings for an assault on a child, where the assault causes 'actual bodily harm' (as defined by case law on s. 47 of the Offences Against the Person Act 1861) or more serious injury.

There is also a duty on the State equivalent to that recognized in relation to Art. 2 in *Osman* v *United Kingdom* (see 1.7.1), where it is aware, or should be aware, of a real and immediate risk that an individual will suffer torture or inhuman or degrading treatment at the hands of another. The State will then have a duty to take reasonable steps to protect the individual from the threat. An example of this approach is to be found in *Re E (A Child)* [2008] UKHL 66, [2009] 1 AC 536. This arose out of sectarian conflict in Northern Ireland. A group of primary school children from Catholic families had to take a route to school through a Protestant area. People in the Protestant area sought to stop this. The parents and their children were confronted by a hostile mob who shouted threats, abuse, and obscenities at them. There were attacks them with missiles, including an explosive device. The response of the police was to create a 'corridor' from police and army vehicles, and to deploy police officers carrying riot shields to escort the families and protect them from missiles. Some of the parents claimed that this action was not robust enough, and more direct action should have been taken to protect the protesters. The House of Lords applied the tests used in *Osman* v *United Kingdom*. It was quite clear that there was a real and immediate risk of behaviour falling within Art. 3, but the court felt that the police had taken reasonable steps to address this, and rejected the parents' claim.

This case demonstrates that the duty on the State under Art. 3, while it is an absolute duty where actions by State agents directly involve behaviour falling with the Article, is subject to a test of 'reasonableness' where the positive duty to protect individuals from other citizens is concerned.

Finally, as with Art. 2, where behaviour falling within Art. 3 has occurred for which the State may bear some responsibility, there is an obligation to carry out a full independent investigation of the circumstances: *Veznedraglou* v *Turkey* (2001) 33 EHRR 59.

QUESTIONS

1 What are 'human rights'? Where do they come from? Does it make sense to talk about such rights other than in the context of a legal system (national or international)?

2 Are human rights 'claim rights' as defined by Hohfeld? If not, what type of rights are they?

3 Why does the ECHR deal almost entirely with political rights? Aren't economic and social rights more important to people in their everyday lives than, for example, freedom of the press?

4 Why do Parliament and the common law not provide sufficient protection for an individual's human rights?

5 How 'absolute' is the right under Art. 2? In what circumstances may it be lawful for a State agent to take someone's life?

6 Is the concept of 'inhuman and degrading' treatment sufficiently clearly defined by the Strasbourg case law?

FURTHER READING

Dworkin, R. (1978), *Taking Rights Seriously*, London: Duckworth

Feldman, D. (2002), *Civil Liberties and Human Rights in England and Wales*, 2nd edn, Oxford: Oxford University Press

Finnis, J. M. (2011), *Natural Law and Natural Rights*, 2nd edn, Oxford: Clarendon Press

Gearty, C. (2007) *Civil Liberties*, Oxford: Clarendon Press

Gearty, C. and Ewing, K. (2000), *The Struggle for Civil Liberties*, Oxford: Oxford University Press

Gorman, J. (2003), *Rights and Reason*, Chesham: Acumen Publishing

Gostin, L. (ed.) (1988), *Civil Liberties in Conflict*, London: Routledge

Halpin, A. (1997), *Rights and Law—Analysis and Theory*, Oxford: Hart Publishing

Harris, D. J., O'Boyle, M., and Warbrick, C. (2008), *Law of the European Convention on Human Rights*, 2nd edn, Oxford: Oxford University Press

Harvey, C. (2004), 'Talking about Human Rights', [2004] EHRLR 500

Hohfeld, W. N. (1913), 'Some Fundamental Legal Conceptions as Applied in Judicial Reasoning', (1913) 23 *Yale Law Journal* 16

Keating, H. (2006), 'Protecting or Punishing Children: Physical Punishment, Human Rights and English Law Reform', (2006) 26 LS 394

Mill, J. S. (1962) (first published 1859), 'On Liberty', in Warnock, M. (ed.), *Utilitarianism*, London: Fontana

Mowbray, A. (2012), *Cases and Materials on the European Convention on Human Rights*, 3rd edn, Oxford: Oxford University Press

National Council for Civil Liberties (1984), 'NCCL Independent Inquiry into the Policing of the Miners' Strike' (Interim Report), National Council for Civil Liberties

Ovey, C. and White, R. C. A. (2010), *Jacobs and White, The European Convention on Human Rights*, 5th edn, Oxford: Oxford University Press

Parpworth, N. (2012), *Constitutional and Administrative Law*, 7th edn, Oxford: Oxford University Press

Rogers, J. (2002), 'A Criminal Lawyer's Response to Chastisement in the European Court of Human Rights', [2002] Crim LR 98

Steiner, J., Alston, P., and Goodman, R. (2007), *International Human Rights in Context*, 3rd edn, Oxford: Oxford University Press

Waldron, J. (ed.) (1984), *Nonsense upon Stilts*, London: Methuen

Waldron, J. (ed.) (1984), *Theories of Rights*, Oxford: Oxford University Press

2

The Human Rights Act 1998: Overview

2.1 Introduction

The purpose of this chapter is to provide an overview of the Human Rights Act 1998 (HRA 1998) and the way in which it operates. Some general conclusions on its effectiveness in relation to the protection of civil liberties and human rights in England and Wales are also drawn. Changes in approach to legislation and its interpretation in both Parliament and the courts which have resulted from the Act are considered. As far as the common law is concerned, the most important effects on the substantive law in the areas covered by this book are dealt with in later chapters. One particular issue receives fuller discussion here, however, which is the development of the doctrine of judicial review, and the way in which that has been affected by the HRA 1998 (see 2.4.1).

In addition, the question of the extent to which the Act fulfils the role of a 'Bill of Rights', as that concept is understood in other jurisdictions, is discussed. A particular issue which is relevant to that discussion is that of 'entrenchment', and the extent to which the HRA 1998 can be said to have any special status different from other legislation. To what extent is it vulnerable to the doctrines of Parliamentary sovereignty and implied repeal? Related to this is the current argument that the Human Rights Act is in need of reform, and should perhaps be replaced by a 'UK Bill of Rights'. The current state of play of this debate is considered at 2.6.3

Finally, the issue of the supervision of the HRA 1998 is considered. What mechanisms are there to review the way in which the HRA 1998 is operating, both at the particular level of its effect on the substantive law, and more generally in encouraging changes in attitude towards the rights which the Act is supposed to protect?

We start, however, by looking at the provisions of the Act itself, the obligations it imposes on 'public authorities' and, in particular, the way in which it makes the rights contained in the European Convention on Human Rights (ECHR) part of the law to which English courts are required to pay attention in reaching their decisions.

2.2 The Human Rights Act 1998

2.2.1 Introduction

What follows is not intended to be a complete discussion of the HRA 1998 and the case law under it. It is an overview, setting out the framework which the

Act provides for the consideration of issues of civil liberties and human rights. Examples of how the courts have used the Act are given, through the use of representative cases rather than a comprehensive survey. As far as the areas on which this book is focused more detailed discussion of the case law on the Act is found in the appropriate chapters later in the book, dealing with specific Articles of the ECHR, and their implementation in English law. In this chapter the main focus is on cases which do not fall within the scope of those other chapters, such as those dealing with the issue of what constitutes a 'public authority'.

The starting point is the structures which are put in place to give effect in English law to the rights contained in the ECHR. The approach of the courts to the use of those structures will then be considered.

2.2.2 The Convention rights

It is important to note that the HRA 1998 does not 'incorporate' the ECHR in its entirety. The rights which are to have effect under the Act are listed in s. 1 and set out in Sch. 1. They are those contained in:

1. Articles 2–12, 14 and 16–18 of the ECHR.
2. Articles 1–3 of the First Protocol.
3. Article 1 of the Thirteenth Protocol.

The content of the Articles which do have effect has been noted in chapter 1 (1.6 and 1.7) and is considered further at the appropriate places elsewhere in the book. Here we will simply note some of the Articles which have not been included.

Article 1 places the obligation on the signatories to the ECHR to 'secure to everyone within their jurisdiction the rights and freedoms defined in' the Convention. In other words, it establishes the UK's obligation under international law to abide by the ECHR. As such, it would not be particularly appropriate for it to have effect in domestic law. There has been more controversy, however, about the exclusion of Art. 13. This states that '[e]veryone whose rights and freedoms as set forth in this Convention are violated shall have an effective remedy before a national authority...'. There was some pressure during consideration of the Bill in Parliament to add this Article to those given effect under the Act. The government resisted this on the basis that the enactment of the Human Rights Act itself met the obligation under Art. 13, and that to include it might cause confusion with the 'remedies' provisions contained in the Act (i.e. ss. 7 and 8). These sections were intended to be exclusive, but if Art. 13 stood alongside them, it would amount to an invitation to the courts to consider remedies going beyond those provided by the Act. More importantly, since Art. 13 requires there to be a remedy wherever there is an infringement of one of the Convention rights, its inclusion would have rendered otiose the restricted concept of an 'unlawful act' as defined in s. 6 (see 2.2.3). Nevertheless, both the Home Secretary and the Lord Chancellor made it clear in the Parliamentary debates that Art. 13 was not wholly irrelevant to cases before the English courts, in that it was open to the court to take account of the case law of the European Court of Human Rights (ECtHR) relating to Art. 13 when deciding what remedies to apply *(Hansard,* HL, 18 November 1997, col. 475; *Hansard,* HC, 20 May 1998, col. 979). It might be relevant, for example, that in some cases the European

Court has taken the view that the finding of a violation of the ECHR is in itself a sufficient remedy, *and that there is no need for financial compensation to be awarded* (e.g. *McLeod* v *United Kingdom* (1999) 27 EHRR 493, para. 65, discussed in chapter 6 (6.4.2)). Presumably, the case law might also indicate the appropriate level of financial compensation for particular types of breach. The issue of the correct approach to compensation under the HRA 1998, and the relevance of case law of the ECtHR to this, is discussed further at 2.2.4.

Article 15, which deals with the power of States to derogate from the obligations under the ECHR, is not included in the Schedule to the HRA 1998, but is dealt with directly under s. 14.

2.2.3 Obligations on public authorities

The primary responsibility for ensuring compliance with the ECHR is placed on 'public authorities' (s. 6 of the HRA 1998). Any public authority which acts in a way which is incompatible with a Convention right will be acting unlawfully, unless required to do so by primary legislation (s. 6(1) and (2) of the HRA 1998). 'Public authority' is not fully defined, but it will clearly cover the police, central or local government departments, health and education authorities, and individuals acting on their behalf. Section 6(3) provides that the phrase includes courts and tribunals. The implications of this are discussed further at 2.2.7.

Section 6 also makes it clear that in some cases it may be the type of action rather than the nature of the organization that is important. Section 6(3)(b) together with s. 6(5) provides that any person certain of whose functions are of a public nature will be a public authority, other than in relation to particular acts which are of a private nature. A university, for example, will be a public authority by virtue of s. 6(3)(b), since some of its activities (e.g., selecting, teaching, and examining students in relation to publicly funded degree courses) are almost certainly of a public nature. Actions taken in relation to privately funded research contracts, however, would probably not fall within the scope of the HRA 1998.

It was assumed in Parliament and has subsequently been confirmed by case law, that s. 6 creates two categories of public authority. The first is an authority which is 'public' in relation to all its activities, and must therefore comply with the ECHR in relation to everything it does. Bodies falling into this category include the police and government departments. These have come to be known as 'core' public authorities (see, e.g. Baroness Hale in *YL* v *Birmingham City Council* [2007] UKHL 27, [2008] 1 AC 95, para. 37). The second category is an authority which is 'public' only in relation to certain of its functions, and only needs to comply with the Convention in relation to those—such bodies have become known as 'hybrid' public authorities. The first category is, for example, required to pay attention to the ECHR in its dealings with employees under their contracts of employment; the second category is not. An alternative analysis might have been that in *all* cases the decision as to whether a body is acting as a public authority should depend on the function being exercised. This has not been accepted by the courts. The House of Lords in *YL* v *Birmingham City Council* has given clear support to the two-fold division into 'core' public authorities, and 'hybrid' authorities which are only 'public' in relation to certain activities. This must now be regarded as settled law.

There has been considerable case law on the meaning and scope of the concept of 'public authority', particularly in relation to 'hybrid' authorities, including two decisions of the House of Lords. The issue has also been the subject of two reports by the Parliamentary Joint Committee on Human Rights. The main issue of principle which has arisen from the cases and the reports is whether the test should be based on the institutional and organizational characteristics of the body under consideration, or whether the focus should be on the nature of the task being performed. The decision of the House of Lords in *YL* v *Birmingham City Council* appears to have settled that the latter approach is the one to be adopted.

The type of problem which arises in defining the limits of the concept of public authority was illustrated by the early decision in *Poplar Housing Regeneration Community Association Ltd* v *Donoghue* [2001] EWCA Civ 595, [2001] 4 All ER 604. The question was whether a housing association providing accommodation on behalf of a local authority was, in so doing, acting as a public authority within s. 6. The Court of Appeal held that the reference in s. 6(3)(b) to 'any person certain of whose functions are of a public nature' did not mean that any person acting on behalf of a public authority was itself a 'public authority'. It would depend on the nature of the act (s. 6(5) limits the scope of s. 6(3)(b) in relation to 'private' acts), and the relationship between the person and the public authority. The renting of property could be an act which was either public or private. For example, the provision of housing by a local authority in accordance with its statutory responsibilities is the act of a public authority. But 'where a small hotel provides bed and breakfast accommodation as a temporary measure, at the request of a housing authority that is under a duty to provide that accommodation' the hotel would not be acting as a public authority (para. 58, p. 619). As Lord Woolf explained (para. 65, p. 621):

> What can make an act, which would otherwise be private, public, is a feature or a combination of features which impose a public character or stamp on the act. Statutory authority for what is done can at least help to mark the act as being public; so can the extent of control over the function exercised by another body which is a public authority. The more closely the acts that could be of private nature are enmeshed in the activities of a public body, the more likely they are to be public. However the fact that the acts are supervised by a public regulatory body does not necessarily indicate that they are of a public nature.

Lord Woolf suggested the position is analogous to that involved in deciding which bodies are susceptible to judicial review, but it is also clear that there is not a complete overlap. The HRA 1998 and the ECHR are serving a different purpose from the procedure of judicial review, and their scope may therefore be wider. On the facts in the *Poplar* case, the Court of Appeal concluded that, taking into account the close links between the housing association and the local authority, the housing association was acting as a public authority.

The Court of Appeal, however, distinguished the *Poplar* case in its subsequent decision in *R (on the Application of Heather)* v *Leonard Cheshire Foundation* [2002] EWCA Civ 366, [2002] 2 All ER 936. A large charitable organization provided accommodation in care homes to residents whose rent was paid by a local authority. The Court of Appeal held that this was not sufficient to mean that the charity was acting as a 'public authority' in the provision of this accommodation. This may be contrasted with the decision in *R (on the Application of A)* v *Partnerships in*

Care Ltd [2002] EWHC 529 (Admin), [2002] 1 WLR 2610. Here the question was whether the managers of a private psychiatric hospital were exercising a 'public function' (therefore making their actions subject to judicial review) in relation to decisions as to the alteration of the care provided in one of its wards. Taking into account both the *Poplar* and the *Leonard Cheshire* decisions, Keith J held that, since the provision of care was directly regulated by the Nursing Homes and Mental Nursing Homes Regulations 1984, which required the provision of adequate staff and treatment facilities, the managers were acting as a 'public authority' as regards this area. He distinguished this area from decisions as to *treatment*.

A full consideration of the concept of 'public authority' was undertaken by the House of Lords in *Parochial Church Council of the Parish of Aston, etc v Wallbank* [2003] UKHL 37, [2003] 3 All ER 1213. The House, reversing the decision of the Court of Appeal, held that a Church of England parochial church council was not a public body for the purposes of the HRA 1998. It was a body concerned with the regulation of the affairs of the church, rather than exercising a public function. Actions taken to carry out repairs to part of a church could not be said to involve the exercise of a public function. This analysis emphasized that it is the nature of what the body is doing in any particular case, that is, its 'function', that is important, more than its institutional status. Strong support for the 'functional' rather than the 'institutional' approach was put forward by the Joint Committee on Human Rights (JCHR) in its 7th Report of 2003–04 ('The Meaning of Public Authority under the Human Rights Act' (2004), HL Paper 39/HC Paper 382). It argued that relying too much on the institutional links will have the effect of providing too limited an approach to the concept of 'public authority', with the decision being likely to rest on 'a number of relatively arbitrary criteria' (p. 52). It preferred the approach taken by the House of Lords in the *Aston* case with its emphasis on 'functions' rather than institutional relationships.

The Joint Committee returned to this issue in its 9th Report of Session 2006–07 ('The Meaning of Public Authority under the Human Rights Act' (2007), HL Paper 77/HC Paper 410). It strongly supported the approach taken in the *Aston* case, in contrast to some more recent decisions, such as *R (Beer)* v *Hampshire Farmer's Markets Ltd* [2003] EWCA Civ 1056, [2004] 1 WLR 233, which seemed to be reverting to the 'institutional analysis'. The Committee was also writing in anticipation of the House of Lords' reconsideration of the issue in a case involving care homes. It strongly advocated a broad approach to the concept of public authority, believing this to be in line with what Parliament had intended, and advocated a rejection of the much narrower approach adopted in cases such as the *Leonard Cheshire* decision.

The House of Lords' decision in this case is reported as *YL* v *Birmingham City Council* [2007] UKHL 27, [2008] 1 AC 95. It concerned the provision of care to an elderly woman. The care was provided by a privately run nursing home, operating as part of a commercial organization, but was paid for by the local authority. In addition to the parties, the House also heard submissions from counsel for the Secretary of State for Constitutional Affairs, Justice, Liberty, and the British Institute of Human Rights, and took written submissions on behalf of Help the Aged, the National Council on Ageing, and the Disability Rights Commission. The tenor of all these submissions, in line with the approach advocated by the Joint Committee, was that the House should adopt a broad test and find that an organization which provided care funded by a local authority should be treated as acting as a public authority for that purpose. In fact the majority of the House (it divided 3:2) rejected that suggestion. While fully supporting the 'functional' analysis, as opposed to that based on 'institutional' status, the majority supported the line taken in the *Leonard Cheshire* case. It took the view that the provision of care by a private company was essentially a contractual arrangement, and not the exercise of a public function. While the local authority had statutory obligations to ensure that care was provided, and would be acting as a public authority in relation to this, that did not apply to a private organization which organized the day-to-day care. A local authority was a 'core' public authority, and in all its activities it had to comply with the HRA 1998—this would include the day-to-day provision of care if it was undertaken directly by a local authority. The position was different, however, where that care was provided by a private body, which could make similar contractual arrangements with individuals and families, in relation to which the HRA 1998 would have no relevance. The minority of the House (Lord Bingham and Lady Hale) found that distinction unacceptable, and would have found for the claimant on this point.

Not surprisingly, given that the government supported the arguments presented to the House of Lords that the care home should be treated as a public authority, legislation was quickly introduced to amend the position. This is contained in the Health and Social Care Act 2008. Section 145 of the Act provides that:

> A person ('P') who provides accommodation, together with nursing or personal care, in a care home for an individual under arrangements made with P under the relevant statutory provisions is to be taken for the purposes of subsection (3)(b) of section 6 of the Human Rights Act 1998 ... to be exercising a function of a public nature in doing so.

'Care home' has the same meaning as in the Care Standards Act 2000, and the 'relevant statutory provisions' are ss 21(1)(a) and 26 of the National Assistance Act 1948 (which deal with the duty of local authorities to provide accommodation, either directly or through voluntary organizations).

As will be seen, this is a very specific reversal of the position following the House of Lords' decision in *YL* v *Birmingham* in relation to care homes. It has no wider implications for the approach to identifying public authorities. In this respect the approach of the majority in *YL* v *Birmingham* remains good law.

An earlier decision of the High Court in *Cameron* v *Network Rail Infrastructure Ltd* [2006] EWHC 1133 (QB), [2007] 3 All ER 241 would seem to fit well with this approach. The judge held that Network Rail, in providing maintenance services for the rail network, was not acting as a public authority. Operating a railway was not an inherently public function, and at the relevant time (the Potters Bar train crash of May 2002) Network Rail no longer had any statutory responsibility for safety.

There has also been a Court of Appeal decision following *YL* v *Birmingham*, which provides an indication of how it will be interpreted and applied. This is *R (Weaver)* v *London and Quadrant Housing Trust* [2009] EWCA Civ 587. In this case the Court of Appeal considered whether the termination of a tenancy in relation to social housing run by a trust, but subsidized by the local authority, was an act of a 'public authority'. The court, and in particular Elias LJ, placed much more emphasis than has been given in previous cases on s. 6(5), which provides that in relation to hybrid authorities acts of a private nature are not within the scope of the HRA 1998. As the court suggested this means that even if a body is found to be a hybrid authority, it is still necessary to look at the particular act under review to decide whether it was public or private. In this case, for example, it was conceded by the Trust that it was a public authority in so far as it had a power to obtain parenting orders or anti-social behaviour orders. This did not, however, decide the issue in relation to the exercise of its power to terminate a tenancy. In deciding that issue, Elias LJ considered first whether the provision of social housing by the Trust was the exercise of a private or public function. He noted that there was a significant element of public subsidy to the Trust, and that the Trust was in effect assisting the local authority to achieve its statutory duties and objectives (paras 68–9). This restricted the freedom of the Trust to allocate properties. The provision of subsidized housing (as opposed to simply providing housing) was the antithesis of commercial activity, and properly described as 'governmental'. The Trust was acting in the public interest and had charitable status, and the regulation to which it was subject was designed in part to further government policy with respect to a vulnerable group in society (para. 71). All of these factors, taken together, indicated that the Trust was, in providing social housing, fulfilling a public rather than a private function. In that context, the act of termination of the tenancy in this case was distinguishable from the similar power in *YL* v *Birmingham*. Here the act was so bound up with the public function of the provision of social housing that in itself it was the exercise of a public function (para. 76). It was distinguishable from the act of terminating a contract, for example, for the cleaning of windows of the Trust's properties, which would readily be seen as the exercise of a private function. Lord Collins agreed with Elias LJ; Rix LJ dissented. The decision was, therefore, that this particular action of terminating a tenancy in relation to social housing was the action of a public authority, and therefore needed to be compliant with the Convention rights, under the HRA 1998.

It will be seen from the above that the decision as to what is and is not a public authority is not a straightforward one. There is a strong subjective element, as indicated by this passage from Lord Mance's opinion in *YL* v *Birmingham* (para. 128):

> The centrally relevant words, 'functions of a public nature', are so imprecise in their meaning that one searches for a policy as an aid to interpretation. The identification of the policy is almost inevitably governed, at least to some extent, by one's notions of what the policy should be, and the policy so identified is then used to justify one's conclusion. Further, given that the question of whether section 6(3)(b) applies may often turn on a combination of factors, the relative weight to be accorded to each factor in a particular case is inevitably a somewhat subjective decision.

Given this subjectivity in the current position, it would be more satisfactory if there were a more general amendment of the Act, going beyond the specific provision relating to care homes in the Health and Social Care Act 2008, to provide clearer guidance to the courts.

Moving to more certain issues, s. 6(3) excludes from the definition of 'public authority' the two Houses of Parliament or 'a person exercising functions in connection with proceedings in Parliament'. The enactment of legislation is thus not within the Act (in line with the general policy of preserving Parliamentary sovereignty), nor are proceedings for contempt of Parliament. The exclusion did not apply, however, to the House of Lords acting in its judicial capacity (s. 6(4)). This is understandable: such an exclusion would have made a nonsense of the otherwise central requirement that courts take account of the HRA 1998 and the ECHR in reaching decisions.

Section 6(6) provides that, although a failure to act is included within the scope of the section, this does not apply to failures to introduce legislation. This is a very important limitation. It means that a government department will not be able to be held to be in breach of the Act simply because there is a gap in the law. An obvious example is the area of privacy (discussed in detail in chapter 6). It is well known that English law provides no general statutory protection for rights of privacy of the kind recognized by Art. 8 of the ECHR. A legal challenge under the HRA 1998 against the Home Office for its failure to provide such protection would, however, be doomed to failure, because of s. 6(6). This is of particular importance in relation to the potential for disputes between individuals relating to breaches of Convention rights. Although the ECHR is primarily concerned with rights as between the individual and the State, in some circumstances it has been used where the infringement has been by another private individual rather than a public authority. This concept of 'horizontal' as opposed to 'vertical' effect has been looked at in chapter 1 (1.7), in relation to the positive obligations imposed under Arts 2 and 3 of the ECHR. It is discussed further at 2.2.7. Under the ECHR case law intervention is achieved in such cases by reference to Art. 1, which, as we have seen, requires signatories to the Convention to 'secure to everyone within their jurisdiction the rights and freedoms defined in' the Convention. Thus, in the case of *A* v *United Kingdom* (1999) 27 EHRR 611 the 9-year-old victim's rights had been most directly infringed by his stepfather, who had beaten him with a garden cane. The UK government was found to be in breach of the ECHR, however, because the English law on offences against the person allowed a defence of reasonable chastisement in relation to such behaviour. In allowing this the government had failed to secure the right of the victim not to be subjected to inhuman and degrading treatment. This illustrates the fact that, although Art. 1 is not included in the Schedule to the HRA 1998, and cannot, therefore, be used to obtain a remedy under that Act, the same result may be achieved by arguing in particular that, for example, the defence of reasonable chastisement should be interpreted in the light of the ECHR so as not to apply to the behaviour in question. If that argument failed, however, the challenge to the gap in the law would have to be taken up via an application to Strasbourg, rather than in the domestic courts.

Following the decision in *A* v *United Kingdom*, the government at one point seemed to feel that the Court of Appeal's decision in *R* v *H* [2002] 1 Cr App R 7, redefining the matters to be taken into account in considering the defence of reasonable chastisement, meant that no further action was necessary. In the end, however, it did reform the law by s. 58 of the Children Act 2004, so that 'reasonable chastisement' can no longer be used as a defence in criminal or civil proceedings for an assault on a child, where the assault causes 'actual bodily harm' (as defined by case law on s. 47 of the Offences Against the Person Act 1861) or more serious injury.

2.2.4 **Proceedings, standing, and remedies**

We have seen that, in legal proceedings relating to the interpretation of legislation or the common law, at least insofar as it affects rights as between the individual and the State, a person can rely on the ECHR and its jurisprudence in support of his or her case. Can proceedings be initiated simply on the basis of alleged infringement of a Convention right, rather than being parasitic on some other action? This is dealt with by s. 7(1)(a) of the HRA 1998. This allows a person to bring proceedings 'in the appropriate court or tribunal' against a public authority which has acted or proposes to act in a way which is contrary to the ECHR. The 'appropriate court or tribunal' is to be determined 'in accordance with rules' (s. 7(2)). By virtue of s. 7(9) this means 'rules made for the purposes of the section' or 'rules of court'. Thus, in the absence of any specially created rules, the normal rules of court will apply.

Whether the ECHR is relied on in proceedings based on some other legal right, or in its own right, however, the person using it must be a 'victim' within the meaning of Art. 34 of the ECHR (s. 7(1), (7)). In *Taylor* v *Lancashire County Council* [2005] EWCA Civ 284, a claim that a provision of the Agricultural Holdings Act 1986 was discriminatory, and incompatible with the ECHR, was rejected because the claimant had not been adversely affected by the provision. Even if the action is for judicial review, standing in this context is to be determined by the definition of 'victim' rather than the normal rules applying to judicial review. Article 34 does not define 'victim' other than to state that it can be an individual, group of people, or non-governmental organization (which could include a private company). The European case law on the definition of a 'victim' indicates that the applicant must have been directly or indirectly affected by the alleged infringement of the ECHR. This means that 'pressure groups' or similar organizations probably will not have standing to bring actions under the HRA 1998, unless they can show that they are acting on behalf of specific individuals who are victims. This is in contrast to the position in relation to judicial review actions where the test of 'sufficient interest' means that representative actions are possible (see, e.g. *R* v *Secretary of State for Social Services, ex p Child Poverty Action Group* [1990] 2 QB 540; *R* v *Secretary of State for Social Security, ex p Joint Council for the Welfare of Immigrants* [1997] 1 WLR 275). The concept of victim has been held to cover those who are potentially at risk of an infringement of their rights, as in *Norris* v *Ireland* (1988) 13 EHRR 186 which concerned a gay man potentially affected by laws penalizing homosexual behaviour). It can also cover family members where the actual victim has died, either as a result of the alleged infringement (as in *McCann* v *United Kingdom* (1995) 21 EHRR 97), or after starting proceedings (as in *Loukanov* v *Bulgaria* (1997) 24 EHRR 121).

Where proceedings are brought under s. 7(1)(a) (i.e. independently of any other legal action) they must be started within one year of the act complained of, unless the court or tribunal concerned considers that a longer period is equitable having regard to all the circumstances (s. 7(5)).

In two important cases the House of Lords has considered the international scope of the HRA 1998. In *Jones* v *Ministry of the Interior* [2006] UKHL 26, [2007] 1 All ER 113 the claimants alleged that they had been tortured while being detained by the police or military in Saudi Arabia. The House held that the defendants (i.e. the authorities in Saudi Arabia) could rely on State immunity, as provided by s. 1(1) of the State Immunity Act 1978, and that such immunity was not disproportionate, nor incompatible with the Art. 6 of the ECHR right to a fair trial. The HRA 1998 could not, therefore, be used by the claimants. By contrast in *R (Al-Skeini)* v *Ministry of Defence* [2007] UKHL 26, [2007] 3 All ER 685 the claimants were Iraqi citizens complaining about the actions of British armed forces in Iraq. In each case a relative of one of the claimants had been killed. The House held that the HRA 1998 applied to acts of UK public authorities wherever they occurred within the jurisdiction of the United Kingdom. This was in line with the statement in Art. 1 of the ECHR imposing responsibility on a State in relation to all those within its jurisdiction. The House held that deaths which had occurred as a result of military action in Iraq did not necessarily fall within the jurisdiction of the United Kingdom, and most of the claims were dismissed. One of the deceased, however, had died while being held in custody by British forces in a military base in Iraq. This fell within the United Kingdom's jurisdiction and the relatives were therefore entitled to bring a claim under the HRA 1998. When the unsuccessful claimants took their case to Strasbourg, the ECtHR took a broader view of 'jurisdiction' (*Al-Skeini* v *United Kingdom* (2011) 53 EHRR 18). It held that jurisdiction outside a State's borders could arise in two situations: first, where State agents (e.g. soldiers) exercise authority and control over individuals, and second, where a State is exercising effective control over a whole area. In this case, although the actions took place outside British military bases, the security operations involved the soldiers exercising authority and control over individuals, and so the applicants did have standing to bring a claim against the United Kingdom for an alleged breach of Art. 2 (right to life) (see also 1.7.1, for further discussion of Art. 2).

The Court of Appeal in *R (on the Application of Smith)* v *Oxfordshire Assistant Deputy Coroner* [2009] EWCA Civ 441, held that where the victim was a soldier who had died from hyperthermia in a military base in Iraq, any inquest into the death was required to be compliant with Art. 2 of the ECHR.

It follows that the HRA 1998 can have relevance to actions which take place outside the United Kingdom, where the actions are those of a UK public authority, and take place in a situation over which the United Kingdom can be said to have jurisdiction (for a recent example, see *Ismail* v *Secretary of State for Defence*, [2013] EWHC 3032 (Admin) where Afghan prisoners of war being held by British troops in Afghanistan were entitled to the protection of the ECHR rights).

As regards remedies, the court or tribunal which finds a breach of a Convention right has a wide discretion. Section 8(1) provides that it 'may grant such relief or remedy, or make such order, within its powers as it considers just and appropriate'. Damages for past breaches, of Convention rights, and injunctions to restrain prospective or continuing breaches, are likely to be the most likely remedies sought and provided. As regards damages, however, s. 8 also contains some limiting provisions. First, damages can only be awarded by a court which has the power to award such compensation in civil proceedings (s. 8(3)). Thus, a Crown Court which finds that the police have acted in contravention of the ECHR as regards a defendant in a criminal trial has no power to award damages to the defendant. Second, the court or tribunal must be satisfied that, taking account of any other remedies or relief given and the consequences of the court or tribunal's decision, damages are necessary in order to provide 'just satisfaction' to the victim (s. 8(3)). The reference to 'just satisfaction' reflects the wording of Art. 41 of the ECHR, which is the provision giving the power to the ECtHR to award damages. The relevance of the ECHR and its jurisprudence in this context is further emphasized by s. 8(4) which requires the court or tribunal to take account of the principles applied by the Convention under Art. 41 in deciding whether to award damages, and if so how much. It has not been uncommon for the ECtHR to find that the decision that there has been a breach of a Convention right is sufficient without the need for monetary compensation beyond the costs of the action. (This has been acknowledged by Silber J in *R (N)* v *Secretary of State for the Home Department* [2003] EWHC 207 (Admin), [2003] HRLR 20, by the Court of Appeal in *Anufrijeva* v *Southwark London Borough Council* [2003] EWCA Civ 1406, [2003] 3 FCR 673, and by the House of Lords in *R (Greenfield)* v *Secretary of State for the Home Department* [2005] UKHL 14, [2005] 2 All ER 240.)

The assessment of damages for human rights violations has been considered in several cases under the HRA 1998. Different approaches have been adopted by different courts. In *R (Mamabakasa)* v *Secretary of State for the Home Department* [2003] EWHC 319 (Admin) it was suggested that an approach based on the compensation awarded by the Parliamentary Commissioner for the Administration (Ombudsman) would be the proper one. More commonly the approach has been on the same basis as in the law of tort, with non-pecuniary loss being compensated as it is in that area. That was the approach supported by the Law Commission in its report 'Damages Under the Human Rights Act' (Report No. 266, 2000) and was followed in *R (Bernard)* v *London Borough of Enfield* [2002] EWHC 2282 (Admin), [2003] HRLR 4. In a full consideration of the issue in *R (KB) MHRT* [2003] EWHC 193 (Admin), [2003] 2 All ER 209, Stanley Burnton J also concluded that this was the right approach, particularly since a breach of a Convention right may well also involve a tort—e.g. Art. 5 and false imprisonment. This view was confirmed by the Court of Appeal in *Anufrijeva* v *London Borough of Southwark*. The Court also noted that English courts ought to be at least as generous in awarding damages as the ECtHR, since otherwise the purpose of the HRA 1998 (reducing the need to take cases to Strasbourg) would be defeated. A more cautious note was sounded by the House of Lords in *R (Greenfield)* v *Secretary of State for the Home Department*. It held that, at least in cases involving infringement of Art. 6 rights (the right to a fair trial), the tort measure was not appropriate. The court should be guided much more by the approach of the ECtHR to such cases—which tended to be to make very modest awards of damages, or no award at all. More generally, there was no need in any case to go beyond what could be recovered at Strasbourg. The purpose of the HRA 1998 in 'bringing rights home' was to make the remedies that would have been available at Strasbourg available in the domestic courts, not to provide better remedies than would be obtained from the ECtHR (para. 19 of Lord Bingham's judgment).

2.2.5 Particular safeguards

Sections 11–13 of the HRA 1998 deal with some particular safeguards of human rights specifically preserved or emphasized. Section 11(a) provides that relying on a Convention right does not restrict any other right or freedom which the person concerned has under the law. Common law and statutory rights continue to exist alongside the ECHR. This will be of particular importance where the rights go beyond those conferred by the ECHR. In relation to discrimination on the grounds of race or sex, for example, the protection afforded by Art. 14 of the ECHR is narrower in scope than that contained in the Equality Act 2010 (see chapter 12). Section 11(a) confirms that those broader rights will still be available, even where a person bases a legal claim at least in part on the HRA 1998.

Section 11(b) similarly preserves the right to bring claims or proceedings which would be available apart from ss. 7 or 9 of the HRA 1998. This may be important in relation to the issue of standing. As we have seen, the ECHR and the HRA 1998 restrict the bringing of claims to those who are 'victims', with that word having a particular and relatively narrow definition. This will not, however, restrict other claims being brought alongside an HRA 1998 claim by those who have standing on some other basis (e.g. under the rules relating to judicial review) even if they fall outside the strict definition of 'victim' under the ECHR.

Section 12 refers to freedom of expression, and was added at a relatively late stage to meet concerns (probably unjustified) that the ECHR, and in particular the privacy protection given by Art. 8, might be used to restrict the press unduly. ECHR case law under Art. 10 (freedom of expression), however, has frequently made reference to the importance of press freedom in democratic societies, and there is no reason to assume that Art. 8 would automatically 'trump' such arguments. Nevertheless, s. 12(4) requires the courts to have 'particular regard to the importance of the Convention right to freedom of expression'. In addition, where the proceedings relate to material which is 'journalistic, literary or artistic', the court must have regard to the extent to which it has or is about to become available to the public, or to which it is or would be in the public interest for it to be published. The court must also have regard to 'any relevant privacy code'. The implications of this part of s. 12 are considered further in chapter 6 (6.9.2).

Section 12(2) and (3) addresses the situation of without-notice applications, and particularly those which might lead to the restriction of publication prior to trial. The subsections require that, generally, notice must be given to the other party before any such relief is granted, and that in any case publication should not be restrained unless the court is satisfied that the applicant is likely to be able to establish at trial that publication should not be allowed. The meaning of the word 'likely' in this section was considered by the House of Lords in *Cream Holdings Ltd* v *Bannerjee* [2004] UKHL 44, [2004] 4 All ER 617. The House disagreed with the Court of Appeal on the interpretation of the word. The Court of Appeal had suggested that it meant whether the claimant had a 'real prospect of success convincingly established', rather than simply 'more probable than not'. Lord Nicholls, giving the main judgment in the House of Lords, however, ruled that in general the approach to s. 12(3) of the HRA 1998 should be that an interim restraint order should not be made unless the applicant's prospects of success were 'sufficiently favourable' to justify an order being made. In most cases the test of 'sufficiently favourable' would be whether the applicant was probably ('more likely than not') going to succeed at trial. There would be some cases, however, where a lower standard would be appropriate—e.g. where the potential adverse consequences of disclosure would be particularly grave, or where a short-lived injunction was needed to enable the court to hear and give proper consideration to an application for interim relief. On the facts of the case before it, the grant of the injunction was not justified and the appeal against it was allowed.

Section 13 of the HRA 1998 was included following concerns by church organizations that it might otherwise restrict decisions taken on religious grounds—such as the refusal to allow gay couples to marry, or the requirement that teachers in church schools are members of the appropriate religion. The section provides that, where a court's determination of a question under the HRA 1998 might 'affect the exercise by a religious organisation...of the Convention right to freedom of thought, conscience and religion, it must have particular regard to the importance of that right'. It is difficult to see that this does in fact add anything in practice to the protection afforded by Art. 9 of the ECHR. This specifically refers to the freedom of a person, 'either alone or in company with others and in public or in private, to manifest his religion or belief in worship, teaching, practice and observance'. This freedom is only subject to limitations prescribed by law and necessary in a democratic society:

> ...in the interests of public safety, for the protection of public order, health or morals, or for the protection of the rights and freedoms of others.

This type of limitation, discussed at greater length elsewhere (see chapter 12 (12.1.2)), means that only restrictions which are 'proportionate' and designed to meet a 'pressing social need' will be permitted. Although it is true that Art. 14 prohibits discrimination in the exercise of Convention rights on grounds of religion, and there might be situations where this would prevail over Art. 9, in practice it was always unlikely that the worst fears of the churches would have been realized. Even if there was a risk that they might, the wording of s. 13 (simply requiring a court to have 'particular regard' to freedom of religion) is not really strong enough to make much impact on the determination of the issue.

2.2.6 Derogations and reservations

The ECHR has always allowed States to make derogations from, or reservations to the Convention rights, in order to deal with emergencies or other special circumstances. A derogation disapplies certain Convention rights completely; a reservation qualifies the right. The UK government, for example, in 1988 made a derogation from the Convention rights as to detention before charge because of the threat of terrorism related to Northern Ireland. This derogation was lifted in April 2001. A further derogation in response to terrorism was, however, made in November 2001, in the wake of the terrorist attacks in New York on 11 September 2001. This allowed for detention without trial in certain circumstances, but was quashed by the House of Lords in *A* v *Secretary of State for the Home Department* [2004] UKHL 56, [2005] 3 All ER 169 (see further chapter 10 (10.6.1)). There are no current derogations by the UK. The only reservation to date by the UK government was made in 1952 in relation to the right to education contained in the First Protocol to the ECHR. This had the effect that the right is guaranteed 'only so far as it is compatible with the provision of efficient instruction and training, and the avoidance of unreasonable public expenditure' (Sch. 3, Pt. II to the HRA 1998).

Sections 14–17 set out procedural matters relating to derogations and reservations, and create the concept of 'designated' derogations and reservations.

The power to initiate such derogations and reservations is given to the relevant Secretary of State, by order. A derogation must be approved by both Houses of Parliament within 40 days of the order (s. 16(3)–(5) of the HRA 1998), otherwise it will lapse. There is no comparable provision in relation to reservations, which are therefore entirely a matter of executive decision (though they must be reviewed by the appropriate Minister every five years—s. 17 of the HRA 1998).

2.2.7 'Vertical' or 'Horizontal' effect

The main purpose of the ECHR is to protect individuals against infringements of their rights by States or State organizations. This is the so-called 'vertical' effect of the ECHR. Thus, it is not generally concerned with rights as between two individuals. Nevertheless, the ECtHR has been prepared to intervene where the domestic law has failed to provide adequate protection for the individual as against other citizens—as where the domestic law against assault cannot be used by the victim, or provides too wide a defence for the attacker (as in *X and Y v The Netherlands* (1986) 8 EHRR 235 and *A v United Kingdom* (1999) 27 EHRR 611). In addition it has been argued that the fact that s. 6 of the HRA 1998 includes courts within the definition of a 'public authority', means that they are obliged more generally to protect individuals from infringement of their human rights by other individuals (the so-called 'horizontal' effect). The argument is that, since the court, as a public authority, has to take decisions in line with the ECHR obligations, this requires it to develop the law in new ways. If it fails to provide protection where an individual's rights have been infringed—even if this is by another individual rather than by a public authority—it will itself be failing in its duty as a public authority. A particular area where this argument was raised prior to the HRA 1998 coming into force was in relation to the protection of privacy (which is recognized under Art. 8). It was suggested that, although English law had previously not recognized any general right of privacy, the HRA 1998 would require it do so as between individuals, or in particular as between an individual and the press, and that this would involve accepting the possible 'horizontal' effect of the rights under the Act. In fact, as will be seen from the full discussion of this area in chapter 6, the courts managed to sidestep this issue by developing privacy rights in the context of the established law on breach of confidence. By using their powers under the HRA 1998 to reinterpret the common law, they did not need to consider the 'horizontal'/'vertical' question. The general point about the effect of s. 6 and how courts will approach their role as a public authority still awaits full clarification. The narrow approach will be to say that s. 6 simply requires them to act in accordance with the ECHR in relation to the conduct and operation of trials and legal proceedings. The broad approach will be to say that the courts should develop the law and recognize new rights and obligations as between individuals, as being in the spirit of the HRA 1998 and the new recognition of the importance of human rights—that is, courts should give the HRA 1998 and the ECHR full 'horizontal' effect.

A final issue which needs to be noted in relation to the approach of English courts in applying European case law is what account they will take of the 'margin of appreciation'. This concept has developed in the ECHR case law as a result of the fact that the Convention is an international treaty. The ECtHR has long recognized that in many areas there are different cultures and traditions, and that it is not appropriate for the Strasbourg Court in every area to set absolute standards for every country in the Council of Europe. This has been applied, for instance, in the area of controls over obscene publications, where the fact that a particular book was sold without control in many countries of Europe did not mean that restricting its availability in England involved an unacceptable restriction of the publisher's freedom of expression (*Handyside* v *United Kingdom* (1976) 1 EHRR 737). The Strasbourg Court thus applied the 'margin of appreciation' allowing, in effect, a discretion to the State to decide exactly how far rights should be protected within its own jurisdiction. Clearly it would be inappropriate for English courts applying the HRA 1998 to adopt such an approach. They have to decide what standard is to be applied, and to refer to a 'margin of appreciation' would be an abnegation of this responsibility (see the comments of Buxton LJ in *R* v *Stafford Justices, ex p Imbert* [1999] 2 Crim App Rep 276). The English courts do, however, need to be aware of the way in which the European Court uses this concept in considering the European case law. Just because the Court, applying the margin of appreciation, has held that in a particular State there was no breach of the ECHR, does not mean that the English court should necessarily take the same view in relation to the United Kingdom. It is free to decide that, although the context of the way in which the infringement of rights occurred in the other State led the Strasbourg Court to a particular conclusion, a stricter protection of rights should operate in this country. This also illustrates another important point about the domestic application of the ECHR and its case law. That is, that the ECHR provides only a *minimum* level of protection, and there is no reason why an English court should not decide that this minimum provides an insufficient level of protection for an individual's rights. The court should approach its task by looking at the broad objectives of the ECHR, interpreting it as a living instrument, capable of different interpretations in different times and in different contexts, but providing the framework upon which the United Kingdom can develop its own system of human rights protection. In practice, however, the English courts have been reluctant to adopt such an approach, taking their lead from Lord Bingham's statement in *R (Ullah)* v *Special Adjudicator* [2004] UKHL 26, [2004] 2 AC 323 that while legislatures may provide protections of rights that go beyond what is required, it is not appropriate for courts to do so by adopting their own interpretation of Convention rights, because (para. 20):

> ...the meaning of the Convention should be uniform throughout the states party to it. The duty of national courts is to keep pace with the Strasbourg jurisprudence as it evolves over time: no more, but certainly no less.

This caution has also been applied to situations where there is no clear ruling from the ECtHR on an issue (see *Ambrose* v *Harris* [2011] UKSC 43; [2011] 1 WLR 2435) but has been the subject of strong academic criticism (see, e.g. E. Bjorge [2013] CLJ 289).

2.2.8 Retrospectivity of the HRA 1998

To what extent does the HRA 1998 apply to actions taken before 2 October 2000? The answer to this question is important to those whose rights were allegedly infringed before that date, but who, for example, still have an appeal route open.

Should the appeal body take into account the HRA 1998 and the Convention rights? As time passes, this issue becomes less important in practice, but is likely to remain an issue there may still be come cases where the issue will arise. The position is governed by s. 22 of the HRA 1998, as interpreted by the House of Lords.

2.2.8.1 The statutory provisions

The issue of retrospectivity is dealt with by s. 22(4) of the HRA 1998. This states:

> Paragraph (b) of subsection (1) of section 7 applies to proceedings brought by or at the instigation of a public authority whenever the act in question took place; but otherwise that subsection does not apply to an act taking place before the coming into force of that section.

The relevant passage of s. 7(1) is as follows:

> A person who claims that a public authority has acted...in a way which is made unlawful by s. 6(1) may...(b) rely on the Convention right or rights concerned in any legal proceedings, but only if he is...a victim of the unlawful act.

Section 6(1) is the provision which makes it unlawful for any public authority to act in a way which is incompatible with a Convention right.

What is the effect of these provisions? It is clear that they are intended only to allow the Act to be used as a defence and not as the basis of a claim. Thus, it is only where someone is or has been the subject of legal action by a public authority that the retrospective aspect of s. 22(4) will apply. In *R (Hurst)* v *London Northern District Coroner* [2007] UKHL 13, [2007] 2 All ER 1035, the House of Lords held that the holding of an inquest did not constitute the bringing of proceedings under s. 22(4). A relative of the deceased challenging the procedure at an inquest was bringing an action against a public authority. The right to initiate actions against a public authority under s. 7(1)(a) is covered by the last part of s. 22(4) which states that, other than in relation to the actions under s. 7(1)(b), 'that subsection' (that is, s. 7(1)) 'does not apply to an act taking place before the coming into force of that section'. In *Hurst's* case this precluded HRA 1998 action by the relative, since the death occurred before the section came into force.

The wording of s. 22(4) taken at face value would have suggested, despite its limitations, a fairly broad scope for the HRA 1998 to have a retrospective effect. In fact, the section has received a relatively restrictive interpretation by the House of Lords. In *R* v *Lambert* [2001] UKHL 37 the House held that standards under the Convention (e.g. Art. 6) could not be applied in relation to an appeal in a criminal case where the trial occurred prior to the HRA coming into force. This had significance not only for standard appeals, but also for the work of the Criminal Cases Review Commission, which looks at alleged cases of miscarriages of justice, sometimes many decades old, and has the power to refer them to the Court of Appeal for reconsideration. Although this restrictive approach to s. 22 was later doubted (see *R* v *Kansal (No. 2)* [2001] UKHL 62), the decision in *Lambert* remains good law, albeit of limited practical importance.

2.3 **The interpretation of legislation**

2.3.1 **Statements of compatibility**

Section 19 of the HRA 1998 requires that, in relation to every government Bill, the Minister in charge of it must make a statement about the Bill's compatibility with the Convention rights. The statement must be made before Second Reading (s. 19(1)) and be in writing (s. 19(2)). There is no such obligation in relation to subordinate legislation or Private Members' Bills. The statement will either be that the Bill is thought to be compatible (a 'statement of compatibility': s. 19(1)(a)), or that, although a statement of compatibility cannot be made, 'the government nevertheless wishes the House to proceed with the Bill' (s. 19(1)(b)).

Current practice is for the statement to be included on the cover of the published version of the Bill. Such statements are not very informative. The one attached to the Terrorism Bill in 2005, for example, simply stated that 'Mr Secretary Clarke has made the following statement under section 19(1)(a) of the Human Rights Act 1998: In my view the provisions of the Terrorism Bill are compatible with the Convention rights'.

There has been only one reported judicial pronouncement on the effect of a statement of compatibility and this was generally dismissive of their significance as far as the courts are concerned. In *R v A* [2001] UKHL 25, [2001] 3 All ER 1, Lord Hope commented (para. 69, p. 24):

> These statements may serve a useful purpose in Parliament. They may also be seen as part of the parliamentary history, indicating that it was not Parliament's intention to cut across a convention right.... No doubt they are based on the best advice that is available. But they are no more than expressions of opinion by the minister. They are not binding on the court, nor do they have any persuasive authority.

It is certainly true that the issue of a s. 19(1)(a) statement is no guarantee that the legislation is in fact compatible with the Convention rights. The Terrorism Bill which became the Terrorism Act 2000 had a statement of compatibility attached to it, but the ECtHR has subsequently found at least one of its provisions incompatible with the Convention (see chapter 10 (10.4.1)). The main purpose of the s. 19(1)(a) statements of compatibility may therefore be said to be to try to ensure that proper account is taken of the Convention rights during the passage of legislation. There is a limitation on their usefulness, however, in that they will only apply to the Bill as it stood at the time that the statement was first made. When, as is inevitably the case with almost all Bills, amendments are made, and provisions are added by the government or otherwise, there is no provision for any statement of compatibility in relation to these changes.

The alternative to a 'statement of compatibility' under s. 19(1)(a) is the statement which recognizes the incompatibility but indicates that the government still wishes to proceed (s. 19(1)(b)). This was used in relation to the Bill which became the Communications Act 2003. The Secretary of State for Culture, Media, and Sport attached the following statement to the Bill:

> I am unable (but only because of clause 309) to make a statement that, in my view, the provisions of the Communications Bill are compatible with the Convention rights. However, the Government nevertheless wishes the House to proceed with the Bill.

Clause 309 related to the power of OFCOM to prohibit broadcast advertisements of a 'political nature'. It was felt that this might infringe Art. 10 of the ECHR. In the event, when the House of Lords came to consider the clause, which became s. 321 of the Communications Act 2003, in *R (on the application of Animal Defenders International)* v *Secretary of State for Culture, Media and Sport* [2008] UKHL 15, [2008] 1 AC 1312, it held that, while the section engaged Art. 10, the restrictions on political broadcasting which it contained were, in the case before it, 'necessary in a democratic society', and therefore not incompatible with the ECHR.

It is not clear what effect a statement of incompatibility under s. 19(1)(b) would have on the interpretation provisions of s. 3 (see 2.3.2). There is nothing in the HRA 1998 to require it to have any effect; nevertheless it must be likely that, if such a statement is made, the courts will not strain as hard as they otherwise might to find an interpretation which is compatible with the ECHR.

The incompatibility statement was not used, perhaps surprisingly, in relation to the Anti-terrorism, Crime, and Security Act 2001, in relation to which a derogation had to be made from Art. 5 of the ECHR because of the provisions as to extended detention of suspected international terrorists (see chapter 10 (10.6.1)). Nevertheless, the s. 19 statement on the front of the Bill simply stated that the view of Mr Blunkett was that its provisions were compatible with the Convention rights.

2.3.2 Human Rights Act 1998, s. 3

Section 3 of the HRA 1998 imposes a duty on courts to read and give effect to both primary and subordinate legislation in a way which is compatible with Convention rights 'so far as it is possible to do so'. Prior to the HRA 1998's coming into force this was an area for speculation as to how the courts would react. Would they be prepared to adopt a more flexible approach to statutory interpretation than in the past, in order to try to make legislation compatible with the ECHR? Or would they be forced into making large numbers of declarations of incompatibility under s. 4 of the HRA 1998? As will be seen, there has been significant use of both powers, though at times it has been unclear which should take precedence. The use of s. 3 will be considered first. The situations in which s. 4 has been used are dealt with at 2.3.3.4.

2.3.3 The courts' response

The attitude towards s. 3 which has been adopted by the courts is illustrated by the following comments of Lord Steyn in *R* v *A* [2001] UKHL 25, [2001] 3 All ER 1 (para. 44):

> ...the interpretative obligation under s. 3 of the 1998 Act is a strong one. It applies even if there is no ambiguity in the language in the sense of the language being capable of two different meanings.... In accordance with the will of Parliament as reflected in

> s. 3 it will sometimes be necessary to adopt an interpretation which linguistically may appear strained. The techniques to be used will not only involve the reading down of express language in a statute but also the implication of provisions. A declaration of incompatibility is a measure of last resort. It must be avoided unless it is plainly impossible to do so.

This suggested that s. 3 introduced a completely new element to the process of statutory interpretation when Convention rights are in issue. In particular, a strained interpretation of the language of a statute, or the implication of matters into it, thus rendering it compatible with the ECHR, is far preferable to the issuing of a declaration of incompatibility.

It is not possible here to deal in detail with all the cases that have considered the operation of s. 3 in relation to the interpretation of statutory provisions. Three House of Lords' decisions on the issue will be looked at first, and then two cases where s. 3 has been used to provide a solution to a procedural problem. This section will conclude with a brief look at some cases where the courts have found that statutes are not incompatible with Convention rights.

2.3.3.1 Section 3 in the House of Lords

The first of the leading House of Lords authorities on the application of s. 3 is *R v A* [2001] UKHL 25, [2001] 3 All ER 1. This case concerned the rules relating to the cross-examination of the complainant in rape cases. This is a matter on which there has been considerable concern, particularly concerning the way in which women complainants have been questioned about their previous sexual behaviour. In order to deal with some of these concerns Parliament enacted in the Youth Justice and Criminal Evidence Act 1999 (1999 Act) some strict rules as to when such questioning might be allowed, thus removing much of the judge's discretion on the issue. The appellant in this case had been charged with rape. His defence was that the complainant had consented, or even if she had not, that he had believed that she had consented. His counsel sought permission under the provisions of the 1999 Act to cross-examine the complainant about an alleged sexual relationship with the defendant in the three weeks before the alleged rape. The judge ruled that such cross-examination was prohibited by s. 41 of the 1999 Act, which does not allow questioning about the complainant's previous sexual relationships other than in strictly limited circumstances. One of these (under s. 41(3)(c)) is that the issue was that of consent, and the behaviour to which the questioning will relate is 'so similar (i) to any sexual behaviour of the complainant which... [it is alleged]... took place as part of the event' which is the subject of the charge, 'or (ii) to any other sexual behaviour of the complainant which... took place at or about the same time as that event, that the similarity cannot reasonably be explained as a coincidence'. The judge, however, ruled that the defendant's proposed questioning did not fall within this.

The House of Lords held that there was a risk of these restrictions interfering with the defendant's right to a fair trial under Art. 6. The provisions of the 1999 Act and in particular s. 41(3)(c), should, therefore, be read under s. 3 of the HRA 1998 'as subject to the implied provision that evidence or questioning which is required to ensure a fair trial under Art. 6 of the ECHR should not be treated as inadmissible'

(Lord Steyn, para. 45, p. 18). The effect of the decision was (Lord Steyn, para. 46, p. 18, in a formulation with which all the other members specifically agreed):

> ...that under s. 41(3)(c) of the 1999 Act, construed where necessary by applying the interpretative obligation under s. 3 of the 1998 Act, and due regard always being paid to the importance of seeking to protect the complainant from indignity and from humiliating questions, the test of admissibility is whether the evidence (and questioning in relation to it) is nevertheless so relevant to the issue of consent that to exclude it would endanger the fairness of the trial under Art. 6 of the Convention. If this test is satisfied the evidence should not be excluded.

This approach, despite Lord Steyn's reference to it as a 'reading' of the statutory provisions, clearly goes beyond giving a particular meaning to the words of the statute. Rather, it requires the effect of a particular provision to be limited by consideration of Art. 6. It is as if the statutory provisions were to be read as having attached to them the qualification 'subject to Art. 6 of the ECHR'. It seems, therefore, that it would be more appropriate to regard this approach as falling within the s. 3 reference to 'giving effect' to statutory provisions in a way that is compatible with the ECHR, as opposed to interpreting the language in a particular way. The particular decision in R v A is open to criticism in that it can be argued to be clearly departing from the intention of Parliament to reduce the discretion of the judge as to the admissibility of evidence in rape cases. Rather than interpreting s. 43 in a way which provides clear guidelines (even if those might extend the scope for admissibility slightly wider than Parliament intended), the decision has been put back fully to the judge to decide on the basis of what is 'fair' within Art. 6. The decision also leaves the field wide open for a defendant against whom a judge has ruled that evidence is inadmissible to challenge this on appeal by arguing that the judge's decision did not comply with Art. 6. The result of this case, therefore, while understandable in terms of what the House of Lords was trying to achieve, does not suggest that it is likely to produce an overall reduction of the unsatisfactory aspects of the current law on rape.

The second case to consider is more directly concerned with the way in which the words of a statute are read, but also shows the House of Lords taking a fairly expansive view of the scope of its powers under s. 3 of the HRA 1998. In R v Lambert [2001] UKHL 37, [2001] 3 All ER 577, the appeal concerned a defendant who had been charged with the possession of cocaine, contrary to the Misuse of Drugs Act 1971. He claimed that he did not know that the bag that he was carrying contained cocaine or any other controlled drug, and wished to rely on the defence under s. 28 of that Act. This provides that, where a person has been proved to have factual possession of a controlled drug, it is then up to that person to prove 'that he neither believed nor suspected nor had reason to suspect that the substance or product in question was a controlled drug' (s. 28(3)(b)(i)). The trial judge directed the jury, in accordance with the accepted view at the time, that this meant that there was a burden of proof on the defendant to establish this defence on the balance of probabilities. The defendant appealed on the basis that this ruling was incompatible with Art. 6 of the ECHR. As is noted (see 2.2.9.2), the House dismissed the appeal on the basis that the HRA 1998 did not apply to appeals from convictions which occurred prior to 2 October 2000. Nevertheless, it went on to consider the substance of the defendant's arguments on compatibility. It accepted that the judge's interpretation of s. 28 was no longer acceptable in the light of the rights given to defendants by Art. 6 of the ECHR, and in particular the presumption of innocence recognized by Art. 6(2). The section could only be rendered compatible by reading it as imposing simply an *evidential* burden on the defendant, rather than a burden of proof. The words 'prove' in s. 28 should, therefore, be read as meaning 'give sufficient evidence to raise an issue'.

The approach in this case is much more a 'reading' of the statutory provision than that taken in *R v A*. What the House is doing in *Lambert* is to say that a particular word should be read as having a particular meaning, even though this is in conflict with its natural meaning, and the way that it has previously been interpreted. Nevertheless the meaning was a *possible* one, and since it had the effect of making the statutory provision compatible it was to be preferred.

There was a series of cases subsequent to *Lambert*, taking varying views as to whether it was correct to interpret a provision in a criminal statute which appears to impose a burden of proof on the defence as only requiring the defence to raise the issue. The position was reviewed by the House of Lords in *Sheldrake v DPP* [2004] UKHL 43, [2005] 1 All ER 237. The case dealt with appeals in two cases, dealing with two statutory provisions, one concerned with a road traffic offence, and the other concerned with an offence under the Terrorism Act 2000. In *Sheldrake* itself, the case concerned provisions of the Road Traffic Act 1988 concerned with drunk driving. Under s. 5(2) of the Act, if a person is found in charge of a motor vehicle with excess of alcohol in his or her blood, it is a defence for him or her to prove that there was no likelihood of him or her driving while still over the limit. The Divisional Court, following *Lambert*, held that s. 5(2) prima facie placed a burden of proof on the defendant. This would, however, be incompatible with Art. 6(2).

The Court therefore interpreted s. 5(2) as imposing simply an evidential burden on the defendant. The House of Lords overturned this decision. It held that the task of the court was 'never to decide whether a reverse burden should be imposed on the defendant, but always to assess whether a burden enacted by Parliament unjustifiably infringes the presumption of innocence' (para. 31, per Lord Bingham). Reviewing the relevant case law of the ECtHR Lord Bingham concluded that (para. 21):

> ...the Convention does not outlaw presumptions of fact or law, but requires that these should be kept within reasonable limits and should not be arbitrary. It is open to states to define the constituent elements of a criminal offence, excluding the requirement of *mens rea*. But the substance and effect of any presumption adverse to the defendant must be examined and must be reasonable. Relevant to any judgment will be the opportunity given to the defendant to rebut the presumption, maintenance of the rights of the defence, flexibility in the application of the presumption, retention by the court of a power to assess the evidence, the importance of what is at stake and the difficulty which a prosecutor may face in the absence of a presumption.

Applying this approach to s. 5(2) of the Road Traffic Act 1988, Lord Bingham took the view that, while it infringed the presumption of innocence, it clearly had a legitimate objective—i.e. 'the prevention of death, injury and damage caused by unfit drivers' (para. 41). Was it, then, an 'acceptable' infringement, applying the tests set out in the paragraph above? Lord Bingham was of the view that it was. The likelihood of the defendant driving was 'so closely conditioned by his own knowledge and state of mind at the material time as to make it much more appropriate for him to prove on the balance of probabilities that he would not have been likely to drive than for the prosecutor to prove, beyond reasonable doubt, that he would' (para. 41). The imposition of the legal burden on the defendant did not go beyond what was necessary.

The other appeal which the House considered in *Sheldrake* ran alongside; the offence of belonging to a 'proscribed organisation' under s. 11 of the Terrorism Act 2000. Where a person has been proved to be a member of such an organization, s. 11(2) provides a defence if the defendant proves that he or she became a member before proscription and has taken no active part in the organization post-proscription. The Court of Appeal held that s. 11(2) did not relate to something which was an element of the offence under s. 11(1), but merely provided an exception to it. Therefore Art. 6(2) was not infringed, but even if it had been, the infringement was 'justified and proportionate' to the legitimate aims of the legislation. The House of Lords disagreed. Lord Bingham noted (para. 51) that a person innocent of any blameworthy conduct could fall within s. 11(1). Requiring such a person to prove a defence would contravene the presumption of innocence. The defendant would also be put in the difficult position of having to prove a negative—i.e. that he or she had not had any involvement with the organization at the relevant time. Moreover, the potential penalty was severe—imprisonment for up to 10 years. The section should therefore be read as only imposing an evidential burden on the defendant.

An earlier, and more restrictive, House of Lords consideration of s. 3 occurred in *In Re S (FC)* [2002] UKHL 10, 14 March 2002. The case concerned the provisions regarding the making of care orders under the Children Act 1989. The challenge under the HRA 1998 was that the Act provided that, once a care order had been made in favour of a local authority, the court could not then intervene, even if the procedures which it had been agreed would take place under the care order were not put into effect. There were allegations that this led to breaches of Arts 8 and 6 of the ECHR. The Court of Appeal found that the relevant provisions of the Children Act 1989 were prima facie incompatible with the Convention rights, but that under s. 3 it was justifiable to read into the Act a power in the court to require a report on progress. The House of Lords, with Lord Nicholls giving the leading speech, held that this was an unacceptable use of s. 3. The purpose of s. 3 was interpretation, not legislation. Nevertheless, he recognized that the boundary between the two was sometimes difficult to draw. However, he concluded that (para. 40):

> For present purposes it is sufficient to say that a meaning which departs substantially from a fundamental feature of an Act of Parliament is likely to have crossed the boundary between interpretation and amendment. This is especially so where the departure has important practical repercussions which the court is not equipped to evaluate.

The approach taken by the Court of Appeal in trying to use s. 3 to produce what Lord Nicholls saw as a change in a fundamental feature of the Children Act 1989 (that is, the fact that the parental responsibilities of a local authority should be left to it to carry out without interference from the courts once a care order has been made) went beyond what was permitted.

The decision in *In Re S (FC)* does not conflict with the views on the application of s. 3 expressed in *R v A*, *R v Lambert*, or *Sheldrake* and the principles which they applied should be regarded as still indicating the way in which the courts should approach their task under s. 3. As indicated, however, it might be argued that *R v A* did change a fundamental aspect of the law of evidence in rape cases, as deliberately determined by Parliament, and that Lord Nicholls' comments quoted above might be thought to lead to the conclusion that this went beyond what was acceptable. There is no indication in his speech, however, that he had any doubts about the approach taken in *R v A*. *In Re S* shows, however, that the House will not be prepared to sanction 'interpretations' which result in the creation of new rights and responsibilities where the consequences of these may not have been thought through, or may give rise to difficulties in practice.

Further confirmation of the commitment of the courts to a bold approach to the use of s. 3 comes from *Ghaidan* v *Mendoza* [2004] UKHL 30, [2004] 3 All ER 411. The case concerned para. 2 of Sch. 1 to the Rent Act 1977. This allows the 'spouse' of a protected tenant to succeed to the tenancy on the death of the tenant. The claimant argued that the provision should be applied to partners who were of the same sex, and not just to husbands and wives or people living together as husband and wife (para. 2(2) of Sch. 1). The House of Lords had held prior to the HRA 1998 that such an interpretation was impossible: *Fitzpatrick* v *Sterling Housing Association* [1999] 4 All ER 705. The question was whether the enactment of the HRA 1998 required a different approach, and in particular whether s. 3 would allow for the interpretation put forward by the claimant. The House found, first, that the provisions of the Schedule, if interpreted literally, unjustifiably discriminated between heterosexual and homosexual couples. They were therefore incompatible with Art. 8 of the ECHR, read with Art. 14. The question, then, was whether the paragraph could be read, using s. 3 of the HRA 1998, so as to apply to homosexual couples. The majority of the House thought that it could. Lord Nicholls indicated that there were limits to what could be done using s. 3. In particular, 'the meaning imported by application of s. 3 must be compatible with the underlying thrust of the legislation being construed' (para. 33). Subject to this, however, a court could, by using s. 3, modify the meaning and effect of primary and secondary legislation (para. 32). In this case (para. 35 (emphasis added)):

> ...the social policy underlying the...extension of security of tenure...to the survivors of couples *living together* as husband and wife [that is, in addition to those who are actually married] is equally applicable to the survivor of homosexual couples living together in a close and stable relationship.

In other words, if 'living together' rather than 'marriage' was the criterion for survivorship, there was no basis for distinguishing between heterosexual and homosexual couples.

As noted, the case indicates the courts' continuing preparedness to use a bold and purposive approach to its interpretation powers under s. 3 of the HRA 1998.

2.3.3.2 **Section 3 and procedural issues**

In two reported cases s. 3 has been used to resolve issues of procedure. In *Cachia v Faluyi* [2001] EWCA Civ 998, the court was concerned with the interpretation of the Fatal Accidents Act 1976. The situation was that the claimant's wife had been killed in a road accident in 1988. In 1991, C issued a writ under the Fatal Accidents Act 1976 on behalf of his wife's estate and her children claiming damages from the defendant who had been driving the car which had hit C's wife. This writ was never served. In 1997, following a change of solicitors, a fresh writ was issued, again claiming damages on behalf of C's wife's children. Their claim was not barred by the relevant limitation period, but the defendant relied on s. 2(3) of the Fatal Accidents Act 1976 which states that '[n]ot more than one action shall lie for and in respect of the same subject matter of complaint'. There was clear previous authority that 'action' encompasses the issue of a writ, even if it has not been served. The Court of Appeal, however, held that to prevent the children bringing their claim in these circumstances would involve an infringement of their right to a trial under Art. 6. Although the ECtHR recognizes the validity of some forms of limitation period or other restrictions on access to the courts (e.g. in relation to vexatious litigants), none of these applied here. In this case, the restriction resulting from s. 2(3) was no more than a 'procedural quirk' (para. 19, p. 197) and did not serve any legitimate aim. Using its powers under s. 3 the court held that 'action' in s. 2(3) should be read to mean 'served process', so that the children's claim was not barred. As Brooke LJ concluded (para. 21, p. 197): 'This is a very good example of the way in which the enactment of the 1998 Act now enables English judges to do justice in a way which was not previously open to us'.

Goode v *Martin* [2001] EWCA 1899, [2002] 1 All ER 620 is also a case concerned with the issue of restrictions on access to the courts. In this case the statutory provisions were contained in secondary legislation, namely the Civil Procedure Rules 1998 (SI 1998/3132) (CPR 1998), rather than in a statute. The claimant had been injured in a boating accident in August 1996. In October 1997, she issued a writ against the defendant, the owner of the boat. A defence was served in November 1997, and then an amended defence, which for the first time gave the defendant's explanation of how the accident occurred, in February 1999. The claimant then wished to serve an amended claim, relying on the facts revealed in the defendant's amended defence. This was in April 2000, however, which was eight months after the expiry of the statutory limitation period (in August 1999). Such an amended claim was only allowable by virtue of CPR 1998, r. 17.4(2). This permits a court to allow an amended claim outside the limitation period 'only if the new claim arises out of the same facts or substantially the same facts as a claim in respect of which the party applying for permission has already claimed a remedy in the proceedings'. The defendant argued that the claimant's amended claim did not meet this test, as it was based on different facts to her earlier claim (albeit facts raised by the defendant). The claim was struck out on this ground by the Master and this was confirmed by the High Court. The Court of Appeal, however, considered that the position was affected by the HRA 1998. The application of the rule contained in CPR 1998, r. 17 had no legitimate aim when applied to the facts of the case. The claimant ought to be able to adopt the version of events put forward by the defendant and argue that even on that basis he had been negligent. It was, therefore, appropriate for the court to use the technique of interpretation under s. 3 of the

HRA as identified by Lord Steyn in *R* v *A*. Thus, it was permissible to read CPR 1998, r. 17.4(2) as if it read 'only if the new claim arises out of the same facts or substantially the same facts as *are already in issue on* a claim in respect of which the party applying for permission has already claimed a remedy' (emphasis added). On this basis the claimant's amended statement of claim should be allowed to proceed.

Two points may be made about this decision. First, it is plain here that, rather than simply interpreting a provision, or implying an overarching principle under which it should operate (as in *R* v *A*), the court is taking full advantage of Lord Steyn's reference to 'the implication of provisions' and reading additional words into the rule. It may be that this is easier in relation to subordinate as opposed to primary legislation, but it appears to open the door to the possibility of courts rewording statutes. It is by no means clear that s. 3 was intended to go this far. Second, the court does not seem to have referred to it the Court of Appeal decision in the pre-HRA 1998 case of *Daniels* v *Walker*, *The Times*, 17 May 2000. In that case, the defendant had raised as one ground of appeal the suggestion that the judge's application of the CPR 1998 as regards the use of expert evidence was in conflict with the right to a fair trial under Art. 6 of the ECHR. The Court of Appeal regarded this as a hopeless suggestion. There was no room for an argument of this kind in relation to the CPR 1998. The provisions of the rules placed an obligation on the court to deal with cases justly. It could not be suggested that the way in which matters are conducted in civil proceedings could contravene Art. 6. It would seem that the Court of Appeal has now turned its back on this view of the CPR 1998. This is to be welcomed. While it is probably true to say that the CPR 1998 *themselves* cannot be said to infringe Art. 6, because they, like Art. 6 itself, require the court to act fairly, the way in which the rules were applied in a particular case could potentially have an unfair effect, as is shown by *Goode* v *Martin*. It is good, therefore, that a less rigid view than that expressed by the Court of Appeal in *Daniels* v *Walker* has now been adopted.

2.3.3.3 Statutes found compatible

There have been several reported cases where the courts have been asked to find legislation incompatible with the ECHR, or to reinterpret it so as to make it compatible, and have refused to do so. A few examples are noted here.

First, in *R (on the Application of Alconbury Developments Ltd)* v *Secretary of State for the Environment* [2001] UKHL 23, [2001] 2 All ER 929, the House of Lords took the view that the various statutory provisions related to planning procedures which involved decision making by the Secretary of State were rendered compatible by the availability of judicial review in relation to these powers. The post-HRA 1998 approach to judicial review is considered further at 2.4.

Second, in *Re K (A Child)* [2001] 2 All ER 719, the Court of Appeal made the point that the fact that a statutory provision might in some circumstances lead to a decision which infringed an individual's rights did not necessarily mean that the provision itself was incompatible. The decision taken under it might be vulnerable as being an action of a public authority which fell foul of s. 6, but the provision itself could be allowed to stand. The case concerned the use of orders placing children in secure accommodation under s. 25 of the Children Act 1989. The court held that these involved a deprivation of liberty and, thus, Art. 5 was engaged, but they could be justified by Art. 5(1)(d) which permits 'the detention of a minor by lawful order for the purpose of educational supervision'. The court must have the requirements of Art. 5(1)(d) in mind whenever it made a secure accommodation order, but the fact that it might in a particular case step outside the area permitted by that provision did not render s. 25 itself incompatible with the ECHR.

In *Poplar Housing Regeneration Community Association Ltd* v *Donoghue* [2001] EWCA Civ 595, [2001] 4 All ER 604, one of the issues before the court was the meaning of 'public authority' under s. 6 of the HRA 1998. This is discussed above (see 2.2.3). The interpretation issue related to s. 21(4) of the Housing Act 1988. The defendant had been housed temporarily by the claimant on behalf of the local authority, pending a decision on whether she was intentionally homeless. The local authority concluded that she was, and this led the claimant housing association to issue a notice that possession of the house was required. Section 21(4) provides that where such a notice has been issued, a court 'shall make an order for possession'. The county court judge, therefore, made such an order. The defendant appealed on the basis that the order infringed her rights to family life under Art. 8 of the ECHR. At the time the defendant had three young children and was expecting a fourth. There was also an Art. 6 issue, in that the mandatory nature of s. 21(4) meant that a court was unable properly to determine her rights, and in particular her rights under Art. 8. The Court of Appeal accepted that the defendant's rights under Art. 8(1) had been infringed. The crucial question was whether the infringement was justified by Art. 8(2). The court concluded that (para. 69, p. 622):

> ...in considering whether Poplar can rely on Art. 8(2), the court has to pay considerable attention to the fact that Parliament intended when enacting s. 21(4) to give preference to the needs of those dependent on social housing as a whole over those in the position of the defendant.

In other words, within the general scheme of housing provision, the rights of the defendant had to give way to the 'rights of others' as recognized by Art. 8. As to the Art. 6 point, there were various routes of appeal against a decision that a person is intentionally homeless (not all of which the defendant had pursued), so there was no breach of this Article either.

As to the interpretation issue, although given its decision that there was no breach of the defendant's rights there was no need to deal with this, the court expressed a cautious view of the powers under s. 3 of the HRA 1998. In particular they should not be used to legislate. The defendant's counsel had suggested that s. 21(4) could be rendered compatible with the ECHR by inserting the words 'if it is reasonable to do so' at the beginning. The Court of Appeal clearly regarded this as being an unacceptable use of s. 3. Whether the same view would be taken now must be more doubtful. The *Poplar* decision preceded those of the House of Lords in *R* v *A* and *R* v *Lambert*, and a wider approach to s. 3 taken by those decisions might well encompass reading words into a statute if the court felt this was necessary to make it compatible (see *Goode* v *Martin* at 2.3.3.2).

The mandatory requirement on a court to impose a life sentence on someone convicted of murder was challenged in *R (on the Application of Lichniak)* v *Secretary of State for the Home Department* [2002] UKHL 47, [2002] 4 All ER 1122. The House of Lords confirmed the decision of the Court of Appeal, holding that the use of a mandatory life sentence together with the system of release on licence, subject to recall, was not incompatible with either Art. 3 or Art. 5 of the ECHR. The system did not reach the level of severity sufficient to engage Art. 3, and was not in practice sufficiently 'arbitrary' to engage Art. 5. The House placed some reliance on the ECtHR decision in *T* v *United Kingdom* (2000) 30 EHRR 121, where it had found that a sentence of 'detention during Her Majesty's pleasure' was not incompatible with Convention rights.

In the cases of *R* v *Rezvi* [2002] UKHL 1, [2002] 1 All ER 801, and *R* v *Benjafield* [2002] UKHL 2, [2002] 1 All ER 815, the House of Lords expressed the view (strictly obiter because the cases fell foul of the non-retrospective nature of the HRA 1998 as determined in *R* v *Lambert* (see 2.3.3.1)) that the confiscation orders under the Criminal Justice Act 1988 and the Drug Trafficking Act 1994, respectively, were not incompatible with the rights to property under Art. 1 of the First Protocol. The Criminal Justice Act 1988 provisions were a 'precise, fair and proportionate response to the important need to protect the public' ([2002] UKHL 1, para. 17) and the Drug Trafficking Act 1994 was a 'fair and proportionate response to the need to protect the public interest' ([2002] UKHL 2, para. 8).

The Hunting Act 2004, which banned hunting with dogs, was considered in *R (Countryside Alliance)* v *Attorney-General* [2008] 1 AC 719. The House of Lords held that the restrictions on the use of land and property contained in the Hunting Act 2004 fell within the scope of Art. 1 to the First Protocol to the ECHR (see chapter 1 (1.6.3.1)), but that they had a legitimate purpose (preventing suffering to wild animals) and were proportionate to that purpose. The Hunting Act 2004 was not incompatible with this part of the ECHR.

2.3.3.4 Declarations of incompatibility

What happens when a court finds that it is impossible to interpret a legislative provision in a way which is compatible with the ECHR? That depends on the level of the court concerned, and whether the legislation is primary or subordinate. If the provision is contained in subordinate legislation, then the court, at whatever level, should treat the provision as ineffective, unless primary legislation 'prevents the removal of the incompatibility' (s. 3(2)(c)). In other words, if a provision in a statutory instrument has to be framed in a particular way because of the requirements of the Act under which the instrument is made, then the court must give effect to it, even if it is incompatible with the ECHR. If, however, the primary legislation does not require the statutory instrument to be framed in a way which is incompatible, then the court should treat it as ineffective. Thus, if magistrates are considering a criminal offence defined in a statutory instrument, which they find to be incompatible and not required by the enabling Act, they should refuse to convict on the basis that the 'offence' is to be treated as a nullity.

In relation to all primary legislation, and subordinate legislation which is incompatible because of the requirements of primary legislation, all courts remain obliged to enforce the relevant provisions, despite their incompatibility. Higher courts, however, are given the power to issue a 'declaration of incompatibility' (s. 4 of the HRA 1998). The courts which have this power are the Supreme Court, the Judicial Committee of the Privy Council, the Court of Appeal, and the High Court (but this does not include the Employment Appeal Tribunal: *Whittaker* v *P and D*

Watson [2002] ICR 1244). Magistrates' courts, Crown Courts, county courts, and employment tribunals do not have the power.

If a court is considering issuing a declaration of incompatibility under s. 4 of the HRA 1998, s. 5 requires that notice should be given to the Crown. The relevant Minister may then be joined as a party to the proceedings. This gives the government the chance to argue against the issue of a declaration before it is made. In criminal proceedings, if a declaration of incompatibility is nevertheless made, the Minister has the power to appeal to the Supreme Court (subject to leave being given by the court issuing the declaration, or the Supreme Court itself).

The issue of a declaration of incompatibility has no effect on the case before the court, or indeed on the legislation which is declared incompatible. If it concerns a criminal offence, for example, other courts will be obliged to continue to convict those charged with the offence, even if the Supreme Court has issued a declaration of incompatibility. In practice, of course, the Crown Prosecution Service may be reluctant to proceed with such cases until there has been some further clarification. Apart from anything else, individuals who have been convicted under legislation which has been declared incompatible are very likely to launch an application to the ECtHR itself.

The main effect of the issue of a declaration of incompatibility, however, is to open up the possibility of taking 'fast-track' remedial action as provided by s. 10 of, and Sch. 2 to, the HRA 1998. This allows (but does not require) a Minister to amend primary or subordinate legislation so as to remove the incompatibility by means of an order approved by both Houses of Parliament. The change may be made retrospective (Sch. 2, para. 1(1)(b)). This is a significant power in relation to primary legislation. Normally, Acts of Parliament can only be changed by full-scale amending legislation. Under the HRA 1998, amendments can be made by the much simpler process of an order laid before and approved by the two Houses. Indeed, in urgent cases, the order can come into effect immediately, subject to later approval by the two Houses (Sch. 2, para. 4). Normally, however, Parliament will have 60 days to consider a draft order before voting on it.

The 'remedial order' power can also be used to remedy an incompatibility identified as a result of proceedings before the ECtHR (s. 10(1)(b) of the HRA 1998).

As of September 2011 there had been 27 occasions on which a court had been moved to issue a 'declaration of incompatibility', though in eight of these the decision to do so was overturned on appeal (Ministry of Justice, 'Responding to Human Rights Judgments', Cm 8162, 2011). This was the case in *R (on the Application of Alconbury Developments Ltd) v Secretary of State for the Environment* [2001] UKHL 23, [2001] 2 All ER 929, which was the first reported example of the issue of a declaration. The case concerned the way in which planning decisions are taken, and in particular the role of the Secretary of State in the decision-making process. The Divisional Court thought that these procedures were incompatible with the right to a fair and public hearing by an impartial and independent tribunal, as guaranteed by Art. 6. It therefore proposed to issue a declaration of incompatibility in relation to various provisions of the planning legislation. On appeal, however, the House of Lords took the view that the procedures were rendered compatible by the availability of judicial review in relation to the Secretary of State's powers. The declarations of incompatibility therefore, did not take effect.

A further example of a case in which a declaration was made but then overturned is *Wilson* v *First County Trust Ltd* [2003] UKHL 40, [2003] 4 All ER 97. This again concerned compatibility with Art. 6. The statutory provision under consideration here was s. 127(3) of the Consumer Credit Act 1974. This provides that a consumer credit agreement cannot be the subject of an enforcement order unless a document containing all the 'prescribed' terms has been signed by the debtor or hirer. The court has no discretion in the matter. Where, therefore, the amount of credit, which was one of the prescribed terms, had been miscalculated and an incorrect figure entered in the document, the court could not enforce the agreement against the debtor, despite the fact that the error had caused no prejudice to any of the parties. The Court of Appeal held that this lack of any power for the court to do justice on the facts of the case, meant that the creditor's rights under Art. 6 were infringed. Section 127(3) was, therefore, incompatible with the ECHR. The issue of a declaration of incompatibility was, however, overturned by the House of Lords, on the basis that, applying the 'retrospectivity' provisions discussed, the Act did not apply to the events which led to the case. Nevertheless, the case is notable for the fact that it exemplifies that the rights guaranteed by the ECHR are available to legal persons, in this case a company, as well as to individuals. It also shows that it is not always the case that the rights dealt with operate solely to protect the individual from the actions of government or large organizations. Here the powers were used to deal with the injustice of an individual being able to gain a benefit by avoiding a credit agreement on the basis of a minor error in the documentation.

The next case to consider was concerned with Art. 5 rather than Art. 6. This was *H* v *North and East Region Mental Health Review Tribunal* [2001] EWCA Civ 415, [2001] 3 WLR 512. The statutory provisions under review were ss 72 and 73 of the Mental Health Act 1983. A mental patient who has previously been ordered to be detained as a restricted patient (in this case following a conviction for manslaughter) can apply to a Mental Health Tribunal to be discharged. Sections 72 and 73 taken together provide that, if the Tribunal is satisfied that the patient is no longer suffering from mental illness, psychopathic disorder, making it appropriate for the patient to be detained for medical treatment, or that it is not necessary for the health or safety of the patient or the protection of others that the patient should receive such treatment, then it shall order release. The complaint of the applicant in this case was that this placed the burden of proof on the patient, which was contrary to Art. 5(1) and (4) of the ECHR. Article 5(1) guarantees the right to liberty, but recognizes that this may legitimately be lost in relation to 'persons of unsound mind' (Art. 5(1)(e)) provided that this 'is in accordance with a procedure prescribed by law'. Article 5(4) provides that everyone deprived of liberty is entitled to 'take proceedings by which the lawfulness of his detention shall be decided speedily by a court'. The Court of Appeal, having considered the domestic cases on the provisions of the Mental Health Act 1983 (e.g. *Reid* v *Secretary of State for Scotland* [1999] 2 AC 513, and *Perkins* v *Bath District Health Authority* [1989] 4 BMLR 145), and the ECHR cases on Art. 5 (e.g. *Winterwerp* v *The Netherlands* (1979) 2 EHRR 387, and *Johnson* v *United Kingdom* (1999) 27 EHRR 296) concluded that the provisions of the Act did in effect impose a burden of proof on the applicant (that is, to prove that he or she was not suffering from a mental illness, etc.) and that this was contrary to Art. 5. It was not possible to read the sections in a way that was compatible with the ECHR, and a declaration of incompatibility was made. On this occasion, the government used its power under s. 10 of the HRA 1998 to issue a remedial order amending the Mental Health Act 1983 provisions (the Mental Health Act 1983 (Remedial) Order 2001 (SI 2001/3712)).

Provisions of the Mental Health Act 1983 were again under consideration in *R(M)* v *Secretary of State for Health* [2003] EWHC 1094 (Admin), [2003] UKHRR 746. On this occasion the court held that ss 26 and 29 of the Mental Health Act 1983 were incompatible with Art. 8 of the ECHR. These provisions operated to make the applicant's father automatically her 'nearest relative', and provided no mechanism for a challenge to this. The applicant alleged that her father had sexually abused her as a child. The government accepted the incompatibility, given that the European Commission on Human Rights had already found to this effect in *JT* v *United Kingdom* [2000] 1 FLR 909, but resisted the making of the declaration because it had plans for the amendment of the relevant provisions under a draft Mental Health Bill. The court did not think that this was a reason to refuse the declaration. The government had known about the incompatibility for some time, but had not yet acted. It was not for the court to speculate as to the content or progress of proposed legislation. In the event, the government announced in March 2006 that it was not proceeding with the Mental Health Bill, which had been under discussion over the previous five years.

In *International Transport Roth GmbH* v *Secretary of State for the Home Department* [2002] EWCA Civ 158, [2003] QB 728, the court was concerned with provisions of Pt. II of the Immigration and Asylum Act 1999 (see chapter 11 (11.3.4)). These were designed to deal with the problems of unlawful immigrants arriving in this country, primarily in lorries, but also in other vehicles. The provisions empower the Secretary of State to issue a penalty notice requiring the person responsible for the vehicle in which unlawful immigrants are found to pay £2,000 for each immigrant. There are also powers for the immigration authorities to detain the vehicle concerned until the penalties are paid. These procedures were challenged as being incompatible with the ECHR. The trial judge held that they were incompatible with Art. 6 and Art. 1 of the First Protocol (see chapter 1 (1.6.3)). On appeal a majority of the court agreed with this conclusion, largely on the grounds that the penalties imposed were disproportionate to the objectives of immigration control that they were designed to assist. The court, therefore, confirmed the trial judge's declaration of incompatibility. No remedial action has as yet been taken in relation to this decision.

Two cases considered the powers of the Home Secretary to set the 'tariff' which those sentenced to life imprisonment must serve before being considered for release. In *R (Anderson)* v *Secretary of State for the Home Department* [2002] UKHL 46, [2002] 4 All ER 1089 the House of Lords held that the power of the Home Secretary (under s. 29 of the Crime (Sentences) Act 1997) to set the tariff for a prisoner serving a mandatory life sentence, was incompatible with Art. 6 of the ECHR. Similarly, in *R (D)* v *Secretary of State for the Home Department* [2002] EWHC 2805 (Admin), [2003] 1 WLR 1315, the High Court held that the powers of the Home Secretary, contained in ss 47 and 49 of the Mental Health Act 1983, to restrict the release of a prisoner who had served the tariff part of a discretionary life sentence, was also incompatible with Art. 6. Decisions as to the length of sentence to be served should be made by a judicial body, and not by a member of the executive.

In *Bellinger* v *Bellinger* [2003] UKHL 21, [2003] 2 All ER 593 the applicant, a post-operative male-to-female transsexual, appealed against a decision that her marriage to her husband was void by virtue of s. 11(c) of the Matrimonial Causes Act 1973 because she was in law regarded as a man. The House of Lords confirmed that the marriage was not valid, but also held that s. 11(c) of the Matrimonial Causes Act was incompatible with Arts 8 and 12 of the ECHR.

Finally, note should be made of the decision of the House of Lords in *A* v *Secretary of State for the Home Department* [2004] UKHL 56, [2005] 2 WLR 87, in which a declaration of incompatibility was made in relation to powers of indefinite detention without trial under the Anti-terrorism, Crime and Security Act 2001. This case is discussed fully in chapter 10 (10.6.1).

These cases show the potential for the use of declarations of incompatibility. There has, however, been some debate about the relationship between ss 3 and 4. Some commentators saw the developments in the use of s. 4 in 2002–03 as an indication that the courts were drawing back from the bold use of s. 3 seen in *R* v *A* [2001] UKHL 25, [2001] 3 All ER 1, and *R* v *Lambert* [2001] UKHL 37, [2001] 3 All ER 577 (see 2.3.3)—see, e.g. D. Nicol, 'Statutory Interpretation and Human Rights after *Anderson*', [2004] PL 273 and 'Gender Reassignment and the Transformation of the Human Rights Act', (2004) 120 LQR 194, and C. Gearty, 'Revisiting Section 3(1) of the Human Rights Act' (2003) 119 LQR 551. A different view was taken by A. Kavanagh in 'Statutory Interpretation and Human Rights After *Anderson*: A More Contextual Approach', [2004] PL 537. The matter was considered by the House of Lords in *Ghaidan* v *Mendoza* [2004] UKHL 30, [2004] 3 All ER 411. The House rejected any suggestion that s. 4 should be used in preference to s. 3. Lord Steyn in particular emphasized that s. 3 is to be regarded as the 'prime remedial remedy and that resort to section 4 must always be an exceptional course' (para. 50). (An annex to Lord Steyn's opinion contains a useful list of all the declarations of incompatibility issued to that date, and all the cases where the interpretative power under s. 3 had been used.)

2.4 Interpreting the common law

Although the HRA 1998 does not specifically state that the common law should be interpreted and developed by the courts in line with the ECHR, this is the effect of ss 2 and 6. Section 6 (see 2.2.3) includes courts within the category of 'public authority', and therefore requires them to act in accordance with the ECHR. Section 2, more directly, requires a court or tribunal in determining any question relating to a Convention right to take into account the cases of the European Court and Commission of Human Rights. The English court is not obliged to follow the decision of the ECHR, but in *Ofulue* v *Bossert* [2008] EWCA Civ 7 the Court of Appeal set out the approach to be adopted (this is in line with that put forward by the House of Lords in cases such as *R (Alconbury Developments Ltd)* v *Secretary of State for the Environment, Transport and the Regions* [2001] UKHL 23 (p. 26) and *R (Ullah)* v *Special Adjudicator* [2004] UKHL 26 (p. 20)). The English court (para. 31):

> ...would have to have very good reasons for departing from Strasbourg jurisprudence. Special circumstances justifying departure might exist if the domestic court were satisfied that the Strasbourg court had misunderstood the effect of domestic law. Moreover, if the rule of domestic law creates a discretion rather than an absolute rule of law, the domestic court might come to the conclusion that the discretion should be exercised in a different way from that in which it was in fact exercised in the case before the Strasbourg court.

That discretion will be greater where the Strasbourg Court has indicated that the situation is one in which it will recognize a 'margin of appreciation' (for which, see 2.2.8) for States to decide how to comply with the Convention obligation. Further consideration of the relationship between ECtHR judgments and the English courts appears in the Supreme Court's decision in *R (Chester)* v *Secretary of State for Justice* [2013] UKSC 63—a case on prisoners' voting rights (see also chapter 1 (1.6.3)). Lord Mance, giving the leading judgment, noted (paras 25–7) that the Supreme Court in *R* v *Horncastle* [2009] UKSC 14, para. 11 had indicated that, while departing from Strasbourg decisions should be rare, in some cases doing so could lead the ECtHR to reconsider its view. Similarly in *Manchester City Council* v *Pinnock* [2010] UKSC 45 Lord Neuberger affirmed that in some cases a 'dialogue' between Strasbourg and the English courts might be appropriate, but that where (para. 48):

> ...there is a clear and constant line of decisions whose effect is not inconsistent with some fundamental substantive or procedural aspect of our law, and whose reasoning does not appear to overlook or misunderstand some argument or point of principle, we consider that it would be wrong for this court not to follow that line.

Applying that approach to the case before him, Lord Mance concluded that (para. 27):

> ...there are limits to this process [of dialogue], particularly where the matter has been already to a Grand Chamber once or, even more so, as in this case, twice. It would have then to involve some truly fundamental principle of our law or some most egregious oversight or misunderstanding before it could be appropriate for this Court to contemplate an outright refusal to follow Strasbourg authority at the Grand Chamber level.

Specific instances of the way in which the courts have undertaken their responsibilities under the HRA 1998 are dealt with throughout the rest of this book. What follows here is a general consideration of the kind of approach which has been adopted. For the most part the attitude may be characterized as 'cautious' rather than 'bold'—as perhaps typified by the incremental approach to the development of 'privacy' rights, discussed in chapter 6 (6.10).

Overall there has been much less case law concerned with the interpretation of the common law, as opposed to statutory provisions. Indeed, the most significant development is probably that of the emergence of a law protecting privacy from the concept of breach of confidence. The impact of *Osman* v *United Kingdom* [1998] EHRR 245, in which the ECtHR held that a blanket immunity in relation to negligence actions against the police was contrary to Art. 6 (right to a fair trial), has not been as significant as might have been predicted in terms of the development of tort law. It was the subject of considerable criticism by academics (e.g. C. Gearty 'Unravelling *Osman*', (2001) 64 MLR 159) and judges (e.g. Lord Browne-Wilkinson in *Barrett* v *Enfield London Borough Council* [1999] 3 All ER 193, p. 198 and Lord Hoffmann, 'Human Rights and the House of Lords', (1999) 62 MLR 159). Moreover, the ECtHR itself seems to have retreated from the position adopted in *Osman* in the later cases of *Z* v *United Kingdom* (2002) 34 EHRR 3 and *TP and KM* v *United Kingdom* (2002) 34 EHRR 2. It may well have had some impact, however, though not explicitly acknowledged, in the House of Lords' decision in *Hall* v *Simons* [2000] 3 All ER 673 to hold that solicitors and barristers should no longer be immune from negligence actions.

One area of the common law does merit further consideration here, however. That is the common law remedy of judicial review. Statistics produced by the Lord Chancellor's Department (now the Ministry of Justice) indicated that the most frequent article of the ECHR pleaded in the first year of the HRA 1998's operation was Art. 6—the right to a fair trial (followed by Arts 5 and 8). It is also important to note that when Art. 6 is raised the courts will look at the full range of potential remedies available to the applicant. In deciding the question of whether there has been an infringement of the rights guaranteed by the Article the appeal process must be looked at, as well as the initial decision. Thus, a decision of a public authority to dismiss an employee by procedures which are not in line with Art. 6 may not involve a breach of the ECHR provided that the employee can challenge the decision in an employment tribunal. Similarly, in *R (on the Application of Alconbury Developments Ltd)* v *Secretary of State for the Environment* [2001] UKHL 23, [2001] 2 All ER 929 (see 2.3.3.4) the fact that the Secretary of State's decision making on planning applications might have been vulnerable under Art. 6 was remedied by the availability of judicial review. Since one of the most common methods of challenging a decision of a public authority is by judicial review, the way in which this remedy is operated by the courts becomes crucial in considering Art. 6 rights.

The traditional approach to 'reasonableness' within judicial review, based on the approach taken in *Associated Provincial Picture Houses* v *Wednesbury Corporation* [1948] 2 KB 223, is limited in its scope. The question to be asked under the *Wednesbury* test is whether any authority in the place of the decision maker could reasonably have come to the same conclusion. In other words the test is one of rationality, and has limited concern with the content of the decision, or whether it operates fairly on the person whom it affects.

The fact that this limited approach might not be satisfactory in the human rights context was explicitly recognized prior to any suggestion of incorporation of the ECHR. In *R* v *Ministry of Defence, ex p Smith* [1996] QB 517 Lord Bingham, in the Court of Appeal, accepted as accurate a reformulation of the *Wednesbury* test suggested by counsel as being appropriate in human rights' cases. While the test is still one of whether the decision is one to which a reasonable decision-maker could have come (p. 554):

> ...in judging whether the decision-maker has exceeded this margin of appreciation the human rights context is important. The more substantial the interference with human rights, the more the court will require by way of justification before it is satisfied that the decision is reasonable.

This accepted an extended scope for review in the human rights context, but was only an incremental step from the *Wednesbury* approach. A further step was taken by Lord Phillips in the Court of Appeal in *R (on the Application of Mahmood)* v *Secretary of State for the Home Department* [2001] 1 WLR 840, in outlining the procedure to be adopted once the HRA 1998 was in force. He suggested that in scrutinizing an executive decision on judicial review the question to ask is (para. 40, p. 858):

> ...whether the decision-maker could reasonably have concluded that the interference was necessary to achieve one or more of the legitimate aims recognised by the Convention. When considering the test of necessity in the relevant context, the court must take into account the European jurisprudence in accordance with section 2 of the 1998 Act.

The test is thus moving towards a decision on whether the rights of the applicant have been infringed, but does not quite go that far. The essence is still whether the decision was *reasonable* rather than whether it was *right*. If the decision-maker could reasonably have concluded that a legitimate aim was being served, but was in fact wrong in that conclusion, the court cannot interfere on this test. There is clearly a strong argument that this is inadequate to satisfy the requirements of Art. 6.

One of the fullest considerations of the issue, and the one that is now being regularly adopted in HRA 1998 cases, is to be found in the judgment of Lord Steyn in *R v Secretary of State for the Home Department, ex p Daly* [2001] UKHL 26, [2001] 3 All ER 433, with which the rest of the House agreed. The case was concerned with a policy of searching prisoners' cells which required the prisoner to be absent even while legal correspondence was being examined. This was held to be in breach of both the common law rights to legal professional privilege and Art. 8 of the ECHR. In looking at the correct approach to judicial review in such cases, Lord Steyn noted the comments of Lord Phillips in *Mahmood*. He stated, however, that it was important to note that where Convention rights were in issue the question of 'proportionality' must be considered. This refers to the fact that the ECtHR has emphasized in many cases that in considering whether a restriction on a Convention right is 'necessary in a democratic society' the question of whether the restriction is proportionate to its objective is very important. As Lord Steyn emphasizes, this 'proportionality' approach is clearly distinguishable from the traditional approach to review. He points to three differences in particular (para. 28):

> First, the doctrine of proportionality may require the reviewing court to assess the balance which the decision maker has struck, not merely whether it is within the range of rational or reasonable decisions. Secondly, the proportionality test may go further than the traditional grounds of review in as much as it may require attention to be directed to the relative weight accorded to interests and considerations.

The third difference is that the approach needs to go further even than the 'heightened scrutiny' test in *ex p Smith* since the ECtHR had found that test to be inadequate in *Smith and Grady* v *United Kingdom* (1999) 29 EHRR 493.

The most important of these differences may well be the first. It seems to be requiring, as indeed the ECtHR's view of Art. 6 would seem to require, that the review assesses the *quality* of the decision, as well as its *reasonableness*. Lord Steyn is at pains to point out that his suggested changes do not mean 'that there has been a shift to a merits review' (para. 28, p. 446). It is simply that in an HRA 1998 case the intensity of the review is heightened by the context. Despite this protestation, however, the test which he is proposing, and is now being adopted, seems to come so close to judging the merit of the decision (that is, did it take proper account of the applicant's Convention rights in deciding whether the restriction on them was proportionate) that it makes very little practical difference.

The conclusion is that the new approach put forward by Lord Steyn has done enough to ensure that the availability of judicial review will generally suffice to satisfy the right under Art. 6 to a proper, independent, review of actions which potentially impinge on Convention rights. Whether this is in fact the case will have to await a consideration by the ECtHR of a case in which it has been applied.

2.5 'Free-standing' human rights?

Although the potential clearly exists within the HRA 1998 for the courts to develop new rights and remedies, not previously recognized by the common law and not arising in the context of the application of statutes, to date the tendency has been to try to make any finding of infringement of human rights 'parasitic' on an existing recognized legal action. This is very clearly the approach of the courts in relation to the arguments for the development of a 'free-standing' right of privacy. As can be seen from the discussion in chapter 6 (6.10), the method used for increasing the scope of the recognition of privacy under English law has primarily been based on developing the existing law of breach of confidence.

In an appropriate case, however, it seems the courts will be prepared to recognize that the existence of a right recognized by the ECHR may require that there is also a need for a remedy, independent of any statutory framework or common law cause of action. In *R (Amin) v Secretary of State for the Home Department* [2003] UKHL 51, [2003] 4 All ER 1284 the applicants were the family of a prisoner in a young offender institution who had been killed by his cellmate. The cellmate's behaviour had previously been known to be dangerous. There was an internal Prison Service inquiry into the death, but the family did not participate in this. An inquest was opened but adjourned pending police inquiries. These led to the prosecution and conviction of the cellmate. Following this the coroner, as she was entitled to do, declined to continue with the inquest. There was also a separate investigation by the Commission for Racial Equality (CRE), focusing on racial discrimination in the prison service, but also looking in particular at the death of the prisoner. This included a one-day public hearing involving the questioning of certain witnesses by counsel for the CRE. The family were offered a limited role within this, but declined to participate. Following this, the family wrote to the Home Office seeking a full public inquiry. This was refused. Application was then made to the High Court for a declaration that the Home Secretary's refusal to hold a public inquiry amounted to a breach of the right to life under Art. 2 of the ECHR.

The judge granted this declaration. The Court of Appeal reversed this decision, but the declaration was restored by the House of Lords.

The main judgment was delivered by Lord Bingham. He reviewed the case law on Art. 2 in the ECtHR, and noted that it was clearly established that the right to life included the right to an investigation of the circumstances of a violent death (para. 20):

> The obligation to ensure that there is some form of effective official investigation when individuals have been killed as a result of force is not confined to cases where it is apparent that the killing was caused by an agent of the state (*Salman* v *Turkey* (2002) 34 EHRR 425 (para. 105))

He also placed considerable reliance on the ECtHR's decision in *Edwards* v *United Kingdom* (2002) 12 BHRC 190, which was another case where a prisoner had been killed by a cellmate—in this case one who was known to be suffering from acute mental illness. The ECtHR held that there was an obligation for the State to investigate such deaths of its own initiative, without relying on the next of kin, for example, to lodge a formal complaint. Moreover, the investigation must be sufficient public scrutiny of the investigation or its results to secure accountability in practice as well as in theory. In all cases the next of kin of the victim should be involved 'to the extent necessary to safeguard his or her legitimate interests' (para. 73 of the ECtHR's judgment).

In the light of the ECtHR's approach to the Art. 2 issues the House of Lords was convinced that the judge had been correct to issue the declaration that an independent public investigation into the death should be held. The inquiries which had been held had not had the clear independence, nor had they sufficiently involved the victim's family.

This is a very important decision in the development of the English courts' approach to the HRA 1998 and Convention rights. Although the issue of a declaration has no binding force on the government, the fact that the House of Lords has been prepared to rule that the HRA 1998 does lead to positive obligations to act to protect rights (as well as negative obligations not to interfere with their infringement) even outside areas covered by the common law or statute, opens up the possibility for a much more pro-active use of Convention rights. It cannot be said, however, that the courts have to date made much use of this possibility.

2.6 **Other issues**

Before concluding this discussion of the HRA 1998, three other issues need consideration. First, there is the question of the extent, if at all, to which the HRA 1998 can be said to be 'entrenched' into the constitution. This is important in relation to its status, and to the balance of power between Parliament and the courts. The second issue is that of the 'oversight' of the HRA 1998, and the procedures that have been, or should be, put in place to monitor its operation and development.

Related to both the first two issues is the question of whether the HRA 1998 should be reformed or replaced. In 2011 the coalition government announced the establishment of a Commission to review and report on this issue and its report was published in December 2012. Although the recommendations of the Commission are unlikely to be acted on in the short-term, if at all, some consideration of the issues raised is discussed at 2.6.3.

2.6.1 Entrenchment

One of the characteristics of a Bill of Rights tends to be that it has a constitutional position at the top of the legislative pile. Because it is dealing with rights that are deemed to be 'fundamental', all other legislation is subordinate to it, and the courts look to it as the ultimate source of authority. Moreover, the Bill is quite likely to be 'entrenched'—that is, subject to a procedure for change which is much more difficult than the ordinary passage of legislation.

This has, however, been one of the traditional areas of difficulty in relation to the debate about a Bill of Rights in the United Kingdom because of the notion of Parliamentary sovereignty, and its corollary the doctrine of 'implied repeal'. UK constitutional law has as one of its fundamental principles the rule that Parliament can do what it likes. As classically stated by Dicey (A. V. Dicey, *An Introduction to the Study of the Law of the Constitution*, 10th edn (London: Macmillan & Co., 1965), pp. 39–40):

> The principle of Parliamentary sovereignty means neither more nor less than this, namely, that Parliament [defined as the 'Queen in Parliament'] has, under the English constitution, the right to make or unmake any law whatever; and, further, that no person or body is recognised by the law of England as having a right to override or set aside the legislation of Parliament.

There are, in theory, no restrictions on what Parliament can enact, and the courts will give effect to any legislation that is properly passed, without regard to its content. This raises a problem for the proponents of a Bill of Rights. If such a Bill is enacted simply as an ordinary Act of Parliament, there is nothing, under the Diceyan view, to stop Parliament in the future from enacting legislation which conflicts with the Bill, and the courts would be obliged to give effect to such legislation. This would significantly reduce, if not destroy altogether, the function of a Bill of Rights as a guarantee of the freedoms contained in it. Thus, if freedom of expression were one of the freedoms recognized, there would still be nothing to stop Parliament enacting a restrictive piece of legislation such as the Video Recordings Act 1984 (see chapter 8 (8.6.2)). Is it not possible somehow to 'entrench' the Bill, so that later legislation will not have this effect?

One answer which might be proposed (and is more or less what has been adopted in the HRA 1998 by virtue of s. 3) is that the legislation enacting the Bill should indicate that subsequent legislation must be interpreted as complying with the Bill, at least unless Parliament specifically indicates otherwise (see for another example of this approach, s. 33(1) of the Canadian Charter of Rights and Freedoms). This retains Parliamentary sovereignty, but requires it to be exercised deliberately in certain fields. The difficulty with this approach is the so-called doctrine of 'implied repeal', most clearly stated by Maugham LJ in *Ellen Street Estates Ltd* v *Minister of Health* [1934] 1 KB 590 (p. 597):

> The Legislature cannot, according to our constitution, bind itself as to the form of subsequent legislation, and it is impossible for Parliament to enact that in a subsequent statute dealing with the same subject-matter there can be no implied repeal.

This approach requires that if two Acts of Parliament are in conflict, the courts should treat the latter as having impliedly repealed the former. Thus, any provision inconsistent with the HRA 1998 contained in subsequent legislation would (subject to s. 3 of the Act) have to be regarded as having repealed the relevant part of the Act, even if this was only done incidentally, rather than deliberately. This doctrine was, however, reconsidered in the case involving the so-called 'metric martyrs'—traders who objected to the replacement of imperial measures of weight with the metric system. In *Thoburn* v *Sunderland City Council* [2002] EWHC 195 (Admin), [2003] QB 151, they challenged the validity of the regulations which introduced the change, partly on the basis of an argument that the part of the European Communities Act 1972 enabling amendments of law, statutory or otherwise, to be made by regulation, had been impliedly repealed by later legislation. The Divisional Court, in rejecting this argument, held that the common law had in recent years recognized a distinction between 'ordinary statutes' and 'constitutional statutes'. The former are subject to implied repeal, the latter are not. The argument is set out in Laws LJ's judgment (para. 62):

> In the present state of its maturity the common law has come to recognise that there exist rights which should properly be classified as constitutional or fundamental: see for example such cases as *Simms* [2000] 2 AC 115 *per* Lord Hoffmann at 131, *Pierson v Secretary of State [1998] AC 539, Leech [1994] QB 198, Derbyshire County Council v Times Newspapers Ltd* [1993] AC 534, and *Witham* [1998] QB 575. And from this a further insight follows. We should recognise a hierarchy of Acts of Parliament: as it were 'ordinary' statutes and 'constitutional' statutes. The two categories must be distinguished on a principled basis. In my opinion a constitutional statute is one which (a) conditions the legal relationship between citizen and State in some general, overarching manner, or (b) enlarges or diminishes the scope of what we would now regard as fundamental constitutional rights. (a) and (b) are of necessity closely related: it is difficult to think of an instance of (a) that is not also an instance of (b). The special status of constitutional statutes follows the special status of constitutional rights. Examples are the Magna Carta, the Bill of Rights 1689, the Act of Union, the Reform Acts which distributed and enlarged the franchise, the HRA, the Scotland Act 1998 and the Government of Wales Act 1998.

As will be seen, Laws LJ includes, not surprisingly, the HRA 1998 within his examples of 'constitutional' statutes. His analysis draws on the effects of the *Factortame* litigation on European law, and in particular *R* v *Secretary of State for Transport, ex p Factortame Ltd (No. 2)* [1991] 1 AC 603. As far as international law is concerned it is clear that the British government, as a result of the United Kingdom's membership of the EU, is obliged to bring English law in line with the requirements of EU law. The British government accepts the jurisdiction of the Court of Justice of the European Union to give definitive rulings on European law. At the domestic level, s. 2(1) of the European Communities Act 1972 acknowledged the direct effect of Community law, without the need for enactment by Parliament (see, e.g. chapter 12 (12.2)). The English courts likewise have accepted this, and regularly refer questions of law to the Court of Justice of the European Union, accepting as binding the rulings of that Court. The final question arises as to what the courts should do if the UK Parliament enacts legislation that is in conflict with European law. The doctrine of Parliamentary sovereignty and implied repeal would have suggested that the UK Act of Parliament should take precedence over the requirements of European law. In *R* v *Secretary of State for Transport, ex p Factortame Ltd (No. 2)*, however, the House of Lords accepted a ruling from the European Court of Justice that it could provide interim relief restraining the Secretary of State for Transport from withholding or withdrawing registration of fishing vessels under regulations made under the Merchant Shipping Act 1988, pending consideration of the validity of that legislation by the European Court. In effect, therefore, European law was being regarded as overriding the provisions of duly enacted legislation. In this area, at least, then, the doctrine of Parliamentary sovereignty has been severely weakened. Of course Parliament could change the position by repealing the European Communities Act 1972, and withdrawing from the European Union, but while the United Kingdom remains a member, it seems that the English courts will give effect to European law, even where this is in conflict with subsequent enactments of the UK Parliament.

This seems to support the view of Laws LJ that some statutes may have a special constitutional status. If this analysis is correct, and it must be recognized that the statements in *Thoburn* are arguably obiter, in that the court found that in any case the alleged inconsistency between the European Communities Act 1972 and the later legislation was not made out, then it seems clear that the HRA 1998 should fall into this special category. Implied repeal of its provisions is on this basis impossible. Nevertheless, the limitation of this argument, even if valid, must be noted. As discussed, the court in *Thoburn* recognized that the government could decide to repeal the European Communities Act 1972 and leave the European Union, and that this could be achieved by an ordinary statute. The special constitutional status of the HRA 1998 would not protect it, therefore, against expressly contradictory provisions in any subsequent legislation.

The most radical solution to this problem would have been to decide that the whole UK Constitution required revision and restatement. A new constitutional document could have been produced setting out the powers of the executive, the courts, and the legislature. In that context it might have been possible to include a Bill of Rights as part of the new constitution, and thus to give it a status distinct from an ordinary piece of legislation. The difficulty with such an approach would have been finding the political will and consensus to embark on such an enterprise. New constitutions are usually the result of conquest, revolution, achieving independence, or, at least, severe internal political pressure for change. The Labour government of 1997–2010 did initiate significant constitutional change in the devolution of power to Scotland and (to a lesser extent) Wales. It clearly did not feel the need, or any pressure for, a constitutional change which would have more generally affected the supremacy of the Westminster Parliament. As a result, the HRA 1998 was enacted as a normal statute. The result of the fact that the issue of entrenchment has not been directly addressed within the HRA 1998 is that the

Act is as potentially vulnerable as any other piece of legislation to at least express, if not implied, repeal, of all or part of its provisions. There are two procedures, however, which attempt to ensure that proper account is taken of the Act in relation to subsequent legislation. First, there is the requirement in s. 19 that in relation to every new Bill the relevant Minister should, before its second reading, make a declaration about compatibility with the ECHR (see 2.3.1). The second way in which the HRA 1998 attempts to ensure that proper account is taken of the ECHR in the operation of legislation is, of course, the interpretation provision of s. 3, (see 2.3.2). This also gives weight to the argument that 'incidental' or 'accidental' repeal of any part of the HRA 1998 will not be allowed, and that is only where Parliament has clearly and deliberately set out to alter its provisions that this will be given effect.

The fact, however, that in the end the HRA 1998 can be amended, and repealed, following normal Parliamentary procedures, with no provision, for example, for special majorities, leads to the conclusion that it does not fully meet the criterion of being 'superior law' which would normally be expected of a Bill of Rights.

2.6.2 **Monitoring the Human Rights Act 1998**

To what extent is there, or ought there to be some overall mechanism for reviewing the way in which the HRA 1998 is operating, both at the particular level of its effect on the substantive law, and more generally in encouraging changes in attitudes towards the rights which the Act is supposed to protect? The HRA 1998 itself provides a mechanism by which an individual whose rights have been infringed can obtain redress. Is there, however, any more general way in which laws, or activities, which appear to be in conflict with Convention rights can be challenged, without the need to identify specific victims?

This area is not dealt with directly by the HRA 1998. The fact that it shares the definition of 'victim' with the ECHR means that the scope for class actions is also limited. The White Paper which preceded the HRA 1998 (*Bringing Rights Home*, Cm 3872, 1997) considered the possibility of establishing a Human Rights Commission, similar to (and perhaps taking over the functions of) the CRE, the Equal Opportunities Commission (EOC), and the Disability Rights Commission (DRC). Such a Commission, it was suggested, might have the power to scrutinize legislation before it is enacted and to seek a ruling from the courts as to whether it would involve, or run the risk of, the infringement of Convention rights. When the HRA 1998 was passed, however, the government decided that such a Commission should not be established immediately, while not ruling out the possibility for the future. In March 2003 the Parliamentary JCHR reported strongly in favour of the establishment of such a Commission (Sixth Report of Session 2002–03, 'The Case for a Human Rights Commission', HC 489–I). In October 2003 the government announced that it had accepted this recommendation, and that firm proposals would be put forward in a White Paper in the spring of 2004, with implementation, possibly, by late 2006. This was done in the Bill which became the Equality Act 2006. The Act provided for the establishment of the Equality and Human Rights Commission (EHRC), and this came into being in the Autumn of 2007. As well as taking over duties of the CRE, EOC, and DRC, the

EHRC has a duty under s. 3 of the Act to 'exercise its functions...with a view to encouraging, and supporting the development of a society in which—...(b) there is respect for and protection of each individual's human rights'. More specifically, by virtue of s. 9:

> The Commission shall, by exercising the powers conferred by [Pt. 1 of the Act]—
> (a) promote understanding of the importance of human rights,
> (b) encourage good practice in relation to human rights,
> (c) promote awareness, understanding and protection of human rights, and
> (d) encourage public authorities to comply with section 6 of the Human Rights Act 1998 (c. 42) (compliance with Convention rights).

Section 11 gives the EHRC a monitoring role in relation to the effectiveness of human rights enactments. This includes advising the government about the effectiveness of existing laws, suggesting amendments, and commenting on proposed changes in the law. Until now, this role has been fulfilled by the Parliamentary JCHR, which in practice appears to be continuing to take the lead in this area.

One gap in the EHRC's powers is that it is not empowered to provide legal assistance to individual claimants bringing human rights actions. Such a power is available to the existing commissions in relation to claims of discrimination, and is an important part of their work. This is continued in relation to the equality legislation by s. 28 of the Equality Act 2006, but the section does not extend to human rights claims not involving discrimination.

Prior to the creation of the EHRC, the role of supervising legislation was taken primarily by the JCHR, and this continues to the most active body in this area. This has as its first term of reference 'to consider matters relating to human rights in the United Kingdom (but excluding consideration of individual cases)'. It also has responsibility in relation to the supervision of remedial orders issued in the wake of a declaration of incompatibility (see 2.3.3.4). The Committee has fulfilled its main role largely by considering proposed legislation (such as the Anti-terrorism, Crime and Security Bill, the Proceeds of Crime Bill and the Police Reform Bill) and issuing reports on its compatibility with Convention rights. The effect of its recommendations seems to have been limited, with few changes to legislation actually following from them. Nevertheless, the Committee does fill a significant part of the role which could otherwise be played by a human rights commission. Moreover, it should be noted that other Parliamentary committees can also play a role in the supervision of legislation. In relation to the Anti-terrorism, Crime and Security Bill, for example, it was also considered by the House of Commons Home Affairs Committee, the House of Lords Constitution Committee, and the House of Lords Select Committee on Delegated Powers and Regulatory Reform. Pre-enactment scrutiny of legislation appears, therefore, to be reasonably well catered for, with the JCHR playing a very important role. What it specifically cannot do is either assist individuals in the way that the CRE, EOC, and DRC have done in the past, or do anything to challenge compatibility once legislation has been passed. Unfortunately, as discussed, it seems that the EHRC will also have only limited scope to contribute to this area.

2.6.3 **Reform of the Human Rights Act 1998**

It is clear that the HRA 1998 has had a significant impact on the law of the United Kingdom. A full assessment of its success or otherwise probably needs to wait a few more years. There have been suggestions from people within the leadership of both the Labour and Conservative parties that the Act operates in a way which is too restrictive of public authorities, for example in the fight against crime and terrorism, and that it should be amended or replaced with a 'Bill of Rights'. Such a Bill might, for example, include 'responsibilities' to be placed on citizens, as well as their 'rights'. A report by the JCHR in August 2008, however, suggested the addition of economic and social rights and third generation rights to those currently recognized by the Convention ('A Bill of Rights for the UK', 29th Report of Session 2007–08, HL Paper 165–1, HC 150–1).

Such an extension would be possible, though politically unlikely. It is clear, however, that there could not be any significant limitation of the HRA 1998 rights in any new Bill, without an impact on the UK government's international obligations under the ECHR, adherence to which is a condition of membership of both the Council of Europe and the European Union. A cynical view of this might be that the fact that politicians see the Act as an effective restraint on their activities in restricting freedom is an indicator of its success. A review of the operation of the HRA 1998 by the Department for Constitutional Affairs (DCA) published in July 2006 (available at http://webarchive.nationalarchives.gov.uk/+/http:/www.dca.gov.uk/peoples-rights/human-rights/pdf/full_review.pdf) concluded that the Act had:

(a) had no significant impact on criminal law, or on the government's ability to fight crime;

(b) had an impact upon the government's counter-terrorism legislation, but the main difficulties in this area (deportation of suspected terrorists) arose not from the HRA 1998, but from decisions of the ECtHR;

(c) had beneficial impact in other areas and had led to a positive dialogue between UK judges and those at the ECtHR;

(d) not significantly altered the constitutional balance between Parliament, the executive, and the judiciary.

It also concluded that the Act had had a generally beneficial impact on the formulation of policy. Perceived problems with the Act arose from 'myths and misperceptions', largely resulting from the way in which the Act was reported and commented on in the media, though also contributed to by deficiencies in training of those working in relevant areas. The Review concluded with a restatement of the government's commitment to the ECHR.

The Home Office also carried out in 2006 a review of the impact of the HRA 1998 on the criminal justice system. This review has not been published in full, but in a response published in January 2007 (Cm 7011) to a report by the JCHR, the Home Office stated that the review 'had found no evidence that the Act itself has interfered with the processes by which public safety is assured' (para. 37). On the other hand there were 'occasions where officials may have acted over-cautiously in applying the Act' (para. 37).

Both the DCA review and that by the Home Office suggest that problems have arisen from the interpretation and implementation of the HRA 1998 rather than from the Act itself or the way it attempts to protect rights. Further discussion of both these reviews is to be found in the JCHR's 32nd Report of Session 2005–06 (HL Paper 278, HC 1716, 7 November 2006).

It is not surprising that over the years of its existence the HRA 1998 has run into criticism from governments. One of the purposes of the Act is to protect the citizen from abuse of his or her rights by the State, so it is almost inevitable that its effect will, in some cases, be to thwart actions which the State wishes to take (as with the indefinite detention without charge or trial of suspected terrorists—see chapter 10 (10.6.1)). The press and other media have also been quick to criticize decisions such as restrictions on the deportation of convicted criminals because of the conflict with their rights to a family life under Art. 8 of the ECHR. Some of the criticisms have been inaccurate and have continued despite the attempt by the DCA in 2006 (see the report at http://webarchive.nationalarchives.gov.uk/+/http:/www.dca.gov.uk/peoples-rights/human-rights/pdf/full_review.pdf) to try to dispel some of the 'myths' that had grown up around it.

At the time of the general election in 2010 both the Conservative and Labour parties were committed to some reform of the HRA 1998. The Liberal Democrats, on the other hand, have been consistent supporters of the Act. As a result, the coalition between the Conservatives and Liberal Democrats had to find a way of resolving their differences on this issue. The document setting out there joint programme in May 2010 (*The Coalition: Our Programme for Government*) contained the following commitment (p. 11):

> We will establish a Commission to investigate the creation of a British Bill of Rights that incorporates and builds on all our obligations under the European Convention on Human Rights, ensures that these rights continue to be enshrined in British law, and protects and extends British liberties. We will seek to promote a better understanding of the true scope of these obligations and liberties.

This commitment was met by the establishment in March 2011 of just such an independent Commission, under the chair of a retired senior civil servant, with eight other members, seven of whom had a legal background. The terms of reference of the Commission were:

> The Commission will investigate the creation of a UK Bill of Rights that incorporates and builds on all our obligations under the European Convention on Human Rights, ensures that these rights continue to be enshrined in UK law, and protects and extend our liberties.
>
> It will examine the operation and implementation of these obligations, and consider ways to promote a better understanding of the true scope of these obligations and liberties.
>
> It should provide advice to the Government on the ongoing Interlaken process to reform the Strasbourg court ahead of and following the UK's Chairmanship of the Council of Europe.
>
> It should consult, including with the public, judiciary and devolved administrations and legislatures, and aim to report no later than by the end of 2012.

As will be seen the terms of reference assumed the United Kingdom's continuing commitment to the ECHR, so any suggestion that we should try to withdraw from this, as has been suggested in some parts of the popular press, was excluded from consideration. To do so would be politically very difficult, affecting, as it would, the United Kingdom's membership of both the Council of Europe and the European Union. In relation to the third term of reference, the 'Interlaken Process' results from a declaration emanating from a meeting of the Council of Ministers in Interlaken, Switzerland, held in February 2010 (available at http://www.eda.admin.ch/etc/medialib/downloads/edazen/topics/europa/euroc.Par.0133.File.tmp/final_en.pdf). This committed the Council of Europe, amongst other things, to further streamlining the work of the ECtHR to ensure that it focuses on the most important cases and deals with those speedily. In connection with this the UK Commission on a Bill of Rights issued interim advice to the UK government in July 2011 (see http://www.justice.gov.uk/downloads/about/cbr/cbr-court-reform-interim-advice.pdf), in advance of the United Kingdom's Chairmanship of the Council of Europe (November 2011–May 2012). It made four recommendations:

- That the government should vigorously pursue reforms designed to ensure that as many as possible of human rights cases are dealt with by domestic courts, and that the ECtHR deals only with 'a limited number of cases that raise serious questions affecting the interpretation or application of the Convention and serious issues of general importance'.

- That 'the government should use its chairmanship to initiate a time-bound programme of fundamental reform'.

- That the government should ensure that such a programme leads to 'a new and effective screening mechanism that allows the Court to decline to deal with cases that do not raise a serious violation of the Convention'.

- That the government should ensure that such a programme deals with the need to revisit the 'the role of the Court in awarding "just satisfaction" '.

The make-up of the Commission, consisting of an almost equal balance of supporters and critics of the HRA 1998 (judging from their previous comments on the subject) made it unlikely that it is going to come forward with radical proposals, and so it proved. The Commission divided 7:2 on the central issue of whether there should be a UK Bill of Rights (*A UK Bill of Rights? The Choice Before Us*, Commission on a Bill of Rights, 2012). Although only 25 per cent of respondents to the Commission's consultation supported such a move, the majority on the Commission proposed that one should be introduced to replace the HRA 1998. This would be desirable in part because it might increase public acceptance and approval, which was seen as being low in relation to the HRA. The minority, in opposing this recommendation, referred to the result of the consultation, but also to the fact that there was no support for such a move in the UK outside England. In the light of increased devolution it felt that any move in this direction should be part of a more general constitutional settlement. Even the majority recognized that it would be sensible to await the results of the Scottish devolution referendum, due in September 2014. The other main recommendations of the majority were:

- Additional rights might be created, for example in the areas of equality, and civil and criminal justice (which the Commission saw as having been under threat from government action in recent years). Socio-economic rights should not, however, be included.

- The balance between courts and Parliament should remain the same (i.e. no power to strike down legislation).
- 'Public authority' should be defined to include private providers of public services.
- Regarding the inclusion of 'responsibilities/duties', rights should be universal and should not be made conditional upon the exercise of responsibilities by the individual concerned.
- The ECtHR needs further reform and the UK government should continue to press for this.

In relation to the last point, to the extent that the perceived difficulties with the HRA stem from the Strasbourg Court and the way in which it operates, the power to change things is not in the hands of the UK government alone. Co-operation with European partners is needed if reforms of the Court or the Convention, or both, are to take place. A small step towards this was taken with the 'Brighton Declaration' of April 2012, which recognized the importance of the principle of 'subsidiarity' (i.e. that local courts may be best placed to take decisions) and that the processes of dealing with the large number of applications to the ECtHR needed further reform. Some of these issues are reflected in Protocol 15 to the Convention, which was opened for signature in June 2013, but which will not come into effect until ratified by all Member States. At the time of writing less than half the States had signed the Protocol, and only one had ratified it.

On the more general issue of the impact of the Bill of Rights Commission's recommendations and any reform of the HRA, given the divisions of opinion on the issue both within and between the political parties forming the current coalition government, it is clear than no firm proposals for reform will come forward prior to the 2015 General Election. Even then, it will take at least a year, and more likely two, for any reform to be put in place. It is likely, therefore, that the HRA 1998 in its present form is going to provide the framework for human rights issues in the United Kingdom for some years to come.

2.7 Conclusions

An overall assessment of the success or otherwise of the HRA 1998 depends on our expectations of it. It is suggested that these should focus on what we would expect a 'Bill of Rights' to achieve. On this there are a number of factors which might be put forward.

First, there is the political effect that the existence of a clear and agreed statement of rights should have. It will be likely to encourage a different way of thinking about issues, both inside and outside Parliament and in the courts. Parliament should be more likely to consider the rights implications of new legislation; the press and other commentators will tend to measure the law, and actions of Parliament, the executive, and the judiciary against the standards set by the Bill;

and the courts will pay attention to the Bill when developing and interpreting the law. These beneficial developments operate at an informal level, changing attitudes and expectations. Second, there should also be more specifically legal benefits. Individuals who feel that their rights have been infringed should have a means of redress provided by the Bill. They will be able to enforce their rights in the courts, or whatever other tribunal is established to adjudicate on issues arising under the Bill.

Has the HRA 1998 provided these benefits? The amount of attention which the Act has received, and the level of awareness of 'rights' issues which it has engendered, suggest that it will have a lasting effect on attitudes and expectations. As far as its effect on Parliament is concerned, it clearly has not stopped Parliament from enacting laws that extend restrictions on freedom (e.g. the Criminal Justice and Police Act 2001 and the Anti-terrorism, Crime, and Security Act 2001), but it has generally meant that these restrictions have been made the subject of judicial supervision. To that extent at least there has been a recognition of the requirements of the ECHR, as there has also in the provisions which specifically limit the exercise of a power to situations where its use is proportional to its objective (see, e.g. s. 5(2) of the Regulation of Investigatory Powers Act 2000).

As far as the courts are concerned, the approach of the judiciary to the HRA 1998 has been largely encouraging. There was some scepticism as to whether the judges would be able to adapt to a different type of law, and to the need to consider the effect of Convention rights more directly than in the past. The argument was that our existing judges are not appropriately trained, and do not have the right background, to deal with the broad political, or quasi-political, issues which inevitably arise in attempting to construe and apply a generally worded Bill of Rights. English judges are used to dealing with narrowly specific issues raised by particular cases, applying or distinguishing precedents, or interpreting closely worded legislation. As has been shown by some of the material in this chapter, and in particular the development of judicial review, the courts have, however, shown a willingness to take on board the new demands made by the existence of a quasi-Bill of Rights within the UK legal system. There are times when they appear perhaps unduly defensive of the common law, arguing that the rights alleged would have been protected even in the absence of the HRA 1998 (see, e.g. Lord Bingham in *R v Secretary of State for the Home Department, ex p Daly* [2001] UKHL 26, [2001] 3 All ER 433), but this does not matter unduly as long as the end result is that protection is provided. The response has been similar to that of the Canadian judiciary when faced with the introduction of the Charter of Rights and Freedoms in 1982. There were some equally sceptical views about how they would deal with it, but with the Supreme Court giving the lead in *Hunter* v *Southam* (1984) 11 DLR (4th) 641 a purposive approach to the interpretation and application of Charter rights was soon established. There is no reason to doubt that the English judiciary, following the lead of the Supreme Court, can be equally successful in dealing with the demands of the HRA 1998. Of course, there will remain those who feel that the background of our judges makes them unsuited to the task of dealing with human rights issues. This school of thought, represented most powerfully by Professor J. A. G. Griffith in *The Politics of the Judiciary*, 5th edn (London: Fontana Press, 1997), argues that judges in the United Kingdom, when they are required to make political choices, do so in a way which is, as a result of their backgrounds, and the position they hold in society, 'necessarily conservative, not liberal' (p. 336). Judges are part of the establishment and will, therefore, tend to support the established order, which in many cases will mean supporting the government. It is too early to say whether these fears will prove justified as regards the judicial approach to the HRA 1998, but, as indicated, the early signs are encouraging. An unduly deferential judiciary would not have been prepared to challenge directly the government's anti-terrorism legislation, as was done in *A v Secretary of State for the Home Department* [2004] UKHL 56, [2005] 2 WLR 87 (discussed further in chapter 10 (10.6.1)).

For individuals too, the HRA 1998 has so far been largely good news, in that they are now able to raise human rights issues, at least as defined by the Convention rights, before the ordinary courts, and those rights are being taken seriously, even if they are not upheld in every case. Doors are opening, for example, to the recognition of rights of privacy (see chapter 6 (6.10)), and to the need for proper consideration of the reasons for violent death, particularly where this has occurred when the victim was in the custody of the State. It is to be hoped that this will continue as the case law on the Act develops and the ideas which it is generating mature. One of the more disappointing areas, however, is that of the exclusion of evidence in criminal trials, where the advent of Art. 6 has led to no discernible change in the operation of s. 78 of the Police and Criminal Evidence Act 1984 (PACE) (see chapter 4 (4.6.4.3)).

Overall, therefore, the HRA 1998 appears to be having a significant and positive effect on the development of civil liberties in the United Kingdom. There is still much to criticize, however. New powers are still being given to the police to deal with suspects, with little by way of balancing of the rights of the individual. Freedom of speech is still the subject of controls which may well be regarded as excessive in relation to official secrets, and the censorship of films and videos. The freedom to engage in public protest operates within a framework which is the subject of close supervision by the police, and may be the subject of somewhat haphazard control as a result of the continued existence of the common law power to control breaches of the peace. Extradition has become difficult to challenge, and deportation orders and asylum claims operate with unsatisfactory appeal procedures.

On balance, the verdict must be that the HRA 1998 has started to produce the benefits that would be hoped for from a Bill of Rights, but that there is still substantial room for improvement. We continue to live in a society which is more restricted than it needs to be (taking account of all realistic threats to its stability), and where the trend in recent years has been for Parliament to subject existing freedoms to further limitation. It is important for those who study the law to be aware of this and to be prepared to argue for the full recognition of the rights contained in the ECHR, and against any further encroachment on our liberties. For in our type of society it is the law, and the way that it is used by governments, that is the means by which, in the main, our freedom is restricted, just as, paradoxically, it is through the law that our rights may be best protected. Those who study and work with the law have a responsibility to try to ensure that the balance is properly struck between such restriction and protection.

QUESTIONS

1 Is the current definition of a 'public authority' in need of revision? If so, how should it be defined? Would it be better for Parliament to provide a list of such authorities, as has been done in the Freedom of Information Act 2000?

2 To what extent can the HRA 1998 apply to disputes between individual citizens?

3 Do you think that the courts have used their power of interpretation of legislation under s. 3 of the HRA 1998 appropriately? Can they be accused of thwarting Parliament's intention and so shifting the constitutional balance between the courts and Parliament?

4 Can action be taken under the HRA 1998 without there being an existing cause of action under the common law or statute?

5 Is the HRA 1998 susceptible to the doctrine of implied repeal, or does it have a special constitutional status which distinguishes it from 'ordinary' statutes?

6 How should the HRA 1998 be reformed, if at all? Should it be replaced with a Bill of Rights? If so, what would such a change achieve?

FURTHER READING

Buxton, R. (2000), 'The HRA and Private Law', (2000) 116 LQR 48

Campbell, D. and Young, J. (2002), 'The Metric Martyrs and the Entrenchment Jurisprudence of Lord Justice Laws', [2002] PL 399

Cane, P. (2004), 'Church, State and Human Rights: are Parish Councils Public Authorities?', (2004) 120 LQR 41

Craig, P. (2001), 'The Courts, the Human Rights Act and Judicial Review', (2001) 117 LQR 589

Dicey, A. V. (1965), *An Introduction to the Study of the Law of the Constitution*, 10th edn, London: Macmillan & Co

Commission on a Bill of Rights (2012), *A UK Bill of Rights? The Choice Before Us*, vols 1 and 2, London: Commission on a Bill of Rights

Croft, J. (2002), *Whitehall and the Human Rights Act 1998—The First Year*, London: The Constitution Unit

Edwards, R. (2002), 'Judicial Deference under the Human Rights Act', (2002) 65 MLR 859

Ekins, R. (2003), 'A critique of Radical Approaches to Rights Consistent Statutory Interpretation', [2003] EHRLR 641

Ewing, K. D. (2004) 'The Futility of the Human Rights Act', [2004] PL 829

Gearty, C. (2001), 'Unravelling *Osman*', (2001) 64 MLR 159

Gearty, C. (2003), 'Revisiting Section 3(1) of the Human Rights Act', (2003) 119 LQR 551

Griffith, J. A. G. (1997), *The Politics of the Judiciary*, 5th edn, London: Fontana Press

Grosz, S., Beatson, J., and Duffy, P. (2000), *Human Rights—the 1998 Act and the European Convention*, London: Sweet & Maxwell

Hunt, M. (1998), 'The Horizontal Effect of the HRA', [1998] PL 423

Kavanagh, A. (2004), 'Statutory Interpretation and Human Rights after *Anderson*: a More Contextual Approach', [2004] PL 537

Kavanagh, A. (2004), 'The Elusive Divide Between Interpretation and Legislation under the Human Rights Act', (2004) 24 OJLS 259

Klug, F. (2003), 'Judicial Deference under the Human Rights Act 1998', [2003] EHRLR 125

Klug, F. and Starmer, K. (2005), 'Standing Back from the Human Rights Act: How Effective is it Five Years On?', [2005] PL 716

Leigh, I. (2002), 'Taking Rights Proportionately: Judicial Review, the Human Rights Act and Strasbourg', [2002] PL 265

Nicol, D. (2004), 'Gender Reassignment and the Transformation of the Human Rights Act', (2004) 120 LQR 194

Nicol, D. (2004), 'Statutory Interpretation and Human Rights after *Anderson*', [2004] PL 273

Oliver, D. (2004), 'Functions of a Public Nature under the Human Rights Act', [2004] PL 329

Phillipson, G. (2003), '(Mis)reading Section 3 of the Human Rights Act', (2003) 199 LQR 183

Raine, J. and Walker, C. (2002), 'The Impact on the Courts and the Administration of Justice of the Human Rights Act 1998', Lord Chancellor's Department Research Series 9/02

Rogers, J. (2003), 'Applying the Doctrine of Positive Obligations in the European Convention on Human Rights to Domestic Substantive Criminal Law in Domestic Proceedings', [2003] Crim LR 690

Steyn, J. (2005) '2000–2005: Laying the Foundations of Human Rights Law in the United Kingdom', [2005] EHRLR 349

Sunkin, M. (2004), 'Pushing Forward the Frontiers of Human Rights Protection: the Meaning of Public Authority under the Human Rights Act', [2004] PL 643

Wade, W. (2000), 'Horizons of Horizontality', (2000) 116 LQR 217

Wadham, J., Mountfield, H., Prochaska, E., and Brown, C. (2011), *Blackstone's Guide to the Human Rights Act 1998*, 5th edn, Oxford: Oxford University Press

3

Personal Liberty (Article 5) I: Stop, Search, and Arrest

3.1 Introduction

One of the hallmarks of a free society is the ability of its citizens to go about their business without the need to explain to anyone in authority what they are doing, and without the fear that they may be subject to arbitrary challenge or arrest. It is recognized in the United States Bill of Rights, in the 4th Amendment, in the Canadian Charter of Rights and Freedoms, ss 7–10, and in the European Convention on Human Rights (ECHR), Art. 5 (see 3.2). This aspect of personal freedom is of great importance. It is sometimes treated as an element of a more general right of privacy, which covers also the freedom to enjoy property, and the freedom from the disclosure of personal secrets. To categorize it in this way, however, runs the risk of downgrading its importance. A person's physical freedom is surely more important than the quiet possession of their home, or the maintenance of their domestic secrets. To interfere bodily with a person strikes at the heart of their individuality. Invasion of bodily integrity is regarded as a most serious offence when committed by one citizen against another. Assaults and related offences are treated as serious crimes, which attract substantial penalties. This may be said to reflect the importance that society attaches to this aspect of the individual's existence. It is therefore reasonable to expect that when similar invasions are authorized on behalf of the State, by, for example, giving its police force the power to stop people, to search them, or to compel them physically (by arrest) to attend a police station, this should only be on the clearest grounds, and in situations of necessity.

This chapter is primarily concerned with the laws which justify such invasions of personal freedom. The majority of the powers discussed are available to police officers only, though in some cases they may be exercised by other officials, or even by private citizens. Under the Police Reform Act 2002 (s. 38 and Sch. 4, Pt. 1) all police forces have the power to employ civilian 'community support officers' (PCSOs), with the authority to exercise some powers on the streets which were formerly limited to the police. The Home Office reported that in September 2012 there were around 14,000 PCSOs employed by forces in England and Wales, though the number has decreased slightly from a figure of over 16,000 in 2010 (perhaps as a result of the recession) (A. Dhani, 'Police Service Strength', HOSB 01/13, Home Office). The largest numbers of PCSOs are to be found in the metropolitan areas, particularly London, with around 3,000. No other force had more than 1,000 PCSOs, though Greater Manchester had 787. At the other end of the scale there were 95 PCSOs for Cumbria and 106 for Bedfordshire. The figures show, however, that the PCSOs are an important part of the policing process, while still small in comparison to the number of serving police officers (around 66,000 across England and Wales).

Among the powers which such officers can use is the power to issue a fixed penalty notice to someone engaging in anti-social behaviour (see 3.4.5). They also have the power to detain a person for 30 minutes pending the arrival of a police officer. From January 2008 a statutory standard set of powers for PCSOs has been provided by the Police Reform Act 2002 (Standard Powers and Duties of Community Support Officers) Order 2007 (SI 2007/3202).

Virtually all the powers discussed in this chapter are based in statutes, many of them being contained in the Police and Criminal Evidence Act 1984 (PACE).

Before moving on to consider those statutory provisions, the context provided by the Human Rights Act 1998 (HRA 1998) will be considered.

3.2 Stop, search, and arrest under the Human Rights Act 1998

Article 5 of the ECHR sets out the standards to be applied in relation to infringements of personal freedom. After stating the general right to 'liberty and security of person', the Article goes on to recognize various exceptions. The one that is most relevant to this chapter is Art. 5(1)(c), which allows deprivation of liberty 'in accordance with a procedure prescribed by law', where it takes the form of:

> ...the lawful arrest or detention of a person effected for the purpose of bringing him before the competent legal authority on reasonable suspicion of having committed an offence or when it is reasonably considered necessary to prevent his committing an offence or fleeing after having done so.

Further, a person who is arrested must be told promptly, and in a language which the person can understand, of the reasons for the arrest (Art. 5(2)). In some circumstances, Art. 5(1)(b) may also be relevant. This covers detention 'in order to secure the fulfilment of any obligation prescribed by law'. Various of the other provisions of Art. 5 are more relevant to the procedures at the police station, and so are discussed in chapter 4.

These are the provisions which must be considered when looking at the possibility of action under the HRA 1998 to challenge the use of stop and search or arrest powers. Are the powers outlined in this chapter justifiable under Art. 5(1)? It is arguable that such powers do not generally involve sufficient deprivation of liberty to engage Art. 5. This was the view of the House of Lords in *R (Gillan)* v *Commissioner of Police of the Metropolis* [2006] UKHL 12, [2006] 2 WLR 537 (para. 25). In contrast, when the case reached Strasbourg (*Gillan* v *United Kingdom* (2010) 50 EHRR 45) the European Court of Human Rights (ECtHR) noted that while the individuals concerned were subject to the stop and search power (para. 57):

> ...the applicants were entirely deprived of any freedom of movement. They were obliged to remain where they were and submit to the search and if they had refused they would

> have been liable to arrest, detention at a police station and criminal charges. This element of coercion is indicative of a deprivation of liberty within the meaning of art.5(1).

The Court found a violation of Art. 8 (right to private life) in this case, and so did not need to decide the Art. 5 issue, but the passage above suggests that if necessary it would have found that Art. 5 was engaged by stop and search (*Gillan* v *United Kingdom* is discussed more fully in chapter 10 (10.4.1)).

In *Austin* v *Metropolitan Police Commissioner* [2009] UKHL 5 the House of Lords held that the detention of a crowd for several hours in the exercise of powers to prevent a breach of the peace did not engage Art. 5, and this was confirmed by the ECtHR in *Austin* v *United Kingdom* (2012) 55 EHRR 14 (this case is discussed more fully in chapter 9 (9.6)). The Article has, however, been held to be applicable to the detention required to carry out a blood test (*X* v *Austria* (1979) 18 DR 154). This would suggest that, if a person is subjected to a search, rather than just stopped and asked questions, then there will be detention sufficient to require justification under Art. 5. Where a stop and search power is based on 'reasonable suspicion', then it may fall within Art. 5(1)(c). Although the suspicion required for stop and search does not necessarily involve suspicion of committing a criminal offence, the approach taken by the European Court in *Brogan* v *United Kingdom* (1989) 11 EHRR 117 (discussed in chapter 10 (10.4.3.2)) may be relevant. Here the Court held that the use of an arrest power with a view to allaying or confirming suspicions was justified by Art. 5(1)(c). This broad approach may well justify stopping and searching based on reasonable suspicion.

The alternative, and the one which would have to be used where the power does not require reasonable suspicion (and where there was no such suspicion in relation to the particular use of the power), would be for the authorities to rely on Art. 5(1)(b). The finding of the European Commission on Human Rights in *McVeigh, O'Neill and Evans* v *United Kingdom* (1981) 5 EHRR 71,that powers to stop and examine entrants to the UK did involve an 'obligation' falling within Art. 5(1)(b), suggests that this may provide a basis for validating stop and search powers.

Even if Art. 5 is not engaged, any stop involving a search will engage Art. 8 (right to respect for private life): see *Gillan* v *United Kingdom*. But Art. 8 allows for infringements where necessary in the interests of public order and the prevention of crime, and most stops and searches based on reasonable suspicion would fall within this (for those not based on such suspicion, see the discussion at 3.4.6).

As regards powers of arrest, these have been considered in a number of cases before the European Court. One of these was the 1990 case *Fox, Campbell and Hartley* v *United Kingdom* (1990) 13 EHRR 157. This concerned arrests under s. 11 of the Northern Ireland (Emergency Provisions) Act 1978, which allowed an arrest without warrant of 'any person suspected of being a terrorist'. The Court made it clear that the mere fact that an arrest took place under this power, which contained no requirement of *reasonable* suspicion, did not make it unlawful. It was necessary to decide in each case whether there was in fact reasonable suspicion. Thus the provision itself cannot be struck down; only particular actions taken under it (para. 31). The Article requires 'reasonable suspicion of having committed an offence', but the Court seemed quite prepared to accept that this would be satisfied by 'reasonable suspicion of being a terrorist' as it had done previously in *Brogan* v *United*

Kingdom. On the facts, however, the government had not produced sufficient evidence to show that there was reasonable suspicion, and so there was a breach of Art. 5(1)(c). In *Murray* v *United Kingdom* (1994) 19 EHRR 193, on the other hand, which concerned the power of the armed forces to detain suspects under s. 14 of the Northern Ireland (Emergency Provisions) Act 1978, the government was able to show, largely as a result of evidence produced in Mrs Murray's civil action against the Ministry of Defence, that there was a basis for the suspicion. Here, therefore, although the power was again expressed in subjective terms, there was no breach of Art. 5(1)(c), because the suspicion, as a matter of fact, was based on reasonable grounds. The fact that the assessment of compliance with Art. 5(1)(c) must be based on the 'particular circumstances of each case' rather than the manner in which the power is expressed was confirmed by the European Court in *O'Hara* v *United Kingdom* (2002) 34 EHRR 32, para. 41.

In *Guzzardi* v *Italy* (1980) 3 EHRR 333, on the other hand, the Court ruled that the reference in Art. 5(1)(c) to the use of arrest to prevent a person committing an offence, only applied in relation to a 'concrete and specified offence' (para. 102). It could not be used to justify a policy of general prevention directed against an individual, or category of individuals, who, like members of the Mafia, for example, are dangerous because of a continuing propensity to commit crimes. Thus, what in effect this part of Art. 5(1)(c) is primarily intended to cover, is the situation recognized, for example, in s. 24 of PACE, where a power of arrest is given in relation to a person reasonably suspected of being about to commit a specific arrestable offence (see 3.5.3.1).

Overall, therefore, it seems that in this area the powers and procedures under English law relating to stop and search and arrest are generally within the scope of what is allowable under Arts 5 and 8 of the ECHR, as interpreted in the cases, and therefore, subject to various specific points raised later in this chapter, not susceptible to challenge under the HRA 1998. It is important to remember, however, that the ECtHR looks at individual cases, not particular rules and procedures. Thus, in the same way that the Court may decide that the way in which a power (which is perhaps too widely framed in domestic law) has been applied in the case before it means that there is no breach of the ECHR, the contrary must also be true. If a power, which is framed in a way which meets the requirement of Arts 5 or 8, is applied oppressively in a particular case, there is then the possibility of a challenge under the ECHR. This would apply equally to the possibility of challenge under the HRA 1998.

A further possibility, to the extent that the powers involve a search of an individual, is that a particular search might involve inhuman or degrading treatment, contrary to Art. 3 of the ECHR, This is most likely to arise, however, where a police officer has acted in a way which goes beyond what is permitted under PACE and its Codes of Practice (e.g. by carrying out a search involving the removal of clothing in a public place). In such situations the individual might have a remedy in any case, on the basis that the actions of the police officer had become 'unlawful', without necessarily needing to use the HRA 1998. The House of Lords in *Wainwright* v *Home Office* [2003] UKHL 53, [2003] 4 All ER 969 (the facts of which are given in chapter 4 (4.1.2)), however, held that there was no breach of the common law in relation to a search by prison officers which did not comply with the Prison Rules. As regards the applicability of the HRA 1998 to such situations, the ECtHR in *Wainwright* v *United Kingdom* (2007) 44 EHRR 40 found that the searches did not reach a level of seriousness to engage Art. 3, but were in breach of Art. 8.

3.3 The Police and Criminal Evidence Act 1984 and its Codes of Practice

The enactment of PACE did not constitute a full codification of police powers, though it was a substantial step towards it. PACE provides the framework for the exercise of powers of stop and search, arrest, and detention (which is discussed in chapter 4). It derived largely from the recommendations of the Royal Commission on Criminal Procedure which reported in 1981 (Cmnd 8092), though it did not follow them precisely. Of almost equal importance in practical terms to the provisions of PACE itself, are the Codes of Practice associated with it. There are currently eight of these Codes, covering stop and search (Code A), entry to premises (Code B), detention and questioning (Code C), identification (Code D), tape recording of interviews (Code E), visual recording of interviews (Code F), arrest (Code G), and the detention and questioning of terrorist suspects (Code H). The most recent versions of Codes A, B, and D came into force on 7 March 2011; Code C and H on 11 July 2012; Codes E and F on 1 May 2010; and Code G on 13 November 2012. Current versions of the Codes are available on the Home Office website (http://www.gov.uk/police-and-criminal-evidence-act-1984-pace-codes-of-practice).

The Codes of Practice provide detailed regulations which in many cases fill out the broad powers contained in PACE, and explain how they should operate in practice. The legal status of the Codes of Practice is set out in ss 60, 66, and 67 of PACE. Sections 60 and 66 simply impose on the Home Secretary the responsibility for issuing the Codes of Practice. Sections 67(9) to (11) deals with their legal status. First, s. 67(11) confirms that the Codes of Practice are admissible in evidence in any legal proceedings (criminal or civil) to which they are relevant. In practice, the most common reference to the Codes of Practice has been in criminal proceedings, where the defendant is arguing that evidence is inadmissible because of a breach of one of the Codes of Practice (see chapter 4 (4.6.3)). Second, a failure by a police officer to comply with the provisions of a Code of Practice will not in itself render the officer liable to any criminal or civil proceedings: s. 67(10). Thus, breach of the Codes of Practice is neither a criminal offence, nor a statutory tort. Nor will it necessarily lead to disciplinary proceedings. Finally, any person, even if not a police officer, who has the duty of investigating criminal offences or charging offenders, must have regard to the relevant provisions of the Codes of Practice: s. 67(9).

The Codes of Practice thus have a legal status, but not such a strong one as the provisions of PACE itself. If, for example, a police officer steps outside the provisions of PACE in carrying out a search, this may well lead to a charge of assault. If a provision of the Code of Practice on stop and search is not followed, however, there is no automatic consequence, other than that the officer may be liable for a disciplinary offence. Breach of the Code of Practice will, however, be relevant, for example, in deciding whether to admit any evidence obtained as a result of the search.

Both the Codes of Practice and PACE must, of course, be considered and inter-preted in the light of the HRA 1998.

3.4 **Stop and search**

3.4.1 **Common law**

The position at common law is that neither a police officer, nor anyone else, has any right to stop a person, unless they are going to arrest them; nor is there any general obligation to answer questions put by a police officer. The rule is illustrated by *Rice* v *Connolly* [1966] 2 QB 414. Rice had been observed for some time by two police officers in the early hours of the morning, walking the streets of Grimsby. A number of burglaries had been committed that night, and the officers were on the lookout for suspects. They eventually challenged Rice, and asked where he was going. He refused to answer, and gave generally unhelpful replies. When asked to go with the officers he refused, and was arrested and charged with obstructing a police officer in the execution of his duty. The Divisional Court allowed his appeal against conviction. Lord Parker stated the legal position in the following terms (p. 419):

> It seems to me quite clear that though every citizen has a moral duty...to assist the police, there is no legal duty to that effect, and indeed the whole basis of the common law is the right of the individual to refuse to answer questions put to him by persons in authority, and to refuse to accompany those in authority to any particular place; short, of course, of arrest.

All that is allowed to the police is to attract a person's attention in order to address a question to them. This may include touching (*Donnelly* v *Jackman* [1970] 1 All ER 987), provided that this does not 'transcend the norms of acceptable behaviour' (*Collins* v *Wilcock* [1984] 3 All ER 374). Physically preventing a person from going away from the officer will clearly be impermissible. In *Collins* v *Wilcock* the officer grabbed the arm of a woman she wished to talk to, in order to stop her from walking off. This was held to exceed that officer's lawful powers.

None of this, of course, prevents the police approaching people in public places and asking them questions—what has become known as a 'stop and account'. But there is no obligation on the individual to answer, and unless there is available a specific statutory power to stop, a police officer cannot lawfully detain a citizen other than by an arrest (arrest is discussed at 3.5).

3.4.2 **General statutory provisions**

A number of statutes contain powers of stop and search. Some general provisions applying to all such powers are now contained in s. 2 of PACE and Code A.

Code A sets out in paras 1.1–1.5 a set of principles applying to the use of stop and search powers. These state that such powers 'must be used fairly, responsibly, with respect for people searched and without unlawful discrimination' (para. 1.1).

They also note that 'failure to use the powers in the proper manner reduces their effectiveness' (para. 1.3). On the other hand, Note of Guidance 1 to Code A notes that citizens have a 'civic' duty to help police officers to prevent crime and discover offenders. Paragraph 2.7 of Code A indicates that a person whom the police officer reasonably suspects to be in *innocent* possession of an item for which there is a power of search may be stopped and searched notwithstanding the fact that there would be no power of arrest. This power should only be used, however, where attempts to secure the co-operation of the person concerned have failed.

An important change introduced into Code A in 2003 is that it now forbids searching with 'consent' where there is no statutory or common law power available (para. 1.5). All searches, with one exception, should take place on the basis of the relevant legal power and follow the provisions of Code A. The one exception relates to the searching of those entering sports grounds or other premises where consent to such a search is a condition of entry (para. 1.5).

3.4.2.1 Reasonable suspicion

Most powers of stop and search (but not all: see 3.4.5) require reasonable grounds for suspicion. These must exist before a person is stopped. There is no power to stop in order to find grounds for carrying out a search (para. 2.11 of Code A). On the other hand, once a person is lawfully stopped, the officer is encouraged to question the person, since this may reveal information which will render a search unnecessary (para. 2.9). The Court of Appeal, in the unreported case of *Samuels* v *Commissioner of Police for the Metropolis*, 3 March 1999, confirmed, however, that a failure to co-operate in answering questions cannot in itself give rise to a reasonable ground for suspicion. The apparent statement to the contrary in *R (Diedrick)* v *Chief Constable of Hampshire* [2012] EWHC 2144 Admin, para. 9, is inconsistent with the earlier Court of Appeal authorities.

The Royal Commission regarded 'reasonable suspicion' as a concept which could not be defined. Some attempt is made, however, in Code A to try to indicate what it does and does not mean. Paragraph 2.2 starts by making it clear that there must be an 'objective' basis to it. The police officer's 'hunch' or 'feeling' about a person is never going to be enough; nor may it be based on 'personal factors' (para. 2.2 of Code A). Thus, 'appearance' (e.g. hairstyle and clothing), or previous convictions cannot be used in isolation, or in combination with each other, as the sole basis for a reasonable suspicion justifying a search. Here, as elsewhere, the police must not discriminate against people on the basis of the 'protected characteristics' recognized by the Equality Act 2010 (e.g. age, race, religion, sex). 'Stereotyped images' that certain persons or groups are more likely to commit offences may also not be used. If, however, an officer has reliable information or intelligence that members of a group or gang identified by, for example, distinctive clothing, jewellery, insignias, or tattoos, habitually carry knives, weapons, or drugs, that distinctive means of identification can be used as the basis for a stop and search (para. 2.6 of and Note 9 to Code A).

Code A gives some examples of factors which may ground reasonable suspicion. Information received (the source does not apparently matter) describing an article or a person may be enough. A person's being 'out of place' has in the past been mentioned by police officers as a basis for suspicion. The current version of Code A does not give any specific recognition of this, but suggests that the suspicion must relate to 'behaviour' so that 'reasonable suspicion can sometimes exist without specific information or intelligence and on the basis of the behaviour of a person' (para. 2.3 of Code A). So if, for example, a person is attempting to hide something on the street at night, this might create a reasonable suspicion of possession of stolen or prohibited articles.

All of this allows the police officer a fair degree of discretion. Provided that some objective basis can be shown for the suspicion, the courts are unlikely to reject it as unreasonable. It is only where the decision is clearly random, or based on a 'hunch' or prejudice, that the officer's action is likely to be regarded as unreasonable. The unreported case of *Black* v *DPP* (11 May 1995) provides an example of a situation where the police officers were held to have acted without sufficient basis for a reasonable suspicion. The police were carrying out a perfectly lawful search of premises on the basis of a warrant issued under the Misuse of Drugs Act 1971 (see chapter 6 (6.4.5.2). The occupier's brother arrived at the premises, and the police immediately purported to detain him for the purpose of searching him for illicit drugs. The basis for the suspicion was said to be that he 'was visiting a well-known drug dealer and that he might be present for the purpose of buying or selling controlled drugs'. The Divisional Court rejected this as forming the basis of a reasonable suspicion. Such a suspicion could clearly not be said to arise merely because a person called at the premises. They might well be there in some lawful capacity such as 'a visitor who called for a catalogue payment, or a door-to-door salesman, or the gas man'. In this case the suspect was known to be a close relative of the occupant—'he therefore had an independent reason to be there, quite apart from any suspicion relating to drugs'. The suspect's resistance to the police's attempts to search him did not, therefore, amount to the offence of obstruction.

The concept of 'reasonable suspicion' is central to the operation of discretionary police powers, and therefore crucial to the freedoms of the citizen. It is disappointing that it remains such a nebulous concept which is not properly explained either by definition or example in the relevant legislation or Codes of Practice, and is dealt with only to a limited extent by case law.

It is relevant to note in this context that the police operation of stop and search powers has been the subject of criticism on the basis that the powers appear to be used disproportionately in relation to particular groups, in particular young black males. Statistics relating to 2010 and published in a Ministry of Justice report in October 2011 revealed that there were seven times more stops and searches of black people per head of population than of white people ('Statistics on Race and the Criminal Justice System 2010', Ministry of Justice, October 2011, available at https://www.gov.uk/government/publications/race-and-the-criminal-justice-system--3)

The Macpherson Report on 'The Stephen Lawrence Inquiry', Cm 4262, 1999 (*Report*), identified this imbalance in the use of stop and search powers as one example of 'institutional racism' within the Metropolitan Police (para. 6.45). 'Institutional racism' was defined in the *Report* (para. 6.34) as:

> The collective failure of an organisation to provide an appropriate and professional service to people because of their colour, culture, or ethnic origin. It can be seen in or detected in processes, attitudes and behaviour which amount to discrimination through unwitting prejudice, ignorance, thoughtlessness and racist stereotyping which disadvantage ethnic minority people.

Initiatives to address these issues since the *Report* do not appear to have had much success in reducing the disproportionate use of stop and search against non-white citizens. The attempts to ensure even-handed and reasonable treatment through the PACE Codes of Practice, therefore, do not seem in the end to have been successful in achieving this aim.

In July 2013 the Home Secretary announced a consultation on the use of stop and search, based in part on concern about the inequality in the use of the power as between different ethnic groups. At the time of writing the outcome of this consultation is not known.

3.4.2.2 Notification provisions

Section 2 of PACE requires certain information to be given to a person who is stopped, if a search is to follow. If the officer stops with a view to searching, but decides, quite properly (s. 2(1)), not to proceed because such a search is unnecessary or impractical, no information has to be given. Until recently, there was a requirement that a record should be made of all stops, including those which were simply 'stop and account'. This was introduced largely in order to ensure that accurate information could be kept as to the ethnic background of those stopped by the police, for whatever reason. It has now been decided, however, that this was imposing an unnecessary burden on officers, and the most recent version of Code A has removed this requirement. Given the statistics on the imbalance in racial terms of the use of stop and search powers, referred to at 3.4.2.1, it is unfortunate that the recording of this information has ceased. It will make it more difficult in future to discover the truth about any alleged biases in the use of powers to stop. A challenge to the decision to cease recording 'stop and accounts' was rejected in *R (Diedrick)* v *Chief Constable of Hampshire* [2012] EWHC 2144 Admin.

Where there is to be a search, the constable must, before starting, take reasonable steps to bring to the suspect's attention:

1. if the constable is not in uniform, the constable's warrant card (s. 2(2), para. 3.9 of Code A);
2. the constable's name, and the police station to which the constable is attached;
3. the object of the proposed search: that is, what is being searched for;
4. the constable's grounds for proposing to make it; and
5. the fact that if a record is made of the search (see 3.4.2.4) the suspect is entitled to a copy.

These procedural requirements have two effects. They require the constable to address explicitly the issue of why the search is being carried out, and whether it is necessary. They also provide the suspect with information that may help to explain what is going on and, therefore, make it less intimidating. This may also provide the basis for action if there is a subsequent wish to challenge the legality of what has been done. Given these benefits, it is unfortunate (though understandable) that the Divisional Court has held in *DPP* v *Avery* [2001] EWHC 748 (Admin), [2002] 1 Cr App R 31 that the power which the police have in certain circumstances to require a person to remove a mask or other face-covering is not a 'search' and, therefore, not subject to the requirements of s. 2 (see further on this, 3.4.6.2).

Where the requirements of s. 2 do apply, a failure to follow them will affect all that follows. Thus in *Osman* v *Southwark Crown Court, The Times*, 28 September 1999 the Divisional Court confirmed that failure by police officers to give their name and station was in itself enough to render a subsequent search unlawful, so that actions taken to resist the search could not amount to an assault on the officers in the execution of their duty. This was confirmed by the Court of Appeal in *R* v *Bristol* [2007] EWCA Crim 3214. An officer who suspected that the defendant had a wrap of drugs concealed in his mouth had grabbed him in a way so as to stop him swallowing, while shouting, 'Drugs search, spit it out'. The defendant resisted, and was charged with obstructing a constable contrary to s. 23(4)(a) of the Misuse of Drugs Act 1971. The Court of Appeal found that the failure by the officer to give his name and station, which could have been done by shouting three words—'Mansson, Charing Cross'— meant that the search was unlawful, and the conviction should be quashed.

3.4.2.3 The conduct of the search

PACE itself says little about how the search should be conducted. The only relevant provision is s. 2(9), which states that a constable conducting a search without arrest may not require a person to remove any clothing in public, other than an outer coat, jacket, or gloves. Paragraph 3 of Code A goes into more detail, operating within the general principle that every reasonable effort should be made to minimize the embarrassment of the person being searched (para. 3.1 of Code A). Co-operation should be sought in every case, even if the suspect initially objects. Reasonable force may, however, be used as a last resort (para. 3.2 of Code A; see also s. 117). In *James* v *Director of Public Prosecutions* [2012] EWHC 1317 Admin it was stated (para. 8) that a 'pat-down' search does not involve the use of force, and nor does touching any part of the body other than 'in sensitive parts' (undefined). Perhaps more surprisingly it was also held that the placing of a hand on the suspect's throat, without applying pressure, did not constitute the use of force (the officer thought, correctly as it proved, that the suspect was concealing drugs in his mouth).

Where the basis of the suspicion justifying the search is that an article has been seen to be slipped into a pocket, the search should be confined to that pocket. Searches for small, easily concealable, articles may justifiably be more extensive. Searches going beyond what is permitted by s. 2(9) should be done out of public view, in a police van, for example, unless the person searched is willing to remove more (Notes for Guidance, note 7). Notes for Guidance, note 7, also indicates that an empty street should still be regarded as being 'in public'. If the search involves the removal of more than outer coat, jacket, gloves, headgear, or footwear it must be carried out by a person of the same sex, and must not take place in the presence of a person of the opposite sex, unless the person being searched specifically requests this (para. 3.6).

The duration of the detention for the purpose of the search should be limited to what is necessary to carry out the search at the place where the person was stopped or nearby (s. 2(8)). As the Notes for Guidance state (note 5), searches in public 'should be completed as soon as possible'.

These controls over the conduct of the search are basically satisfactory, except to the extent that they allow the person being searched to 'opt out' of the restrictions.

In the absence of any method for ensuring that consent was genuinely given, the 'consent' exceptions leave wide open the possibility of people being too timid, or unsure of their rights, to object to what the police want to do, and for this to be subsequently interpreted as 'consent'.

3.4.2.4 Procedures following a search

Once a search has been carried out there is an obligation on the constable to make a record of it in writing, unless it is not practicable to do so (s. 3(1)). The limitation of 'impracticability' will apply, for example, in a situation of public disorder, where the number of searches to be conducted, or the general situation, will effectively preclude the keeping of records (see also para. 4.1 of Code A).

The record must be made on the spot if at all possible, or if not, as soon as practicable thereafter (s. 3(2)).

The record may be made electronically or on paper (para. 4.1 of Code A). The police have a standard form for the recording of searches, the 'national search record', which should normally be used.

The content of the record is spelt out in s. 3(6), and para. 4.3 of Code A. It must include the identity of the constable (if the search is in connection with terrorism or it is reasonably believed that disclosure of names might endanger the officers concerned, the officers' warrant number and duty station should be recorded—para. 4.4 of Code A); the object of, and grounds for, the search; and the date, time, and location. There is no requirement to record the name or address of the person searched, but a note must be made of the person's ethnicity. This should be on the basis of the person's self-defined ethnicity, though the ethnicity as perceived by the officer making the search should also be recorded if this differs from the self-definition. These recording requirements were significantly reduced by the Crime and Security Act 2010, as part of the aim of reducing the bureaucratic burden on the police (see, e.g. P. Strickland and S. Almandras, *Crime and Security Bill*, HC Research Paper 09/97).

The person searched is entitled to a copy of the record, on request, at any time within three months of the search (s. 3(7), (9)). This period was reduced from 12 months by the Crime and Security Act 2010.

These requirements are an attempt to provide safeguards against the improper use of police powers of stop and search. Whether they do so to any great effect is open to question.

There are also provisions of a similar kind relating to searches of vehicles.

3.4.3 The PACE powers

The procedures outlined at 3.4.2.4 apply to virtually all powers to stop and search. PACE itself introduced new powers, and these are to be found in ss 1 and 4. Only the powers to stop vehicles, and to stop and search individuals are discussed here. The Act also gives powers to search vehicles.

3.4.3.1 Stolen or prohibited articles

The main stop and search power is contained in s. 1(2). The Act does not, in fact, generally use the word 'stop'. The relevant provision in s. 1 states that a constable may 'detain' a person or vehicle for the purpose of a search to which the section applies. This is consistent with the procedures outlined at 3.4.2.4, which make it clear that a 'stop' or 'detention' can only take place where there are reasonable grounds for suspicion justifying a search. In relation to vehicles, s. 3(9) provides that only a constable in uniform has the power to stop vehicles. The general power of a constable to stop vehicles is discussed further at 3.4.6.1.

Section 1(2) gives a constable the power to search any person for stolen or 'prohibited' articles, or 'any article to which subsection 8(A)' of s. 1 applies. Stolen articles are not further defined, so anything which constitutes stolen goods for the purpose of the Theft Act 1968 is presumably covered (s. 24 of the Theft Act 1968: this includes goods obtained, e.g. by blackmail or criminal deception). 'Prohibited articles' are defined in s. 1(7) of PACE. There are two main categories. The first is 'offensive weapons'. The second is various articles which may be used in relation to offences under the Theft Act 1968.

'Offensive weapon' is defined in s. 1(9) of PACE, to mean any article made or adapted for use for causing injury to persons, or intended by the person in possession of it for such use by that person or another. This is based on the similar definition of offensive weapon used in the Prevention of Crime Act 1953. It is clear that it covers articles which are in themselves 'offensive', such as guns and flick-knives. It was held in *R* v *Vasili* [2011] EWCA Crim 615 that such an article which has a dual purpose, in this case a flick-knife which could also be used as a lighter, remains an offensive weapon. The definition also covers innocent items which have been adapted for causing personal injury, such as a bicycle chain attached to a handle (creating a flail), or a screwdriver sharpened to a spike. Finally, and most controversially, it covers everyday, unadapted items, which are capable of being used to cause injury. Most of the contents of the kitchen drawer, or the toolbox, will come into this category. Such items become prohibited articles when they are in the possession of a person whose intention is that the article should be used for causing injury. Thus, a constable, in order lawfully to stop and search for such an item, must have reasonable suspicion not only of the fact that the person to be searched has possession of the article, but also of that person's state of mind in relation to the use of the article. It is difficult to see that this could ever be the case, unless the article has *already* been used for such a purpose. Section 1(8A) brings within the stop and search power a specific type of potentially offensive weapon, that is any article which has a blade or is sharply pointed, other than a folding pocket knife with a blade of three inches or less. A folding knife which can be locked open comes within the scope of s. 1(8A): *Harris* v *DPP*; *Fehmi* v *DPP* [1993] 1 All ER 562. It is an offence under s. 139 of the Criminal Justice Act 1988 to be in possession of such an article in a public place, unless the person in possession can prove that there was a good reason or lawful authority for this. The burden of proof is thus on the possessor to prove an innocent reason for having it in a public place. It was held in *L* v *DPP* [2002] 2 All ER 854 that this 'reverse burden' was not contrary to Art. 6 of the ECHR. Section 1(8A) of PACE applies to 'any article in relation to which a person has committed, or is committing, or is going to commit an offence under s. 139 of the Criminal Justice Act 1988'.

The second category of prohibited article is defined in s. 1(7)(b) and (8) of PACE. It covers articles made or adapted for use, or intended by the possessor for use, in connection with the commission of the following Theft Act 1968 offences: burglary

(s. 9), theft (s. 1), taking a motor vehicle without authority (s. 12), or obtaining property by deception (s. 15). The Criminal Justice Act 2003 added to this list offences under s. 1 of the Criminal Damage Act 1971 (destroying or damaging property). It could cover, therefore, a crowbar, skeleton keys, car keys, credit cards, or again, virtually any item from a standard domestic toolbox, provided the relevant purpose can be established.

Finally, the s. 1 power covers any firework which is in a person's possession in contravention of a prohibition imposed by the fireworks regulations.

In order to exercise the power under s. 1 of PACE, a constable must have reasonable grounds for suspecting that the person to be searched has possession of one of the articles outlined above (s. 1(3)). The 'reasonable suspicion' will have to be determined as explained in 3.4.2.1. The power may be exercised in any public place. This means any place to which the public, or a section of the public, has access, on payment or otherwise, as of right or by virtue of express or implied permission (s. 1(1)). It includes, therefore, not only the street, but shops, football or other sports stadiums, theatres, cinemas, or clubs. It would also presumably cover public libraries, museums, and art galleries. In relation to places other than the street, the constable must have a right to be on the premises. The power under s. 1 gives a constable no general right to enter premises without the permission of the occupier. There appears, however, to be an exception to this in that s. 1(1) also states that the power may be exercised in any other place, not being a dwelling, to which 'people have ready access'. There are two situations which this will cover. First, it will allow a search to be carried out on premises which are sometimes open to the public, but are not open at the relevant time. An obvious example would be a car park, which is only open when adjacent shops are open (see, e.g. *Marsh* v *Arscott* (1982) 75 Cr App R 211). Second, it would seem to apply in a situation where, in order to attempt to avoid an anticipated search, a suspect steps off the street into a nearby garden. In order to give any effect to this provision, it must be assumed that the constable will be regarded as having an implied licence to go on to the premises to carry out the search. (Powers of entry to premises are discussed more fully in chapter 6.)

The possibility of a search taking place in a garden is dealt with further in s. 1(4). If the constable wishes to search a person who is in a garden or yard, or on other land, which in either case is attached to a dwelling, a search is only permissible if the constable has reasonable grounds for suspecting that the person does not live in the dwelling, and is not on the land with the express or implied permission of someone who lives in the dwelling. Thus, a person approached on the street by a constable can escape the possibility of a search by moving to their own front garden, or that of a friend or relation who would consent to their being there. This confirms that the extension of the power to areas to which the public has 'ready access' is designed primarily to deal with the situation of the person trespassing in order to escape the attentions of the police.

Finally, if a search carried out under the s. 1 powers leads to the discovery of an article which a constable has reasonable grounds to believe to be an article of a kind which may be searched for *under the section*, that article may be seized (s. 1(6)). If drugs, for example, are found, this section gives no power to seize them. Strictly speaking, it seems that another search should be undertaken, and the suspect notified accordingly. In practice, however, it seems highly unlikely that any court would exclude evidence which has been obtained in this way. (For the power to exclude evidence, see chapter 4 (4.6.4).) The situation can also probably be regularized by an arrest, and the use of the consequent general power of seizure under s. 32 (see 3.5.4.1), or possibly by the use of the general power under s. 19 (see chapter 6 (6.6.2)) or s. 51 of the Criminal Justice and Police Act 2001 (see chapter 6 (6.4.5.1)). This assumes that the reference in s. 19 to things found 'on premises' can include things found in the possession of a person who is on the premises ('premises' being defined to include 'any place': s. 23).

3.4.3.2 Road checks

The general police powers to stop vehicles are discussed at 3.4.6.1. Section 4 of PACE gives a specific, though rather limited power to the police to establish road checks. This will allow the police to stop either all vehicles, or vehicles selected by any criterion (s. 4(2)), in order to check on who is travelling in the vehicle (not to search for property). Essentially, therefore, this is a power to stop vehicles randomly, without the need for any reasonable grounds in relation to any particular vehicle in relation to which the power is exercised. This is a serious inroad into the freedom of individuals to go about their business without arbitrary interference. The Royal Commission thought, however, that this might be justified in situations of emergency (Cmnd 8092, para. 3.32). It is, however, a power which, if the detention is sufficient to bring the power within the scope of Art. 5, might be open to challenge under the HRA 1998, because of the lack of any requirement of reasonable suspicion. In practice, however, these powers do not appear to cause problems. Authorization must normally be given by an officer of at least the rank of superintendent, and details of the procedures and powers are set out in s. 4 of PACE. They are not, however, discussed further here.

3.4.4 Other statutory powers

Powers of stop and search arise under a variety of statutes. A list of the powers is given in an Annex to Code A. There is only space to consider two of these here, namely the powers under the Misuse of Drugs Act 1971, and the Sporting Events (Control of Alcohol, etc.) Act 1985. In addition, police powers in relation to breath tests are considered.

3.4.4.1 Misuse of Drugs Act 1971, s. 23

This is one of the most commonly used powers of stop and search. In 2011–12, for example, around 50 per cent of all stops and searches (i.e. 546,800 out of 1,095,700) were for drugs ('Police Powers and Procedures England and Wales 2011/12', Home Office, April 2013). The next most commonly used power (at 20 per cent) was the power to search for stolen goods. Until 2002–03 stops for stolen goods had generally exceeded those for drugs, and there is no clear explanation for the change. Section 23 empowers any constable to carry out a search of a person whom the constable has reasonable grounds to suspect is in possession of a controlled drug. The person may be detained for the purpose of carrying out the search (s. 23(2)(a)). A 'controlled drug' is one defined as such in s. 2 of, and Sch. 2 to, the Act. It will currently include, among many other substances, cannabis, heroin, cocaine, crack, LSD, and ecstasy.

The power can be exercised anywhere: it does not have to be in a public place. Thus, police officers who have entered private premises in the execution of a search warrant relating to stolen goods, for example, will be entitled to search a person found on those premises who is reasonably suspected to be in possession of a controlled drug.

Nothing is said in the section about the way in which the search should be carried out, but the general provisions outlined above will apply. Paragraph 3.3 of Code A, in noting that where there is a search for a particular article it may only be reasonable to search the pocket into which it has been seen to be slipped, goes on to say that:

> In the case of a small article which can be easily concealed, such as a drug, and which might be concealed anywhere on the person, a more extensive search may be necessary.

For the use of force in relation to a search for drugs, see *James* v *Director of Public Prosecutions* [2012] EWHC 1317 Admin, discussed at 3.4.2.3. There is nothing in the section to prevent the search, if taking place in private, from being a strip search (i.e. involving the removal of more than outer clothing). An 'intimate search' is, however, prohibited by s. 53(1) of PACE (see chapter 4 (4.5.3.2)).

There is also power to stop and search a vehicle, on reasonable suspicion that controlled drugs may be found in it (s. 23(2)(b)). This presumably is also available where the drugs are suspected to be on a person in the vehicle.

Anything found in the course of a search under s. 23 which appears to the constable to be evidence of an offence *under the Act* may be seized. If offensive weapons or stolen goods are found, this section gives no power to seize them. As noted at 3.4.3.1, however, there are other powers which may justify seizure, and it is in any case unlikely that any court will refuse to admit evidence which has been obtained in this way.

Intentional obstruction of a constable exercising powers under this section is an offence (s. 23(4)).

3.4.4.2 The Sporting Events (Control of Alcohol, etc.) Act 1985

This Act is unusual in that it makes unlawful in certain circumstances the possession of articles which may normally be carried quite legally in a public place (though local authorities do now have the power to designate public areas in which it is prohibited to *consume* alcohol: ss 12 and 13 of the Criminal Justice and Police Act 2001). It was directed primarily at the problems of football violence, which were seen as being fuelled by alcohol. As a result it is made an offence to be in possession of alcoholic drinks while in certain types of vehicle travelling to certain sporting events (ss 1 and 1A). A power to stop and search relevant vehicles travelling to or from a designated sporting event is given to constables by s. 7(3), and is exercisable on reasonable grounds for suspicion that an offence under s. 1 is being or has been committed.

In addition, it is an offence to be in possession of alcoholic drinks, or any drink container (full or empty) which is capable of causing injury to a person struck by it, while present at a designated sporting event, or while entering or trying to enter a designated sports ground (s. 2(1)). A constable who has reasonable grounds to suspect that a person is committing or has committed an offence under the Act may search that person.

Somewhat surprisingly, no specific power to seize items is given in connection with either of these search powers. If an arrest follows the search, however, a power of seizure will arise under s. 32 of PACE (see 3.5.4.1). It may also be possible to rely on the general seizure power under s. 19 of PACE or s. 51 of the Criminal Justice and Police Act 2001 (chapter 6 (6.4.5.1)).

As noted, these provisions represent an unusual infringement on personal freedom. The possession of alcohol is not normally illicit. The powers are presumably thought justifiable because of (a) their limited scope as regards times and place; and (b) the magnitude of the problem they were passed to address.

Section 2A creates a similar offence in relation to fireworks or similar devices (e.g. distress flares). The same powers of stop and search apply to this offence.

3.4.4.3 **Breath tests**

It is in this context that there have been the most frequent calls in recent years for the police to have the power to stop motorists at random. Concern over the quantity of deaths and injuries on the roads attributable to alcohol has for some reached a stage where it outweighs the rights of the individual to be free from arbitrary detention. The current powers to require breath tests do not go this far, however, and are contained in the Road Traffic Act 1988. There is no power to require a vehicle to be stopped in order for a breath test to be carried out. If the power under s. 163 (see 3.4.6.1) is used, however, grounds for carrying out a breath test may quickly arise (see, e.g. *Steel* v *Goacher* [1983] RTR 98, where the smell of alcohol on the driver's breath after he had stopped gave rise to a reasonable suspicion justifying a test).

Section 6 of the Road Traffic Act 1988 sets out the situations where a constable has the power to require a person to provide a specimen of breath, and thus to be detained for this purpose. All the grounds require reasonable suspicion on the part of a constable. First, a constable in uniform may require a breath test on the basis of reasonable suspicion that a person is, or has been, driving or attempting to drive a motor vehicle on a road or other public place, and that the person either has alcohol in their body, or has committed a moving traffic offence (s. 6(1)(a) and (b)). These provisions also apply to a person reasonably suspected of being, or having been in charge of a motor vehicle, in the same way as to a suspected driver. Second, if a road accident has occurred, any constable may require any person who there are reasonable grounds to believe was driving, or attempting to drive, or in charge of a vehicle at the relevant time, to provide a specimen of breath. In relation to this power, the person may, if the constable thinks fit, be required to give the specimen at a police station specified by the constable.

A person who has been required to provide a specimen of breath may be detained at a police station, in order to stop them driving whilst still intoxicated, and thus committing an offence under s. 4 or s. 5 of the Act (s. 10). The power will continue until a constable decides that the person would no longer be committing such an offence by driving.

There are further powers in relation to the taking of samples of breath, blood, or urine, under s. 7 of the Act. These powers will generally follow an arrest, and be exercised at a police station. They are not considered further here.

3.4.5 **Penalty notices**

A different type of power was created by Pt. I of the Criminal Justice and Police Act 2001. This gives the police the power, in certain circumstances to issue a 'penalty notice' to someone over 10 whom a uniformed constable has reason to believe has committed a 'penalty offence' (s. 2). The relevant offences are set out in s. 1, and are mainly minor offences related to public disorder. They include a number of offences connected with drunkenness, such as s. 12 of the Licensing Act 1872 (being drunk on a highway, in a public place, or in licensed premises), s. 91 of the Criminal Justice Act 1967 (disorderly behaviour while being drunk in a public place) and various offences under the Licensing Act 2003 concerned with the sale of alcohol to children. The list also includes trespassing on a railway, or throwing stones at trains (ss 55 and 56 of the British Transport Commission Act 1949), throwing fireworks in a public place (s. 80 of the Explosives Act 1875), and wasting police time (s. 5(2) of the Criminal Law Act 1967). Some more serious offences, such as theft, criminal damage, and the offence under s. 5 of the Public Order Act 1986 (see chapter 9 (9.4.6)) have been added to the list. These were originally excluded in the face of strong opposition in order to ensure that the Bill became law.

Although this type of fixed penalty has been used previously in relation to certain strict liability road traffic offences, this use is clearly a major extension. The police will have the power, not only to arrest, but also to decide guilt. As is the usual case with such schemes, the person to whom a notice is given can ask to be tried for the alleged offence, rather than paying the penalty (s. 4). Where the penalty is paid, payment is made to the chief executive of the local justices, rather than to the police.

3.4.6 **Powers not requiring reasonable suspicion**

As we have seen, in general powers of stop and search must be based on reasonable suspicion. The police are not as a rule allowed to stop people on a random or arbitrary basis as they go about their business. This is an important freedom. Nevertheless, there are three statutes which give the police the power to stop, and in two cases to search, vehicles or people, without the need for reasonable suspicion. The first is a long-standing power which is now contained in the Road Traffic Act 1988. The others are of more recent origin, and are limited to situations concerning serious crime, or terrorism.

3.4.6.1 **Road Traffic Act 1988, s. 163**

The widest power which is given to any police officer to stop citizens is contained in s. 163 of the Road Traffic Act 1988. Section 163(1) simply states:

> A person driving a motor vehicle on a road must stop the vehicle on being required to do so by a constable in uniform.

Section 163(2) contains a similar provision applying to bicycles, and s. 163(3) makes it an offence to fail to comply with a direction to stop.

Note that the power under s. 163 is not in itself dependent on any reasonable suspicion on the part of the constable. The stop may apparently be entirely at random.

The question may be asked as to why, if this is the case, is there the need for the provision as to road checks in s. 4 of PACE? Could the police not simply use s. 163 of the Road Traffic Act 1988? Part of the answer to this lies in s. 4(2) of PACE. This refers to a road check under s. 4 as being a specific use of the power under s. 163. The effect is that if the police want to set up a road check for one of the purposes covered by s. 4(1), they must use the procedures there set out. If they wish to carry out a road check for other purposes, for example to check on compliance with the regulations concerning safety belts, they may simply rely on s. 163, and the limitations and procedures contained in s. 4 are inapplicable. The power to stop in s. 163 is complemented by the powers in ss 164 and 165, to require the driver of a vehicle to produce certain documentation, such as a driving licence, certificate of insurance, and 'MOT' test certificate of roadworthiness.

There is no power, however, to require the driver of a vehicle to take part in a 'census' of cars travelling on a particular road: *Hoffman* v *Thomas* [1974] 2 All ER 277.

The most recent consideration of this power by an English court (in its incarnation as s. 159 of the Road Traffic Act 1972) was in *Lodwick* v *Sanders* [1985] 1 All ER 577. The two members of the Divisional Court agreed that the section gives a constable a *power* to require the driver of a vehicle to stop (as was stated in *R* v *Waterfield* [1963] 3 All ER 659), and does not simply impose a *duty* on the motorist to stop (as was suggested in *Steel* v *Goacher* [1983] RTR 98). Once stopped the driver is under a duty to remain at a standstill at least until the constable has had the opportunity to exercise the powers under ss 164 and 165. The constable will, however, only have the power physically to detain the vehicle, for example by seizing the ignition key, where there are reasonable grounds (which may have arisen after the vehicle has been stopped) to believe the vehicle to be stolen. This will in effect amount to an arrest of the driver, and the procedures relevant to arrest (see 3.5) should be followed. Two Scottish cases in 1999 considered s. 163. In *McNee* v *Ruxton* [1999] GWD 28–1354 it was held that the evidence of offensive weapons found in a car following a s. 163 stop was admissible. The power under s. 163 was very wide and there was nothing to suggest that the police officers were acting outwith those powers. In *Stewart* v *Crowe* [1999] SLT 899, as part of Christmas crackdown on drink-driving, all vehicles on a particular road were stopped under s. 163, and the drivers asked to take a breath test. If they refused, they were let go unless the officer smelt alcohol on their breath. The appeal court upheld this use of s. 163. It was a general and unrestricted power and the only limitation was that it should not be used oppressively. A general campaign where all vehicles were stopped, as opposed to vehicles being selected arbitrarily or at random, was not oppressive, as it did not operate unfairly against any particular citizen.

These Scottish decisions only add to the uncertainty surrounding this power, and its distinction from a power of random stop and search seems quite narrow.

Given this, one would have thought that Parliament would at some stage have taken the opportunity to clarify exactly to what situations it was intended to apply. It is also a power which might be vulnerable to challenge under Art. 5 of the ECHR (though the period of detention may be insufficient to engage this Article) or more feasibly Art. 8, on the basis that the breadth of the provision means that it is insufficiently 'prescribed by law' (see the discussion of *Gillan* v *United Kingdom* in chapter 10 (10.4.1)).

3.4.6.2 Criminal Justice and Public Order Act 1994, s. 60

This power arises where a senior police officer, of at least the rank of inspector, reasonably believes that incidents involving serious violence may take place within his area, and that an authorization under the section is expedient to prevent this, or that people are carrying dangerous instruments or offensive weapons in his police area without good reason. The officer may issue a written authorization which will bring into force certain stop and search powers in that area, for up to 24 hours. If an inspector gives the authorization then an officer of at least the rank of superintendent must be informed as soon as it is practicable. The powers exist, therefore, for a limited period, but this may be extended for a further 24 hours if it appears that this would be expedient in the light of offences which have been, or are reasonably suspected to have been, committed 'in connection with any activity falling within the authorisation' (s. 60(3)).

Once an authorization is in force, any constable in uniform has the power to stop and search any pedestrian for offensive weapons or dangerous instruments (s. 60(4)). 'Offensive weapon' has the same definition as in s. 1(9) of PACE (see 3.4.3.1). 'Dangerous instrument' means 'instruments which have a blade or are sharply pointed'. This is a broad definition, which will cover knives of all types, skewers, swords, axes, etc. The constable may also stop any vehicle and search the vehicle, its driver, and any passengers, for such articles. In neither case is there any need for the constable to have 'reasonable suspicion' that such articles are in the possession of the person searched, or in the vehicle. Random searching is permitted, as is the routine searching, for example, of every person passing along a particular street. Failure to stop when required is an arrestable offence (s. 60(8)). Dangerous instruments, or articles which the constable reasonably suspects to be offensive weapons, which are found during a search may be seized (s. 60(6)).

This power is a particularly broad one, which can only be justifiable if it is used in a way which is strictly limited in place and time, and in connection with very serious incidents. Following the decision of the ECtHR in *Gillan* v *United Kingdom* (discussed in chapter 10 (10.4.1)) on a similar power under the Terrorism Act 2000, s. 60 was subject to challenge on the basis that its breadth means that it is not sufficiently 'prescribed by law' for the purposes of Art. 8. This argument was rejected in *R (Roberts)* v *Commissioner of Metropolitan Police* [2012] EWHC 1977 Admin, on the basis that the issue of an authorization required 'reasonable suspicion' on the part of the issuing officer, and the search power itself was more limited in scope than that considered in *Gillan* v *United Kingdom*. Even so, *Gillan* v *United Kingdom* makes it clear that its use will engage Art. 8, so that any search conducted under it will need to be proportionate to the objectives of the section (as was accepted in *R (Roberts)* v *Commissioner of the Metropolitan Police*). In other words, the power will need to be used with sensitivity if it is not to appear oppressive.

Use of the power is subject to the provisions of s. 2 of PACE and Code A, for example as to the information to be given prior to the search, and the conduct of the search itself (see 3.4.2.2–3.4.2.4).

An additional power was added to s. 60 by the Crime and Disorder Act 1998 (s. 25), and revised by the Anti-terrorism, Crime, and Security Act 2001 (s. 94). It is now contained in s. 60AA of the Criminal Justice and Public Order Act 1994 (CJPOA 1994) and, when an authorization under s. 60 is in force, empowers a constable in uniform to require a person to remove any item which the constable reasonably believes the person is wearing 'wholly or mainly for the purpose of concealing his identity'. The section also provides for the seizure of such items when the constable reasonably believes that the person intends to use them to conceal identity (s. 60AA(2)). This includes seizure where the items are not being worn, but are discovered during the course of a search. There is, however, no specific power of search in relation to such items—the discovery must, therefore, be in the course of a search instigated for another purpose.

The main addition introduced by the 2001 Act was to enable an officer of at least the rank of inspector to give an 'authorisation' relating specifically to the power under s. 60AA where the officer:

> ...reasonably believes
>
> (a) that activities may take place...in his police area...that are likely to involve the commission of offences, and
>
> (b) that it is expedient, in order to prevent or control the activities, to give an authorisation under this subsection.

It will be seen that, although the power to give an authorization is predicated on the existence of a 'reasonable belief', the grounds themselves are much wider than those which apply to an authorization under s. 60, and so broadly stated as to make any possibility of challenge (e.g. by judicial review) unlikely. As is the case with s. 60, the authorization must be in writing (s. 60AA(6)), and, if given by an inspector, must be notified to a superintendent (or above) (s. 60AA(5)). A superintendent has the power, where offences have been committed, or are reasonably suspected to have been committed, in relation to the activities to which the authorization relates, to extend it for a further 24 hours (s. 60AA(4)).

The target of this power was said by the relevant minister at the time of its original introduction to include 'youths, with balaclavas covering their faces, who hijack cars and drive them at high speed around housing estates' (*Hansard*, Commons Standing Committee B, 9 June 1998, col. 804). It was also recognized, however, that it could be used against hunt saboteurs, or other demonstrators. The first reported case on its use involved an animal rights activist, demonstrating near a dog-breeding site. In *DPP* v *Avery* [2001] EWHC 748 (Admin), [2003] 1 Cr App R 31 it was alleged that the exercise of the power was unlawful because the constable had not complied with the requirements of s. 2 of PACE, concerning giving the constable's name and the grounds of the exercise of the power. The Divisional Court, however, held that the power under this provision was not a power of search, and that, therefore, it did not fall within the scope of s. 2 of PACE.

The exercise of the power was in any case self-explanatory, and nothing would be gained by the person being told by the constable 'that he believed that the person was concealing his identity'. Moreover, any interference with liberty involved was justified by the legitimate objectives of the provision, so that it did not offend against the HRA 1998. This may well be so, but the power is clearly one which needs sensitivity in its use, so that it is only used where there is a genuine attempt to conceal identity, rather than masking for religious or other legitimate reasons (such as the avoidance of pollution). In this context Note for Guidance 4, in Code A to PACE notes that:

> … [m]any people customarily cover their heads for religious reasons—for example, Muslim women, Sikh men, Sikh or Hindu women, or Rastafarian men or women. A police officer cannot order the removal of a head or face covering except where there is reason to believe that the item is being worn by the individual wholly or mainly for the purposes of disguising, not simply because it disguises identity.

This effectively limits the power to situations where the officer has reason to believe that the head or face covering has not been adopted for genuine religious reasons and should go some way to meeting the objections of the religious groups concerned. Where there may be religious sensitivities Code A states that the officer should permit the item to be removed out of public view. Where practicable this should also be out of sight of anyone of the opposite sex to the person concerned.

There is no power for the constable to remove a mask by force, but a refusal to comply with a request is a summary offence, for which, of course the constable may arrest.

3.4.6.3 **Terrorism Act 2000, ss. 44–7**

The powers under these sections were originally added to the previous terrorism legislation by the CJPOA 1994. They were similar to the power under s. 60 of the CJPOA 1994, discussed at 3.4.6.2, in that they provided for random and routine searching for limited periods, and within a specified area. They had to be modified significantly following the decision of the ECtHR in *Gillan* v *United Kingdom*. Since they are concerned with terrorism, full discussion of this power is left to chapter 10 (10.4.1).

3.5 **Arrest**

The powers that have been considered so far only authorize a very limited period of detention; that is, sufficient to carry out a search, to ask questions with a view to deciding whether or not a search is necessary, or to carry out a breath test. If the police wish to detain people in order to question them about their suspected involvement in a criminal offence, or in order to remove them from the scene of a disturbance, for example, this can only be done by using a power of arrest.

As is noted in 3.2, powers of arrest are subject to the provisions of Art. 5 of the ECHR, and the effect of these are noted at the appropriate points below.

PACE contains no definition of what amounts to an arrest, so this remains a matter to be determined largely by the common law. No particular words or procedures are necessary. Section 28 of PACE assumes that an arrest can take place simply by a constable informing a person that they are under arrest. There are cases prior to the Act which suggest that this may not be enough in itself to constitute an arrest. In *Genner* v *Sparks* (1705) 6 Mod Rep 173, 1 Salk 79, for example, it was held that a statement that a person was under arrest, which was followed by the immediate departure of the proposed arrestee, would be ineffective. Some physical contact, albeit simply a touch, was needed. Thus, a police officer who shouts at a suspect who is on the other side of the street 'you are under arrest', does not effect an arrest. If, on the other hand, the person to whom the words are spoken acquiesces in the arrest, and goes with the officer, it would seem that no physical contact is necessary: *Russen* v *Lucas* (1824) 1 C&P 153. It is not clear whether these decisions should still be regarded as good law on this point, but although the issue of when an arrest occurs has been discussed in later cases (e.g. *R* v *Inwood* [1973] 1 WLR 647, *R* v *Brown* [1976] 64 Cr App R 231, *Pedro* v *Diss* [1981] 2 All ER 59, and *Murray* v *Ministry of Defence* [1988] 2 All ER 521), none of them has contradicted the principles stated above. If the arrest is constituted by physical detention, any physical restraint going beyond what is necessary to attract a person's attention, and any involuntary detention beyond the period justified by the exercise of the powers in the previous section, will constitute an arrest. If the procedures outlined below are not followed, it will be unlawful.

Where a person has initially been questioned with consent, it may be more difficult to decide when an arrest has taken place. A person may voluntarily 'help the police with their inquiries' either on the street, or at a police station, without being arrested. It may be difficult in such situations to identify the point in time when an arrest occurs. What is clear from s. 29 of PACE, and para. 3.21 of Code C, however, is that as soon as a constable has decided that there are lawful grounds for arresting a person, and that the constable would not allow that person to leave police custody, then the person should immediately be told that he or she is under arrest.

There was no Code of Practice dealing with arrest for the first 20 years that PACE was in force, but one came into effect on 1 January 2006, namely Code G. In addition, some provisions of Code A (e.g. 'reasonable suspicion' (see 3.4.2.1)) and Code C (as noted) are relevant, and ss 28–31 of PACE deal with some procedural issues.

No particular formality is required in order to place somebody under arrest. As we have seen, the mere fact of physical detention, or the use of words indicating that an arrest has taken place, is sufficient. Where the arrest is by physical detention, the person must immediately be told that he or she is under arrest: s. 28(1). This is so even where the fact of arrest is obvious (s. 28(2)). The constable placing handcuffs on a suspect who has been caught robbing a bank is still obliged to say 'you are under arrest'. This particular form of words does not need to be used. In *R* v *Brosch* [1988] Crim LR 743, the Court of Appeal approved the statement of Stephenson LJ in the pre-PACE case of *R* v *Inwood* that 'there is no magic formula; only the obligation to make it plain to the suspect by what is said and done that he is no longer a free man'. In *Brosch* it was held to be enough that the person effecting the arrest (in this case the manager of a restaurant) grabbed the suspect's shoulder and said 'stay there'. This approach was followed in *Adler* v *CPS* [2013] EWHC 1968 (Admin) where an off-duty police officer arrested someone he had observed breaking a car window. It was found that he had indicated that he was 'detaining' the suspect and although he had not used the word 'arrest', the arrest was lawful. In *Dawes* v *DPP* [1994] RTR 209, an arrest was effected by a device (fitted by the police) which trapped the suspect in a car which he was attempting to steal.

Whatever the manner of the arrest, there is also an obligation to tell the person arrested the grounds for the arrest (s. 28(3)—which fulfils the similar obligation contained in Art. 5(2) of the ECHR). This must be done at the time of the arrest, or as soon as practicable thereafter, though there is no requirement that it should be done by the arresting officer: *Dhesi* v *Chief Constable of the West Midlands Police, The Times*, 9 May 2000, CA. The requirement remains even if the grounds for arrest are obvious (s. 28(4)). Thus, in the example of the bank robber the constable must not simply say 'you are under arrest', but 'you are under arrest for robbery'. The only exception to either of these requirements recognized by the Act is where the person escaped from custody before it was reasonably practicable to fulfil them. The obligation to give reasons for the arrest, has, however, been considered in several cases since the Act came into force. The Divisional Court in *Edwards* v *DPP* (1993) 97 Cr App R 301 held that if a reason is given, it must be a valid one. A constable had purported to arrest a person for 'obstruction', an offence which did not carry any power of arrest. The court ruled that, although the constable might have had other valid grounds for the arrest, the fact that a specific invalid ground was cited rendered the arrest unlawful. The court also noted that 'giving correct information as to the reason for an arrest is a matter of the utmost constitutional significance where a reason can be and is given at the time'. Similarly, in *Wilson* v *Chief Constable of Lancashire Constabulary*, 23 November 2000, unreported, the Court of Appeal held that, where facts were known to the police which could have been made known to the arresting officers, it was unfair to arrest for an unidentified offence that took place at some unspecified time and place. An arresting officer's minimum obligation was to give a suspect sufficient information to allow the suspect opportunity to respond. On the other hand, provided that correct information is given about the actual arrest, the fact that there is another *motive* for the arrest will not, it seems, necessarily render the arrest unlawful. In *R* v *Chalkley* [1998] QB 848, the police arrested the defendant on suspicion (for which there were reasonable grounds) of offences involving credit-card fraud. The real motive for the arrest, however, was to allow the police to gain access to the defendant's home and to install a listening device, with a view to acquiring evidence of serious robberies. The credit-card charges were never proceeded with. The Court of Appeal took the view that the arrest was lawful (p. 872):

> ...a collateral motive for an arrest on otherwise good and stated grounds does not necessarily make it unlawful. It depends on the motive.

In particular, where the motive is to assist the investigation of a far more serious crime, then this was legitimate. That this was the case had been indicated by the House of Lords in *Christie* v *Leachinsky* [1947] AC 573, where it was recognized that it was permissible in some circumstances to use a 'holding charge' to allow the detention of a suspect while more serious offences were investigated. Before any questioning takes place in relation to the more serious offence, however, the suspect must be arrested for that offence, or at least made aware of the true nature of the investigation: *R* v *Kirk* [1999] 4 All ER 698, CA.

As to the language that must be used, in *Brosch* it was held that the statement 'you're on drugs, aren't you' made immediately prior to the arrest was sufficient to indicate the grounds. This was presumably treated as being made 'at the time of' the arrest. In *Dawes* (the 'car-trap' case), the police were held to have arrived sufficiently quickly after the suspect was trapped to fulfil the requirement of notification 'as soon as practicable'. The Divisional Court noted, however, that if there was a possibility that the police might be slow to respond in such a situation, it might be prudent:

> ...to consider whether it would be practicable to put something in the car which would advise persons detained that they were under arrest and the reason why they were under arrest.

In *DPP* v *Hawkins* (1988) 88 Cr App R 166, the court had to consider the situation where the giving of reasons was impracticable at the time of the arrest. Hawkins had violently resisted arrest, and this clearly brought the case within the 'impracticability' exception. He was taken to a police station, but even then was not told of the grounds for his arrest. It was held that this rendered the arrest unlawful, but that this did *not* mean that the police officers were not acting in the execution of their duty when they apprehended Hawkins and took him to the police station. In effect, the arrest appears to remain lawful until a point has been reached where it is practicable to give reasons. The failure to do so at that stage is not retrospective. This does not correspond to the most obvious reading of the wording of s. 28, which states:

> ...no arrest is lawful unless the person arrested is informed of the ground for the arrest at the time of, or as soon as is practicable after, the arrest.

It may well be argued, however, that the literal reading would make things too difficult for the police in dealing with those who violently resist arrest (see D. Birch, [1988] Crim LR 742). Hawkins' only remedy would thus appear to have been to sue the police for false imprisonment in relation to any detention *subsequent* to the point where it was practicable to give reasons. The decision in *Hawkins* was distinguished in *Edwards* v *DPP*, on the basis that in the latter case an invalid reason had been given at the time of the purported arrest. This might suggest that the police officer is safer giving *no* reason for the arrest, rather than risking giving an invalid one. It is important to remember, however, that the suspect's behaviour in *Hawkins* rendered the giving of a reason at the time of the initial arrest 'impracticable'. This was held not to be the case in *Edwards*. It follows that, if it is practicable to give a reason at the time of the arrest, but none is given, then the arrest is invalid from the start. The application of the obligation in Art. 5(2) of the ECHR to give reasons for an arrest was considered in *Fox, Campbell, and Hartley* v *United Kingdom* (1990) 13 EHRR 157. This concerned arrests under s. 11 of the Northern Ireland (Emergency Provisions) Act 1978, which allowed an arrest without warrant of 'any person suspected of being a terrorist'. The ECtHR accepted that the purpose of the requirement in Art. 5(2) was to enable the person to be in a position to challenge the arrest. Telling the applicants that they were being arrested because they were suspected of being terrorists was not sufficient for this purpose; but subsequent questioning over the next 7–8 hours in relation to specific criminal acts, and membership of proscribed organizations, was sufficient to indicate the reason for the arrest, and met the requirements of Art. 5(2) (paras. 41–3). What is required in terms of content and promptness must be assessed in each case 'according to its special features' (para. 40). A similar approach was taken in *Murray* v *United Kingdom* (1994) 19 EHRR 193, which concerned the power of the armed forces to detain suspects under s. 14 of the 1978 Act. The European Court decided that, in the light of the fact that shortly before her questioning Mrs Murray's brothers had been convicted in the United States of offences connected with the purchase of weapons for the Provisional IRA, and of the evidence as to the questions which she was asked (para. 77):

> ...it must have been apparent to Mrs Murray that she was being questioned about her possible involvement in the collection of funds for the purchase of arms for the Provisional IRA by her brothers in the United States.

These decisions suggest that the requirement of Art. 5(2) may not in fact be as strict as that contained in s. 28 of PACE, in that it is apparently acceptable under the ECHR that the information as to the reasons for an arrest can be given over a period of time, and indirectly.

Whether what happened in *Hawkins* would also be acceptable is more doubtful. If, as seems likely, the failure *ever* to give reasons for the arrest in this case amounted to a breach of Art. 5(2), then Hawkins should have a right to compensation, by virtue of Art. 5(5). That he had no effective remedy might well amount to a breach of the ECHR, which could therefore now, if such a situation was to arise, form the basis of an action under the HRA 1998.

A person who is arrested should be cautioned as to the right to remain silent, and its consequences (para. 3 of Code G; see also chapter 4 (4.5.1)), unless such a caution has been issued immediately prior to the arrest, or it is impracticable because of the person's condition or behaviour.

3.5.1 Power of arrest at common law

The only power of arrest under the common law relates to 'breaches of the peace'. A constable may arrest a person who is causing a breach of the peace, or who is behaving in such a way as to lead the constable reasonably to apprehend an imminent breach of the peace, or who, where a breach has occurred, behaves in a way which leads the constable reasonably to believe that a breach will recur (*R* v *Howell* [1982] QB 416). The leading authorities are the House of Lords' decisions in *Albert* v *Lavin* [1981] 3 All ER 578 and *R (Laporte)* v *Chief Constable of Gloucestershire* [2006] UKHL 55, [2007] 2 All ER 529 (discussed more fully in chapter 9 (9.6)). In *Albert* v *Lavin* the defendant tried to push into a bus queue. An off-duty policeman tried to stop him, and when the defendant resisted, purported to arrest him for a breach of the peace. The defendant was charged with assaulting a police officer in the execution of his duty. The House of Lords upheld the conviction, and in so doing set out the powers that exist in relation to arrest for breach of the peace in the following terms (Lord Diplock, p. 880):

> [E]very citizen in whose presence a breach of the peace is being, or reasonably appears to be about to be, committed, has the right to take reasonable steps to make the person who is breaking or threatening to break the peace refrain from doing so; and those

> reasonable steps will include detaining him against his will. At common law this is not only the right of every citizen, it is also his duty

What is a 'breach of the peace'? For such an ancient concept, with case law going back to at least the eighteenth century, it is surprising that there is no absolutely certain answer. The definition which appears to be most widely accepted currently is that given by Watkins LJ in *R v Howell* [1982] QB 416 (p. 427):

> We are emboldened to say that there is a breach of the peace whenever harm is actually done or is likely to be done to a person or in his presence his property or a person is in fear of being so harmed through an assault, an affray, a riot, unlawful assembly or other disturbance.

Mere rowdiness, then, does not constitute a breach of the peace. (It may constitute an offence under the Public Order Act 1986: see chapter 9 (9.4.6)). Something in the way of actual or potential harm to a person or property is needed. A much broader definition was used by Lord Denning in *R v Chief Constable of the Devon and Cornwall Constabulary, ex p Central Electricity Generating Board* [1982] QB 458. He claimed (p. 471) that there is a breach of the peace 'whenever a person who is lawfully carrying out his work is unlawfully and physically prevented by another from doing it'. The other members of the Court of Appeal, however, did not follow this definition, finding on the facts that violence was likely, and that the police could intervene on this basis. The *Howell* approach thus seems to be the one to follow.

A breach of the peace can take place on private premises to which the public are admitted (*Thomas v Sawkins* [1935] 2 KB 249), or even in a residence (*R v Lamb* [1990] Crim LR 58; *Demetriou v DPP* [2012] EWHC 2443 Admin).

The imminence of an apprehended breach of the peace will be a question of fact in each case. In *Moss v McLachlan* [1985] IRLR 77 Skinner J referred to the need for a 'close proximity both in place and time'. In that case a distance of one-and-a-half miles, which could have been covered in less than five minutes by car, was held to be sufficiently proximate to allow powers to prevent a breach of the peace to be used. In *R (Laporte) v Chief Constable of Gloucestershire* the House of Lords viewed the facts of *Moss v McLachlan* as being at the limits of 'imminence', which should be interpreted as meaning 'about to happen'.

The Court of Appeal, in two cases subsequent to *Moss v McLachlan*, emphasized that the power to arrest on the basis of an *apprehended* breach of the peace, that is where no breach of the peace has yet occurred, and where the person arrested has not acted unlawfully, is exceptional, and should only be used where clearly necessary. In *Foulkes v Chief Constable for Merseyside* [1998] 3 All ER 705 it was used in relation to a man trying to re-enter his own house in the course of a family dispute. The Court of Appeal held that this was not a proper use of the power. The same approach was taken in *Bibby v Chief Constable of Essex, The Times*, 24 April 2000, where the power had been used to arrest a bailiff who was trying to seize goods to meet a judgment debt. The Court of Appeal, following the line taken in *Foulkes*, and by the Divisional Court in *Redmond-Bate v DPP* [1999] Crim LR 998 (which is discussed further in chapter 9 (9.6)) set out the following conditions for the use of the power:

(i) There must be the clearest of circumstances and a sufficiently real and present threat to the peace to justify the extreme step of depriving of his liberty a citizen who was not at the time acting unlawfully.

(ii) The threat must come from the person who was to be arrested.

(iii) The conduct must clearly interfere with the rights of others.

(iv) The natural consequence of the conduct must be violence from a third party.

(v) That violence must not be wholly unreasonable.

(vi) The conduct of the person arrested must be unreasonable.

Applying this to the case before it the Court of Appeal held that the arrest of the bailiff had been unlawful. The House of Lords in *R (Laporte)* v *Chief Constable of Gloucestershire* confirmed that the power to arrest to prevent an anticipated breach of the peace should only be used against a person acting lawfully when no other means of preventing the breach is possible.

The ECtHR has held in *Steel and ors* v *United Kingdom* (1998) 28 EHRR 603 that the power to arrest for a breach of the peace does not in principle involve any infringement of Art. 5 of the ECHR. It will depend on how it is used in particular circumstances. This decision and the English case law relating to the power to arrest for a breach of the peace are discussed further in the context of the law relating to demonstrations in chapter 9 (9.6).

3.5.2 Arrest under warrant

The police may obtain, from a justice of the peace, a warrant for arrest in relation to any person who has, or is suspected of having, committed an indictable offence: s. 1(1), (4) of the Magistrates' Courts Act 1980. In practice, however, the powers available to arrest without warrant under PACE and other statutes are so extensive that the police have little need to use this power, and it is not discussed further. It should be noted, however, that in *McGrath* v *Chief Constable of the Royal Ulster Constabulary* [2001] UKHL 39, [2001] 4 All ER 334, the House of Lords held that the fact that a warrant had been mistakenly issued in the name of someone who was not in fact a 'suspect' did not make the arrest of the person named unlawful. In this case a person had given another person's name when convicted of an offence, and then failed to appear for sentencing. A warrant was issued in the false name, and that person was arrested. The arresting officer was, however, entitled to act on the basis of the information on the warrant, in the absence of any indication on its face that it might be inaccurate. Indeed, it seems that an attempt to arrest the real absconder on the basis of this warrant would have been unlawful, since he was not the person named in it.

3.5.3 Powers of arrest under PACE

Police powers of arrest changed significantly as from 1 January 2006, when the amendments to PACE included in Pt. 3 of the Serious Organised Crime and Police Act 2005 came into force. Prior to that, the main power of arrest under PACE related to 'arrestable offences'. The concept of the arrestable offence had become rather complex. It was defined by s. 24 of PACE, in part by reference to the maximum sentence which an offence carried (at least five years' imprisonment), and in part by a list of specific offences set out in a Schedule to PACE. There was also a power, under s. 25 of PACE, to arrest for *any* offence, provided that certain conditions were met. There were also some arrest powers provided by particular statutes (e.g. the Public Order Act 1986) for offences which were not 'arrestable' within the PACE definition. In truth, the situation had become over-complicated, and the rationale behind the different categories of arrest power had been lost. A review of police powers was carried out in 2004 by the Home Office, and a consultation paper, 'Modernising Police Powers to Meet Community Needs' (Home Office, August 2004) was produced. This suggested that the category of 'arrestable offence' should disappear and that the police should always have the power to arrest for any offence, provided that it was 'necessary' to do so. It is this proposal that was enacted, by means of a reform of s. 24 of PACE, and the repeal of s. 25.

3.5.3.1 The arrest power, PACE, s. 24

A constable may arrest without warrant anyone:

1. who is, or is reasonably suspected to be, about to commit an offence (s. 24(1)(a), (c)); or

2. who is, or is reasonably suspected to be, in the act of committing an offence (s. 24(1)(b), (d)); or

3. who is guilty of committing an offence (s. 24(3)); or

4. who is reasonably suspected to be guilty of having committed an offence (s. 24(2), (3)) (whether or not an offence has actually been committed).

In each case, the test for reasonable suspicion will be the same as in relation to the power to stop and search (see 3.4.2.1). In *Alanov* v *Chief Constable for Sussex* [2012] EWCA Civ 234 the Court of Appeal emphasized that while the threshold for reasonable suspicion is not high, there must be some basis for linking the suspect to the offence. Following a rape in which the victim was attacked from behind (and so was unable to give a detailed description), a man in a nearby flat was found washing his genitals. His partner had lied about his presence on the property. There was, however, insufficient evidence on which to base a reasonable suspicion that he had committed the rape.

In addition, the power to arrest must only be exercised where the constable has reasonable grounds to believe that it is necessary to do so. Where an offence has been committed, or is suspected, but an arrest is not necessary, then the appropriate course will be for the suspect's details to be taken and a summons issued. The grounds which will support a belief that an arrest is necessary are set out in s. 24(5), and further explained in Code G, paras 2.4–2.9. Providing one of the grounds set out in s. 24(5) exists, the arrest will be lawful; there is no need for an arresting office to consider whether an alternative course of action might be appropriate: *Hayes* v *Chief Constable of Merseyside Police* [2011] EWCA Civ 911.

The grounds set out in s. 24(5) fall into three main categories relating to the identity of the suspect, the behaviour of the suspect, and the needs of the investigation. Looking at the first category, the constable will be entitled to arrest if, for example, the suspect's name cannot be readily ascertained, or no satisfactory address (needed for service of a summons) has been given. Equally, if the constable has reasonable grounds to doubt that a name given is correct, or that an address is satisfactory for service, he may arrest. Mr and Mrs Duck who decide to name their son 'Donald' should be aware that this may make him more likely to be arrested; those tempted to rename their cottage 'Buckingham Palace' should also be aware of the problems which this may create in this respect.

Paragraph 2.9 of Code G suggests that in some circumstances mobile fingerprinting might be used to ascertain identity, and so avoid the need to arrest

Turning to the second category, the constable will have power to arrest on the basis of a reasonable belief that this is necessary to prevent the person arrested 'causing physical injury to himself or any other person'; or causing loss or damage to property; or committing an offence against public decency in a situation where members of the public cannot reasonably be expected to avoid the person (s. 24(5)(c)(iv), (6)); or causing an unlawful obstruction of the highway (s. 24(5)(c)(v)). The constable also has a power to arrest on the basis of a reasonable belief that this is necessary to protect a child or 'other vulnerable' person from the person arrested (s. 24(5)(d)). This cannot be simply because the suspect might assault the vulnerable person, since this is already covered by s. 24(5)(c)(i). What other reasons for protection there might be, however, is not clear. Paragraph 2.9(d) of Code G does not assist greatly, other than by referring generally to the vulnerable persons 'physical or mental health or welfare'. Such a situation might perhaps arise where the arrested person is a man suspected of committing a sexual offence in relation to a member of his family, who might suffer psychological harm unless the suspect was removed (see D. Clark, V. Bevan, and K. Lidstone, *The Investigation of Crime*, 3rd edn (London: Butterworths, 2003), p. 270).

The arrest will also be regarded as necessary where the constable has reasonable grounds to believe that the suspect will otherwise suffer physical injury (s. 24(5)(c)(ii)). This type of 'protective' arrest is unusual in that it does not depend on what the suspect says or does, but on what might be done to the suspect. Presumably, the power is there to deal with the situation where the commission of an offence leads to a hostile reaction from other members of the public who have witnessed what happened (see Code G, para. 2.9(c)(ii)). The driver, for example, who as a result of careless driving has knocked down and injured a child, may need to be removed from the scene rather than being left to the mercies of the passers-by.

The final two reasons for arrest relate to the police investigation. They recognize that arrest may be necessary:

- to allow the prompt and effective investigation of the offence or of the conduct of the person in question; or
- to prevent any prosecution for the offence from being hindered by the disappearance of the person in question.

It seems likely that these two reasons for arrest will be the ones which the police will rely on with most frequency (see, e.g. *Hayes* v *Chief Constable of Merseyside Police* [2011] EWCA Civ 911).

The breadth of the power of arrest means that it will be up to the individual officer to decide whether it is appropriate to use it in any particular situation. Code G provides the following guidance:

1.2 The exercise of the power of arrest represents an obvious and significant inter-ference with the Right to Liberty and Security under Article 5 of the European Convention on Human Rights set out in Part I of Schedule 1 to the Human Rights Act 1998.

1.3 The use of the power must be fully justified and officers exercising the power should consider if the necessary objectives can be met by other, less intrusive means. Absence of justification for exercising the power of arrest may lead to challenges should the case proceed to court. It could also lead to civil claims against police for unlawful arrest and false imprisonment. When the power of arrest is exercised it is essential that it is exercised in a non-discriminatory and proportionate manner which is compatible with the Right to Liberty under Article 5.

This places a considerable responsibility on the constable, who may have to make a decision very quickly. It is likely that there will cases challenging the use of arrest as disproportionate, so that it will be up to the courts to provide further guidance.

It is important to remember that in all cases the person arrested must have been a suspect *before* the above 'reasons' for an arrest arise. This is illustrated by a case under the old s. 25 power. In *G v DPP* [1989] Crim LR 150, G was at a police station for the purpose of making a complaint. He was asked for, and gave, his name and address, but the officer did not believe that this was correct. G became abusive and was arrested for disorderly behaviour under s. 29 of the Town Police Clauses Act 1847 (which was not an 'arrestable' offence at that time). The arrest was held to be unlawful, because G was not a suspect at the time he was asked to give his name and address. The actions which might have constituted the offence took place subsequently.

It should be noted that these powers are similar to what is permitted by Art. 5(1)(c) of the ECHR, which recognizes the legitimacy of arrest for *any* offence where a person is reasonably suspected of having committed an offence, or when it is reasonably considered necessary to prevent his committing an offence, or fleeing after having done so.

The constable's powers under s. 24 of PACE are wider than those of the private citizen. Only a constable has the power under (1). In relation to (4), the private citizen only has such a power where an arrestable offence has actually been committed: s. 24(5) (confirmed in *R v Self* [1992] 3 All ER 476); the constable on the other hand may arrest where there are reasonable grounds to suspect that such an offence has been committed. The question of what amounts to 'reasonable suspicion' has been considered above (see 3.4.2.1) in the context of stop and search powers. There is also some case law on the issue in the context of arrest.

The case of *Castorina v Chief Constable of Surrey* [1988] NLJ 180 was concerned with the pre-PACE power of arrest under the Criminal Law Act 1967, but it was clear that the Court of Appeal thought that the same principles should apply to s. 24 of PACE, despite the slightly different wording of the arrest provision. A woman had been arrested following a burglary at a company from which she had recently been dismissed, and against which it was thought the woman might bear a grudge. She was released without charge, and sought damages for wrongful arrest and false imprisonment. The Court of Appeal criticized the trial judge who had defined the test of whether the arrest was lawful as being whether there was an 'honest belief founded on reasonable cause leading an ordinary cautious man to the conclusion that the person arrested was guilty of the offence'. In addition the judge had felt that the 'ordinary man' would not have arrested without seeking further information from the suspect. The Court of Appeal regarded this as too stringent a test. The question was not whether there was an honest belief in the suspect's guilt, but whether there was a *suspicion* based on reasonable grounds that the suspect *might* have committed the offence. Once there were such reasonable grounds, then, as indicated previously by the House of Lords in *Holgate-Mohammed v Duke* [1984] 1 AC 437, the question whether there should be an arrest or further inquiries was a matter of discretion to be tested on the basis of the principles for executive discretion established by *Associated Provincial Picture Houses* v *Wednesbury Corporation* [1948] 1 KB 223. This means that the decision to arrest must be made taking into account relevant matters excluding the irrelevant; it must be made for a proper purpose; and it must not be one that no reasonable officer (taking account of the relevant considerations) could have made. *Holgate-Mohammed* v *Duke* confirmed that an arrest in order to detain for questioning was made for a legitimate purpose.

The application of this test is illustrated by the decision of the Court of Appeal in *Plange* v *Chief Constable of South Humberside Police, The Times*, 23 March 1992. There it was held that, in the highly unusual situation where a constable has reasonable grounds to suspect a person, but knows that there is no possibility that a charge will be brought, an arrest would be unlawful, because the arresting officer would be acting on 'some irrelevant consideration or for an improper purpose'. Similarly, even though there are objectively reasonable grounds for suspicion, if there is no evidence that the arresting officer in fact thought that an arrestable offence had been committed, then the arrest will be unlawful: *Chapman* v *DPP* (1988) 89 Cr App R 190.

This case, somewhat surprisingly, was not referred to in *O'Hara* v *Chief Constable of the Royal Ulster Constabulary* [1997] 1 All ER 129. The House of Lords here had to consider whether the instructions of another officer could provide the arresting officer with reasonable grounds for suspicion in making an arrest. In other words, if a senior officer says to a constable, 'arrest that man!', will the constable be acting lawfully in doing so? The case was concerned with an arrest under s. 12(1)(b) of the Prevention of Terrorism (Temporary Provisions) Act 1984, but the House specifically stated that its comments were relevant to other arrest powers based on reasonable suspicion, and in particular s. 24 of PACE. The House held that the simple instruction from a superior officer was *not* sufficient in itself to provide reasonable grounds for suspicion. The wording of the provisions required that the arresting officer had personal knowledge of sufficient relevant information to found a reasonable suspicion. This might come from a briefing by the superior officer, or information from an informant, or personal observation. If, however, the arresting officer did not have personal knowledge of this kind, then the arrest would be unlawful. On the facts, however, it was held that there was sufficient evidence for the court to find that the briefing which the arresting officer in the case had apparently been given did provide a basis for reasonable suspicion. Subsequently, the Court of Appeal has held, purporting to follow *O'Hara* v *Chief Constable of the Royal Ulster Constabulary*, that reliance on an entry on the police national computer was likely to provide the necessary objective justification for an arrest: *Hough* v *Chief Constable of Staffordshire* [2001] EWCA Civ 39.

The ECtHR confirmed that the approach taken by the House of Lords on this issue is in line with the requirements of Art. 5: *O'Hara* v *United Kingdom* (2002) 34 EHRR 32. The Court emphasized that the reasonableness of the suspicion on which an arrest must be based 'forms an essential part of the safeguard against arbitrary arrest and detention laid down in Art. 5(1)(c) of the Convention' (para. 34). This requires 'the existence of some facts or information which would satisfy an objective observer that the person concerned may have committed the offence, though what may be regarded as reasonable will depend on all the circumstances of the case' (para. 34). On the other hand (para. 36):

> It may also be observed that the standard imposed by Article 5(1)(c) does not presuppose that the police have sufficient evidence to bring charges at the time of arrest. The object of questioning during detention under sub-paragraph (c) of Article 5(1) is to further the criminal investigation by way of confirming or dispelling the concrete suspicion grounding the arrest. Thus facts which raise a suspicion need not be of the same level as those necessary to justify a conviction, or even the bringing of a charge which comes at the next stage of the process of criminal investigation.

These statements, indicating the current view of the European Court, should form the basis for consideration of the issue by the English courts when faced with the question of whether the exercise of an arrest power meets the obligation under the HRA 1998 to comply with Art. 5.

The most recent consideration of the 'reasonable suspicion' issue in the context of arrest is the Court of Appeal decision in *Cumming* v *Chief Constable of the Northumbria Police* [2003] EWCA Civ 1844, *The Times*, 2 January 2004. Here it was held that, where one out of a specific group of people was likely to have committed an offence, there could be reasonable grounds for arresting all of them. The Court relied on *Castorina* and on *Fox, Hartley, and Campbell* v *United Kingdom*, but did not, surprisingly, refer to *O'Hara* v *United Kingdom* (though it did mention the House of Lords' decision in *O'Hara*). It emphasized that, in applying the third question under *Castorina*, that is, whether the discretion to arrest accorded with *Wednesbury* reasonableness, full weight must be given to Art. 5 of the ECHR (para. 43). Nevertheless, the court felt that in all the circumstances the arrests were justifiable on the basis of the facts as they appeared to the police at the time.

3.5.3.2 **Arrest by private individuals**

The powers of arrest possessed by those other than police constables are now set out in s. 24A of PACE. They are more limited than those of the police. They apply only to indictable offences, not to all offences. They may be used in respect of a person who is, or is reasonably suspected of being, in the act of committing an indictable offence. Where such an offence has actually been committed (not simply where it is suspected—see *R* v *Self* [1992] 3 All ER 476), a person reasonably suspected of having committed it may be arrested.

All the above is subject to the person concerned reasonably believing that it is 'necessary' for certain specified reasons, and that it is not reasonably practicable for a constable to make the arrest instead. The reasons for which an arrest may be necessary are set out in s. 24A(4), and are to prevent the person arrested:

(a) causing physical injury to himself or any other person;

(b) suffering physical injury;

(c) causing loss or damage to property; or

(d) making off before a constable can assume responsibility for him.

3.5.4 Powers and procedures following arrest

The powers and procedures to be followed after an arrest are set out in ss 30–2 of PACE. These do not, however, apply to a person arrested for a breach of the peace, since this is not an 'offence' within the meaning of PACE—*Williamson* v *Chief Constable of the West Midlands* [2003] EWCA Civ 337, [2004] 1 WLR 14. The Court of Appeal thought that it was nevertheless good practice for people who had been arrested for a breach of the peace to be dealt with as if they were subject to the relevant provisions of PACE.

3.5.4.1 Power of search

When any person has been arrested other than at a police station, a constable may carry out a search of the person on three grounds. First, there is a power of search where the constable has reasonable grounds for believing 'that the person arrested may present a danger to himself or others' (s. 32(1)). The power is not further explained, but presumably is intended primarily to enable the police to discover any weapon which the person might have in his or her possession. It would also presumably cover harmful drugs, if there is thought to be a danger of the arrested person attempting suicide. Section 32(8) allows the seizure and retention of anything which the constable has reasonable grounds to believe the arrested person might use to cause physical injury 'to himself or any other person'.

Second, a constable may search for anything which might be used by the arrested person to escape, on the basis of reasonable grounds for believing that some such thing is concealed on the person (s. 32(2)(a)(i)).

Third, a constable may search for evidence of *any* offence, not just the offence for which the arrest took place, on the basis of reasonable grounds for believing that such evidence is concealed on the person arrested (s. 32(2)(a)(ii)).

In relation to the last two powers, they are limited to what is reasonably required in order to discover what is suspected to be concealed (s. 32(3)). In relation to either power the constable may seize and retain anything discovered (other than an item subject to legal privilege (for which see chapter 6 (6.7.1.1)) which the constable has reasonable grounds for believing might be used to assist the arrested person to escape, or is evidence of, or has been obtained in consequence of, the commission of any offence (s. 32(9)).

None of the powers under s. 32, however, authorizes the constable to require the removal in public of more than an outer coat, jacket, or gloves (s. 32(4); compare the powers in relation to stop and search (see 3.4.2.3)). Certain powers to enter and search premises also arise as a consequence of arrest, under ss 18 and 32. These powers are discussed in chapter 6 (6.4.3.2).

3.5.4.2 Procedure following arrest

The basic procedure following arrest, and any search that may have taken place as a result, is for the arrested person to be taken to a police station (assuming that the arrest has taken place elsewhere) (s. 30(1)). There is also a power, however, under s. 30A, for the officer to release the arrested person on bail, subject to the requirement that they attend a police station at a specified time. Where the person is taken to a police station, this should happen 'as soon as practicable'. Generally the police station should be a 'designated police station' (s. 30(2)), which in practice will mean one of the larger police stations in the area (s. 35). There is an exception, however, if the period of custody is likely to be relatively short (less than six hours), and the constable is working in an area covered by a station which is not designated (s. 30(3) and (4)). The constable may also take the person to a non-designated station in two other situations: first, where an individual constable has carried out the arrest, or taken charge of the arrested person (e.g. following a citizen's arrest), and has no assistance from other officers available (s. 30(5)(a)); and, second, where the constable thinks that there is a risk of injury to the arrested person, the constable, or someone else, if the person has to be taken to a designated station (s. 30(5)(b)). These are exceptional cases, however, and in any case, a person who is first taken to a non-designated station should be moved to a designated station, or released, within six hours. This is to ensure that the proper procedures relating to detention, which require the supervision of a custody officer (see chapter 4 (4.2.1)), are carried out, where any extended period of detention occurs.

A final situation in which the arrested person need not be taken to a designated station is where the constable decides before arrival that it is no longer necessary to keep the person under arrest (s. 30(7)). This might occur, for example, where a person arrested under s. 24, with the arrest being 'necessary' because they have failed to give satisfactory identification or may be a danger to others (see 3.5.3.1), decides to give a satisfactory name or address, or no longer appears to be a danger to anybody. Release in this way should be recorded by the constable (s. 30(8)). Thus, all arrests should be recorded, either upon arrival at a police station (see chapter 4 (4.2)), or upon previous release.

It was noted above that, under the normal procedures, the arrested person should be taken to a designated station as soon as practicable. Section 30(10) recognizes one particular situation where delay may be justified. This is where the presence of the arrested person is required elsewhere, in order to carry out investigations which it is reasonable should take place immediately. This would be the case, for example, where the police wish to search premises immediately after the arrest, and wish to have the arrested person present. The reasons for any such delay must be recorded as soon as the arrested person arrives at a police station (s. 30(11)).

The purpose of s. 30 is to ensure that the arrested person is received as soon as possible into the system of detention, and its associated safeguards, which is set out in Pt. IV of the Act (and discussed in chapter 4). The fact that some exceptions are allowed, however, might encourage the police to try to find reasons for delay so that they can question the person, or obtain other information, before entering the realm of compulsory access to legal advice, and tape-recorded interviews. As is seen in chapter 4 (4.5.2.1), amendments to the Codes of Practice have been introduced to counter this by extending the notion of what constitutes an 'interview', and to reduce the advantages to the police of using the 'mobile interview room' (that is, a police car), to take the 'scenic route' to the police station. Some of the problems which still exist for the arrested person, however, are shown by *R* v *Kerawalla* [1991] Crim LR 451. The arrest took place in a hotel room, and Kerawalla was questioned there for some time. It was held that he had not been wrongly deprived of his right to legal advice under s. 58 of PACE, because this right only applied to people in custody at a police station. Moreover, although the police were in breach of their duty under s. 30 to bring Kerawalla to a police station as soon as practicable, this breach was not such as should render the evidence obtained from the questioning at the hotel inadmissible. Although the Court of Appeal emphasized the point that in this case they did not think there was any bad faith involved on the part of the police, and that they were not delaying taking the suspect to the police station simply to avoid his having access to legal advice, the decision can only act as an encouragement to the police to stretch the limits of s. 30 as far as possible.

It is not clear that the HRA 1998 will be of much assistance to a person dealt with as in *Kerawalla*. Unless the detention following arrest extends long enough to fall foul of Art. 5(3) of the ECHR, which requires an arrested person 'to be brought promptly before a judge or other officer authorised by law to exercise judicial power', such action by the police may well not infringe a Convention right. On the other hand, it clearly would be open to a court to rule that an arrest which was followed by undue delay in bringing the suspect to the police station was no longer 'lawful' within Art. 5(1)(c) and, therefore, provide a remedy on that basis. The approach in *Kerawalla*, however, is not encouraging as regards the likelihood of the courts making such a ruling. Nor is there any case law on the Convention which would appear to assist in supporting such a line.

3.6 Challenging the police

There are various ways in which an allegation that the police have exceeded or abused their powers as regards stop and search, or arrest, can be pursued. Civil actions, official complaints, and attempts to have evidence excluded may all be appropriate in particular cases. The most frequent complaints of this kind, however, arise out of procedures during detention. Discussion of these issues is therefore left until chapter 4 (4.6).

QUESTIONS

1   Is the approach to the scope of the right to liberty in Art. 5 of the ECHR taken by the House of Lords in *R (Gillan)* v *Commissioner of Police of the Metropolis* appropriate? Shouldn't the police need to justify any interference with an individual's freedom to walk along a public highway?

2   What is 'reasonable suspicion' for the purposes of stop and search or arrest? Are the limits placed on the use of subjective views by Code C satisfactory?

3   If a power of the kind which exists under s. 60 of the CJPOA 1994 is needed, do the provisions of s. 60 sufficiently limit its scope?

4   Given that the police now have the power to arrest anyone whom they reasonably suspect is committing or about to commit an offence, is there any need for the common law power to arrest for a breach of the peace?

5   Are the requirements as to the information that must be given to a person who is arrested sufficient in the light of the way in which they have been interpreted by the English and Strasbourg courts?

FURTHER READING

Austin, R. (2007), 'The New Powers of Arrest: Plus Ça Change: More of the Same or Major Change?', [2007] Crim LR 459

Bottomley, K. Comena, C., Dixon, D., Gill, M., and Wall, D. (1992), *The Impact of PACE*, Hull: University of Hull

Cape, E. (2003), 'The Revised PACE Codes of Practice: A Further Step Towards Inquisitorialism', [2003] Crim LR 355

Clark, D., Bevan, V., and Lidstone, K. (2003), *The Investigation of Crime*, 3rd edn, London: Butterworths

Lustgarten, L. (2002), 'The Future of Stop and Search', [2002] Crim LR 603

Macpherson, W. (1999), 'The Stephen Lawrence Inquiry: Report on an Inquiry by Sir William Macpherson of Cluny', Cm 4262, TSO

Ministry of Justice (2011), 'Statistics on Race and the Criminal Justice System 2010', October 2011 (available at https://www.gov.uk/government/publications/race-and-the-criminal-justice-system--3)

Royal Commission on Criminal Procedure (Philips Commission) (1981), 'Report', Cmnd 8092, HMSO

Sanders, A. and Young, R. (2010), *Criminal Justice*, 4th edn, Oxford: Oxford University Press

Zander, M. (2003), *Police and Criminal Evidence Act 1984*, 4th edn, London: Sweet & Maxwell

4

Personal Liberty (Article 5) II: Detention and Questioning

4.1 Introduction

This chapter continues the consideration of issues raised in chapter 3. While that chapter was concerned, however, with the initial decision to stop a person, and prevent them from departing, this chapter looks at the issues arising from more extended detention, generally at a police station. The focus here is on the grounds for such extended detention prior to charge, and the procedures which must be adopted in relation to it. The chapter does *not* deal with the procedures after a charge has been made, or after a person has been convicted. Both may involve deprivation of liberty, but the civil liberties issues are different where someone is either facing a specific charge, or has been convicted of an offence. They are not discussed further in this book, except to the extent that one of the 'remedies' for a breach of a person's pre-trial rights may be to claim that the trial itself is thereby rendered unfair. This raises the issue of the right to a fair trial guaranteed by Art. 6 of the European Convention on Human Rights (ECHR). The main consideration of this Article is to be found in chapter 5, but some reference will be found here as to how it has been applied in relation to such matters as the 'right to silence', or the right of access to legal advice, of those under suspicion of having committed an offence. What we are principally concerned with here, however, are the rights of a citizen who is a 'suspect' but against whom the police do not have sufficient evidence to charge with an offence.

The Police Reform Act 2002 (PRA 2002) includes provisions which allow some of the police powers dealt with in this chapter to be exercised by civilian 'detention officers'. They may, among other things, be empowered to search detained persons, to take fingerprints and certain samples without consent, and to take photographs. There are no precise figures as the number of detention officers, but statistics in relation to the position as at the end of September 2012 gave a figure of just over 4,000 'designated officers', which will include detention officers, across the whole of England and Wales (A. Dhani, 'Police Service Strength', HOSB 01/13, Home Office, January 2013).

4.1.1 Reasons for extending detention prior to charge

Why should the police have the power to detain prior to charge? The main purpose of such detention is to enable the suspect to be questioned, with a view to deciding whether there is sufficient evidence to bring a charge, or to obtaining such evidence, for example, in the form of a confession. The need to obtain evidence, however, cannot in itself justify the deprivation of liberty involved. It is not thought right to give the police compulsory powers of detention in relation to witnesses to criminal offences. Such people are perfectly entitled to refuse to co-operate with the police. Of course, if the matter goes to trial, the witness can be compelled to attend to give evidence, and may be in contempt of court for failing to do so. At the stage of acquiring evidence in the course of an investigation, however, the fact that such people may be in possession of vital information is not thought sufficient to entitle the police to force them to submit to questioning. In a limited range of situations it may be an *offence* to fail to give information. For example, under s. 19 of the Terrorism Act 2000 it is an offence in certain circumstances not to provide information about a belief or suspicion that an offence has been committed under ss 15–18 of the Act (mainly concerned with the funding of terrorism). A more general provision of this kind, covering information likely to be of assistance in preventing acts of terrorism, or in apprehending offenders, was added to the Terrorism Act 2000 by s. 117 of the Anti-terrorism, Crime, and Security Act 2001, and now appears as s. 38B of the Terrorism Act 2000. A person may be arrested under s. 24 of the Police and Criminal Evidence Act 1984 (PACE) in relation to either of these offences. In these limited circumstances, therefore, it is possible for the police to detain and question someone who is not directly involved in the commission of an offence, but may have relevant information.

In general, however, the special powers of detention given in relation to suspects must be justified by the suspicion itself. As can be seen in chapter 3, for an arrest the police must have reasonable grounds for believing that the person was in some way involved in criminal activities. Because there is such a belief, and therefore the reasonable possibility that the person has committed a criminal offence for which they will have to stand trial, it is acceptable that, in certain circumstances, the police should be able to detain the person with a view to obtaining the evidence they need to proceed. Such detention will only be for a restricted period of time, however, and is subject to a variety of procedural safeguards.

4.1.2 The Human Rights Act 1998: context

The main provisions of the ECHR which are relevant to detention and questioning are Arts 3, 5, 6, and 8.

Looking first at Art. 5, the provision which may justify the undoubted deprivation of liberty which is involved in the procedures discussed in this chapter is Art. 5(1)(c). This permits:

> …the lawful arrest or detention of a person effected for the purpose of bringing him before a competent legal authority on reasonable suspicion of having committed an offence or when it is reasonably considered necessary to prevent his committing an offence or fleeing after having done so.

This confirms that, generally speaking, only suspects can be the subject of compulsory powers of detention and questioning. Alongside this, reference must also be made to Art. 5(3), which deals with the need for judicial supervision of detention authorized by Art. 5(1)(c). This states:

> Everyone arrested or detained in accordance with paragraph 1(c) of this Article shall
> be brought promptly before a judge or other officer authorised by law to exercise
> judicial power.

The combination of these two Articles means that, although detention is possible
for the purpose of questioning suspects, it needs 'prompt' approval by someone
exercising judicial authority. The United Kingdom fell foul of this requirement
in *Brogan* v *United Kingdom* (1989) 11 EHRR 117 (discussed further in chapter 10,
(10.4.3.2)) when terrorist suspects were detained for periods of between four
and seven days on the authorization of the Home Secretary. This was found by
the European Court of Human Rights (ECtHR) not to meet the requirements of
Art. 5(3). Judicial approval of continued detention must be part of the procedure at
a relatively early stage, though the Court did not specify a particular time limit. It
noted, however, that in the French text of Art. 5(3) the word used is *'aussitôt'*, which
confirmed the connotation of immediacy. This aspect of the detention powers
considered in this chapter must therefore be given careful consideration.

As regards treatment while in detention, Art. 3, which prohibits 'torture' and
'inhuman or degrading treatment' is relevant. It has been fully discussed in
chapter 1 (1.7.2). As is discussed there this covers not only physical abuse, but can
also extend to such things as a failure to provide proper toilet facilities or medical
treatment.

Where treatment does not reach the level of seriousness to breach Art. 3, it may
engage the right to respect for private life under Art. 8 (see, e.g. *Wainwright* v *UK*
(2007) 44 EHRR 40). But breaches of this right will be justifiable if they are necessary in the interests of the prevention of crime, and are proportionate to that objective. Article 8 is discussed further in chapter 6.

Turning to Art. 6, this guarantees the right to a fair trial. It was confirmed by the
European Court in *Saunders* v *United Kingdom* (1997) 23 EHRR 313 that, as had been
suggested in *Funke* v *France* (1993) 16 EHRR 297:

> ... [a]lthough not mentioned in Article 6 of the Convention, the right to silence and
> the right not to incriminate oneself, are generally recognised international standards
> which lie at the heart of the notion of a fair procedure under Article 6.

This has implications, therefore, for procedures prior to trial, and in particular
what can be required of a suspect who is being questioned, and what implications, if any, a court may subsequently draw from a suspect's silence when being
questioned.

The case law on this area is discussed in more detail in chapter 5, but in *Saunders*
it was held that information obtained from the applicant under a compulsory questioning procedure during a Companies Act 1985 investigation by the Department
of Trade and Industry should not have been used in a subsequent criminal trial (see
now s. 59 of and Sch. 3 to the Youth Justice and Criminal Evidence Act 1999). In
Murray v *United Kingdom* (1996) 22 EHRR 29, on the other hand, it was held that it
was legitimate in certain circumstances for a court to draw adverse inferences from
a suspect's silence under questioning, provided that the suspect had had proper
access to legal advice.

With these constraints over detention and questioning powers in mind, we can now turn to the statutory framework within which such powers operate.

4.1.3 The PACE framework

The powers and responsibilities of the police, and the rights of those detained prior to charge, are now primarily governed by Pts IV and V of PACE, and Code C. For the relationship between the statute and the Code, see chapter 3 (3.3). PACE places much of the responsibility for ensuring that the provisions of the Act and the Code are complied with on to the shoulders of the 'custody officer' (see 4.2.1), who is in charge of the 'custody record' which should provide documentary evidence as to what was done in relation to each suspect in detention. Here, as in other parts of the Act, the main method of trying to achieve a balance between police powers and the freedoms of the citizen, is by the use of record keeping, to attempt to ensure that the limits are not overstepped. There are, however, in this part of the Act some positive rights given to those detained, most importantly the right of access to legal advice, under s. 58 (see 4.4.2).

The Code of Practice, as will be seen at 4.4.4, goes into considerable detail on the conditions of detention, spelling out, for example, the details of the type of meals to be provided. The problem here, however, is that there are no very effective methods of enforcement (see 4.6).

The procedures that follow are described as they apply to an adult, of sound mind, who understands English. Special rules operate in relation to various categories of particularly vulnerable suspect, but for reasons of space these are not dealt with here.

4.2 Preliminary procedures at the police station

As we have seen, people arrested away from a police station must normally be taken to a designated police station without delay (see chapter 3 (3.5.4.2)). Some people may be arrested at the police station. For example, if the police have been interviewing somebody who has been attending the police station voluntarily, and a constable decides that, if the person wanted to leave, that would no longer be allowed, the person must be arrested (s. 29). There must also be grounds for an arrest, of course. As soon as the arrested person arrives at the police station, or the person at the station is arrested, they become the responsibility of the custody officer.

4.2.1 The custody officer and the custody record

Appointment of custody officers is the responsibility of the chief officer of police for the area (that is, normally, the chief constable) though the power may be delegated (s. 36). The custody officer will almost always be a sergeant. No officer of lower rank may be appointed as a custody officer (s. 36(3)), though in some circumstances a constable may temporarily act as a custody officer (s. 36(4), (7)). Officers of the rank of sergeant or above who are not custody officers may also act as such in the same circumstances. Each designated police station will generally have a number of custody officers, so that there will always be one on duty. There is no legal obligation on a chief constable, however, to appoint more than one per station: *Vince* v *Chief Constable of the Dorset Police* [1993] 2 All ER 321.

It is the responsibility of the custody officer to open a custody record in relation to any person brought to the police station under arrest, or arrested at the police station (para. 2.1 of Code C). This will act as a 'log book' of the person's time at the police station. All entries must be timed and signed by the maker (para. 2.6 of Code C). The detainee, and the detainee's legal representative, have a right to a copy of the custody record for 12 months after release (para. 2.4A of Code C), and there is also a right, on giving notice, to inspect the original (para. 2.5 of Code C).

4.2.2 Information to be given at the start of detention

When an arrested person comes under the supervision of a custody officer, certain information must be given immediately (para. 3.1 of Code C). This information relates to, first, the right to have someone informed of the arrest (see 4.4.1); second, the right to legal advice (see 4.4.2); and third, the right to consult the Codes of Practice (which must be available at every police station). It should be made clear that these are continuing rights, which may be exercised at any time during custody.

The custody officer must also provide the person with a written notice. This should set out the above three rights, and in addition draw attention to the right to a copy of the custody record (see 4.2.1) and arrangements for obtaining legal advice (para. 3.2 of Code C). A further written 'notice of entitlements' should be given, dealing with such matters as visits during custody, provision of meals and other facilities, and the conduct of interviews (Note 3A of Code C). Just to make sure that all this is done, the person must be asked to sign the custody record acknowledging receipt of the various notices. A refusal to sign must be noted on the custody record.

These procedures are obviously better than nothing, but they are no guarantee that the person actually understands the entitlements, let alone is put in a position to enforce them. For many people who have just arrived at a police station under arrest, reading documents containing lists of rights is likely to be a low priority, and a request to sign, issued by a confident custody officer, is likely to be construed as an order to be obeyed, without necessarily much attention being paid to what is being signed. All this may well happen without any attempt to manipulate the procedures on the part of the police; they are no safeguard at all against an officer or officers who decide to act in bad faith.

Research soon after the implementation of PACE found that in 42.9 per cent of cases observed, the rights were read 'too quickly/incomprehensibly/incompletely' (see A. Sanders and L. Bridges, 'Access to Legal Advice and Police Malpractice' [1990] Crim LR 494). It seems that the situation may have improved subsequently, but there are still doubts about whether suspects properly understand what they are being told (see A. Sanders and R. Young, *Criminal Justice*, 4th edn (Oxford: Oxford University Press, 2010), pp. 231–9 for a useful summary of the relevant research).

4.2.3 **The decision to detain**

The first obligation of the custody officer, having issued the above information, is to decide whether the person is to be detained. This is governed by s. 37 of PACE and Art. 5(1)(c) of the ECHR. Under Art. 5(1)(c) all that is required is that there should be reasonable suspicion that the person has committed an offence (though as is seen below there are strict limits on how long a person can be held on this basis before being brought before a judge—see 4.3). If the custody officer decides that there is no such reasonable suspicion then, of course, the person must be released forthwith. The requirements of s. 37 of PACE are rather more complex.

The custody officer must first decide whether there is sufficient evidence to charge the person with the offence for which the arrest was made (s. 37(1)). If there is, then the person should be charged. Cape, however, has suggested that in practice custody officers routinely ignore this part of s. 37, and that suspects are regularly detained without charge when there is in fact already sufficient evidence on which to charge (E. Cape, 'Detention Without Charge: What Does Sufficient Evidence to "Charge" Mean?' [1999] Crim LR 874).

The presumption is that, where the suspect is charged, release from custody (with or without bail) will follow, unless there are particular reasons for continued detention, as specified in s. 38. This aspect of police procedures is not considered further here. If the custody officer decides that there is insufficient evidence for a charge, then, again, the starting point is release with or without bail. In two circumstances, however, the custody officer may authorize continued detention. The first is where there are reasonable grounds for believing that this is necessary to secure or preserve evidence relating to an offence for which the person is under arrest. There may be a risk, for example, that the suspected thief, if released, will dispose, or arrange for the disposal, of the stolen goods. The second, and most frequently used, ground for continued detention before charge is where the custody officer has reasonable grounds to believe that this is necessary in order to obtain evidence by questioning the person. The reasonable grounds in this case are likely to come largely from the investigating officer, who will no doubt seek to convince the custody officer that a period of questioning will result in a confession, or the obtaining of other evidence which will link the suspect sufficiently to the crime to justify a charge. Paragraph 3.4 of Code C, makes it clear that the custody officer should not invite any comment from the detainee either on the arresting officer's account of the arrest, or as to the decision to detain. If unsolicited comments are made, then they should be noted on the custody record. The custody officer should, however, resist the temptation to ask questions, or get involved in a dialogue with the detainee, concerning the detainee's involvement in any offence, or continued detention. Such an exchange is likely to constitute an 'interview', and therefore be subject to the protective provisions which apply in these circumstances (see 4.5.2).

If the decision is to detain, the custody officer must make a written record of the grounds (s. 37(4)). This should normally be done in the presence of the detainee, who should also be told of the grounds for the detention (s. 37(5)). This need not be done, however, if the detainee is at the time incapable of understanding what is said, or is violent or likely to become violent, or is in urgent need of medical attention (s. 37(6)). A detainee who is not in such a state must then be asked to sign the custody record to indicate whether legal advice is wanted or not. The custody officer must ensure that the signature is in the right place. If legal advice is requested, then the procedures in para. 6 of Code C, will come into play (see 4.4.2).

4.2.4 Search of detainees

Section 54(1) gives power to the custody officer to make an inventory, which will be included in the custody record and should be signed by the detainee (para. 4.4 of Code C), of everything in the possession of a detained person, including items taken from the person on arrest. Following changes to s. 54 made by the Criminal Justice Act 2003, the making of a record, and the extent of any record, is now at the custody officer's discretion, whereas it used to be obligatory. It remains, however, obligatory to *ascertain* what is in the possession of the detainee. A search may be carried out (by a constable of the same sex as the detainee) in order to facilitate this, though an intimate search or a search requiring the removal of more than outer clothing must follow the procedures in Annex A to Code C (discussed at 4.5.3.2). Note 4A to Code C states that the search need not be made if the person is clearly only to be detained for a short period, and is not to be placed in a cell. In that case the custody record should be endorsed 'not searched', and the detainee asked to sign. If the detainee refuses to sign, the custody officer will be obliged to compile an inventory.

The custody officer may normally seize and retain any item in the possession of the detainee (s. 54(3)). Clothes and personal effects (which does not include cash or other items of value (para. 4.3 of Code C)), however, may only be seized where there are reasonable grounds to believe that the detainee may use them to cause physical injury, to damage property, to interfere with evidence, or to assist escape (s. 54(4)(a)). Any clothes or personal effects which the custody officer has reasonable grounds to believe may be evidence relating to an offence (not necessarily that for which the person is detained) may also be seized (s. 54(4)(b)). The detainee, unless violent or likely to become violent, or incapable of understanding what is said, should be told the reasons for any seizure of property (s. 54(5)).

An additional power of search or examination was added by the Anti-terrorism, Crime, and Security Act 2001, and now appears as s. 54A of PACE. It empowers an inspector to authorize a search or examination for the purpose of ascertaining the detainee's identity, and in particular 'whether he has any mark that would tend to identify him as a person involved in the commission of an offence'. The offence may be one committed outside the United Kingdom, and the power is clearly in part intended to assist in the identification of those suspected of involvement in international crime, including terrorist offences. An intimate search (see 4.5.3.2) is not permitted under this power. Any mark discovered may be photographed. Neither the search nor the photography requires the consent of the detainee.

4.3 Time for detention

The period for which a person may be detained without charge as part of a criminal investigation is never without limit. The Anti-terrorism, Crime, and Security

Act 2001 did allow for indefinite detention without charge in relation to certain non-UK citizens who could not be deported (because there was no 'safe' country which would take them), but who were suspected of being 'international terrorists' and, therefore, regarded as dangerous to leave at large. This power, which was found by the House of Lords to be incompatible with the ECHR, is discussed further in chapter 10 (10.6.1). Constraints on the time for lawful detention are to be found in the case law on Art. 5 of the ECHR, which will have effect under the HRA 1998, and in PACE itself. Under PACE, the maximum period differs according to whether the person is being held under the terrorism provisions (see chapter 10 (10.4.3.2)), on suspicion of an indictable offence (see 4.3.3), or for any other offence (see 4.3.2).

4.3.1 The 'relevant time'

In calculating the permitted period of detention without charge under PACE, it is obviously important to identify the point when time starts to run. This is referred to in the Act as 'the relevant time', and is defined in s. 41. The standard situation is where a person is arrested and then taken to a police station. The relevant time is arrival at the police station (s. 41(2)(d)). Note that if the person is taken to a station other than a designated station (see chapter 3(3.5.4.2)), time still starts to run from arrival at that station. If arrival at the police station has been delayed, either legitimately, for example, to enable a search of premises to be carried out in the presence of the suspect, or illegitimately, as in *R v Kerawalla* [1991] Crim LR 451 (see chapter 3 (3.5.4.2)), the time prior to arrival will not count towards the period of detention.

In relation to a person arrested at a police station, the time of arrest is the relevant time (s. 41(2)(c)).

Special provisions apply where a person is arrested outside the police area in which their arrest is sought. If the arrest takes place in another police area in England and Wales, and the person is not questioned about the offence in that police area, the relevant time is normally the time at which the person first arrives at a police station in the area where the arrest was sought (s. 41(2)(a), (3)), subject to a 'safety-net' provision, whereby if the person is not taken to such a police station within 24 hours of the arrest, time will start to run anyway. If the person *is* questioned in the other police area, then the standard rule will apply, that is, the relevant time will be the time of first arrival at a police station, wherever situated. Thus if a suspect sought in Area A is arrested in Area B, and questioned in a police car which takes the suspect to a police station in Area C, before being moved to Area A, the relevant time will the time of arrival at the station in Area C.

Where the arrest takes place outside England and Wales (e.g. in Scotland) the relevant time will be either the time at which the arrested person arrives at a police station in the area where arrest was sought, or 24 hours after the person's arrival in England or Wales, whichever is the earlier (s. 41(2)(b)).

Finally, there is the situation where a person is being detained by the police in police Area A, and arrest of the person for another offence is sought in police Area B, so that the person is taken from A to B for the purpose of being questioned about that offence, not having been questioned about it in Area A. The relevant time is then either 24 hours after leaving the place of detention in A, or the time of arrival at a police station in B, whichever is the earlier (s. 41(5)).

As is clear from the above, rather complicated, provisions it is quite possible for a person to be in police detention for up to 24 hours before time starts to run against the police. Although there will be limitations on the power to question the detainee in this preliminary period, the additional time must be borne in mind when considering the statutory periods of permissible detention prior to charge. When considering the period of detention for the purposes of Art. 5, however, it would seem that time will start to run immediately from the point at which the person's liberty is restricted, which will normally be when he or she is arrested.

Section 41(6) provides that where a person is referred to hospital for medical treatment, any period during which that person is questioned either in transit to or from the hospital, or at the hospital, is to count towards his or her period in detention, but that any other period (e.g. while that person is undergoing medical treatment) is not to do so. It was noted in *Littlejohn v South Wales Police* [2008] EWHC 301 (Admin) that, read literally, this could lead to a very extended period. In the case before it a suspect had been arrested on suspicion of having swallowed a bag or bags containing drugs. He was sent to hospital in case the bags burst, endangering his life. The intention was that he should remain under observation until the bags passed through his system. It was expected that this would happen within 72 hours, but in fact the suspect had no bowel motions for a two-week period. The medical staff at the hospital were unwilling to keep him there, as they did not regard him as needing treatment. The police sought to continue his detention. The Divisional Court granted a writ of *habeas corpus* ordering his release. It was reluctant to decide exactly how s. 41(6) should operate, but clearly in this case the fact that there was medical opinion to the effect that he no longer required treatment or supervision meant that it no longer applied to the suspect, and he had to be released. One of the members of the court suggested that if a person was kept at hospital against that person's will, then any such period should count towards the maximum period for which he or she could be detained (para. 34), but was not prepared to give a decision, which on the facts was not needed, to clarify that point.

A similar issue arose in *R (Chief Constable of Greater Manchester) v Salford Magistrates' Court* [2011] EWHC 1578 (Admin) in relation to suspects who are released on bail. Police practice had been that when a suspect was released on bail prior to the maximum time for which detention had been authorized having expired (e.g. six hours after the relevant time), then when they reported back to the police station they could be detained for the remainder of the unexpired period (e.g. in this case, 18 hours) without any further authorization. In *R (Chief Constable of Greater Manchester) v Salford Magistrates Court* [2011] EWHC 1578 (Admin) the judge held that this was incorrect, and that, on the proper interpretation of the statutory provisions, time continued to run during the period of bail. The effect of this was that, if a person reported back after the period for authorized detention had expired, the police could only detain that person further if there was new evidence on the basis of which the suspect could be re-arrested, so that time could start to run again. This decision caused much consternation as far as the police were concerned, since it conflicted with generally accepted practice. An appeal to the Supreme Court was initiated but abandoned when Parliament amended s. 47 of PACE to make it clear that any period during which a person is released on bail does not count towards the authorized period of detention (Police Detention and Bail Act 2011). The police may, therefore, when a person surrenders to bail, detain them for any unexpired period of authorized detention which was available prior to the release on bail. The Act is stated to have retrospective effect. It is possible that it might be open to challenge in this respect as being in conflict with Art. 7 of the ECHR, but the general view seems to be that because the amendment does not create any criminal liability or impose any punishment it would not do so (see the comments by the Home Secretary at *Hansard*, HC, 7 July 2011, vol. 530, pt. 184, col. 1686). At any rate there has to date been no challenge to this provision.

4.3.2 The standard period of detention

Section 41(7) states that in general a person who is in police detention 24 hours after the relevant time must be charged or released. The exceptions to this are noted at 4.3.3–4.3.4. The police may not obtain another 24 hours by releasing and re-arresting. Section 41(9) prohibits a person released (other than on police bail) under s. 41(7) from ever being re-arrested without warrant for the same offence, unless new evidence has come to light. Arrest for a slightly different offence may well be permissible, however. For example, a person released after being detained in relation to suspected importing of cannabis might be re-arrested for possession with intent to supply. This would be likely not to be regarded as an abuse, unless the police were clearly acting in bad faith (see, e.g. *R v Great Yarmouth Magistrates, ex p Thomas* [1992] Crim LR 117, dealing with custody limits after charge).

4.3.2.1 Reviews of detention

Just because the custody officer has decided that detention is justified does not mean that the investigating officers automatically have 24 hours to question the suspect. Regular reviews of the need for continued detention must be held. These will be conducted by a 'review officer', who must be an officer of at least the rank of inspector, who is not directly involved with the investigation (s. 40(1), (2)). In *R v Chief Constable of Kent, ex p Kent Police Federation* [2000] Crim LR 854 it was held that the review should be carried out in the presence of the detainee, and not by means of a video link. The effect of this decision was reversed by s. 73 of the Criminal Justice and Police Act 2001 (CJPA) which inserted new ss 40A and 45A into PACE. Section 45A provides for regulations to be issued by the Home Secretary permitting the review to be carried out by 'video-conferencing' where such facilities are available. The video-conferencing power was piloted in police stations in one area (Alton and Winchester) (see SI 2003/2397) during 2003–04. The results of the pilot were to be evaluated by the Home Office, but no conclusions have been published. No regulations have been made to apply the power more generally. In the absence of video-conferencing, if it is not 'reasonably practicable' for an officer of at least the rank of inspector to be present, s. 40A provides for review by telephone. The first review will generally take place not later than six hours after detention was first *authorized* (s. 40(3)(a)). This means when the custody officer decided to detain under s. 37(3) (see 4.2.3), not 'the relevant time'. Subsequent reviews must take place at intervals of not more than nine hours (s. 40(3)(b), (c)). Generally, then, unless there is a significant gap (i.e. at least nine hours) between 'the relevant time' and the decision to detain, there will be at least two reviews during the standard 24-hour period of detention. It was established in *Roberts* v *Chief Constable of the Cheshire Constabulary* [1999] 2 All ER 326 that, if a review does not take place at the proper time, the detainee will be entitled to compensatory damages for false imprisonment. It is irrelevant whether or not, if the review had taken place at the proper time, the detainee would have been released. R's detention should have been reviewed at 5.25 a.m. but the review did not take place until 7.45 a.m. The Court of Appeal upheld an award of damages of £500 for R's false imprisonment during the intervening 2 hours 20 minutes—though it commented that the judge's award was high, particularly given the fact that R had apparently been asleep throughout the relevant period.

A review may be postponed if it is not practicable to carry it out at the required time (s. 40(4)). The Act does not limit the kinds of circumstances which might lead to impracticability, but does specify two particular situations where postponement will be justified. The first of these is where the detainee is being questioned by a police officer, and the review officer is satisfied that the interruption necessary for a review would prejudice the investigation. The investigating officer who is on the brink of obtaining a confession need not break off for the purposes of a review. The second situation is where there is no review officer readily available. Both these possibilities allow a fair scope for police discretion in carrying out reviews, though the reasons for any postponement must be recorded on the custody record (s. 40(7)), and the review must be carried out as soon as it becomes practicable to do so (s. 40(5)).

In carrying out the review, the review officer must consider the same issues, and follow the same procedures as the custody officer does in dealing with the initial decision to detain (see 4.2.3). Continued detention will only normally be justified therefore, where there are reasonable grounds for believing that it is necessary either to secure or preserve evidence relating to an offence for which the person is being detained, or to obtain such evidence by questioning (s. 37(2)). Before reaching such a decision, however, the review officer must give the detainee (unless asleep), or the detainee's solicitor (if available), the opportunity to make representations about the detention (s. 40(12)). Such representations may be oral or in writing (s. 40(13)), although the review officer is not obliged to hear oral representations from the detainee, if the officer considers that the detainee is unfit to make such representations (s. 40(14)). Where the review is carried out by video-conferencing or by telephone, any written representations may be transmitted by 'facilities... for the immediate transmission of written representations', if they are available. This presumably means by fax or email, as indicated by para. 15.11 of Code C.

Code C recommends that, where a detainee is likely to be asleep at the time when the next review is due, the review officer should bring it forward, so that the detainee will be able to make representations (Note 15C of Code C) (cf. the case of *Roberts* as discussed). As noted, reviews may be carried out over the telephone, as provided by s. 40A. Paragraphs 15.9–15.11 of Code C detail the procedures to be used in relation to such a review.

There is, of course, likely to be tension in some cases between the requirements of the review officer, and those of the investigating officer, who may be of the same or higher rank than the review officer. If a conflict arises as to what is to be done in relation to a detainee, the review officer should immediately refer it to an officer of at least the rank of superintendent, who is responsible for the police station where the review is being carried out (s. 40(11)). This senior officer will presumably have the last word as to what is to happen in the case.

It would seem likely from the approach taken in *Brogan* v *United Kingdom* (1989) 11 EHRR 117 (discussed in detail in chapter 10 (10.4.3.2)) that the standard 24-hour period of detention before release or charge would be regarded as being permissible under Art. 5 of the ECHR, given that a person charged and kept in custody is to be brought before the next sitting of the magistrates (s. 46 of PACE).

4.3.3 The extended period: indictable offences

Detention without charge beyond the normal 24 hours is permissible in certain situations. One of these is where at least one of the offences for which the detainee has been arrested is an indictable offence.

Under the original version of PACE, no detention beyond 24 hours was permissible unless the person was being detained in relation to a 'serious arrestable offence'. This was a rather complex category of offences, but covered all the most serious ones, such as murder, rape, and other serious assaults. It could also include any arrestable offence (for which see chapter 3 (3.5.3)), if the consequences were sufficiently serious (e.g. a large-scale theft, or extensive criminal damage). The Criminal Justice Act 2003 changed the position, so that an initial 12 hours' detention beyond the initial 24 could be approved by a superintendent in relation to any arrestable offence. Further amendment was made by the Serious Organised Crime and Police Act 2005, following proposals contained in the Home Office's consultation paper published in the summer of 2004—'Modernising Police Powers to Meet Community Needs', Home Office. As from 1 January 2006, extended periods of detention, up to 96 hours, have been available in relation to any *indictable offence*. This was a significant extension of the power of extended detention. There is, of course, an obligation under the HRA 1998 to use the power proportionately. This means that the police officers and magistrates' courts who take the decisions in this area should continue to use the power only for the most serious offences, comparable to those which were 'serious arrestable offences' under the previous law.

Where the detainee has been arrested for an indictable offence, the maximum possible period of detention without charge is extended from 24 hours to 96 hours, that is, up to four days. Such extensions are subject to special procedures, however, and detention beyond 36 hours will always require the approval of a magistrates' court. As far as Art. 5 of the ECHR is concerned, the addition of 12 hours to the standard period of 24 hours would previously have been regarded as being justified by the seriousness of the offence. Whether this would be the case if the power is used in relation to a low-level indictable offence (e.g. a theft of a few pounds), must be open to question. Any detention beyond 36 hours will require the agreement of a magistrates' court, and this judicial involvement is likely to satisfy the requirements of Art. 5(3) (see the discussion of *Brogan* v *United Kingdom* (1989) 11 EHRR 117 in chapter 10 (10.4.3.2)). The exact extent of the use of these powers is difficult to determine. The official figures published by the Home Office only give overall figures for the use of powers to extend detention beyond 24 hours when no charge follows ('Police Powers and Procedures England and Wales 2011/12', Home Office, April 2013). They show a significant increase in the use of this power in recent years. In 2004–05 the figure for this category was 1,132, and increased to 2,459 in 2005–06, before falling back to 1,826 in 2006–07. These figures are much higher than for the years prior to 2004–05, showing an increase of around 100 per cent. The highest figure pre-2004 was in 1998–99 when 710 people were detained, and in general the figure had been in the 600s. It is difficult to avoid the conclusion that the increase in the use of the power is a reflection of the change in 2004 which allowed to power to be used in relation to any arrestable offence, whereas prior to that it was only available in relation to serious arrestable offences. The threshold changed (at the start of 2006) to any indictable offence. This seems to have led to a further increase in the use of extended detention. The figure for 2011–12 was 4,420.

As regards the use of the power to extend detention beyond 36 hours on the authority of a magistrates' court, the Home Office's figures indicate the full use of this power. In 2011–12, 478 warrants of extended detention were requested and 15 were refused. Again this figure has increased significantly following the change in the threshold for the use of this power. Prior to 2004–05 the figure of applications per year was around 300, so there has been an increase of more than 50 per cent. It is still a tiny proportion of the total of those arrested (0.04 per cent). In 2011–12, 60 per cent of those detained under a magistrates' court warrant for extended detention were subsequently charged. This percentage has remained fairly constant for a number of years.

The initial power to extend detention beyond 24 hours must be exercised by an officer of at least the rank of superintendent who is responsible for the police station at which the person is detained. As well as having reasonable grounds to believe that at least one of the offences for which the detainee is under arrest is an indictable offence, the officer must also have reasonable grounds for believing that the continued detention is necessary to secure or preserve evidence relating to an offence (not necessarily the indictable offence) for which the detainee is under arrest, or to obtain such evidence by questioning (s. 42(1)(a)). These, of course, are the same grounds which justify an initial decision by the custody officer to detain, and the decision by the review officer to continue detention up to 24 hours. The officer approving extended detention, however, must in addition have reasonable grounds for believing that the investigation is being conducted 'diligently and expeditiously' (s. 42(1)(c)). Before reaching a decision, the officer, as is also the case in relation to a review officer during the initial 24 hours, must allow the detainee or the detainee's solicitor to make representations orally or in writing about the detention (s. 42(6), (7), (8)). If after this the officer is satisfied on reasonable grounds of all the matters specified in s. 42(1), then the officer may authorize continued detention up to 36 hours from the 'relevant time' (see 4.3.1). The power cannot be exercised, however, before the second review of detention under s. 40 (see 4.3.2.1) has been carried out, or more than 24 hours after the relevant time (s. 42(4)). It cannot be used pre-emptively at an early stage of detention, therefore, nor retrospectively, to legitimate unauthorized detention beyond 24 hours.

If a decision to continue detention is made, it is the duty of the officer authorizing it to inform the detainee of the grounds, and to record them in the detainee's custody record (s. 42(5)).

At the expiry of 36 hours from the relevant time the detainee must either be charged, kept in detention in accordance with a magistrates' warrant under s. 43

(below), or released (s. 42(10)). If released, the detainee may not be re-arrested without warrant for the same offence, unless new evidence has become available justifying a further arrest (s. 42(11)).

After the initial 36 hours of detention, the control of continued detention changes significantly. Whereas up to this point it may be regarded as essentially an administrative procedure operated by the police, the introduction of supervision by the magistrates' courts at this stage indicates that it then becomes a judicial decision. As discussed, this is important in the context of compliance with the requirements of Art. 5 of the ECHR.

The application for a warrant of further detention is governed by ss 43–45. It must be made to a magistrates' court, which is defined as being 'a court consisting of two or more justices sitting otherwise than in open court' (s. 45(1)). The application may be made at any point before the expiry of 36 hours from the relevant time. If, however, it is not practicable for a magistrates' court to sit before the expiry of this time, but will become so within the next six hours, the application may be made before the expiry of those six hours (s. 43(5)). In effect, therefore, a person can be detained, in certain circumstances, for up to 42 hours from the relevant time, before being brought before the magistrates. The court has a power to dismiss an application which it thinks it would have been reasonable to make before the expiry of the 36 hours (s. 43(7)). In *R v Slough Magistrates' Court, ex p Stirling* (1987) 151J P 603, the Divisional Court held that s. 43(7) constitutes a requirement, rather than a discretion to dismiss the application if it appears that an earlier application would have been reasonable.

The application must be supported by an information (a copy of which must be supplied to the detainee) outlining the reasons for arrest, the progress of the investigation, and the reasons for believing that continued detention is necessary (s. 43(14)). The detainee must be present at the hearing, and is entitled to be legally represented. The grounds for issuing a warrant of further detention are the same as those for authorizing continued detention (s. 43(4)). The warrant, if issued, may extend the period of detention by up to 36 hours (s. 43(11), (12)). If it is refused, the detainee must be charged or released, unless there is still a period of previously authorized detention which has not expired (s. 43(15), (16)). No further application for an extension may be made after a refusal, however, unless new evidence has subsequently come to light (s. 43(17)). Similarly, a person who is released at the expiry of a warrant of further detention may not be re-arrested for the same offence unless new evidence has come to light since the release (s. 43(19)).

If the police wish to extend a warrant of further detention, this is possible, but a new application and information will need to be submitted, and there will have to be a further hearing before a magistrates' court, in relation to each extension (s. 44). The maximum period for any one extension is 36 hours, and no extension may extend the period beyond 96 hours from the relevant time. Ninety-six hours is therefore the maximum period for which anyone can be detained without charge, other than those arrested under the Terrorism Act 2000 (see chapter 10 (10.4.3.2)).

4.3.4 **The extended period: the terrorism provisions**

There are powers to detain without charge beyond 96 hours in relation to those being held in connection with terrorism. These powers are dealt with in chapter 10 (10.4.3.2).

4.4 **Conditions during detention**

4.4.1 **The right to have someone informed**

One of the effects of police detention is isolation from friends and family. A person who has been arrested on the street and taken to a police station, may well be concerned that no one will know what has happened. PACE deals with this by generally giving a detained person the right to let someone know of the arrest, and the place of detention (s. 56(1)). This right is one of those which the custody officer is obliged to draw to the attention of the detainee (para. 3.1 of Code C; see 4.2.2). Only one communication is allowed. If the detainee is moved to another location, however, the s. 56 right may be exercised again (s. 56(8)). The communication may be to a friend, a relative, or any other person known to the detainee, or likely to take an interest in the welfare of the detainee. If the detainee's first choice cannot be contacted, two alternatives may be nominated: if neither of these can be contacted, it is at the custody officer's discretion whether further attempts are allowed (para. 5.1 of Code C).

Delay in the exercise of this right is governed by s. 56(2)–(7). It will only be allowed where a person is detained under the 'terrorism provisions' (discussed in chapter 10 (10.4.3.3)), or for an indictable offence. This is another power for which the threshold was reduced from a 'serious arrestable offence' to an indictable offence by the Serious Organised Crime and Police Act 2005 (see 4.3.3), as from 1 January 2006. It can only be authorized by an officer of at least the rank of inspector. The authorization of delay may be given orally, but should be confirmed in writing as soon as possible (s. 56(4)). There are three sets of conditions which may justify delay in relation to an indictable offence. The first is where the authorizing officer has reasonable grounds for believing that telling the named person of the arrest would lead to one of four consequences, which are:

1. interference with, or harm to, evidence connected with an indictable offence;

2. interference with, or physical injury to, other persons;

3. the alerting of other persons suspected of having committed an indictable offence; or

4. hindrance of the recovery of property obtained as a result of an indictable offence.

All these consequences clearly have the potential for impeding the police investigations, but that does not have to be believed to be the case before delay is authorized.

The second set of conditions for delay relates specifically to drug trafficking. Where the offence for which the person is under arrest is a drug-trafficking offence (for which see the Drug Trafficking Act 1994), delay will be permissible if there are reasonable grounds to believe that the recovery of the proceeds of the trafficking will be hindered by telling the named person of the arrest (s. 56(5A)(a) of PACE).

The third set of conditions for delay relates to confiscation orders under Pt 2 of the Proceeds of Crime Act 2002, which allows the courts to make such orders in relation to the proceeds of criminal conduct. Delay will be permissible where there are reasonable grounds for believing that the detainee has benefited from the offence (which must, of course, be an indictable offence), and the recovery of that benefit will be hindered by telling the named person of the arrest.

The grounds for delay are also set out in Annex B to Code C, though it is not made clear there that the police objection to communication must relate to the person named. In other words the decision to delay should not be a general one that this detainee is not to be allowed to communicate with anyone. In each case the question asked should be: 'Would communication with this named person be likely to result in one of the consequences justifying delay?' It is not clear whether the detainee who, for example, initially names a suspected accomplice, should, if that is thought to be unacceptable, be allowed an alternative to whom the police would not object. The wording of the Act does not require the police to allow this, and the Code of Practice is silent on the issue.

If delay is authorized, the detainee must be told the reason, which must also be noted on the custody record (s. 56(6) of PACE). If the reason ceases to exist, the detainee should be told of this, and given the opportunity to exercise the right at this stage (para. 6 of Annex B to Code C). In any case, where the detainee is under arrest for an indictable offence delay in the exercise of this right must never extend beyond 36 hours from the 'relevant time' (see 4.3.1) (s. 56(3)).

The right in s. 56 will be satisfied by the passing of a message by the police, but para. 5.6 of Code C also provides that the detainee should normally be allowed to communicate with one person directly by telephone or letter. Before such communication takes place, however, the detainee should be told that, unless it is to a solicitor, it may be listened to or read, and used in evidence (para. 5.7 of Code C). This privilege may be denied by an officer of at least the rank of inspector who considers that its exercise may result in one of the consequences listed earlier as justifying a delay under s. 56.

There is nothing in Art. 5 or Art. 6 of the ECHR which appears to relate to this right, and there is no case law under the Convention dealing with it. It is unlikely, therefore, that a claim relating to refusal or delay in the exercise of this right would get very far under the HRA 1998. An improper refusal or delay which does not fall within the conditions laid down in PACE (e.g. if the right were delayed in relation to an offence which was not an indictable offence) would, however, have the potential of rendering continued detention unlawful.

4.4.2 The right of access to legal advice

This right is contained in s. 58. It has proved to be one of the most significant provisions of PACE in terms of litigation relating to it. This is not surprising. The right of the detained citizen to legal advice and representation is fundamental to a fair system of criminal justice. The balance of power between a professional police force, highly trained in techniques of questioning, and operating on home ground (that is, the police station), and the private individual, in unfamiliar and threatening circumstances, can only be equalized by allowing the detainee professional legal advice.

The right arises where a person has been arrested and is being held in police custody in a police station or other premises (s. 58(1)). It does not apply in relation to a person who has been arrested in connection with a drink-driving offence and is asked to provide a specimen of breath, urine, or blood. There is no right to delay provision of the specimen until legal advice has been obtained (*DPP* v *Billington* [1988] 1 WLR 535, and *Kennedy* v *DPP* [2002] EWHC 2297 (Admin), [2004] RTR 6). As regards the meaning of 'held in police custody', in *R* v *Kerawalla* [1991] Crim LR 451, in effect applying the definition of 'police detention' contained in s. 118(2), it was held to mean that the right only arises where a person has been taken to a police station and is under the supervision of a custody officer. Thus, in that case, where questioning had taken place in the hotel room where Kerawalla had been arrested, he had no right of access to legal advice. It is true that some other aspects of s. 58 would be difficult to comply with (e.g. noting the request in the custody record), if it applied prior to arrival at a police station. Section 58(1) is, however, broad enough to allow for a different interpretation, and the result is unfortunate in that it may encourage the police to delay arrival at a police station (subject to the requirements of s. 30, see chapter 3 (3.5.4.2)), simply with a view to being able to question before the detainee has had access to legal advice. This will particularly be the case if any evidence thus acquired is held to be admissible, as in *Kerawalla*. This may, however, be affected by Art. 6 of the ECHR, applied via the HRA 1998. The right to a fair trial has been held to include, in certain circumstances, the right to legal advice during questioning. In the Scottish case of *Ambrose* v *Harris* [2011] UKSC 43, [2011] 1 WLR 2435 the Supreme Court, reviewing the Strasbourg jurisprudence, held that the right to legal advice should arise from the moment an individual was being questioned as a suspect, rather than simply a witness. Whether evidence obtained prior to legal advice being available should be admissible was, however, to be determined by considering whether to admit it would overall breach the individual's right to a fair trial under Art. 6. It should not be automatically excluded. (Article 6 is discussed further in chapter 5.)

Under the PACE provisions, the detainee must be informed of the right of access to legal advice on arrival at the police station, and, as we have seen at 4.2.2, be given a written statement referring to it. A poster advertising the right is to be prominently displayed in the charging area of every police station (para. 6.3 of Code C). If the right is declined, the suspect should be told of the right to speak to a solicitor on the telephone (para. 6.5 of Code C). A suspect who continues to waive the right to legal advice should be asked to give reasons for so doing. There is no obligation to provide reasons (Note 6K to Code C), but if any are given they should be recorded on the custody record (para. 6.5 of Code C).

Prior to 1 January 2006 the only situation where the right to legal advice could be delayed was where the suspect was being held in connection with a 'serious arrestable offence' or under the terrorism provisions. Most of those in police custody were therefore entitled to exercise the right at any time. The abolition of the category of serious arrestable offence by the Serious Organised Crime and Police Act 2005 (see 4.3.3), however, means that the delay is possible where a person is being held in relation to any indictable offence (or under the terrorism provisions). Potentially this could lead to an increase in the use of the delaying power. For other reasons, outlined below, however, it is unlikely that there will in practice be extensive use of it. The terrorism provisions are discussed in chapter 10 (10.4.3.3); what follows relates solely to those under arrest for indictable offences.

The maximum period of delay is 36 hours from the 'relevant time' (see 4.3.1) (s. 58(5)). It may only be authorized by an officer of at least the rank of superintendent (s. 58(6)). The procedures to be followed, and the conditions justifying delay, are virtually the same as for the right to have someone informed under s. 56 (see 4.4.1). The fact that delay is justified in relation to one of the rights, however, does not automatically mean that it will be justified in relation to the other (*R v Parris* (1988) 89 Cr App R 68). In addition, the following differences in wording should be noted. First, whereas in s. 56 the conditions for delay refer to 'telling the named person', under s. 58 the more general formulation of 'the exercise of the right' is used. In other words, it would appear at first sight that the police objection should be a general one, and not related to the particular legal adviser the detainee wishes to consult. The Court of Appeal in *R v Samuel* [1988] QB 615, however, thought that the reasonable belief that, for example, the solicitor might (albeit unwittingly) transmit information useful to the detainee's accomplices, must be related to the particular adviser that the detainee wishes to consult. They thought that it would only be very rarely that the police officer could have such a reasonable belief in relation to a solicitor. This is now spelt out by para. 3 of Annex B to Code C, which states that:

> Authority to delay a detainee's right to consult privately with a solicitor may be given only if the authorising officer has reasonable grounds to believe the solicitor the detainee wants to consult will, inadvertently or otherwise, pass on a message from the detainee or act in some other way which will have any of the consequences [which if reasonably suspected justify delaying access].

This is further reinforced by Note of Guidance B3 which states that:

> A decision to delay access to a specific solicitor is likely to be a rare occurrence and only when it can be shown that suspect is capable of misleading that particular solicitor and there is more than a substantial risk that the suspect will succeed in causing information to be conveyed which will lead to one or more of the specified consequences.

If this is the case, then the suspect should be offered access to another solicitor, which might be the duty solicitor.

The second difference in wording from s. 56 arises where the police rely on the first set of conditions, dealing with the possible harmful consequences of exercising the right. Section 58(8) specifies that the reasonable grounds for belief that this will happen must relate to the exercise of the right 'at the time that the person detained desires to exercise it'. The police objection must therefore be more specific as to time in relation to this right, as opposed to the s. 56 right. The reason for this is that the right under s. 58 is a continuing one, which can be exercised at any time, whereas the right under s. 56 can only be exercised once (unless the detainee is moved to a different location).

Annex B to Code C specifies that access to a solicitor may not be denied on the grounds that the solicitor might advise the detainee not to answer any questions (para. 4). This is a most important provision, for this is one of the things which the police will be most concerned about if legal advice is allowed, even though this may now lead to adverse inferences being drawn at trial. Quite rightly, however, as long as the suspect's right of silence is regarded as having some importance, the police should not be able to weaken it further by preventing access to a lawyer who will make sure that the suspect knows exactly what the situation is, and will advise silence, if that appears to be the most appropriate course. As can be seen (see 4.6.4.3), incriminating statements, made in the absence of a legal adviser, have frequently been excluded by the courts as 'unfair evidence' under s. 78 of PACE.

If delay of access to legal advice is authorized, then the detainee must be told the reason, and it must be recorded on the custody record (s. 58(9)). Once the reason for delay ceases to exist, then access to legal advice should be allowed immediately (s. 58(11)).

In practice, these powers to delay access to legal advice are very rarely used. This is probably the result of a combination of the restrictive approach taken in *Samuel* (as discussed) and various decisions of the ECtHR (discussed at 4.5.1.3) which have emphasized the importance of access to legal advice in ensuring the right to a fair trial under Art. 6 of the ECHR. Early research on PACE (pre-*Samuel*) showed the power to delay being used in about 1 per cent of cases (D. Brown, Home Office Research Study No. 104, 1987). Subsequently, a study of 12,500 cases found no examples of the use of the power (T. Bucke and D. Brown, Home Office Research Study No. 174, 1997). This does not mean, however, that all detainees receive legal advice, since many do not ask for it. In the 1997 study by Bucke and Brown the highest level of requests for legal advice over a year was in 1995–6. In that year 40 per cent of detainees asked for advice, and 34 per cent actually received it. Thus, less than half of all detainees actually sought legal advice, and only just over a third received it. The difference between the two figures does not result from any formal refusal of access under s. 58, but from other difficulties, such as the availability of the solicitor requested or other delay, or from the detainee having had a change of mind about needing advice. The reasons why detainees do not initially seek advice or later cancel a request are likely to be various. Some may feel, for example if caught 'red-handed', that there is little point in receiving advice; others may feel that they are so clearly 'innocent' that there will be no need for legal advice in order to convince the police of this (indeed, seeking legal advice might be seen by such suspects as indicating that they have something to hide). Concerns about likely delays may lead some to feel that the quickest way out of the police station is to decline the opportunity of receiving legal advice. There is also some evidence that the police not infrequently 'play' on these types of feeling in a way which discourages a request for advice, or encourages a request to be withdrawn (see A. Sanders and R. Young, *Criminal Justice*, 4th edn (Oxford: Oxford University Press, 2010), pp. 235–9).

New procedures for dealing with a detainee's request for legal advice took effect from April 2008, and are set out in Note 6B to Code C. These distinguish between the detainee who is in a position to pay for legal advice, and those who rely on publicly-funded advice. As regards a detainee who wishes to pay for legal advice, he or she should be given the opportunity to consult a specific solicitor or another solicitor from the same firm. If this solicitor is unavailable, two further choices can be made. Beyond that, any further attempt to contact a specific solicitor is at the discretion of the custody officer. Where these procedures fail to identify a solicitor able to give advice, or in any case where the detainee is seeking publicly funded advice, initial access to legal advice is to be by means of a phone call to a Defence Solicitor Call Centre (DSCC) authorized by the Legal Services Commission (LSC). The DSCC will determine whether legal advice should be limited to telephone advice, or whether a solicitor should attend. Telephone advice will be appropriate if the detainee is being held in relation to a non-imprisonable offence, or following arrest for failing to appear in court, or in relation to a drink-driving offence, or following a breach of bail conditions. Apart from this the Code does not indicate how the DSCC should exercise its discretion to decide whether attendance is appropriate. It does suggest, however, that the fact that the police intend to interview or hold an identification parade will be relevant, as will the ability of the detainee to communicate by telephone, the eligibility of the detainee to assistance from an appropriate adult, or allegations of serious mistreatment by the police. The intention of these changes is clearly to increase the number of cases where advice will be given purely on the telephone.

When advice is given in person, and a solicitor arrives at the police station, there is no obligation on the police to provide the solicitor with any information. The report of the Royal Commission on Criminal Justice, Cm 2263, July 1993 (*Runciman Report*) recommended that solicitors should automatically see, and if possible be given a copy of the custody record on arrival, and on departure (*Runciman Report*, ch. 3, para. 51). They should also be able to hear the tapes of any interviews, and be informed of the general nature of the case, and the prima facie evidence against the suspect (*Runciman Report*, ch. 3, paras 52 and 53). These procedures have not been incorporated into the Code.

If a solicitor arrives at a police station to see a particular detainee, that person must be told of this, even if he or she is being interviewed at the time (para. 6.15 of Code C). The detainee should be asked if he or she wishes to see the solicitor. This must be done even if the suspect has previously declined legal advice. The fact that the solicitor attended, and the decision of the detainee, should be recorded in the custody record.

The solicitor has no *right*, however, to enter the police station to see a client: *Rixon v Chief Constable for Kent*, *The Times*, 11 April 2000 (CA). The right lies with the client, and it is the client who must take action in the event that a police refusal to allow a solicitor to enter the station affects the client's right to legal advice.

Some concerns have been expressed about the quality of legal advice. The more regular use of telephone advice, as is now encouraged by the Code, increases the risk that the confidentiality of the discussions between solicitor and client will be compromised. On several occasions, the ECtHR has emphasized the importance of such confidentiality (e.g. *S v Switzerland*, 28 November 1991, and *Brennan v United Kingdom* (2002) 34 RHRR 18). In *R (La Rose) v Commissioner of the Metropolis* [2001] EWHC 553 (Admin), *The Times*, 17 August 2001, however, the Divisional Court found that there was no breach of the applicant's rights in the fact that he had had to use a telephone that was on the custody sergeant's desk. Other police officers were in the custody suite at the time. The applicant had taken the phone as far from the desk as its cord would permit, and had, on his solicitor's advice, given only 'yes' and 'no' answers to her questions. The court noted that there was no suggestion that anyone had attempted to eavesdrop on the conversation. It seems likely, however, that the applicant was inhibited in the advice that he could receive by the situation in which it was given, and there was clearly a strong risk, if not the actuality, of solicitor/client confidentiality being prejudiced. It is certainly arguable that the Strasbourg Court would have taken a different view of this situation.

The only legal right is to advice from a 'solicitor'. Solicitors' firms have always made considerable use of non-solicitor advisers to assist those being detained by the police, and this has been another source of concern about the quality of the advice given. Estimates of the frequency with which this occurs have at times been as high as between 40 per cent and 50 per cent of police station attendances (L. Bridges and J. Hodgson, 'Improving Custodial Legal Advice', [1995] Crim LR 104). Subsequent research (relating to 1995–96) showed a figure of about 16 per cent (T. Bucke and D. Brown, Home Office Research Study No. 174, p. 26). The reduction is at least partly explicable by the introduction of an 'accreditation' scheme (set up by the Law Society and the Legal Aid Board in 1995, and now run by the LSC), under which non-solicitor advisers are required to be trained and to have passed assessments (though 'probationary' representatives may still act while being trained). Bridges and Choongh's survey of the effect of this scheme suggests that it resulted in some improvement in the quality of advice given (L. Bridges and S. Choongh, 'Improving Police Station Legal Advice', Law Society Research Study No. 31, 1998).

Paragraph 6.12 of Code C provides that accredited or probationary representatives under the above scheme should be treated as 'solicitors' in terms of access to their clients. They should be allowed access unless 'an officer of the rank of inspector or above considers that such a visit will hinder the investigation of crime'. Some factors which might lead to such a decision are set out in para. 6.13 of Code C. In addition to being satisfied as to the identity and status of the representative, the officer may take a view as to whether the representative is 'of suitable character' (e.g. a person with a criminal record is unlikely to be 'suitable'). The officer should also take into account any matters contained in a written letter of authorization provided by the solicitor for whom the adviser is acting. It was held by the Court of Appeal in *R (Thompson)* v *Chief Constable of the Northumbria Constabulary* [2001] EWCA Civ 321, [2001] 4 All ER 354 that it was not permissible for a chief constable to impose a 'blanket' ban on a representative. A decision had to be made in relation to a particular investigation, on a 'case-by-case' basis. The representative in this case was a former police officer, who had been dismissed for making sexually discriminatory comments, and was at the time appealing against his dismissal. The Court of Appeal recognized that the situation might be 'uncomfortable' for Thompson or his former fellow officers, but this was not a relevant consideration. The chief constable could issue advice to his officers as to the character of a representative, but the decision must be taken by the appropriate officer in relation to a particular investigation.

There has also been some concern over the extent to which legal advisers, including solicitors, properly protect their client's interests in the police station. Research by Baldwin for the 1993 Royal Commission on Criminal Justice (J. Baldwin, 'The Role of Legal Representatives at Police Stations', RCCJ Research Study No. 3, HMSO, 1992) found that advisers were often passive, and tended to assist the police rather than their clients. Similar conclusions were drawn by McConville and Hodgson (M. McConville, and J. Hodgson, 'Custodial Legal Advice and the Right to Silence', RCCJ Research Study No. 16, HMSO, 1993), who found that advisers were only intervening on behalf of the client in 20–22 per cent of cases. A rather more positive view, however, was taken by Bridges and Choongh ('Improving Police Station Legal Advice'). They found that in 78 per cent of the cases which they observed where an intervention by the adviser was called for, some intervention was made on behalf of the client. Nor did they observe the adviser acting as a 'third interviewer' for the police, as Baldwin had done. As noted, they suggest that some improvement in the situation may be attributable to the scheme of accreditation of non-solicitor legal advisers introduced in 1995, as discussed.

4.4.3 The terrorism provisions

The powers of the police to delay exercise of the right to have someone informed, and the right to legal advice, where the detainee is held under the terrorism provisions, are dealt with in chapter 10 (10.4.3.3).

4.4.4 Other conditions

Paragraphs 8 and 9 of Code C contain detailed provisions on the conditions of detention, and the treatment of detainees. Paragraph 8 covers such matters as the state of the cells, access to toilet and washing facilities, provision of meals, and exercise.

Paragraph 9 deals primarily with the provision of medical treatment, where a detainee appears to be ill, or otherwise in need of medical attention. It also contains a general provision (para. 9.2) relating to complaints by, or on behalf of, a detainee, of improper treatment. If such a complaint is made, or if an officer thinks that improper treatment may have occurred, a report must be made as soon as possible to an officer of at least the rank of inspector, who is not connected with the investigation. If the improper treatment concerns a possible assault, or unreasonable use of force, then the police surgeon should also be called.

The provisions in paras 8 and 9 are of great importance to the individual detainee, and promote a standard of civilized treatment which is clearly desirable. A person in detention for questioning is simply a suspect, and is entitled to be kept in conditions which are as comfortable as possible, and to be treated well. It must be noted, however, that there is very little in the way of sanctions in relation to breaches of these provisions, unless, perhaps, they are sufficiently serious to amount to 'inhuman and degrading treatment' under Art. 3 of the Convention. The application of Art 3 in this context has been discussed in chapter 1 (1.7.2) Where the breaches are less serious than this, a failure to comply with the provisions in paras 8 and 9 will not make the detention unlawful, nor will there be any remedy in damages against the police officers responsible. Even if it is argued that incriminating evidence was obtained while a person was detained in conditions which fall below those required, the evidence is unlikely to be excluded unless the breaches are serious, and it can plausibly be argued that the statements would not have been made had the breaches not occurred (see 4.6.4). A formal complaint under the police complaints procedure is probably all that can be done in most cases to back up the rights given by paras 8 and 9 (see 4.6.3).

4.5 Obtaining evidence during detention

The purpose of detaining a suspect is almost always to obtain evidence. There are three principal ways in which this can be done: by questioning, by taking samples for analysis, and by identification procedures (identity parades, etc.). All three are governed by PACE and its Codes. Before looking at how they operate, and the extent to which the rights of the detainee are protected, however, the use of the 'caution' and the right to silence must be considered.

4.5.1 Cautions and the right to silence

4.5.1.1 Caution: content and procedures

At various stages in the investigation of a crime the police are obliged to issue a caution to a suspect, in effect reminding the suspect of the right to silence, and its consequences. The rules relating to cautioning are not contained in PACE itself, but in the Codes, particularly para. 10 of Code C.

A caution must be given whenever a suspect is to be questioned about an offence, regarding the involvement or suspected involvement of the suspect in that offence. Questioning for other purposes, such as to establish the suspect's identity or address, can take place without a caution as can an investigation which does not involve questioning, such as a search (para. 10.1 of Code C). A caution will normally be required when a suspect is questioned prior to arrest; when a suspect is arrested; and where a suspect in police detention is to be questioned, or further questioned. It is the responsibility of the interviewing officer to make sure that, when there is a resumption of questioning following a break, the detainee realizes that the questioning is still taking place under caution. The safest procedure is probably for the caution to be repeated.

The normal form of the caution is set out in para. 10.5 of Code C. It is to be given in the following terms:

> You do not have to say anything. But it may harm your defence if you do not mention when questioned something which you later rely on in court. Anything you do say may be given in evidence.

In situations where adverse inferences may not be drawn from silence (that is, where a suspect has asked for legal advice but access has been delayed), however, a different form of caution must be used. This is set out in para. 2 of Annex C to Code C:

> You do not have to say anything, but anything you do say may be given in evidence.

The difference relates to the fact that where interviewing takes place before legal advice has been made available no adverse inferences may be drawn from the detainee's silence. If statements are made during such an interview, however, they may be admissible, subject to the overall 'fairness' requirement of s. 78 of PACE (discussed at 4.6.4): *R v Ibrahim* [2008] EWCA Crim 880.

The most important matter is not the precise words used, but whether the suspect understands their significance. Minor deviations from the above formulae will not matter, as long as the gist of the caution is communicated (para. 10.7). If it appears to the officer issuing the caution that the suspect does not understand what it means, then the officer should explain it in his own words (Note 10D to Code C).

A record of the caution should be made in the officer's pocket book, or in the interview record, as appropriate (para. 10.13 of Code C). This is important, since evidence resulting from an interview not under caution may well be excluded (see 4.6.4.3).

Two cases emphasize the need for the use of cautions in connection with police undercover operations. In *R v Christou* [1992] QB 979 the police had set up a shop which purported to be a genuine business dealing in jewellery. All transactions in the shop were video-recorded. The defendants were recorded dealing in stolen goods. It was argued that their conversations with the undercover officers managing the shop were in effect interviews, and that a caution should have been given (which would, of course, have destroyed the police officers' 'cover'). The Court of Appeal held that the conversations were outside the scope of the Codes, which were directed towards protecting the individual from abuse and pressure from police officers, who are perceived to be in a position of authority, leading to the possibility of the suspect being intimidated or undermined. The factual situation in this case meant that no such pressure or intimidation could possibly arise. In reaching this conclusion, however, the court issued the following warning (p. 991):

> It would be wrong for the police officers to adopt or use an undercover pose or disguise to enable themselves to ask questions about an offence uninhibited by the requirements of the Code and with the effect of circumventing it.

This warning was followed in *R v Bryce* (1992) 95 Cr App R 320. An undercover police officer visited the defendant who was selling a car. The officer asked a series of questions which were clearly directed towards establishing that the car was stolen. They culminated in the direct question 'How long has it been nicked?', to which the defendant was reported to have answered 'two to three days'. The defendant was then arrested. The Court of Appeal held that this series of questions ran the risk of offending against the caveat in *Christou*. Since the conversation was disputed, and, unlike the exchanges in *Christou* had not been recorded, it should not have been admitted.

The principles which lie behind the use of the caution derive from the idea of the 'right to silence'. That is, the right of any suspect not to answer questions, and not to give evidence at trial. What is the basis of the right to silence? It relates to two other principles which are regarded as being of fundamental importance in the English criminal justice system. The first is the presumption of innocence. No one is guilty, until *proved* to be so. Moreover, the burden of proof is always on the prosecution: *Woolmington* v *DPP* [1935] AC 462. Thus, suspects or defendants are under no obligation to provide any explanation of their behaviour, or any other evidence: the prosecution must prove guilt beyond reasonable doubt.

The second, and related, principle is that a person cannot be compelled to make a self-incriminating statement. It is thought wrong to put people into the position where they are forced to condemn themselves out of their own mouths.

4.5.1.2 The right to silence

The right to silence has been a controversial issue in recent years. It was thought that 'experienced criminals' and terrorists who had been trained to resist interrogation could 'play the system' by keeping silent, safe in the knowledge that no adverse inference could be drawn at any subsequent trial. They might also produce a new line of defence at trial which the police would have had no opportunity to explore, if it was not mentioned during initial questioning. These concerns gave rise to calls for the right to silence to be amended. This was done to a limited extent in the Northern Ireland (Criminal Evidence (Northern Ireland) Order 1988 (SI 1988/1987)). Similar proposals for England and Wales were put forward by a Home Office Working Party in 1989. What was proposed was not, of course, that the suspect should be physically forced to speak. Rather, the suggestion was that a failure to answer questions, provide information, or give evidence, could be matters from which the court would be entitled to draw adverse inferences in appropriate cases. The knowledge that such inferences could be drawn might then be expected to lead to suspects, and their legal advisers, being less ready to rely on silence as a means of defence to police inquiries.

The majority of the members of the 1993 Royal Commission on Criminal Justice recommended that the position as regards the right of silence, and the inferences to be drawn from silence, should remain unchanged (*Runciman Report*, ch. 4, para. 22). Nevertheless, on 6 October 1993, the then Home Secretary, Michael Howard, announced at the Conservative Party Conference that he intended to remove the 'so-called right to silence'. In the end the right was modified by s. 34 of the Criminal Justice and Public Order Act 1994 (CJPOA). This provides that a court may draw 'such inferences…as appear proper' (s. 34(2)) (including, therefore, inferences of guilt) if the accused (s. 34(1)):

(a) at any time before he was charged with the offence, on being questioned under caution by a constable trying to discover whether or by whom the offence had been committed, failed to mention any fact relied on in his defence in those proceedings; or

(b) on being charged with the offence or officially informed that he might be prosecuted for it, failed to mention that fact.

Sections 36 and 37 contain similar provisions relating to the accused's failure to account for objects, substances, or marks on his person or clothing, or in his possession, or for his presence at a particular place. Sections 34–37 have all been amended by s. 58 of the Youth Justice and Criminal Evidence Act 1999, so as to provide that no inferences shall be drawn if at the relevant time the suspect 'had not been allowed an opportunity to consult a solicitor'. It is the *opportunity* that is important: inferences may be drawn if the suspect has simply decided not to seek legal advice. As noted (see 4.4.2), s. 58 came into force on 1 April 2003.

The effect of ss 34–37 is that the suspect is still entitled to say nothing, but to do so has now become risky. It may mean that a later defence will not be believed. Moreover, a judge is entitled to point out to the jury that it may draw inferences adverse to the defendant from the lack of explanation provided when first questioned. Initial research has suggested that the change in the law has had a 'marked impact' on what happens in the police station (T. Bucke, R. Street, and D. Brown, 'The Right of Silence: The Impact of the Criminal Justice and Public Order Act 1994', Home Office Research Study No. 199, 2000, p. 69). The use of the right to silence was found to have fallen from 32 per cent to 21 per cent in London, and from 21 per cent to 14 per cent elsewhere.

The amendments to the law contained in ss 34–37 of the CJPOA 1994 did not, therefore, abolish the 'right to silence' but they have reduced its effectiveness. There is undoubtedly as a result increased pressure on suspects to reply to police questioning. The change has tilted the balance of power in the police station further in favour of the police questioner. Whether this is a justifiable movement will depend on a view as to the direction in which the balance was tilting prior to the enactment of the change. It seems unlikely, however, that the current procedures render the possibility of wrongful convictions less likely.

There have been a large number of cases on the operation of ss 34–37 of the CJPOA 1994, most of them focusing on the way in which the judge should direct the jury. A selection of the main decisions will be looked at here.

In *R v Cowan* [1996] 1 Cr App R 1 Lord Taylor CJ, commenting on the specimen direction issued by the Judicial Studies Board set out five 'essentials' which needed to be highlighted:

(a) The judge will have told the jury that the burden of proof remains upon the prosecution throughout and what the standard required is.

(b) It is necessary for the judge to make clear to the jury that the defendant is entitled to remain silent. That is his right and his choice.

(c) An inference from failure to give evidence cannot on its own prove guilt. That is expressly stated in s. 38(3) of the Act.

(d) Therefore the jury must be satisfied that the prosecution have established a case to answer before drawing any inferences from silence.

(e) If, despite any evidence relied on to explain his silence, or in the absence of any such evidence, the jury conclude the silence can only sensibly be attributed to the defendant's having no case to answer or none that would stand up to cross-examination, they may draw an adverse inference.

In *R v Argent* [1997] Cr App R 27 the Court of Appeal dealt with the reasons why the accused might have remained silent, or failed to mention a relevant fact, during interview. This might be because of legal advice to that effect, and this could be taken into account by the jury. In looking at the circumstances in which the silence occurred, however, the jury should not be restrictive (p. 33):

> Matters such as the time of day, the defendant's age, experience, mental capacity, state of health, sobriety, tiredness, knowledge, personality and legal advice are all part of the relevant circumstances: and these are only examples of things which may be relevant.

One of the most common reasons is likely to be legal advice. If this is the reason given, however, it does carry with it a disadvantage. As was confirmed in *R v Bowden* [1999] 2 Cr App R 176, once this reason is put forward then this amounts to a waiver of the legal professional privilege which otherwise protects communications between solicitor and client. This means that the solicitor can be called as a witness to explain the basis on which the advice was given, and asked questions more generally about what passed between client and solicitor.

The situation in *Condron* involved the fact that the defendants' solicitor had advised them not to answer police questions. The defendants (who were husband and wife) had been arrested on suspicion of various drugs offences relating to the supply of heroin. The solicitor's advice to remain silent, as he confirmed at the trial, was based on the fact that he felt that they were not in a fit state to be interviewed, as a result of their suffering the symptoms of heroin withdrawal. The police's medical examiner did not agree, and the interviews took place, with the defendants answering 'no comment' to each question. At the trial, the defendants produced innocent explanations of the transactions which the police had witnessed, and which had led to their arrest. The trial judge directed the jury that they could draw adverse inferences from the defendants' silence at interview if they thought it 'proper to do so'. The defendants were convicted. On appeal the Court of Appeal held that the judge had properly allowed the evidence of the 'no comment' interviews to be given. As regards his direction to the jury, the court thought that it would have been 'desirable' if he had directed them more strongly in relation to the drawing of inferences, in the way suggested by Lord Taylor in *Cowan*, that is (p. 7):

> If despite any evidence relied upon to explain his silence or in the absence of any such evidence, the jury conclude the silence can only be sensibly attributed to the defendant's having no answer or none that would stand up to cross-examination, they may draw an adverse inference.

But despite this defect in the summing-up, the Court of Appeal did not think that the conviction was 'unsafe', and so the appeal was dismissed. The defendants applied to the ECtHR, alleging infringement of their right to a fair trial under Art. 6. The European Court in *Condron v United Kingdom* (2001) 31 EHRR 1 adopted the same approach as it had done in *Murray (John) v United Kingdom* (1996) 22 EHRR 29 (see 4.1.2). It confirmed that there is no absolute right to silence, but that since the right lies at the heart of the notion of a fair procedure under Art. 6 particular caution was required before using silence against an accused (para. 56). Silence cannot be used as the sole or main basis for conviction. But an accused's silence in a situation which clearly called for an explanation could be taken into account in assessing the persuasiveness of other evidence produced by the prosecution.

Turning to the facts of the instant case it was important that the Condrons (unlike John Murray) had had access to a solicitor throughout the time when they were being questioned. This was a safeguard against any compulsion to speak which might arise from the terms of the caution (as discussed). At the same time, the trial court needed to give appropriate weight to legal advice to remain silent. The European Court felt that the judge's direction had not properly reflected the balance between the right to silence and the drawing of adverse inferences which the Court had suggested in *Murray*. In particular, given the reasons for silence put forward by the defendants, that is their solicitor's genuine belief in their unfitness to be questioned, it was *essential* rather than merely *desirable* (as the Court of Appeal had suggested) that the judge should have given the strong direction (as quoted) on when an adverse inference can be drawn. Getting the direction right was vitally important in a jury trial, where no reasons are given for the jury's decision. This also meant that the defect at trial could not be remedied on appeal, as suggested by the government, since the Court of Appeal had no means of knowing whether or not the defendants' silence played a significant role in the decision to convict. Moreover, the Court of Appeal was focusing mainly on whether the convictions were 'safe', and this did not take adequate account of the right to a fair procedure which was what was guaranteed by Art. 6. The European Court therefore found that the Condrons had been denied a fair hearing in breach of Art. 6(1).

Following the decision of the ECtHR in *Condron*, the English Court of Appeal showed some equivocation about giving effect to it. In some cases, the court seemed happy to accept reliance on legal advice as a valid basis for ruling out adverse inferences, as long as the reliance was thought to be genuine: for example *R* v *Betts & Hall* [2001] Cr App R 257. In others, for example *R* v *Smart* [2002] EWCA Crim 772, [2002] Crim LR 684, a more restrictive approach was adopted, giving weight to whether there were other justifications for the decision to remain silent. The ECtHR returned to the issue in *Beckles* v *United Kingdom* (2003) 36 EHRR 13. The defendant had remained silent on legal advice. The ECtHR found that the judge had failed to direct the jury properly.

In particular, the judge had suggested that there was no independent verification that the solicitor had advised silence, whereas this did appear in the record of the police interview. Moreover, the judge had failed to emphasize that the jury should only draw adverse inferences where they considered the silence consistent only with guilt. There had, therefore, been a breach of the applicant's Art. 6 right to a fair trial. This was, therefore, a further confirmation of the position taken in *Condron*.

Following this decision of the ECtHR, the Criminal Cases Review Commission referred Beckles' conviction back to the Court of Appeal: [2004] EWCA Crim 2766, [2005] 1 All ER 705. The court, in quashing the conviction, ruled that where a defendant claims to have remained silent on legal advice, the jury should be directed that, if they believe that the defendant genuinely *and reasonably* relied on such advice, then they should not draw any unfair inference from the silence. The court came to this conclusion in trying to resolve the apparent conflict between the decision in *Betts & Hall*, which posed a test simply of 'genuineness' of reliance, and those of *R* v *Howell* [2003] EWCA Crim 1, [2005] 1 Cr App R 1 and *R* v *Knight* [2003] EWCA Crim 1977, [2004] 1 Cr App R 117, which required consideration of whether there was any other justification underlying the legal advice (such as mental disability, intoxication, shock, or the need to refer to documents). Following the line taken in *R* v *Hoare & Pierce* [2004] EWCA Crim 784, [2005] 1 Cr App R 355, the court in *Beckles* required that the reliance on legal advice must not only be genuine, but also *reasonable*. The view seemed to be that this was consistent with the ECtHR's approach. It clearly is not. That approach is based on the defendant's *only* reason for silence being that he has no answer to the questions, or no answer that would stand up to cross-examination. As the ECtHR put it in *Beckles* (para. 62), the jury must be allowed to consider fully 'whether the applicant's reason for his silence was a genuine one, or whether, on the contrary, his silence was in effect consistent *only* with guilt and his reliance on legal advice to stay silent merely a convenient self-serving excuse' (emphasis added). Once it is accepted that the reliance on legal advice is a genuine reason for keeping silent, questions of reasonableness, or whether there are other reasons for not answering, should not arise. The defendant has a genuine reason other than guilt for his silence, and therefore his silence is not consistent only with his guilt. The introduction by the Court of Appeal of tests of reasonableness is therefore inconsistent with the approach of the ECtHR. It is to be hoped that at some point the Supreme Court may have an opportunity to remedy this. Otherwise, further recourse to Strasbourg is likely to be necessary.

A procedure that is not infrequently adopted as a result of legal advice is that the suspect puts forward a prepared statement at the start of the interview, and then refuses to answer any questions. It was confirmed by the Court of Appeal in *R* v *Knight*, that it was inappropriate to allow the drawing of any adverse inference where the defendant had disclosed his full defence in a prepared statement, and then refused to answer questions, provided that the statement was wholly consistent with the defendant's subsequent testimony at trial.

4.5.1.3 The privilege against self-incrimination

As regards self-incrimination, an earlier exception to this was created by the Criminal Justice Act 1987, in relation to the investigation of serious frauds. The House of Lords in *Smith* v *Director of the Serious Fraud Office* [1992] 3 All ER 456 undertook a lengthy analysis of the right to silence, and the rule against self-incrimination. It concluded that the inquisitorial regime which Parliament had approved in the Criminal Justice Act 1987, allowed the Director of the Serious Fraud Office to obtain by compulsion (that is, it would be an offence to refuse to answer) responses to questions which might be self-incriminating (although the use to which such responses could be put is strictly limited: s. 2(8) of the Criminal Justice Act 1987). The operation of this type of provision was considered by the ECtHR in *Saunders* v *United Kingdom* (1997) 23 EHRR 313. It was confirmed by the European Court that, as had been suggested in *Funke* v *France* (1993) 16 EHRR 297:

> Although not mentioned in Art. 6 of the Convention, the right to silence and the right not to incriminate oneself, are generally recognised international standards which lie at the heart of the notion of a fair procedure under Article 6.

In *Saunders* the applicant had been the subject of a Department of Trade and Industry investigation under the Companies Act 1985. This gave powers to the inspectors to require answers to questions, a refusal to comply being liable to be treated as if it were a contempt of court (s. 436 of the Companies Act 1985). Saunders co-operated with the inspectors, and provided information. Transcripts of his answers to questions were subsequently used in a criminal prosecution against Saunders, and he was convicted. Saunders complained to the ECtHR. Both the Commission and the Court held that the procedures adopted infringed Art. 6, in that it involved a marked departure 'from one of the basic principles of a fair procedure' (that is, the right not to incriminate oneself) ((1997) 23 EHRR 313, p. 340):

> The public interest cannot be invoked to justify the use of answers compulsorily obtained in a non-judicial investigation to incriminate the accused during the trial proceedings.

Procedures, therefore, which combine a system of questioning where it is obligatory to answer, with the possibility of the use of those answers in subsequent proceedings, will offend against Art. 6. The government response to this was to enact

s. 59 of, and Sch. 3' to, the Youth Justice and Criminal Evidence Act 1999 which provide that, in relation to various statutory powers requiring compulsory answers to questions, including those under s. 434 of the Companies Act 1985 and s. 2 of the Criminal Justice Act 1987, the answers given may not be used as evidence in a subsequent criminal prosecution (other than for perjury).

A different type of situation involving compulsion to answer questions was considered by the Privy Council in the Scottish case *Brown* v *Stott* [2001] 2 All ER 97.

The defendant had been arrested at a supermarket in relation to the theft of a bottle of gin. The officers smelt alcohol on her breath. She then indicated that her car was in the supermarket car park. She was asked who had been driving it at 2.30 a.m. (i.e. at about the time she would have arrived at the car park). This was a question which, by virtue of s. 172(2)(a) of the Road Traffic Act 1988 she was obliged to answer. Failure to do so would constitute a criminal offence, punishable with a fine of up to £1,000. The defendant said that she had been driving. She was then given a breath test and charged with driving with an excess of alcohol. At trial she objected to evidence of her answer as to who was driving being used against her. She was convicted, but the Scottish appeal court allowed her appeal, holding that in the light of Art. 6(1) of the ECHR and the privilege against self-incrimination, she should not have been required to answer the question. The prosecution appealed to the Privy Council, which took a different view. It noted that the privilege against self-incrimination was not specifically recognized by Art. 6, but had been implied by the court as one of the factors (together with the right to silence) which might prejudice the right to a fair trial. While the right to a fair trial was unqualified, the same could not be said of those rights which were implied rather than specifically stated. In relation to such rights it was appropriate for the court to consider whether any proposed restriction of them was 'reasonably directed by the national authorities towards a clear and proper objective' and represented 'no greater qualification than the situation calls for' ([2001] 2 All ER 97, p. 115, per Lord Bingham). In this case, the problems of death and injury caused by road accidents had led the government to impose a scheme of regulation over vehicle users. There was, therefore, a clear 'public interest' motive underlying s. 172. The question was, therefore, whether the section constituted a 'proportionate' response to the problem. The Privy Council felt that, taking into account that s. 172 involved a simple answer to one question, which would not necessarily involve the admission of any criminal liability, and that all who own or drive motor cars are aware that they are subject to a regulatory regime which does not apply to others, the requirement to answer could be justified. It was not, therefore, unfair to allow the evidence of the answer to be given at trial, and there was no breach of Art. 6.

While it is clear that if the Privy Council's decision had gone the other way it would have caused severe practical problems for those charged with enforcing road traffic law, it appeared to be out of line with the approach which had been taken by the ECtHR. In *Saunders* v *United Kingdom*, for example, in a passage quoted by Lord Bingham in *Brown* v *Stott*, the Court commented that ((1997) 23 EHRR 313, para. 74, emphasis added):

> ...the general requirements of fairness contained in art 6, *including the right not to incriminate oneself,* apply to criminal proceedings in respect of all types of criminal offences without distinction from the most simple to the most complex. The public interest

> cannot be invoked to justify the use of answers obtained in a non-judicial investigation to incriminate the accused during trial proceedings.

This approach would seem to indicate that the Strasbourg Court might have taken a different view to that of the Privy Council in this situation. Certainly, where more serious offences are involved, the Court confirmed, in a decision handed down a few weeks after *Brown* v *Stott*, that the imposition of a penalty for a failure to answer questions can amount to a breach of the ECHR. In *Heaney and McGuiness* v *Ireland* (2001) 33 EHRR 12 the applicants had been arrested in connection with the investigation of an explosion. They were asked to account for their movements at a particular time but refused to do so. As a result they were convicted of an offence under s. 52 of the Offences Against the State Act 1939, for which they were sentenced to six months' imprisonment. The ECtHR recognized that the right to silence and the privilege against self-incrimination are not absolute (para. 47). It also considered the Irish government's argument that s. 52 was a proportionate response to the continuing terrorist and security threat. Nevertheless, quoting the paragraph from *Saunders* v *United Kingdom*, the Court held that the security and public order concerns could not 'justify a provision which extinguishes the very essence of the applicants' rights to silence and against self-incrimination guaranteed by Article 6(1) of the Convention' (para. 58). In the sixth edition of this book it was suggested that, if a government's attempts to deal with threats of terrorism and public disorder were insufficient grounds to justify the breach in this case, it must surely be debatable whether the objective of enforcing road traffic law which was relied on by the Privy Council in *Brown* v *Stott* should be sufficient to justify s. 172 of the Road Traffic Act 1988. In *O'Halloran* v *United Kingdom* (2008) 46 EHRR 21, however, the Strasbourg Court took just such a line. There were two applicants in this case. Both had been required, under s. 172 of the Road Traffic Act 1988, to state who had been the driver at a particular time of a vehicle registered in their name, in relation to alleged speeding offences. One of the applicants had complied, but argued that this 'confession' should have been inadmissible as evidence against him, because it was supplied under constraint. The other applicant had refused to comply, and had been convicted of the offence of failure to supply the details. He alleged that he had been punished more harshly for this offence than if he had been convicted of the alleged speeding. The Strasbourg Court reviewed its previous case law in this area and noted that (para. 53):

> ...in all the cases to date in which 'direct compulsion' was applied to require an actual or potential suspect to provide information which contributed, or might have contributed, to his conviction, the Court has found a violation of the applicant's privilege against self-incrimination.

This did not mean, however (para. 53):

> ...that any direct compulsion will automatically result in a violation. While the right to a fair trial under Article 6 is an unqualified right, what constitutes a fair trial cannot be the subject of a single unvarying rule but must depend on the circumstances of the particular case.

The Court then reviewed all the circumstances of the cases before it. It clearly placed some weight on the view, also expressed by Lord Bingham in *Brown* v *Stott*, that it was relevant that owning a motor vehicle is a voluntary activity. Thus (para. 57):

> Those who choose to keep and drive motor cars can be taken to have accepted certain responsibilities and obligations as part of the regulatory regime relating to motor vehicles, and in the legal framework of the United Kingdom, these responsibilities include the obligation, in the event of suspected commission of road traffic offences, to inform the authorities of the identity of the driver on that occasion.

It also noted the limited nature of the information which the police could require under s. 172, i.e. simply the identity of the driver. Having regard to this, and to its decision in the rather similar case of *Weh* v *Austria*, the Court concluded (paras. 62–3):

> Having regard to all the circumstances of the case, including the special nature of the regulatory regime at issue and the limited nature of the information sought by a notice under section 172 of the Road Traffic Act 1988, the Court considers that the essence of the applicants' right to remain silent and their privilege against self-incrimination has not been destroyed.

Accordingly, there has been no violation of Article 6(1) of the Convention.

While it is understandable that the practicalities of road traffic law carried significant weight with the Strasbourg Court, as they had with the Privy Council, it is to be hoped that this decision does not indicate any significant retreat from the very strong position on the privilege against self-incrimination which the Court has previously adopted.

4.5.2 Interviews

The main method by which the police gain, or attempt to gain, evidence from a suspect is by means of interviews. Such questioning is controlled by various provisions in PACE and Code C. The protective provisions only apply, however, to something which is properly classified as an 'interview'. It is necessary, therefore, to start with the definition of this concept, before moving on to look at how it is regulated.

4.5.2.1 Meaning of an 'interview'

The concept of the interview was not defined in the original version of the PACE Codes. There was a certain amount of case law on the issue, some of which will still need to be considered, but the starting point is now para. 11.1A of Code C. It states that:

> An interview is the questioning of a person regarding his involvement or suspected involvement in a criminal offence or offences, which, under paragraph 10.1 [of Code C], must be carried out under caution.

Paragraph 10.1 requires a caution to be given where there are grounds to suspect a person of an offence and the answers to questions (or the suspect's failure or refusal to answer questions) may be given in evidence to a court in a prosecution. Questioning which is not directed to this end but is, for example, to establish a person's identity, or the ownership of a vehicle, or to assist in the conduct of a search of a person or property, will not, therefore, constitute an 'interview'.

The current definition of an interview follows criticism of the previous definition by the 1993 Royal Commission on Criminal Justice (*Runciman Report*, ch. 3, para. 10). The Court of Appeal in *R v Cox* (1992) Cr App R 464, had had considerable difficulty interpreting this definition, which tried to draw a distinction between questioning about a criminal offence on the one hand (which constituted an interview), and questioning to obtain information or an explanation of facts, or 'in the ordinary course of the officer's duties', on the other (which would not constitute an interview). The distinction proved unworkable, and has therefore been abandoned. The definition as it now stands seems to envisage a very broad definition of an interview. It is, at any rate, established that an interview can occur away from a police station (*R v Maloney and Doherty* [1988] Crim LR 523, and *R v Fogah* [1989] Crim LR 141); nor is it necessary for the officer concerned to be intending to conduct an interview. In *R v Sparks* [1991] Crim LR 128, what started out as an informal 'chat' between an officer not involved in the investigation and the suspect, was capable of being regarded as an interview when the conversation elicited damaging admissions from the suspect.

On the other hand, a conversation instigated by the suspect in which the police did not ask questions but simply recorded what was said, was held not to be an interview by the Court of Appeal in *R v Menard* [1995] 1 Cr App R 306. In the Court's view the hallmark of an interview is 'questioning', and since on the facts of the present case this did not occur, there was no interview. The definition will also exclude the situation where the questioning is directed to a person who is not *at that stage* a suspect, but who might become one, depending on the answer to the questions. This is because the definition of an interview is tied to the requirement to caution, and this only arises where there are grounds to suspect a person of an offence. This corresponds to the approach in *R v Absolam* (1989) 88 Cr App R 332, p. 336, where Bingham LJ defined an interview as a 'series of questions directed by the police to a *suspect*' (emphasis added). The grounds for suspicion must be objectively 'reasonable' (*R v Shah* [1994] Crim LR 125, CA). It was held by the Court of Appeal in *R v James* [1996] Crim LR 650, that the test was the same as that for the power of arrest (see chapter 3 (3.5.3.1)), and this was confirmed by *R v Blackford*, 17 February 2000, CA. It is not the case, however, that all comments addressed to a person against whom there are reasonable grounds for suspicion will amount to an interview. Thus, in *R v Maguire* (1989) 90 Cr App R 115 the accused was arrested near the scene of a burglary, and was thus a suspect. In the police car, an officer said to him: 'Look, you've both been caught. Now tell us the truth.' This was held simply to be an invitation to the suspect to explain himself, and did not constitute an interview. This would presumably still be the case under Note 11.1A.

Finally, to conclude with one point of much greater certainty, para. 11.1A of Code C specifically provides that procedures in relation to breath tests, etc. under s. 7 of the Road Traffic Act 1988, do not constitute interviewing for the purposes of the Code. Such powers, even where they lead to the compulsory provision of evidence which will form the basis of a criminal prosecution, are unlikely to be found to involve a breach of Art. 6 of the ECHR. This is because the ECtHR has consistently, from the case of *Funke* v *France* (1993) 16 EHRR 297 onward, drawn a clear distinction between statements on the one hand and *physical* evidence, in the form of documents, samples, etc. on the other. It has taken the view that the compulsory provision of such physical evidence does not involve a breach of the rights to silence or against self-incrimination.

4.5.2.2 Conduct of an interview

Paragraph 11.1 of Code C provides that, once a decision to arrest has been taken, a suspect must not generally be interviewed about the offence other than at a police station. The only exceptions are where the delay involved in taking the suspect to a police station would be likely to lead to one of the consequences which justifies delaying exercise of the right to have someone informed under s. 56(5) (see 4.4.1).

The conduct of the interview, in terms of duration, breaks, provision of meals, etc. is governed by para. 12 of Code C. For example, in any 24 hour period the detainee should normally be allowed at least eight hours' rest (para. 12.2).

An important aspect of the interview procedure is the continuing right to private legal advice, and to have a legal adviser present during an interview (paras 6.1 and 11.2 of Code C). Any request for legal advice, and the action taken on it, must be recorded (para. 6.16 of Code C).

The right to legal advice will apply unless a decision has been taken to delay access under s. 58(8) or (8A) (see 4.4.2). Otherwise, in relation to an interview with a detainee who wants legal advice, the interview should not start unless one of the conditions set out in para. 6.6 of Code C is satisfied. There are four of these. The first arises where an officer of at least the rank of superintendent has reasonable grounds for believing that delay will involve an immediate risk of harm to persons or serious loss of, or damage to, property (para. 6.6(b)(i) of Code C). A detainee suspected of having planted a bomb, for example, may need to be questioned about its location. Once sufficient information has been obtained to avert the risk, however, questioning should stop until the detainee has received legal advice (para. 6.7 of Code C). The second condition is where an officer of at least the rank of superintendent has reasonable grounds to believe that to await the arrival of a solicitor who has been contacted and has agreed to attend would cause unreasonable delay to the progress of the investigation (para. 6.6(b)(ii) of Code C). Before reaching such a decision the officer should, where practicable, obtain an estimate of the likely delay from the solicitor. If the solicitor is on the way to the station, or about to set off, it will not normally be appropriate to begin the interview. If it appears that it will be necessary to start the interview before the solicitor's arrival, the solicitor should be told how long the police are prepared to wait, so that alternative arrangements for legal advice may be made by the solicitor (Note 6A to Code C). If legal advice is delayed on one of the above grounds, then no adverse inferences may be drawn from silence during the interview. As regards the other grounds, dealt with next, adverse inferences *may* be drawn, because they apply in situations where there has been no denial of the *opportunity* for legal advice.

The third condition justifying interviewing before legal advice has been given arises where the solicitor nominated by the detainee is unavailable. This may be because the solicitor cannot be contacted, or is unwilling to attend. The detainee must also have declined to see the duty solicitor, if one is available (para. 6.6(c) of Code C). The interview may then start immediately, subject to the approval of an officer of at least the rank of inspector.

In all the above cases, where the detainee has asked for legal advice and the interview is begun in the absence of a legal adviser, this must be recorded on the interview record (para. 6.17 of Code C). The fourth situation in which an interview may be started or continued without legal advice in relation to a suspect who has previously asked for such advice is where the suspect has had a change of mind (para. 6(6)(d)). Approval for interviewing to start or continue must be given by an officer of at least the rank of inspector (though this may be done by telephone) (Note 6I to Code C). The inspector has an obligation to inquire into the reasons for the change of mind. If approval is given, confirmation of the agreement of the suspect, the change of mind and any reasons given for it, and the name of the authorizing officer must be recorded in the taped or written interview record at the beginning or recommencement of the interview.

If a solicitor arrives at a police station to see a particular detainee, there is an obligation on the police to inform the detainee of this, even if the detainee has previously declined legal advice (para. 6.15 of Code C). The right to legal advice is that of the client to receive it, however, not of the solicitor to give it. Thus, it was held by the Court of Appeal in *Rixon* v *Chief Constable of Kent, The Times*, 11 April 2000 that a solicitor who had been refused access to a client in a police station had no cause of action against the police. It is not clear whether the right to be told of the solicitor's willingness to advise applies where the solicitor has contacted the police station by telephone rather than in person. In *R* v *Chahal* [1992] Crim LR 124, the detainee, who had indicated that he did not want a solicitor, was not told of telephone calls from a solicitor who had been instructed by his family. It was held by the Court of Appeal that he had no right to be told of the calls. This decision was reached on the basis of the original Code, which did not have a provision equivalent to the current para. 6.15. The wording of para. 6.15 is in terms of the solicitor being physically present at the police station. This would suggest that the police have no obligation to inform the detainee of telephone calls. It is submitted, however, that the spirit of para. 6.15 suggests that as a matter of practice the police should do so.

A solicitor who is present at an interview may only be required to leave if their conduct prevents the investigating officer properly questioning the detainee (para. 6.9 of Code C). Challenging an improper question, or advising the detainee not to answer, or seeking to give the detainee further legal advice, are not grounds for requiring the solicitor to leave (Note 6D to Code C). On the other hand, answering questions on the detainee's behalf, or providing written replies for the detainee to quote, may well provide such justification. An investigating officer who thinks that a solicitor is behaving in a way which justifies exclusion, should stop the interview and consult either a superintendent, if available, or an officer of at least the rank of inspector who is not connected with the investigation. This senior officer should speak to the solicitor, and then decide whether to allow the solicitor to continue to be present at the interview. If the decision is taken to exclude the solicitor, the detainee must be given the chance to consult another solicitor, who will have the opportunity to be present when the interview continues (para. 6.10 of Code C). These provisions indicate the seriousness with which the right to legal advice is treated within the Code. Only where there is clear misconduct is the solicitor of the detainee's choice to be excluded, and even then the detainee is not to be prejudiced more than necessary. The interview should not continue until a new solicitor is available to advise the detainee, and attend the interview.

4.5.2.3 **Record of interview**

In most cases nowadays interviews are recorded on tape. Detailed procedures relating to this are contained in Code E. This is designed to encourage confidence in the procedure on the part of the detainee, and to ensure security. The system has advantages for both the detainee and the police, in that the police will not be able to put words into the detainee's mouth, but incriminating statements which appear on the tape will be difficult to deny.

Within police stations the use of tape recordings will satisfy the more general requirement under para. 11.7 of Code C, of the contemporaneous recording of interviews. Where recording facilities are not available, however, a written record will need to be made. The details of the procedures to be followed are set out in paras 11.7–11.14 of Code C. As is the case with a tape-recorded interview, a written record must give the details of the location of the interview, the time it starts and finishes (including any breaks), and the names of all those present. It may take the form of a precise record of the words used, or a summary. If it is not practicable to make the record during the interview itself, it must be made as soon as practicable thereafter. The person interviewed should be given the chance to read and sign the record. This allows the detainee to indicate any inaccuracies. The detainee's solicitor, if present, should also be given the opportunity to read and sign the record.

These procedures are regarded by the courts as very important. As will be seen, in discussing the exclusion of evidence under s. 78 (see 4.6.4.3) one of the most common grounds for excluding evidence of incriminating statements has been that a proper contemporaneous record was not kept. Such a record is regarded as greatly increasing the reliability of the evidence. As a result, the current version of Code C includes a requirement of a written record even as regards statements made outside the context of an interview (para. 11.13 of Code C). Any comments made by a suspect, even if unsolicited, should be recorded in writing. The record should be timed and signed by the officer making it. The suspect should also be given the opportunity to read and sign the record, in the same way as for an interview record. This extension of recording requirements to 'non-interview' statements reduces the possibility of the police relying on evidence of statements supposed to have been made at the time of arrest, or before arrival at the police station. The courts will not be prepared to accept the evidence of the police officer on its own; they will expect it to be backed up by a written contemporaneous record.

Further discussion of these requirements, and the effects of police failure to comply with them can be found at 4.6.4.3, in relation to exclusion of evidence under s. 78 of PACE.

4.5.3 **Fingerprints, searches, and samples**

Fingerprinting has long been an important element in police detection, as a means of linking a specific individual to a crime. The development in recent years of so-called 'genetic fingerprinting' has made samples of blood or other bodily fluids of perhaps even greater importance. The technique relies on matching DNA profiles, which are very unlikely to be the same for different people. It has become an important part of investigation and prosecution procedures.

The issue looked at here is the extent to which the police have the power to take fingerprints, or samples, from a suspect to aid their inquiries. Extensive searching, including bodily orifices, may also be justified in looking for evidence of drug offences, for example. Such procedures of sampling and search obviously involve a major intrusion into the bodily integrity of the suspect. They would constitute serious assaults if carried out without consent, or specific lawful authority. In relation to the HRA 1998, the most relevant provision is Art. 3 of the ECHR prohibiting 'inhuman or degrading treatment'. A non-consensual intimate search would be very likely to fall within the definition of such treatment. Other, lesser, searches, if carried out in inappropriate circumstances (e.g. in public or by a member of the opposite sex) might also do so. Most types of search will engage the Art. 8 right to respect for an individual's private life (see *Gillan* v *United Kingdom* (2010) 50 EHRR 45, discussed in chapter 3 (3.2)). Although Art. 8(2) allows for the infringement of this right 'for the prevention of disorder or crime', the interference would have to be 'necessary' and proportionate in order to be justified. These issues are discussed further at various points below as the details of the powers are dealt with. The powers of the police in this area are covered by ss 55 and 61–65 of PACE; para. 4 of and Annex A to Code C; and paras 4–6 of Code D. As will be seen, the way in which the appropriate balance between the rights of the citizen and the powers of the police is struck is by reference to recording and notification procedures, the level of seniority of the officer given the power of authorization, and the seriousness of the offence. Thus the most intrusive procedures need the authorization of an officer of at least the rank of inspector, and are available only in relation to indictable offences. Many of the powers in this area used to require authorization by a superintendent. This was, however, reduced to inspector by the CJPA 2001. The change has obvious practical advantages for the police, but it must at the same time be seen as reducing, even if slightly, the protection afforded to the detainee. The same is true of the reduction of the level of seriousness of the offence from the original 'serious arrestable offence' to the current 'indictable offence'. This change was made with effect from January 2006 by the Serious Organised Crime and Police Act 2005. (For further discussion of the abolition of the concept of the serious arrestable offence, see chapter 3(3.5.3).)

4.5.3.1 Fingerprinting and photographs

The power to take fingerprints from a detainee is governed by s. 61. Where possible this should be done with the consent of the detainee, which must be given in writing (s. 61(2)). If consent is not forthcoming, the police may take fingerprints without consent if the person is detained at a police station in connection with a recordable offence (s. 61(3)). Prior to 2004, the approval of an inspector was required for the exercise of this power, but this requirement was removed by the Criminal Justice Act 2003. The taking of fingerprints now seems to be a matter of routine, and not linked to any particular suspicion that the fingerprint evidence will assist in the investigation of the crime. Where consent is not given, reasonable force may be used (s. 117). Any person who is fingerprinted should be told the reasons beforehand (para. 4.7 of Code D), and that the prints may be the subject of a 'speculative search' (that is, checked against police records) s. 61(7A). The fact that the necessary information has been given to the detainee should be recorded on the custody record (s. 61(8)). The detainee should also be told about the procedures for destruction, which are discussed at 4.5.3.5.

Non-consensual taking of fingerprints is unlikely to be regarded as sufficiently serious in itself to breach Art. 3 of the ECHR. Nor would it be likely to be held to infringe privacy under Art. 8 to a greater extent than is necessary for the purposes of crime prevention.

A general power to take photographs of detainees, without consent if necessary, was added to PACE by the Anti-terrorism, Crime, and Security Act 2001, and now appears as s. 64A. This replaced the position as previously stated in para. 4 of the previous version of Code D that photographs should generally only be taken with the consent of the detainee, other than in exceptional circumstances, and then only under the authorization of a superintendent. There is also a power to require the removal, or if necessary to remove, any covering over the head or face of the detainee in order to take the photograph. The photograph can be used for the 'prevention or detection of crime, the investigation of an offence or the conduct of a prosecution'. As with the power of search under s. 54A (see 4.2.4) 'offence' here includes offences committed outside the United Kingdom. Part of the justification for the power is, therefore, to assist in the identification of those wanted for offences abroad, and in particular terrorist offences. The power is stated generally, however, and so is not limited to such situations.

As with fingerprinting, it is likely that these powers would not be held to be sufficiently serious to infringe Art. 3, and would fall within the justification for interference with the right under Art. 8. The provisions relating to the removal of head coverings also clearly raise the possibility of an infringement of the right to the manifestation of a person's religion under Art. 9; again, however, it is likely that they would fall within the permitted restrictions set out in Art. 9(2).

4.5.3.2 **Strip searches and intimate searches**

The general power of search and seizure at the time when the initial decision to detain is made is discussed at 4.2.4. A strip search, which means any search involving the removal of more than outer clothing, may be authorized by a custody officer who reasonably believes that it is necessary in order to remove an article which a person would not be allowed to keep (para. 4.1 of Code C, and para. 10 of Annex A to Code C). This includes articles of clothing or personal effects which the custody officer has reasonable grounds for believing may be evidence of an offence. Underwear stained with blood, or other substances requiring scientific analysis, might well fall into this category. As long as the search takes place in private, and only in the presence of officers of the same sex as the suspect, then it is unlikely to be regarded as being in breach of either Art. 3 or Art. 8 of the ECHR. In *Wainwright v Home Office* [2003] UKHL 53, [2003] 4 All ER 969 the House of Lords held that strip searches of people visiting a relative who was on remand did not involve a breach of Art. 3 or Art. 8, despite the fact that they had not followed the approved procedure under the Prison Rules. The claimants had, for example, been asked to uncover virtually all of their bodies at the same time; the female claimant had been searched in a room that was not private because it had an uncurtained window; and the penis of the male claimant had been touched by an officer and the foreskin lifted. The male claimant was awarded damages for battery at common law as regards the touching of his penis, but both also claimed breaches of Arts 3 and 8. They were distressed by their treatment and the male claimant suffered post-traumatic stress disorder. Lord Hoffmann, delivering the leading speech, held that the treatment, other than the battery as regards the male, had not reached a sufficient level of seriousness to engage Art. 3 (para. 49). As regards Art. 8, the actions of the prison officers had appeared to involve negligent rather than intentional breaches of the rules and there was no necessity for a remedy in damages to be available in such a situation (para. 51). The ECtHR, however, disagreed as to Art. 8: *Wainwright* v *United Kingdom* (2007) 44 EHRR 40. Although the actions of the officers were 'in accordance with law' and were carried out for a legitimate objective (controlling access to drugs in prisons) (para. 47), they were not proportionate to that objective (para. 48):

> Where procedures are laid down for the proper conduct of searches on outsiders to the prison who may very well be innocent of any wrongdoing, it behoves the prison authorities to comply strictly with those safeguards and by rigorous precautions protect the dignity of those being searched from being assailed any further than is necessary. They did not do so in this case.

As a result the actions were not 'necessary in a democratic society'. Damages of €3,000 were awarded to each of the applicants. As a result of this decision the police now need to ensure that when strip searches are used the procedures and limitations set out in Code C are scrupulously observed.

An intimate search may only be authorized by an officer of at least the rank of inspector. The definition of an intimate search is contained in s. 65, where it is defined as 'a search which consists of the physical examination of a person's body orifices, other than the mouth'. This includes, therefore, searches of the ears and nose, as well as the vagina and rectum. The removal of a search of the mouth from the category of 'intimate search', effected by the CJPOA 1994, followed a recommendation to this effect by the 1993 Royal Commission on Criminal Justice (*Runciman Report*, ch. 2, para. 30). The mouth had become a common hiding place for drugs, resulting in the adoption by the police of procedures such as those approved by the Court of Appeal in *R* v *Hughes*, *The Times*, 12 November 1993. A police officer had held on to the defendant's jaw with one hand, and the outside of the defendant's nostrils with the other, as a result of which the defendant spat out a wrapper containing cannabis. This was held not to constitute an intimate search, even though a search of the mouth would at the time have fallen into this category. The change in the law makes it easier for the police to use more direct methods of recovering things hidden in a suspect's mouth.

The justifications for allowing an intimate search are two, namely to recover items which might be used to cause physical injury, or to recover a Class A drug (as defined in s. 2(1) of the Misuse of Drugs Act 1971) (s. 55(1)). The authorizing officer must have reasonable grounds for believing that something falling into one of these categories will be found, and that it cannot be found without an intimate search (s. 55(2)). In relation to a search for drugs, the officer must also have reasonable grounds to believe that it was in the possession of the detainee with appropriate criminal intent prior to the arrest (s. 55(1)(b)(ii)). Only intention to supply, or to evade customs restrictions will be sufficient: mere possession is not enough (s. 55(17)). The authorization must be given or confirmed in writing (s. 55(3)).

In general an intimate search may only be carried out by a doctor or nurse. If, however, in relation to a search which is not simply a search for drugs, the authorizing officer thinks that it is impracticable (perhaps because of the urgency of the situation) to have the search carried out by a doctor or nurse, it may be made by a police officer of the same sex as the detainee. If the search is simply for drugs, it must not take place at a police station, but at a hospital, a doctor's surgery, or 'some other place used for medical purposes' (s. 55(8)).

Although the grounds justifying an intimate search are narrow, the range of items which may be seized as a result of such a search is rather wider. As regards evidence, the custody officer may seize anything found in the course of the search which the officer has reasonable grounds to believe may be evidence relating to *any* offence (s. 55(12)). In addition, items which the officer believes (reasonable belief is not necessary) may be used to cause injury, damage property, interfere with evidence, or assist escape, may be seized. The detainee must normally be told the reason for the seizure (s. 55(13)), but there does not appear to be any requirement to record this. On the other hand, the extent of any intimate search, and the justification for it, must be noted on the detainee's custody record.

An intimate search carried out without consent, and with the use of 'reasonable force' (as permitted by s. 117 of PACE) clearly has the potential to constitute 'inhuman or degrading treatment' under Art. 3 of the ECHR. This is particularly so where the search involves the vagina or rectum, rather than the ears or nose (or indeed the mouth, even though this is no longer an intimate search). It seems likely, however, that the English courts will accept the necessity of such searches in limited circumstances. They will want to be sure, nevertheless, that there really was no alternative, and that the search was carried out with the minimum of force and with all other possible safeguards for the suspect in place. A similar approach would be likely as regards any challenge under Art. 8, on the grounds of infringement of privacy.

4.5.3.3 Intimate samples

An intimate sample is now defined in s. 65 as:

1. a sample of blood, semen or any other tissue, fluid, urine or pubic hair;
2. a dental impression;
3. a swab taken from a person's genitals, or from a person's body orifice other than the mouth.

The 1993 Royal Commission on Criminal Justice recommended, responding to suggestions to this effect from the police, that saliva should be classified as a non-intimate sample, which can be taken without consent, primarily because of its usefulness in DNA profiling (*Runciman Report*, ch. 2, para. 29). It also suggested that dental impressions, which were not dealt with anywhere, should be added to the list of intimate samples (*Runciman Report*, ch. 2, para. 31).

The taking of intimate samples, which is governed by s. 62, is such an intrusion into a person's bodily integrity, that, with one exception, which is dealt with below, they may only be taken with consent, which must be given in writing. Even then it will only be lawful if authorized (either before or after consent has been attained: *R v Butt* (1999) Crim LR 414) by an officer of at least the rank of inspector, who has reasonable grounds for suspecting that the detainee is involved with a recordable offence, and for believing that the sample will tend to confirm or disprove such involvement. A recordable offence is one punishable with imprisonment, or specified in the National Police Records (Recordable Offences) Regulations 2000 (SI 2000/1139). It thus covers a very wide range of offences. Prior to the CJPOA 1994, the power to take intimate samples had existed only in relation to serious arrestable offences. The 1993 Royal Commission on Criminal Justice recommended that the police should have the power to take intimate samples with the permission of the suspect in any case, partly because such samples may be used to eliminate a person from suspicion, as well as suggesting guilt (*Runciman Report*, ch. 2, para. 32). The authorization for the taking of a sample must be made or confirmed in writing, and the detainee must be informed of the authorization and the grounds for it. If the detainee consents, the sample may then be taken, though if it is to be of anything other than urine it must be taken by a doctor (s. 62(9)). A dental impression must be taken by a registered dentist. The authorization, the grounds, and the consent, should be recorded in the detainee's custody record (s. 62(7), (8)).

The detainee, of course, may refuse to allow the sample to be taken. There is no power to override this consent and take a sample by force, nor does refusal in itself constitute an offence (unlike the position in relation to the drink-driving procedures under s. 7 of the Road Traffic Act 1988). If, however, there is such a refusal to give an intimate sample, then in any subsequent criminal proceedings the court is empowered to draw 'such inferences from the refusal as may appear proper' (s. 62(10)). Because of this, para. 6 of Code D requires the detainee to be warned of the effects of a refusal, and sets out an appropriate form of words (Note 6D to Code D):

> You do not have to provide this sample/allow this swab or impression to be taken, but I must warn you that if you refuse without good cause, your refusal may harm your case if it comes to trial.

The extension of the scope of the power to take intimate samples, with consent, to the majority of offences, together with the fact that adverse inferences may be drawn from such a refusal, has considerably weakened the position of the suspect in this area. Indeed, given the very intrusive nature of procedures to take intimate samples, it may be questioned whether sufficient weight is now given to the rights of the suspect to resist such intrusions on personal privacy, and bodily integrity.

The fact that consent is required, however, probably means that the procedures would not be considered as involving any breach of Art. 3 of the ECHR, or of amounting to a disproportionate invasion of privacy under Art. 8, provided that there is full compliance with the procedures and safeguards set out in the legislation and the Code of Practice.

The one situation where a blood sample can be taken without consent is to be found in s. 56 of the PRA 2002, which authorizes a doctor, at the request of the police, to take blood samples without consent from a person involved in a road accident who is unconscious or incapacitated. Although the justification of this power is to assist in the control of drink-driving, it must be open to challenge under Art. 8. The use of evidence obtained from such a sample might also be said to infringe the privilege against self-incrimination, and thus be contrary to Art. 6 (see 4.5.1.3), though the ECtHR's more relaxed approach to physical incriminating evidence, as opposed to incriminating statements, means that this is probably unlikely. (Cf. *Jalloh* v *Germany* (2007) 44 EHRR 32—drugs obtained by administration of emetic to suspect allowed to be used in evidence against him. See also the discussion of *O'Halloran* v *United Kingdom* (at 4.5.1.3) which would suggest a similar conclusion.)

4.5.3.4 Non-intimate samples

These are defined in s. 65 as:

1. a sample of hair other than pubic hair;
2. a sample taken from a nail or from under a nail;
3. a swab taken from any part of a person's body other than a part from which a swab taken would be an intimate sample;
4. saliva;
5. a footprint or a similar impression of any part of a person's body other than a fingerprint or palm print.

The taking of a non-intimate sample is less intrusive than an intimate sample, but may still involve unpleasant, painful, or degrading procedures. As a result, the normal procedure will be to seek consent, which must be given in writing (s. 63(2)). If such consent is not forthcoming, then an officer of at least the rank of inspector may authorize the taking of the sample, and reasonable force may be used. A sample of non-pubic hair may be taken by plucking, as opposed to cutting (s. 63A(2)).

The grounds for authorizing the taking of a non-intimate sample without consent are the same as those in relation to taking an intimate sample with consent (see 4.5.3.3). In other words, the power will not arise at all unless the detainee is suspected of involvement in a recordable offence. The notification and recording procedures under s. 63 are the same as for the taking of intimate samples under s. 62.

There is no sanction for refusal to provide a non-intimate sample by a detainee who is being held in relation to an offence which is not a recordable offence. Since there is no specific provision in s. 63 comparable to that in s. 62 allowing adverse inferences to be drawn from a refusal, it must be assumed that the court would have no power to draw such inferences.

The non-consensual taking of a non-intimate sample, though clearly less intrusive than an intimate search (see 4.5.3.2) might nevertheless be considered to be sufficiently degrading to fall within the scope of Art. 3 of the ECHR. Depending on the circumstances, and in particular the seriousness of the offence under investigation, it might also amount to a disproportionate infringement of privacy under Art. 8. There is, therefore, some scope for an HRA 1998 challenge to the use of these powers.

4.5.3.5 Destruction of fingerprints and samples

Where a person is cleared of an offence, or if it is decided not to prosecute, or to discontinue a prosecution, s. 64 of PACE provided that any fingerprints or samples which had been taken must be destroyed. The value of this provision was considerably reduced by the House of Lords' decision in *Attorney-General's Reference No. 3 of 1999* [2001] 2 AC 91. Evidence (derived from a sample) which should have been destroyed under s. 64 was used in a subsequent investigation to identify a suspect, from whom a fresh sample was then taken. The Court of Appeal held that, because s. 64 prohibited the use of information obtained from the original sample, the evidence of the new sample was inadmissible. The House of Lords disagreed. The section specifically stated that information obtained directly from the original sample was inadmissible; but it did not state that fresh information obtained from that sample, contrary to s. 64, was also inadmissible. In that situation the question of admissibility was for the judge to decide, using s. 78 of PACE (see 4.6.4.3) if necessary. The effect of this decision was given a statutory basis by the amendments to s. 64 introduced by s. 82 of the CJPA 2001, although these provisions have now been reformed following the decision of the ECtHR in *S and Marper* v *United Kingdom* (1998) 48 EHRR 50. Under the revisions introduced by s. 82 the obligation to destroy samples or prints where the suspect has been cleared of an offence was removed entirely. Such samples might be used, but only 'for purposes related to the prevention or detection of crime, the investigation of an offence or the conduct of a prosecution' (s. 64(1A), as substituted by s. 82 of the CJPA 2001). Moreover, samples supplied voluntarily, for example for the purposes of elimination, can also be retained where the donor of the sample has given consent to their retention.

These procedures for the retention of samples taken from those not proceeded against or acquitted were challenged under the HRA 1998 in *R (S)* v *Chief Constable of Yorkshire* [2004] UKHL 39, [2004] 4 All ER 139 (this case is also often referred to by the name of one of the other applicants—'Marper'). The House of Lords found that, in so far as the procedures interfered with the right to private life under Art. 8, they were justifiable and proportionate as a means of achieving the public benefit of the effective investigation and prosecution of serious crime. The House also rejected an argument that Art. 14 was infringed because the provisions involved an unlawful discrimination between innocent people suspected of crime, and innocent people who had never been so suspected. The applicants took their complaint to Strasbourg, and the decision of the ECtHR was handed down in *S and Marper* v *United Kingdom* (2008) 48 EHRR 50. The Court considered the position in relation to the retention of samples, DNA profiles derived from such samples, and fingerprints. Although it recognized that fingerprints contained less information that samples or DNA profiles, the retention of all three categories of material raised private life concerns under Art. 8 (paras 77 and 86). In other words Art. 8 was engaged, and the government needed to justify the retention under Art. 8(2). In relation to the question whether the rules contained in the revised s. 64 met the requirement that the interference should be 'in accordance with law', the Court noted that there was a need in relation to this type of intrusion on private life to have (para. 99):

> ...clear, detailed rules governing the scope and application of measures, as well as minimum safeguards concerning, *inter alia*, duration, storage, usage, access of third parties, procedures for preserving the integrity and confidentiality of data and procedures for its destruction, thus providing sufficient guarantees against the risk of abuse and arbitrariness.

It agreed with the applicants that the some of the wording of s. 64 was expressed in general terms and liable to extensive interpretation. It did not reach a final decision on this issue, however, in the light of its overall conclusions on other grounds which were in favour of the applicants' arguments.

There was no doubt that the measures had a 'legitimate aim' under Art. 8, namely the prevention of crime. The remaining issue was whether the procedures were 'necessary in a democratic society'. The Court noted that more restrictive approaches to the retention of this type of material were adopted in other Member States, and that even within the United Kingdom, the Scottish system did not allow for the indefinite retention of samples, etc. England, Wales, and Northern Ireland appeared to be the only jurisdictions 'to allow the indefinite retention of fingerprint and DNA material of any person of any age suspected of any recordable offence'. Its conclusion was that (para. 125):

> ...the blanket and indiscriminate nature of the powers of retention of the fingerprints, cellular samples and DNA profiles of persons suspected but not convicted of offences, as applied in the case of the present applicants, fails to strike a fair balance between the competing public and private interests and that the respondent State has overstepped any acceptable margin of appreciation in this regard.

There was, therefore, a violation of Art. 8.

The UK government's response was to enact Chapter 1 of the Protection of Freedoms Act 2012, in the form of new ss 63D–O and 63U to PACE. These establish a regime similar to that operating in Scotland. They provide that DNA *samples* (e.g. blood, urine, and saliva) will never be retained for more than the six months necessary to ensure that a satisfactory DNA profile has been obtained and loaded on to the National DNA Database. In relation to DNA *profiles* and fingerprints the relevant period will depend on whether or not there had been a conviction, the type of offence, and the age of the suspect:

- Convicted adults, including those receiving a caution, warning or reprimand: indefinite retention, whatever the nature of the offence.
- Convicted juveniles (under 18): indefinite retention for serious offences; for first minor offence, five years, or custodial sentence given, that sentence plus five years; indefinite retention for second offence.
- Unconvicted adults and juveniles:
  - in relation to serious offences, three years, extendable by two years on the order of a district judge;
  - in relation to minor offences for which a person is tried and acquitted, until the finding of not guilty;
  - in relation to those with a prior conviction for a recordable offence, indefinite detention, unless the first offence was a minor offence committed under the age of 18;
- Terrorism and national security: any material may be retained for three years, with the possibility of the police seeking extensions to this.

These proposals are a clear improvement on the previous situation. Questions still remain, for example, as to whether indefinite retention is proportionate in relation to all convictions. Under this scheme a person who had accepted a caution in relation to a minor traffic offence would have their DNA profile kept on the database indefinitely.

4.5.4 **Identification by witnesses**

In some situations the police will want to confirm their suspicions by asking for identification of a suspect by a witness or victim. There are four ways in which this can be done. The relevant procedures are set out in para. 3 of Code D, and Annexes A–D to Code D. The four methods are:

(a) video identification;

(b) identification parade;

(c) group identification; or

(d) confrontation.

The current version of Code D and the Annexes came into effect on 7 March 2011. Prior to 2002, an identification parade was the preferred method. A change introduced in April 2002 gave equal status to video identification and an identification parade. The change was said to 'recognise the developments in the value and use of video identification since it was first introduced into the Code in 1991' (Foreword to the booklet issuing the revision (Home Office, 2002)). It is also clear that it is thought that video identification may be quicker and easier to arrange. It is likely that video identification will come to replace identification parades as the main method used.

The procedures will be under the control of an officer of at least the rank of inspector, who is not involved in the investigation, and who is referred to as 'the identification officer' (para. 3.11 of Code D). The current version of para. 3, however, provides that many of the arrangements for the conduct of an identification procedure can be carried out by 'civilian' employees of the police force, rather than by police officers themselves.

Identification by means of photographs, photofit, identikit, etc. must not be used if the suspect is known, and available to take part in an identification. If the identity of the suspect is not known, then such pictures may be used, and the procedure set out in Annex E to the Code should be followed. It is not discussed further here, since it is unlikely to involve any infringement of human rights. A power to photograph detainees is given by s. 64A (see 4.5.3.1).

4.5.4.1 **Choosing an identification procedure**

Whenever a suspect disputes an identification by a witness, an identification procedure must be held, unless it would be impracticable or would serve no useful purpose (e.g. where the suspect is well-known to the witness) (para. 3.12). The choice of which type of identification procedure lies with the officer in charge of the investigation, in consultation with the identification officer. The initial choice should be between a video identification or an identification parade. Full information should be given (orally and in the form of a written notice) to the suspect as to the procedure chosen, the availability of legal advice, and the consequences of refusal to take part (e.g. that this fact may be given in evidence at trial), along with various other matters set out in para. 3.17. If the suspect refuses the procedure first offered, the reason for the refusal should be given and representations may be made by the suspect or the suspect's legal adviser as to why another procedure should be used. The decision in the end lies with the identification officer (para. 3.15).

If the suspect refuses to take part in the procedure chosen then the identification officer may make arrangements for a covert video identification or a covert group identification (para. 3.21 of Code D). It is very important, however, that all the relevant procedures set out in Code D are followed in such a case. In *Perry* v *United Kingdom* (2004) 39 EHRR 3 the ECtHR found a breach of Art. 8 in relation to a case where covert filming had taken place and then been used for identification purposes without following all the procedures in the version of Code D applicable at the time (1997). The applicant, who had been convicted of armed robbery partly on the basis of this identification evidence, was awarded damages of £1,000.

4.5.4.2 Video identification

The detailed procedures for a video identification are set out in Annex A to Code D. The set of images used must include at least eight people in addition to the suspect. As well as being of similar appearance, they must be shown, as far as possible, in the same positions or carrying out the same set of movements. What is clearly envisaged is a series of images of each person in turn, including the suspect, rather than a shot of the group as a whole. The suspect or the suspect's solicitor should have a chance to see the images before it is shown to the witness, and to raise any objections, which should be met if possible. Before being shown the images the suspect or the suspect's solicitor should be provided with details of the first description of any witness who is to attend the identification. The suspect may not be present when the witness views the images, but the suspect's solicitor is entitled to be there. If the solicitor or a representative of the solicitor is not able to be present, or if the suspect is not legally advised, then the video identification should itself be recorded on video.

The Annex also contains procedures to ensure that there is no communication between witnesses about the images. Each witness should see the set of images at least twice, but may see the whole or part as many times as they wish, and can ask for a particular image to be frozen.

4.5.4.3 Identification parades

The detailed procedure for these is in Annex B to Code D. These include matters such as the minimum number of people (at least eight in addition to the suspect), and the fact that the suspect may choose where to stand in line. Other procedures, such as the need for the suspect or the solicitor to be given a copy of the witness's first description, and the opportunity to object to the arrangements, are similar to those applying to a video identification. The suspect is entitled to have a solicitor or friend present at the parade.

A video recording, or if this is impracticable, a colour photograph should be taken of the parade, a copy of which should be made available on request to the suspect or the suspect's solicitor.

4.5.4.4 Group identifications

If the officer in charge of the investigation thinks a group identification would, in the particular circumstances, be more satisfactory than a video identification or a parade, and the identification officer thinks that it is practicable, a group identification may be offered. If the suspect refuses, then a covert group identification may be arranged. In either case the identification should take place in a place where there are likely to be significant numbers of other people, such as a shopping centre or a bus station, or some other similar public place. Detailed procedures are set out in Annex C to Code D.

4.5.4.5 Confrontation

This may take place without the suspect's consent, if none of the other three procedures is practicable. The procedure is governed by Annex D to Code D. It should normally take place in the police station, and in the presence of the suspect's solicitor (unless this would cause unreasonable delay).

4.6 Challenging the police

The recognition of rights is of little value to the citizen unless the infringement of such rights is backed up with effective sanctions. In English law the remedies for police misbehaviour are now fourfold, namely, civil action, action under the HRA 1998, official complaint, or exclusion of evidence.

4.6.1 Civil action

The traditional remedy of the citizen unlawfully detained by State authorities is the writ of *habeas corpus*. It is, however, of little practical use in relation to police powers of stop and search, arrest, or detention for two reasons. First, the writ is mainly concerned with whether the correct procedure has been followed. As will have been noted, many decisions in this area are based on reasonable suspicion or belief, and this is notoriously difficult to challenge. Second, the periods of detention without charge are in most cases relatively short, a matter of a day or two at most. An application for the writ will normally be adjourned for 24 hours. Once a person has been released or charged, then the writ of *habeas corpus* becomes irrelevant. It has, however, been much more frequently used in relation to detention prior to deportation and extradition proceedings, and so a more detailed consideration of the writ is left to chapter 11, which is concerned with these issues.

Similar problems of timing apply to using judicial review, though there are some circumstances where it can be appropriate—e.g. *Caetano v Commissioner of Police for the Metropolis* [2013] EWHC 375, where an application for judicial review was successful in a challenge to the police's decision to issue a caution.

Civil actions in tort for trespass to the person, in the form of an assault, or false imprisonment may also be possible. The action for 'misfeasance in public office' is also a possibility (see *Kuddus v Chief Constable of Leicestershire* [2001] UKHL 29, [2001] 3 All ER 193). These may be taken after the event, and may provide damages for the claimant. Their success will depend on showing that the police have acted beyond the scope of any statutory or common law power. A failure to comply with the provisions of one of the PACE Codes of Practice will not be sufficient. The most likely bases for the claim will be either that there was no justification for an arrest, search, or detention, or that excessive force was used. If the tort is proved, however, exemplary damages may be available. The rules relating to the award of exemplary damages are set out in the two House of Lords' decisions *Rookes* v *Barnard* [1964] AC 1129, and *Cassell & Co.* v *Broome* [1972] AC 1027. These cases limited the availability of such an award to two situations. The one that is relevant here is where there has been oppressive, arbitrary, or unconstitutional action by servants of the government. 'Servants of the government' will include police officers. This issue was considered by the Court of Appeal in *Holden* v *Chief Constable of Lancashire* [1986] 3 All ER 836. The plaintiff had been unlawfully arrested, and held in a police cell for 20 minutes. There was no use of excessive force, or other improper conduct, other than the fact that the arrest had no lawful justification. The judge withdrew the issue of exemplary damages from the jury (this is one area where it is common for a civil action to be heard before a jury), on the basis that there was no 'oppressive' or 'arbitrary' conduct by the police. The Court of Appeal ruled that this was wrong. The categories set out by the House of Lords were disjunctive. In other words, there could be an award of exemplary damages where there was unconstitutional conduct, even though this was not accompanied by any oppression or arbitrariness. In coming to this conclusion, the Court of Appeal was also reluctant to hold that every unlawful action by the police, no matter how well-intentioned, justifies exemplary damages.

The whole issue of the appropriate level of damages, including exemplary damages, in actions against the police was given detailed consideration by the Court of Appeal in *Thompson* v *Commissioner of Police for the Metropolis* [1997] 2 All ER 762. The case arose out of concern about the high level of some awards, and the court issued a 14-point set of guidelines which a judge should have in mind when directing a jury on this issue. It might well be appropriate for such direction to be delayed until after the jury has reached its decision on liability. The judge would normally have heard submissions from counsel on the issue of damages in the absence of the jury.

The main elements in these guidelines (which are too extensive to quote in full) are first, that basic compensatory damages for unlawful detention should start at about £500 for the first hour, increasing thereafter on a decreasing scale, so that for a 24-hour detention, a sum of about £3,000 would be appropriate. Aggravated damages should be awarded where there were features of the case which meant that the basic award would provide insufficient compensation. Such damages might be appropriate where there had been 'humiliating circumstances at the time of the arrest' or where any subsequent conduct was 'high-handed, insulting, malicious or oppressive'. Aggravated damages would be likely to start at about £1,000, but would not normally amount to as much as twice the level of the basic damages. Basic and aggravated damages together are intended to provide the claimant with 'fair compensation'. They are not intended as punishment, although aggravated damages 'would in fact contain a penal element as far as the defendant is concerned'. The jury should be reminded of this effect of aggravated damages when considering, in appropriate cases, the possibility of exemplary damages. Exemplary damages should only be awarded where the combination of basic and aggravated damages provides inadequate punishment in the circumstances. The jury should be reminded that such damages provide a 'windfall' to the claimant and, if paid out of police funds, eat into money which might otherwise be applicable for the benefit of the public. The sum awarded should be no more than was required to mark the jury's disapproval of the oppressive or arbitrary behaviour. As to the amount, the Court felt that exemplary damages would be unlikely to be less than £5,000. Beyond this:

> ...the conduct must be particularly deserving of condemnation for an award of £25,000 to be justified, and the figure of £50,000 should be regarded as the absolute maximum, involving officers of at least the rank of superintendent.

As an overall check on the level of the award:

> ...it will be unusual for the exemplary damages to produce a result of more than three times the basic damages being awarded (as the total of the basic aggravated and exemplary damages) except...where the basic damages are modest.

Thus if the basic damages are £10,000 and aggravated damages £5,000, then exemplary damages should not normally exceed £15,000 (producing a total of £30,000 (£10,000 × 3)).

In one of the cases before it, the Court of Appeal reduced an award of £200,000 exemplary damages for wrongful arrest, false imprisonment, and assault to £15,000 (on top of compensatory damages of £20,000). In the other, which concerned false imprisonment, assault, and malicious prosecution, the overall award of £51,500 was upheld. The court said that it would have increased the compensatory damages from £1,500 to £20,000 (including £10,000 aggravated damages) and reduced the exemplary damages from £50,000 to £25,000. The resulting figure of £45,000 was, however, sufficiently close to the overall jury award for this to fall within the jury's 'margin of appreciation'. The court therefore allowed the £51,500 to stand.

It will be noted that in this case the court did not follow its own guidance given earlier as to the relationship between the basic award, exemplary damages, and the overall sum awarded. This would have produced exemplary damages of not more than £10,000, in order to keep within an overall award of not more than three times the basic award. This perhaps indicates that the guidelines, though detailed, should not be treated as 'rules', and that juries (and the appeal courts) still retain a broad discretion to award a sum which is appropriate in all the circumstances.

Despite the apparent concern about the high level of awards which lay behind this case, in cases where the conduct was unconstitutional, then exemplary damages could be considered, but there should probably be some other impropriety on the part of the police before such an award would be appropriate. If exemplary damages are not awarded, then, as is shown from the cases listed in the leading work on this topic (R. Clayton and H. Tomlinson, *Civil Actions Against the Police*, 3rd edn (London: Thomson Sweet & Maxwell, 2004), ch. 14, especially pp. 610–13), the amount awarded in terms of compensation is likely to be relatively small. Generally speaking, the awards have been below £5,000.

4.6.2 Action under the Human Rights Act 1998

It has been noted at various points that there may be a potential for challenging powers as being in breach of the HRA 1998, because they are not

'Convention-compatible'. To the extent that the challenge is against a statutory power itself (as opposed to the way in which the power has been exercised) then, of course, the best that can be obtained is a 'declaration of incompatibility' (s. 4 of the HRA 1998; and see chapter 2 (2.3.3.4)), which is of limited use. If the challenge is that powers have been exceeded in a way that contravenes the ECHR (e.g. an intimate search being carried out improperly in a manner that breaches Art. 3 or Art. 8 of the ECHR), then damages may be awarded (s. 8 of the HRA 1998). The issue of the quantum of damages in relation to actions under the HRA 1998 is discussed in chapter 2 (2.2.4). The principles outlined there, derived from the case law, indicate that the successful claimant will not receive an award any larger than that available in a comparable tortious action, and might well be in line with the awards made by the ECtHR which tend to be smaller.

4.6.3 Official complaints

PACE introduced a framework for a system of complaints against police misconduct, which is now contained, in a revised form, in the PRA 2002. In so far as the individual complainant is concerned such systems are of limited use, in that they do not provide compensation, or any other redress, for those who are the victims of such misconduct. Of course, as with those who have suffered from the criminal activities of others, victims may gain some satisfaction simply from seeing the malefactor brought to book. In a more general way, however, the existence of an effective complaints procedure can be an instrument for the promotion of civil liberties, in that it may act as a deterrent to the police from stepping outside their legitimate powers. Its most significant role may therefore be in controlling temptation, rather than punishing offenders.

Up until 2004, the complaints system was under the supervision of the Police Complaints Authority (PCA), which was set up under provisions contained in PACE. There were criticisms, however, in that, although the PCA was an independent body, it had no resources to carry out its own investigations, and had to rely on police forces to do this. This led to the perception of the police investigating themselves, and a consequent lack of confidence in the system. New proposals were put forward in a framework document published by the Home Office in December 2000, entitled 'Complaints Against the Police: Framework for a New System'. The objectives of the new system included increased public confidence and trust in the police and in the complaints system as a whole; quicker resolution of complaints; improved communications with complainants; and the improved collection, collation, and reporting of data. The proposals were given effect by Pt. 2 and Sch. 3 to the PRA 2002, which provide for the establishment of an Independent Police Complaints Commission, to replace the PCA. The new arrangements came into force in April 2004. In what follows, all statutory references are to the PRA 2002, unless otherwise stated.

4.6.3.1 Independent Police Complaints Commission

The Independent Police Complaints Commission (IPCC) is an independent body consisting of a chairman (appointed by the Queen) and ten members (appointed by the Secretary of State), none of whom shall previously have been a police officer

(s. 9). It has a general role in supervising the operation of the complaints system, but also has the facilities to carry out its own investigations.

The first level at which a complaint will be dealt with will generally be, however, that of the chief constable (or in London the Commissioner) of the police force of which the officer against whom the complaint is made is a member. (In the following paragraphs, references to the 'chief constable' should be taken to include the Metropolitan Police Commissioner, and the Commissioner of Police for the City of London.)

4.6.3.2 Procedures for complaints

Complaints may be received by the chief constable, the police authority, or the IPCC. In all cases there is a duty to ensure that the complaint is recorded, and to ensure that relevant evidence is preserved. It is then necessary to determine who is the 'appropriate authority' for the purposes of the investigation of the complaint (Sch. 3, para. 1). In general this will be the chief constable. The only exception is where the complaint is against an officer above the rank of superintendent. In this case the appropriate authority is the police authority for the chief constable's area (s. 29(1)). The Act makes provision for informal resolution of complaints in certain circumstances. This is not available, however, unless the complainant consents, and the appropriate authority is satisfied that even if the complaint was proved no criminal or disciplinary proceedings against the officer would be appropriate (Sch. 3, para. 6). Complaints involving allegations of significant breaches of PACE or the Codes of Practice seem unlikely to be appropriate for informal resolution. In that case, the appropriate authority must appoint an officer to carry out a formal investigation. This officer can be from the same or another force. Where the officer under investigation is above the rank of superintendent, the investigating officer must not be a person under that officer's direction or control.

Some complaints must be referred to the IPCC. These include where the misconduct alleged resulted in death or personal injury (Sch. 3, para. 4), or where the Secretary of State has by regulations provided that the investigation of the complaint should be so supervised. At the time of writing no regulations had been issued, but similar regulations under the previous system covered assaults occasioning actual bodily harm; offences under s. 1 of the Prevention of Corruption Act 1916; and serious arrestable offences. Other complaints may be referred to the IPCC on the basis of the gravity of the subject matter or any other exceptional circumstances. The IPCC also has the power to require a complaint to be referred to it.

Where a complaint has been referred to the IPCC which it considers needs to be investigated, there are four possible procedures. The IPCC must decide which should be adopted taking into account the seriousness of the case and the public interest (Sch. 3, para. 15). The four possible procedures are:

(a) investigation by the appropriate authority on its own behalf;

(b) investigation by that authority under the supervision of the IPCC;

(c) investigation by that authority under the management of the IPCC; and

(d) investigation by the IPCC itself.

Where the investigation is *supervised* by the IPCC, it holds a veto over the selection of the investigating officer (Sch. 3, para. 17). Where the investigation is *managed* by the IPCC, the investigating officer, who must again be approved by the IPCC, will also be under its direction and control (Sch. 3, para. 18).

The biggest change introduced by the new system is, however, that IPCC has the power to conduct investigations itself, using its own staff, who, for these purposes are given the relevant powers attaching to police officers (Sch. 3, para. 19). These include powers of arrest, detention for question, search of persons or premises, and seizure of evidence. For the first time, the police will be seen to be being fully investigated by an external body.

Once an investigation is complete, a report must be made, with a view to deciding whether any disciplinary or criminal proceedings should follow. In the case of investigations supervised, managed, or conducted by the IPCC the report will go to that body. For other investigations it will go to the appropriate authority. If it appears that a criminal offence has been committed, the case must be referred to the Director of Public Prosecutions. In other cases it is up to the appropriate authority to decide what action, if any, to take. In cases where the IPCC has been involved in the investigation, it retains supervisory powers over the authority's decision, and can direct that disciplinary proceedings should be brought (Sch. 3, para. 27). Where the IPCC has not been involved, the appropriate authority's decision may be the subject of an appeal by the complainant to the IPCC (Sch. 3, para. 25).

In addition to the above, the procedures set out in Sch. 3 contain provisions designed to ensure that all complaints are properly recorded, and that complainants are fully informed at all stages of the progress of their complaint and its outcome. There are also various points at which complainants can appeal to the IPCC in relation to the way in which the complaint is being dealt with.

4.6.3.3 Position of the complainant

In the past, a complaint has been unlikely to lead to either disciplinary or criminal proceedings. Between 1985 and 1994 there were 116,451 fully investigated complaints, but only 11,065 (9.5 per cent) resulted in disciplinary action of any kind ('PCA 10—Police Complaints Authority—The First Ten Years', HMSO, 1995, p. 9). Subsequent figures showed a similar pattern. In 1999–2000, 8,048 complaints were formally investigated, but only 714 (9 per cent) were substantiated, and only 353 officers had disciplinary charges proved against them (Home Office Statistical Bulletin, 14/00). Again, in 2000–01, 9,842 complaints were investigated, 903 (9 per cent) were substantiated, and 152 officers had disciplinary charges proved against them (Home Office Statistical Bulletin, 21/01). A successful complaint provided nothing in the way of direct compensation for the officer's wrongdoing. Moreover, statements made during a formal investigation would not be available in any subsequent civil action, since they were held to be potentially protected by public interest immunity: *Neilson* v *Laugharne* [1981] 1 QB 736, *Conerney* v *Jacklin* [1985] Crim LR 234, *Peach* v *Metropolitan Police Commissioner* [1986] QB 1064, and *R* v *Chief Constable of West Midlands Police, ex p Wiley* [1995] 1 AC 274.

A further hazard for the complainant was that the complaint might be regarded as defamatory, and action taken for libel by the police officer concerned: *Conerney* v *Jacklin*. This, and certain other difficulties noted by Clayton and Tomlinson (*Civil Actions against the Police*, 2nd edn (London: Sweet & Maxwell, 1992), pp. 74–5) led to the conclusion that there was very little advantage in making a formal complaint against the police. Moreover, the low level of success of such complaints meant that the threat of one being brought was unlikely to be a deterrent for a police officer considering bending or breaking the rules set out in PACE and its Codes of Practice.

The reforms introduced by the PRA 2002 addressed some of the above issues, but by no means all of them. Much depends on the way in which the IPCC carries out its responsibilities, and whether it is seen as operating as a genuinely independent check on the police. The initial reports of the IPCC (from 2004–05 onwards) showed that the level of complaints increased. In the first year there was a 44 per cent increase, with further increases on top of that of 15 per cent and 12 per cent in subsequent years. This at least suggests that there was increased public confidence in the new complaints system, which was one of the objectives of the reform. This is confirmed by the continued increase in complaints each year. In 2008–09 there was a further 8 per cent annual rise, to 31,747 complaints, as compared to 22,898 in 2004–05. The numbers have stabilized or slightly reduced since then, with the figure for 2011–12 being 30,143 ('Police Complaints Statistics 2011-12', IPCC, October 2012). Research carried out by the IPCC and reported in its 2008–09 Annual Report found that 88 per cent of respondents thought that the IPCC would handle complaints fairly, though the percentage among ethnic minority respondents was lower, at 77 per cent.

The percentage of substantiated allegations was initially higher than under the old system (2004–05: 13 per cent; 2005–06: 12 per cent; 2006–07: 11 per cent) but still quite small. In 2011–12 the equivalent figure was 12 per cent, so the position seems to be fairly consistent and stable.

Overall the introduction of the IPCC was a considerable improvement over the previous complaints regime. There are still concerns, however, about the number of complaint being received, and the low percentage of cases where complaints are upheld.

4.6.4 **Exclusion of evidence**

The fact that in certain circumstances a court may be prepared to exclude evidence produced by the prosecution is important for the citizen. Of course, a court should primarily be concerned with issues of relevance and reliability; but even where evidence is relevant and reliable, there may be circumstances where the defendant can justifiably claim that it should not be used, because of the manner or the circumstances in which it has been obtained. A clear example of this is where the evidence has been obtained by torture. In *A v Secretary of State for the Home Department (No. 2)* [2006] UKHL 71 the House of Lords held that there was an absolute prohibition on using evidence acquired by torture. The case was one involving alleged involvement in terrorism, where some of the evidence came from interrogations which took place outside the United Kingdom, and conducted by foreign agencies. If the defendant in such a case raises the possibility of evidence having resulted from torture, the prosecution does not have to prove beyond reasonable doubt that it was not obtained in this way, but the court must consider, using a 'balance of probabilities' test whether torture was involved. If it decides that it was, then any evidence obtained in this way must be excluded.

A power to exclude evidence may go some way to ensuring that the rights of the citizen to be treated properly by the police and other investigating authorities are upheld. There are two sections under PACE which give the courts the power to exclude evidence. Section 76 is concerned solely with confessions, broadly defined in s. 82(1) as including:

> ...any statement wholly or partly adverse to the person who made it, whether made to a person in authority or not and whether made in words or otherwise.

This does not include wholly exculpatory statements, even if they may be used against the defendant at trial (e.g. to demonstrate inconsistency or evasion): *R v Hasan* [2005] UKHL 22, [2005] 4 All ER 685. Section 78, on the other hand, is concerned with all types of evidence, including confessions.

4.6.4.1 **Section 76(2)(a): oppression**

If a confession appears to have been obtained as a result of oppression, then, whether or not it is thought to be reliable, it should be excluded, unless the prosecution can prove beyond reasonable doubt that it was not so obtained. The matter may be raised either by the defence, or by the court itself (s. 76(3)). 'Oppression' is defined as including 'torture, inhuman or degrading treatment, and the use or threat of violence (whether or not amounting to torture)'. Fortunately, the thumb-screw and the rack are not commonly found in British police stations—though as indicated above the issue of evidence obtained by torture may arise where British courts are considering evidence obtained from outside the jurisdiction, which may particularly arise in terrorist investigations.

Interrogation procedures falling short of torture, but involving prolonged physical discomfort, or sensory deprivation, would almost certainly be regarded as constituting 'inhuman or degrading treatment'. This was the view of the ECtHR in relation to procedures of this kind used in Northern Ireland (see *Ireland v United Kingdom* (1979–80) 2 EHRR 25). In *R v Fulling* (1987) 85 Cr App R 136 the Court of Appeal expressed the view that it was unlikely that oppression could occur without some impropriety on the part of the police. The court referred to the *Oxford English Dictionary* definition of it as involving:

> ...exercise of authority or power in a burdensome, harsh, or wrongful manner; unjust or cruel treatment of subjects, inferiors, etc, or the imposition of unreasonable or unjust burdens.

In this case the alleged oppression was that a police officer had told the defendant, who had been held in police custody for two days, that her lover had been having an affair with another woman, who happened to be in the next cell. The defendant then confessed, on the basis that this was the only way in which she would be released from custody. The Court of Appeal held that the trial judge had been right to rule that this was not a case of oppression.

There are, in fact, very few examples of the courts finding the existence of oppression. One is *R v Beales* [1991] Crim LR 118, where the confession was obtained as result of an interview in which the defendant had been 'hectored and bullied from first to last', and which had included deliberate misstatements of the evidence by the interviewing officer in order to put pressure on the defendant. The trial judge ruled that this constituted oppression, though the confession might also have been excluded on grounds of unreliability.

4.6.4.2 Section 76(2)(b): unreliability

As with oppression the issue of unreliability may be raised by either the defence or the court. It arises where a confession was or may have been obtained from a person:

> ...in consequence of anything said or done which was likely, in the circumstances existing at the time, to render unreliable any confession which might be made by him in consequence thereof.

Once the issue is raised, the burden is on the prosecution to prove beyond reasonable doubt that the confession was not obtained in this way. It is not enough to show that the confession is reliable. The test is whether what happened to produce the confession was *likely* to render it unreliable. Thus, in *R v Cox* [1991] Crim LR 276 the Court of Appeal quashed a conviction because the judge had allowed evidence of a confession which he considered reliable, whereas he should have considered the question of whether the failure to follow the correct procedures (in this case interviewing a juvenile in the absence of an appropriate adult) made it likely that a confession made in those circumstances would be unreliable. Although the section refers to 'any confession', it should be read as meaning 'any such' or 'such a' confession (*Re Proulx* [2001] 1 All ER 57). The focus should, therefore, be on the confession that was made, not on some other hypothetical confession that might have been made.

It is clear that one situation to which s. 76(2)(b) will apply is where there has been conduct by the police, in the form of threats or inducements, which puts pressure on a defendant, but which falls short of oppression. It need not necessarily involve any impropriety: *R v Fulling* (1987) 85 Cr App R 136. An indication that the offence would be treated as one 'more for the attention of doctors than judges' might well have been regarded as an inducement to admit guilt: *R v Delaney* (1988) Cr App R 338 (indecent assault).

The statement or behaviour which leads to the confession need not come from the police. It will be most likely to lead to unreliability if it emanates from a person in authority, such as a parent, or a teacher, but it does not have to do so. In *R v Harvey* [1988] Crim LR 241 it came from the co-defendant. The defendant's own conduct, however, cannot trigger the operation of the section: *R v Goldenberg* (1988) 88 Cr App R 285 (defendant was a drug addict).

Other conduct which has led to exclusion under s. 76(2)(b) includes a failure to comply with the requirements of Code C. In *R v Doolan* [1988] Crim LR 747, for example, there was a failure to caution before interview. Failure to allow access to a solicitor may also render a confession unreliable: *R v Chung* (1991) 92 Cr App R 314.

4.6.4.3 Section 78: unfairness

Section 78 was included in PACE at a relatively late stage in its Parliamentary proceedings, as a government response to an attempt by Lord Scarman to get an even broader exclusionary power included. Its effect is to give to any court a power to exclude evidence if:

> ...it appears to the court that, having regard to all the circumstances, including the circumstances in which the evidence was obtained, the admission of the evidence would have such an adverse effect on the fairness of the proceedings that the court ought not to admit it.

There was some scepticism at the time as to the extent to which the courts would be prepared to use this discretion, particularly in the light of the very limited exclusionary rule which existed under the common law on the basis of the House of Lords' decision in *R v Sang* [1980] AC 402. All the members of the Lords in this case were prepared to recognize that there should be the possibility of excluding evidence on the basis of unfairness, but did not present any uniform view as to what circumstances might justify this. Oppression was probably enough, but the fact that the evidence was obtained as a result of the activities of an *agent provocateur* would not in itself merit exclusion.

In fact, contrary to expectations, s. 78 has been used in many cases. Part of the reason for this is that it quickly became established that the section could be used to exclude *any* evidence, including confessions and other incriminating statements, which might at first sight have seemed to be the exclusive preserve of s. 76. It also became established fairly early on, in *R v Samuel* [1988] QB 615, that the section was a self-contained provision which should be interpreted within its own terms, rather than being regarded as simply restating the common law (as had been suggested by Watkins LJ in *R v Mason* [1987] 3 All ER 481). A recent example of its use is to be found in *R v Newell* [2012] EWCA Crim 650, [2012] 1 WLR 3142. The trial judge had allowed cross-examination on inconsistencies between a statement on a form completed by the defendant's advocate as part of a plea and case management hearing and the defendant's defence at trial (where he was represented by a different lawyer). The Court of Appeal held that information provided in a plea and case management hearing was intended (para. 33):

> ...primarily as a means for the provision of information to enable a judge actively to manage the case up to and throughout the trial, and the parties to know the issues that have to be addressed and the witnesses who are to come.

It was important that the defence should not become over-cautious in providing information. In that context, in general, the trial judge should normally exercise the discretion under s. 78 to exclude evidence of statements on forms completed as part of the plea and case management hearing. Allowing such evidence to be used against the defendant should be the exception (as in, e.g. *R (Firth) v Epping Justices* [2011] EWHC 388 (Admin), [2011] 1 WLR 1818).

The early decision on s. 78 in *R v Samuel* [1988] QB 615 was important in establishing one of the main grounds on which exclusion has subsequently been justified: that is, on the basis that there have been 'significant and substantial' breaches of the Act, or a Code of Practice, or both. The case was in fact concerned with breach of a statutory provision (that is, the right of access to legal advice), but it was subsequently confirmed by the Court of Appeal in *R v Keenan* [1989] 3 All ER 599, that a breach of the Code could in itself justify exclusion (in this case, failure to keep proper records of interviews, as required by Code C).

The fact that the breach must be 'significant and substantial' means that it is unlikely that breaches of the detailed provisions of the Codes concerning such things as the provision of meals will be sufficient (see, e.g. *R v Brine* [1992] Crim LR 122). In fact, the vast majority of cases under s. 78 have been concerned with just two types of breach, namely, breach of the provisions concerning access to legal advice under s. 58, and breach of the provisions of Code C concerning the requirements to make contemporaneous records of interviews, and to show these to the suspect (e.g. *R v Canale* [1990] Crim LR 329, *R v Walsh* (1990) Cr App R 161, *R v Scott* [1991] Crim LR 56, and *R v Sparks* [1991] Crim LR 128). Other breaches as regards, for example, breath tests (*Hudson* v *DPP, The Times*, 28 May 1991, and *DPP v Godwin* [1991] RTR 303), or identification procedures (*R v Nagah* [1991] Crim LR 55) can, however, lead to exclusion. On the other hand, it was held in *Stanesby* v *DPP* [2012] EWHC 1320 (Admin) that the fact that an officer who was told by the defendant that he was on medication for depression, and who should therefore have summoned an 'appropriate adult' to support the defendant (PACE Code C, para 1.4)), had carried out a breath test without doing so did not render the breath test inadmissible.

Even if there has been a significant and substantial breach this does not, however, lead to automatic exclusion. In a number of cases the courts have refused to exercise the power to exclude evidence because the breach did not 'make any difference' to what had happened, and the evidence was not, therefore, unfair. In reaching this decision the courts are not saying that the evidence is *reliable* despite the breach: reliability or not is generally irrelevant to s. 78. What they are saying is, for example, that the confession would have occurred even if the correct procedures had been followed. In *R v Alladice* [1988] Crim LR 608, for example, the defendant had wrongfully been refused access to a solicitor. His own evidence at the trial, however, made it clear that he was well aware of the right to remain silent, and that a solicitor might well have advised him to say nothing. There was no reason to suppose that he would not have confessed if he had had access to a solicitor. The same view was taken in *R v Dunford* (1990) 140 NLJ 517 and in *R v Dunn* (1990) 91 Cr App R 237, where the presence of a solicitor's clerk during an interview which was not recorded justified admitting the evidence of the interview.

Unlawful actions by the police in the course of obtaining evidence will not automatically render it inadmissible: the judge still has discretion under s. 78. This was the ruling of the House of Lords in *R v Khan* [1996] 3 All ER 289. The police had obtained evidence by planting a surveillance device on private property, which had almost certainly involved trespass and criminal damage. The House of Lords did not think that this illegality was anything more than one of the factors to be considered by the judge in exercising the s. 78 power. On balance, there was no unfairness to the accused in admitting the evidence.

Khan's case was considered by the ECtHR, but before this judgment is discussed, it should be noted that the Court of Appeal took a similarly restricted view of the use of s. 78 in *R v Chalkley* [1998] 2 All ER 155. This case also involved surreptitious recording of the defendant's conversations at his home. The Court of Appeal held that s. 78 does not involve a 'balancing exercise' similar to that undertaken in deciding whether to stay proceedings. The test is simply whether it is fair to admit the evidence in the light of the effect it will have on the proceedings. The way in which the evidence was obtained is only relevant insofar as it goes to the *quality* of the evidence. As indicated, the operation of s. 78 was considered by the ECtHR in *Khan v United Kingdom* (2001) 31 EHRR 45. The Court held that Khan's right to privacy under Art. 8 of the ECHR had been infringed, because the powers of the police to enter premises and plant 'bugging' devices were not 'prescribed by law' as required by Art. 8(2)—though this defect was subsequently remedied by the provisions of the Police Act 1997 (see chapter 5 (5.3.2)). As regards Khan's allegation that the refusal to exclude the evidence under s. 78 amounted to an infringement of his right to a fair trial under Art. 6(1), the Court held by a majority of 6:1 that there was no infringement. It referred to its earlier decision in *Schenk v Switzerland* (1988) 13 EHRR 242, in which, dealing with similar factual circumstances, it made clear that Art. 6 does not lay down particular rules on the admissibility of evidence. The fact that evidence has been obtained improperly does not therefore, of itself, require that it should be excluded. The test is whether the proceedings as a whole, including the way in which the evidence was obtained, are fair. The Court noted that the case did not involve entrapment or any inducement to make admissions. It also noted that the applicant had had an opportunity at each stage of the criminal proceedings to challenge the use and authenticity of the recordings, and that the courts did have a 'discretion' to exclude it under s. 78 of PACE if the admission would have given rise to unfairness.

The European Court's decision in *Khan* thus gives support to the narrow approach to s. 78 taken by the House of Lords and by the Court of Appeal in *Chalkley*. It is in some ways difficult to reconcile, however, with the European Court's decision in *Condron v United Kingdom* (2001) 31 EHRR 1 (see 4.5.1.2), where it laid stress on the fact that in exercising its appellate jurisdiction the Court of Appeal needed to look beyond whether the conviction was 'safe' to consider whether the proceedings as a whole were fair. The approach taken by the House of Lords in *Khan* and the Court of Appeal in *Chalkley* seem to sit more comfortably with an approach which says 'is this conviction safe?' rather than 'were the proceedings fair?' Indeed at one point Auld LJ in *Chalkley* made this point specifically stating that (p. 172):

> ...[t]he court has no power under the substituted s. 2(1) [of the Criminal Appeal Act 1968] to allow an appeal if it does not think the conviction unsafe but is dissatisfied in some way with what went on at the trial.

Although this very narrow view of the power of the Court of Appeal to overturn a conviction must be taken to be of dubious authority in the light of the later decisions in *R v Mullen* [1999] 3 WLR 777 (discussed in chapter 11 (11.3.3.2)) and *R v Smith* [2000] 1 All ER 263), the above cases still suggest that the English and European courts may have a different view as to what amounts to 'fairness of proceedings'. This was, however, denied by the House of Lords in *R v P* [2001] 2 All ER 59, p. 70, and in *R v Loosely; Attorney-General's Reference (No. 3 of 2000)* [2001] UKHL 53, [2001] 4 All ER 897. This case was concerned with situations of alleged 'entrapment', and in particular whether the narrow English approach to this (as exemplified by *Sang*) should be considered as having been modified by the requirements of Art. 6. The ECtHR decision in *Texeira de Castro v Portugal* (1998) 28 EHRR 101 held that there would be a breach of the right to a fair trial if, as they found had occurred in that case, a person was incited by undercover police officers to commit an offence which he would otherwise not have committed. The applicant, who had no previous criminal record, had supplied heroin to the officers. The Court regarded it as significant that the applicant had no 'predisposition' to criminal activity. In the subsequent English case of *Nottingham City Council* v *Amin* [2000] 2 All ER 946, a taxi-driver who was outside his licensed area picked up two plain-clothes police officers who hailed him. The Court of Appeal held that the case of *Texeira de Castro* v *Portugal* did not lead to the conclusion that the evidence of the police officers should be excluded under s. 78. The defendant had not been 'prevailed upon or overborne or persuaded or pressured or instigated or incited to commit the offence' ([2000] 2 All ER 946, p. 954), and the magistrate had been wrong to exclude the evidence. Similarly, in *R* v *Shannon* [2001] 1 WLR 51, the Court of Appeal held that the trial judge had not acted incorrectly in refusing to exclude the evidence of conversations covertly recorded by a journalist posing as an Arab sheikh in the trial of the defendant for the supply of cocaine and cannabis. The test was whether the journalist had incited the offences or merely provided the setting in which the defendant took the opportunity to commit them. In the circumstances the defendant had not been denied a fair trial.

These decisions were reviewed by the House of Lords in *Loosely.* The approach taken in both *Amin* and *Shannon* was largely approved. The appeal itself concerned two cases. In one (*Loosely*) the defendant had on three occasions been approached by an undercover police officer and asked if he could supply heroin. On each occasion the defendant did so. In the second case (the *Attorney-General's Reference*) the defendant had been approached about the purchase of cheap (contraband) cigarettes, which he was willing to buy. Subsequently, the defendant was asked if he could supply heroin. He did so, but alleged that this was only as part of his desire to maintain what he saw as a good supply of cheap cigarettes, and he was on record as saying in the course of the transactions 'I am not really into heroin myself' ([2001] UKHL 53, para. 92, [2001] 4 All ER 897, p. 921). The House distinguished between the two cases. The general principles applied are not easy to discern from the various speeches, but Lord Nicholls' statement that 'ultimately the overall consideration is always whether the conduct of the police or other law enforcement agency was so improper as to bring the administration of justice into disrepute' (para. 25; p. 905) probably sums up the view of the House fairly accurately. In considering this the nature of the offence may be relevant, since some offences require more pro-active techniques (e.g. where the activities are generally difficult to detect). It is also relevant, as suggested in the earlier cases, whether the officer actively instigated the offence, or merely provided the opportunity for its commission. The previous criminal record of the defendant was, however, unlikely to be relevant.

As to the cases before it, the House held that the judge at Loosely's trial had correctly exercised his discretion in allowing the evidence of the conversations with the defendant to be given. In the *Attorney-General's Reference*, on the other hand, the trial judge had correctly decided to stay proceedings, as an abuse of process. The House confirmed that a stay of proceedings, rather than exclusion under s. 78, should be the normal approach where the police had overstepped the mark in relation to 'entrapment'. It was also specifically asked in the *Attorney-General's Reference* whether the powers under s. 78 and to stay proceedings had been modified by Art. 6 of the ECHR. Here the House was unanimous in holding that no modification of approach was required, and that English law was thus in line with the ECtHR's approach to this issue. Whether this is in fact so will have to wait until some future case on the issue goes to the Strasbourg Court, but it remains the case that the English approach appears to be somewhat more restrictive in its interpretation of 'unfairness' than that of the ECtHR as expounded in *Texeira de Castro*.

4.6.4.4 The relevance of bad faith

Despite the relatively narrow approach to s. 78, there is no doubt that the courts are considerably influenced by what they regard as 'bad faith' on the part of the police. Trickery by the police will in some cases lead to exclusion under s. 78 even if there has been no breach of the Act or Codes of Practice. In *R v Mason* [1987] 3 All ER 481, the police had told the defendant and his solicitor that the defendant's fingerprints had been found near to the scene of the crime. This was quite untrue, and the defendant's subsequent confession was ruled inadmissible. 'Bad faith' does not necessarily consist of a deliberate trick, however. Awareness on the part of the police that they are acting outside their lawful powers may well be enough: *Matto v DPP* [1987] Crim LR 641. Conversely, in some cases, the courts have been prepared to condone deceit by the police. In *R v Bailey* [1993] 3 All ER 513, a blatant piece of play acting was approved by the Court of Appeal. The investigating officers and the custody officer played out a conversation in front of the defendants, in which the custody officer, appearing to act against the wishes of the investigating officers, insisted in placing the two defendants in the same cell. In fact, the investigating officers wanted the defendants together, as the cell was bugged. The defendants, lulled into a false sense of security, engaged in a conversation which contained a number of damaging admissions, and was recorded. The Court of Appeal found nothing wrong in what the police had done, even though it was clearly a means of circumventing the fact that they could not question the defendants further (because they had both already been charged). The approach in *Bailey* has been followed post-HRA 1998 in *R v Mason* [2002] EWCA Crim 385, 13 February 2002, CA. Similarly, in *R v Smurthwaite* (1993) 98 Cr App R 437 the evidence of tape-recorded conversations between an undercover police officer pretending to be a contract killer, and the defendant who was seeking to arrange the murder of his wife, was admitted. The Court of Appeal thought that the judge was right to admit the evidence, since there was no pressure placed on the defendant to arrange the murder, and he could not be said to have been enticed into committing an offence which he would not otherwise have committed. The use of covert listening devices in a police station was considered by the ECtHR in *PG and JH v United Kingdom* (2008) 46 EHRR 51. In this case they had been used in order to obtain samples of the suspects' speech. The Court held that the use of the devices infringed the suspects' right to respect for private life under Art. 8. This was because the use of such devices was not regulated by any statutory regime, and the infringement could not, therefore, be said to be 'in accordance with law', even if its objectives would have been justifiable. The position has now changed by virtue of the controls over covert surveillance contained in the Regulation of Investigatory Powers Act 2000, which is dealt with in chapter 6 (see 6.5.3). The actions taken by the police in *Bailey*, *Mason*, and *Smurthwaite* would now fall to be regulated by that Act.

   If bad faith can be shown, this may well override the fact that a breach might not otherwise be regarded as substantial, or that it made no difference. In *R v*

Alladice, for example, where, as we have seen, the confession was held admissible because the breach was thought to have made no difference to the defendant, Lord Lane commented that 'if the police had acted in bad faith, the Court would have had little difficulty in ruling any confession inadmissible under s. 78'. The unreported cases of *R* v *Hall* (1994) (Leeds Crown Court), and *R* v *Stagg* (1994) (Central Criminal Court) provide other examples of the police overstepping the mark. In both cases an undercover policewoman 'befriended' a man charged with murder, and obtained incriminating information. In both cases the trial judge refused to allow the evidence thus obtained to be given at the trial. The emotional context in which the evidence was obtained made it unfair to allow it to be admitted. Moreover, in *Hall* some of the questioning had clearly been used as a means of circumventing the provisions of Code C. This approach shows that, despite protestations to the contrary, the power to exclude evidence is at times used to discipline the police. The knowledge that a deliberate failure to follow the correct procedures might well lead to evidence being excluded under s. 78 must have some effect in encouraging adherence to them, and the influence of the section must be regarded as having been a beneficial one in respect of the protection of the rights of the suspect while in police custody. It should be noted, however, that the actual methods of obtaining evidence used in *Stagg* and *Hall* would now fall under the Regulation of Investigatory Powers Act 2000 (see chapter 6 (6.5.3)). Provided that the procedures set out in that Act have been followed, the chances of such evidence being excluded under s. 78 will be greatly reduced, if not extinguished altogether.

QUESTIONS

1 Is the threshold for the application of the rights under s. 3 of the ECHR set at the right level by (a) the English courts, and (b) the ECtHR?

2 Do the roles of the custody officer, and the independent reviewer of continued detention, provide sufficient protection for the person detained during the period when authorization is entirely in the hands of the police?

3 Is the period of 96 hours' detention without charge in relation to all indictable offences, other than terrorism offences, too long? Or too short?

4 To what extent are the 'right to silence' and the privilege against self-incrimination still a part of the English criminal justice system?

5 Are the new provisions for retention of DNA profiles and fingerprints compatible with Art. 8 of the ECHR?

6 Where someone is aggrieved by actions of the police taken against them, what action is likely to be most successful in seeking redress?

FURTHER READING

Balding, D. J. and Donnelly, P. (1994), 'The Prosecutor's Fallacy and DNA Evidence', [1994] Crim LR 711

Baldwin, J. (1992), 'The Role of Legal Representatives at Police Stations', Royal Commission on Criminal Justice Research Study No. 3, HMSO

Berger, M. (2007), 'Self-incrimination and the ECtHR: Procedural Issues in the Enforcement of the Right to Silence', [2007] EHRLR 514

Bridges, L. and Choongh, S. (1998), 'Improving Police Station Legal Advice', Law Society Research Study No. 31, Law Society

Bridges, L. and Hodgson, J. (1995), 'Improving Custodial Legal Advice', [1995] Crim LR 104

Bucke, T. and Brown, D. (1997), 'In Police Custody: Police Powers and Suspects' Rights under the Revised PACE Codes of Practice', Home Office Research Study No. 174, Home Office

Bucke, T., Street, R. and Brown, D. (2000), 'The Right of Silence: The Impact of the Criminal Justice and Public Order Act 1994, Home Office Research Study No. 199, Home Office

Cape, E. (1999), 'Detention Without Charge: What Does Sufficient Evidence to "Charge" Mean?', [1999] Crim LR 874

Cape, E. (2002), 'Incompetent Police Station Advice and the Exclusion of Evidence', [2002] Crim LR 471

Cape, E. (2003), 'The Revised PACE Codes of Practice: A Further Step Towards Inquisitorialism', [2003] Crim LR 355

Clayton, R. and Tomlinson, H. (2004), *Civil Actions against the Police*, 3rd edn, London: Thomson Sweet & Maxwell

Dennis, I. (2002), 'Silence in the Police Station: the Marginalisation of Section 34', [2002] Crim LR 25

Farrington, D. (1993), 'Unacceptable Evidence', (1993) 143 NLJ 806

Home Office (2000), 'Complaints Against the Police: Framework for a New System', Home Office

Home Office (2004), 'Modernising Police Powers to Meet Community Needs', Home Office

Jennings, A., Ashworth, A. and Emerson, B. (2000), 'Silence and Safety: the Impact of Human Rights Law', [2000] Crim LR 879

McConville, M. and Hodgson, J. (1993), 'Custodial Legal Advice and the Right to Silence', Royal Commission on Criminal Justice Research Study No. 16, HMSO

Ormerod, D. and Birch, D. (2004), 'The evolution of the discretionary exclusion of evidence' [2004] Crim LR 138

Phillips, C. and Brown, D. (1998), 'Entry into the Criminal Justice System: a Survey of Police Arrests and their Outcomes', Home Office Research Study No. 185, Home Office

Police Complaints Authority (1995), 'PCA 10—Police Complaints Authority—The First Ten Years', HMSO

Runciman Report (1993), 'Royal Commission on Criminal Justice', Cm 2263, HMSO

Sanders, A. and Bridges, L. (1990), 'Access to Legal Advice and Police Malpractice', [1990] Crim LR 494

Sanders, A. and Young, R. (2010), *Criminal Justice*, 4th edn, Oxford: Oxford University Press

Zander, M. (2003), *Police and Criminal Evidence Act 1984*, 4th edn, London: Sweet & Maxwell

5

Right to a Fair Trial: Article 6

5.1 Introduction

This chapter focuses on the right to a fair trial. The first part is concerned with the obligations imposed on States by Art. 6 of the European Convention on Human Rights (ECHR) in relation to this right. The second half of this chapter (5.4 onwards) focuses on a particular threat to a fair trial, in the form of the reporting of imminent or current legal proceedings, which may raise a risk that the outcome of those proceedings will be adversely affected. This is dealt with in English law primarily by the offence of contempt of court. The last section deals with a particular type of contempt related to the extent to which a court can compel a journalist to disclose his or her source.

Article 6 imposes on States the obligation to provide a fair procedure for the determination of all civil rights and obligations, and all criminal charges. This requires:

- a fair and public hearing;
- within a reasonable time;
- before an independent and impartial tribunal.

This overall right to a fair trial is absolute, and cannot be limited by a State even if it feels there are legitimate grounds to do so. The various elements which support the right, however, such as the right of access to legal advice, or the right to remain silent, may be qualified by proportionate steps to meet a legitimate objective. This was the view of the Privy Council in *Brown v Stott* [2001] 2 All ER 97 and confirmed by the European Court of Human Rights (ECtHR) in *O'Halloran v United Kingdom* (2008) 46 EHRR 21 (these cases are discussed in more detail in chapter 4 (4.5.1.3)).

The Article distinguishes between civil and criminal procedures. Where a person is facing a criminal charge, more detailed and specific obligations are imposed on the State under Art. 6(2) and (3), which do not apply to civil proceedings. The order of treatment here, therefore, is to deal first with those provisions which apply to *all* proceedings, and then to deal with those which are particular to the criminal process.

5.2 Obligations applying to all proceedings

5.2.1 Open justice

Article 6(1) refers to 'public' hearing. This implies that all legal proceedings should be open to the press and public. Justice should be seen to be done. There are, however, exceptions, which are referred to in the Article, which may mean that some or all of the proceedings may justifiably be held in private. This is where it would be 'in the interests of' one or more of the following:

- morals;
- public order;
- national security;
- protecting juveniles;
- protecting the private life of the parties;
- other special circumstances where publicity would prejudice the interests of justice.

The final category might apply, for example, where a defendant was facing two separate trials. Reporting of the first trial might unfairly prejudice the second, so that it would be appropriate not to allow reporting of the first (though the press might still be allowed to attend on the understanding that there was to be no publication until after the second trial). Further discussion of the reporting of trials is to be found in the section of this chapter dealing with contempt of court (5.4).

The wording of Art. 6(1) suggests that judgment should *always* be given in public. In *B & P v United Kingdom* (2002) 34 EHRR 19, however, the court accepted that in certain situations, in this case because the decision involved children, it may be justifiable for judgment to be given in private (see also *Sutters v Switzerland* [1984] Series A, No. 74 where it was held that the judgment could be delivered in writing rather than being read in open court).

5.2.2 'Determination' of rights and obligations

The rights under Art. 6 only apply to proceedings which constitute a 'determination' of an individual's rights. Proceedings which may relate to a person's rights, but do not finally determine them, may not need to meet all the criteria set out in the Article. So in *Fayed v United Kingdom* (1994) 18 EHRR 393, a Department of Trade and Industry inspection and report did not have to comply with Art. 6, since it was primarily a fact-finding exercise, even though legal proceedings by other authorities might follow. As was noted in chapter 2 (2.3.3.4), in *R (on the Application of Alconbury Developments Ltd) v Secretary of State for the Environment* [2001] UKHL 23, [2001] 2 All ER 929, it was held that planning decisions taken by a Minister did not need to comply with Art. 6 because they were susceptible to judicial review, with this providing the 'determination' of the relevant rights. Prior to the Human Rights Act 1998 (HRA 1998), the ECtHR had found in *W v United Kingdom* (1986) 10 EHRR 293, which was a case about children in care, that the availability of judicial review was inadequate, because it looked only at the procedural aspects, and did not consider the merits of the case. As discussed in chapter 2 (2.4.1), under the HRA 1998 the remedy of judicial review in human rights cases has developed so that it does approach a merits review. Even if it does not go that far, in *Bryan v United Kingdom* (1995) 21 EHRR 342, another planning case, the ECtHR held that it was satisfactory if the judicial review covered the particular ground on which the applicant was seeking to challenge a planning decision—in this case, error of law.

This approach to the requirement of a 'determination' means, for example, that internal disciplinary procedures initiated by an employer against an employee do not necessarily need to be compatible with Art. 6 (though it may be good practice for them to be) in any situation where the employee will have access to an Employment Tribunal if he or she is dissatisfied with the outcome of the internal proceedings.

5.2.3 'Within a reasonable time'

There are clear links here with the obligations under Art. 5 in relation to criminal procedures to bring an individual before a court with appropriate speed. These are discussed in chapter 4 (see 4.1.2). Under Art. 6, the ECtHR has set out in number of cases the approach to taken to the question of whether there has been undue delay in the overall length of proceedings. So, in *Pelissier v France* (2000) 30 EHRR 715, for example, the Court stated the approach as follows (para. 67):

> The reasonableness of the length of proceedings is to be assessed in the light of the particular circumstances of the case, regard being had to the criteria laid down in the Court's case law, in particular the complexity of the case, the applicant's conduct and the conduct of the competent authorities.

The application of these principles has led to findings against the United Kingdom in a number of cases. Examples include *Mitchell v United Kingdom* (2003) 36 EHRR 52 (contract action—nine and a half years), *Henworth v United Kingdom* (2005) 40 EHRR 33 (murder trial plus retrials—6 years, with the applicant in custody throughout), *King v United Kingdom* (2005) 41 EHRR 2 (tax proceedings—14 years). In the end the court will make an assessment based on the overall circumstances, with no one particular factor being conclusive.

5.2.4 Independent and impartial tribunal

This is at the centre of the right to a fair trial. Unless the court or tribunal is independent of both sides to the case, so that it can decide without fear or favour, then justice will not be done, nor be seen to be done. That is why it is important that judges do not hold office at the discretion of the executive, and the reason why it is necessary that procedures for removing a judge from office should be onerous, and rarely used. In *Starrs v Ruxton* [2000] HRLR 191 the Scottish High Court of Justiciary considered the position of 'temporary sheriffs' who heard criminal cases in the Scottish system. These judges were appointed by the Secretary of State, but the Lord Advocate had a strong input in the annual decision as to whether a judge's post should be renewed. The Lord Advocate was a member of the Scottish Executive, and was also the head of the prosecution service in Scotland. The Court held that the lack of security of tenure of these judges, and the perception that their continued employment might depend on the decisions they reached, meant that they could not be seen to be 'independent', so that the requirements of Art. 6 were not met. The procedures for appointing such judges in Scotland were subsequently revised to make them compatible with the Article.

Another example of a tribunal which was found not to meet the required standard of independence was considered in *Findlay* v *United Kingdom* (1997) 24 EHRR 221. This concerned courts-martial. A soldier was tried for offences involving threatening fellow soldiers at gun-point following a heavy drinking session. The court-martial was convened by the local commanding officer, a Major-General, who appointed the members of the tribunal, and the prosecuting and defence counsel, all of whom were officers under his command. The soldier pleaded guilty to various charges and was sentenced to 2 years' imprisonment, and sentence confirmed by the Major-General. The court found that this procedure did not meet the requirement of a fair and impartial tribunal. The procedure for courts-martial was changed by the Armed Forces Act 1996 to meet this objection.

Problems may arise in a jury trial, if there is evidence of bias within the jury. In *Sander* v *United Kingdom* (2001) 31 EHRR 44 one member of a jury had sent a note to the judge complaining that some other members had made racist jokes about Asians, the ethnic group to which the applicant belonged. The next day a note was sent from all jurors denying any racial bias, and a note from the juror who was thought to have made the racist comment, attempting to explain his behaviour. The judge issued directions to the jury that it was to try the case on the evidence, but allowed the trial to continue. The applicant was convicted. The ECtHR held that his Art. 6 rights had been infringed. It was clearly concerned that the juror who had complained had been intimidated by the others, and also noted that the letter of 'explanation' suggested that racist comments had in fact been made. Much stronger action had been required by the judge to counteract the perception of bias; he probably should have stopped the trial. By contrast, in the earlier case of *Gregory* v *UK* (1998) 25 EHRR 577, on rather similar facts, but where the evidence of racist comments was much less clear, the Court was satisfied that the actions of the judge in issuing strong directions to the jury had been sufficient to counteract any perception of bias.

5.2.5 'Equality of arms'

Article 6 contains a specific provision relating to the provision of legal advice for criminal defendants, which is noted at 5.3.5. More generally the right to fair trial may require the provision of legal advice in any proceedings, including civil proceedings, to ensure that one side is not an unfair advantage. This is the so-called 'equality of arms' principle. Two contrasting ECtHR cases involving defamation actions illustrate the approach of the court. In *McVicar* v *United Kingdom* (2002) 35 EHRR 22, a journalist was successfully sued by Linford Christie, the athlete, over allegations of use of performance-enhancing drugs. The journalist claimed that his defence had been hindered by the lack of legal aid, and the consequent lack of legal representation (he had acted in person for the most part). The ECtHR held that there was no breach of Art. 6—the defendant was 'a well-educated and experienced journalist who would have been capable of formulating cogent argument' (para. 53), and, in all the circumstances, was not 'prevented from presenting his defence effectively to the High Court...by his ineligibility for legal aid' (para. 62).

A different conclusion was reached, however, in *Steel and Morris* v *United Kingdom* (2005) 41 EHRR 22. The defendants here were individuals who had distributed leaflets critical of McDonald's, the fast-food chain. They were sued for libel by

McDonald's. This resulted in the longest ever trial, lasting 313 days. McDonald's succeeded in their claim, and the judge awarded a total of £60,000 in damages. The defendants' appeal failed, and they sought redress from Strasbourg, alleging, among other things, a breach of Art. 6. The Court distinguished this case from *McVicar*, largely on the basis of the disparity of resources available to the two sides in *Steel and Morris*. Whereas in *McVicar*, the dispute was essentially between two individuals (though the claimant was considerably more wealthy than the defendant), in *Steel and Morris* it was a large multi-national corporation taking action against private individuals. As the court noted (para. 16), the defendants claimed to be:

> ...severely hampered by lack of resources, not just in the way of legal advice and representation, but also when it came to administration, photocopying, note-taking, and the tracing, preparation and payment of the costs and expenses of expert and factual witnesses. Throughout the proceedings McDonald's were represented by leading and junior counsel, experienced in defamation law, and by one or two solicitors and other assistants.

All of this meant that there was a disparity of resources which could not have failed to give rise to unfairness (para. 69). The denial of legal aid deprived the defendants 'of the opportunity to present their case effectively before the court and contributed to an unacceptable inequality of arms with McDonald's' (para. 72). There was, therefore, a breach of Art. 6.

5.3 **Rights applying to criminal proceedings**

The first point to note is that the question of whether proceedings are criminal or civil is not to be determined solely by the categorization of the domestic jurisdiction. The ECtHR regards this as an autonomous concept—in other words, it reserves to itself the decision as to whether proceeding fall within the 'criminal' section of Art. 6. In *Engel v The Netherlands* (1976) 1 EHRR 647 the court identified three criteria which were relevant to this decision (para. 82):

- the labelling by the state—if the proceedings are labelled as criminal by the state, this will generally be conclusive. If they are not, the Court will also look at:
- the nature of the offence; and
- the severity of the potential penalties.

Applying these criteria the Court found that 'disciplinary' offences within a code applying to soldiers were 'criminal' when the penalties involved significant deprivation of liberty. This approach has subsequently been used to find that proceedings relating to breaches of prison discipline were criminal: *Ezeh and Connors v United Kingdom* (2004) 39 EHRR 1. In *Öztürk v Germany* (1984) 6 EHRR 409 the Court held that the State's 'decriminalization' of certain motoring offences, which were still punishable by a significant fine, did not take them outside the scope of the protections for criminal proceedings contained in Art. 6.

5.3.1 **Presumption of innocence**

Article 6(2) states that 'Everyone charged with a criminal offence shall be presumed innocent until proved guilty according to law'. The burden of proof is thus on the prosecution to prove its case. This is a principle which has been long recognized in English criminal law, and indeed has been described as its 'golden thread': *Woolmington* v *DPP* [1935] AC 462, at pp. 481–2. As noted in chapter 4 (4.5.1.3), the ECtHR has nevertheless been prepared to recognize that in some situations it may not be a breach of Art. 6(2) to require the accused to bear the burden in relation to facts relied upon as a defence to a charge: *O'Halloran* v *United Kingdom* (2008) 46 EHRR 21.

The presumption of innocence has also been held to imply the right of suspects to remain silent, and not to incriminate themselves: *Funke* v *France* (1993) 16 EHRR 297; *Saunders* v *United Kingdom* (1997) 23 EHRR 313. The details of this approach and its limitations are discussed in chapter 4 (4.5.1.2 and 4.5.1.3).

5.3.2 **Information about charge**

Article 6(3)(a) requires that anyone charged with a criminal offence is 'to be informed promptly, in a language which he understands and in detail, of the nature and cause of the accusation against him'. There is clearly overlap here with the requirement in Art. 5(3) that a person who is arrested should be given similar information. This is discussed in chapter 3 (3.5) where it is noted that, 'promptly' does not necessarily mean 'immediately', and provided the information is given within a reasonable time of charge, the obligation will probably have been satisfied.

The requirement of using a language which the suspect understands was found to be infringed in *Brozicek* v *Italy* (1989) 12 EHRR 371. The applicant had been arrested in Italy for tearing down the flags of a political party. He was released and returned to Germany, where he lived. He did not speak or understand Italian. He was sent letters in Italian, informing him that he was to be charged with various offences in Italy. The applicant replied, in German, asking for the relevant information to be supplied in German. This did not happen, and the applicant was eventually convicted by an Italian court, in his absence, of various offences. The ECtHR held that his Art. 6 right to a fair trial had been broken by the failure to comply with Art. 6(3)(a).

5.3.4 **Time and facilities to prepare defence**

Article 6(3)(b) states that an accused must have 'adequate time and facilities for the preparation of his defence'. It has been held that provided the accused's lawyer has the relevant information, then there will be no breach of this obligation: *Kamasinki* v *Austria* (1991) 13 EHRR 36.

An example of a failure to comply is to be found in *Hadjianastassiou* v *Greece* (1993) 16 EHRR 215. The Greek court gave its decision in outline on 22 November. The defendant had to lodge an appeal by 27 November, but the full reasons for the court's decision were not made available until 10 January. Once the appeal had been lodged, no additional legal arguments could be raised. The ECtHR held that the applicant's rights under Art. 6(3)(b) had not been complied with.

5.3.5 **Right to defence and access to legal advice**

Article 6(3)(c) states that a defendant has the right:

> To defend himself in person or through legal assistance of his own choosing, or if he has not sufficient means to pay for legal assistance, to be given it free when the interests of justice so require.

As discussed in chapter 4 (4.5.1.2) delaying access to a lawyer may amount to a breach of this right in a situation where adverse inferences may be drawn from silence, or incriminating statements used against the suspect: *Murray* v *United Kingdom* (1996) 22 EHRR 29. More generally, the Court has held that free legal representation should be made available wherever an individual's liberty will be at threat from a conviction: *Benham* v *United Kingdom* (1996) 22 EHRR 293. The implication is that free legal advice need not be provided where the available penalty is only a fine, or some other penalty falling short of imprisonment. The overall test is whether the 'interests of justice' require the provision of such advice. The proposals put forward by the UK Government during 2013 to restrict access to legal aid in criminal cases (for which see the Ministry of Justice website at https://www.gov.uk/government/policies/making-legal-aid-more-effective) will have to be measured against this aspect of Art. 6.

In *Artico* v *Italy* (1980) 3 EHRR 1 there was a breach of this provision where a court nominated lawyer failed to take any active steps on behalf of the applicant, and the court failed to respond to requests to appoint a replacement.

5.3.6 **Rights to examine witnesses**

Article 6(3)(d) gives the defendant in a criminal trial the right:

> To examine or have examined witnesses against him and to obtain the attendance and examination of witnesses on his behalf under the same conditions as witnesses against him.

In *Saidi* v *France* (1994) 17 EHRR 251 the applicant was charged with drugs and homicide offences. The case against him was primarily based on identification evidence from three witnesses, but the applicant was given no opportunity to challenge these witnesses. He was convicted, and his appeals rejected. The ECtHR held that the failure to allow the applicant to confront the witnesses constituted a breach of Art. 6(3)(d).

The ECtHR has on a number of occasions considered the situation where witnesses are allowed to give evidence anonymously. While not ruling out such evidence entirely, the court has expressed the view that 'a conviction should not be based either solely or to a decisive extent on anonymous statements': *van Mechelen* v *The Netherlands* (1997) 25 EHRR 647, para. 55. In that case, anonymous witnesses were questioned by the judge, but not defence lawyers, and this was held to be a breach of Art. 6(3)(d). In the United Kingdom the issue came to a head in *R* v *Davis (Iain)* [2008] UKHL 36. It had become quite common practice in trials to allow witnesses who feared that they might suffer reprisals, and were therefore reluctant to give evidence unless they were allowed to do so anonymously, to give evidence, for example, from behind a screen, as had happened in *Davis*. The House of Lords, following the approach taken by the ECtHR, ruled that this was generally unacceptable, and that other than in exceptional circumstances (which probably should be determined by Parliament rather than the courts), anonymity should not be allowed. Parliament responded by passing the Criminal Evidence (Witness Anonymity) Act 2008, which does allow anonymous evidence in certain closely defined circumstances.

5.3.7 Free assistance of interpreter

Article 6(3)(e) provides that any person charged with a criminal offence has the right 'to have the free assistance of an interpreter if he cannot understand or speak the language used in court'.

The United Kingdom was found to be in breach of this provision in a case where the defendant had pleaded guilty, but no adequate interpretation provision was made at the sentencing stage of the proceedings: *Cuscani v United Kingdom* (2003) 36 EHRR 2.

The obligation to provide free interpretation applies even if the defendant is convicted. The attempt by the German government to recover the costs of interpretation from those convicted was held to be a breach of Art. 6(3)(e) in *Luedicke, Belkacem and Koc v Germany* (1978) 2 EHRR 149.

5.4 The offence of contempt of court

The requirement of trial before an 'impartial' tribunal needs particular care when decisions are to be taken by a jury, as in most criminal trials for serious offences in the UK. Issues can also arise where one of the parties to an action has a legitimate interest that information to be disclosed to a court is not given wider circulation. Against this, is the fact that journalists, broadcasters, and internet bloggers frequently obtain copy from reporting or commenting on civil and criminal cases, or other matters involving legal issues. This might be, for example, a sensational murder trial, a defamation action involving a celebrity, or a challenge to the legality of actions taken by a government department. Local newspapers, too, regularly report even quite minor legal cases. Most of the time this causes no problems, but such reporting is not without its restrictions, generally imposed to ensure the 'proper administration of justice', or in Art 6 terms, a 'fair trial'. In a number of situations there are specific statutory controls over the reporting of legal proceedings. More generally, such reports and discussions are subject to the law on contempt of court. One of the main objectives of such controls, and this applies particularly to contempt of court, may be to prevent prejudice to a current or future trial—that is to make sure that the parties to an action receive a fair trial in accordance with Art. 6 of the ECHR.

5.4.1 The nature of the offence

The offence of contempt of court is unusual. It can be both civil and criminal in character. In its civil form it is concerned with people who disobey court orders (e.g. injunctions). In looking at contempt as part of the right to a fair trial under Art. 6, we are more concerned with it in its criminal form, which is relates to the proper administration of justice in court proceedings (both civil and criminal). Although contempt is a type of criminal offence, it is not dealt with by the normal criminal process. In some circumstances the court which has been affected by an alleged contempt will deal with the matter itself, even if it is not a court which normally has criminal jurisdiction. Often, however, the Attorney-General will initiate proceedings in the Queen's Bench Division. It is always dealt with summarily, rather than on indictment, and procedural matters are governed by Ord. 52 of the Rules of the Supreme Court, as re-enacted in Sch. 1 to the Civil Procedure Rules. This strange character is perhaps a result of the rather obscure origins of the offence. It has been suggested that the power to deal with contempts originated in the Court of the Star Chamber, and was then appropriated by the ordinary courts (H. Street, *Freedom, the Individual and the Law*, 5th edn (Harmondsworth: Penguin, 1982), p. 147). Whatever the truth of this, it is clear that by the middle of the eighteenth century the offence was sufficiently well established for the Lord Chancellor, Lord Hardwicke, to identify three different ways of committing it. These were 'scandalizing the court itself', 'abusing parties who are concerned in causes', and 'prejudicing mankind against persons before the cause is heard' (*Roach v Garvan* (1742) 2 Atk 469). These categories can still be found to exist as types of contempt in the modern law. It is clear from them that 'contempt' is not being used here as a synonym for 'disrespect'. It is not the dignity of the judges which is being protected by contempt of court, but the authority and integrity of the judicial process.

5.4.2 Common law and statute

The origins of contempt lie in the common law. Onto this, however, a number of statutory provisions have been grafted, most notably the Contempt of Court Act 1981 (CCA 1981). Unfortunately, this piece of legislation, which was introduced as a liberalizing measure following criticisms in the ECtHR (see 5.4.5), did not codify the law. Moreover, the courts have shown a willingness in recent years to breathe new life into the common law. As a result, the student of this area often has to grapple with a confusing mixture of statutory and common law rules. This is true, for example, of the next issue to be considered, i.e. What is a 'court'?

5.4.3 What is a 'court'?

For there to be contempt, there must be a court for the accused to be in contempt of: what is a 'court' for these purposes? Any of the standard courts of the civil or criminal justice systems will clearly be covered, from magistrates' courts, to the Supreme Court. What of all the other bodies, however, which exist in the modern legal system to decide issues of fact and law? We have numerous specialist tribunals, for example industrial tribunals, social security appeal tribunals, mental health review tribunals, etc. They are part of our legal system, and may perform similar tasks to the general courts but they are not described as 'courts'. Does this remove them from the scope of contempt of court?

The answer to this is to be found in a mixture of case law and statute. The issue was first addressed in *Attorney-General v BBC* [1980] 3 All ER 161. The BBC was planning to show a film about a religious sect called the Plymouth Brethren. The Brethren alleged that this would prejudice a case which they had pending before a local valuation court. This was a body which decided issues relating to the rating of property ('rates' being a form of local taxation). The Attorney-General sought an injunction on behalf of the Brethren to restrain the alleged contempt. The main issue was whether the local valuation court could be regarded as a 'court' for contempt purposes. The Queen's Bench Division and the Court of Appeal both thought that it could. The House of Lords took a different view. It approached the issue on the basis that it was the *function* of the body which was important, rather than the *label* attached to it. The fact that this body was labelled as a 'court' could not be conclusive. In fact the House thought that it was exercising a purely *administrative* function within the rating system. To be a court, it would have had to be exercising a *judicial* role. On that basis, there could be no contempt of a local valuation court.

This approach was followed by Parliament in the CCA 1981. Section 19 defines a court as 'any tribunal or body exercising the judicial power of the State'. This definition had to be applied in *Pickering* v *Liverpool Daily Post* [1991] 1 All ER 622. Pickering was trying to prevent publicity about a pending hearing by a mental health review tribunal, which was to decide on whether he could be released from a mental hospital. He argued that adverse publicity might influence the tribunal, prejudicing his chance of a fair hearing, and thus constituting contempt of court. The Court of Appeal overruled an earlier decision (*Attorney-General v Associated Newspapers Group plc* [1989] 1 All ER 604) of the Divisional Court that a mental health review tribunal was not a court within the definition of s. 19. The view of the Court of Appeal (with which the House of Lords agreed) was that, since the tribunal was an independent body, which was required to act judicially on the basis of evidence, and had the power to decide matters affecting the liberty of individuals, it should be regarded as exercising the judicial power of the state. It was, therefore, a 'court' for the purposes of s. 19. Thus, the proposed publications could potentially amount to contempt. On the facts, however, the House of Lords found that they would not, and refused the injunction.

Similar tests to those used in *Pickering* were applied by the Divisional Court in *Peach Grey & Co.* v *Summers* [1995] 2 All ER 513 in considering the status of an industrial tribunal. As was anticipated by most commentators, the view taken was that an industrial tribunal (now an 'employment' tribunal) is a 'court' for the purposes of contempt. In addition to the points listed above in relation to mental health review tribunals, it was noted that employment tribunals have legally qualified chairmen, and must give reasons for their decisions, which can be appealed on points of law to the Employment Appeal Tribunal, and thence to the Court of Appeal. There was no doubt that such tribunals exercise a judicial rather than an administrative function, and are thus 'courts'. It is only those bodies which are not concerned primarily with the determination of individual rights, but rather with matters such as the distribution of resources (as, perhaps, is the case with social security appeal tribunals), which will not be regarded as courts for these purposes. The fact that the definition refers to the judicial power of the *state* means that the disciplinary tribunal of a professional body will not be a 'court' for the purposes of the Act: *General Medical Council* v *BBC* [1998] 3 All ER 426.

5.4.4 **Penalties and remedies for contempt**

The traditional method of punishment for contempt was imprisonment. For civil contempts this could mean imprisonment until the contempt was 'purged', i.e. until the contemnor apologized and agreed to abide by the order of the court. A stubborn individual could languish in prison indefinitely. The position is now governed by s. 14 of the CCA 1981.

Section 14 provides that committal to prison for contempt shall always be for a fixed period. The indefinite aspect of purging contempt has thus disappeared, though a contemnor might still shorten the fixed term by apologizing and agreeing to comply with the court's wishes. The maximum term for a committal by a superior court, which for these purposes includes a county court (s. 14(4A)), is two years. The limit for an inferior court is one month. There is also a power to fine for contempt, which is in practice the more commonly used penalty. Here the inferior court is limited to a fine of £1,000; there is no limit for superior courts.

It is also possible to seek an injunction to restrain a threatened criminal contempt. This is a further distinction between contempt and other criminal offences. In general the courts are reluctant to issue an injunction to restrain the commission of a criminal offence, on the basis that if the threat of the criminal penalties for committing the offence is not enough to deter the potential criminal, issuing an injunction is likely to be futile. In relation to contempt, the wish to ensure the due administration of justice apparently outweighs this argument, and both interim and permanent injunctions can issue. For interim injunctions, pending the full hearing of the case, the standard rules for balancing the interests of the parties derived from *American Cyanamid Co.* v *Ethicon* [1975] AC 396 apply. The claimant has to show an arguable case; once this is done the court must decide whether the 'balance of convenience' is for or against the issue of an injunction.

5.4.5 **Contempt and the Human Rights Act 1998**

The main focus for discussion of the compatibility of the law on contempt of court with the HRA 1998 is on the relationship between Art. 6 and Art. 10 (freedom of expression). To what extent can freedom of expression be restricted in the interests of ensuring a 'fair trial'?

Article 10(2) allows for restrictions on freedom of expression to the extent necessary in a democratic society to maintain 'the authority and impartiality of the judiciary'. The meaning of this phrase was considered in *Sunday Times* v *United Kingdom* (1979) 2 EHRR 245. The ECtHR ruled that 'the judiciary' here did not simply mean 'judges', it also encompassed 'the machinery of justice' and 'the judicial branch of government' (para. 55). This included the rights of litigants (para. 56). On this basis it was possible that, in addition to the avoidance of bias in proceedings, various other matters could come within the scope of the reasons for restriction permitted by Art. 10(2), such as the protection of parties from undue pressure, avoiding 'trial by newspaper' and avoiding disrespect for the processes of law.

Most of the areas covered by the English law of contempt will thus come within the scope of a 'legitimate aim'. There are, however, as we shall see, some areas of contempt where it could be argued that the restrictions are not sufficiently clearly defined to be said to be 'prescribed by law'. In addition, in all cases it will be necessary to demonstrate that the restriction is 'necessary in a democratic society'. This means that the restriction must reflect a 'pressing social need' and be proportionate to the legitimate aim being pursued.

In the ECHR cases the ECtHR has recognized that this is an area where, within the above constraints, individual countries will be allowed a 'margin of appreciation' as to the level of restriction. As indicated in chapter 2 (2.2.8), this cannot operate in the same way for an English court applying Art. 10 under the HRA 1998. The court will have to decide what the standard is to be for this jurisdiction. The fact that the European Court has recognized the possibility of a margin of appreciation means, however, that English courts may well not be swift to depart from standards already established, particularly where these are part of the statutory controls in this area. The most likely area for intervention is in those areas of contempt where the common law governs the controls. These issues are discussed further at the relevant points later in this chapter.

The general approach which should be taken in applying Art. 10 to this area is best demonstrated by the ECtHR's decision in *Sunday Times v United Kingdom* (the thalidomide case). The application to the European Court arose out of the House of Lords' decision in *Attorney-General v Times Newspapers Ltd* [1974] AC 273. The background to the case was that the distributors of the drug thalidomide, which it was alleged caused the birth of malformed babies, were being sued for negligence by some of the parents of these babies. The pre-trial proceedings were very drawn out, and *The Sunday Times* decided to campaign on behalf of the plaintiffs. They published an article which was severely critical of the defendants, Distillers. It said that the thalidomide children shamed Distillers, and criticized them for relying on the strict letter of the law. Whatever the position as regards negligence, *The Sunday Times* asserted that the company could afford a much more generous offer of compensation than it had so far been prepared to make. *The Sunday Times* then published a further article which alleged that Distillers had in any case been negligent in distributing the drug. The House of Lords held that this prejudgment of the specific issue which was to be decided in the action by the parents against Distillers amounted to a contempt of court, irrespective of whether it was likely to have an influence on the judge or judges hearing the case. *The Sunday Times* applied to the European Commission alleging an infringement of Art. 10. The Commission found that there was a breach of Art. 10 and referred the case to the Court. The Strasbourg Court's decision ((1979) 2 EHRR 245) was, by 11 votes to 9, in agreement with that of the Commission.

The first issue which the Court addressed was whether the restriction in this case could be said to be 'prescribed by law'. The applicants argued that the idea that 'prejudgment' was in itself contempt, irrespective of the effect on any particular case, was a novel one. For a restriction on behaviour to be prescribed by law it must be possible for citizens to assess beforehand with a reasonable degree of certainty the consequences of their acting in a particular way. The Court agreed with this approach (para. 49) but felt that, in the circumstances, there had been sufficient indication in previous cases (in particular *Hunt v Clarke* (1889) 58 LJQB 490) of the dangers of prejudgment to alert the applicants to the risk of contempt on these grounds (para. 52).

Next the Court considered whether the restriction had an aim which was 'legitimate' under Art. 10(2). As discussed, it came to the conclusion that it did.

The final issue was whether the interference was 'necessary in a democratic society'. The Court adopted the same approach as that which it had previously taken in the obscenity case of *Handyside v United Kingdom* (1976) 1 EHRR 737 (see chapter 8 (8.2)). Thus, while the ECHR does not set out an absolute standard, and individual countries will be allowed a 'margin of appreciation', the restriction must, as noted, respond to a 'pressing social need'; it must be 'proportionate to the legitimate aim pursued'; and the reasons given to justify it must be 'relevant and sufficient under Article 10(2)' (para. 62). To reach a conclusion on these matters the Court had to examine all the circumstances surrounding the issue of the injunction against *The Sunday Times*.

The Court noted that at the time of the injunction there had already been considerable pressure on Distillers from other quarters, including Parliamentary debates, to settle the claim on more beneficial terms. The article itself was, the Court thought, couched in moderate terms, and was not completely one-sided. Moreover, at the time when the article was proposed to be published, negotiations had been proceeding for several years, and the case had not yet reached the stage of trial.

In this context, the Court's role was to balance the public interest in freedom of expression against the need to maintain the authority of the judiciary. This was in contrast to the view of at least some of the House of Lords that the prejudgment rule was absolute, and that the House could not get involved in trying to balance the competing interests. The Court was required to take a different approach, and consider the public interest in the debate on the thalidomide tragedy, which was a matter of undisputed public concern, raising 'fundamental issues concerning protection against and compensation for injuries resulting from scientific developments' (para. 66). The Strasbourg Court's conclusion was that taking into account all the matters noted above, there was in this case no pressing social need sufficient to outweigh the public interest in freedom of expression. The restraint was not proportionate to the legitimate aim pursued, and was not necessary in a democratic society for maintaining the authority of the judiciary.

The response of the UK government to this decision was, eventually, to pass the CCA 1981. To what extent did this Act meet the criticisms of the ECtHR? Particular points on this issue will be noted later in the chapter. In some ways, however, the Act went further than necessary. The Strasbourg Court did not go so far as to say that prejudgment without prejudice to a particular case should never be contempt. On the contrary it specifically recognized the protection of the administration of justice in general as a legitimate aim of restriction. Nor was the introduction of a much stricter *sub judice* rule by means of the concept of 'active' proceedings (see 5.4.6.2) a requirement of the Court. The Court's main criticism was the failure to balance public interest issues. The response to this was the inclusion of s. 5 of the CCA 1981, headed 'Discussion of public affairs', which is discussed at 5.4.8.1. As will be seen, however, s. 5 probably does not meet all the Court's concerns. There is, therefore, scope for challenge to some aspects of the CCA 1981 under the HRA 1998, as well as to the common law rules.

5.4.6 **The Contempt of Court Act 1981**

As discussed, this Act was introduced primarily as a liberalizing measure following criticism of the English law of contempt in the ECtHR. It also took account of some of the recommendations of the Phillimore Committee on Contempt of

Court ('Report of the Committee on Contempt of Court', Cmnd 5794, 1974). Its main liberalizing provisions were the reduction in the scope of the *actus reus* of contempt (see 5.4.7), the shortening of the period of time when legal proceedings are deemed to be *sub judice* (see 5.4.6.2), and the introduction of a defence of public interest (see 5.4.8.1).

5.4.6.1 The strict liability rule

Contempt of court was always unusual in that it was one of the few common law offences of strict liability (i.e. there was no need to prove any intention or reckless-ness against the defendant in respect of the consequences of the actions alleged to amount to contempt). The CCA 1981 retained this feature of the law, but limited its scope. The relevant provisions are ss 1 and 2(1). Section 1 states that the 'strict liability rule' means:

> ...the rule of law whereby conduct may be treated as a contempt of court as tending to interfere with the course of justice in particular legal proceedings regardless of intent to do so.

The phrase 'regardless of intent to do so' is slightly ambiguous. It could mean 'where there is no intent to do so', or 'whether or not there is intent to do so'. The second meaning is probably what was intended, so that the strict liability rule could be used in a situation where contempt *was* intended. Recently, however, the tendency has been to prosecute such cases as common law contempt by virtue of s. 6(c) of the Act (see 5.2.4). The strict liability rule may thus end up only being used where the contempt is clearly unintentional.

Section 2(1) states that the strict liability rule applies 'only in relation to pub-lications'. This means that in relation to other types of behaviour which might amount to criminal contempt, for example disrupting court proceedings, the pros-ecution will now have to prove an intent to interfere with the administration of justice. A 'publication' is defined in the section as including any:

> ...speech, writing, broadcast or other communication in whatever form, which is addressed to the public at large or any section of the public.

Private letters, conversations, telephone calls, etc. are not within the scope of the strict liability rule. Whether there is publication to a section of the public will be a question of fact in each case. Circulation of a publication amongst a small group of people, for example the members of a club, might escape. On the other hand in *Re Lonhro plc* [1989] 2 All ER 1100 (see 5.4.7.7), a copy of a newspaper was circulated to between 2,000 and 3,000 people on a mailing list. There seems no doubt that this would have been regarded as a publication even if the newspaper had not also been put on general sale.

Most of the CCA 1981 is concerned with the strict liability rule. Accordingly, where the prosecution is prepared to prove intent, the Act will become largely irrelevant.

5.4.6.2 Active proceedings

One of the main criticisms of the pre-Act law, particularly from the point of view of journalists, was the uncertainty as to when it started to operate. At what point did a case become *sub judice* so that any comment about it, or reporting of it, ran the risk of being in contempt? The most commonly used phrase to describe the position was that proceedings had to be 'pending or imminent'. This did not, however, require any formal steps towards the initiation of proceedings to have been taken. In *R* v *Savundranayagan and Walker* [1968] 1 WLR 1761 Salmon LJ thought that contempt could operate in a situation in which 'it must surely have been obvious to everyone' that a person was about to be arrested. The press objected that this left it in an impossible situation as regards the investigation of suspected wrong-doing at a time when the authorities had not yet decided to act. The CCA 1981, adapting a recommendation of the Phillimore Committee, attempts to avoid this uncertainty through the concept of 'active proceedings'.

Section 2(3) says that the strict liability rule applies only to 'active proceedings'. These are then defined in Sch. 1 to the Act.

Criminal proceedings become active once any formal step has been taken. This can be an arrest, the issue of a warrant for arrest or a summons, the service of an indictment, or the charging of a suspect. They cease to be active after an acquittal, or conviction and sentence, or if the proceedings are discontinued in any other way, for example release without charge (otherwise than on bail).

Civil proceedings become active when arrangements are made for the hearing, or, if no previous arrangements are made, when the hearing begins. In relation to High Court actions, the effective date will generally be when the case is set down for trial. Note that this 'setting down' does not involve the fixing of a specific date for the hearing. Civil proceedings in other courts, for example the county courts, will become active when a date for the hearing is set. In either case, the proceedings will remain active until the action is concluded, or withdrawn.

Appellate proceedings, either criminal or civil, are treated as separate actions. They become active from the time at which an intention to appeal is formally indicated, i.e. by giving notice of appeal, or applying for leave to appeal. There may thus be a gap between the trial and the launch of an appeal when a case is for a time 'inactive'. Appeal proceedings cease to be active once concluded. If, however, the appeal court refers the case back to the lower court, proceedings in the lower court at once become active again.

Although the position under the CCA 1981 is a great improvement on the common law as far as certainty is concerned, journalists and editors may still need to take care, particularly in relation to criminal proceedings. The onus will be on them to make appropriate checks to make sure that no arrest warrant has been issued, and that no one has been charged in relation to a case. If, for example, a suspect is being questioned at a police station, but has not been arrested or charged, a newspaper may decide to publish a story about the case. If between the paper being printed, and its distribution around the country, a charge is made, the proceedings will become active, and the publication potentially liable for contempt. The newspaper may then escape liability only if it is possible to rely on the defence of innocent publication under s. 3, which is discussed at 5.4.8.2.

5.4.7 *Actus reus* of contempt

A publication will not amount to contempt under the strict liability rule simply because it refers or relates to active proceedings. It must also run the risk of affecting those proceedings. The test is set out in s. 2(2) of the Act:

> The strict liability rule applies only to a publication which creates a substantial risk that the course of justice in the proceedings in question will be seriously impeded or prejudiced.

There are three elements of this definition which require discussion: the nature of a 'substantial risk'; the requirement that the risk relates to 'the proceedings in question'; and the type of publication which will give rise to a risk of serious impediment, or prejudice.

5.4.7.1 Substantial risk

A 'substantial' risk does not mean a 'very big risk': *Attorney-General* v *English* [1983] 1 AC 116. It means a risk that is not remote. This was discussed in *Attorney-General* v *News Group Newspapers* [1986] 2 All ER 833. The England cricketer Ian Botham had brought an action for libel against a newspaper. At a time when this action was set down for trial, and thus 'active', he discovered that another newspaper was intending to publish similar defamatory statements. The Attorney-General sought an injunction to restrain this publication on the basis that it amounted to contempt, in that it would prejudice Botham's original libel action. The trial judge granted the injunction, but it was lifted by the Court of Appeal. The court ruled that 'substantial' related to the proximity of the risk. A risk might be remote in place or time. For example, an article published in a local newspaper in Devon would be unlikely to affect a trial taking place in Newcastle, many hundreds of miles away. In Botham's case the remoteness related to time. Although the case had been set down for trial, it was clear that it was not likely to take place for at least another 10 months, by which time, as Sir John Donaldson MR commented 'many wickets will have fallen, not to mention much water having flowed under many bridges, all of which would blunt any impact of the publication'.

A similar approach was taken in *Attorney-General* v *ITN* [1995] 2 All ER 370. A person had been arrested in connection with a murder. A television news broadcast, and the first editions of a number of newspapers, reported the fact that the arrested person was a convicted IRA terrorist, who had escaped from prison while serving a sentence for murder. This information was clearly highly prejudicial to the person arrested. Nevertheless, it was held that the 'ephemeral nature' of the brief broadcast, the small circulation of the newspapers (none being more than 2,500 copies), and the length of period until the trial (9 months), meant that the risk of prejudice was not 'substantial'. In the view of Leggatt LJ (p. 383): 'when the long odds against the potential juror reading any of the publications is multiplied by the long odds against any reader remembering it, the risk of prejudice is, in my judgment, remote.' In *Attorney-General* v *Times Newspapers* [2012] EWHC 3195 (Admin), although the publication by a national newspaper of information about a killing and the previous convictions of the suspect was potentially seriously prejudicial the risk was again held not be substantial because either the suspect would plead guilty, or there would be sufficient delay before trial to minimize the risk (also taking into account the circulation of the newspaper and the relatively small chance of a juror having been a reader). By way of contrast, in *Attorney-General* v *BBC, The Times*, 26 July 1996, the Divisional Court held that, despite a 6-month gap between publication and trial, there could still be a substantial risk of prejudice. The offending comments were made on the popular television show *Have I Got News for You?*, and related to the sons of Robert Maxwell (Ian and Kevin) who were awaiting trial for alleged fraud. Comments were made to the effect that they were 'heartless scheming bastards'. The court felt that the words were 'strikingly prejudicial' and went to the heart of the case which the jury were to try. It was also relevant that they were used on television in a programme which was repeated the next day, and that both speakers and victims were 'much in the public eye'. Taking all this into account, the risk of prejudice was substantial, and both the BBC and the production company were fined £10,000.

5.4.7.2 Proceedings in question

The risk must relate to the 'proceedings in question' (s. 2(2)). This refers to the definition of the strict liability rule in s. 1, which says that it applies to interference with 'particular legal proceedings'. In other words, the strict liability rule, in contrast to the position under the common law (see 5.2.4), does not apply to publications which might have an adverse affect on the administration of justice in general, rather than in a particular case. For example, criticizing judges for lack of impartiality could not be contempt under the strict liability rule, though it might on other grounds. The same would be true of a publication commenting on a completed case which might discourage potential witnesses from coming forward in future cases which are not active.

5.4.7.3 Nature of risk

Third, the risk must create a substantial risk of *serious impediment or prejudice*. The qualification 'serious', like the adjective 'substantial', was added to the common law test by the CCA 1981. It indicates that the courts should not be concerned with trivial or technical contempts. Only when the outcome of a legal action is likely to be affected should contempt be found. What kind of publication is likely to have that effect? There are a number of categories:

1. publications which prejudge the outcome of a case;
2. publications which may prejudice a jury against a party;
3. publications which criticize a party to a legal action; and
4. publications which pre-empt the legal rights of parties to an action.

In some situations a publication may have more than one of the above effects.

5.4.7.4 Prejudgment

The risk from prejudgment will only arise where the case is to be heard by magistrates or a jury. Judges are said to be able to ignore such publications, and are thus not likely to be prejudiced by them. Prejudging a civil action will therefore rarely amount to contempt under the strict liability rule. This is one of the changes introduced by the CCA 1981. In *Attorney-General* v *Times Newspapers Ltd* [1974] AC 273 (the thalidomide case) the House of Lords had held that prejudging a civil action could be contempt, since 'trial by newspaper' had an adverse effect on the administration of justice generally, irrespective of its effect on the particular case. Following criticism of this decision by the ECtHR (see 5.4.5), the CCA 1981 restricted strict liability contempt to the situation where particular proceedings are likely to be affected. In relation to criminal proceedings, any assumption of guilt on the part of the accused will almost certainly be regarded as contemptuous. In the pre-CCA 1981 case of *R v Bolam* (1949) 93 SJ 220, the *Daily Mirror* described the defendant in a murder trial as a 'vampire' and stated that he had committed other murders. This was regarded as a very serious contempt, warranting the committal of the editor to prison. There is no doubt that it would also be contempt under the strict liability rule. The press needs to be particularly careful where there has been a well-publicized manhunt, culminating in an arrest. In 1980 the arrest of Peter Sutcliffe led to statements, encouraged by a police press conference, that the so-called 'Yorkshire Ripper', who had murdered a number of women, had been caught. Sutcliffe subsequently confessed, so there was no actual prejudice to his trial, but the risk of prejudice was surely such that the Attorney-General could have obtained convictions if he had been prepared to act. A similar result based on 'hypothetical' prejudice (in this case because the person about whom the prejudicial material was published was never brought to trial) occurred in *Attorney-General v MGN Ltd* [2011] EWHC 2074 (Admin). In this case the newspaper reporting related to a murder of a young woman, Joanna Yeates, which had attracted a lot of attention. The police arrested her landlord, Christopher Jefferies. Two newspapers, the *Daily Mirror* and *The Sun* then published a number of articles which were very prejudicial towards Mr Jefferies, suggesting *inter alia* that he was a 'voyeur' who spied on his tenants, that he was a suspect in the murder of another young woman, that he had stalked a woman of similar age and appearance to Miss Yeates, and that he had been given the nickname 'Hannibal Lecter' by an other of his tenants. Another man, Vincent Tabak, was then arrested and confessed to killing Miss Yeates. At his subsequent trial he was convicted of murder. The Attorney-General brought action against the two papers, arguing that the publications were in contempt under the strict liability rule. The court had no doubt that 'vilification of a suspect under arrest' could fall within the rule (para. 31):

> At the simplest level publication of such material may deter or discourage witnesses from coming forward and providing information helpful to the suspect, which may, (depending on the circumstances) help immediately to clear him of suspicion or enable his defence to be fully developed at trial.

It concluded that the articles in both newspapers constituted contempt under the strict liability rule.

In *Attorney-General v MGN Ltd* [1997] 1 All ER 456 contempt was alleged, despite that fact that the trial concerned had been stayed by the judge because of the adverse publicity, so that there was no actual prejudice to the defendant. This concerned the prosecution for assault of Geoffrey Knights, who had previously achieved some notoriety in the tabloid press as a result of his relationship with the well-known television actress, Gillian Taylforth. Amongst other things they had been involved as unsuccessful plaintiffs in a libel action following their arrest for alleged indecent behaviour in a car on the A1, an action which had received extensive publicity. There had also been reports from time to time of other incidents of alleged violent behaviour by Mr Knights, and that he had a prison record for violence. In the April and May prior to the start of the latest prosecution a number of newspapers had run stories about the incidents which had led to the charges. These were, as Schiemann LJ put it ([1997] 1 All ER 456, p. 466):

> ...all written in typical graphic tabloid style. They include large banner headlines, large photographs of all...those involved in the incident. There is a measure of exaggeration in the description of the injuries sustained...and the language used is undoubtedly emotive.

A trial date had been fixed for October, but in September Mr Knights' counsel applied for a stay of proceedings on the basis that the pre-trial publicity made it impossible for Mr Knights to have a fair trial. This application was successful. Subsequently the Attorney-General brought contempt proceedings against a number of newspapers. The court set out a number of principles to be adopted in such cases, most of which either repeated the statutory tests or established common law rules. One of these was that each publication must be looked at separately. In other words the cumulative effect of a number of publications should not be considered: the particular publication under consideration must itself create a substantial risk of serious prejudice. On the other hand, it is equally true that:

> ...the mere fact that, by reason of earlier publications, there is already some risk of prejudice does not prevent a finding that the latest publication has created a further risk.

Applying this approach to the articles concerned, all of which were published in the April or May prior to the scheduled trial, the court did not think that any one of them individually created a substantial risk that the course of justice in the proceedings would be seriously impeded or prejudiced. The contempt proceedings therefore failed in relation to all the publications. In arriving at this conclusion the court was at pains to stress that it did not cast any doubt on the correctness of the judge's decision to stay the proceedings. As Schiemann LJ explained:

> A consequence of the need in contempt proceedings, in which respondents face imprisonment or a fine, to be sure, and to look at each publication separately and the need in trial proceedings to look at the risk of prejudice created by the totality of publications can be that it is proper to stay proceedings on the ground of prejudice albeit that no individual is guilty of contempt.

This confirms that the cumulative effect of a series of articles, even if they all appear in the same newspaper, cannot be taken into account in establishing the *actus reus* of contempt. Each publication must be considered in its own right.

In *Attorney-General* v *Birmingham Post* [1998] 4 All ER 49 the Divisional Court considered the question of whether the fact that a publication *during* a trial had led the judge at the trial to stay proceedings meant that the publication was automatically in contempt. It took the view that this was not necessarily the case, since the questions asked by the trial judge when considering a stay, and those asked by the Divisional Court in considering an application under the CCA 1981, were not identical. Nevertheless, Simon Brown LJ commented that he found 'it difficult to envisage a publication which has concerned the judge sufficiently to discharge the jury and yet is not properly to be regarded as a contempt' ([1998] 4 All ER 49, p. 59).

In the case before the court it was held that the publication had been in contempt, and the newspaper was fined £20,000.

5.4.7.5 Problems arising from jurors' use of the internet

The growth in internet use has raised two particular situations which may give rise to the possibility of contempt by jurors. They are first, members of a jury using social media to comment on the case which they are trying, and second the use of the internet to discover information relevant to the case which has not been included in the evidence presented to the court (e.g. information about any previous convictions of the accused). Both of these situations were considered in *Attorney-General* v *Davey* [2013] EWHC 2317. This involved two cases. In the first, Davey had been empanelled on a jury to hear a case of alleged sexual activity with a child. He used his Facebook page to post a message saying, *inter alia*: 'I've always wanted to Fuck up a paedophile & now I'm within the law'. In the second case, Beard was a jury member on a lengthy fraud trial. He used the internet to investigate the background to the case, and discovered that there were around 1,800 victims of the alleged fraud—a fact which he disclosed to other jury members. This, and other information which Beard had discovered, did not form part of the evidence to be presented to the jury.

In both cases the court concluded that there was a substantial risk of prejudice to the administration of justice. Both defendants were convicted, and sentenced to imprisonment for two months. The court noted that although steps were taken to try to ensure that jurors are aware of what they can and cannot do as regards use of the internet, there was an argument that jurors should also be handed a notice setting this out and indicating the penal consequences of a breach. The court invited the Criminal Procedure Rules Committee and the Judicial College to consider introducing the giving of a written notice of this kind as standard practice.

5.4.7.6 Prejudice without prejudgment

Prejudicing a jury against a defendant in criminal proceedings can occur without there necessarily being an implication of guilt. Particular care must be taken over the publication of photographs, especially where identity is in issue. This is the case even where the defendant is a well-known celebrity, whose image might be thought to be widely known. This was the view of the High Court of Judiciary in the Scottish case of *Scottish Daily Record* v *Thomson* [2009] HCJAC 24, where the defendant was a well-known footballer, awaiting trial for assault. The risk here is the potential effect on witnesses who may be giving identification evidence.

Publication of photographs on the web can also give rise to difficulty, as shown by *Attorney-General* v *Associated Newspapers Ltd* [2011] EWHC 418 (Admin). On the day that the jury were empanelled in murder trial, two newspapers published on their website a photograph of the defendant holding a pistol with his finger on the trigger. In both cases the photographs were available for a number of hours before being removed. Despite the fact that the judge had warned the jury not to look for information relevant to the case on the web, and that there was no evidence that any of them had done so, the court found both newspapers guilty of contempt, and fined them £15,000 ([2011] EWHC 1894 (Admin)).

Revealing details of the defendant's past life may also constitute contempt. In the pre-CCA 1981 case of *R* v *Thompson Newspapers Ltd, ex p Attorney-General* [1968]

1 All ER 268, it was held to be contempt to refer to the defendant in a trial for incitement to racial hatred, as a former 'brothel-keeper, procurer and property racketeer'. It may be, however, that the wording of s. 2(2) has relaxed the law in this area. In *Attorney-General* v *Times Newspapers Ltd, The Times*, 12 February 1983 (the *Fagan* case), actions for contempt were brought against a number of newspapers commenting on the prosecution of Michael Fagan who was accused of, among other things, burglary in Buckingham Palace. Descriptions of him as a drug addict, a glib liar, and a potential suicide, were held not to amount to contempt. Lord Lane commented that 'jurors were to be credited with more independence of mind than was sometimes suggested'. It may well be that the new qualifications of 'substantial' and 'serious' contributed to this decision. In *Attorney-General* v *Guardian Newspapers Ltd (No. 3)* [1992] 3 All ER 38, the Divisional Court held that a statement that a defendant in criminal proceedings was awaiting trial on other charges did not *necessarily* create a substantial risk of serious prejudice. The way in which the information had been presented in this case (the defendant was one of a group, and not named) meant that the risk of a juror being affected by it was insignificant.

Note that prejudice against a party can affect the prosecution as well as the defence. One of the newspapers involved in the *Fagan* case had stated that the prosecution had dropped a charge which was in fact being pursued. This could clearly have prejudiced the jury if the report had led them to think that the prosecution was so unsure of its case that it had at one point abandoned the charge altogether.

The jury must also be protected against emotional reporting which might influence its attitude towards one of the parties. In 1981, soon after the CCA came into force, a trial took place in Leicester of Dr Leonard Arthur, who was accused of the attempted murder of a Down's syndrome baby (John Pearson) in his care. The prosecution alleged that the regime which the doctor had prescribed had hastened the baby's death. While the trial was in progress the *Sunday Express* published an article written by its editor, Sir John Junor. It read as follows (*The Times*, 17 November 1981):

> In the three grim days of his short, sad life, mongol baby John Pearson was given no nourishment. His parents had rejected him. So instead of being fed he was drugged. Even then, we know he fought tenaciously for life. Without a chance of success. And so he died. Unloved, unwanted. I blame no one. I condemn no one. And I make no comment on the case in Leicester Crown Court.

Although there was no direct suggestion of guilt, nor any comment on Dr Arthur himself, the Divisional Court had no doubt that this constituted contempt under the CCA 1981. Watkins LJ thought that 'in this trial, more than most, it was essential that extraneous, irrelevant, and emotional influences should not reach the minds of jurors, lest they influenced the jury improperly, and denied Dr Arthur a fair trial'. Sir John Junor was fined £1,000, and Express Newspapers £10,000.

5.4.7.7 **Criticizing parties**

The third type of prejudice is where the publication criticizes one of the parties to a legal action. This can operate in relation to either civil or criminal proceedings, and may be prejudicial in two ways. First, it may deter potential witnesses from coming forward. For example, statements that a prosecution ought not to have been brought, or that a particular defence is morally unsupportable (though technically available), might have the effect of making potential witnesses for the prosecution or defence respectively reluctant to give evidence. Second, it may discourage the parties themselves from pursuing their legal rights. In this form it has been found more commonly in relation to civil proceedings. In *Vine Products v Green* [1966] Ch 484, Buckley J recognized that comment on a pending action could amount to contempt if it was:

> ...likely in some way or other to bring pressure to bear upon one or other of the parties to the action, so as to prevent that party from prosecuting or from defending the action, or encourage that party to submit to terms of compromise which he otherwise might not have been prepared to entertain, or influence him in some other way in his conduct in the action, which he ought to be free to prosecute or to defend, as he is advised, without being subject to such pressure.

This type of contempt was considered in detail in *Attorney-General v Times Newspapers Ltd* [1974] AC 273 (the thalidomide case). The distributors of the drug thalidomide, which it was alleged caused the birth of malformed babies, were being sued for negligence by some of the parents of these babies. The pre-trial proceedings were very drawn out, and *The Sunday Times* decided to campaign on behalf of the plaintiffs. They published an article which was severely critical of the defendants, Distillers. It said that the thalidomide children shamed Distillers, and criticized the company for relying on the strict letter of the law. Whatever the position as regards negligence, *The Sunday Times* asserted that the company could afford a much more generous offer of compensation than it had so far been prepared to make.

The House of Lords was unanimous that, in some circumstances, criticism of parties could amount to contempt. Their Lordships were not in agreement, however, as to what type of criticism would have this effect, nor as to how the law should apply to *The Sunday Times* article. In relation to publications (as opposed to private pressure) the distinction was drawn between fair and temperate criticism, and holding a party up to public obloquy. The former was permissible, the latter contempt. To this extent the quotation from Buckley J given above was probably too widely stated. As Lord Reid pointed out, it would surely not be contemptuous to urge Shylock in Shakespeare's *Merchant of Venice* not to insist on his pound of flesh. The difficulty in drawing the line, however, is shown by the fact that three of their Lordships (Reid, Cross, and Morris) felt that *The Sunday Times* was on the right side of it, whereas Lords Diplock and Simon felt that the article constituted contempt.

5.4.7.8 Pre-emption

The final way in which the *actus reus* of contempt may be committed under the strict liability rule is if the publication pre-empts the rights of one of the parties to a legal action. This category of contempt arose out of the litigation resulting from the British government's attempts to ban the publication of the book *Spycatcher* (see chapter 7 (7.7.2)). It was first recognized by the Court of Appeal in *Attorney-General v Times Newspapers Ltd* [1987] 3 All ER 276 (*The Independent* case). The Attorney-General had obtained interlocutory injunctions against two newspapers, *The Observer* and *The Guardian*, restraining them from publishing information or extracts drawn from *Spycatcher*. While these injunctions were still in force, *The Independent*, and two other newspapers, published extracts and summaries from the book. The Attorney-General brought an action for contempt. In a preliminary action to determine whether contempt could occur in such a situation, the Court of Appeal held that it could, a view that was subsequently confirmed by the House of Lords (*Attorney-General v Times Newspapers Ltd* [1991] 2 All ER 398). This was not because the injunctions against *The Observer* and *The Guardian* had any direct effect on other newspapers: they did not. The potential liability of *The Independent* was based not on breach of an injunction, which would have been civil contempt, but on interference with legal proceedings, i.e. criminal contempt.

The reason for this was that the action against *The Observer* and *The Sunday Times* was for breach of confidence. The material contained in *Spycatcher* had been obtained in circumstances alleged to imply confidentiality, and the newspapers were breaking that confidence by their threatened publication. *The Independent*, by revealing the information which was said to be confidential, was prejudicing the Attorney-General's chance of success against *The Observer* and *The Sunday Times*. Once confidential material has been put into the public domain, even as a result of a wrongful action, its quality of confidence is lost, and the courts will not intervene to restrain further publication. *The Independent* had put some of the information into the public domain, and thus prejudiced the Attorney-General's action. The only remaining problem was that the proceedings against *The Observer* and *The Sunday Times* were not 'active' at the time when *The Independent*'s article was published. The Attorney-General had to argue therefore that the editor of *The Independent* had intentionally committed the contempt, and was liable at common law. This aspect of the case is discussed at 5.2.4.

The approach taken in *The Independent* case was followed in *Attorney-General v Observer Ltd* [1988] 1 All ER 385 (which concerned the question of whether a library could supply a copy of *Spycatcher* without being in contempt), and discussed further in *Re Lonrho plc* [1989] 2 All ER 1100. In this case the Secretary of State for Trade had decided not to publish a report by Department of Trade inspectors into a successful take-over bid for Harrods, the London department store, pending consideration of the case by the Director of Public Prosecutions and the Serious Fraud Office. He also decided not to refer the case to the Monopolies and Mergers Commission. Lonrho, which had been an unsuccessful bidder for Harrods, sought judicial review of these decisions. The application succeeded at first instance, but was overturned on appeal. While a further appeal to the House of Lords was pending, Lonrho received a copy of the inspectors' report, and arranged for its publication in a special edition of *The Observer* (which Lonrho owned). Some 200,000 copies were distributed, and some were sent to members of the House of Lords due to hear the appeal. The Attorney-General brought proceedings for contempt, which were heard by a special panel of the House of Lords exercising original, rather than appellate, jurisdiction.

The House held that the possible grounds for contempt were prejudgment and pre-emption. On prejudgment, the House took the view that in the light of the ECtHR decision in the *Sunday Times* thalidomide case (see 5.2.2), and the CCA 1981, prejudgment on its own could not amount to contempt. It would only do so if it was likely to have an effect on the trial. Here there were no witnesses or jury to affect, and it was unlikely that the Secretary of State would be influenced in pursuing his appeal. That left pre-emption as the only possible type of contempt. Here the circumstances were superficially similar to *The Independent* case, in that information which the government wished to keep secret had been revealed. In this case, however, there was no injunction restraining publication, and the central issue was not 'confidentiality', but whether the Secretary of State had acted lawfully in deferring publication. There might be other remedies for what had been done, for example breach of copyright, but the publication did not constitute contempt.

The *actus reus* of this type of contempt was again fully discussed in *Attorney-General* v *Punch* [2002] UKHL 590, [2003] 1 All ER 289. This was another case which arose out of the activities of the former member of the MI5, David Shayler (see chapter 7(7.6.6.3)). The Attorney-General believed that Shayler was supplying to certain newspapers confidential material obtained from documents unlawfully retained by him when he left MI5. He initiated an action against Shayler and Associated Newspapers. He also obtained an interim injunction restricting further disclosures or publications pending trial. Subsequently, Shayler wrote several articles for *Punch* magazine. *Punch* was not a party to the original action and, therefore, not directly affected by the original injunction. The Attorney-General took action against the editor of the magazine for contempt of court, on the basis that some of the articles published were covered by the injunction. Silber J found the editor guilty of contempt and imposed a fine of £5,000. The editor appealed.

The Court of Appeal allowed the appeal on the basis that the purpose that the Attorney-General was trying to achieve, i.e. the protection of confidential material, could not apply where the relevant material had already been published. On a further appeal by the Attorney-General, however, the House of Lords took a different view from the Court of Appeal. The House thought that the Court of Appeal had incorrectly focused on what the Attorney-General's purpose had been in seeking the injunction, rather than on what the *court's* purpose had been in granting it. In this case the court's purpose had been to preserve the confidentiality of the material *specified in the order*. If, therefore, a publication disclosed information specified in the order then the *actus reus* of contempt would be committed, since the purpose of the order would thereby be thwarted. It was irrelevant that the order might be drawn in over-wide terms in relation to the objectives of the claimant (i.e. here, the protection of national security).

As regards the question of obtaining the Attorney-General's permission, the House of Lords did not regard this as objectionable, since a refusal by the Attorney-General could always be challenged by application to the court for a variation of the order. The permission requirement involved a 'simple, expeditious and inexpensive' procedure which might well avoid the necessity of an application to the court. The decision of the House led to the restoration of the trial judge's decision, and the re-imposition of the fine of £5,000.

The result of these decisions seems to suggest that the pre-emption category of contempt will be limited to cases concerning confidentiality. In other cases, different remedies will probably be available. A useful comparison was drawn in the Court of Appeal in *The Independent* case ([1987] 3 All ER 276), with defamation. If an interim injunction is issued in a defamation action against one publisher, and a third party then publishes the same libel, there is no contempt. The claimant can sue the third party, and the action against the original defendant is in no way compromised. It is only where, as with breach of confidence, the action of the third party has the effect of destroying what is being protected by the injunction, and rendering the claimant's rights nugatory, that contempt has a role to play.

It is unclear, however, how these principles should be applied where an injunction is issued which purports to apply universally, rather than simply to the parties before the court, as was done in *Venables* v *News Group Newspapers Ltd* [2001] 1 All ER 908 (discussed in chapter 6 (6.10.2)). Presumably, for there to be criminal contempt, the court should still ask whether the publication thwarts the purpose of the injunction, and whether it was published with the relevant *mens rea* (for which see 5.4.9). It seems, however, that in these circumstances a newspaper which has knowledge of the injunction and publishes information, not in the public domain, which is likely to contravene the purpose of the injunction will commit 'civil' rather than 'criminal' contempt (see 5.4.1). This was the approach taken by Dame Elizabeth Butler-Sloss in *Attorney-General* v *Greater Manchester Newspapers Ltd, The Times*, 7 December 2001. The *Manchester Evening News* had published information which was in the judge's view likely to lead to the identification of the two men that the injunction issued by her in *Venables* v *News Group Newspapers* was intended to protect. Although the information concerned was contained in a government publication and on a website, it was not sufficiently accessible to be regarded as being in the 'public domain'. The newspaper was, therefore, in contempt simply for breaching the injunction, rather than, as would be the case in criminal contempt, for prejudicing the administration of justice.

One issue of uncertainty in relation to contempt and confidentiality was clarified in *Jockey Club* v *Buffham* [2002] EWHC 1866 (QB), [2003] QB 462. In this case Gray J considered the application of criminal contempt in relation to a *final* injunction relating to confidential material. He held that the category of contempt based on a third party interfering with the purpose of an injunction issued against one of the parties to an action had no application where the injunction was final. The essence of that category of contempt was interference with the course of justice in the relevant proceedings, and if the proceedings were concluded there could be no such interference.

5.4.8 Defences

5.4.8.1 Defence of public interest

One of the criticisms of the English law of contempt which was made by the ECtHR in the *Sunday Times* thalidomide case was that it paid too little attention to competing public interests, which might go in favour of publication. The government responded by including such a defence in s. 5 of the CCA 1981. This is entitled 'Discussion of public affairs':

> A publication made as or as part of a discussion in good faith of public affairs or other matters of general public interest is not to be treated as a contempt of court under the strict liability rule if the risk of impediment or prejudice to particular legal proceedings is merely incidental to the discussion.

The section does not strictly speaking operate as a defence, in that the burden of proof is on the prosecution: *Attorney-General v English*. In other words, once the defence has raised the issue of public interest it is up to the prosecution to try to prove that the publication was not in good faith; did not relate to public affairs or other matters of public interest; or that the risk of prejudice was not merely incidental to the discussion.

The operation of s. 5 has been discussed in several cases. The most important of these is the House of Lords' decision in *Attorney-General v English*. This case, like the *Sunday Express* case discussed at 5.4.7.5, was concerned with the trial of Dr Leonard Arthur on a charge of attempted murder of a Down's syndrome baby. On the third day of the trial the *Daily Mail* published an article by Malcolm Muggeridge in support of Mrs Marilyn Carr, a 'pro-life' candidate in a Parliamentary election. Mrs Carr had been born without arms, but had managed to lead a very normal life despite this handicap. The article asserted that if a baby like Mrs Carr was born today 'someone would surely recommend letting her die of starvation, or otherwise disposing of her'. Later in the article it was also suggested that 'mongoloid' (i.e. Down's syndrome) babies would be destroyed 'before or after birth'. The subject matter of the article clearly related very closely to the allegations made against Dr Arthur. The House of Lords had no doubt that it created a substantial risk of serious prejudice under s. 2(2). Nevertheless, the House felt that it avoided being in contempt because it was protected by s. 5. To write an article supporting Mrs Carr without referring to the allegations about current medical practice would, as Lord Diplock put it, depict Mrs Carr as 'tilting at imaginary windmills'.

In the course of finding that the *Daily Mail* was not in contempt, the House made various other comments on s. 5. First, the requirement that the risk of prejudice is 'merely incidental' does not mean that the comments have to be necessary to the discussion. It does not matter that other words or phrases could have been used, as long as the risk is no more than an incidental consequence of expounding the main theme. Second, it was regarded as important that the article made no reference to the Arthur trial (indeed Malcolm Muggeridge claimed to be unaware that the trial was taking place). A contrast was drawn by Lord Diplock with the *Sunday Times* thalidomide case, where the whole point of the articles was to put pressure on Distillers. The suggestion seems to be that s. 5 would not have protected *The Sunday Times*. This is ironic in that one of the main reasons for including s. 5 was to meet the criticisms of the approach in the thalidomide case by the ECtHR.

In at least one later case, the courts have been prepared to allow s. 5 to be used even where a particular case is referred to. In the *Fagan* case the *Mail on Sunday* had published an article suggesting that there had been a homosexual liaison between Fagan and the Queen's police bodyguard. The Divisional Court thought that could clearly create a risk of prejudice within s. 2(2). The issue of the safety and security of the Queen was, however, a matter of serious public concern, and the court was prepared to regard the risk of prejudice as merely incidental to the discussion of this matter.

In *Attorney-General v Guardian Newspapers* [1992] 3 All ER 38, the Divisional Court held, obiter, that in the context of a discussion about the propensity of judges to impose reporting restrictions in fraud trials (which was clearly a matter of public interest), a possibly prejudicial reference to a particular case, where reporting had been restricted because the accused was awaiting trial on other charges, was merely incidental to the discussion.

The precise scope of s. 5 is still uncertain. The decision of the House of Lords in *Attorney-General* v *English* is the leading authority, but seems to envisage a fairly restricted role for the defence. The Divisional Court's approach in the *Fagan* case appears more liberal, but the extent to which other courts feel inhibited by the comments in the *English* case in using the section remains to be seen. It is certainly arguable that s. 5, particularly if restrictively interpreted, does not really meet the criticisms of the ECtHR in *Sunday Times* v *United Kingdom*. The section does not on its face require the courts to 'balance' one interest against another in the way suggested by the European Court. Moreover, it gives no special recognition to freedom of expression, or the importance of the press in a democracy. The risk is, therefore, that the weight will still be on the side of restricting publication. The effect of s. 3 of the HRA 1998, however, should be to encourage the courts to adopt a liberal interpretation, rather than a restrictive one, in giving effect to the principles contained in Art. 10 of the ECHR, and in s. 12 of the HRA 1998 itself. If that is done, then s. 5 may in the end have the effect of incorporating the approach required by the European Court.

5.4.8.2 **Other defences**

The CCA 1981 provides three other defences under the strict liability rule, in ss 3 and 4. These are innocent publication (s. 3(1)), innocent distribution (s. 3(2)), and contemporary reports of proceedings (s. 4(1)).

The defences in s. 3 are substantial re-enactments of provisions previously contained in s. 11 of the Administration of Justice Act 1960. They are true defences, in that the burden of proof is specifically stated to be on the defence (s. 3(3)). Given that a conviction for contempt carries with it the potential for two years' imprisonment it may be that under the approach taken by the House of Lords in *Sheldrake* v *DPP* [2004] UKHL 43, [2005] 1 All ER 237 (see chapter 2 (2.3.3.1)), the courts would use their power under s. 3 of the HRA 1998 to interpret s. 3(3) of the CCA 1981 as imposing only an evidential burden on the defendant.

Section 3(3) protects the innocent publisher of contemptuous material, who does not know, and has no reason to suspect, that proceedings are active at the time of the publication. This might protect the editor in the situation referred to in 5.4.6.2, where a charge takes place between the finalizing of a story and its appearance on the streets. The editor will have to show, however, that all reasonable care has been taken. This might mean, for example, that the editor who knows that someone is helping the police with their inquiries, should check with the police as to the likelihood of a charge being made, before proceeding with a story on the case.

The defence of innocent distribution under s. 3(2) is aimed at protecting people like newsagents, who are 'publishers' of the newspapers, magazines, etc. which they sell, and so potentially liable under the strict liability rule if any of those publications contain prejudicial material. The section provides a defence if it can be proved that at the time of the distribution the distributor did not know, and had no reason to suspect, that the publication contained anything which would fall foul of the strict liability rule. As with s. 3(1), it must be shown that all reasonable care has been taken.

The third defence, in s. 4(1), was a new one. It removes from the scope of the strict liability rule fair and accurate reports of legal proceedings held in public, provided that they are published contemporaneously and in good faith. The requirement of contemporaneity means, for example, that a report of a case heard a year previously which is published at a time when someone involved in the case is again before the courts would not be protected by s. 4(1).

The section covers all proceedings held in public, so in theory this would allow the reporting of matters discussed in open court, but in the absence of the jury (such as an argument as to the admissibility of evidence). Such a publication would undoubtedly have been treated as contempt prior to the Act (cf. *R* v *Evening Standard Co. Ltd* [1954] 1 All ER 1026). Now it will not be so, unless it can be said that the publication was not 'in good faith'. It seems likely that a court would expect an experienced reporter or editor to recognize the prejudicial nature of such a publication, and so regard such action as not in good faith. In addition, the court does have the power under s. 4(2) to issue a specific order postponing potentially prejudicial reports of proceedings. This is discussed further at 5.2.5.

5.4.9 Common law contempt

The application of the common law of contempt to publications is preserved by s. 6(c). This states that nothing in ss 1–5 of the CCA 1981 'restricts liability for contempt of court in respect of conduct intended to impede or prejudice the administration of justice'. In other words, if the prosecution can prove intent then the question is whether the publication would have been contemptuous if it were not for the provisions of the CCA 1981. If the answer is yes, then the provisions relating to the strict liability rule become irrelevant. The survival of this form of contempt alongside the CCA 1981 raises the potential for confusion, as illustrated by *Yousaf* v *Luton Crown Court* [2006] EWCA Crim 369, where a Crown Court judge, intending to use the common law, made reference to s. 2 of the CCA 1981. The resulting confusion for the defendant's counsel and others involved in the proceedings led to the convictions for contempt being quashed by the Court of Appeal.

The significance of the availability of common law contempt was first recognized in *The Independent* case (see 5.4.7.7). The Court of Appeal was satisfied that the publication was prejudicial because it pre-empted the Attorney-General's action for breach of confidence against *The Observer* and *The Guardian*; but there were no proceedings in that action which were 'active' within Sch. 1. Nevertheless, the Court of Appeal said that *The Independent* could still be liable if the editor could be said to have had an intention to prejudice. This meant a specific intention, not simply recklessness. On the other hand, the Court of Appeal said that intention must be approached here in the same way as in other areas of the criminal law. On the basis of the homicide cases of *R* v *Moloney* [1985] 1 All ER 1025, and *R* v *Nedrick* [1986] 3 All ER 1, intention could be (but did not have to be) inferred if the editor could be shown to have foreseen the prejudice as a virtual certainty as a result of the publication. On this basis the case was sent back to the trial judge, who found the editor of *The Independent* guilty of contempt (*In Re Attorney-General* v *The Observer Ltd and Guardian Newspapers Ltd, The Times*, 9 May 1989). The editor's evidence had shown that although he did not desire to be in contempt, he was aware that the publication would do precisely what the court had said should not be done, and that a person should not knowingly frustrate the purpose of the court, because this would interfere with the administration of justice.

In the case of *Attorney-General* v *Observer Ltd* [1988] 1 All ER 385, it was held that intention does not require that it was the publisher's purpose or desire to cause prejudice. In that case it was ruled, following *The Independent* case, that it would be contempt under the common law for a library to stock a copy of *Spycatcher*. A slightly different line was taken by the majority of the Court of Appeal in *Attorney-General* v *Punch* [2001] EWCA Civ 403, [2001] 2 All ER 655 (the facts of which are given at 5.4.7.7). They held that the Attorney-General needed to prove that the editor knew 'that the publication would interfere with the course of justice by defeating the purpose underlying the injunctions' (para. 115, p. 684), and that the editor may have misunderstood the Attorney-General's purpose. The House of Lords, however, disagreed with the Court of Appeal's approach to the intention issue in this case: [2002] UKHL 590, [2003] 1 All ER 289. In the light of its view on the *actus reus* of the offence (see 5.4.7.7) it held that the editor must have appreciated that what he was doing was precisely what the order was intended to prevent. This was, therefore, knowing interference with the administration of justice, and contempt under the common law. The penalty imposed by the trial judge (i.e. a fine of £5,000) was restored.

The common law has also been relied on where there was a risk of prejudice to a criminal trial. In *Attorney-General* v *News Group Newspapers* [1988] 2 All ER 906 (*The Sun* case), *The Sun* had taken up the case of an eight-year-old alleged to have been raped by a doctor, supporting both financially and through its columns a private prosecution (which in fact resulted in the doctor's acquittal). Before these proceedings became active *The Sun* published on successive days articles attacking the doctor in very emotive language. His photograph was printed on the front page. Watkins LJ could not accept that an experienced editor 'could have failed to have foreseen that the material which he published...would incur a real risk of prejudicing the fairness of a trial of Dr. B'. On this basis the editor of *The Sun* was guilty of contempt under the common law.

These cases dealt with the role of the common law when there are no active proceedings. It is unclear whether proceedings must nevertheless be 'pending or imminent' (the old common law test for strict liability contempts). Watkins LJ in *The Sun* case doubted whether it was necessary, and a two-judge Divisional Court split on the issue in *Attorney-General* v *Sport Newspapers* [1992] 1 All ER 503.

Intentional contempt can operate alongside strict liability contempt. This possibility was recognized by the House of Lords in *Re Lonrho* [1990] 2 All ER 1100, though it was not applied as the House did not think there was any contempt at all. In *Attorney-General* v *Hislop* [1991] 1 QB 514, the Court of Appeal said that articles published by the magazine *Private Eye* were intended to put improper pressure on Mrs Sonia Sutcliffe (the wife of the 'Yorkshire Ripper') to discontinue a libel action against the magazine. The libel proceedings were active, and the articles therefore constituted contempt under both the common law, and the strict liability rule.

This increase in the use of common law contempt, particularly in situations where the strict liability rule can also apply, is worrying. One of the important reforms contained in the CCA 1981 was the introduction of the defences under ss 4 and

5. Both of these only operate under the strict liability rule. If the Attorney-General chooses to use the common law instead, as in *Attorney-General* v *Hislop*, then these defences are unavailable. The danger of this happening is increased by the broad definition of 'intention', as capable of being inferred from 'foresight'. Although this definition is in line with that operating in other areas of criminal law, it is submitted that there is a case here (given that Parliament has specifically provided for strict liability in certain circumstances) for limiting intention to 'purpose'. This would be in line with the restriction of the availability of the defences to the situation where the publisher acts in good faith. A deliberate attempt to affect the outcome of proceedings by improper means cannot be regarded as being published 'in good faith'. On the other hand, the fact that an editor has foreseen a possible risk of prejudice should not automatically preclude reliance on s. 5 if the matter is one of public concern. This situation is one which may be affected by the HRA 1998. In applying the common law of contempt the courts will now be obliged to take account of ECHR jurisprudence on the area which, as we have seen, clearly requires them to balance the relevant public interests. Although the fact that common law contempt will always involve an 'intentional' contempt which may weight the balance in favour of restriction, the public interest in freedom of expression cannot be ignored entirely. It is certainly arguable that in a case where the common law is being used in relation to a situation which could have been dealt with under the CCA 1981, the HRA 1998 should now lead the court to take into account the public interest before deciding whether the offence has been proved.

The wide use of the common law also threatens another advantage of the CCA 1981, i.e. the certainty introduced to the *sub judice* rule by the concept of 'active' proceedings. Indeed, if the obiter suggestions in *The Sun* case, and *Attorney-General* v *Sport Newspapers*, that proceedings need not even be 'imminent', are taken up, the law will run the risk of being even more uncertain than prior to the CCA 1981. This is another situation which might be affected by the HRA 1998. One of the requirements of Art. 10(2) is certainty. If a publisher is unable to be certain at the time of publication whether proceedings are sufficiently close for the Divisional Court to decide that a contempt may be committed, then there is a strong argument that the law is insufficiently certain to allow it to be used to penalize the publisher. It may well be, therefore, that the HRA 1998 will have the effect of curtailing the development of the common law of contempt, and encourage the Attorney-General to rely on the CCA 1981. That this might be the approach taken was, however, contradicted by the response of the Attorney-General, Lord Goldsmith, in the Autumn of 2003, in relation to widespread stories in the media that a girl had been raped by certain unnamed footballers. Although no formal action had been taken against anyone, he was reported as saying (*The Guardian*, 1 October 2003):

> Although there have not yet been any arrests, and there may not be any, if there are to be criminal proceedings...editors should not engage in conduct, nor publish material, including comment, that may create a substantial risk of serious prejudice to the course of justice in these proceedings.

Although Lord Goldsmith was here using the language of s. 2 of the CCA 1981 (i.e. strict liability contempt), since at the time there were no 'active' proceedings, the only possible basis for an action for contempt in relation to publications at that time would have been under the common law.

The strict line being taken with the media by Lord Goldsmith was to some extent undermined the following month when the Home Secretary, Mr Blunkett, made some comments following the arrest of a person on suspicion of involvement in terrorism, which could be read as presuming guilt, in that he suggested that the person had an established link to Al-Qa'ida (see *The Guardian*, 29 November 2003). The Attorney-General responded by saying that he would investigate what Mr Blunkett had said, but this, not surprisingly, did not lead to any further action.

5.4.10 **Disobeying court rulings**

As noted at 5.4.1, the main restrictions on publications arise out of criminal contempts, which are likely to have an effect on the outcome of proceedings. The CCA 1981 also recognizes two situations where a publication may amount to civil contempt, in that it involves disobedience to a court order.

5.4.10.1 **Section 4(2): reports of proceedings**

We have seen that under s. 4(1) of the CCA 1981, contemporaneous reports of legal proceedings may generally be published without fear of contempt. Under s. 4(2) the court has a power in certain circumstances to order the postponement of the publication of such reports. The grounds for postponement are that the report would create a substantial risk to the administration of justice in the proceedings which are the subject of the report, or to other proceedings pending or imminent. Note that the power is only to postpone, not to impose a permanent ban. This was confirmed recently by the Court of Appeal in *Re Times Newspapers* [2007] EWCA Crim 1925, where the trial judge had purported to make a s. 4(2) order postponing indefinitely any reporting of a question and answer given in open court by one of the accused. The Court of Appeal held that this was *ultra vires*. The appropriate way to achieve the judge's objective would have been an order under s. 11 of the CCA 1981 (see 5.4.10.2).

The circumstances in which it is envisaged that the s. 4(2) power might need to be used is where, for example, evidence has been heard in the absence of the jury, in order to decide on its admissibility, or where there are other proceedings pending which involve one of the parties to the current proceedings, and which might be adversely affected by reports of them.

This new power was seized on with some avidity by courts at all levels, and in 1983 a Practice Note was issued to try to curb what was seen as an over-use of the section. The requirements laid down by the Lord Chief Justice were:

(a) the order should be put into writing by the judge or the clerk of the court;

(b) it should be in precise terms, indicating its scope;

(c) it should state the time at which it will cease to have effect; and

(d) it should state the specific purpose of making the order.

A 'blanket order' at the start of the trial postponing all reporting should not generally be made. The court should limit the scope of the order to what is necessary to prevent prejudice: *R v Horsham Justices, ex p Farquharson* [1982] QB 762. It was confirmed by the Divisional Court in *R v Clerkenwell Magistrates' Court, ex p Telegraph plc* [1993] 2 All ER 183 that the press and other news media should normally be allowed to make representations to the judge or magistrate who is considering making an order. The magistrate in this case had refused to hear anyone apart from the parties. Although it was within his discretion to act in this way, the Divisional Court indicated that representatives of the media would generally be in the best position to represent the public interest in reporting proceedings, which was clearly a factor of which the magistrate or judge needed to take account. The order issued by the magistrate was quashed, and the case returned to him for reconsideration.

Where a valid order is made, any breach of it will amount to contempt. In the *Horsham Justices* case, Lord Denning argued that breach of a s. 4 order should only constitute contempt if it created a risk of prejudice. The majority of the Court of Appeal, however, ruled that the breach was in itself contempt, irrespective of any effects of the publication, and this must be regarded as representing the current position. It was accepted as being so by Brooke J in *Attorney-General v Guardian Newspapers* (p. 48), although this case also made it clear that criticizing the making of a s. 4(2) order, rather than breaking its terms, cannot in itself be regarded as contempt. It is not clear, however, that the principle that breach of an order 'automatically' leads to contempt would be held to be 'Convention compatible' under the HRA 1998. The ECHR cases in this area require restrictions on freedom of expression to be both 'proportionate' to the legitimate aim pursued and to take account of all the relevant public interests. This suggests that there should in every case be a balancing of arguments as to whether a particular publication should be penalized as contemptuous, even if it has involved breach of a s. 4(2) order. It may well be, therefore, that the approach taken by Lord Denning in the *Horsham Justices* case will now be the one which should be preferred.

Despite the attempts by the Attorney-General and the Lord Chief Justice to indicate that s. 4 orders should be made with caution, they have continued to cause problems for the press and broadcasters. In *Re Central Independent Television plc* [1991] 1 All ER 347, the judge made an order restricting reporting so that the jury who had to spend the night in a hotel considering their verdict, would be able to watch television and listen to the radio. The Court of Appeal ruled that this was not an appropriate use of the power. The objective of the order could have been achieved by restricting the jurors' access to the broadcasts, and it was not therefore necessary in the interests of the administration of justice. Similarly, in *ex p Telegraph plc* Lord Taylor emphasized the careful nature of the balance to be made between the 'competing public considerations of ensuring a fair trial and of open justice' (p. 976), and that restrictions should only be imposed where 'necessary'. This did not simply mean asking whether the imposition of restrictions was the only way to avoid the risk, but also whether the risk was one which was sufficiently serious for it to be necessary in the interests of justice to avoid it. Applying that approach, the Court of Appeal reduced the scope of the judge's order so that it applied simply to the identities of the accused, and not to any other material. The issue of postponing the reporting of any proceedings which took place in the absence of the jury should be considered if and when it arose.

The need for a balancing of the issues was also emphasized in *R v Beck, ex p Daily Telegraph* [1993] 2 All ER 177. Beck had been a social worker in charge of children's homes in Leicester. He was charged with a large number of offences involving sexual and physical abuse. As a result of the number of charges, the trial was split into three. The judge at the first trial made a s. 4(2) order, because of the risk of prejudice to the subsequent trials. On appeal, the Court of Appeal accepted that there was a substantial risk of this kind. This was not the end of the matter, however, because the public interest in the reporting of trials had also to be considered. In the circumstances of this case, the court felt (p. 182):

> [t]here must ... inevitably be widespread public concern, not only in Leicester but generally, over the circumstances in which those in public service have the opportunity to commit such offences, and why, notwithstanding complaints on the part of the victims, nothing whatever was done about it. Is it right in those circumstances, we ask ourselves, that this trial should proceed without the public having any opportunity of knowing what is going on?

Having balanced this consideration against the risk of prejudice to the defendant, the court concluded that the s. 4(2) order should be lifted. In other words, the freedom of expression arguments outweighed those concerned with the administration of justice. This approach was developed by Lindsay J in *MGN Pension Trustees Ltd* v *Bank of America National Trust and Savings Association* [1995] 2 All ER 355. In this case the s. 4(2) order was sought in civil proceedings concerning breach of trust, where some of the defendants were likely to be tried on criminal charges of fraud, arising out of the same facts. Lindsay J identified three questions which had to be asked (p. 361):

> (i) is there a substantial risk of prejudice to the administration of justice in the criminal trials; if so, (ii) does it appear to be necessary for avoiding that risk that there should be made some order postponing publication of report of the civil actions and if so (iii) ought the court in its discretion to make any and, if so, what order.

'Necessary' in the second question means more than merely 'convenient': it requires that prejudice cannot be avoided without an order. The third question allows the judge to consider the broader issues of public interest of the kind used in *Beck*, so that even if there is a risk which can properly be described as substantial, which could only be avoided by making an order, it does not automatically follow that a postponement order should be made. On the facts, however, Lindsay J held that there was not in this case a 'substantial risk of prejudice', so that the argument for an order fell at question (i).

The requirements to balance the needs of justice, and the defendant's right to a fair trial under Art. 6 of the ECHR, against the potential infringement of the Art. 10 rights of the press, was again emphasized in *The Telegraph Group plc* [2001] EWCA Crim 1075, [2001] 1 WLR 1983. In deciding whether to make an order the court should ask: (a) whether the publication of the relevant material would create a 'not insubstantial' risk to the administration of justice; if so (b) whether a s. 4(2) order was 'necessary' to eliminate the risk; and if so, (c) whether the risk should nevertheless be tolerated as the 'lesser of two evils' (para. 22).

5.4.10.2 Section 11: matters not disclosed in court

Section 4 deals with the restriction of the reporting of matters disclosed in court. Section 11 recognizes a power in certain situations to forbid the publication of matters which were *not* disclosed in the course of a trial. The section says that where a court has the power to allow information to be withheld from the public during the course of proceedings, and exercises that power, then it may also give directions prohibiting the publication of that information outside the court. There must be a deliberate decision that information should not be given. Matters that simply have not been referred to cannot be included within in a s. 11 order. This is the effect of the Court of Appeal's decision in *Re Trinity Mirror plc* [2008] EWCA Crim 50, where the judge at a sentencing hearing made a s. 11 order in relation to disclosure of information which might identify the children of the defendant. The Court of Appeal held that this was not an appropriate use of the power, and the order was *ultra vires*.

Section 11 does not give any guidance as to when the court has the power to keep things secret within the court. This falls to be determined by the common law. Such a power has been recognized in relation to blackmail trials (*R v Socialist Worker* [1975] QB 637), and trials involving national security issues (*Attorney-General* v *Leveller Magazine* [1979] 1 All ER 745), but the categories are presumably not closed. It was held in *R v Westminster City Council, ex p Castelli, The Times*, 14 August 1995, however, that it was not appropriate to use the power simply in order to protect the privacy of a litigant. Applicants for judicial review of a decision by a local authority in relation to its duties under the Housing Act 1985 wished to prevent the fact that they were HIV-positive being published in reports of the case. The judge refused to make an order under s. 11. In *R v Hasan (Aytach)* [2005] UKHL 22, [2005] 2 AC 467 the Court of Appeal had purported to make an order under s. 11 preventing the disclosure of certain information disclosed in the Crown Court trial other than in a complete report of the judgment or in a legal journal. The House of Lords held that it had no power to make such an order, where it related to evidence which had been given in open court, and had been referred to by the judge in his summing up. A slightly different approach was taken by the Court of Appeal in *Re Times Newspapers*. In the course of a trial under the Official Secrets Act 1989 the judge had made an order under s. 8 of the Official Secrets Act 1920 allowing the exclusion of the public from the giving of any evidence that might prejudice national security. By mistake, during the defendant's evidence in chief, a question and answer were given which should have formed part of the *in camera* proceedings. The judge purported to deal with this by an order under s. 4(2) of the CCA 1981 but, as discussed (see 5.4.10.1) the Court of Appeal held that this was inappropriate, since it could not justify a ban extending beyond the end of the trial. The Court of Appeal thought, however, that a s. 11 order could have been made to achieve the same result, because (para. 23):

> . . . [t]he question and answer fell within the category of evidence that the judge had ordered should be withheld from the public by his ruling under section 8(4) of the OSA. It was open to him to make an order under section 11 of the CCA that embraced the question and answer, notwithstanding that the question and answer had, by mistake, been heard in public.

The Court of Appeal does not seem to have been referred to the House of Lords' decision in *Hasan's* case. If it had, it would have been expected that it would have distinguished it. The fact that it did not means that the decision on this point in

Re Times Newspapers must be of doubtful authority, since it could be regarded as being *per incuriam*.

Turning to examples of situations where such an order is clearly appropriate, in *R v Socialist Worker* witnesses in a blackmail trial were allowed to be identified as 'Mr X' and 'Mr Y'. The judge indicated that they were not to be identified in any publication outside the court. The *Socialist Worker* purported to identify the witnesses. This was held to amount to contempt under the common law in that it would deter potential blackmail victims from giving evidence in the future, and in any case flouted the authority of the court. It would now constitute contempt as a breach of a s. 11 direction. It is unclear whether it would *automatically* do so in the same way as a breach of s. 4. In *Attorney-General v Leveller* a failure to comply with a direction not to disclose the name of an army officer identified in court as simply 'Colonel B', was held by the House of Lords not to constitute contempt, since the direction was made before the colonel gave evidence, and that evidence had made his identity obvious. The court had not re-issued the direction after this evidence had been given, and there was therefore no contempt in publishing the colonel's real name. It is to be hoped that the courts would adopt the same approach to a breach of a s. 11 direction.

In *Re Times Newspapers*, the judge also made an order under s. 11 preventing publications that would, or might, reveal evidence which had been subject to his *in camera* order. The Court of Appeal held that there was no power to make an order in relation to material which 'might' have this effect. It commented that such an order (para. 31):

> ...would appear to cover a publication based on speculation but which did not make it plain that it was mere speculation as to the evidence that was given *in camera* that was, in fact, wholly inaccurate. We do not consider that such a publication could fall within the wording of section 11. It would not be the publication of the name or matter withheld. Nor would prohibition be necessary for the purpose for which the name or matter was withheld, namely to prevent it becoming known to the public in the interests of national security.

The judge's order under s. 11 was amended to remove the word 'might'.

A direction under s. 11, if valid, may be permanent in its effect, and so there is no need to indicate how long it is to last. In all other respects, however, the issue of the direction should follow the requirements of the 1983 Practice Note, outlined at 5.4.10.1 in relation to s. 4.

5.4.10.3 **Challenging orders under ss 4(2) and 11**

The method of challenging an order under either s. 4 or s. 11 will depend on the court issuing it. If it is made by magistrates, or some other inferior court which is subject to the jurisdiction of the High Court, the appropriate method of challenge is by judicial review. In *R v Arundel Justices, ex p Westminster Press* [1985] 2 All ER 390, for example, a s. 11 direction issued by magistrates was held to be *ultra vires*, in that it related to information which had been disclosed in the proceedings. If, however, the order is issued during a trial on indictment, judicial review will not be available, because the High Court has no jurisdiction over the Crown Court: *R v Central Criminal Court, ex p Crook, The Times*, 8 November 1984. There was for a time, therefore, no way of challenging an order issued by a Crown Court judge. Now, however, s. 159 of the Criminal Justice Act 1988 gives a right of appeal to the Court of Appeal in this situation. Where such an appeal takes place the Court of Appeal should decide the issue on its merits, not simply review the judge's exercise of his discretion. This was the view of the Court of Appeal in *R* v *Beck, ex p Daily Telegraph plc* [1993] 2 All ER 177, p. 180, and was confirmed by the same court in *The Telegraph Group plc* [2001] EWCA Crim 1075, [2001] 1 WLR 1983. This seems to mean that there are more extensive powers of review in relation to a Crown Court judge's decision than that of a magistrate, where the means of challenge is by judicial review. It seems hard, however, to justify such a distinction between the two types of proceedings.

5.5 Protecting journalists' sources

Journalists will generally claim that it is necessary for the proper performance of their role that they are allowed to keep their sources secret. The argument is that they will not get information, for example, about abuses of power within government, or dubious business practices, unless insiders feel able to reveal what is going on without the risk of their identity being disclosed. Journalists will, however, run the risk of being in contempt if they refuse to reveal the name of a source in legal proceedings. The need to provide journalists with some protection has long been recognized, but this is now given statutory form in s. 10 of the CCA.

The section allows a person to refuse to disclose 'the source of information contained in a publication for which he is responsible', unless it is 'necessary in the interests of justice or national security, or for the prevention of disorder or crime'.

The precise scope of the section has been considered in a number of cases since the Act. Some of the decisions have taken a broad view as to its application. The overall effect, however, has been to narrow down the number of situations in which the journalist or publisher will be protected.

Looking first at the positive side, it was held in *Secretary of State for Defence* v *Guardian Newspapers* [1985] AC 339, that the section applied to an indirect disclosure of a source. The Secretary of State had brought an action to recover a document from *The Guardian*, which had been leaked from his department. *The Guardian* resisted this action, although the document was clearly the property of the Ministry of Defence, on the basis that markings on it would probably enable the Ministry to identify the source of the leak. The House of Lords agreed that, although in this case even *The Guardian* itself was unaware of the identity of its informant, it was entitled to plead s. 10 to avoid indirectly disclosing this information. As we shall see, however, the House felt that on the facts the Secretary of State was able to bring his claim within one of the exceptions to the section.

The section requires the disclosure to be 'necessary' if one of the exceptions is to apply. In *Maxwell* v *Pressdram* [1987] 1 All ER 656 the Court of Appeal emphasized that this did not mean 'important' or 'relevant'. In this case the information was sought in order to show that the defendants in a libel action had made false statements either recklessly or knowingly, and had persisted in a defence of 'justification' simply to avoid an interim injunction. The Court of Appeal thought that these matters could adequately be dealt with by the trial judge in his direction to the jury as to the availability of aggravated or exemplary damages, and that disclosure was, therefore, not necessary.

The rest of the reported decisions on s. 10 have tended to go in favour of disclosure. First, in *Secretary of State for Defence* v *Guardian Newspapers* the House of Lords held that the interests of national security could prevail even if it was agreed that the leaked document did not prejudice it. It was enough that a civil servant in the Ministry of Defence might have leaked a document for the national security issue to be raised.

Second, in *Re an Inquiry under the Company Securities (Insider Dealing) Act 1985* [1988] AC 660, the House of Lords held that the interests of the prevention of crime did not require the person seeking disclosure to identify any particular crime or crimes that might be committed. It was enough if disclosure might help generally in the prevention of future insider dealing, etc.

Third, in *X Ltd* v *Morgan Grampian (Publishers) Ltd* [1991] 1 AC 1, the House of Lords again held that the interests of justice were not limited to interests arising in the course of legal proceedings. It covered also the ability to exercise important legal rights. Lord Bridge gave the following example:

> [I]f an employer of a large staff is suffering grave damage from the activities of an unidentified disloyal servant, it is undoubtedly in the interests of justice that he should be able to identify him in order to terminate his contract of employment, notwithstanding that no legal proceedings may be necessary to achieve that end.

With respect to Lord Bridge, this seems in itself to open a gaping hole in the protection afforded by s. 10. Taken together with the other two House of Lords decisions it would mean that the situations in which journalists would now be able to rely on the protection of the section would be very small in number. (See also T. R. S. Allan, 'Disclosure of Journalists' Sources, Civil Disobedience and the Rule of Law' [1991] CLJ 131.) The issues raised by this case were considered by the ECtHR in *Goodwin* v *United Kingdom* (1996) 22 EHRR 123. The full facts were that the journalist, William Goodwin, had received confidential and sensitive information about the financial position of T Ltd. Goodwin telephoned T to check the accuracy of what he had received, and to solicit comments from the company, with a view to publication of an article in a magazine. T Ltd at once obtained an injunction restraining the publication of any of the information held by Goodwin. The company also wished, however, to trace the source of the leak of the information. It obtained from the High Court an order directing Goodwin to disclose his source. Goodwin refused to do so, and was subsequently held by the judge to be in contempt. Goodwin appealed against the order to disclose his source, but this was rejected by both the Court of Appeal and, as we have seen, the House of Lords. Goodwin was fined £5,000 for his contempt by the High Court. He then appealed to the ECtHR, claiming a breach of Art. 10. The Commission upheld this claim, and the European Court agreed, by a majority of 11 to 7, that there was a breach of this Article ((1996) 22 EHRR 123). The Court took the view that the requirement to disclose a source 'in the interests of justice' was sufficiently well established to be regarded as being 'prescribed by law'. It also held that the order of the court was taken in pursuit of a legitimate aim, i.e. the protection of the rights of T Ltd. The crucial issue, therefore, was whether the order to disclose was 'necessary in a democratic society' for the protection of those interests. The Court noted that the 'protection of journalistic sources is one of the basic conditions for press freedom' (para. 39). Consequently an order to disclose a source 'cannot be compatible with Article 10 of the Convention unless it is justified by an overriding requirement in the public interest' (para. 39). The Court noted that the main objective of maintaining the confidentiality of the information concerning T Ltd's business had been achieved by the issue of injunctions prohibiting publication. In that context, was it also necessary to require disclosure of the source? The Court did not think so (para. 45):

> On the facts of the present case, the Court cannot find that T's interests in eliminating, by proceedings against the source, the residual threat of damage through the dissemination of the confidential information otherwise than by the press, in obtaining compensation and in unmasking a disloyal employee or collaborator were, even if considered cumulatively, sufficient to outweigh the vital public interest in the protection of the applicant journalist's source.

The means adopted were, in other words, disproportionate to the legitimate ends being pursued, and there was therefore a violation of Goodwin's right to freedom of expression under Art. 10.

This decision gave strong support to the right of journalists not to disclose their sources, other than in the most pressing cases. It confirms that this right is part of the right to freedom of expression. English courts applying s. 10 of the CCA in future, as a result of the HRA 1998, will be required to pay careful attention to the approach taken by the ECtHR in this case. Cases post-*Goodwin* have not, however, always seen the English courts being keen to uphold the refusal to disclose.

In *Saunders* v *Punch* [1998] 1 All ER 231 Lindsay J did refuse to order disclosure, though without placing any great weight on *Goodwin*, other than adopting a passage from it relating to the 'high importance' in a democratic society of the journalist's right to refuse disclosure. But he came to his decision on the basis of the English cases, rather than as a result of applying Art. 10 of the ECHR. The applicant had sought disclosure because an article in *Punch* magazine suggested that notes of meetings between the applicant and his solicitor might have been revealed. The judge, however, thought that an injunction restraining further publications of the same kind provided adequate protection for the applicant, and that the balance of interests was, therefore, against requiring the magazine to reveal its source. Similarly, in *John* v *Express Newspapers* [2000] 3 All ER 257 the Court of Appeal (again without relying on Art. 10 of the ECHR) overturned a judge's order for disclosure where a newspaper had obtained a draft of junior counsel's opinion in pending legal proceedings. The judge had attached more significance than was justified on the facts to the interests of justice and the need to protect legal professional privilege.

In *Camelot Group plc* v *Centaur Communications Ltd* [1998] 1 All ER 251, by contrast, disclosure was ordered (or rather the return of documents which would have the effect of enabling the claimant to identify the source). The case concerned the 'leaking' of draft accounts of Camelot which runs the National Lottery. The information caused considerable bad publicity for the company and attracted criticism from the government. The Court of Appeal, in considering whether the material should be returned, did pay careful attention to the European Court's decision in *Goodwin*, as well as the views of the House of Lords in *X Ltd v Morgan Grampian (Publishers) Ltd* [1991] 1 AC 1. It came to the somewhat surprising conclusion that both courts were applying the same principles, and that the main difference probably came from their respective view of the facts. Applying these principles, it held that s. 10 of the CCA should not be used to restrict the return of the documents to Camelot. In coming to this conclusion, the court felt that it was relevant that there was no great public interest in the early publication of accounts, which in any case would have been published by the company a week later. Against that Camelot had a legitimate interest in identifying an untrustworthy employee. The potential 'chilling' effect on what is communicated to journalists unable to guarantee anonymity to their sources, was dismissed on the basis that there never has been a 'blanket' rule protecting such sources, and that disclosure of the source has always been possible in some cases.

This decision is disappointing in that it pays lip service to the importance of the press in a democratic society, but then concentrates far too closely on the facts of the individual case without fully recognizing the wider implications of compelling a journalist to disclose a source. The *Goodwin* decision should have been seen as giving a message to the English courts about their approach to this issue, as displayed in *X Ltd v Morgan Grampian (Publishers) Ltd*; instead it was treated as just one court's view of a particular set of circumstances, and carrying no particularly strong weight in applying domestic law. It was to be hoped that the coming into force of the HRA 1998 might have led to a reconsideration of the English courts' approach, with a recognition that decisions of the ECtHR need to be given more weight than those of the House of Lords, difficult as it may be for that change to be accepted. The opportunity for such a reconsideration occurred in *Ashworth Hospital Authority v MGN* [2002] UKHL 29, [2002] 4 All ER 193. The case concerned the publication in a newspaper published by MGN of information concerning Ian Brady, the 'Moors Murderer', who was being held at Ashworth Hospital, where he was on hunger strike. The article included extracts drawn from the hospital's database. There was no doubt that the material had been unlawfully downloaded from the database and passed to the journalist who wrote the article. The hospital obtained an order from the High Court ordering MGN to explain how it came into possession of Brady's medical records, and to identify any employee of the hospital and anyone else who was involved in enabling MGN to acquire such possession. The appeal against this order was heard in December 2000—that is, after the HRA 1998 had come into force.

The Court of Appeal had no doubt that, apart from the provisions of s. 10 of the CCA 1981 and Art. 10 of the ECHR, the hospital had the right to the information which it sought. What was the effect of s. 10 on this? The court specifically considered the question of whether the interpretation of the protection to journalists afforded by s. 10 adopted by the English courts was too narrow in the light of the European Court's approach to the area under Art. 10. The conclusion to which Lord Phillips MR came was as follows ([2001] 1 All ER 991, para. 97, p. 1012):

> I consider that Schiemann LJ [in the *Camelot* case] correctly identified that the European Court differed from the English courts in its view of the implications that non-disclosure would have for the plaintiff company. At the same time I am inclined to accept Mr Browne's submission that the decisions of the European Court demonstrate that the freedom of the Press has in the past carried greater weight in Strasbourg than it has in the courts of this country.

He noted that the European Court in *Goodwin* had taken the view that it was only in 'exceptional circumstances where vital public or individual interests are at stake' that an order requiring the disclosure of a journalist's sources could be justified. Nevertheless (para. 99):

> ...[t]he disclosure of confidential medical records to the Press is misconduct which is not merely of concern to the individual establishment in which it occurs. It is an attack on an area of confidentiality which should be safeguarded in any democratic society. The protection of patient information is of vital concern to the National Health Service and, I suspect, to health services throughout Europe. This is an exceptional case. If the order...discourages Press sources from disclosing similar information in the future, this will be no bad thing.

Thus, while giving slightly more acknowledgement to the importance of Art. 10 than has been the case in previous decisions, on the facts the conclusion (with which the rest of the court agreed) was that the sources should be disclosed. Laws LJ, in agreeing with Lord Phillips' conclusion, dissociated himself from any suggestion that in some circumstance it might be a good thing to impose a 'chilling effect' on the Press by requiring the disclosure of sources. The 'public interest in the non-disclosure of Press sources is constant' and does not vary with the type of information concerned (para. 101, p. 1012). Disclosure of such sources is always prima facie contrary to the public interest. The question is simply in all cases 'whether there is an overriding public interest, amounting to a pressing social need, to which the need to keep Press sources confidential should give way' (para. 101, p. 1012). On the facts, there was such an overriding public interest in this case.

There was a further appeal to the House of Lords ([2002] UKHL 29, [2002] 4 All ER 193). The House upheld the decision of the Court of Appeal, making two main points. First, that for the purposes of the procedural rules relating to disclosure, it was not necessary that the person against whom the order was sought should be a 'wrongdoer' who had committed a tort, breach of contract, crime, or other legal wrong. It was enough that the person had become 'involved' in the wrongdoing. Second, the House emphasized that the consequence of s. 10 of the Contempt of Court Act 1981 and Art. 10 of the ECHR (as interpreted in *Goodwin* v *United Kingdom*) was that the ordering of the disclosure of a journalist's sources could only be justified where the necessity for it was 'convincingly established' and following the 'most careful scrutiny by the Court' (para. 61). The situation must be exceptional if disclosure of sources is to be justified (para.

66). On the facts, however, Lord Woolf CJ, who delivered the leading speech, concluded (para. 66):

> The care of patients at Ashworth is fraught with difficulty and danger. The disclosure of patients' records increases that difficulty and danger and to deter the same or similar wrongdoing in the future it was essential that the source should be identified and punished. This was what made the orders to disclose necessary and proportionate and justified.

Thus, the House of Lords confirmed that the identity of the source should be disclosed. In coming to this conclusion Lord Woolf referred to the comments of Lord Phillips about the discouragement of disclosure being 'no bad thing'. Lord Woolf felt that this comment had been misinterpreted and simply meant that the wrongful disclosure of medical records was to be discouraged, rather than that the chilling effect of an order was 'no bad thing' (para. 65). It seems, therefore, that the approach of Laws LJ is to be regarded as correctly stating the position.

Following the decision of the House of Lords, the *Daily Mirror* disclosed its source. This turned out to be, not an employee of the hospital, but a freelance investigative journalist, Robin Ackroyd, who had in turn received the information from one or more employees at the hospital. Ackroyd had been paid by the *Daily Mirror*, but had not paid his sources anything for their information. It seems that their motives were purely the desire to reveal what they considered to be bad practice at the hospital as regards the treatment of Ian Brady. The Hospital sought an order compelling Ackroyd to disclose his source, but he refused. Gray J granted the Hospital's order without a full hearing of the issues, because he felt that the situation was covered by the decision of the House of Lords in the previous action. The Court of Appeal disagreed: *Mersey Care NHS Trust* v *Ackroyd* [2003] EWCA Civ 663, [2003] EMLR 36. It felt that Ackroyd's position was distinguishable. The decision in the action against the *Daily Mirror* was partly based on the assumption that there had been wrongdoing by an employee of the hospital in disclosing information for money. This was not in fact the case. The majority of the Court of Appeal felt that there was, in the new situation, an arguable case that the disclosure was justified in the public interest. Moreover, Ackroyd's position was distinguishable from that of the *Daily Mirror*. He had been involved previously in the exposure of (unrelated) ill-treatment of patients at Ashworth, which had been confirmed by an inquiry chaired by a judge. His activities as an investigative journalist were clearly dependent on being able to guarantee the anonymity of sources. A requirement to disclose in this case could have a chilling effect, which might outweigh the social need to preserve identity of sources. Finally, the Court unanimously took the view that the lapse of time since the disclosure (and the fact that there appeared to have been no similar disclosures since) might well tip the balance in favour of rejecting the order. It was wrong, therefore, for the judge to have issued the order without a full hearing of the issues. The Court of Appeal ordered that the case should proceed to trial. At the trial the judge accepted many of the points raised by the Court of Appeal in the preliminary action ([2006] EWHC 107). He found that there were significant factual differences between the positions of *Ackroyd* and *MGN*. In particular he noted that (para. 197):

...the hospital no longer contends that the source acted for money, with the result that I have had to find afresh what the purpose of the source was, and to re-assess the risk of further disclosures now, in the light of that fact, and in the light of the absence of any similar disclosures since 1999. The extent of the disclosure by the source was more limited than was previously understood to be the case. I have not found that the source was one of a number of people limited to 200, but that it is impossible to say how large the group is. I have not found that the source was probably an employee, although he or she may have been, and even if it was an employee, the numbers who have left the hospital since 1999 represent about a third of those who worked there in 1999. So the likelihood of the hospital being able to obtain the redress it seeks against the source is correspondingly diminished. In addition, the stance of Ian Brady has changed, and I have not found that the disclosure was made without his consent. Finally, unlike the courts in the MGN action, I have heard the evidence of Mr Ackroyd and have concluded that he was a responsible journalist whose purpose was to act in the public interest.

The lapse of time was also significant. He came to the conclusion that (para. 194) there was, in 2006, when he heard the case, no 'pressing social need that the sources should be identified', and that an 'order for the disclosure of the Defendant's sources would not be proportionate to the pursuit of the hospital's legitimate aim to seek redress against the source, given the vital public interest in the protection of a journalist's source'.

The Hospital appealed against this decision. The Court of Appeal held that the judge had taken into account all the relevant considerations ([2007] EWCA Civ 101, [2007] HRLR 19). There was no basis on which it could properly interfere with the balance which he struck (para. 81). The judge's decision to refuse to order disclosure was upheld (para. 85).

This judgment is clearly more favourable to journalists than some of the earlier decisions discussed. It is important that the Art. 10 issues have now been put in the forefront of discussion, with it being on the person seeking disclosure to convince the court that such disclosure would be necessary and proportionate (para. 80).

Less encouraging, however, was the approach of the Court of Appeal in *Financial Times Ltd v Interbrew SA* [2002] EWCA Civ 274, [2002] EMLR 446. Here, the Court of Appeal, purporting to apply the approach adopted by the Court of Appeal in *Ashworth* (and making very little detailed reference to *Goodwin v United Kingdom*), again held that the protection of press sources was overridden on the facts of the case. Here the order related to the return of documents relating to a takeover bid. The publication had created a 'false market' in the shares of the companies. Although it was recognized that the presumption was that disclosure should not be ordered, this case was again found to be one in which disclosure should be ordered. This was largely because of the risk of repetition, and the fact that the motives of the source were clearly 'maleficent' (Sedley LJ, para. 55). Leave to appeal was refused, and the decision was noted with approval by the House of Lords in the *Ashworth Hospital* case, which considered it to be another example of an 'exceptional' situation where disclosure was justified. When the case was considered by the Strasbourg Court, however, it held that there had been a violation of Art. 10: *Financial Times Ltd v United Kingdom* (2010) 50 EHRR 46. Although the order was 'prescribed by law' and had a 'legitimate aim' (the protection of the rights of others and of the disclosure of information received in confidence' (para. 58), it went beyond what was 'necessary in a democratic society'. The Court's conclusion was that (para. 71):

> [A]s in the *Goodwin* case, Interbrew's interests in eliminating, by proceedings against X, the threat of damage through future dissemination of confidential information and in obtaining damages for past breaches of confidence were, even if considered cumulatively, insufficient to outweigh the public interest in the protection of journalists' sources.

As a result of this re-affirmation of *Goodwin* by the Strasbourg Court, the Court of Appeal's decision in *Ackroyd*'s case provides the best indication of the way in which cases should be dealt with by the English courts in the future.

QUESTIONS

1   Is it justifiable that Art. 6 of the ECHR gives more extensive protection to criminal proceedings, as opposed to civil? What reasons might be given for this?

2   Is it satisfactory that some of the provisions of Art. 6 may be held to be overridden, where there is a justifiable reason (see, e.g. *O'Halloran* v *United Kingdom*)?

3   Why should there be controls over the reporting of legal proceedings? Why can't juries be trusted to ignore irrelevant information or argument?

4   Does the CCA 1981 meet the criticisms of the English law of contempt made by the ECtHR in the thalidomide litigation?

5   Is it satisfactory that common law contempt exists alongside the CCA 1981? Shouldn't 'intentional' contempt be brought within the legislative provisions?

6   Are the powers of the court to control publication of information about legal proceedings under ss 4(2) and 11 of the CCA 1981 compatible with the rights of a free press under Art. 10 of the ECHR?

7   Does s. 10 of the CCA 1981 provide sufficient and appropriate protection for journalists' sources?

FURTHER READING

Auld, Lord Justice (2001), *A Review of the Criminal Courts of England and Wales*, London: TSO

Barendt, E. and Hitchens, L. (2000), *Media Law Cases and Materials*, Harlow: Longman

Cram, I. (ed) (2010), *Borrie and Lowe's Law of Contempt*, 4th edn, London: Butterworths

Devonshire, P. (2003), '*Spycatcher* Returns to the House of Lords', (2003) 119 LQR 384

Eady, D. and Smith, A. T. H. (2005), *Arlidge, Eady and Smith on Contempt*, 3rd edn, London: Sweet & Maxwell

Haralambous, N. (2004), 'Investigating Impropriety in Jury Deliberation: A Recipe for Disaster?', (2004) 68 J Crim L 411

Miller, C. J. (2000), *Contempt of Court*, 3rd edn, Oxford: Oxford University Press

Phillimore, Sir Henry (1974), 'Report of the Committee on Contempt of Court', Cmnd 5794, HMSO

Robertson, G. (1993), *Freedom, the Individual and the Law*, 7th edn, Harmondsworth: Penguin

Robertson, G. and Nicol, A. (2008), *Media Law*, 5th edn, London: Penguin

Runciman Report (1993), 'Royal Commission on Criminal Justice', Cm 2263, HMSO

Smith, A. T. H. (2003), 'Third Parties and the Reach of Injunctions', (2003) 62 CLJ 241

Spilsbury, S. (2003), *Media Law*, London: Cavendish Publishing

Stone, R. (1988), 'Intentional Contempt and Press Freedom', (1988) 138 NLJ 423

6

Article 8: Right to Respect for Private Life

6.1 Introduction

Article 8 of the European Convention on Human Rights (ECHR) protects the right to respect for a person's private and family life, home, and correspondence. It is probably the most wide-ranging of all the rights in the Convention, covering such things as intrusions by the police onto private property, telephone tapping and surveillance, prisoners' rights to correspondence with their lawyers, the rights of aliens not to be deported, the right of access to information on abortion, and the right not have details of one's private life revealed by the press. This chapter does not attempt a comprehensive coverage of all the case law which is encompassed by Art. 8, though some of the areas are discussed in other chapters. This chapter starts by looking at some general issues, and then focuses on police powers of entry, search and seizure, and the privacy rights of the individual as against the press.

6.2 General issues

Article 8 is a qualified right. An interference by a public authority with this right will be justifiable if it is:

- in accordance with law; and
- necessary in a democratic society in the interests of:
  - national security;
  - public safety;
  - the economic well-being of the country;
  - the prevention of disorder or crime;
  - the protection of health or morals; or
  - the protection of the rights and freedoms of others

The requirement that the interference is 'in accordance with law' means, according to the European Court of Human Rights (ECtHR) that the law must be adequately accessible and foreseeable, that is, formulated with sufficient precision to enable the individual—if need be with appropriate advice—to regulate his or her conduct (see, e.g. *Gillan v United Kingdom* (2010) 50 EHRR 45, para. 76). The test of 'necessity in a democratic society' will include the requirement that the interference is

proportionate to the achievement of whichever of the legitimate grounds for interference (as listed in Art. 8(2)) is being used to justify it.

Article 8 not only requires the State to refrain from interfering with an individual's private life, etc. it also imposes a positive duty on a State to ensure that other
citizens do not unduly infringe those rights. The requirement here, as with other
positive obligations under the ECHR, will be to take reasonable steps to ensure
protection of the rights. In the areas covered by the rest of this chapter, the sections on entry, search and seizure, and surveillance, are largely concerned with a
State's negative duties, whereas the protection of individuals against press intrusion relates to the positive duty on a State to protect one citizen against the acts of
another.

6.3 Entry, search, and seizure

This section is primarily concerned with the situations where the law allows the
police, or other officials of the State, to enter a person's land, or to seize a person's
property, without permission, and the justifications for such infringements of the
individual's rights. It also deals with an area of increasing importance—that of surreptitious surveillance by the police or security services. This covers such things
as the tapping of telephones, the placing of 'bugging' devices on private premises,
or eavesdropping on private conversations by remote means. Some of these procedures will involve direct infringement of property rights; all involve potential
infringements of an individual's privacy and, therefore, are likely to raise issues of
compatibility with Art. 8. The order of treatment will be to look first at the situations where powers are given to interfere directly with an individual's property,
and then at the more indirect surveillance procedures.

6.4 Land and premises: rights of entry

The first group of powers to be considered relate to land and premises. We are looking here at powers which allow the police or others to enter premises against the
wishes of the owner, or other person having exclusive possession, and, in some
cases, to search those premises. The powers to seize things which are found on the
premises are considered at 6.6.

6.4.1 Trespass and licence

We are concerned in this chapter with entries without permission which, if they
take place without lawful authority, will amount to the tort of trespass. The tort
will not, however, be committed, if there is an express or implied licence to enter.
Express licences do not create too many problems. A police officer may be invited
in, for example, to discuss a possible criminal offence. It should be noted, however,
that an express licence can be created by conduct. In *Faulkner v Willetts* [1982]

Crim LR 453, the invitation to a police officer was deemed to have been made when the appellant's wife, having opened the door, and been told the reason for the officer's visit, left the door open and walked back into the house. No words of invitation to enter were uttered, but there was held to be an express licence to enter, created by conduct. Paragraph 5.1 of Code B of the Police and Criminal Evidence Act 1984 (PACE), however, requires that where a police officer wishes to carry out a search with consent, such consent should be given in writing on a special Notice of Powers and Rights. This notice is to be used, if practicable, wherever premises are to be searched by the police (para. 5.7 of Code B; see 6.4.3.2).

A licence to enter may also be implied in some situations. The scope of such an implied licence is limited, however. In *Robson* v *Hallett* [1967] 2 QB 939 it was held that there is an implied licence to go to the front door of a house where the entrant has legitimate business with the occupier. Entry to a front garden for this purpose will not, therefore, be a trespass. The purpose of the licence is to enable the entrant to deliver things to the premises, or to attract the attention of the occupier, and will presumably, therefore, also apply to the common parts of blocks of flats, in so far as these are not already 'public places' (see, e.g. *Knox* v *Anderton* (1983) 76 Cr App R 156 and *Rukwira* v *DPP* [1993] Crim LR 882).

An implied licence will not arise if the occupier makes it clear that particular visitors are not welcome. A notice stating 'Police Keep Out' would be likely to be effective for this purpose. Both an express or implied licence can be terminated by clear words indicating that it has been withdrawn. In *Lambert* v *Roberts* [1981] 2 All ER 15, for example, the words 'this is private property: you are trespassing' were held sufficient to terminate a licence. Mere verbal abuse of the visitor, however, may not be enough: *Snook* v *Mannion* [1982] Crim LR 601.

Once a licence has been withdrawn, the visitor who is already on the premises must be given a chance to leave. Reasonable force may then be used to expel the trespasser: *Davis* v *Lisle* [1936] 2 KB 434. If the trespasser is a police officer, forcible ejection will not amount to the offence of assault on a police constable in the execution of his duty, because the failure to comply with the termination of the licence will take the officer outside the scope of any lawful duty (*Davis* v *Lisle*). (The whole issue of licences in this context is discussed more fully in R. Stone, *The Law of Entry, Search, and Seizure*, 5th edn (Oxford: Oxford University Press, 2013), pp. 2–9.)

6.4.2 **Entry without warrant: common law**

As far as the police are concerned, the position as to entry to premises under the common law, against the wishes of the occupier, is governed by s. 17(5) and (6) of PACE. Section 17(5) states that, subject to subsection (6), 'all the rules of common law under which a constable has power to enter premises without a warrant are hereby abolished'. Subsection (6) then preserves 'any power of entry to deal with or prevent a breach of the peace'. This would appear to mean that the only power under the common law which is available to the police is therefore the power in relation to breaches of the peace. This interpretation of s. 17 was, however, rejected by the House of Lords in *R (on the Application of Rottman)* v *Commissioner of Police for the Metropolis* [2002] UKHL 20, [2002] 2 All ER 865. In this case the House of Lords held that s. 17 was really only concerned with powers of entry to arrest, and that the power to enter and search premises following an arrest (see, e.g. *Ghani* v *Jones* [1969] 3 All ER 1700) survived the enactment of PACE (though subject to ss 18 and 19 of that Act in relation to offences committed in England and Wales). This meant that the police did have a power, which they had purported to exercise in this case, to search the premises of a person who had been arrested under a warrant for extradition.

In practice, however, it is the breach of the peace power which provides the main non-PACE power of entry for the police. The meaning of 'breach of the peace' is discussed in chapter 3 (see 3.5.1). The same definition will apply here. How exactly does the power operate?

The power was considered in some detail in *Thomas* v *Sawkins* [1935] 2 KB 249. A public meeting was being held on private premises. It had previously been made clear to the police that their presence was not welcome. Nevertheless, two officers attended, and entered the premises where the meeting was held. It was clear that they did not have the permission of the organizers to be there, and so were not present on the basis of any licence. Indeed, one of the stewards of the meeting attempted to eject one of the officers, who resisted, with the assistance of his fellow officer. This led to a private prosecution for assault being brought against one of the officers. The Divisional Court was called on to decide whether the police officers' presence was lawful. It was held that it was. The case established that the police have the power to enter premises to deal with actual, or reasonably anticipated, breaches of the peace. The officers had such a reasonable apprehension in this case, so their presence was lawful, and their resistance to being expelled could not constitute an assault on the steward. This decision might be open to question in the light of the stress placed by the House of Lords in *R (Laporte)* v *Chief Constable for Gloucestershire* [2006] UKHL 55, [2007] 2 All ER 529 (see chapter 9 (9.6)) on the need for an anticipated breach of the peace to be 'imminent'—i.e. about to happen—before any action can be taken by the police. At the time the officers entered, or were asked to leave, the premises, was such a breach imminent? *Thomas* v *Sawkins* was not discussed in *Laporte*'s case.

This power applies not only to premises to which the public has been invited, but also to purely domestic situations. *McLeod* v *Commissioner of Police for the Metropolis* [1994] 4 All ER 553 concerned a dispute between husband and wife as to the removal of the husband's property from the matrimonial home following the break-up of their marriage. The husband, accompanied by police officers, went to the house to enforce a court order instructing the wife to hand over his property. The wife was not present, but the police went on to the property with the husband. It was held that they were entitled to do so provided that they reasonably believed that a breach of the peace was likely in the 'near future'.

Mrs McLeod took her complaint to the ECtHR (*McLeod* v *United Kingdom* (1999) 27 EHRR 493), alleging a breach of Art. 8. The Court held (perhaps surprisingly given the limited case law on the issue) that the power to enter private premises without a warrant to deal with or prevent a breach of the peace was defined with sufficient precision to meet the criterion of being 'in accordance with law' as required by Art. 8(2). Moreover, the police officers in this case were clearly pursuing the legitimate aim of preventing disorder or crime. The fundamental question, therefore, was whether English law, as applied by the Court of Appeal in this case, had struck a fair balance between Mrs McLeod's right to respect for her private life and home, and public interest in crime prevention. Two points were important. First, the court order did not empower Mr McLeod to enter the premises to recover his property, but rather required Mrs McLeod to hand it over. The police officers had not checked on what the court order did or did not allow. Second, once the police officers had become aware that Mrs McLeod was not on the premises it should have been clear to them that there was little or no risk of crime or disorder occurring. The use of the power in this case was, therefore, disproportionate to the end being pursued, and did amount to a breach of Art. 8 (though the Court did not award any compensation under Art. 50).

It is important to note that, although this case went in Mrs McLeod's favour, this was only on the basis of the particular circumstances in which the power had been used. The Court confirmed that the police were, in appropriate circumstances, entitled to enter and remain on private domestic premises to deal with actual or reasonably apprehended breaches of the peace without this necessarily involving any infringement of Art. 8 (see also the arrest cases of (*R* v *Lamb* [1990] Crim LR 58 and *Demetriou* v *DPP* [2012] EWHC 2443 Admin)).

The common law also recognized a general power of entry available to any citizen where a person called out for assistance against an attacker: *Handcock* v *Baker* (1800) 2 Bos & P 260. The powers of the police in this context, to the extent that they go beyond the power to deal with a breach of the peace, are now governed by s. 17(1)(e) of PACE (see 6.4.3.1). People other than police officers, however, presumably still have a power of entry on this basis under the common law.

6.4.3 Entry and search without warrant: PACE

PACE gives powers of entry and search without warrant to the police under three sections, namely, ss 17, 18, and 32. The first of these is concerned primarily with powers of arrest, the latter two deal with powers to enter and search premises in order to obtain or secure evidence. These powers will generally fall within the objective of preventing disorder or crime within Art. 8, and will be compatible with that Article, provided that they are used in a way which is proportionate to that objective.

6.4.3.1 Entry for the purpose of arrest, etc

Section 17 gives a number of powers of entry and search, mainly in connection with the exercise of powers of arrest. In each case the constable entering the premises must have reasonable grounds for believing that the person sought is on the premises (s. 17(2)(a)). First, the power is given to effect an arrest under warrant, or to execute a warrant of commitment under s. 76 of the Magistrates' Courts Act 1980 (this concerns those in default to the court, e.g. for not paying a fine). Second, the power may be used to arrest for any indictable offence (s. 17(1)(b)). Third, there are two summary public order offences in relation to which premises may be entered to effect an arrest, (s. 17(1)(c)). These are offences under s. 1 of the Public Order Act 1936 (prohibition on wearing political uniforms, see chapter 9 (9.4.8.4)), and s. 4 of the Public Order Act 1986 (fear or provocation of violence, see chapter 9 (9.4.5)). It is not clear why these particular offences justify this special power of entry, particularly given the powers in relation to a breach of the peace noted at 6.4.2. Fourth, as regards various 'squatting' offences under ss 6, 7,

8, and 10 of the Criminal Law Act 1977, s. 144 of the Legal Aid, Sentencing, and Punishment of Offenders Act 2013, and s. 76 of the Criminal Justice and Public Order Act 1994 (CJPOA 1994), s. 17(1)(c) of PACE gives a power of entry to carry out an arrest to an officer in uniform. It is easier to see the justification for this than the power relating to the public order offences, since 'squatters' are almost inevitably going to be on private premises. Fifth, the police may enter to arrest for offences under s. 4 of the Road Traffic Act 1988 (driving under the influence of drink or drugs) or s. 163 of the same Act (failure to stop). Sixth, there is a power to enter to arrest in relation to an offence under s. 27 of the Transport and Works Act 1992 (offences relating to drink or drugs). Seventh, there is a power of entry to arrest in relation to various summary offences related to the prevention of harm to animals under the Animal Welfare Act 2006, and for an offence under s. 61 of the Animal Health Act 1981 (rabies). Eighth, s. 17(1)(ca) gives a power of entry to arrest a child or young person who has been remanded or committed to local authority accommodation under s. 23(1) of the Children and Young Persons Act 1969. Finally, a power of entry is given to recapture a person who is 'unlawfully at large' and whom the police officer is pursuing. This will apply to those who have escaped from arrest, imprisonment, or other lawful custody. The application of the provision to persons detained under the Mental Health Act 1983, and the meaning of 'pursuit' were considered by the House of Lords in *D'Souza v DPP* [1992] 1 WLR 1073. A woman, who had a history of mental illness, had discharged herself from hospital after being detained under s. 6(2) of the Mental Health Act 1983. She went home. The police decided that she was 'unlawfully at large' and went to her home to 'recapture' her. The woman's husband and daughter forcibly resisted the police's entry, and were charged with assaulting a police officer in the execution of his duty. They were convicted, and the daughter appealed. The House of Lords held that the mother was within the scope of s. 17(1)(d), but the power under that section had to be exercised while 'in pursuit'. There was no evidence of a pursuit in this case. The police had simply formed an opinion as to where the woman was, and had gone to those premises to apprehend her. They were not in the execution of their duty when forcing entry, and the case was remitted to the Crown Court with a direction to dismiss the charge against the daughter. This case confirms that the provision applies to mental patients. It also limits the scope of the power, however. It cannot be used unless there is some pursuit of the fugitive. The result seems to be that the position under PACE is much the same as under the common law concept of entry in 'hot pursuit': *McLorie v Oxford* [1982] QB 1290.

In *O'Loughlin v Chief Constable of Essex* [1998] 1 WLR 374, the Court of Appeal held that the police should give reasons for the entry before exercising the right of entry by force under s. 17. The simple refusal to allow entry when reasons had not been given did not in itself justify the immediate use of force.

There is a final power of entry and search under s. 17(1)(e) which is not related to arrest. This is for the purpose of saving life or limb, or preventing serious damage to property and obviously covers the area which fell under the common law power recognized in *Handcock v Baker* (1800) 2 Bos & P 260 (see 6.4.2). It is unusual in that its exercise is not dependent on any reasonable belief or suspicion on the part of the police officer. Presumably, then, a genuine belief that entry without consent is necessary for one of the specified purposes is sufficient. There is no reason why the power should be this broad. It would have been perfectly satisfactory to make the power available here, as with the other powers in s. 17(1), only where the constable had reasonable grounds for believing it was necessary. Indeed, Art. 8(2) of the ECHR, which would presumably provide legitimacy for this power on the basis of its use to protect the rights of others, would almost certainly require that it should only be exercised on the basis of reasonable suspicion, in order to meet the requirement of being 'necessary in a democratic society'. Abuse of the power, therefore, would run the risk of challenge under the Human Rights Act 1998 (HRA 1998). The extent of the power under this subsection to enter to 'save life or limb' was considered in *Syed* v *DPP* [2010] EWHC 81, [2010] Cr App R 34. The police had gone to a house following a report of a disturbance from a member of the public. When they arrived there was no evidence of a disturbance. The appellant spoke to the officers on the threshold and told them that he had had a verbal argument with his brother. He became evasive when further questions were asked. The police sought entry on the basis of s. 17(1)(e), saying that they were concerned for the welfare of those on the premises. The appellant reacted violently, assaulting the officers. He was convicted of assaulting a police officer in the execution of his duty. On appeal, his conviction was quashed. The power under s. 17(1)(e) was meant to deal with serious cases, as indicated by its language. Concern for the welfare of someone on the premises was too low a threshold for the power to become available. The officers had, therefore, not been acting in the course of their duty in seeking entry under this power.

All the powers to search under s. 17 are limited to what is reasonable for the purpose for which the power of entry is exercised. Once the person sought, for example, has been discovered and apprehended, no further search will be justified under s. 17. If the police wish to search further in order to find evidence, or a weapon used by the person arrested, for example, they will have to rely on one of the other powers justifying search without warrant, under s. 18 or s. 32 (see 6.4.3.2).

6.4.3.2 Entry and search after arrest for an indictable offence

Under the original version of PACE there were two powers of entry and search without warrant, following an arrest. Section 18 covered arrests for arrestable offences. Section 32 gave a power in relation to any arrest. The changes brought in by the Serious Organised Crime and Police Act 2005, and effective from 1 January 2006, made the threshold for both sections an arrest for an indictable offence. The scope of s. 18 was therefore broadened, while s. 32 was narrowed. It means that there is now no power of entry following arrest in relation to, for example, the offence of assaulting a police officer (under s. 89 of the Police Act 1996), since this is triable only summarily.

There remain other differences in which the two powers may be used, in particular as regards the premises that may be entered, and the time of the entry. These will be examined.

The power under s. 18 has been widely used. The premises to which it relates are those which are occupied or controlled by the person who has been arrested. It is not enough that the police have a reasonable belief in such 'occupation or control'. In *Khan* v *Metropolitan Police Commissioner* [2008] EWCA Civ 723 the person arrested had given the police a false name and address. The police carried out a search of the named premises, relying on s. 18. The Court of Appeal upheld the view of the trial judge that the search was unlawful, so that the owner of the premises was entitled to damages for trespass.

The word 'controlled' is not defined. It may well cover a person's place of work, for example, thus permitting the search of an office, or locker. Does a landlord, however, 'control' premises which are let out to tenants? The word is not clear, and is potentially wide in scope. The vagueness that it entails is unfortunate. The power is to be supervised by an officer of the rank of inspector or above (s. 18(4)). Unless the power is exercised immediately following an arrest away from a police station, the inspector should give the officer who is to carry out the search a written authorization which can be taken and shown to anyone on the premises to be searched (s. 18(4); *R v Badham* [1987] Crim LR 202). Paragraph 6.7 of Code B provides for a standard form of Notice of Powers and Rights which should, if practicable, be used for this purpose. This is discussed further below. It is not sufficient for the authorization simply to be recorded in the inspector's notebook: *R v Badham*. Section 18(7) also requires the inspector to record the grounds for the search and the evidence sought. Where the person in occupation or control of the premises is in police custody at the time of the search, a record of the authorization, the grounds for the search, and the evidence sought, should be included in the custody record (s. 18(8)).

It will often be the case that the police officer arresting a suspect away from a police station will want to search premises under the s. 18 power immediately, and before taking the suspect to the police station. This is permitted by s. 18(5), where it is necessary for the effective investigation of the offence. In this case the officer conducting the search must, as soon as practicable, inform an officer of the rank of inspector or above that the search has taken place. That officer will then make the records relating to the search referred to above.

The power under s. 18 is to search premises on which there are reasonable grounds to believe there is evidence of the offence for which the suspect has been arrested, or of an indictable offence connected with or similar to that offence. 'Connected with' would include, for example, searching for evidence of the theft of a gun which had been used in a robbery for which the suspect was arrested. 'Similar to' would cover the situation, for example, where a person arrested for using a stolen credit card was suspected of having other stolen cards at home. It will not apply if, after arrest, the police, perhaps as a result of questioning the suspect, have reasonable grounds to believe that evidence of some totally unconnected offence will be found on premises. If the police wish to search under the s. 18 power in that situation they will have to arrest for the second offence.

The power may not be used to search for evidence which is subject to legal privilege (see 6.7.1.1). It can, however, be used to search for evidence for which it will not normally be possible to obtain a search warrant, that is, 'excluded' material (see 6.7.1.2) or 'special procedure' material (see 6.7.1.3).

The search must not extend beyond what is reasonably required for the purpose of discovering the evidence sought (s. 18(3)). If it is stolen computers, it will not be legitimate, therefore, to search desk drawers. If the items sought are small and easily hidden, however, for example, documents or drugs, there will be virtually no limit to the search. Once the items sought have been found the search should cease (para. 6.9A of Code B).

Section 32 gives a power to enter, following arrest for an indictable offence, in relation to the premises on which the arrest took place, or which the arrested person left immediately prior to the arrest. The power is broader than that under s. 18 in this respect, in that the premises do not have to be under the occupation or control of the arrested person. They may belong to an innocent third party who is not in any way subject to suspicion on the part of the police.

The power is to enter and search for evidence of the offence for which the person was arrested, and the officer concerned must have reasonable grounds for believing that such evidence will be found on the premises. This is narrower than s. 18 which, as we have seen, allows searches for evidence of 'connected' or 'similar' arrestable offences.

The wording of s. 32 does not indicate when the power may be used. In particular, it is not stated whether it must be used immediately following the arrest. In *R v Badham* [1987] Crim LR 202 the police tried to rely on the power as justifying an entry and search some four hours after the arrest. The Crown Court judge refused to accept this as a legitimate use of the power. Although it will be difficult to tell exactly where the line is to be drawn, the section does not confer an open-ended power to return to search premises where an arrest took place. It is intended to be an 'immediate' power. Any delay on the part of the police will, therefore, need very clear justification. It is submitted that once the arrested person has been taken to a police station the power under s. 32 should be regarded as expired. If the police subsequently wish to carry out a search, they will have to rely on s. 18 (if available), or seek a warrant.

6.4.3.3 Conduct of searches

Paragraph 6 of Code B sets out various provisions which apply to all searches. Searches should take place 'at a reasonable hour', unless this would be likely to frustrate the purpose of the search (para. 6.2). No definition is given of what is 'a reasonable hour'. A previous version of Code B stated that in deciding this, regard should be had as to when there is likely to be anybody on the premises. It stated that times when people are likely to be asleep should be avoided, unless this would be likely to frustrate the purpose of the search. In other words, it suggested that, unless there is good reason to act otherwise, searches should take place during the daytime, at a time when the premises are likely to be occupied by someone with power to grant entry. The requirement from Art. 8(2) of the ECHR and associated case law that infringements of private life can only be justified to the extent that they are necessary in democratic society, and proportionate to the aim being pursued, adds weight to such an approach. The current version of Code B omits these comments, but they would appear to remain relevant. The meaning of a 'reasonable hour' was considered by the Divisional Court in *Kent Pharmaceuticals Ltd v Director of the Serious Fraud Office* [2002] EWHC 3023 (Admin). The Court took the view that a search of domestic premises at 6 a.m. was at 'a reasonable hour'. Although Lord Woolf, LCJ, had some concerns about entering premises occupied by a family at such an early hour of the morning, he felt that it was also important the residents of the premises should be present when the warrant was executed. Since many people leave their home for work early in the morning, a search at 6 a.m. was not overall 'unreasonable'. In other words, it seems that the early hour of search was regarded as being beneficial to the householder, as it makes it more likely that he or she will be present at the time of search. It seems unlikely, however, that those families who do not normally rise until 7 a.m. or later would regard a knock on the door and a demand for entry at 6 a.m. as particularly reasonable. It must be also be questionable whether it would meet the requirements of Art. 8. In *Redknapp* v *City of London Police Commissioner* [2008] EWHC 1177 (Admin), [2009] 1 All ER 229, a warrant had been executed at a family home at 6 a.m. The Divisional Court refused to find that this was 'unreasonable' in the absence of specific evidence as to the operational needs of the exercise of the warrant. The Court appeared to be adopting a presumption of 'reasonableness', rebuttable by evidence to the contrary.

On arrival at the premises the officer in charge should normally attempt to communicate with someone who is entitled to grant access, and explain the authority under which entry is sought (para. 6.4 of Code B). The officer's identity should be given, and, if the officer is not in uniform, the officer's warrant card shown. The purpose of the search, and the grounds for undertaking it should also be stated (para. 6.5 of Code B). None of the above need be done, however, where the premises are known to be empty, or there are reasonable grounds for believing that to alert the occupants would frustrate the object of the search, or endanger the police officers or others (para. 6.4 (i)–(iii) of Code B). Reasonable and proportionate force may be used to gain entry in such cases, or where the occupier has refused to allow entry, or cannot be communicated with (para. 6.6 of Code C).

Once entry has been gained, the officer in charge should, if practicable, give the occupier a Notice of Powers and Rights, in the standard form set out in para. 6.7 of Code B. This should be done before any search begins, unless there are reasonable grounds for believing that to do so would frustrate the object of the search, or endanger the police officers or others (para. 6.8 of Code B). If the premises are unoccupied a copy of the Notice should be left in a prominent position.

The Notice should set out the power under which the search is taking place, and the extent of the powers of search and seizure being relied on. The rights of the occupier, and of the owner of any property seized, should be explained, as well as the possibility of compensation for damage, and where applications for this should be directed. Finally the Notice should state that a copy of the Code is available for inspection at any police station (para. 6.7 of Code B).

Paragraph 6.10 of Code B emphasizes that searches should be conducted 'with due consideration for the property and privacy of the occupier', and with 'no more disturbance than necessary'. If the occupier wants a friend, neighbour, or other person to witness the search this should generally be allowed (para. 6.11 of Code B). There is no need to delay a search for this purpose, however, and the officer in charge may refuse the request if there are reasonable grounds for believing that to comply would seriously hinder the investigation.

Finally, premises which have been entered by force, should be left secure (para. 6.13 of Code B).

We see here the general pattern of protection under PACE and its Codes of Practice repeated. The citizen is protected against the police by the requirements that the exercise of the powers is supervised by an officer of a particular rank (in the case of s. 18, an inspector); that the police follow certain procedures; and that the citizen is given the fullest possible information. All of the protective provisions are subject to exceptions, however, and it must be debatable how effective they are likely to be in deterring abuse by police officers. If followed they would be likely to render any search compatible with Art. 8.

6.4.4 Entry and search under warrant: general provisions

In this section we consider further the situations where the wishes of the occupier of premises may be overridden by the need for the police to obtain evidence in relation to an investigation. Whereas the powers under ss 18 and 32 are dependent on there having been an arrest, in some cases the police may wish to search for evidence which is likely to form the basis of an arrest. Alternatively, other restrictions on the availability of the powers to search without warrant may apply, even though the police have a suspect in custody. The premises in question may not be those on which the arrest took place, and may also not be under the occupation or control of the person arrested. In these situations, in order to gain access to the premises other than by consent, the police will have to seek some sort of judicial authority, generally from a magistrate, for entry and search, in the form of a 'warrant'.

Sections 15 and 16 of PACE set out procedures which should be followed in relation to all applications for, and exercise of, powers of entry and search under warrant. Section 15(1), which is headed 'Search warrants—safeguards', states that 'an entry on or search of premises under a warrant is unlawful unless it complies with this section and section 16 below'. The Court of Appeal in *R v Longman* [1988] 1 WLR 619 had some difficulty in deciding to what 'it' referred. Was it the warrant, or the entry, or the search? The Divisional Court in *R v Central Criminal Court, ex p AJD Holdings* [1992] Crim LR 669, however, took the view that an invalid warrant could render a search based on it unlawful. Moreover, it was accepted in *R v Chief Constable of Lancashire, ex p Parker and McGrath* [1993] Crim LR 204 that a breach of the provisions in s. 16 as to the information to be provided to the occupier at the time of the search, could render the whole search unlawful. The implication is that 'it' in s. 15 refers to all three elements, that is, the warrant, the entry, and the search. All must comply with the various requirements of ss 15 and 16 for the entry and search to be lawful. This approach also receives some support from *Kent Pharmaceuticals Ltd v Director of the Serious Fraud Office* where Lord Woolf, LCJ, in the Divisional Court noted the problem, but without deciding the issue, adopted the interpretation most generous to the applicants, i.e. 'that all the requirements of sections 15 and 16 have to be complied with if a warrant is to protect a search and the seizure of goods within premises to which it relates' (para. 16). In *R (Bhatti) v Croydon Magistrates Court*, ([2010] EWHC 522 (Admin), [2011] 1 WLR 948) Elias LJ reviewed the authorities since *Longman* and concluded that the better view was that expressed above—that 'it' in s. 15 refers to the whole process of entry under warrant, and not simply the warrant itself. He noted that this was the view taken by the Divisional Court in both *R v Chief Constable of the Warwickshire Constabulary, Ex p Fitzpatrick*, [1999] 1 WLR 564 and R v *Chesterfield Justices, Ex p Bramley* [2000] QB 576. The point may now be taken to be settled.

6.4.4.1 Procedures for application for a warrant

Section 15 is primarily concerned with the procedures to be followed in applying for a warrant. These are supplemented by the provisions of para. 3 of Code B. No application should generally be made without the authority of an officer of at least the rank of inspector (para. 3.4 of Code B). In a case of urgency, however, the senior officer on duty may give the authorization. An application should not be made on the basis of anonymous information for which corroboration has not been sought (para. 3.1 of Code B). In any case, the officer concerned should take reasonable steps to check the accuracy of the information. Reasonable inquiries should be made to establish the nature of the premises, whether anything is known about the occupier, and whether the premises have been previously searched and, if so, how recently (para. 3.3 of Code B). The nature and location of the articles sought should be ascertained as specifically as possible (para. 3.2 of Code B). All this should be done before the application is made. The application will be made *ex parte*, so the person whose premises are to be searched will have no opportunity to challenge the application at this stage. It must be supported by information in writing (s. 15(3)). There should be full disclosure of all relevant information (e.g. that the warrant is being sought in connection with a private prosecution: *R v Zinga* [2012] EWCA Crim 2357). In particular, the constable applying must make clear the power under which the warrant is sought, the grounds for the application, the premises to be entered and searched, and, so far as is possible, the articles or persons being sought (s. 15(2), (2A)). Note that where the application is for an 'all premises' warrant under s. 8 of PACE, slightly different requirements apply. These are dealt with at 6.4.5.1. The judge or magistrate receiving the application may ask questions which the officer should answer on oath (s. 15(4)). Questions may be asked about the reliability of the police sources, but there is no need to disclose the identity of an informant (Note 3A to Code B). There is no provision in the Act or Code for the recording of exchanges between the issuing magistrate and the officer applying for the warrant. The failure to keep such a record was criticized by the court in *R (Austen) v Chief Constable of Wiltshire* [2011] EWHC 385 (Admin), para. 49, which clearly felt that it should be standard practice to do so.

No particular form is required for a warrant (*R v IRC, ex p Rossminster* Ltd [1980] AC 952). It must state, however, the name of the applicant, the date of issue, the enactment under which it is issued, the premises to be searched, and, as far as practicable, what is being sought (s. 15(6)). Two copies must be made, and certified as such (s. 15(7) and (8)). More copies may be required in relation to a warrant issued under s. 8 of PACE which covers multiple premises or allows multiple entries (see 6.4.5.1).

6.4.4.2 Execution of warrant

The provisions of para. 6 of Code B, discussed at 6.4.3.3, apply to an entry and search under warrant. In addition, the following particular provisions apply to the execution of a warrant. A warrant will generally authorize entry on one occasion only (s. 15(5)), which must take place not more than three months after the issue of the warrant (s. 16(3)). The time limit used to be one month, but was changed by the amendments contained in the Serious Organised Crime and Police Act 2005. A Home Office Consultation document of August 2004 (see chapter 3 (3.5.3)) suggested that the one-month time limit was 'arbitrary' and that the question of duration could be left to the discretion of the issuing magistrate or judge, according to the circumstances (para. 3.9). There seems to have been no particular evidence that the one-month limit caused problems, and the change that has been made simply substitutes one arbitrary time limit for another. The justification is presumably that with the advent of warrants issued under s. 8 of PACE allowing multiple entries (see 6.4.5.1) a longer time period was justified. It is not clear that the change was needed in relation to all search warrants.

Unless it is a case of urgency, if the search might have an adverse effect on relations with the local community, then the local police/community liaison officer must be consulted before the search takes place.

A warrant may be executed by any constable (that is, not necessarily by the officer who obtained it) (s. 16(1)). It may authorize others to accompany the constable (s. 16(2)). This allows for experts to go on to the premises with the police in appropriate cases. They should be there to assist, however, rather than to direct the search. The control of the search, and decisions as to what is to be seized, must remain that of the police: *R v Reading Justices, ex p South West Meat Ltd* [1992] Crim LR 672.

The occupier, if present at the time, must be given a chance to inspect the warrant (*R v Longman* [1988] 1 WLR 619), and be given a copy of it (s. 16(5)). If the original warrant had schedules attached to it, specifying the items sought, a failure to supply these with the copy of the warrant given to the occupier renders the search unlawful: *R v Chief Constable of Lancashire, ex p Parker and McGrath* [1993] Crim LR 204. If the occupier is not present, but some other person appears to be in charge of the premises, the obligation in s. 16(5) applies to that person (s. 16(6)). If the premises are unoccupied, a copy of the warrant must be left in a prominent place (s. 16(7)).

A warrant which has been executed should be endorsed with the results of the search, indicating whether what was sought was found, and whether anything else was seized (s. 16(9)). An endorsed warrant, or one which has expired before being executed, must be returned to the court which issued it, and kept for 12 months (s. 16(11), (12)). During that period it must be made available for inspection on request by the occupier of the premises to which it relates (s. 16(12)).

The case of *Hepburn* v *Chief Constable of Thames Valley Police* [2002] EWCA Civ 1841 confirmed that the exercise of a warrant to search premises for drugs does not of itself give a power to detain and search any person found on the premises. The police will have to show that they have reasonable suspicion that the person concerned is in possession of drugs and then exercise their powers of personal search under s. 23 of the Misuse of Drugs Act 1971 (see chapter 3 (3.4.4.1)). In *Hepburn* the police did not have such a reasonable basis for suspicion and the claimant succeeded in an action for assault and false imprisonment.

Hepburn was distinguished by the Divisional Court in *DPP* v *Meaden* [2004] EWHC 3005 (Admin), [2004] 4 All ER 75, where the search warrant covered the search of people, as well as premises. Officers were entitled in those circumstances to confine individuals on the premises to particular rooms and to use reasonable force in so doing.

6.4.5 **Entry under warrant: the powers**

In *Entick* v *Carrington* (1765) 19 State Tr 1029, 95 ER 807, Lord Camden CJ emphasized that if a power of entry is alleged, then the judges must decide by looking 'into the books' to see 'if such a justification can be maintained by the text of the statute law, or by the principles of common law'. The case was one of a number (see also *Wilkes* v *Wood* (1763) 19 State Tr 1153, *Leach* v *Money* (1765) State Tr 1002, and *Wilkes* v *Lord Halifax* (1769) 19 State Tr 1406) in which the government had tried to use general search warrants to enter and search the premises of publishers of anti-government newspapers. The courts had no doubt that such general warrants had no legal validity, and that the entries therefore constituted trespasses. These cases were one of the highlights of the courts' upholding of individual rights against the power of the State. They led to a situation in English law whereby the power to obtain search warrants was strictly limited, and arose only where specifically granted by statute for a particular purpose. The requirement of Art. 8 that such powers are 'in accordance with law', and used for a legitimate, and identifiable, objective imposes a similar requirement.

This situation was obviously advantageous as far as civil liberties were concerned, but gave rise to certain anomalies. In particular, where an offence existed at common law, rather than under statute, there would not generally be any power for the police to obtain a warrant to search for evidence. In *McLorie* v *Oxford* [1982] QB 1290, for example, it was held that the police had no power to enter private premises to seek evidence relevant to an offence of attempted murder. The Royal Commission on Criminal Procedure which was the precursor to PACE recommended that in relation to serious offences this gap should be filled ('Report', Cmnd 8092, 1981, para. 3.42). This was done, though not in precisely the way in which the Royal Commission recommended, by s. 8 of PACE.

Section 8 of PACE has been reformed, following the 2004 Home Office Consultation (see chapter 3 (3.5.3)), by the Serious Organised Crime and Police Act 2005, so as to allow for warrants giving entry to unspecified premises under the control of a suspect, and for more than one entry under the same warrant. These provisions are examined in detail below, but it is arguable that they have led to a significant weakening of the principle of specificity set out in *Entick* v *Carrington*. The s. 8 warrants are not the broad executive-issued orders condemned in that case, but they do give the police much broader powers than has ever previously been the case. It is unlikely that the ECtHR would find that these powers in themselves breach Art. 8, but their use in inappropriate situations might well do so.

6.4.5.1 **PACE, s. 8**

The section allows the police to obtain a search warrant from a Justice of the Peace. The procedures in ss. 15 and 16, and Code B, outlined in 6.4.4, will apply. Section 8 only applies where there are reasonable grounds for believing that an indictable offence has been committed. As noted, the original purpose of this power was to allow for a warrant to search for evidence of serious offences. To that end, the original version of PACE limited the power to 'serious arrestable offences'. As discussed in chapter 3, this concept has been abandoned, so that now the power is a very wide one, applying to all indictable offences. It will now, therefore, overlap with many of the more specific statutory powers, for example under the Theft Act 1968 and the Misuse of Drugs Act 1971. It remains to be seen whether the police in future make greater use of the s. 8 power than the specific powers. It will be up to the issuing magistrate to ensure that the power is not used inappropriately.

The power given by a s. 8 warrant is to enable a search to be made for material which is likely to be of substantial value to the investigation of the indictable offence, and which will be admissible evidence at trial (s. 8(1)). The material must not fall into one of the protected categories, that is legally privileged, excluded, or special procedure (see 6.5).

In some circumstances the police may now seek a warrant in relation to multiple premises, or allowing multiple entries to the same premises. These changes were introduced by the Serious Organised Crime and Police Act 2005 and follow on from the suggestions contained in the Home Office Consultation Paper, 'Modernising Police Powers to Meet Community Needs', published in August 2004. The justifications for the changes were related to developments in crime and technology since PACE was enacted (para. 3.2): 'Evidence and the proceeds of crime can be moved very quickly between locations to thwart investigations'. As the Consultation Paper also noted, 'Applying repeatedly for warrants owned by the same individual can cause delay and impede investigations' (para. 3.3). In relation to multiple entries, it was suggested that complex IT and financial fraud cases can require an 'extended police presence'. The idea is that it would be better to let the police leave and return under the same warrant, rather than having to remain on the premises for lengthy periods.

Section 8(1A) makes it clear that the application for a warrant seeking entry to a number of sets of premises may either specify all those premises, or specify all premises 'occupied or controlled by a person specified in the application'—the latter being designated an 'all premises warrant'. It was stated, obiter, in *Redknapp* v *City of London Police* [2008] EWHC 1177 (Admin), [2009] 1 All ER 229 that one warrant can included both a specific premises warrant and all premises warrant. Where the application is for an all premises warrant, the magistrate must be satisfied that the nature of the offence under investigation and the items sought renders this type of warrant 'necessary' (s. 8(1B)(a)). The magistrate must also be satisfied that it is not 'reasonably practicable' to specify all the premises which might need to be searched (s. 8(1B)(b)). Section 16(3A) requires that where an all premises warrant is being executed, no premises unspecified in the warrant may be entered without the written authorization of an officer of at least the rank of inspector. Paragraph 6.3B of Code B requires this officer to be one not involved in the investigation.

As regards warrants allowing multiple entries, these are dealt with by s. 8(1C) and (1D). The magistrate must be satisfied that the multiple entries are 'necessary' to achieve the purpose for which the warrant is issued. This is a clear reflection of the requirements of Art. 8. The number of entries may be limited to a specified number, or unlimited, provided that they take place within 3 months of the issue of the warrant. Section 16(3B) provides that no premises may be entered for a second or subsequent time without the written authorization of an officer of at least the rank of inspector. Paragraph 6.3A of Code B requires the officer to be one not involved in the investigation.

In addition to being satisfied that there are reasonable grounds for believing that material satisfying the above conditions is to be found on premises specified in the application, the magistrate must also be satisfied, on reasonable grounds, that one of a number of further conditions is met. These conditions relate to the necessity of using a warrant to gain access to the material, and are set out in s. 8(3). They are:

1. that it is not practicable to communicate with one or other of the persons entitled to grant entry to the premises, or access to the material;

2. that entry to the premises will not be granted without a warrant being produced; and

3. that unless the police can gain immediate entry on arrival at the premises, the purpose of the search may be frustrated, or seriously prejudiced.

It must be clear from the application which of the above grounds the police are relying on. In *Redknapp* v *City of London Commissioner* the application failed to state which of the s. 8(3) conditions was being relied on. All of them were listed on the pro forma application, but none had been deleted by the police. Because of this the court could not be satisfied that the magistrate had been reasonably satisfied of any of the conditions, and the warrant was invalid.

The conditions do not mean that a warrant can only be issued under s. 8 where other means have been tried, or would be bound to fail (which is the position under s. 9; see 6.7.2): *R* v *Billericay Justices and Dobbyn, ex p Frank Harris Coaches Ltd* [1991] Crim LR 472. On the other hand, in *R* v *Guildhall Magistrates' Court, ex p Primlaks Holdings Co.* (1988) 89 Cr App R 215, the Divisional Court emphasized the Draconian nature of the power under s. 8. As a result it is imperative that the magistrate to whom the application for a warrant is made does not simply accept assertions by the police that there are reasonable grounds for belief in relation to the various matters set out above. The magistrate must be satisfied independently of such assertions, on the basis of the information presented. In the instant case, where the premises in relation to which the warrant was sought were the offices of a firm of solicitors, the material was almost certain to be legally privileged, or special procedure material. Moreover, it was very difficult to accept that it was impossible to communicate with the solicitors in order to gain access, or that the solicitors would have been likely to dispose of the material on being given notice of the police's interest. The correct procedure on the part of the police would have been to seek a production order under s. 9 (see 6.7.2). A different approach may be justified where it is the firm of solicitors itself which is under investigation: *R* v *Crown Court at Leeds, ex p Switalski* [1991] Crim LR 559 (discussed further at 6.7.2.1).

The procedure to be adopted when a warrant under s. 8 is sought and there is a risk that items subject to legal privilege may be included was considered by the Divisional Court in *R* v *Chesterfield Justices, ex p Bramley* [2000] 1 All ER 411. The following guidelines were put forward. First, if the officer applying for a warrant did not volunteer information regarding legal privilege it was up to the magistrate to make inquiries. The magistrate had to be satisfied that there were no reasonable grounds for suspecting that material sought included items subject to legal privilege. In executing a warrant the constable must not go beyond what is necessary to achieve its purpose, but otherwise can seize any items unless there are reasonable grounds to believe that they are subject to legal privilege. The constable is not, however, obliged to accept a claim of legal privilege at face value—inspection of the item will generally be necessary to test the claim. Although some sorting and sifting of documents can take place on the premises, in some cases involving large quantities of material it may be necessary to take it away. In this case, the material is 'seized' and if it later transpires that it was not covered by the warrant (e.g. because it is legally privileged) then it must be returned immediately, and there may well be liability in damages to the owner for the wrongful seizure. The seizure of the other items is not rendered unlawful, however, by such wrongful seizure of some items. Finally, the court recognized that attention should be paid to the right of privacy under Art. 8 of the ECHR. This meant that the wording of the statute should be interpreted strictly.

The procedures suggested in *Bramley* have now been supplemented, and to some extent superseded, by Pt. 2 of the Criminal Justice and Police Act 2001. This provides additional powers of seizure wherever a person is lawfully on premises and finds something which the person has reasonable grounds for believing is or may be something 'for which he is authorised to search on those premises' (s. 50(1)). The provisions which are set out in ss. 50–70 and Schs 1 and 2 are not particularly clearly drafted. Their effect is, however, that if it is not reasonable to determine on the premises whether the items about which the suspicions are held are actually liable to seizure, they may be taken away in order for that determination to be made off the premises. The power also applies where the suspect material is 'comprised in something else' (such as a computer) which the person has no power to seize (s. 50(2)). The factors which are relevant to whether it is practicable to carry out any necessary examination on the premises are set out in s. 50(3), and include the length of time, the number of people needed, and whether the determination would involve damage to the property. There is a duty to give notice of the exercise of these powers to the occupier (s. 52), and a power to challenge the seizure by application to a Crown Court judge is given by s. 59. This provision of judicial supervision of the powers, albeit after the event, is presumably thought sufficient to satisfy the requirements of the ECHR in this area. The provision of s. 19(6) of PACE precluding the seizure of items reasonably believed to be legally privileged does not apply to a seizure under s. 50(2). Section 54, however, deals with what should happen to legally privileged material. Such material must generally be returned as soon as it is discovered, but there is an exception where the material cannot reasonably be separated from other property, the seizure and retention of which is lawful. There is a similar provision requiring the return of excluded and special procedure items in s. 55, but this is in addition subject to s. 56 which provides, in the same way as s. 19 of PACE, that such material may be retained if it is evidence of an offence and it is necessary to retain it 'in order to prevent its being concealed, lost or destroyed' (s. 56(3)).

These provisions were enacted to deal with practical problems faced by the police in exercising their powers of search and seizure. There is no doubt, however, that they extend the infringements on the privacy rights protected by Art. 8. The question will be whether they, or their exercise, can be regarded as 'proportionate'. The ECtHR's approach to this issue is exemplified by *Niemietz* v *Germany* (1993) 16 EHRR 97. In this case the warrant had allowed the search of a lawyer's office. The Court held that the use of forcible search powers in these circumstances involved a breach of the right to privacy, and was not 'necessary in a democratic society'. The power, which took no account of, for example, the requirements of professional confidentiality, which might need special protection, was disproportionate to its purposes. As far as English law is concerned, the provisions of PACE dealing with legally privileged and special procedure material will generally satisfy these requirements but the extended powers under the 2001 Act in relation to such material must raise the possibility of incompatibility. It will be necessary for the police to use these powers with discretion, if they are not to be found to be 'disproportionate'. There is also the possibility, in addition to the possible infringement of Art. 8, that the new powers to retain legally privileged material could cause problems with Art. 6. If, in a particular case, the legally privileged material which was seized and retained related to an ongoing case, it might well be arguable that this infringed the right to a fair trial. Although the 'access' provisions of s. 21 of PACE (see 6.6.3) will apply to material seized under these powers, since this is required to be 'under the supervision of a constable' it might well not be adequate in relation to legally privileged material.

6.4.5.2 Other statutory powers

Many statutes give the police powers to obtain warrants to enter and search premises (see, e.g. R. Stone, *The Law of Entry, Search, and Seizure*, 5th edn, Oxford: Oxford University Press, 2012 ch. 5). The most frequently used are those relating to stolen goods (s. 26 of the Theft Act 1968), drugs (s. 23 of the Misuse of Drugs Act 1971), and pornography (s. 3 of the Obscene Publications Act 1959, see chapter 8 (8.5.1.2)). The procedures set out in ss 15 and 16 of PACE must be followed. All the provisions are in a fairly standard form, requiring the police to convince a Justice of the Peace that there are reasonable grounds for believing that the items sought are on the premises specified. In relation to these powers, the use of a search warrant is not so much a 'last resort' as it is under s. 8 of PACE. The conditions set out in s. 8(3) (see 6.4.5.1) do not need to be satisfied; it is enough that the relevant items are believed, on reasonable grounds, to be on the premises.

There are also various powers which allow the police to obtain a warrant to enter in order to inspect premises. Examples include para. 25 of Sch. 3 to the Local Government (Miscellaneous Provisions) Act 1982 (in relation to sex shops) and s. 15 of the Theatres Act 1968 (where a performance of a play is suspected of involving the commission of an offence under the Act). Since these powers do not involve any search of the premises, they are not covered by ss 15 and 16 of PACE. There is no reason, however, why the relevant provisions of Code B should not be followed as indications of 'best practice', even though there is no statutory obligation to do so.

6.4.6 Special powers

Two statutes give the police special powers of entry which do not depend on a warrant issued in the normal way. These are now to be found in the Terrorism Act 2000 and the Police Act 1997. The second of these, in particular, may be regarded as having made a significant extension to police powers.

The Terrorism Act power is dealt with in chapter 10 (10.4.4.1). The Police Act 1997 is dealt with at 6.5.2.

6.5 Surveillance

In recent years there has been increasing statutory regulation of activities which have always taken place, but without a clear legislative framework. These include such things as telephone tapping, the use of 'bugging devices' in premises, and the covert recording of conversations. All of these activities will prima facie involve infringements of 'privacy' as protected by Art. 8 of the ECHR. The move towards legislative control of these activities, which may be carried out by or on behalf of the police, HM Revenue and Customs, the security services, or other government agencies, has been largely prompted by the need to ensure compatibility with Art. 8. In particular, the Article requires that any intrusion into privacy should be 'in accordance with the law'; as has been noted, this has been interpreted by the ECtHR as requiring that there should be a clear legal framework, either under the common law or statute. The area will be considered in three sections—interception of communications, placing and use of 'bugs' on private property, use of covert human intelligence sources.

6.5.1 Interception of communications

The starting point in this area is the case of *Malone* v *Metropolitan Police Commissioner* [1979] Ch 344, in which Malone brought an action in the High Court challenging the legality of a police telephone tap. Sir Robert Megarry held that he had no cause of action. There was no general right to privacy under English law and the tapping procedure had involved no trespass or other interference with Malone's property. Malone took his case to Strasbourg, where it was held by the ECtHR that the United Kingdom was in breach of its obligations under Art. 8 of the ECHR primarily because the law did 'not indicate with reasonable clarity the scope and manner of exercise of the relevant discretion conferred on the public authorities': *Malone* v *United Kingdom* (1985) 7 EHRR 14, para. 79. The infringements of Malone's privacy were, therefore, not 'in accordance with law'. The response of the UK government was to enact the Interception of Communications Act 1985, which established a statutory scheme for the control of telephone tapping and other interception of communications carried out by the police and the security services. This has now been replaced by Pt. I of the Regulation of Investigatory Powers Act 2000 (RIPA 2000).

6.5.1.1 Regulation of Investigatory Powers Act 2000, Pt. I

The Act came into force in October 2000. It is supported by a Code of Practice issued under s. 71 of the Act.

Section 1 of the RIPA 2000 makes it an offence 'intentionally and without lawful authority' to intercept communications by a postal service or a telecommunications system. This offence extends to voicemail messages, even after they have been accessed by the intended recipient: *R* v *Edmondson* [2013] EWCA Crim 1026 (a case arising out of the alleged phone hacking by journalists at the *News of the World*). An interception will be lawful if it is done with consent (s. 3), or under the authority of a warrant issued under the Act (s. 5). The offence extends to private telecommunications systems in response to the ECtHR's decision in *Halford* v *United Kingdom* (1997) 24 EHRR 523, where a police officer complained about the tapping of her internal phone. Since the 1985 Act did not extend to private systems the United Kingdom was found in breach of Art. 8. The RIPA 2000 also defines 'telecommunications system' sufficiently widely to cover mobile phones (including text-messaging), email, and pagers (s. 2(1)).

The authorization of interceptions is governed by ss 5–16. The power to issue a warrant authorizing an interception lies with the Home Secretary (though in some exceptional cases with a 'senior official' (see s. 7(2)). The application for such a warrant must come from one of a list of people specified in s. 6. These include the Director-General of the Security Service, the Chief of the Secret Intelligence

Service, the Commissioners of HM Revenue and Customs, the Director of the National Crime Agency, and the Metropolitan Police Commissioner. Other Chief Constables in England and Wales are not included. The Code of Practice (para. 2.1) refers to applications from police forces outside the Metropolitan Police Area being routed through the National Criminal Intelligence Service. This should presumably now be taken to refer to the National Crime Agency. Applications from Special Branch should go through the Metropolitan Police Special Branch. The warrant is only to be issued if the Home Secretary believes that it is 'necessary' for certain specified purposes (as set out in s. 5(3)) and that 'the conduct authorized by the warrant is proportional to what is sought to be achieved by that conduct' (s. 5(2)). This wording, which is different to that used in the 1985 Act, was clearly included with the HRA 1998 in mind, and the requirements of the ECtHR that infringements of rights under Art. 8 should be no more than is 'necessary in a democratic society' to achieve a legitimate objective specified in the Article. The purposes identified in s. 5(3) are:

(a) the interests of national security;

(b) preventing or detecting serious crime;

(c) safeguarding the economic well-being of the United Kingdom; or

(d) giving effect to an international mutual assistance agreement in circumstances equivalent to those falling within (b).

The two main concerns about these purposes are the definition of serious crime and the vagueness of purpose (c), both of which seem to give more latitude than may be desirable to the Home Secretary or those applying for a warrant. 'Serious crime' is defined in s. 81(3) in the following, alternative, terms:

(a) that the offence or one of the offences that is or would be constituted by the conduct is an offence for which a person who has attained the age of twenty-one and has no previous convictions could reasonably be expected to be sentenced to imprisonment for a term of three years or more;

(b) that the conduct involves the use of violence, results in substantial financial gain or is conduct by a large number of persons in pursuit of a common purpose.

This is wide enough to include any battery. The final phrase of (b) runs the risk of covering those involved, for example, in the organization of demonstrations, which may incidentally constitute relatively minor public order offences. It is to be hoped that the tests of 'necessity' and 'proportionality' will be sufficient to prevent the inappropriate use of interception warrants. The Code of Practice deals with this in paras 2.4 and 2.5, which state:

2.4 Obtaining a warrant under the Act will only ensure that the interception authorised is a justifiable interference with an individual's rights under Article 8 of the European Convention of Human Rights (the right to privacy) if it is necessary and proportionate for the interception to take place. The Act recognises this by first requiring that the Secretary of State believes that the authorisation is necessary on one or more of the statutory grounds set out in section 5(3) of the Act. This requires him to believe that it is necessary to undertake the interception which is to be authorised for a particular purpose falling within the relevant statutory ground.

> 2.5 Then, if the interception is necessary, the Secretary of State must also believe that it is proportionate to what is sought to be achieved by carrying it out. This involves balancing the intrusiveness of the interference, against the need for it in operational terms. Interception of communications will not be proportionate if it is excessive in the circumstances of the case or if the information which is sought could reasonably be obtained by other means. Further, all interception should be carefully managed to meet the objective in question and must not be arbitrary or unfair.

The contents of the warrant are dealt with by s. 8. It must specify as the target for the interception either one individual or a single set of premises. It should also contain schedules setting out the details of addresses, numbers, apparatus, etc. to be used in identifying the communications to be intercepted. The duration is governed by s. 9. The default period is three months from issue, but it may be renewed an unlimited number of times (provided the Home Secretary continues to believe it to be necessary). Where a senior official has issued the warrant as a matter of urgency (under s. 7(2)(a)), it will last for only five days. In relation to renewed warrants based on 'national security' or 'economic well-being' grounds, the period is six months.

Supervision of the operation of the above system is by an independent Interception of Communications Commissioner, who must have previously held high judicial office (s. 57). This continues a system established under the 1985 Act. The current Commissioner is Sir Paul Kennedy, formerly a Court of Appeal judge. The Commissioner is obliged to report annually to the Prime Minister, with the report being received by Parliament and published. The powers of the Commissioner are supervisory to the system as a whole, and do not extend to taking action in relation to particular warrants. The 2012 Annual Report indicated that there had been 3,362 warrants issued during that year, an increase of 16 per cent over the previous year ('Report of the Interception of Communications Commissioner for 2012', HC 571, 2013—available at http://www.iocco-uk.info/docs/2012%20Annual%20Report%20of%20the%20Interception%20of%20Communications%20Commissioner%20WEB.pdf). The Commissioner noted that 55 errors had been reported to him—mainly involving transposition errors in relation to telephone numbers or 'other technical reasons' (2012 Annual Report, p. 16). This was an increase from 42 in 2011, and of over 100 per cent from 2010. The Commissioner commented that 'any increase in errors is extremely regrettable and I have stressed to those involved the importance of reminding staff of the need to comply with the legislation, and to reform procedures where necessary to minimise the risk of errors being repeated' (2012 Annual Report, p. 17).

The only route of complaint for those dissatisfied with the operation of the above systems is to a Tribunal established under s. 65 of and Sch. 3 to the RIPA 2000. Again, this continues a system established by the 1985 Act. The members of the Tribunal must have held 'high judicial office'. Section 67(2) makes it explicit that the Tribunal is to operate on the principles of 'judicial review'. This means that its focus will be tend to be on procedure rather than substance though, as noted in chapter 2, where human rights issues are involved, judicial review now comes close to a merits review (2.4.1). If the Tribunal finds that there has been some impropriety, it has the power to quash a warrant, order the destruction of any information obtained by it, and to award compensation. Although this appears to give the Tribunal significant powers, because interceptions are by their nature secret, and evidence obtained from them is inadmissible in legal proceedings (s. 17), it will be rare that an individual will be aware what has happened, and therefore be in a position to complain. Moreover, there is no further appeal from a decision of the Tribunal (s. 67(8)). The scheme of supervision established by the RIPA 2000, though it would probably satisfy the ECtHR in relation to compatibility with Art. 8 (see *Christie* v *United Kingdom* (1994) 78–A DR E Com HR 119), thus provides little assistance for an individual whose privacy has been infringed.

In 2010 the Tribunal received 164 complaints, and upheld six. This is reported in the 'Report of the Interception of Communications Commissioner for 2010', HC 1239, 2010, at para. 9.4 (no figures are given in the 2012 Report). One of the cases concerned abuse of RIPA surveillance powers by a local authority, rather than in connection with the interception of communications. In general the information available about the complaints to the Tribunal and its decision is vague and unhelpful.

6.5.2 The Police Act 1997—'bugging' private premises

This Act was passed in March 1997 and was brought into force over the following two years. The section of the Act which is relevant to this chapter is Pt. III, headed 'Authorization of Action in Respect of Property', which came into force in February 1999. It was enacted largely in response to the case of *R* v *Khan* [1996] 3 All ER 289, and the fact that the procedures there revealed were likely to be susceptible to challenge under the ECHR, as was confirmed in *Khan* v *United Kingdom* (2001) 31 EHRR 45 (see chapter 4 (4.6.4.3)). The effect of this part of the Act is to give to the police powers to enter and interfere with property, and to carry out surveillance by means of wireless telegraphy, without the need for a warrant. These powers came to be known in the debates on the Act as the powers to 'bug and burgle'. Such actions, which would otherwise be unlawful, are made lawful if covered by an authorization (s. 92). The powers are similar to those given to the security and intelligence services which, however, generally have to act under warrants issued by the Home Secretary (see, e.g. s. 5 of the Intelligence Services Act 1994). The procedures under the Police Act 1997 are subject to the supervision, and to a certain extent the control, of special 'Surveillance Commissioners', headed by a 'Chief Surveillance Commissioner' (s. 81(1) of the RIPA 2000). They are all appointed by the Prime Minister from the ranks of senior judges (s. 91(1)). Section 63 of the RIPA 2000 also provides for the appointment of 'Assistant Surveillance Commissioners' who must hold or have held office as a Crown Court judge or circuit judge. The powers are also supplemented by a Code of Practice issued under s. 71 of the RIPA 2000.

The power to issue an authorization under these provisions rests, *inter alia*, with the chief officer of police, or the Director-General of the Serious Organised Crime Agency (s. 93(5)). The discussion here will focus on the powers of the chief constable, or Commissioner (in London). In a case of urgency, where it is not reasonably practicable to obtain an authorization from the chief officer, it may be issued by an officer of the rank of assistant chief constable, or equivalent (s. 94). The application for an authorization must come from a member of the chief officer's force.

The basis on which an authorization may be issued is that the authorizing officer believes that the action is necessary because it will be of substantial value in the prevention or detection of 'serious crime', and that the action is proportional to what is sought to be achieved (s. 93(2)). Serious crime is defined in s. 93(4). Conduct which involves one or more offences will constitute a serious crime if:

(a) it involves the use of violence, results in substantial financial gain or is conduct by a large number of persons in pursuit of a common purpose; or

(b) the offence or one of the offences is an offence for which a person who has attained the age of twenty-one and has no previous convictions could reasonably be expected to be sentenced to imprisonment for a term of three years or more.

This definition is very similar to that used in the RIPA 2000 (see 6.5.1), and in the same way has caused concern in that the reference in (a) to 'a large number of persons in pursuit of a common purpose' would seem to cover, for example, the activities of environmental protesters, who might commit minor offences under the Public Order Act 1936, or obstruct the highway. The then Conservative government gave assurances that this type of offender is not the Act's target, but the language is clearly wide enough to cover such people.

An authorization will normally be in writing, though in a case of urgency it may be given orally (provided that it is given by the chief officer in person, and not, e.g. by an assistant chief constable) (s. 95(1)). A written authorization will last for three months; an oral authorization, or one issued by an assistant chief officer, will last for 72 hours. Either type of authorization may be renewed, in writing, for a further three months. There is no limit on the number of such renewals that may be made. A duty on the authorizing officer to cancel an authorization which is no longer needed is imposed by s. 95(6).

As soon as an authorization is given, a Commissioner should be given notice of it in the prescribed form (s. 96 and the Police Act 1997 (Notification of Authorisations, etc.) Order 1998 (SI 1998/3241)). This does not prevent action being taken immediately on the authorization, however, other than in the circumstances described below. The Commissioner has the power to quash or cancel an authorization if satisfied that there were no reasonable grounds for believing that the conditions for its issue were satisfied, or that they have ceased to apply (s. 101). Where the Commissioner quashes an authorization, the destruction of any records of information obtained may be ordered. This does not apply, however, to records required for pending criminal or civil proceedings. The police may, therefore, have gained the material they need, even though the authorization is found by the Commissioner to be *ultra vires*.

The circumstances in which action on an authorization must await the approval of a Commissioner are set out in s. 97. There are two categories of circumstances, one relating to the nature of the property specified; the other relating to the type of information which may be obtained. As regards the first category the need for approval arises where the authorizing officer believes that any of the property specified:

1. is used wholly or mainly as a dwelling or as a bedroom in a hotel; or
2. constitutes office premises.

The second category arises where the authorizing officer believes that the action authorized is likely to result in any person acquiring knowledge of:

1. matters subject to legal privilege;
2. confidential personal information; or
3. confidential journalistic material.

These categories are defined in ss 98–100. The definitions are very similar to those relating to legally privileged, excluded, and journalistic material under PACE (see 6.7.1).

Having received an authorization which indicates that the authorizing officer believes that it falls within the above provisions of s. 97, the Commissioner must, as soon as reasonably practicable, give written notice to the authorizing officer as to whether the authorization is approved or refused.

This safeguard of prior approval by a Commissioner goes some way to meeting the concerns expressed about the extensive nature of the power to 'bug and burgle' given by these provisions. Unfortunately, the effect is rather spoilt by s. 97(3) which provides that the requirements for prior approval do not apply where the authorizing officer believes that the case is one of urgency. The belief does not have to be based on reasonable grounds. Frequent use of this provision will make the safeguards provided of little use. It is encouraging that the Code of Practice specifically states that 'an authorisation is not to be regarded as urgent where the need for an authorisation has been neglected or the urgency is of the authorised officer's own making' (para. 5.6) and that 'the urgency provisions should not be used routinely' (para. 6.15). Moreover, an officer relying on the urgency ground must, in the notification to the Commissioner, explain the reasons why the case is thought to be urgent (see para. 6.15). It is not clear how effective in practice these exhortations and requirements are in controlling the use of the urgency provisions.

The route for complaints about to the exercise of these powers is to the Tribunal established under the RIPA 2000 (see 6.5.1.1). The scope for complaint, however, is likely to be reduced by the fact that these powers are, by their nature, concerned with covert operations. If carried out properly there is no reason why the person who is the subject of them need ever know that they have been used (unlike the situation in relation to the use of a normal search warrant). It may well be only if material acquired by use of the powers is used as evidence in legal proceedings that the fact of their use becomes known. The basis for the use of the material is not, however, necessarily to acquire admissible evidence. The criterion for the issue of the authorization, as indicated, is that it will be of substantial value in the prevention or detection of serious crime. It may thus be used simply to gather intelligence about actual or potential criminal activity, rather than providing material which can be used directly as a basis for a criminal charge against a particular person. It is the covert nature of these powers, combined with the limited role for judicial approval, that makes them so controversial as an addition to the armoury of police powers.

Appeals against a decision of a Commissioner by an authorizing officer, in relation to a decision to quash or cancel an authorization, are to be made to the Chief Surveillance Commissioner (ss 104–07).

Finally, the Chief Commissioner is given a supervisory role in relation to the operation of the provisions (s. 107), as part of which the Chief Commissioner is required to make an annual report to the Prime Minister.

The powers given by this part of the Police Act 1997 must be regarded as being at the limit of what is acceptable in a democratic society, or even beyond that limit. Indeed it is questionable whether the degree of judicial involvement would be regarded as sufficient to meet the standards laid down by the ECtHR in relation to powers of entry to private property. In *Funke* v *France* (1993) 16 EHRR 297, for example, customs officials had searched the applicant's house using powers given by Art. 64 of the French Customs Code. The ECtHR found the search to be in breach of Art. 8 of the ECHR, in that it went beyond what could be regarded as 'necessary in a democratic society' for dealing with international fraud. In particular, the absence of any requirement for a judicial warrant meant that the other restrictions on the power were 'too lax and full of loopholes for the interferences in the applicant's right to have been strictly proportionate to the legitimate aim pursued'. In relation to the Police Act 1997, it must be doubtful whether the role of the Commissioners would constitute sufficient judicial supervision to satisfy the ECtHR. This was not the view, however, of the Court of Appeal in *R* v *SL* [2001] EWCA Crim 1829, [2002] Crim LR 584 where it supported the trial judge's view that the (pre-RIPA 2000) provisions of the 1997 Act were compatible with Art. 8.

6.5.3 **Covert surveillance**

This area is now regulated by Pt. II (ss 26–48) of the RIPA 2000. There are two associated Codes of Practice, one dealing with covert surveillance (which also covers the powers under the Police Act 1997 as discussed) and one dealing with the use of covert human intelligence sources. The provisions were enacted primarily to ensure that covert surveillance activities could be made immune from challenge under the HRA 1998. There is no necessity, as the Codes of Practice make clear, for the authorization procedures to be used, since the surveillance will not generally involve any otherwise unlawful actions, but if they are, it is anticipated that this will remove the possibility of a challenge under Art. 8 of the ECHR.

Section 26 identifies three types of behaviour that are covered by the Act: directed surveillance; intrusive surveillance; and the conduct and use of covert human intelligence sources. 'Surveillance' is partially defined in s. 48 to include:

(a) monitoring, observing or listening to persons, their movements, their conversations or their other activities or communications;

(b) recording anything monitored, observed, or listened to in the course of surveillance; and

(c) surveillance by or with the assistance of a surveillance device.

'Directed surveillance' is covert but not 'intrusive' surveillance, undertaken for the purposes of a specific investigation or operation, and likely to result in the obtaining of private information about a person. Surveillance is 'intrusive' if it relates to the surveillance of what is happening in residential premises or in a private vehicle, and either involves the presence of an individual in the premises or vehicle, or is carried out by means of a surveillance device. Normally, the device will be in the premises or vehicle, but surveillance may nevertheless be intrusive if the device 'consistently provides information of the same quality and detail as might be expected to be obtained from a device actually present on the premises or in the vehicle' (s. 26(5)).

The definition of what is meant by a 'covert human intelligence source' is spelt out in s. 26(8). Such a source will establish or maintain a relationship with a person for the covert purpose of using the relationship to obtain access to information, or provide such access to another, or for the covert purpose of disclosing information obtained from the relationship. Police actions of the type which occurred in the cases of *R* v *Hall* (1994) (Leeds Crown Court) and *R* v *Stagg* (1994) (Central Criminal Court) discussed in chapter 4 (4.6.4.4), would clearly fall within this definition. It is also likely to cover the actions of most police informers.

The Act provides a system of authorization in ss 28–32. As regards directed surveillance, an authorization can be given by 'individuals holding such offices, ranks or positions with relevant public authorities as are prescribed for the purposes of this subsection by an order under this section' (s. 30(1)). In the case of the police, the relevant rank is superintendent, or in cases of urgency, inspector (SI 2000/2417). The grounds on which authorizations may be granted are similar to those applying to the interception of communications (see 6.5.1). Thus, the authorization must be 'necessary' and 'proportionate' and the grounds include national security and the economic well-being of the United Kingdom. The 'crime' to be prevented or detected does not, however, have to be 'serious' and s. 28(3) also includes 'public safety', 'public health', and tax collection within the grounds. In addition there is a power for the Secretary of State to add to the purposes for which directed surveillance may be authorized by Order.

The authorization of the use of covert intelligence sources under s. 29 is virtually identical to that applying to directed surveillance. The power lies with the same officials and the same grounds justifying an authorization apply. The main difference is that the person authorizing the use of the source must believe that there are appropriate arrangements in place for the supervision of the operation of the source (s. 29(5)).

The basis for the authorization of intrusive surveillance is slightly stricter (s. 32). The power to authorize lies with the Secretary of State or 'senior authorising officers', who in relation to the police are chief constables. The requirements of necessity and proportionality apply, but the grounds are limited to national security, the economic well-being of the United Kingdom, and 'serious crime' (defined as in relation to the interception of communications—see 6.5.1.1).

In relation to directed surveillance or covert sources, the authorization should normally be in writing, and will take effect as soon as issued. It will last for three months in relation to directed surveillance, or 12 months in relation to covert sources, but with the possibility of renewal (s. 43(3)). In urgent cases the authorization may be given orally, but will only last for 72 hours (s. 43(3)).

The authorization procedure in relation to intrusive surveillance is similar to that applying under the Police Act 1997. That is, normally approval must be sought from a Surveillance Commissioner before the authorization can take effect. The Commissioner must be satisfied that the relevant grounds exist for the issue of the authorization (s. 36(4)). The authorizing officer can appeal to the Chief Surveillance

Commissioner against a refusal to confirm the authorization. Once approved, the authorization will normally last for three months, with the possibility of renewal (s. 43(3)).

A person aggrieved by the use of any of the above powers can take a complaint to the Tribunal established under the RIPA 2000, and discussed above in relation to the interception of communications (see 6.5.1.1). There is no other route of complaint.

These procedures are an improvement on the situation prior to 2000, in that there is at least a statutory framework for the operation of powers which almost by definition will involve infringements of privacy. The controls over them are open to criticism, in terms of the vagueness of some of the grounds on which they can be exercised, and the lack of independent supervision. This is particularly true of the powers relating to directed surveillance and covert sources where, unlike intrusive surveillance, there is no involvement of the Surveillance Commissioners. Although, as with the other powers discussed in this section, there are problems as to whether individuals will be aware that their rights have been infringed, at some point it is likely that aspects of this regime will face challenge. The exclusive jurisdiction of the Tribunal means that it is unlikely that they will come before the domestic courts, but an appeal to Strasbourg must be a strong possibility.

6.6 Personal property: seizure powers

In this section the focus is on the powers of the police to seize personal property. Whereas an entry and search of premises involves an intrusion into the individual's physical space, a seizure power has the effect of removing property from the possessor's control at least temporarily. In some cases the seizure, if it is of illicit goods rather than simply evidence, may be a precursor to forfeiture or destruction.

6.6.1 Seizure following personal search

The powers of the police in relation to seizing items found in the exercise of stop and search powers, or following arrest, are noted in chapter 3. Seizure of items found on persons in police detention is covered in chapter 4 (4.2.4).

All items seized under any of the above powers are subject to the general provisions in PACE concerned with the retention of seized property, which are discussed at 6.6.3.

6.6.2 Seizure following lawful entry

To some extent the power of police to seize property after lawful entry will depend on the power which is being relied on. Most statutory powers will indicate what items the police may search for and seize. In the case of s. 26 of the Theft Act 1968 for example, the power is to seize any items which the constable believes to be stolen goods (the belief does not have to be reasonable). Under s. 3 of the Obscene Publications Act 1959, it is to seize any articles which the constable has reason to believe to be obscene, and kept for publication for gain, and any documents relating to a trade or business carried on at the premises. Under s. 23 of the Misuse of Drugs Act 1971, controlled drugs may be seized if the constable has reasonable grounds to believe an offence has been committed in relation to them. Documents relating to a transaction which was or would be an offence under the Act may also be seized. Finally, under s. 8 of PACE the power is simply to seize anything for which a search has been authorized, that is 'relevant evidence', likely to be of substantial value to the investigation, and not consisting of protected material (see 6.7.1). As will be seen there are subtle variations between all these powers. It is necessary in every case to check the detail of the particular statutory provision giving the seizure power.

In addition to the powers attached to each provision, however, a general seizure power is given in s. 19 of PACE. This arises whenever a constable is lawfully on premises. This may be on the basis of consent, entry without warrant (see 6.4.2 and 6.4.3), or entry under a warrant. The constable does not need to be aware of the lawful basis for being on the premises: *Foster* v *Attard* (1985) 83 Cr App R 214. Two categories of item may be seized. The first is items which the constable has reasonable grounds for believing have been obtained in consequence of the commission of an offence (e.g. stolen goods) (s. 19(2)). The second category is items which the constable has reasonable grounds for believing are evidence in relation to any offence (not necessarily one which the constable is investigating) (s. 19(3)). Thus, the constable executing a warrant to search for stolen goods who comes across a gun, or controlled drugs, will almost certainly be entitled to seize them. The only other requirement, which applies to both categories, is that the constable must have reasonable grounds for believing that seizure of the items is necessary in order to prevent them being concealed, lost, altered, or destroyed, or in the case of items in the first category, damaged. The power under s. 19(3) was interpreted in a slightly surprising way in *Cowan* v *Metropolitan Police Commissioner* [2000] 1 WLR 254. The police were investigating allegations that the owner of a van had been sexually abusing children in the back of it. They seized the van in order to search it and carry out various tests on it. The owner brought an action claiming damages for what he alleged was an unlawful seizure. The van constituted 'premises' for the purpose of s. 19 of PACE but the owner claimed that this did not legitimate seizing the van, as opposed to searching it. The police relied on the common law and on s. 19(3) of PACE. The Court of Appeal held that the seizure was justified and lawful on either ground. As far as s. 19(3) was concerned there was no reason why the word 'anything' in the section should not include 'everything' where the nature of the premises made it physically possible for the whole of the premises to be seized and detained.

There is a general limitation in s. 19(6) applying to all powers of seizure under any enactment. This is that the power may not be used to seize items which a constable has reasonable grounds for believing to be subject to legal privilege (see 6.7.1.1). This must now be considered, of course, alongside the power contained in s. 50 of the Criminal Justice and Police Act 2001, which will in certain circumstances justify the seizure and retention of legally privileged material (see 6.4.5.1). Section 19 makes no mention of the other categories of protected material, that is excluded, or special procedure material. Items coming within these categories may be seized under the s. 19 power, even though it is generally impossible to obtain a search warrant in relation to them (s. 9; see 6.5.1). There seems no good reason why the s. 19 power should extend to such items. The fact that it does gives a clear encouragement to the police to gain entry to premises where they feel that excluded or special procedure material may be found, on the basis of some other lawful pretext, and then hope to 'come across' the material in the course of their searches. The supplementary powers to seize and retain such items given by the Criminal Justice and Police Act 2001 (see 6.4.5.1) can only add to such concerns.

Code B adds little to the Act's provisions in relation to seizure. The one addition is in para. 7.4. This deals with where an officer decides not to seize an item because of an explanation given by the person in possession of it. If the constable nevertheless has reasonable grounds for believing that the item has been obtained in consequence of the commission of an offence, the person must be told of this, and that if the property is disposed of, this may give rise to civil or criminal proceedings. The most likely situation for this to occur is where goods which are believed to be stolen are in the hands of an innocent purchaser. Whether the purchaser has acquired rights of ownership over the goods will depend on the civil law; if they are still stolen, any dealing with them may amount to the tort of conversion, or the criminal offence of handling.

Somewhat surprisingly, and contrary to the recommendations of the Royal Commission on Criminal Procedure (Cmnd 8092, para. 3.47), there is no general obligation on the police to provide a receipt for seized items as a matter of course. Where, however, property has been seized under s. 50 of the Criminal Justice and Police Act 2001 there is an obligation under s. 52 of that Act to give the occupier of the premises a written notice setting out what has been seized and under what power, and giving information about the procedures for challenging the seizure. And under s. 21(1) of PACE a person who was the occupier of the premises at the time of seizure, or who had custody and control of any item immediately prior to seizure, is entitled to demand a record of what was seized. There is no time limit on this demand; it may be made at the time of the search or at any time thereafter. The police must provide the information within a reasonable time of the demand (s. 21(2)). The information may enable the individual concerned to enforce rights of access to the material under s. 21 (see 6.6.3), or to make a claim for recovery of it, for example under the Police (Property) Act 1897.

Code B requires a detailed record of every search to be kept at the relevant sub-divisional police station (paras 8.1 and 9.1). The record should include details of the place, time, and authority for the search, and the names of the officers who conducted it. The names of any persons on the premises at the time should be noted, and a list made of all articles which were seized, and why. Finally, if force was used, the reason for this should be given, and details provided of any damage caused, and the circumstances in which it occurred. This record would clearly be very useful to any person who subsequently wishes to make a claim or complaint against the police. There is, however, no statutory right of access to it, so it must be regarded as being primarily intended for use by the police. Of course, once a legal action has been started, access to the record could no doubt be obtained through the normal procedures of disclosure.

6.6.3 Retention of, and access to, seized property

In relation to property seized by the police under any statutory power, the right of the police to retain the property, and the right of the individual to have access to it, is normally governed by s. 22 and s. 21 of PACE, respectively. Where property has been seized under s. 50 of the Criminal Justice and Police Act 2001, however, there are special provisions in ss 53–70 of that Act relating to retention, and the means by which the property can be recovered. The focus here is on the standard procedure under the PACE provisions. These cover seizures as a result of a personal search, as well as in the course of a search of premises. The initial seizure must have been lawful for the powers of retention under s. 22 to arise: *R v Chief Constable of Lancashire, ex p Parker and McGrath* [1993] Crim LR 204. The basic principle set out in s. 22(1) is that the police may retain seized property for as long as is necessary in all the circumstances. This vague formulation gives the police a fair degree of room to exercise discretion. Section 22(2) gives some examples of situations where retention will be justified. These are where the property is required as evidence, or for forensic examination, or other investigation in connection with an offence. If this is the reason for retention, then the original property may not be kept if a copy or photograph would be sufficient (s. 22(4)). Property may also be retained in order to establish its lawful owner, where there are reasonable grounds for believing that it has been obtained in consequence of the commission of an offence.

Where the justification for the original seizure was that the property might be used to cause physical injury, to damage property, to interfere with evidence, or to assist in escape from police detention, it may only be retained while the person from whom it was seized is in police custody, or the custody of a court, and has not been released on bail (s. 22(3)).

If property is retained for the purpose of investigating an offence then s. 21 provides for rights of access to it. If it is retained for other purposes, for example because it is thought to constitute an obscene article and therefore to be liable to forfeiture, the statute gives no right of access, and para. 7.17 of Code B states that access should not be granted if:

> ...the officer in charge of an investigation has reasonable grounds for believing this would:
>
> (i) prejudice the investigation of any offence or criminal proceedings; or
>
> (ii) lead to the commission of an offence by providing access to unlawful material such as pornography.

The rights in s. 21 are given to the person who had custody or control of the property before it was seized. Such a person, or someone acting on his or her behalf, has two rights. First, there is a right, on request, to have access to the seized property under the supervision of a constable. Second, there is a right, on request, to a photograph or copy of the property. This may be done by allowing the person making the request access to the property for this purpose, again under the supervision of a constable, or by providing a photograph or copy within a reasonable time (s. 21(4), (7)).

Where the police's power to retain property has expired, it must generally be returned to the person from whom it was seized, even if the police continue to suspect that it may constitute the proceeds of drug trafficking, or be stolen: *Webb v Chief Constable of Merseyside* [2000] 1 All ER 209, *Costello v Chief Constable of Derbyshire* [2001] EWCA Civ 381, and *Gough v Chief Constable of the West Midlands*

[2004] EWCA Civ 206, *The Times*, 4 March 2004. The action taken for recovery may be by initiating proceedings for a civil remedy, by application for judicial review, or by recourse to the Police (Property) Act 1897. These remedies are discussed further at 6.8.

6.7 Personal property: production orders

In certain situations an individual can be compelled to produce material for inspection by, or surrender to, the police. This may arise under general police powers, for example in relation to obtaining evidence from computers (s. 20 of PACE; see 6.7.2.1), or from an order issued by a court as a result of an application by the police. PACE significantly extended the police's powers to obtain evidence by means of a search warrant (that is, under s. 8; see 6.4.5.1). This raised concern in certain quarters that the power might be used to search for confidential material in the offices of solicitors, social workers, doctors, or voluntary agencies. This concern was met by creating three statutorily defined categories of protected material. In relation to this material, the police would not be able to obtain an ordinary warrant, under PACE or any other statute, but would have to go through a special procedure laid down in PACE, which, if successful, would result in a court order for production of the material to the police. The rest of this section looks at the categories of protected material, and the orders which can be made.

This type of procedure is, of course, less intrusive than the search warrant. It still involves infringements of both property and privacy rights. The property is not seized, but has to be handed over under compulsion, with refusal generally constituting contempt. It will in most cases contain confidential information, disclosure of which may infringe the privacy of the person producing the material, and anyone mentioned in it. It is important, therefore, to look carefully at the protected categories, and the procedures for disclosure, to make sure that they go no further than is necessary in meeting the legitimate aims of police investigations.

6.7.1 Protected material

The three categories of protected material recognized in PACE are legally privileged material, excluded material, and special procedure material. Access to items which are subject to legal privilege cannot be obtained at all. Excluded and special procedure material cannot be obtained by means of an ordinary search warrant, though, as we have seen, it may be seized if discovered in the course of a lawful search (s. 19 of PACE; see 6.6.2).

6.7.1.1 Legal privilege

The definition of 'items subject to legal privilege' is contained in s. 10. The category is intended to protect the confidentiality of communications between client and legal adviser. 'Legal adviser' means a professionally qualified lawyer—the courts have refused to extend the concept to other professions (see, e.g. *R (Prudential plc) v Special Commissioner of Income Tax* [2013] UKSC 1—accountant giving legal advice).

In relation to communications between client and legal adviser the view is taken that the public interest in allowing advice to be given as freely as possible, outweighs the advantages which might accrue to police investigations if access to such communications were allowed. The policy may be seen as being linked to the right to silence, and the privilege against self-incrimination. A person must be free to communicate with a solicitor or barrister without restraint, including the admission of facts which might appear incriminating. The same policy underlies the right of access to legal advice in s. 58 of PACE (see chapter 4 (4.4.2)).

The definition in s. 10 is primarily concerned with 'communications'. This word is undefined, but presumably covers letters, recorded telephone calls or conversations, and electronic messages. Two categories of communication are covered. First, there are those which are made between a professional legal adviser and the client, or any person representing the client, in connection with the giving of legal advice. The advice does not have to relate to any proposed legal proceedings. Second, there are communications made for the purposes of actual or contemplated legal proceedings. In relation to this category, the range of people who may be involved is wider. As well as communications between the client, or the client's representative, and the legal adviser, those between the client, representative, or adviser, and any other person are covered. Communication between the legal adviser and a prospective witness would, for example, come within this definition.

A third category covers items which are not in themselves communications, but are enclosed with or referred to in such communications. The items must have been made in connection with the giving of legal advice, or for the purposes of actual or contemplated legal proceedings. An example of non-documentary material falling within this category occurred in *R v R* [1994] 4 All ER 260. The defendant had provided a blood sample to his doctor, and his solicitors had arranged for scientific analysis of this. The scientist who carried out this analysis was subsequently called as a witness for the prosecution, and her evidence was admitted. The Court of Appeal held that the blood sample, which had been given for the purpose of the defendant's defence, fell within s. 10(1), and was therefore subject to legal privilege. The scientist's evidence should not have been admitted.

In relation to all three categories the privilege only arises where the items concerned are in the possession of a person who is entitled to possession of them; but it extends to any such person, not just the legal adviser and client. Suppose that a solicitor, who is acting for a client charged with causing death by dangerous driving, sends a letter, together with a specially prepared plan of the scene of the accident, to prospective witnesses, asking the witnesses to mark where they were standing at the time of the accident. The solicitor then sends copies of the replies to the client. The letters and the maps would be legally privileged in the hands of the solicitor, the witnesses, and the client.

The case law on s. 10 has generally been restrictive of its scope. In *R v Crown Court at Inner London Sessions, ex p Baines and Baines* [1987] 3 All ER 1025, it was made clear that not every document on a client's file will be subject to legal privilege. Straightforward records of transactions, such as conveyancing documents, do not fall within s. 10. The communications or items must relate to the giving of advice, or to legal proceedings. Thus, in *R v Manchester Crown Court, ex p Rogers* [1999] 1 WLR 832, the Divisional Court held that legal privilege does not extend to records of time on an attendance note, on a time sheet or fee record (since they were not 'communications'), nor to a record of an appointment made since, although this was a 'communication', it was not, 'without more to be regarded as made in connection with legal advice' (Lord Bingham, p. 839). This approach is in line with the policy reasons for the privilege outlined. A person cannot therefore keep material out of the hands of the police by the simple expedient of giving it to a solicitor for safe-keeping. The material may attract some protection as being within the 'excluded' or 'special procedure' categories which will be discussed, but it will not receive the much stronger protection of legal privilege.

A broader restriction of the scope of the privilege derives from the decision of the House of Lords in *Francis and Francis* v *Central Criminal Court* [1988] 3 All ER 775. This case arose under the provisions of the Drug Trafficking Offences Act 1986, which used the definition of legal privilege from s. 10 of PACE. The focus here was on s. 10(2) which removes the privilege from items 'held with the intention of furthering a criminal purpose'. The police were seeking correspondence and attendance notes held by a firm of solicitors relating to property transactions undertaken by one of their clients. The suspicion was that, although the client was probably innocent of any impropriety, the money for these transactions derived from drug-trafficking activities on the part of one of the client's relatives. The question was whether the relative's criminal purpose could remove the privilege from the documents, which were in the possession of the solicitors. The majority in the House of Lords followed the common law decision in *R v Cox and Railton* (1884) 14 QBD 153 which denied the protection of legal privilege where communications were intended to further the client's criminal purpose, even where the communications were in the possession of the innocent solicitor. The House felt that the 'holding' and the 'intention' in s. 10(2) should similarly be considered disjunctively. On this basis, the fact that a third party had an intention to further a criminal purpose was sufficient to remove the privilege. This has a potentially very restrictive effect on the scope of s. 10. Where police are searching for evidence of a criminal offence it is likely that someone will have a criminal purpose in relation to it. Lord Goff, however, thought that the privilege would still apply to communications by a client to a solicitor which, unknown to the solicitor, contained false statements, which might lead to the offence of perjury being committed in legal proceedings. On this basis he was able to uphold the decision, though not the reasoning, in the Divisional Court's decision in the earlier case of *R v Crown Court at Snaresbrook, ex p DPP* [1988] 1 All ER 315. Here the police had argued that a legal aid application which was in the hands of the local Law Society was not privileged, because it was thought to contain untrue statements. The Divisional Court had held that the criminal intention under s. 10(2) must be that of the 'holder'. Following *Francis and Francis* this is clearly wrong, but the decision would still stand on the basis of the approach by Lord Goff, as noted.

6.7.1.2 Excluded material

This is the second most highly protected type of material. As will be seen, in general, excluded material can only be obtained by the police where there was a search warrant power prior to PACE which would have allowed access to it. The fact that it constitutes evidence of a serious offence will not in itself be enough to allow access. Its protected status arises from the fact that it is held in confidence, and that it consists either of personal records, human tissue or tissue fluid, or journalistic material. It is defined in s. 11.

The first type of excluded material consists of personal records. They must have been acquired or created in the course of a person's work, or for the purposes of a paid or unpaid office, and they must be held in confidence. 'In confidence' means held subject to an express or implied undertaking as to secrecy, or to a statutory restriction on disclosure (e.g. under the Official Secrets Acts, or the Data Protection Act 1998). Personal records for this purpose are records of any kind concerning an identifiable person (living or dead), which relate to the person's physical or mental health; spiritual counselling or assistance given or to be given to the person; or other counselling or assistance given or to be given to the person for the purposes of personal welfare, by a voluntary organization, or by someone who from their work has responsibilities for the person's welfare, or is responsible for supervising the person under a court order. All medical records, and those held by clergymen, probation officers, social workers, or voluntary organizations such as the NSPCC or the Samaritans, are likely to be covered. In *R v Crown Court at Cardiff, ex p Kellam*, *The Times*, 3 May 1993, for example, it was held that a hospital's record of mental patients' movements, made for the purposes of National Insurance, was excluded material. The record could be said to 'relate to' the patients' mental health, and so fell within s. 12(a). Educational records and personnel files will only be covered if their contents fall within the above categories, which will by no means always be the case. The details of a person's salary or bank account would not be excluded material.

The second category of excluded material is human tissue or tissue fluid (this includes blood, semen, saliva, etc.). It must have been taken for the purposes of diagnosis or medical treatment, and be held in confidence. If a sample has been taken for the purposes of a criminal investigation, rather than for treatment or diagnosis, it will not be excluded material.

The third category of excluded material is journalistic material, consisting of documents or records, which is held in confidence. 'Journalistic material' is, rather unhelpfully, defined in s. 13 as material acquired or created for the purposes of journalism. This obviously covers the work of reporters working for newspapers, radio, or television, but does it cover the freelance writer collecting material for a book, or the person producing a newsletter for a club or a small group of enthusiasts? The Act provides no help in answering these questions. It does make it clear, however, in s. 13(3) that it includes unsolicited material sent to a journalist by someone who intends that this should be used for the purposes of journalism. For journalistic material to be excluded material, as well as being held in confidence when access is sought, it must have been held in confidence continuously since it was first acquired or created for the purposes of journalism. It has to be in the possession of someone who acquired or created it for the purposes of journalism (s. 13(2)). It does not, however, have to be held continuously by a journalist.

A document received by a journalist in confidence for the purposes of journalism, and then passed in confidence to an expert for an opinion, and then returned to the journalist, will be excluded material while it is in the hands of the journalist. It will lose this status while with the expert, but during that time will almost certainly be special procedure material.

6.7.1.3 **Special procedure material**

This is the material with the lowest level of protection. It is defined in s. 14. Any journalistic material which is not excluded material is special procedure material. It does not have to be held in confidence. Photographs of people engaged in a riot, for example, have been held to fall into this category: *R v Bristol Crown Court, ex p Bristol Press and Picture Agency* (1986) 85 Cr App R 190. The other type of special procedure material consists of items which are not legally privileged or excluded material, but have been acquired or created in the course of a person's work, or for the purposes of a paid or unpaid office, and are held in confidence. There are special provisions relating to employees and associated companies in s. 14(3)–(6), but these do not affect the basic scope of the protection. Examples of material which has been held to come into this category include the accounts of a Youth Association (*R v Central Criminal Court, ex p Adegbesan* [1986] 3 All ER 113), conveyancing documents in the possession of a solicitor (*R v Crown Court at Inner London Sessions, ex p Baines and Baines* [1987] 3 All ER 1025), and details of bank accounts (*R v Crown Court at Leicester, ex p DPP* [1987] 3 All ER 654).

6.7.1.4 **Reasons for protection**

The reasons for giving legally privileged material special protection have been considered at 6.6.2. As regards excluded and special procedure material the reasons are more complex. Leaving aside journalistic material for the moment, it might be thought that the central element is 'confidentiality', since both types of material require this. The special status given to this material is concerned with providing protection for the confidential relationship which exists, for example, between doctor and patient, probation officer and defendant, and, in some cases, employer and employee. This is not enough in itself, however, since it would not explain the difference between excluded and special procedure material. There cannot be degrees of confidentiality: either material is held in confidence or it is not. The additional factor is the privacy of the person who is the subject of the material. Here it does make sense to talk of degrees of privacy: the details of a person's sex life may well be regarded as deserving greater protection than the details of their bank account. The first will be likely to be excluded material; the second only special procedure material.

The justifications for protecting journalistic material are different. Privacy is not really an issue here. The protection is based more on the public interest in a free press. In this context, it is desirable that journalists should be able to gather sensitive information about possible criminal activities without needing to worry that the police will be able to search their premises. Furthermore, where information is given in confidence to a journalist, it is desirable that the source should be fully protected (compare s. 10 of the Contempt of Court Act 1981). If such protection were not available, the journalist would not get the information. The best way of giving the protection is by making the information 'excluded material', and thus making it very difficult for the police to gain access to it.

6.7.2 **Orders for production**

As has already been noted, material which is legally privileged is beyond the reach of the police. Excluded material or special procedure material consisting of documents or records cannot be obtained by means of an ordinary search warrant (s. 9(2)), but may be accessible by means of a production order, or in extreme cases a search warrant, issued by a circuit judge. This procedure for access was introduced by PACE, but has subsequently been applied in other contexts.

6.7.2.1 PACE

The procedure for access to excluded or special procedure material under PACE is set out in Sch. 1. The police must make an application to a circuit judge, rather than a magistrate. Notice of the application must be given to the person in possession of the material sought. It need not be given to anyone else, such as, for example, the person under investigation: *R* v *Crown Court at Leicester, ex p DPP* [1987] 3 All ER 654; nor is a bank, for example, which receives notice of an application concerning a particular account, obliged to notify its customer: *Barclays Bank* v *Taylor* [1989] 3 All ER 563. The notice should set out the general nature of the offences under investigation (e.g. 'fraud', 'riot', 'wounding'), and the address of the premises where the material is alleged to be (*R* v *Central Criminal Court, ex p Carr* (1987) (unreported)). It should also give sufficient information identifying the material to enable the person on whom the notice is served not to 'conceal, destroy, alter or dispose' of it without the permission of either a judge or the police (Sch. 1, para. 11; *R* v *Central Criminal Court, ex p Adegbesan* [1986] 3 All ER 113). A problem with this requirement arose in *R (on the Application of NTL Group Ltd)* v *Crown Court at Ipswich* [2002] EWHC 1585 (Admin), [2003] QB 131. The Divisional Court had to consider a potential conflict between the powers to order the production of special material under PACE and the provisions of the RIPA 2000. The police had obtained an order under s. 9 of PACE in relation to emails stored by the applicant, a telecommunications company. Paragraph 11 of Sch. 1 to PACE, as we have seen, required the applicant not to conceal, destroy, alter, or dispose of the relevant material. The applicant believed that the only way in which it could comply with the order was to intercept the emails and forward them to a different address, but also believed that this would constitute an offence under the RIPA 2000 (see 6.5.1.1). The Court of Appeal, however, held that the para. 11 of Sch. 1 to PACE provided sufficient authority to meet the requirements of s. 1(5) of the RIPA 2000.

Once the notice has been given under PACE, there will then be a 'with notice' hearing, at which the police will try to convince the judge that one of two sets of 'access conditions' is met. It was stated in *R* v *Crown Court at Lewes, ex p Hill* (1990) 93 Cr App R 60 that the judge has a discretion to allow the person under investigation to be heard, even if someone else is in possession of the material. Moreover, since where material is in the hands of a third party who is not under investigation, the respondent may well not have any interest in challenging the application at the hearing, there is a strong duty on the applicant to ensure that all relevant material, including material adverse to the applicant, is before the judge. The judge must have sufficient information on which to decide whether the access conditions have been met: it is not acceptable for the judge simply to accept police assertions to that effect. This point was strongly confirmed by the Court of Appeal in *R* v *Central Criminal Court, ex p Bright* [2001] 2 All ER 244. It is not enough for the judge to consider whether the decision of the constable making the application was 'reasonable' or 'susceptible to review on Wednesbury grounds' (p. 259). Since the judge acted as the safeguard between the police and the person from whom material was sought, it was essential that the judge should be 'personally satisfied that the statutory requirements have been established' (p. 259).

The first set of access conditions (Sch. 1, para. 2) applies only to special procedure material, and follows fairly closely the requirements of s. 8 of PACE (see 6.4.5.1). As with the s. 8 power, the threshold for availability of access has been reduced from a serious arrestable offence, to an indictable offence. This, again, is a significant extension of the availability of a power which was previously thought to be exceptional. There must be reasonable grounds for believing that an indictable offence has been committed, that special procedure material comprising relevant evidence is on the premises, and that it is likely to be of substantial value to the investigation. It was felt in *R v Crown Court at Southwark, ex p Sorsky Defries* [1996] Crim LR 195, that the judge could not have been so satisfied when he took only 15 minutes to come to a decision. The judge must also be satisfied that other methods of obtaining the material, for example a straightforward request for access, have been tried without success, or have not been tried because it appeared that they were bound to fail. Finally, the judge must be satisfied that production of, or access to, the material would be in the public interest, having regard to the likely benefit to the police's investigation, and the circumstances under which the material is held.

The question of the public interest has been considered in several cases. In *R v Bristol Crown Court, ex p Bristol Press and Picture Agency* (1986) 85 Cr App R 190, the police were seeking access to photographs of rioting taken by press photographers. It was argued that it was contrary to the public interest to allow access, because this would prejudice the impartiality of the press, and would increase the likelihood of attacks on journalists and photographers covering such events. It was held that the press's impartiality would not be compromised where the material was handed over under compulsion, and that since the photographs were presumably taken with a view to publication, people photographed engaging in criminal activity would be just as likely to attack the photographer on this basis, as on the basis that the photographs would end up in police hands. A similar line was taken in *Re an Application under s. 9 PACE, The Independent,* 27 May 1988. These cases indicate a fairly restrictive role for the concept of public interest in these situations. That is confirmed on a more general basis by the comments of Glidewell LJ in *R v Central Criminal Court, ex p Carr* (1987) (unreported, but see R. Stone, 'PACE: Special Procedures and Legal Privilege' [1988] Crim LR 498, at 502), where he said:

> If documents of the kinds referred to in the information are on any applicants' premises, it is obvious that they are likely to be of substantial value to the investigation, that some or all of them will be relevant evidence, and therefore that it is in the public interest that such documents should be produced.

This suggests that the issue of 'public interest' may well be subsumed in the decision as to the usefulness and evidential relevance of the material sought. The suggestion was confirmed in *R v Crown Court at Northampton, ex p DPP* (1991) 93 Cr App R 376. The judge, to whom an application for a production order had been made, had held that a receipt held by a firm of solicitors was special procedure material, which would be of substantial evidential value in relation to a serious arrestable offence. He refused to issue an order for production, however, on the basis that it would be contrary to the public interest in that it would be using a 'sledgehammer to crack a nut'. On the Director of Public Prosecutions' application for judicial review of this decision, it was held that once the judge had decided that a serious arrestable offence (this being the test at the time) had been committed it was not consistent for him to reach the conclusion that it was contrary to the public interest to grant access.

It seems, therefore, that although the schedule appears to be clearly worded so as to require the judge to consider whether, notwithstanding the fact that the material would be of substantial value to the investigation and relevant evidence, it might be contrary to the public interest to allow access to it, in practice these decisions point to the conclusion that the main issue with which the judge needs to be concerned is whether the material relates to an indictable offence. Once this is answered in the affirmative, the other elements of the first set of access conditions, and in particular the finding that disclosure is in the public interest, will follow almost as a matter of course.

This cannot be what Parliament intended. In *ex p Bright* the Court of Appeal attempted to find a way out of this situation. The case arose out of the attempts by the former MI5 officer, David Shayler, to reveal information about the operation of the security services, and in particular alleged malpractice by those services. He had been in communication with various newspapers, which had published letters from him, and this led to a police application under PACE for the production of certain files, documents, etc. relating to Shayler held by the newspapers concerned. The judge to whom the application was made issued the order, but the newspapers appealed. The Court of Appeal, for various reasons, allowed the appeal in all but one case. As regards the 'public interest' issue, Judge LJ considered the case of *R v Crown Court at Northampton* and the argument made by counsel for the police based on it, to the effect that once the judge had found that an order was in the public interest, it could not be refused. Judge LJ did not accept this. He pointed out that the issues which could be taken into account under the 'public interest' heading were very limited under the wording of the statute. Second, he noted that the wording of para. 1 of Sch. 1 states that if the judge finds that the access conditions are fulfilled 'he may', not must, make an order. Thus he suggests that even where the access conditions, including the 'public interest', are found to exist, the judge still has a discretion whether to issue the order. In exercising this discretion he could take account of, for example ([2001] 2 All ER 244, p. 261):

> ...the effect of the order on third parties, and any consequent damage to them, or the antiquity of the matters under investigation, or an unexplained re-investigation of matters formally investigated many years earlier, or that, notwithstanding that the offence under consideration is serious, the result of the prosecution would inevitably be a nominal sentence because of circumstances personal and particular to the potential defendant.

In addition, the judge might, in appropriate cases, also take account of 'fundamental principles', such as, in relation to journalistic material, 'the potential stifling of public debate' or, where a person is ordered to produce or give access to material, 'the risk of imposing an obligation requiring the individual to whom the order is directed to incriminate himself'. Indeed, Judge LJ would have made the risk of self-incrimination an 'automatic' ground for refusing the order; the other two members of the court, while broadly agreeing with his approach, thought that it was only a matter for consideration in the exercise of the discretion. In setting out his approach, Judge LJ was careful to base his judgment on common law principles, rather than the ECHR, but it is notable that the last two principles noted would clearly be relevant to Art. 10 and Art. 6, respectively. The case was decided before the HRA 1998 came into force; it would now be more likely that a court would be prepared to base an argument along these lines more squarely on the Convention (and consequently, perhaps, to accept Judge LJ's view on 'self-incrimination' rather than that of the majority).

The approach taken in *Bright* has the advantage of allowing the judge to take into account a wide range of interests, and does have the effect of removing the 'nullification' of the public interest considerations which seemed to be implied by *R v Crown Court at Northampton*. It does so, however, by giving a very limited definition to the public interest criterion under the statute, and then allowing in broader considerations under the guise of the judge's overall discretion. Again, it must be doubtful whether this is quite what Parliament intended, but since it has the effect of giving a much fuller scope for the consideration of civil liberties issues than appeared to be the case under the previous case law, the decision is to be welcomed. This is particularly so now that the threshold for a production order is no longer a serious arrestable offence, but simply an indictable offence. The approach suggested in *Bright* clearly allows the judge to decide whether the use of the power is proportionate in relation to the potential infringement of the privacy rights (under Art. 8 of the ECHR) of the person subject to the order. It might well be the case that an attempt to use this procedure in relation to a relatively minor offence would be thought disproportionate.

The second set of access conditions (Sch. 1, para. 3) allows an order to be made in relation to either special procedure or excluded material. The conditions are satisfied if there are reasonable grounds to believe that the relevant material is on the premises specified, and that, but for s. 9(2) of PACE, it would have been possible and appropriate for a search warrant to have been issued. Section 9(2) makes ineffective any search warrant power in a statute passed before PACE, in so far as it would have enabled access to be gained to legally privileged, excluded, or special procedure material. So if, for example, a blood sample constituting excluded material has been stolen, then it would have been possible, but for s. 9(2), to have obtained a warrant under s. 26 of the Theft Act 1968 to search for it. An order may therefore be granted under the second set of access conditions. It is important to note that, although the second set of access conditions is limited to situations where there was an existing search warrant power, the offence being investigated does not have to be an indictable one, the material sought does not need to be relevant evidence, and there is no question of the public interest to consider. It is also important to remember that, where a search warrant power is contained in legislation passed after PACE, it will allow access to both excluded and special procedure material, unless the later Act itself states otherwise. The Public Order Act 1986, for example, makes no reference to excluded and special procedure material, so the search warrant power contained in s. 24 of that Act can be used to obtain access to such material, without needing to use Sch. 1 of PACE.

A circuit judge who is satisfied that one or the other set of access conditions is fulfilled, may make an order directing the person who appears to be in possession of the material to produce it to a constable, or to give a constable access to it (Sch. 1, para. 4). If the material is held electronically, the order will be construed as directing the person to produce it in a visible and legible form in which it can be taken away (in other words, a print-out), or to give the constable access to the material in a form in which it is visible and legible (e.g. as a display on a computer screen: Sch. 1, para. 5). The order must give at least seven days for compliance (Sch. 1, para. 4). Failure to comply will be treated as a contempt of the Crown Court, thus enabling the person who refuses to be fined or imprisoned (para. 15).

Anything produced and taken away is to be treated as having been seized by a constable, so that the access and retention provisions under ss 21 and 22 of PACE (see 6.6.3) will apply to it.

As a last resort, Sch. 1 provides that in certain circumstances a search warrant may be issued in relation to excluded or special procedure material (para. 12). As Macpherson J commented in *R* v *Maidstone Crown Court, ex p Waitt* [1988] Crim LR 384:

> The special procedure under s. 9 and sch. 1 is a serious inroad upon the liberty of the subject. The responsibility for ensuring that the procedure is not abused lies with circuit judges. It is of cardinal importance that circuit judges should be scrupulous in discharging that responsibility. The responsibility is greatest when the circuit judge is asked to issue a search warrant

Before issuing a warrant the judge must first be satisfied that one of the sets of access conditions is met. In addition the judge must be satisfied that one of a number of further conditions set out in para. 14, and justifying the issue of a warrant, has been met. The first two are similar to conditions which apply under s. 8, that is that it is impracticable to communicate with the person entitled to grant entry to the premises, or the person entitled to grant access to the material. It was held in *R* v *Crown Court at Leeds, ex p Switalski* [1991] Crim LR 559 that 'practicable' does not mean simply feasible, or physically possible. The judge can consider not only the available means of communication but also all the circumstances, including the nature of the inquiries and the person against whom they are directed. In this case a warrant had been issued against a firm of solicitors which was itself under investigation, and this was upheld by the Queen's Bench Division in an action for judicial review. It was emphasized in *R* v *Southampton Crown Court, ex p J and P* [1993] Crim LR 962, however, that it will be unusual for a warrant to be issued against a firm of solicitors. In this case the Divisional Court quashed the warrant on the basis, *inter alia*, that the need for a 'without notice' application had not been made out. A similar view was taken in *ex p Sorsky Defries*, where the warrant was sought in relation to a firm of accountants.

The third condition which may justify the issue of a warrant arises where the material sought is subject to a statutory restriction on disclosure, and is likely to be disclosed in breach of this if the warrant is not issued. This would apply, for example, to journalistic material which was covered by the Official Secrets Acts.

The fourth condition is where service of notice of an application for an order might seriously prejudice the investigation. This would be the case where there was reason to believe that the person in possession of the material would destroy or dispose of it, notwithstanding the provisions of para. 11, or that the person would alert others involved in a criminal operation.

Finally, where the second set of access conditions is satisfied, and an order under para. 4 has not been complied with, a warrant may be issued (para. 12(1)(b)). This does not apply where the order was based on the first set of access conditions. In this case, as previously noted, an action for contempt of court is the only sanction (para. 15).

In relation to either set of access conditions, reforms of Sch. 1 contained in the Serious Organised Crime and Police Act 2005 mean that, as from 1 January 2006, a warrant covering multiple premises, including an 'all premises' warrant, may be obtained, in the same way as is possible under s. 8 (see 6.4.5.1). There is no power, however, to obtain a warrant allowing multiple entries.

If a warrant is issued it will be subject to the general provisions of PACE and Code B, in the same way as any other search warrant. In addition, however, Code B contains some special provisions which apply to searches under a warrant issued under Sch. 1. An officer of at least the rank of inspector should take charge of the search, which should be carried out 'with discretion and in such a manner as to cause the least possible disruption to any business or other activities carried out on the premises' (para. 6.14 of Code B).

Once on the premises, the officer should make sure that material cannot be taken from the premises without the officer's knowledge, and then ask for the material to which the warrant applies to be produced. If there is an index to files on the premises, this may be consulted, and any files which from this appear to contain material sought may be inspected. A physical search should be a last resort, to be used only where there is a refusal to produce the material sought, or to allow access to the index; or where the index appears to be inaccurate or incomplete; or if for any other reason the officer in charge has reasonable grounds for believing that a search is necessary to find the material sought (para. 6.15 of Code B).

6.7.2.2 The Terrorism Act 2000

Schedule 5 to the Terrorism Act 2000 contains powers to obtain search warrants and production orders in relation to material sought in the course of a terrorist investigation. These powers are dealt with in chapter 10 (10.4.4.2).

6.8 Remedies

If there have been breaches of proper procedures by the police in relation to any of the powers discussed in this chapter a formal complaint is, of course, possible, as described in chapter 4 (4.6.3). It is also possible, however, to use civil remedies. In particular, it is necessary to consider actions under the HRA 1998, in tort, judicial review, and the Police (Property) Act 1897.

6.8.1 The Human Rights Act 1998

Any challenge to powers of entry and search and seizure under the HRA 1998 will be based on an infringement of the right to privacy and family life under Art. 8

of the ECHR. As long ago as 1959, however, the Commission, in rejecting a claim as inadmissible, recognized that lawfully authorized searches and seizures would generally fall within Art. 8(2), which permits invasions of such rights where 'necessary in a democratic society...for the prevention of disorder or crime' (App. No. 530/59, Yearbook, vol. 3, p. 190). In the case of *Chappell* v *United Kingdom* (1990) 12 EHRR 1 the ECtHR considered an application relating to the exercise of what was then called an 'Anton Piller' order, but is now under the Civil Procedure Rules simply a 'search order'. This is a kind of 'civil search warrant' commonly used in connection with intellectual property actions: see, for example, R. Stone, *The Law of Entry, Search, and Seizure*, ch. 10. The Court held that it did not involve any infringement of Art. 8, despite the fact that there were some breaches in procedure. It is possible, however, to challenge the issue of a search warrant under Art. 8, as is shown by *Niemietz* v *Germany* (1993) 16 EHRR 97, discussed at 6.4.5.1, if the powers go beyond what is 'necessary in a democratic society'. Most powers under English law, which are based on the authority of a warrant, and take account of special considerations such as legal or other professional privilege, will be likely to meet the standards of Art. 8.

A search which takes place other than on the basis of a warrant will, perhaps, be more likely to be challenged. This was the case in *Funke* v *France* (1993) 16 EHRR 287, discussed at 6.5.2, where a customs search power was not based on the issue of a warrant.

As far as powers to seize property are concerned, these will generally be justified by Art. 1 of the First Protocol to the ECHR. This states that:

> ... [e]very natural or legal person is entitled to the peaceful enjoyment of his possessions. No one shall be deprived of his possessions except in the public interest and subject to the conditions provided for by law and by the general principles of international law.
>
> The proceeding provisions shall not, however, in any way impair the right of a State to enforce such laws as it deems necessary to control the use of property in accordance with the general interest or to secure the payment of taxes or other contributions or penalties.

The power to confiscate obscene publications under the Obscene Publications Act 1959 (see chapter 8 (8.5.1.2)) was held to be justified under the second paragraph of this Article in *Handyside* v *United Kingdom* (1976) 1 EHRR 737. The case also made it clear that temporary seizures of property, falling short of permanent confiscation, do not fall within the scope of the Article.

6.8.2 **Tortious actions**

Where there has been an unlawful entry on to property there will clearly be the possibility of an action for trespass. A police search under such circumstances, however, may well also involve the unlawful use of force against occupants, and so lead to actions for assault, or false imprisonment. This was the basis of the action in *White* v *Metropolitan Police Commissioner*, *The Times*, 24 April 1982, where £20,000 exemplary damages was awarded to both the plaintiffs as a result of the use of 'excessive, unreasonable and unnecessary force' by the police in the course of a search. Where trespass is relied on, it is not necessarily the case that the entry needs to be unlawful from the beginning. If the police act in excess of their powers following a lawful entry, this may well have the effect of turning them into trespassers: *Six Carpenters' Case* (1610) 8 Co Rep 146a. Despite some comments of Lord Denning to the contrary in *Chic Fashions v Jones* [1968] 2 QB 299, there seems no doubt that as far as the retrospective effect of unlawful actions after entry is concerned, as Clayton and Tomlinson conclude (*Civil Actions Against the Police*, 3rd edn (London: Thomson Sweet & Maxwell, 2004), p. 257), 'the doctrine remains good law'. Once the police are regarded as trespassers, this may well have the effect of rendering any further action taken by them unlawful. As indicated in the *White* case, exemplary damages will be available if the police were aware of the fact that they were exceeding their powers, or use excessive force. The award of such damages will, of course, be subject to the guidelines set out by the Court of Appeal in *Thompson v Commissioner of Police for the Metropolis* [1997] 2 All ER 762, discussed at chapter 4 (4.6.1).

Tortious actions may also be brought in relation to seizure of, or damage to, property which has occurred in the course of an unlawful search and seizure. The torts of trespass to goods, conversion, and negligence, may all be relevant here. Whatever the basis of the action, the remedies are governed by the Torts (Interference with Goods) Act 1977, which provides for three categories of remedy (s. 3(2)):

(a) an order for the delivery of the goods, and payment for any consequential damage; or

(b) an order for the delivery of the goods, but giving the defendant the alternative of paying damages by reference to the value of the goods together in either case with payment for any consequential damage; or

(c) damages.

The first of these is available only at the court's discretion, but the plaintiff may choose between the other two (s. 3(3)(b)).

6.8.3 Judicial review

When property has been seized lawfully by the police, but their right to retain it is disputed, then there are some authorities which hold that the appropriate remedy is to seek judicial review of the police action. This was the view taken in *Allen v Chief Constable of Cheshire*, *The Times*, 16 July 1988, where the issue was refusal of access to seized documents. A similar approach was taken in two cases concerned with the attempt to recover property, namely, *R v IRC, ex p Rossminster* [1980] AC 952, and *Roandale v Metropolitan Police Commissioner* [1979] Crim LR 254 (see chapter 8 (8.5.1.2)). In *R v Chief Constable of Warwickshire, ex p Fitzpatrick* [1999] 1 All ER 65, however, it was held that challenges to the legality of seizure should be made by a private law action rather than judicial review. This approach seems to have been accepted as appropriate by the Court of Appeal in the subsequent cases of *Webb v Chief Constable of Merseyside* [2000] 1 All ER 209, and *Costello v Chief Constable of Derbyshire* [2001] EWCA Civ 381, [2001] 3 All ER 150.

In *Webb* money had been seized as the suspected proceeds of drug trafficking. He was not convicted of any offence, but the police refused to return the money.

Webb took proceedings in the county court, at which the police sought to prove, on the balance of probabilities, that the money was the proceeds of drug trafficking and so should not be returned. This argument was successful at trial, but the decision was overturned by the Court of Appeal. It held that the only powers of forfeiture were those that existed under statute, and these depended on a conviction. Provided that Webb could establish that he had at least a possessory title to the money at the time it was seized, then the police could not resist his claim, and were bound to return the money to him. The same principle was applied in *Costello* v *Chief Constable of Derbyshire*. The property here was a car which was believed to be stolen. It was seized from Costello, but he was never charged with any offence. The car was retained by the police for purposes legitimated by s. 22 of PACE until 5 January 1997. At that point Costello sought the return of the car but it was refused. He later brought an action in the county court to recover it. The police resisted this on the basis that the car was undoubtedly stolen and that Costello must have been aware of this. Even though the true owner could not be identified, the car should not be returned to Costello. The police succeeded at trial, but on appeal the court applied the principle used in *Webb*. In other words, it held that if Costello had a possessory title at the time of the seizure he had a better right to the car than the police, and in the absence of the real owner, was entitled to have it returned to him. The only exception to this principle, which was based on the House of Lords' decision in *Tinsley* v *Milligan* [1994] AC 340, was if the transfer would in itself involve illegality. If, for example, the property was a gun, or drugs, the police would be able to resist a claim for its return. That was not the case here, however, and Costello was entitled to succeed.

It would seem, therefore, that judicial review will now only be the appropriate remedy for achieving access under s. 21 of PACE, where this has been denied. Where property is retained as a result of an unlawful seizure, or, following a lawful seizure, is not returned to the person from whom it was seized, then a civil claim is the appropriate means of redress.

6.8.4 **The Police (Property) Act 1897**

Where goods are in the possession of the police as a result of investigations into a suspected offence, this Act, as amended by the Police (Property) Act 1997, provides a summary procedure whereby the owner can reclaim them. This will be most relevant where property which has been lawfully seized is retained after the conclusion of legal proceedings, without being made subject to any order for confiscation or forfeiture. The owner can apply to the magistrates' court for an order for the delivery of the property (s. 1(1)). If ownership is in doubt the court must order delivery to the person appearing to it to be the owner. The existence of the Act does not, however, preclude the use of ordinary civil proceedings to determine ownership, and these are to be preferred if there is a real legal dispute as to who is the owner: *Lyons* v *Metropolitan Police Commissioner* [1975] QB 321. Equally, if an order under s. 1(1) of the Act has been made, any person claiming to be the true owner can challenge this by initiating civil proceedings. There is, however, a time limit of six months from the making of the order for such proceedings to be taken (s. 1(2)). The taking of proceedings under the Police (Property) Act 1897 does not preclude the bringing of subsequent civil proceedings: *Webb* v *Chief Constable of Merseyside* [2000] 1 All ER 209.

6.9 **Protecting private information**

As Glidewell LJ stated in *Kaye* v *Robertson* (1991), 'it is well-known that in English law there is no right to privacy'. This was true at the time, and was in contrast to many other jurisdictions where such a right is specifically recognized, and protected. In the United States, for example, there are specific torts dealing with privacy infringements of particular types, as well as a more general constitutional protection. The HRA 1998 changed the situation in the UK, however. As noted at 6.1, Art. 8 of the ECHR states that 'everyone has the right to respect for his private and family life, his home and his correspondence'. This raised the possibility, much discussed when the HRA 1998 was being considered by Parliament, that the English courts may at last develop a general right of privacy. It is argued at 6.10 that they have, by a slightly tangential route, reached that position in relation to the publication of information about an individual's private life. Prior to this development, claimants in the UK who felt that their privacy had been infringed had to make do with a range of other causes of action, none of which was specifically designed to deal with this right.

As noted at 6.2, the scope of Art. 8, the right to respect for private life, is broad. The focus in this part of this chapter is on the conflict between the activities of the press and individual privacy. The following working definition is therefore adopted, to indicate the scope of what is to follow in the rest of this chapter, and the approach to the discussion. The right to privacy will here be treated as:

> ...the right to prevent, or to be compensated for, the unauthorized acquisition or publication of secret personal information.

With this narrow definition to work with, we must now turn to the issue of why this right is thought to need protecting. Leaving aside the question of physical intrusions, which are objectionable in their own right, why do people object to the 'unauthorized acquisition or publication of secret personal information'? Publication of personal secrets may, of course, cause embarrassment, or even financial loss, if it results in damage to a business, for example (as might be the case if the information concerned relates to previous criminal convictions, or failure to pay debts). It does not necessarily do so. Many people are sensitive about their salary, yet publication of the details of it will in most cases cause them no measurable harm. We would still, no doubt, wish to include this within our definition of an infringement of privacy. When we turn to the acquisition of information, without publication, the problem becomes if anything more difficult. Of course, if the acquirer intends to benefit from the information, or to use it against the person to whom it refers, then there are clear grounds for objection. What about simple acquisition, however, where no further use is made of the information: is this still an invasion of privacy? We would no doubt wish so to categorize the behaviour of the person who deliberately, secretly, and undetected, watches a neighbour undressing, or the deliberate eavesdropper, who secretly listens in to a private conversation simply out of nosiness. What of the unintentional eavesdropper, however, who happens to overhear a conversation on private premises; or the person who just happens to look out of the window at the time the neighbour is undressing? In the latter two cases the effect on the people observed or overheard is exactly the same as in the first two, and yet the first two seem much more serious, even though the victim's privacy has not been invaded to any greater extent than by the unintentional overhearing or observation. Even the latter two situations will become more serious, however, if the person who has innocently intruded then makes use of the information so acquired.

It is suggested that the answers to the questions posed in the previous paragraph are as follows. All the situations outlined involve an invasion of privacy, since that concept must be defined from the point of view of the 'victim' rather than the 'invader'. We will only regard infringement of privacy as needing the protection of the law, however, if the invasion is deliberate (or perhaps reckless, or even negligent), or if the invader makes use of any information acquired as a result of the infringement. Even then, there will be a need to provide for defences, so that, for example, the disclosure of wrongdoing which can only be achieved by an invasion of the privacy of the wrongdoer is not prevented. There is also the problem of whether the development of a 'public interest' defence should mean that those who are in the 'public eye' should be entitled to less protection, in relation to their privacy, than the ordinary private individual. If the answer is yes, as it is in the United States (see *New York Times* v *Sullivan* (1964) 376 US 254), then the question arises as to how you identify a 'public person'. Should it mean anyone who attracts media attention (including, e.g. the victims of crimes or natural disasters), or only those who choose to put themselves in the public eye, such as politicians and entertainers?

With these general issues in mind, we now turn to the ways in which privacy may be protected under current English law. The word 'privacy' will, of course, be used throughout in the sense given in the working definition set out above, unless otherwise indicated.

6.9.1 **Privacy and press freedom**

There has been much controversy in the past few years relating to the relationship between a developing law of privacy on the one hand and the freedom of the press on the other. Two particular issues have dominated discussion.

The first issue is the suspicion that judges are developing a law of privacy 'by the back door' without appropriate Parliamentary scrutiny. This issue does in fact date back to the passage of the HRA 1998, and concerns about the possible effects on the freedom of the press were reflected in s. 12 of the Act, which is discussed at 6.9.2. Matters came to a head in 2010–11 with concerns over the use of so-called 'super-injunctions' which prohibited the press from even reporting the fact that an injunction had been granted. This led to an investigation by committee, whose membership included lawyers working for media organizations, and which was chaired by Lord Neuberger MR. The committee produced a report

which was published in May 2011. It is available at http://www.judiciary.gov.uk/
publications-and-reports/reports/civil/committee-reports-super-injunctions. The
report found that super-injunctions had been used less extensively than had been
claimed, and issued guidance as to when it might be appropriate for such injunctions to be used. Since then the issue seems to have subsided.

The other area of controversy has been the so-called 'phone-hacking' scandal
involving, primarily, the *News of The World*, which closed following revelations
that its staff had been involved in hacking into the messages on a mobile phone
belonging to a murdered teenage girl. The extent of this practice, which involved
clear infringements of privacy, and probably criminal behaviour, was the subject of
a public inquiry chaired by Lord Leveson. Another consequence of the scandal has
been revisions to the make-up and operation of the Press Complaints Commission.
The Leveson Report and its outcome are dealt with at 6.12.

We turn first, however, to the legal rules relating to the protection of privacy,
initially under the common law, and more recently under the HRA 1998.

6.9.2 Privacy under the Human Rights Act 1998

The possibility that Art. 8 could be used to control media intrusions into individual privacy was much discussed at the time when the HRA 1998 was proceeding through Parliament. The scope for using Art. 8 in this way had been tested
in the application to the ECHR in 1995 by Earl Spencer and his wife (*Spencer* v
United Kingdom [1998] 25 EHRR CD 105). The complaint related to publication of
newspaper articles dealing with the alleged eating disorders suffered by Countess
Spencer, together with photographs of her taken without permission. The European
Commission on Human Rights ruled that the application was inadmissible, because
it felt that the applicants had not exhausted the possible domestic remedies. In particular it held that the remedy of breach of confidence should have been pursued
prior to seeking a remedy at Strasbourg. In coming to this conclusion, however, the
Commission recognized that it was possible that Art. 8 could provide a remedy in
this situation ([1998] 25 EHRR CD 105, p. 112):

> On the facts as presented by the parties, the Commission would not exclude that the
> absence of an actionable remedy in relation to the publications of which the applicants
> complain could show a lack of respect for their private lives. It has regard in this respect
> to the duties and responsibilities that are carried with the right of freedom of expres-
> sion guaranteed by Article 10 of the Convention and to Contracting States' obligation
> to provide a measure of protection to the right of privacy of an individual affected by
> others' exercise of their freedom of expression.

Although this statement was not a part of the Commission's decision, it nevertheless indicated the potential for the use of Art. 8 in this context. This potential has
been confirmed by later cases, and in particular by *von Hannover* v *Germany* (2005)
40 EHRR 1 in which the Court ruled that there was an infringement of the privacy
of Princess Caroline of Monaco by the publication of photographs of her in the
German press. The material made no contribution to any debate of public interest,
and in this situation the Princess's Art. 8 rights prevailed over the press's right to
freedom of expression.

These decisions are ones which the English courts ought to 'take into account', by virtue of s. 2 of the HRA 1998, when considering any relevant application of the ECHR in English law.

The door was therefore open for the courts to use Art. 8 as a means of controlling media intrusions on the privacy of individuals through the publication of articles or photographs. What were the factors which might have restrained the courts in developing the law in this way?

First, there is the issue of whether they were prepared to apply the Convention rights where the dispute is between private individuals, rather than between an individual and a public authority. That is the question of 'horizontal' rather than 'vertical' effect, discussed in chapter 2 (2.2.7). The *Spencer* and *von Hannover* cases clearly indicated that it would be appropriate to do so—treating the failure of the State to provide protection in this area via its courts as a breach of its positive duty under Art. 8 (see 6.1).

A second issue was the operation of s. 12 of the HRA 1998, which was inserted largely as a response to concerns that Convention rights might be used too eagerly by the courts against the media. The section contains provisions requiring the notification wherever possible of the person against whom relief is sought (in other words discouraging injunctions obtained by without-notice applications) (s. 12(2)), and discouraging restraint prior to publication (s. 12(3)). The most important provision in this context, however, is s. 12(4), which states that:

> ...[t]he court must have particular regard to the importance of the Convention right to freedom of expression and, where the proceedings relate to material which the respondent claims, or which appears to the court, to be journalistic, literary or artistic material (or to conduct connected with such material), to—
>
> (1) the extent to which—
>
>   (i) the material has, or is about to, become available to the public; or
>
>   (ii) it is, or would be, in the public interest for the material to be published;
>
> (2) any relevant privacy code.

Much of this simply restates what was in any case likely to be a court's approach to balancing the rights under Art. 10 (freedom of expression) and Art. 8 (privacy). The Convention case law has regularly emphasized the importance of the media as the guardians of the public interest, so that restrictions of its Art. 10 rights should be approached with great caution. The final provision (s. 12(4)(b)), however, relating to the need to take into account 'any relevant privacy code' goes somewhat further. It seems to suggest that it is only where self-regulation through a privacy code has failed in a particular case that the court should consider intervening to restrain or compensate for publication. It does not, of course, impose an obligation on the court not to act where the privacy code is still potentially in play, but it might have a chilling effect, and may discourage claimants from trying to use the law at an early stage.

In fact the case law under the HRA 1998 has shown the courts creating a 'privacy' right initially through the development of the law relating to breach of confidence, rather than as an independent right. This has had the advantage, among other things, of not requiring the court to address the 'horizontal' effect issue. If the privacy right is attached to an existing situation where it is recognized that there is a right of action between individuals then the problem does not arise—the courts as public authorities are simply developing existing law in a way which is compatible with the Convention rights.

The relationship between breach of confidence and privacy will, therefore, be considered first, followed by other possible actions which might be brought in order to protect privacy rights.

6.10 Breach of confidence and privacy

For some years the action for breach of confidence has been the main method for developing the protection of privacy in English law. Its use for the rather different purpose of protecting government secrets is discussed in chapter 7 (7.7). The order of treatment here will be to look first at the law prior to the HRA 1998, and then at the way in which it has developed further under the influence of that Act.

6.10.1 Breach of confidence prior to 2 October 2000

The use of breach of confidence to protect the privacy of the individual can be traced back to *Prince Albert* v *Strange* (1849) 1 Mac and G 25. Queen Victoria and Prince Albert, for their amusement, had occasionally made drawings and etchings of subjects of private and domestic interest to themselves, and not intended for publication. Although the precise course of events is obscure, it seems that unauthorized copies from some of the etchings were made by an employee of a printer to whom the etchings had been entrusted by the plaintiff. These copies had found their way into the hands of the defendant, who proposed to exhibit them. The Court of Chancery held that the plaintiff was entitled to an injunction to restrain the publication, since the defendant must have obtained them as a result of a breach of confidence. Similarly in *Argyll* v *Argyll* [1967] Ch 302 it was held that the Duchess of Argyll could obtain an injunction to prevent newspapers from revealing the secrets of her marriage, which had been disclosed to them by the Duke. The Duke had broken the confidence that exists between marriage partners, and his wife was entitled to take action to restrain any further disclosure. The case confirmed that the breach of confidence action can arise independently of any rights derived from property and contract, and is therefore a separate cause of action.

Secrets of sexual relationships may be confidential even if they take place outside marriage. This was confirmed by *Stephens* v *Avery* [1988] 2 All ER 477, where the disclosure related to a lesbian relationship in which the plaintiff had been involved. This case also discussed the limitations of the right to restrain breaches of confidence. It is well established that disclosures which are in the 'public interest' will not be restrained, even if they breach a confidence. The person who is told 'in confidence' about criminal activities need have no hesitation in disclosing them (at least to the proper authorities). In *Stephens* v *Avery* it was suggested by the defence that this should also apply to the disclosure of 'immoral' activities. The court accepted that a duty of confidence would not apply to 'matters which have a grossly immoral tendency' (p. 480), but it refused to categorize a lesbian relationship, or indeed any sexual conduct between consenting adults, as falling into that category.

The public interest defence goes wider than the disclosure of 'iniquity'. In *Lion Laboratories* v *Evans* [1985] QB 526 it was held to legitimize disclosure of information about the problems with the operation of a machine used for carrying out breath tests on motorists. In *X* v *Y* [1988] 2 All ER 648, however, it was held not to justify the disclosure of the names of doctors who were suffering from AIDS, this information having been obtained from confidential medical records. The doctors' privacy was thus protected, but this was as much on the basis of the public interest in maintaining the confidentiality of hospital records, as the doctors' individual rights.

In *Hellewell* v *Chief Constable of Derbyshire* [1995] 1 WLR 804 it was suggested, obiter, by Laws J, that breach of confidence could be used to restrain the publication of photographs:

> If someone with a telephoto lens were to take from a distance with no authority a picture of another engaged in some private act, the subsequent disclosure of the photograph would, in my judgment, as surely amount to a breach of confidence as if he had found or stolen a letter or diary in which the act was recounted and proceeded to publish it. In such a case, the law should protect what might reasonably be called a right of privacy, although the name accorded to the cause of action would be breach of confidence.

The case concerned photographs taken of a man while he was in police custody which local shopkeepers had asked the police to supply for use by their security staff to reduce shoplifting. The applicant was unsuccessful in his application for an interim injunction to prevent the circulation of his photograph because the court held that a 'public interest' defence would be bound to succeed at trial. The comments of Laws J, however, indicated the possibility of the further development of the law in this area.

The possibility of using breach of confidence to protect private telephone calls was indicated by the Court of Appeal in *Francome* v *Mirror Group Newspapers* [1984] 2 All ER 408, which concerned an action to prevent the *Daily Mirror* from publishing secretly obtained tapes of telephone conversations, alleged to reveal breaches of Jockey Club regulations, and possibly criminal offences. Although only dealing with the matter at the interlocutory stage, and therefore not needing to reach a final decision, they regarded the issue of the confidentiality of telephone conversations as arguable, particularly when the eavesdropping occurred by means of an illegal tap. (This area is now partially covered by provisions of the Regulation of Investigatory Powers Act 2000, considered earlier in this chapter, at 6.5.1.1.)

The ground work had, therefore, been done, prior to the HRA 1998, in establishing the possibilities for breach of confidence as a protection for privacy. We must now turn to the way in which the law has developed under the Act.

6.10.2 Breach of confidence under the Human Rights Act 1998

The first of a number of important cases was *Douglas* v *Hello! Ltd* [2005] 4 All ER 128. The case concerned arrangements for the wedding of two film stars—Michael

Douglas and Catherine Zeta Jones. The couple had contracted with *OK!* magazine for it to provide exclusive pictures of the wedding. No other media representatives were to be present, and all those providing services at the wedding and the reception had confidentiality clauses in their contracts. Guests were asked not to take photographs or videos. After the wedding it transpired that *Hello!* magazine had obtained unauthorized photographs of the wedding which it was proposing to publish. Action was brought both by the Douglases and by *OK!* magazine. As the case progressed it became ever clearer that these two actions, though related, needed to be treated separately. Initially, however, both claimants sought an injunction restraining publication, which was granted. The Court of Appeal had to consider whether this interim injunction should be continued, pending the trial of the full action between the claimants and *Hello!* The three judges all came to the decision that it should not, but for slightly varying reasons.

First, as regards the basis of the action, all three were agreed that the tort of breach of confidence potentially applied to the situation. There was less clarity about the extent to which 'confidentiality' could be taken. It clearly applied to those who knew that they were dealing with confidential material, even if they had not been placed under a specific obligation of confidence (see the comments of Lord Goff in *Attorney-General* v *Guardian Newspapers Ltd (No. 2)* [1990] 1 AC 109, p. 281, discussed at 8.7.2). Could it extend beyond such a situation? Sedley LJ was prepared to go so far as to say that 'we have reached a point at which it can be said with confidence that the law recognises and will appropriately protect a personal right of privacy' [2001] 2 All ER 289, para. 110, p. 316, although he later recognized that this is 'grounded in the equitable doctrine of breach of confidence' (para. 125, p. 320). The other two members of the court (Brooke and Keene LJJ) were less clear on this issue, though both recognized that the boundaries between a right of confidentiality and a right of privacy were becoming blurred. The case, therefore, gave weight to the further development of breach of confidence in protecting privacy.

In coming to these conclusions, only Brooke LJ made any reference to the reference in s. 12(4) to a 'privacy code'. Having noted the Press Complaints Commission's Code of Practice, which recognized the need to respect privacy in cl. 3, he commented that this, together with the statutory provisions meant that (para. 94, p. 314):

> ... [a] newspaper which flouts cl. 3 of the code is likely in those circumstances to have its claim to an entitlement to freedom of expression trumped by Art. 10(2) considerations of privacy.

Brooke LJ was also the only one of the judges to give any serious consideration to the possibility of a privacy right existing independently of breach of confidence.

As regards the question of whether the injunction should be continued, there were two aspects which needed to be considered. First, there was the traditional common law approach. This required the court to consider whether the claimant has an arguable case and, if so, where the 'balance of convenience' lay between claimant and defendant as regards interim injunctive relief (*American Cyanamid Co.* v *Ethicon Ltd* [1975] AC 396). Second, there were the provisions of s. 12 of the HRA 1998 (as discussed). Section 12(3) affects the first part of the *American*

Cyanamid test, in that it requires the court not to issue an interim injunction which will affect freedom of expression unless the claimant is likely to succeed at trial (though it has subsequently been doubted whether this makes any significant difference to the test: Sir Andrew Morritt VC in *Imutran Ltd* v *Uncaged Campaigns Ltd* [2001] 2 All ER 385, at para. 17, quoted by Lord Woolf in *A* v *B and C* [2002] EWCA Civ 337, para. 11). Brooke LJ thought that the claimants had established that they were likely to succeed, but that the 'balance of convenience' was in favour of *Hello!*. Damages would be an adequate remedy for the claimants, given that the wedding was not 'private' in the light of the publicity appearing in *OK!*. Sedley LJ came to a similar conclusion, but based his decision more closely within the context of Arts 10 and 8 of the ECHR and the need to balance the right of privacy against that of freedom of expression. Keene LJ was more dubious about the likelihood of success on the part of the claimants but felt that in any case the balance was against prior restraint of publication.

The effect of this decision was, therefore, to indicate that the law was continuing to develop, but because it was dealing only with interim proceedings, and because of the varying approaches as between the members of the court, did not give a clear picture of the status of privacy rights within the law of confidentiality. Nor was this issue particularly advanced when the case returned to the High Court for decision: [2003] EWHC 786 (Ch), [2003] 3 All ER 996. Lindsay J held that the case could be decided without embarking on any consideration of the question of any general law of privacy. He felt that this would be more appropriately dealt with by Parliament. The judge held that the photographic representation of the wedding deserved protection as a 'trade secret'—there was therefore a breach of 'commercial confidence' (as regards both *OK!* and the Douglases) when *Hello!* magazine published the unauthorized photographs. He did not feel that s. 12 of the HRA 1998 operated to prevent liability in these circumstances, taking into account in particular the fact that *Hello!* had acted in breach of the Press Complaints Council's code of practice (which is referred to as a relevant issue in s. 12). He also held that there was a breach of the Data Protection Act 1998 in sending the photographs to the magazine's London office over ISDN telephone lines. As regards quantum, at a separate hearing ([2003] EWHC 2629 (Ch)), he awarded £1,033,156 to *OK!* for the breach of its commercial confidence, and the consequent loss in sales. To the Douglases he awarded £3,750 each for the distress resulting from the breach of confidence, and £50 each for the breach of the Data Protection Act 1988. It is at this point that it becomes clear that the case is concerned with two differing aspects of 'breach of confidence'. The Douglases were in effect using breach of confidence to protect privacy; *OK!* was using it to obtain compensation for a breach of its commercial rights. The decision of Lindsay J was appealed by *Hello!*. By the time the appeal was heard, the House of Lords had handed down its decision in *Campbell* v *MGN Ltd* [2004] UKHL 22, [2004] 2 All ER 995, discussed at 6.10.3, and the Court of Appeal had to take account of the views expressed there. They confirmed that the Douglases' privacy had been breached, and the level of the award to them. As regards *OK!*, however, the Court held that *Hello!* had not in fact committed any breach of commercial confidence. The photographs which it had used did not belong to *OK!*—on the contrary, it had acquired its own photographs. *OK!*'s only right was to use the photographs authorized for the purpose by the Douglases. *Hello!*'s actions did not interfere with that right, and the award to

OK! was overturned. A further appeal to the House of Lords dealt only with *OK!*'s action. In an analysis which is not relevant to the development of privacy law, the House overturned the Court of Appeal decision and restored Lindsay J's award to *OK!*: *OBG Ltd* v *Allan* [2007] UKHL 21, [2007] 4 All ER 545.

This lengthy litigation reaffirmed the centrality of 'confidence' to this area of law, even post-HRA 1998. But the relatively low award made to the Douglases for distress perhaps indicates that, unless there is a strong 'commercial' element (as there was in this case), actions for breach of confidence may not attract sufficient damages to justify the risk of legal action.

The next case to consider is *Venables* v *News Group Newspapers* [2001] 1 All ER 908. Here the applicants were two young men who had been convicted when children of the murder of a toddler. The case had received immense publicity, and there was considerable controversy about the length of time which they should spend in custody. In 2000, when they reached the age of 18, a decision on this issue was made by the Lord Chief Justice which made it likely that the applicants would be released in the relatively near future. It was thought that they would need, for their own protection, to be given new identities when released. They sought permanent injunctions preventing the publication of any information which would reveal their true identities.

The case came before Dame Elizabeth Butler-Sloss, in the Family Division of the High Court. She rejected the argument that the ECHR was irrelevant because the claim was not against a 'public authority'. In the light of the jurisprudence of the ECtHR (e.g. *Glaser* v *United Kingdom* [2000] FCR 193) and the approach taken in *Douglas* v *Hello!*, she had no doubt that she had to apply Art. 10 to the case. This did not, however, 'encompass the creation of a free-standing cause of action based directly upon the articles of the Convention' (para. 27, p. 918). The duty on the court 'is to act compatibly with Convention rights in adjudicating upon existing common law causes of action' (para. 27, p. 918). This clearly supported the view that privacy rights could only be developed within existing legal actions, rather than independently.

As regards the jurisdictional basis for the issue of an injunction, Dame Elizabeth recognized that the situation was novel. The starting point was the freedom of the press as recognized by Art. 10 of the ECHR and s. 12 of the HRA 1998. Restraint could only be justified if it fell within the exceptions recognized in Art. 10(2). She found support, however, for jurisdiction in the law of confidentiality. She noted that in *Douglas* v *Hello!* both Brooke and Keene LJJ referred to the fact that the law of breach of confidence was in the process of developing. It was already established (by *Attorney-General* v *Guardian Newspapers (No. 2)*) that confidence can arise independently of any transaction or relationship between the parties, for example 'when confidential information comes to the attention of the media, in circumstances in which the media have notice of its confidentiality' (para. 81, p. 933). This would apply, for example, to an individual's medical reports which fell into the hands of the press. From here she felt it was possible to make the step to the following proposition (para. 81, p. 933):

> In my judgment, the court does have the jurisdiction, in exceptional cases, to extend the protection of confidentiality of information, even to impose restrictions on the press, where not to do so would be likely to lead to serious physical injury, or to death, of

> the person seeking that confidentiality, and there is no other way to protect the applicants other than by seeking relief from the court.

This meant that the requirement of the restriction of Art. 10 being 'prescribed by law' was met. The question whether restraint was 'necessary in a democratic society' was answered by the risk to the applicants if their identity was revealed. This might involve infringements of their rights under Art. 2 (life) or Art. 3 (torture or inhuman and degrading treatment) of the ECHR, from which no derogation was possible. There was a strong and pressing social need that their confidentiality be protected. Finally, the issue of injunctions was 'proportionate' to the legitimate aim of protecting the rights of the applicants. The need to protect them from serious and possibly irreparable harm met that requirement. In coming to this conclusion, Dame Elizabeth did not feel that she was opening the door too far for actions based on confidentiality (para. 85, p. 934):

> I do not see that this extension of the law of confidence, by the grant of relief in the exceptional circumstances of this case, [i]s opening a door to the granting of general restrictions in the media in cases where anonymity would be desirable. In my judgment, that is where the strict application of Art. 10(2) bites. It will only be appropriate to grant injunctions to restrain the media where it can be convincingly demonstrated, within those exceptions, that it is strictly necessary.

In particular, she expressed doubts as to whether it would be appropriate to grant injunctions to restrict the press in the present case if it were only Art. 8 that was likely to be breached. It was the potential infringements of Arts 2 and 3 that gave real weight to the case.

Finally, because of the exceptional nature of the case, the injunctions were issued to last for the life of the applicants, and were expressed to apply 'to the world' and not just to the parties to the case. Both of these aspects were exceptional, in particular the scope of the injunctions. A dictum of Lord Eldon in *Iveson* v *Harris* (1802) 7 Ves 251, p. 257, 32 ER 102, p. 104 to the effect that 'you cannot have an injunction except against a party to the suit', had generally been followed for nearly 200 years. The requirement to act in accordance with the ECHR introduced by the HRA 1998 meant, however, that 'we are entering a new era'. It was appropriate for the injunctive relief to 'be granted openly against the world' (para. 100, p. 939).

The outcome of this case does not directly support the development of any broad right of privacy. The extension of confidentiality was specifically related to protecting Art. 2 and Art. 3 interests rather than Art. 8. Nevertheless, the fact that judges were prepared to expand the law in this way on the basis of the HRA 1998 indicated the scope for future development. A similar approach was taken in a subsequent case, again involving a person who, as a child, had murdered another, where an injunction was issued to protect the secret identity both of the woman convicted of the offence and of her grown-up daughter: *X, a Woman Formerly Known as Mary Bell* v *O'Brien* [2003] EWHC 1101 (QB), [2003] EMLR 37. In this case, however, it was held that there was no real threat to the life of the claimant, so that the injunction was based on the threats to her mental health, the protection of which fell within the scope of Art. 8.

The limitations of privacy as against the freedom of the press were further explored in the rather different case of *A v B and C* [2002] EWCA Civ 337, [2002] All ER 545. This concerned an attempt by a leading footballer, the captain of a Premier League club, to prevent publication in a newspaper of the details of extra-marital sexual relationships with two women. The women themselves were the sources of much of the information acquired by the newspaper. The Court of Appeal, refused to confirm an interim injunction that had been obtained by A. A's rights to confidentiality did not, in these circumstances, outweigh the right to freedom of the press. The sexual relationships concerned were 'transient', and any confidentiality was weakened by the women's wish to disclose information about them. To prevent them from doing so would infringe their rights to freedom of expression. Moreover, A, as a leading footballer was a public figure and a 'role model' in whose activities there would be a legitimate public interest. In all the circumstances the continuation of the injunction would be an 'unjustified interference with the freedom of the press'.

This case indicated a strong presumption in favour of publication, particularly in relation to 'public figures'. Subsequent cases have shown, however, that the courts are prepared to be quite restrictive as to what may be published even about such figures.

6.10.3 The *Naomi Campbell* case

Probably the most important case in the development of English privacy law to the point it has reached today is the House of Lords' decision in *Campbell v Mirror Group Newspapers Ltd* [2004] UKHL 22. This case was the full hearing (rather than an interim action) of a claim by Naomi Campbell, a well-known fashion model, for damages for breach of confidence in relation to articles and photographs of her published in the *Daily Mirror* newspaper. These had been designed to contradict her previous assertions that she was not a drug addict by revealing details of her attendance at meetings of Narcotics Anonymous and publishing photographs of her leaving such meetings. At trial the judge held that the information was protected by confidentiality. Nevertheless, the claimant was a public figure, and the *Daily Mirror* was entitled to 'put the record straight' about her previous denials of drug addiction. This did not extend, however, to allowing it to publish the details of her attendance at the Narcotics Anonymous meetings or the photographs of her leaving a meeting. Balancing the rights under Art. 8 against those under Art. 10, the claimant was entitled to damages. The judge awarded a total of £3,500 (including £1,000 aggravated damages)—which the editor of the *Daily Mirror* dismissed as a 'derisory' figure. The Court of Appeal took a different view. It held that the exposure of Ms Campbell's deception of the public was in the public interest, and that publication of all the information, including the photographs, was a legitimate, if not essential, part of the 'journalistic package'. Journalists should be allowed 'reasonable latitude' in the manner of reporting, once it is accepted that publication of a story is in the public interest.

Ms Campbell appealed to the House of Lords which, by a majority of three to two, overturned the Court of Appeal and restored the judge's order. Lord Hope indicated that the decision was finely balanced between Arts 8 and 10, but he concluded that the publication of the fact that Ms Campbell was being treated by

Narcotics Anonymous, the details of the treatment, and the photographs, went beyond what was justifiable and constituted an invasion of privacy entitling her to damages (para. 125). The test applied was the reaction of a person of 'ordinary sensibilities' if information of this kind was published about them (para. 99). The photographs seem to have weighed particularly heavily with Lord Hope (para. 121) and Baroness Hale (para. 155) in tipping the balance in the claimant's favour. Lord Carswell did not share this view (para. 170), but was influenced by the fact that the publications ran the risk of causing a significant setback to Ms Campbell's recovery from addiction (para. 169). It is also worth noting the comment of Lord Nicholls (who was part of the dissenting minority) that the continued use of 'confidence' in this area is at times uncomfortable, and that better terminology when discussing cases involving disclosures about an individual's private life would be 'misuse of private information' (para. 14).

The particular sensitivity of photographs in considering a breach of Art. 8 (which seemed to be an important part of the decision of the House of Lords in favour of Naomi Campbell in *Campbell* v *MGN*) was confirmed by the decision of the ECtHR in *von Hannover* v *Germany* (2005) 40 EHRR 1. The ECtHR found that German law had inadequately protected Princess Caroline of Monaco in relation to the publication of photographs of her engaged in everyday activities in public places—e.g. riding a horse, shopping, on a skiing holiday, playing tennis with one of her children. This indicates that, simply because a person is in a general sense a 'public figure', this does not mean that it is legitimate to publish any photographs of them.

The Mirror Group took the decision in *Campbell* v *MGN* to Strasbourg (*MGN* v *United Kingdom* [2011] 53 EHRR 5). The ECtHR confirmed that there had been no breach of Art. 10 in the finding of the House of Lords that the publication of the information about Naomi Campbell involved a breach of confidence, contrary to Art. 8. The ECtHR did find, however, a breach of Art. 10 in the fact that the costs which MGN had had to pay were almost doubled (to over £1 million) as a result of the action being funded on a conditional fee arrangement, which allowed the lawyers to charge a 'success fee' uplift of up to 100 per cent on their actual expenses. This finding is not, however, directly relevant to the development of privacy under English law.

6.10.4 Case law post-*Campbell* v *MGN*

The principles applied by the House of Lords in *Campbell* v *MGN* were considered in relation to rather different circumstances in *Re S (A Child) (Identification: Restriction on Publication)* [2004] UKHL 47, [2004] 4 All ER 683. The claimant was a child whose mother was on trial for the murder of his brother. He successfully sought an injunction from the High Court preventing any publicity in relation to the trial which might enable him to be identified, but this was later modified to exclude any reporting of proceedings in open court. This modification was upheld by the Court of Appeal. The House of Lords noted that both Art. 8 and Art. 10 were engaged in this situation, but that, following Campbell, neither article had automatic precedence over the other. An 'intense focus' on the comparative importance of the specific rights being claimed was needed. The 'proportionality' test had to be applied to each right. Applying this approach, the House of Lords attributed great importance to the freedom of the press to report the progress of a criminal trial without any restraint. It therefore upheld the modified injunction, with the result that there was no restriction on publication of the identity of the claimant's mother, or of photographs of her or her deceased son.

Three further Court of Appeal decisions deserve note. The first is *Ash* v *McKennitt* [2006] EWCA Civ 1714, [2007] 3 WLR 194. This concerned the attempt by Niema Ash to publish a book revealing information about a former friend, the Canadian folk-singer Loreena McKennitt. There was evidence that Ms McKennitt was fiercely protective of her privacy. The Court continued the process of limiting the scope of the decision in *A* v *B and C* as to the legitimacy of revealing information about 'public figures'. Following comments to the same effect in *Campbell* v *MGN* it did not accept that a person who happened to be in the public eye, or even to have been adopted (without seeking this) as a 'role model', was thereby unable to protect his or her privacy (para. 65). It emphasized again the distinction between matters 'of public interest' and 'in the public interest', which seemed to have been weakened in *A* v *B and C*. The material in this case came into the first category. Nor could Ms Ash claim that she was simply telling 'her story', and that preventing this would unduly restrict her Art. 10 rights. The majority of the information used—and this was presumably the reason why a publisher would want to publish the book—was based on disclosures about things said or done by Ms McKennitt. The conclusion was that the Court upheld the trial judge's decision in favour of Ms McKennitt, forbidding the disclosure of the private information.

The second Court of Appeal decision is *Associated Newspapers Ltd* v *Prince of Wales* [2006] EWCA Civ 1776, [2007] 2 All ER 139. The case concerned the publication by the *Mail on Sunday* of extracts from a journal produced by the Prince of Wales relating to one of his foreign visits. It has apparently been his practice over the last 30 years to produce a handwritten journal of personal observations in relation to each foreign visit, and for these to be then copied and circulated, in confidence, to friends, and possibly to others, such as politicians, media people, journalists, and actors.

The journal in question related to the Prince's visit to Hong Kong at the time of the hand-over to the Chinese, and contained some blunt views on some of the Chinese leaders. The trial judge held that the disclosure of the journal to the newspaper was a breach of the Prince's rights under Art. 8, and a breach of confidence. This approach and result was approved by the Court of Appeal. In other words, it held that the Art. 8 issue could be looked at separately from the breach of confidence, thus indicating further that the right to privacy is starting to be recognized as an independent right separate from confidentiality. In relation to both grounds for complaint the Court of Appeal also held that the Prince's right to keep the material secret was not outweighed by Art. 10. The conclusion of the Court, stated in para. 74 was that:

> . . . even if one ignores the significance of the fact that the information published had been revealed . . . in confidence, we consider that the judge was correct to hold that Prince Charles had an unanswerable claim for breach of privacy. When the breach of the confidential relationship is added to the balance, his case is overwhelming.

This amounts to an acknowledgement, at least at the level of an obiter dictum, that privacy rights can exist independently from breach of confidence. This trend has continued in subsequent cases.

Murray v *Express Newspapers plc* [2008] EWCA Civ 446 involved the author of the Harry Potter books, J. K. Rowling. She had been photographed with her husband and children in a public street, on the way to and from a local café, on a family outing. The claim was brought on behalf of her son, David, who was at the time about 19 months old, and was being wheeled in a buggy. One photograph showed David's face, the clothes he was wearing, his size, the style and colour of his hair, and the colour of his skin. All the photographs were taken covertly with a long lens. The family were unaware that the photographs had been taken, until the one showing David appeared in a magazine, at which point they sought an injunction, in David's name, restraining the publication of that or any similar photographs. The trial judge struck out the claim, on the basis that the claimant's Art. 8 rights were not engaged by the taking of a photograph in a public place. The Court of Appeal disagreed. While the issue might be different in relation to J. K. Rowling herself, her son could arguably have an expectation of privacy even in a public place. The Court remitted the case for trial, though it was subsequently settled. The decision, while only on an interlocutory point, and not determining whether there was in fact a breach of privacy, goes some way to indicating that the English courts will follow the lead given by Strasbourg in *von Hannover*, as regards photographs, even when taken in a public place. The case also indicates that Art. 8 can be engaged even where the claimant was unaware of the intrusion, and would not have been able to appreciate its nature (because of his age) even if he had been aware of it.

Further support for the development of a fully fledged privacy right came with the decision of the High Court in *Mosley* v *News Group Newspapers Ltd* [2008] EWHC 1777 (QB). Max Mosley was at the time the head of the FIA, the governing body for Formula 1 motor racing. He had organized a sex-party involving several prostitutes. At the party he and the women engaged in relatively mild sado-masochistic acts. One of the women had been approached by the *News of the World* and had, in response, secretly recorded and filmed some of the party. The newspaper then published an article headlined 'F1 boss has sick Nazi orgy with 5 hookers', purporting to give details of the party. It published a further article the following week. Mr Mosley sued for breach of privacy.

The judge held that the party was an event in relation to which the claimant had a reasonable expectation of privacy. Did the public interest in disclosure of these events outweigh the privacy right? In this respect the judge's finding that there was in fact no 'Nazi' theme to the party, though German had at times been spoken, and a modern German military uniform worn. As he commented (para. 122):

> I have come to the conclusion (although others might disagree) that if it really were the case, as the newspaper alleged, that the claimant had for entertainment and sexual gratification been 'mocking the humiliating way the Jews were treated', or 'parodying Holocaust horrors', there could be a public interest in that being revealed at least to those in the FIA to whom he is accountable. He has to deal with many people of all races and religions, and has spoken out against racism in the sport. If he really were behaving in the way I have just described, that would, for many people, call seriously into question his suitability for his FIA role.

In the absence of this aspect of the events, the judge could not identify any public interest in the exposure of the lawful sexual activities of a public figure.

He awarded the claimant damages of £60,000. Although the press has been critical of this decision, there was no appeal. Mr Mosley sought a ruling from the ECtHR that people who were about to be 'exposed' in newspapers should be given advance notice, and a chance to respond. The ECtHR ruled that there was not a breach of Art. 8 in the failure of English law to provide such a right: *Mosley* v *United Kingdom* [2011] 53 EHRR 30.

6.10.5 Setting the boundaries for privacy

It is clear from the above decisions that, although public figures have less protection than ordinary members of the public, even they have a right to a private life, and not all details about their activities may be published. It is not enough that the information may be of interest to the public; the publication must be in the public interest, in that, for example, it exposes the hypocrisy of the public figure. The most recent cases, both in Strasbourg and in the English courts, have started to indicate limits to the right to privacy.

In Strasbourg the decisions in *von Hannover* v *Germany (No. 2)* (2012) 55 EHRR 15 and *Springer* v *Germany* (2012) 55 EHRR 6 are worthy of note. In the first case, again concerning a photograph of Princess Caroline of Monaco, it was held that the link to the accompanying story about the ill health of her father, Prince Rainier, meant that there was sufficient of a public interest element to justify the publication. In the *Springer* case a German newspaper had published stories about the arrest and conviction of a famous television actor on drugs charges (relating to cocaine). The German courts had held that the case would not have been reported if the person involved had not been famous, and that there was therefore an infringement of his privacy. The ECtHR disagreed and, in this case, held that the Art. 10 rights of the press outweighed the actor's privacy right. In coming to their conclusions in these two cases, which were heard at the same time, the court indicated that the following factors are relevant in reaching a decision on the right balance between Art. 8 and Art. 10:

- Did the article contribute to a debate of general interest?
  - This will depend on the circumstances of the case, but public interest can cover not only politics or criminal offences but also sport and entertainment. It would not, however, cover, for example, the marital difficulties of a president or the financial difficulties of a singer.
- How well known is the person concerned and what is the subject of the report?
  - There appears to be three categories here, i.e. politicians, other public figures, and private individuals, with an increasing right to privacy. But even in relation to politicians and public figures, publication of photographs or commentary relating exclusively to the details of their private life, and having the sole aim of satisfying the curiosity of the readership, is unlikely to be justifiable.
- The prior conduct of the person concerned.
  - This will include whether the information has been published elsewhere. The fact that the person has previously co-operated with the press, or

courted publicity, is relevant, but not an automatic defence in relation to new publications.

- The method of obtaining the information and its veracity.
  - Did the journalists act 'in good faith' and in accordance with the 'ethics of journalism'? Was the information accurate, reliable, and precise?
- In relation to photographs, the circumstances in which they were taken.
  - Was there consent? Was the photo taken without their knowledge, by subterfuge or other illicit means? For private individuals, in particular, a photo may be more substantial interference than a written article.
- The content, form, and consequences of the publication.
  - This will include the way in which the photo or report was published (e.g. how much prominence it was given, how it was headlined); the way in which the person was represented; and the extent of dissemination (e.g. national or local).
- Where publication has been restrained, the severity of any sanction imposed.
  - This will be relevant to the proportionality of the interference with freedom of expression.

These guidelines constitute the first attempt by the Strasbourg Court to establish a framework for the balancing of the rights between Art. 8 and Art. 10 and are likely to be important in relation to future cases involving this issue. If a domestic court properly considers the above, it is likely that the ECtHR will apply the 'margin of appreciation', and allow the domestic decision to stand, rather than reaching its own conclusion. It is perhaps also significant that both the cases in which these principles appear involve a decision in which Art. 10 took precedence over Art. 8. This could be taken as indicating that we are now seeing a reversal of the previous trend in which Art. 8 always seemed to 'win'.

In the UK as well, there is evidence of the dominance of Art. 8, epitomized by the *Campbell* case, starting to weaken. Several of the relevant cases involve the disclosure of sexual indiscretions by footballers, but the first to note concerned a different issue. Much of the above case law has illustrated the expanding role for the concept of privacy. In *Author of a Blog* v *Times Newspapers* [2009] EWHC 1358 (QB), a serving police officer who wrote a blog under an assumed name detailing aspects of current policing, drawn from his own experience, sought to prevent *The Times* from revealing his identity. His request for an injunction was refused. Blogging was a public activity, and while the claimant might wish to preserve his anonymity, there was no reasonable expectation of privacy. In coming to this conclusion the court made reference to the Court of Appeal's decision in *Napier* v *Pressdram Ltd* [2009] EWCA Civ 443, where it had been held that there was no confidentiality surrounding the outcome of complaints against a firm of solicitors which had been considered by the Law Society.

In the first of the 'footballer' cases, *Terry* v *Persons Unknown* [2010] EWHC 119 (QB), John Terry, at the time the captain of the England football team, sought an injunction to restrain the publication of details of sexual relationship with the former girlfriend of another footballer. The judge refused the injunction, noting the obligations under s. 12(3) of the HRA (see 6.9.2) and that there was a likelihood that at trial the defendants would be able to show a 'public interest' in the publication, outweighing the claimant's Art. 8 right. The judge was also clearly influenced by the fact that the action appeared to be being brought on the claimant's behalf by his business partners, and that the claimant seemed more concerned about the impact of the publication on his commercial interests, i.e. his sponsorship by firms, than his own privacy. In two other recent cases the courts have refused to restrict publications on privacy grounds. In *Hutcheson v News Group Newspapers* [2011] EWCA Civ 808 the Court of Appeal upheld a refusal by the trial judge to issue an injunction to prevent a newspaper revealing that the claimant had a 'second family' which his wife, their children, and his son-in-law (a well-known 'celebrity chef') did not know about. The public interest in this case was related to the fact that it was alleged that the claimant, while working for his son-in-law's company, had secretly misused its funds to support his second family. In *Ferdinand v MGN* [2011] EWHC 2454 (QB) the court refused an injunction to the Manchester United and England footballer Rio Ferdinand. The paper wished to disclose information about a lengthy relationship with a woman which had taken place while he also had a long-term girlfriend whom he subsequently married. The public interest related to the fact that the existence of this relationship appeared to conflict with public statements by Ferdinand at the relevant time that he was faithful to his girlfriend, and had put any 'cheating' on her behind him.

Footballers do not always fail in seeking an injunction. In *CTB v News Group Newspapers* [2011] EWHC 1232 (QB) a Premiership footballer succeeded in obtaining an injunction restraining the publication of information about a sexual relationship. The court did not find any countervailing public interest in this. The injunction was to a large extent undermined, however, by the fact that the footballer's name was widely disseminated on *Twitter*, and was also revealed by a Member of Parliament in the House of Commons, under the protection of Parliamentary privilege. The court, in refusing to accept that this meant that the injunction should be discharged, indicated quite clearly that English law in this area has moved beyond 'confidentiality' to protecting privacy itself. It has long been held that once the confidential nature of information has been lost, there is nothing for the claimant to protect (see, e.g. *BBC v HarperCollins Ltd* [2010] EWHC 2424 (Ch)—no injunction to prevent the publisher revealing the identity of 'Stig' the anonymous driver on the television programme *Top Gear*, because the name was already in the public domain). But as the judge put it in *CTB v NGN* in the hearing to consider the application to lift the injunction in the light of the fact that the name had been disclosed in other ways ([2011] EWHC 1334 (QB), para. 3):

> It is obvious that if the purpose of this injunction were to preserve a secret, it would have failed in its purpose. But in so far as its purpose is to prevent intrusion or harassment, it has not failed. The fact that tens of thousands of people have named the claimant on the internet confirms that the claimant and his family need protection from intrusion into their private and family life. The fact that a question has been asked in Parliament seems to me to increase, and not to diminish the strength of his case that he and his family need that protection. The order has not protected the claimant and his family from taunting on the internet. It is still effective to protect them from taunting and other intrusion and harassment in the print media.

The injunction remained in place, despite the fact that the name of the footballer had been widely revealed, including in television news broadcasts.

The general trend of the law in this area has been to extend the scope of privacy rights, and in some cases to set quite a high threshold of 'public interest' in relation to publication of information about public figures (though this seems to have been weakened in some of the 'footballer' cases). One thing is, however, clear, which is that the media need to be very careful about the use of photographs which are not necessary as part of any public interest which may attach to a story.

6.11 Other actions to protect privacy

In addition to the action which has developed from breach of confidence, there are some other remedies which may be relevant to protecting privacy, in the sense of non-disclosure of private information. If the information is untrue, then an action for defamation may be possible. In some circumstances, if disclosure of a document or photograph is involved, the law of copyright may prevent a newspaper or broadcaster publishing its contents (see, e.g. *Ashdown* v *Telegraph Group Ltd* [2001] EWCA Civ 1142, [2001] 4 All ER 666). There is not space to deal with these actions here. One further possibility will, however, be explored further, i.e. the use of the Data Protection Act 1998 to protect privacy.

6.11.1 The Data Protection Act 1998

This piece of legislation, which replaced the Data Protection Act 1984, provides limited protection for privacy in relation to personal information. It forms the UK response to the requirements of the EC Data Protection Directive, which was agreed in 1995. Originally the Act applied only to information stored electronically, but it now applies also to paper-based records. All those who hold such data ('data controllers') are obliged to comply with the 'data protection principles' set out in Sch. 1 to the Act. There are eight principles in all, of which the first six are most relevant to the subject matter of this chapter:

(a) Personal data shall be processed fairly and lawfully... [Schs 2 and 3 set out conditions which must be met before data can be processed—e.g. the consent of the data subject, the performance of a contract].

(b) Personal data shall be obtained only for one or more specified and lawful purposes, and shall not be further processed in any manner incompatible with that purpose or those purposes.

(c) Personal data shall be adequate, relevant and not excessive in relation to the purpose or purposes for which they are processed.

(d) Personal data shall be accurate and, where necessary, kept up to date.

(e) Personal data processed for any purpose or purposes shall not be kept for longer than is necessary for that purpose or those purposes.

(f) Personal data shall be processed in accordance with the rights of data subjects under this Act.

'Personal data' means:

> ...data which relate to a living individual who can be identified—
>
> (a) from those data, or
>
> (b) from those data and other information which is in the possession of, or is likely to come into the possession of, the data controller, and includes any expression of opinion about the individual and any indication of the intentions of the data controller or any other person in respect of the individual.

'Processing', in relation to personal data, means:

> ...obtaining, recording or holding the...data or carrying out any operation or set of operations on the data, including—
>
> (a) organisation, adaptation or alteration...
>
> (b) retrieval, consultation or use...
>
> (c) disclosure... or
>
> (d) alignment, combination, blocking, erasure or destruction

The first two principles control the acquisition of personal information, requiring that it should be done 'fairly and lawfully' and only for specified purposes. The second principle, taken with principles five and six, controls the use to which personal information can be put. The idea is that the person on whom information is being held (the 'data subject') should know the purpose for which it is being held, and should be able to object to its use for any other purpose.

The primary methods for ensuring compliance with the Act lie with the Information Commissioner. The Commissioner has powers of registration, investigation, and supervision, backed up by criminal sanctions. There are, however, also rights for a data subject to seek compensation through the courts in relation to losses caused by any contravention by a data controller of the requirements of the Act (s. 13). The action requires that actual loss be proven, so that breach of privacy involved in the unauthorized disclosure of personal information is not actionable per se. Damages can, however, include compensation for distress. Where the contravention relates to the use of the data for 'journalistic', 'literary', or 'artistic' purposes, then distress can be compensated without the need to show other loss. To this extent, breaches of privacy by the media are compensatable under the Act. Sir David Calcutt suggested that there was greater potential for using data protection legislation in this context ('Review of Press Self-Regulation', Cm 2135, 1993, para. 7.46). Commenting on the 1984 Act he suggested that the government should give:

> ...[f]urther consideration to the extent to which the Data Protection Act may contain provisions which are relevant for the purposes of misrepresentation or intrusion into personal privacy by the press.

An example of an attempt to use this Act in a 'privacy' case is *Campbell* v *MGN* the facts of which are given at 6.10.3. The High Court held that an additional basis on which Ms Campbell could recover damages was that the details of her therapy and the photographs with their captions were sensitive personal data falling within the scope of the Act. The exception in s. 32, which provides that where data are processed only for the purposes of journalism, literature, or art, then they are exempt from all of the data protection principles, other than one dealing with taking precautions against unauthorized or unlawful processing, or accidental loss or damage (principle seven), was held to apply only to pre-publication processing. The Court of Appeal, however, regarded this interpretation of s. 32 as 'illogical' and reversed the High Court's decision on this issue. It held that the exemption for journalism in the section applied to the publication of personal data, as well as to the pre-publication processes. The House of Lords did not address this issue when it considered the case (see 6.10.3), and so it must be assumed that the Court of Appeal's analysis stands.

This attempt to use the Data Protection Act 1998 was unsuccessful, but in *Douglas v Hello! Ltd (No. 6)* [2005] 4 All ER 128 (see 6.10.2) the High Court did hold that the transmission of photographs of the claimants' wedding constituted a breach of the Data Protection Act 1998, albeit one that only attracted an award of nominal damages.

It seems, therefore, that this Act will have a role, though probably a minor one, in developing the protection of privacy under English law.

6.12 The 'Leveson Report' and proposals for reform

In the Spring of 2011 a major scandal erupted in relation to the invasion of privacy by newspapers. It became clear that some journalists had been obtaining private information by hacking, or paying others to hack, into the mobile phones not only of celebrities but also of the victims of crimes and their families. There had been prosecutions in relation to actions of this kind in 2007, relating to the Sunday newspaper, the *News of the World* (see, e.g. *The Guardian*, 26 January 2007 at http://www.theguardian.com/media/2007/jan/26/newsoftheworld.pressandpublishing). In 2011, however, it became clear that the practice was much more widespread than had first appeared. The subsequent furore led to the closure of the *News of the World*, by its parent company, News International. The Government then announced a public inquiry into this and related issues, to be chaired by Sir Brian Leveson, a Court of Appeal judge. His report was issued in the Autumn of 2012 ('An Inquiry Into The Culture, Practices And Ethics Of The Press', HC 780-1, Stationery Office, 2013).

The extensive recommendations are too wide-ranging to discuss in detail here, but some of the main ones were:

1. There should be an independent regulatory body (the 'Board') for the press (replacing the current Press Complaints Commission (PCC))

2. The Board should consist of a majority of people who are independent of the press. It should include people with experience of the industry such as former editors or senior or academic journalists, but should not include any serving editor (unlike the current Press Complaints Commission which, until recently, was chaired by a serving editor). It should not include

any serving member of the House of Commons or any member of the government.

3. The Board should establish and enforce a standards code for the press.

4. There should be an arbitration system to deal with complaints by members of the public against the press.

Most of the above has been accepted by the press and the main political parties. Most controversially, however, the Leveson Report recommended that the system should be underpinned by law. In Recommendation 27 it states:

> In order to meet the public concern that the organisation by the press of its regulation is by a body which is independent of the press, independent of Parliament and independent of the Government, that fulfils the legitimate requirements of such a body and can provide, by way of benefit to its subscribers, recognition of involvement in the maintenance of high standards of journalism, the law must identify those legitimate requirements and provide a mechanism to recognise and certify that a new body meets them.

This clearly envisages legislation to establish the framework of the new system proposed, and this is confirmed by implication in Recommendation 33, which states:

> In passing legislation to identify the legitimate requirements to be met by an independent regulator organised by the press, and to provide for a process of recognition and review of whether those requirements are and continue to be met, the law should also place an explicit duty on the Government to uphold and protect the freedom of the press.

This has proved to be the most controversial aspect of the recommendations. The main political parties have proposed a Royal Charter backed up by legislation as the mechanism for implementing the Leveson recommendations, with the safeguard that any change to the system would have to be approved by a two-thirds majority of both Houses of Parliament. The press is adamant that there should be no legislative back-up, seeing this as an insidious assault on the principle of a free press. At the time of writing the government has achieved approval from the Privy Council for its Royal Charter, but the press appears to be proceeding with the establishment of its own independent regulator (the Independent Press Standards Organisation ('IPSO'). IPSO is unlikely to seek authorization under the Charter, and so will operate outside the Government's proposed scheme. The impact of all this on the protection of privacy, and the balance between privacy and freedom of expression, remains uncertain.

QUESTIONS

1 Does Art. 8 of the ECHR provide sufficient protection against unreasonable searches of premises by the police?

2 What is the difference between the powers of entry given by ss 18 and 32 of PACE? Could one or other of them be repealed? Or should they be consolidated?

3   Does the introduction of search warrants which can apply to multiple premises, and justify repeated entries, mean that the prohibition on 'general' search warrants established by *Entick* v *Carrington* has been significantly weakened?

4   Are the procedures for the supervision of, and challenge to, the exercise of powers of interception of communications, or covert surveillance, sufficient to provide protection for the citizen? How might they be improved?

5   Why is 'journalistic' material given special protection under the powers to obtain access to material in the course of a criminal investigation? Is this status justified?

6   Should those who deliberately place themselves in the public eye have any right to complain if the media reveal information they would rather have kept secret?

7   Has English law now developed a law of privacy, in relation to publications, which exists independently of any breach of confidence?

8   Does the current approach of the English courts to privacy issues give sufficient weight to the public interest in the freedom of the press?

FURTHER READING

Amos, M. (2002), 'Can We Speak Freely Now? Freedom of Expression under the Human Rights Act', [2002] EHRLR 750

Calcutt, D. (1990), 'Report of the Committee on Privacy and Related Matters', Cm 1102, HMSO

Calcutt, D. (1993), 'Review of Press Self-Regulation', Cm 2135, HMSO

Clayton, R. and Tomlinson, H. (2004), *Civil Actions Against the Police*, 3rd edn, London: Thomson Sweet & Maxwell

Feldman, D. (1986), *The Law Relating to Entry, Search and Seizure*, London: Butterworths

Fenwick, H. and Phillipson, P. (2000), 'Breach of Confidence as a Privacy Remedy in the Human Rights Act Era', (2000) 63 MLR 660

Finch, E. (2002), 'Stalking the Perfect Stalking Law: An Evaluation of the Efficacy of the Protection from Harassment Act 1997', [2002] Crim LR 703

Foster, S. (2011), 'Balancing Privacy with Freedom of Speech: Press Censorship, the European Convention on Human Rights and the Decision in *Mosley* v *United Kingdom*', (2011) 16 *Communications Law* 100

Mirfield, P. (2001), 'Regulation of Investigatory Powers Act 2000: Part 2: Evidential Aspects', [2001] Crim LR 91

Robertson, G. and Nicol, A. (2008), *Media Law*, 5th edn, Harmondsworth: Penguin

Schreiber, A. (2006), 'Confidence Crisis, Privacy Phobia: Why Invasion of Privacy Should be Independently Recognised in English law', (2006) 2 *Intellectual Property Quarterly* 160

Sims, A. (2005), ' "A Shift in the Centre of Gravity": The Dangers of Protecting Privacy Through Breach of Confidence', (2005) 1 *Intellectual Property Quarterly* 27

Singh, R. and Strachan, J. (2002), 'The Right to Privacy in English Law', [2002] EHRLR 129

Stone, R. (1988), 'PACE: Special Procedures and Legal Privilege', [1988] Crim LR 498

Stone, R. (2012), *The Law of Entry, Search, and Seizure*, 5th edn, Oxford: Oxford University Press

Zuckerman, A. A. S. (1990), 'The Weakness of the PACE Special Procedure for Protecting Confidential Material', [1990] Crim LR 472

7

....

Freedom of Expression (Article 10) I:
Official Secrets and Freedom of Information

7.1 The meaning of 'freedom of expression'

This is the first of several chapters in which issues relating to the control of freedom of expression are discussed. It is appropriate at this point to indicate what is meant here by 'expression', and why that word has been chosen in preference to 'speech'. One reason is that Art. 10 of the European Convention on Human Rights (ECHR) refers to 'expression' but there are also some substantive reasons for the choice.

'Speech' may be taken to refer to the most obvious forms of expression, such as writing books, or articles, making speeches, or broadcasting. It is clear, however, that in most modern democracies, access to forms of expression for the most effective promotion of ideas, or points of view, is limited. In particular, the control of content in relation to newspapers, and broadcasting, is in the hands of a very small group of people, even at the editorial level. At the level of ownership, the range is reduced even further, with a small number of individuals and organizations owning the major newspapers, and controlling significant areas of broadcasting. In this situation, the possibility of an individual, or group of individuals, being able to promote a particular idea, or point of view, becomes very limited. In order to do so, the attention of the mass media has to be attracted, so that they are prepared to give time or space to the reporting of the arguments being put forward. One way in which this may be done is through the use of social media, in particular *Twitter*, where issues being debated online will often be picked up by the national media. Another, and more traditional way of attracting media attention, is by organizing a 'demonstration'. Events in Eastern Europe over the past ten or more years, and more recently the uprisings in the Arab world of Spring 2011 onwards (the 'Arab Spring') have clearly indicated the power of the street demonstration as a force for change. Even in the United Kingdom, we can find examples of the power of the demonstration. The strength of feeling shown against the 'Poll Tax' or 'Community Charge' at the beginning of the 1990s in the form of marches and processions, was probably a contributing factor to the government's decision to change its policy. Protests about the export of live animals, or against the building of new roads, may have the dual purpose of direct action, intended to stop or delay a particular activity, and of drawing attention to an issue—i.e. animal welfare, and environmental protection. More recently, there have been major demonstrations about globalization, and cuts in public services. It seems right to include these forms of putting forward views alongside 'speech' in the strict sense, and to use the wider term 'expression'. The issues relating to the relationship between demonstrations and freedom of expression are discussed further in chapter 9 (9.1).

The use of this term also makes it clear that 'artistic' expression, such as painting, photography, sculpture, and music is included. Such work may at times carry an overt or explicit political message, but even if it does not do so, arguments for its restriction should be clearly justified. A further type of 'expression' concerning which there may be debate about the extent to which it should be protected is 'commercial speech'—e.g. advertising. The issue was considered by the High Court in *R (British American Tobacco)* v *Secretary of State for Health* [2004] EWHC 2493 (Admin). The applicants were challenging regulations controlling tobacco advertising. The High Court noted that commercial speech, while less fundamental than political or artistic speech, was nevertheless protected by Art. 10 of the ECHR. Restrictions needed to be justified, but on the facts the controls contained in the regulations were proportionate to the objective of protecting public health. Commercial speech is treated here as falling within the scope of 'expression'.

In this book, therefore, the term 'expression' is used to include virtually all ways in which a person may put forward a point of view, an argument, or an artistic idea, or show support for a cause. Two types of action which might come within this definition are, however, specifically excluded. First, the donation of money to support a political cause is not dealt with under this heading. That restrictions on such actions can be treated as a fetter on expression is shown by *Bowman* v *United Kingdom* (1998) 26 EHRR 1, where statutory limitations on the amount that non-candidates could spend on Parliamentary elections was held to restrict the freedom of expression of an anti-abortion candidate who wished to support pro-life candidates, and therefore to infringe Art. 10 of the ECHR. (The UK position was amended by Pt. VI of the Political Parties, Elections, and Referendums Act 2000.) A similar position was taken by the US Supreme Court in *Buckley* v *Valeo* (1976) 424 US 1, as to the scope of the First Amendment. The concentration here, however, is on more direct forms of expression. The second type of action which is excluded is where its primary aim is to cause harm or damage to other people or property, for example, by planting a bomb, even though the objective of such an action may be to attract attention to a cause, and show support for it. Although it would be possible to treat such actions as 'expression' but to use their consequences, or intended consequences, as a justification for restriction, the view is taken here that they should not be regarded as having surmounted even the first hurdle towards achieving that special status that is generally given to speech, and expression.

7.2 Arguments for the protection of freedom of expression

Many constitutions give protection of freedom of speech or expression a high status. In the US Bill of Rights, for example, it appears in the First Amendment, and is included in the first substantive section of the Canadian Charter of Rights and Freedoms (that is, s. 2). This recognition early in these constitutional documents may well be taken to indicate that this freedom is regarded as having particular importance. Why should that be? What arguments can be put forward which suggest that the freedom of expression should have this degree of importance? A variety of such arguments may be proffered, but just three of the most commonly used are looked at here.

7.2.1 'Argument from truth'

In his essay 'On Liberty' (first published in 1859) John Stuart Mill devoted one chapter to 'the Liberty of Thought and Discussion' in which he discussed the freedom of the press and freedom of speech in some detail. The argument which he developed at some length as to why this freedom should be protected has come to be known as the 'argument from truth'. The basis of the argument is that nobody has a monopoly on truth. In particular, he asserted that the majority in a society have no right to suppress the views of the minority, however much they dislike them. An example might be drawn from the area of science, where the prevailing orthodoxy on the nature of the Universe has changed over the centuries, and even now there are debates as to the exact details of its origins. At no point would it have been right to say that, just because a majority of people took the view that one particular theory was correct, all opposing theories were incorrect. Mill's argument is that this approach should apply to political, moral, and philosophical views as well. Unorthodox and minority views must be allowed to be expressed, because there is a chance that they may be 'the truth' or may enable us to get nearer to it. If people disagree with them, they should attack with counter-arguments, not with suppression. Further, Mill argues, even if it is the case that the orthodox view is correct, it is much better that it should be tested against other possibilities than that it should be accepted unquestioningly.

The one exception which Mill allows to this free expression of ideas and opinions, is where it may lead to direct harm to others ('On Liberty', ch. III):

> An opinion that corn-dealers are starvers of the poor, or that private property is robbery, ought to be unmolested when simply circulated through the press, but may justly incur punishment when delivered orally to an excited mob assembled before the house of a corn-dealer, or when handed about among the same mob in the form of a placard.

Restriction of freedom of expression on these grounds is considered further in chapter 9.

As will be seen, the argument from truth has most relevance to the expression of ideas and opinions. It is more difficult to apply it to straightforward factual reporting, and very difficult in relation to artistic expression. Nevertheless, within its limitations, the argument from truth is a powerful one, and those who support the suppression of unpopular viewpoints need to put forward convincing reasons (such as the likelihood of direct harm resulting) why the argument should not apply to protect freedom of expression.

7.2.2 Argument from self-fulfilment

Another widely favoured argument in favour of freedom of expression is based on the idea that such freedom is an important aspect of an individual's self-fulfilment. This argument may be broader than the argument from truth, in that it will clearly cover not only the expression of beliefs or opinions, but also artistic expression. On the other hand, it will be more difficult to include purely factual information within its scope. Does the freedom to publish the details of government contracts for the purchase of office furniture really contribute to anybody's self-fulfilment?

The argument is based on the assumption that individual self-fulfilment is a desirable objective, and one that should take precedence over other considerations which might lead to restrictions on freedom of expression. It also has connections with the idea that expression is intimately tied up with the nature of humanity. We are distinguished from the animals because of our superior abilities to communicate, and to express our feelings in a variety of ways. If we restrict our ability to express ourselves in this way, we are to some extent denying our humanity, and prejudicing our full development as individuals.

A limitation of this reason for justifying free expression is that it is difficult to regard it as giving any special status to free speech, over and above other activities which may contribute to self-fulfilment. The freedom to have children, or to learn a foreign language, may also contribute to this aim for particular individuals. Freedom of expression thus becomes just one amongst a number of civil libertarian objectives, and this does not seem to give it the status as a particularly significant freedom which many would argue that it should have.

7.2.3 Argument from democracy

The third argument looked at here is based on an assumption that there is an agreement on the value of democracy. Once that premise is accepted then certain consequences for freedom of expression will follow almost automatically. By democracy is meant a political system which in some way takes account of the wishes of the people in decisions about how they are to be governed and by whom. In the United Kingdom this is achieved, for example, by the right to vote in general elections to Parliament, which must take place at least once in every five years.

If the participants in a democracy are to be able to exercise their rights as citizens effectively, there are two consequences for freedom of expression. First, there must be the widest possible scope for the exchange of opinion about the society in which the voters are living, the ways in which it operates, and changes which might be made. Only by having the opportunity to consider and debate alternatives to the status quo can the individual citizen be in a position to exercise the responsibilities attached to that membership of the society meaningfully and effectively. The repression of political and philosophical views (broadly defined) is the antithesis of democracy, and the two cannot properly co-exist. Second, the citizen in a democracy requires not only opinions and viewpoints, but also factual information. For example, the citizen cannot make an informed judgment about whether one system of health care is better than another, without the factual information which may make it possible to consider the costs and benefits of the two alternatives. This applies not only to information which may be produced or held by a government, but also to any information, whatever its source, which may have an input into the citizen's decisions about the manner and form of government which should operate, and who should be in charge of it. What is more difficult to include within this justification for freedom of expression is purely artistic work. Of course, many books, plays, films, etc. may be said to have an influence on how the citizen views the world, and society; but it would be difficult to argue that this was the case in relation to every piece of sculpture, every painting, every magazine, every novel, and every television show which is available in a modern society. The argument from democracy is undoubtedly at its strongest in relation to material which has a clear political content, and becomes weaker the more divorced from relevance to the citizen's democratic responsibilities the expression becomes.

7.2.4 Conclusion

The arguments outlined above are not the only ones which can be put forward in favour of freedom of expression but they are some of the most commonly used. As will be seen, none of them supplies a complete case for allowing freedom to all categories of expression. Between them they cover most areas. At times, however, it has to be accepted that there is no special argument justifying freedom for a particular type of expression. At this stage, and the area of pornography may be one where this is the case, the supporter of freedom has to rely on more general civil libertarian arguments, such as that a State has no right to use force (e.g. through the criminal law) to control behaviour, unless that behaviour causes harm to others. This line of argument can again be traced back to John Stuart Mill and 'On Liberty' (see 1.1).

A good extended overview of the arguments for giving freedom of expression special protection may be found in E. Barendt *Freedom of Speech*, 2nd edn (Oxford: Oxford University Press, 2005), ch. I.

7.3 Arguments for and against official secrecy

The arguments in favour of a freedom to publish information about the workings of government are most obviously based on the argument from democracy. This justification for free speech clearly supports the making available of as much information as possible to enable citizens to exercise their democratic responsibilities. It also supports the acceptance of wide-ranging criticism of governments and government officials.

The argument from truth may also be relevant to this area, in the sense that information gathered by the government may contribute towards the search for the truth on various matters. If, for example, a government department is conducting scientific research for military purposes, some of the results of that research may be of value to the wider scientific community. In this way it may contribute towards the avoidance of errors by others, and progress towards discovery of 'the truth' on a particular issue. It should therefore be possible to allow it to be published, unless there are clear reasons why this would, for example, be damaging to the national interest.

Those who argue for restrictions in this area (that is, most governments), generally do so on one of three grounds, or some combination of them.

First, it may be argued that certain types of government information need to be kept secret on grounds of 'national security'. This applies most obviously to matters of defence, where it can most convincingly be argued that disclosure of military secrets may put the whole country 'at risk'. The problem is, however, that the phrase 'national security' has no clear definition. Because the courts have for the most part been prepared to take the word of the government of the day that a particular matter involves issues of 'national security', without exploring that question for themselves, there is very little in the way of case law to provide any guidance. The only specific items which we can say that the concept covers are:

1. the defence of the realm (*The Zamora* [1916] 2 AC 77);

2. the prosecution of war (*The Zamora* [1916] 2 AC 77);

3. the disposition of the armed forces (*Chandler* v *DPP* [1964] AC 763);

4. nuclear weapons (*Secretary of State for Defence* v *Guardian Newspapers* [1984] 3 All ER 601); and

5. the activities of the security and intelligence services (*Attorney-General* v *Guardian Newspapers Ltd (No. 2)* [1988] 3 All ER 852).

The first four of these are all related to 'defence'. The two main categories are thus defence, and activities related to the security and intelligence services. The courts are often prepared, however, to recognize that there may be a further category of 'other matters of national security'. It does not seem possible to define this category further, and so the limits of this argument for restriction of freedom of expression are destined to remain uncertain. (See further on this issue, R. Stone, 'National Security versus Civil Liberty', in F. Patfield and R. White (eds), *The Changing Law* (Leicester: Leicester University Press, 1990).)

A second argument for control is that too free a flow of information may prejudice the government's dealings with other countries or international organizations. This would be to the detriment of the country as a whole. It may also give an unfair advantage to those who might seek to make a profit out of economically sensitive information (e.g. the discussion with other countries about possible devaluation of the currency, or alteration of interest rates). This line of argument has some force, but it only relates to a fairly narrow area of government information.

The third, and more general, argument is that for the process of government to be carried on too much in the open does not lead to good government. One aspect of this relates to the discussions and debates that may take place between civil servants, or between Ministers and civil servants, before a decision is taken on a particular policy, or course of action. It is argued that the participants in such discussions may be inhibited in what they will say, if they feel that this will be disclosed and open to scrutiny. Such inhibition will encourage cautious and self-conscious discussion which will not be in the interests of good government, and as a consequence, not in the interests of the country as a whole.

None of the arguments outlined above provides a convincing justification for wholesale restrictions on the freedom to publish information about government, though each of them has weight in relation to particular areas. They should, however, be kept in mind during the following discussion of the current restrictions which operate under English law, in order to consider the extent to which those restrictions may be able to be justified by one or other of them.

It will be of particular interest to consider how far the above arguments will still affect access to information even under the Freedom of Information Act 2000, which has the aim of increasing the availability of a wide range of government and publicly held information. This is discussed at 7.9.

7.4 **Official secrecy and the Human Rights Act 1998**

Article 10 of the ECHR sets out the right to freedom of expression. It allows this freedom to be restricted, however, for various legitimate reasons set out in Art. 10(2). This includes controls which are in the interests of 'national security, territorial integrity or public safety'. The first of these is the main one which is likely to be of relevance in relation to restrictions on the publication of 'official secrets'. The European Court of Human Rights (ECtHR) has not, however, given any clearer indication of what is encompassed by 'national security' than have the English courts. The *Spycatcher* cases (see 7.7.2) indicate, however, that the issue is justiciable as far as the Court is concerned. The approach taken by the English courts in applying the Human Rights Act 1998 (HRA 1998) in this area has, therefore, been along the same lines to those adopted previously, as outlined in 7.3.

A further legitimate aim for restriction recognized by Art. 10(2) is the 'prevention of disorder or crime'. As we shall see, some information which may affect criminal investigations is treated as being an 'official secret', and restriction on publishing it may be justified on the basis of this aim.

Finally, Art. 10(2) also recognizes the legitimacy of 'preventing the disclosure of information received in confidence', and in some situations this can be used to cover government information (see 7.7).

The ways in which the various provisions of Art. 10(2) may be able to be used to justify restrictions in this area are discussed in more detail at the relevant points later in this chapter (e.g. 7.6.3.3, 7.6.6.3, 7.7.1, and 7.8).

7.5 **The Official Secrets Acts 1911–1920**

The main controls over freedom of expression in relation to official secrecy are contained in various criminal offences contained in the Official Secrets Acts 1911–1989. The Official Secrets Act 1989 (OSA 1989) established a system of controls which need to be looked at separately. It repealed parts of the earlier legislation. In this section, the focus will be on the surviving provisions of the Official Secrets Acts 1911 and 1920.

7.5.1 **The Official Secrets Act 1911**

The Official Secrets Act 1911 was a piece of legislation passed through Parliament in a day, as a result of a panic about espionage, and the activities of foreign, and specifically German, agents. It was, and to the extent that it is still in force, still is, a very widely drafted Act, creating a range of offences. The most important surviving provision in relation to freedom of expression is s. 1. This is labelled in the Act 'Penalties for spying', and it was towards espionage activities that it was clearly directed, providing, amongst other things, offences appropriate for those attempting to acquire sensitive information from military establishments, or communicating such information to agents of a foreign power. It was held in *Chandler* v *DPP*

[1964] AC 763, however, that despite the heading, the scope of the section was wide enough to cover 'sabotage', certainly, and probably any activities that fell within its wording. It has, nevertheless, mainly been used in cases related to espionage. It was clearly intended to be used for serious offences, since it carries a penalty of up to 14 years' imprisonment. The communication offence is the one that is, of course, most relevant to freedom of expression. The offence is committed where:

> ...any person for any purpose prejudicial to the safety or interests of the State...communicates to any other person any secret official code word, or pass word, or any sketch plan, model, article, note, or other document or information which is calculated to be or might be or is intended to be directly or indirectly useful to an enemy.

There are three main issues to consider in relation to this offence: first, what is meant by a purpose prejudicial to the safety or interests of the State; second, what is meant by 'communicates'; and third, what type of information is covered.

In relation to the first issue, the Act itself provides some guidance as to how this may be established. Section 1(2) makes it clear that no specific act showing such a purpose need be proved, and indeed that it may be inferred from 'the circumstances of the case', the defendant's conduct, or the defendant's 'known character'. Furthermore, where the communication offence is charged, and the information relates to a 'prohibited place' (as defined in s. 3), the burden of proof shifts, and a prejudicial purpose is assumed unless the defendant proves otherwise. A 'prohibited place' in effect means any premises used by the armed forces, or by the government for purposes connected with defence.

The meaning of the phrase 'purpose prejudicial' was considered in *Chandler* v *DPP*. The defendants were members of the Campaign for Nuclear Disarmament (CND), who had been involved in the organization of a demonstration at a military airfield occupied by the US Air Force. The plan was to enter the airfield and disrupt its operation by sitting on the runways, etc. The defendants were charged with conspiracy to commit an offence under s. 1(1)(a) of approaching, or entering, a prohibited place (which the airfield was) for a purpose prejudicial to the safety or interests of the State. One line of defence raised was that the activities of the defendants were not connected with 'spying', and were therefore outside the scope of s. 1. As we have seen, however, that point was rejected by the House of Lords. A second defence argument related to the fact that, from their own point of view, the defendants did not have a purpose which was prejudicial to the State's interests. On the contrary, their intention was to try to rid the country of nuclear weapons. They argued that this would make this country, and the world a safer place, and was therefore clearly 'in the interests of the State'. The reaction of the House of Lords to this argument was that, although it could not be said that in every case the courts should simply accept the word of the government as to what constitute the interests of the State, in this case they were concerned with the disposition of the armed forces. In this area, the courts had to accept that this was a matter which was within the exclusive discretion of the Crown. In other words it was not a justiciable issue suitable to be left to a jury. There was no scope, therefore, for consideration of the broader arguments of the defendants as to what were the interests of the State. The jury did have a role, the House felt, however, in that once the 'interests of the State' had been determined, the jury would have to decide whether or not the defendant's purpose was prejudicial to those interests. On the facts of the case this, in reality, left the jury with little to do. The government stated that it was in the interests of the State that the airfield should not be disrupted. The defendants' avowed intention was to disrupt the airfield. The way that the interests of the State were stated thus effectively pre-empted the only issue to be left to the jury, and made a verdict of guilty almost inevitable.

The second issue of interpretation in s. 1 is what is meant by 'communicates'? Again, the Act itself provides some indication. Section 12 states that communication includes 'transfer' or 'transmission'. It is not necessary, therefore, that the recipient of the communication should read it, or understand it. The physical handing over of a document from one person to another is enough to amount to 'communication' under this section. The reason for this interpretation is easy to see, since it would be clearly very difficult to prove that information given to an enemy agent, who might well simply be acting as a courier, was in all cases read and understood. Nevertheless, as with the interpretation of 'interests of the State' it allows a broader scope to the offence than might have been expected at first reading.

The third issue of interpretation relates to what information is covered. The basic requirement is simply that the information needs to be 'useful to an enemy'. In *R v Parrott* (1913) 8 Cr App R 186, the defendant was alleged to have communicated information to a person in Germany. He argued that since the United Kingdom was not at that time at war with Germany, and Germany was not therefore an 'enemy', he could not be said to have communicated information 'useful to an enemy'. This argument was rejected, Phillimore J ruling that:

> When the statute uses the word 'enemy' it does not mean necessarily someone with whom this country is at war, but a potential enemy with whom we might some day be at war.

This is again a wide interpretation. The real answer to Parrott's argument, however, is surely that the phrase 'useful to an enemy' refers to the nature of the information, not the person to whom it is communicated. Any information which, if it fell into the hands of an enemy would be useful, is within the scope of s. 1. The information does not, therefore, need to be 'official' information, or secret information. It can be of any kind, provided that an enemy might find it useful, and if it is communicated to anyone for a purpose prejudicial to the safety or interests of the State, then an offence will have been committed.

This means, for example, that if a civil servant goes home and tells her husband of some matter which she has come across at work, and this is something which an enemy would find it useful to know, then an offence under s. 1 may well have been committed. The only additional point that the prosecution has to establish is that the communication to the husband was for a 'purpose prejudicial'. This may be possible to prove, even if the husband is a perfectly loyal and discreet citizen, who would not think of passing on the information to anyone else. For all the government has to do is to certify that any disclosure of information of this kind is prejudicial, and on the basis of the approach in *Chandler*, a jury would be obliged to find the offence made out.

Given this wide scope, s. 1 of the Official Secrets Act 1911 is potentially a very restrictive provision, which could quite easily be used against a wide range of disclosures concerning the operations of government made by the press. It is arguable, for example, that *The Guardian*'s disclosures in 'the *Tisdall* case' (*Secretary of State for Defence* v *Guardian Newspapers* [1985] AC 339) about the arrangements for the announcement of the arrival of cruise missiles into this country could have come into this category. Control of prosecutions under the Official Secrets Act 1911 is, however, in the hands of the Attorney-General (by virtue of s. 8), and in general prosecutions have only been taken or approved in cases which would be agreed to concern espionage, or related activities. A recent example is the prosecution in 2008 of a soldier, Daniel James, who had been working as an interpreter for a senior officer in the British army in Afghanistan. He was Iranian-born, and was found to have been in communication with an Iranian military attaché in Kabul. He was convicted under s. 1 of the Official Secrets Act 1911 of communicating information useful to an enemy, and was jailed for 10 years (see, e.g. *The Times*, 29 November 2008).

The two notable exceptions to this approach are, first, *Chandler* and, second, the so-called 'ABC' trial in 1978 which arose out of an interview between a journalist (Campbell) and a former soldier (Berry), which had been arranged by another journalist (Aubrey). (This case is not reported, but see A. Nicol, 'Official Secrets and Jury Vetting', [1979] Crim LR 284.) At one stage Aubrey, Berry, and Campbell were all charged with s. 1 offences, despite the fact that there was no suggestion that any of the three intended to pass any information to an enemy. The judge at their initial, abortive trial made it clear that he did not regard this as an appropriate use of s. 1, particularly as some of the information related to prohibited places, and the burden of proof as regards 'prejudicial purpose' thus shifted to the defendants. At the second trial the Attorney-General dropped the s. 1 charges, and proceeded only on the less serious offences contained in s. 2.

The existence of the offence under s. 1 of the Official Secrets Act 1911 is thus more of a potential threat to, than an actual restriction on, freedom of expression; but the fact that its use in a way that is not repressive is dependent on the discretion of the Attorney-General is unsatisfactory. There is no reason why the offence could not be reformulated in more specific language, so that it covered only those activities connected with espionage which were clearly its original and intended target.

This wide scope is also what lays s. 1 open to challenge under the HRA 1998. Article 10 of the ECHR allows restrictions on freedom of expression in the interests of national security, and to the extent that s. 1 is concerned with espionage and related activities it would almost certainly be regarded as an acceptable restriction. The wider scope for the section opened up by *Chandler* v *DPP* [1964] AC 763 might well be regarded as disproportionate and going beyond what is necessary in a democratic society (particularly given the likely existence of alternative, less serious offences under other legislation which could generally be used to deal with the behaviour in question). If this issue were to come before the courts it would be interesting to see if any court below the Supreme Court felt able to say that the effect of s. 3 of the HRA 1998 was that the interpretation of s. 1 adopted in *Chandler* should be narrowed; there seems little doubt, however, that the Supreme Court itself would be compelled to limit the scope of the House of Lords' earlier decision.

7.5.2 **The Official Secrets Act 1920**

Section 1 of the Official Secrets Act 1920 contains offences related to the unlawful retention of documents, and similar matters. These are of little practical importance, and in any case do not strike directly at freedom of expression. Section 7 of the Act is, however, a provision which should be noted, in that it has the potential of considerably widening the effect of s. 1 of the Official Secrets Act 1911.

The section is headed 'Attempts, incitements, etc.', and its concern is acts of preparation for, or assistance with, any of the offences under either the 1911 or 1920 Acts. It makes it an offence to attempt to commit any such offence, or to solicit, incite or endeavour to persuade another person to do so, or to aid or abet its commission. Thus far it adds little or nothing to the general criminal law provisions about participation in crime. In addition, however, it is an offence if a person 'does any act preparatory to the commission of an offence' under either of the Acts. It was confirmed in *R v Oakes* [1959] 2 QB 350 that this is a separate offence from the 'aiding and abetting' offence. An example of its use is to be found in *R v Bingham* [1973] QB 870. Mr Bingham was an RAF officer who had been convicted of various offences under the Official Secrets Act 1911. His wife then published her story in various newspapers, revealing that it had been her idea that she and her husband should pass information to the Soviet Embassy, in order to try to resolve their financial problems. She had, in fact, made the first contact with the Embassy. She said that it had been their intention that only false information should be passed on. As a result of this disclosure, she was convicted of an offence under s. 7. The Court of Appeal upheld her conviction, ruling that, provided that she realized the possibility that harmful information might pass, as they felt she must have done, she had sufficient *mens rea* for the offence. In the course of his judgment, Lord Widgery made clear the wide scope of the *actus reus* of this offence ([1977] QB 870, p. 875):

> ...this is a very special kind of offence based on a section which was passed no doubt by Parliament to fill what was otherwise a gap in the law. It contemplates something which is even more remote from the substantive offence than an attempt to commit it.

Under the general criminal law on attempts, set out in the Criminal Attempts Act 1981, only actions which come very close to the commission of the full offence count as attempts. For example, if you leave home with a loaded gun in your pocket, intending to kill the Prime Minister, you will not at that stage be guilty of attempted murder. Nor will you be so, if having lain in wait for your victim, five minutes before he arrives you change your mind, and abandon your plan. The way that this is expressed in s. 1(1) of the Criminal Attempts Act 1981, is to say that the actions must be 'more than merely preparatory' to the commission of the offence. Under s. 7 of the Official Secrets Act 1920, however, merely preparatory acts do amount to an offence. The problem is to know exactly what this means. In Mrs Bingham's case, for example, when did she first commit an offence? When she tried to make contact with the Embassy? When she looked up the address of the Embassy? When she bought paper and ink in order to write to them? When she left the house in order to buy paper and ink for this purpose? It is submitted that all the above could be regarded as preparatory acts, and that provided that Mrs Bingham could be proved to have had the required intention at the relevant time, she could have been convicted.

This, then, is another example of the way in which the criminal offences under the Official Secrets Acts 1911 and 1920 are much wider in scope, and much easier for the prosecution to prove, than would normally be regarded as appropriate elsewhere in the criminal law. It has already been noted that this is the case in relation to the presumptions as to 'prejudicial purpose' in s. 1(2) of the Official Secrets Act 1911. This difference in approach has been discussed fully by Professor D. G. T. Williams in 'Official Secrecy and the Courts' (in P. Glazebrook (ed.), *Reshaping the Criminal Law* (London: Stevens, 1978)). It may be considered justifiable to the extent that the Official Secrets Acts are concerned with acts akin to treason, and which threaten the very security of the State. Similar arguments are used for the extension of the scope of the criminal law in relation to terrorist activities. The Terrorism Act 2006, for example, contains 'preparatory' offences similar to s. 7 of the Official Secrets Act 1920 (see chapter 6, (6.5.2)). As we have seen, however, the offences under the Official Secrets Acts 1911 and 1920 potentially cover behaviour which has nothing to do with national security, and depend on prosecutorial discretion for their proper use. As a result, there is a strong argument that the normal standards of the criminal law should apply, or that the offences themselves should be much more narrowly defined.

7.6 **The Official Secrets Act 1989**

7.6.1 **Background**

The offences looked at in 7.5 are, at least ostensibly, directed towards spying. There is, of course, concern, amongst governments in particular, that a wider category of official information than is encompassed by this should be subject to restrictions on disclosure. Under the Official Secrets Act 1911 this was achieved primarily through the provisions of s. 2. This was a very widely drafted section which in effect made it an offence to disclose any official information without authority. 'Official information' covered any information to which 'Crown servants' (for example, a civil servant, army officer, or police officer) obtained access in the course of their work. The information did not need to have anything about it which would render its disclosure harmful to the nation. In *R v Crisp and Homewood* (1919) 82 JP 121 it was held that details of army clothing contracts could not be revealed without authorization, even though this information had no military significance. As long ago as 1972, after a thorough review of the section, the Franks Committee ('Report and Evidence of the Committee on Section 2 of the Official Secrets Act 1911', Cmnd 5104, 1972) recommended its repeal because of its 'catch-all' nature, and its unacceptably wide drafting. The Committee recommended its replacement with a new statute containing much more closely defined offences, which would not depend on prosecutorial discretion for its proper operation. Several attempts were made during the 1970s and 1980s to achieve this, both by government and by private members, but all failed, for a variety of reasons. Increasing pressure from the press for reform was fuelled by three cases. The first of these was the 'ABC' trial, referred to at 7.5.1. The outcome of this trial was that after six weeks all three defendants were found guilty, but the two journalists were given a conditional discharge, and the former soldier a suspended six month prison sentence. Since the costs of the trial were estimated at something in the region of £150,000, many felt that the case represented a considerable overreaction by the authorities, and emphasized the problems with s. 2 of the Official Secrets Act 1911.

The other two cases, which occurred in the early 1980s, both concerned civil servants in the Ministry of Defence. Sarah Tisdall was a relatively low-ranking official who was unhappy about the way in which information about the arrival of US cruise missiles into this country was being presented to Parliament. She leaked certain documents to *The Guardian*, which published one of them. Ms Tisdall was traced as the source of the leak and was charged under s. 2. She pleaded guilty, and was sentenced to six months' imprisonment. Many felt that, even if it was right that she should be convicted, the sentence was disproportionate to the offence.

The third case, which arose shortly afterwards, concerned a high-ranking civil servant, Clive Ponting, who was an Assistant Secretary. He was again concerned about the way information was being given to Parliament, in this case concerning the sinking of the Argentine ship, the *General Belgrano*, by a British submarine during the Falklands war in 1982. Ponting passed information, not to the press, but to a sympathetic Member of Parliament (MP). Once again, the ministry managed to identify Ponting as the source, and he was charged with the unauthorized disclosure of official information under s. 2. He attempted to run a defence that it was his public duty to disclose the information. The trial judge, however, ruled that his official duty overrode any such duty, and that the 'interests of the State' under s. 2 could be equated with the interests of the government of the day. It appeared that a conviction was inevitable, but the jury acquitted (*R v Ponting* [1985] Crim LR 318). This was taken as indicating that the jury felt that it was inappropriate for Ponting to have been charged with a criminal offence for acting as he did.

The cases of *Tisdall* and *Ponting* demonstrated the severe difficulties that lay in the way of a civil servant 'whistleblower' who wanted to draw attention to wrongdoing, or malpractice, within a government department. The criticisms which the cases aroused also made it very difficult for the Attorney-General to continue to use s. 2. It had been almost totally discredited. The government once again tried to grasp the nettle of reform. A White Paper was published on 'Reform of Section 2 of the Official Secrets Act 1911', Cm 408, 1988 (White Paper), and an Official Secrets Bill based on it was introduced into Parliament. This became the OSA 1989.

Further reforms relevant to this area have taken place through legislation to deal with the protection of 'whistleblowers' (i.e. the Public Interest Disclosure Act 1998), and to provide for 'freedom of information' in certain circumstances (see 7.9).

7.6.2 Categories of information under the Official Secrets Act 1989

The OSA 1989, and the White Paper on which it was based, take the same basic approach to reform as was suggested by the Franks Committee. Instead of trying to provide a single comprehensive definition of 'official information', the Act sets out a number of specific categories of information, the disclosure of which may need to be controlled. If a certain piece of information falls within a category it may also need to be considered whether its disclosure would be 'damaging'. Finally, there may be a defence available in some circumstances.

There are four main categories of information dealt with under the Act, namely:

1. security and intelligence (s. 1);
2. defence (s. 2);
3. international relations (s. 3); and
4. criminal investigations (s. 4).

7.6.2.1 Security and intelligence

This covers any 'information, document or other article' which relates to 'security or intelligence'. 'Security or intelligence' means 'the work of, or in support of the security and intelligence services or any part of them': s. 1(9). Any information held or transmitted by those services is covered. The Act does not, however, make it clear which services are meant. The Security Service Act 1989 relates to MI5, which is concerned mainly with counter-espionage, and this would certainly be covered. The same is true of MI6, the Secret Intelligence Service, which is mainly concerned with operations abroad, and has been given statutory recognition by the Intelligence Services Act 1994. Whether the activities of the police Special Branch, or its anti-terrorist squad, or the intelligence divisions of the armed forces, are also covered, is uncertain. It is submitted, however, that the wording of the Act is wide enough to cover the work of any State service which is concerned with matters similar or related to the work of MI5 or MI6.

7.6.2.2 Defence

This is defined in s. 2(4). It covers virtually all matters relating to the armed forces, their weapons, and equipment. It also covers the more general matters of 'defence policy and strategy and military planning and intelligence'. This obviously includes all the work of the Ministry of Defence. A final category brings in all arrangements for the maintenance of essential supplies and services that would be needed in time of war. Arrangements of this kind are to some extent dealt with by local authorities. As we shall see, however, local government employees are not generally within the scope of the Act's provisions.

7.6.2.3 International relations

This category is defined in s. 3(5). It means relations between States and international organizations, or between either or both. It includes matters which are internal to another State or organization, but which are capable of affecting the United Kingdom's relations with another (not necessarily the same) State or organization. Two types of international organization which would clearly be covered would be any of the organs of the United Nations, or any of the institutions of the European Union. It is assumed, though the opposite interpretation is at least possible, that 'international organizations' does not include multinational companies.

7.6.2.4 Crime and special investigations

There are three categories of information here, though they are to some extent related. The first category is unlike any of the other categories in ss 1–4, in that it is defined in terms of the effects of disclosure. It covers any information, document, or article the disclosure of which has, or if unauthorized would be likely to have, one of three results, namely:

1. the commission of an offence; or

2. the facilitation of an escape from legal custody, or prejudice to the safekeeping of persons in custody; or

3. impeding the prevention or detection of offences, or the apprehension or prosecution of offenders.

The second main category within s. 4 relates to information obtained as a result of the interception of communications under a warrant issued under s. 5 of the Regulation of Investigatory Powers Act 2000 (RIPA 2000). This Act gives the Home Secretary the power to authorize phone 'taps', in fairly closely defined circumstances. It is discussed further in chapter 6 (6.5.1.1). This category within s. 4 also covers any information relating to an authorized interception, or any document or article held or used in connection with such an interception.

The third category within s. 4 covers any information obtained through the exercise of a warrant issued under s. 3 of the Security Service Act 1989 or s. 5 of the Intelligence Services Act 1994, or an authorization issued under s. 7 of the 1994 Act. These provisions provide for the Secretary of State to authorize members of MI5 (the OSA 1989) or MI6 (the Intelligence Services Act 1994), to engage in otherwise unlawful activities such as entering on property to inspect, photograph, or remove documents, or to plant a bugging device. Any information relating to such action, or obtained by such action, falls within the scope of s. 4 of the OSA 1989.

7.6.2.5 Information not covered

It is important to note that certain categories of information which might have been expected to appear are omitted from this list. The Franks Committee, for example, recommended that Cabinet documents should be subject to restriction. The government, however, took the view that to include them as a category in their own right would suggest that the criminal law was being used to protect against political embarrassment (para. 32 of the White Paper). Similarly economic information, and information provided to the government in confidence (for example, tax returns), is not covered unless it falls within one of the specific categories listed above (paras 33–5 of the White Paper).

7.6.3 Concept of 'damaging' disclosure

It was an important plank in the reform of s. 2 of the Official Secrets Act 1911, that under the new legislation, only disclosures which were 'damaging' would be caught by the criminal law. The existence of this limitation on the scope of the Act was used as a justification for saying that there was therefore no need for defences of 'public interest', or 'prior disclosure'. It could not be in the public interest to disclose damaging information. As regards previous publication, the government suggested that this would be a factor, though not a conclusive one, in deciding whether a further disclosure could be regarded as damaging (paras 62–4 of the White Paper).

The concept of the damaging disclosure operates differently in relation to the four categories of information in ss 1–4 of the Act, so each of them must now be looked at again in turn to see exactly what publications are prohibited. As will be seen the emphasis here is not primarily on the nature of what is disclosed, but the effects of disclosure. It may, therefore, be relevant to look at the questions of to whom the disclosure is made, and where it takes place.

It should also be noted that 'disclosure' of a document or article is defined in s. 12 so as to include 'parting with possession' of it. There is a similarity here with the definition of 'communication' under the Official Secrets Act 1911 (see 7.5.1).

In this section the phrases 'Crown servant' and 'government contractor' are frequently used. These are defined in s. 12 of the Act, and discussed further at 7.6.4.

7.6.3.1 Security and intelligence

There are two situations to consider here, depending on who is doing the disclosing. Where the discloser is a member of the security services, or a person who has been notified as being subject to the provisions of s. 1(1), then there is no need for the prosecution to prove actual or potential damage. Disclosure by such a person of any information falling within the category of 'security and intelligence', and acquired in the course of the person's work, is automatically an offence. It would be an offence under this section, therefore for James Bond to tell Pussy Galore the colour of the tie that 'M' had been wearing that morning (see Ian Fleming, *Goldfinger*). Such a result comes close to retaining the catch-all nature of the old s. 2 of the Official Secrets Act 1911, and does little to support the commitment to criminalize only 'damaging' disclosures. The justification is that the work of a member of the security or intelligence services is so confidential that any breach of that confidentiality must be regarded as damaging, no matter what is disclosed. This assertion remains as unconvincing in relation to s. 1 of the OSA 1989 as it did in relation to s. 2 of the Official Secrets Act 1911. Indeed, the government itself seemed to have accepted in *Attorney-General* v *Blake* [2000] 4 All ER 385 (discussed at 7.7.3), that in certain circumstances information acquired by a member of the security services can lose its confidentiality.

The second situation is where the disclosure is by a person who is, or has been, a Crown servant or government contractor, but is not a member of the security or intelligence services. This would cover civil servants working in the Home Office or the Foreign and Commonwealth Office, for example, who might be engaged on matters related to security or the gathering of intelligence. A disclosure by such a person will be damaging if it causes damage to the work of the security and intelligence services (s. 1(4)), or if it is of information, or a document or article, the unauthorized disclosure of which would be likely to cause such harm. It will also be damaging if, although the disclosure of the particular information, document, or article would not in itself cause harm, it falls within a class or description of information, documents, or articles the unauthorized disclosure of which would be likely to have such an effect. This final category has the potential of greatly widening the scope of the Act, and considerably reducing its liberalizing effect. Its inclusion is presumably based on a similar line of argument to that used in *Secretary of State for Defence* v *Guardian Newspapers*. Here the view was taken that although disclosure of the document leaked by Sarah Tisdall and published by *The Guardian* was not in itself prejudicial to national security, any unauthorized disclosure of documents by civil servants working in the Ministry of Defence would potentially have this effect. It was in the interest of national security, therefore, that no such disclosures should occur, no matter what the content of the particular document disclosed. The adoption of this line of reasoning in s. 1(4) of the OSA 1989, in defining the damaging nature of a disclosure by reference to the 'class' to which the information, document, or article, belongs, rather than by its content, is unfortunate, in that it considerably weakens the government's argument that disclosures in the public interest need no special protection, because only disclosures which are clearly damaging will be caught by the Act. To the extent that it precludes a consideration of whether the restriction of a particular disclosure is 'necessary' to protect national security, and whether the measures taken are 'proportionate' to that objective, it raises the possibility of a challenge under the HRA 1998, on the basis of an infringement of Art. 10.

7.6.3.2 Defence

The offence under s. 2, concerning information relating to defence, is committed where there is a damaging disclosure of any information, document, or article falling within this category, to which the discloser has or had access by virtue of being, or having been, a Crown servant or government contractor. A disclosure of information in this category is damaging if it has, or is likely to have, any of the following effects:

(a) damage to the capability of any part of the armed forces to carry out their tasks;

(b) loss of life, or injury to members of the armed forces;

(c) serious damage to the equipment or installations of those forces;

(d) danger to the interests of the United Kingdom abroad;

(e) serious obstruction to the promotion or protection by the United Kingdom of those interests; or

(f) danger to the safety of British citizens abroad.

It is not clear whether the 'loss of life' in (b) relates only to members of the armed forces. The strict grammatical reading would lead to its covering any loss of life, but the rest of the subsection is entirely concerned with the armed forces.

7.6.3.3 International relations

Once again, it is current or former Crown servants, or government contractors, who may commit the offence of making a damaging disclosure of information falling within the category of 'international relations'. The discloser must have, or have had, access to the information, document, or article, as a result of holding such a position. The damaging effects here are those listed under (d), (e) or (f) in 7.6.3.2 in relation to defence.

Where the offence is based on the fact that the material is likely to have one of these effects if disclosed (rather than having had such an effect), the fact that it was received in confidence from another State, or an international organization, may be sufficient in itself to establish this likelihood (s. 3(3)(a)). It is also possible, of course, to establish the likely damaging effect from the 'nature or contents' of such material (s. 3(3)(b)).

It is not clear that the general restriction on the publication of information relating to 'international relations' meets any of the legitimate aims for restricting freedom of expression specified in Art. 10(2) of the ECHR. Some material within this category might fall into the category of 'national security' but not all of it would. To the extent that the disclosure of information might prejudice the safety of UK citizens abroad, it might be argued that 'public safety' is raised. Section 3 is, nevertheless, the hardest provision to fit within the legitimate reasons for restriction, and therefore might be susceptible to challenge under the HRA 1998.

7.6.3.4 Crime and special investigation powers

Reference to the definition of material within the category of 'crime' (see 7.6.2.4), will show that it is based on the harmful effects of disclosure. As a result, there is no further definition of 'damaging' disclosure in relation to this class of material. In a formal sense this is untidy, in that it is out of line with the general approach of defining a broad category of material, and then identifying damaging disclosures within that category, which is used in ss 1–3. It has little significance of substance, however, and this part of s. 4 fits in with the general policy of the White Paper and the OSA 1989, that disclosures should be judged by their effects, or potential effects, as much as by the type or origin of the material which is disclosed.

In relation to special investigation powers, however, the position is different. As regards information relating to interception of communications, or warrants or authorizations under the Security Service Act 1989 and the Intelligence Services Act 1994, the definition in s. 4(3) of the material covered is purely in terms of the type of material or its content. There is no reference here to the effects of disclosing the material. It is surprising, therefore, to find that there is no definition of damaging disclosure as regards material within s. 4(3). The justification for this approach as regards interceptions appears in paras 30 and 53 of the White Paper. Paragraph 30 gives two reasons why disclosure might be harmful. The first is that '[t]he effectiveness of interception would be much reduced if details of the practice were readily available'. The second is that interception involves interference with the privacy of those whose communications are subject to it: 'Such interference is acceptable in the public interest only if those responsible for interception maintain the privacy of the information obtained'. Paragraph 53 refers to the reasons set out in para. 30, and then asserts that 'no information obtained by means of interception can be disclosed without assisting terrorism or crime, damaging national security or seriously breaching the privacy of private citizens'. Therefore, it is concluded, no specific test of harm is needed in relation to the disclosure of this category of material.

This argument would have more force if s. 4(3) was concerned solely with the content of any interception. As we have seen, however, the section also covers 'any information relating to the obtaining of information by reason of any such interception'. It cannot seriously be argued that all disclosures of information falling within this definition are damaging, since the Commissioner appointed previously under the Interception of Communications Act 1985, and now under the RIPA 2000, to monitor its operation annually issues reports indicating, for example, the number of warrants issued under the Act, the general areas to which they related (drugs, serious crime, etc.) and their effectiveness (that is, the number of arrests which resulted). In the light of this it is hard to accept that a definition of damaging disclosure in respect of this category could not have been devised.

Much the same considerations apply to information relating to warrants or authorizations issued under the Security Service Act 1989 and the Intelligence Services Act 1994. The argument would presumably be that, as with information emanating from members of the security and intelligence services, under s. 1, any disclosure is harmful. Here again, however, the Acts themselves provide for Commissioners who are to supervise, amongst other things, the operation of the warrant system, and make annual reports to the Prime Minister which are laid before Parliament. Disclosure of the information contained in these reports is, presumably, not harmful. There seems no reason, then, why there should not be in this section a definition of 'damaging disclosure' as well. There is clearly scope here for an argument under s. 3 of the HRA 1998 that s. 4(3) of the OSA 1989 should be interpreted as only applying to information the disclosure of which would be damaging to the prevention of crime or terrorism, or would seriously breach the privacy of individual citizens.

7.6.4 Crown servants and government contractors

The principal obligations under ss 1–4 of the OSA 1989 are placed on Crown servants and government contractors. These are defined in s. 12 of the Act.

Crown servants include all government Ministers, but not all MPs. MPs who act as part of a Ministerial private office therefore will not fall in this category. Anyone employed in the civil service in whatever capacity, from a permanent secretary in the Foreign and Commonwealth Office, to a counter-clerk in a local office of the Department for Social Security, is a Crown servant. Less obvious groups who come within the s. 12 definition, are all members of the armed forces, and all police officers. Civilians employed by the police are also specifically included (s. 12(1)(e)), thus giving statutory recognition to the view taken in *Loat* v *Andrews* [1986] ICR 679 in relation to s. 2 of the Official Secrets Act 1911. Section 12(1)(f) and (g) give a power to 'prescribe' that other people, or groups of people, are to be regarded as Crown servants for the purposes of the Act. This has been used, for example, to bring within its scope people concerned with nuclear energy, such as employees of British Nuclear Fuels plc, and the Atomic Energy Authority. It has also been used in respect of non-governmental organizations or bodies, such as the staff of the National Audit Office, and the Parliamentary Commissioner for Administration (Official Secrets Act 1989 (Prescription) Order 1990 (SI 1990/200)).

A 'government contractor' is defined as any person (not being a Crown servant) who 'provides, or is employed in the provision of, goods and services' to the people or organizations specified in s. 12(2)(a). This includes all government departments, and the armed forces. Under s. 12(2)(b) the Secretary of State may certify that suppliers under certain international agreements or arrangements should also be regarded as government contractors.

7.6.5 The private citizen and the press

As can be seen above, the offences under ss 1–4 of the OSA 1989 are all directed against members of the security service, Crown servants, and government contractors. While stopping such people from disclosing information is a restriction on freedom of expression, these provisions do not operate as a direct attack on the press. The fact that civil servants and others are reluctant to leak information may, of course, mean that the press cannot get access to, and publish, some stories that it would like to. More direct controls are, however, contained in ss 5 and 6 of the OSA 1989. These apply to disclosures by people other than Crown servants and government contractors.

It should be noted, however, that the OSA 1989 gives no special status to the press. The ECtHR, on the other hand, has often stated that it is a basic principle of the right to freedom of expression that the special position of the press as a guardian of the public interest should be recognized (e.g. *Observer and Guardian* v *United Kingdom* (1992) 14 EHRR 153, para. 59). Under the OSA 1989 the press is treated in exactly the same way as any other private individual in possession of government information. This is a point on which a challenge under the HRA 1998 might well be expected, if a prosecution under the OSA 1989 fails to give proper weight to the position of the press.

7.6.5.1 Information resulting from unauthorized disclosures or entrusted in confidence

The test of whether a private individual of any sort, including a journalist or editor, commits an offence by disclosing material, depends primarily on how the material was acquired. There are four ways in which information, or a document or article is acquired which may mean that a further disclosure will amount to an offence:

(a) where the material was acquired as a result of a disclosure in contravention of s. 1 of the Official Secrets Act 1911 (see 7.5.1) (s. 5(6));

(b) where the material was acquired as a result of an unauthorized disclosure at some stage by a Crown servant or government contractor (s. 5(1)(a)(i));

(c) where the material was entrusted to the recipient in confidence, or with a reasonable expectation of confidence, by a Crown servant or government contractor (s. 5(1)(a)(ii));

(d) where the material was acquired as a result of an unauthorized disclosure at some stage by a person to whom it had been entrusted as in (c) above.

The disclosure of material falling within (a) is an offence if it is made without lawful authority, and the discloser knows, or has reasonable cause to believe, that it has been communicated in breach of s. 1 of the Official Secrets Act 1911. As will be recalled, this means it must be material which is communicated for a purpose prejudicial to the safety or interests of the State, and which is, or is intended to be, useful to an enemy (see 7.5.1).

In relation to material falling within categories (b), (c), or (d), above, the offence will depend to some extent on the content of the material. If it comes within ss 1, 2 or 3 of the Act, that is security and intelligence, defence, or international relations, it will be an offence to disclose it without lawful authority, if the disclosure is 'damaging' as defined in ss 1, 2, or 3, and the discloser has the required mental element. This is that the discloser knows, or has reasonable cause to believe, that the material is protected against disclosure under the OSA 1989, and that the disclosure would be damaging.

If the material falls within s. 4 of the Act, that is, crime and special investigation powers, then the offence is the same as outlined in the previous paragraph, except that the prosecution has no need to prove that the disclosure was damaging, or that the discloser knew or had reasonable cause to believe that it would be damaging. The discloser must still be shown to have been aware, or to have had reasonable cause to believe, that the material was protected against disclosure under the OSA 1989.

How might these offences work in practice? Suppose a Minister gives an MP information relating to defence, in confidence. This might well be authorized, since Ministers will be taken to have wide powers of self-authorization. What would be the position if the MP then leaks the information to a journalist, and it is published in a newspaper? If the disclosure of the information is damaging, then the MP will commit an offence because of the breach of confidence (category (c), above), and the journalist and newspaper will commit an offence, because of the earlier breach of confidence (category (d), above), provided that in each case the prosecution can prove the relevant mental element.

To take another example, *The Guardian*, in publishing the document sent to it anonymously by Sarah Tisdall (see 7.6.1), might well commit an offence under the OSA 1989. The document was disclosed without authority by a Crown servant, and so fell within category (b) above. It clearly related to defence. The editor of *The Guardian* would only escape liability if its publication of the document was found not to be damaging, or the editor was found not to have had reasonable grounds to believe that it had been sent to him without lawful authority (which is unlikely), or not to have known, or had any reasonable grounds to believe, that the disclosure would be damaging (which is more possible). It was clear from *Secretary of State for Defence* v *Guardian Newspapers*, that there was general agreement that the disclosure of the document which *The Guardian* published was not harmful to the national interest, and it would be difficult to see it as being 'damaging' within s. 2(2) of the OSA 1989. On the other hand, there is the risk that a court might interpret s. 2(2)(c) as covering such a situation. This makes damaging the disclosure of any material the unauthorized disclosure of which would be likely to be damaging under s. 2(2)(a) or (b). That is, it might be argued that although this particular disclosure of this particular document was not damaging, the disclosure of documents of this kind was always potentially damaging. This was the kind of argument which found favour with the House of Lords in *Secretary of State for Defence* v *Guardian Newspapers*. It is not so obviously applicable to s. 2 of the OSA 1989 as it is to s. 1, where there is specific reference to the likely effects of disclosing material of the same 'class' as that actually disclosed (s. 1(4)(b)), but the general history of statutory interpretation in relation to Official Secrets Act provisions does not lend encouragement to an expectation that a narrow interpretation would be adopted (see, e.g. D. G. T. Williams, 'Official Secrecy and the Courts'). It is to be hoped, however, that the interpretation provision in s. 3 of the HRA 1998 would lead the courts to adopt a narrower interpretation, as being more in line with the requirements of Art. 10 of the ECHR.

As will be seen, then, the question of whether the press is significantly less subject to restraint under s. 5 of the OSA 1989 than it was under s. 2 of the Official Secrets Act 1911, will depend to a large extent on the concept of the 'damaging' disclosure, and in particular how this is interpreted by the courts.

7.6.5.2 Information entrusted in confidence to other States or international organizations

The government was concerned about the possible risks of disclosure where information was given to other States or international organizations, and then found its way back into the British press. This was not dealt with in the White Paper, but is addressed in s. 6 of the OSA 1989. The section applies to material relating to security or intelligence, defence, or international relations. Material falling within s. 4 of the OSA 1989 (crime and special investigations) is not therefore covered. The material must have been communicated in confidence by or on behalf of the United Kingdom to another State or international organization. If it comes into a person's possession as a result of having been disclosed without the authority of that State or organization (or a member of it), then a disclosure by that person may constitute an offence, if it is a damaging disclosure. The discloser must know, or have reasonable cause to believe, that it is material to which the section applies, and that its disclosure would be damaging.

Unusually for the OSA 1989, there is here a defence of previous disclosure. Under s. 6(3) if the material has previously been made available to the public (and presumably this does not simply mean the public within the United Kingdom) with the authority of the relevant state or organization, then no offence will be committed.

7.6.6 Defences

The Act is fairly limited in the defences which it allows, and for most offences there is only one that is available.

7.6.6.1 Awareness of nature of material or likelihood of damage

For Crown servants and government contractors it is generally a defence for the discloser to prove lack of knowledge, or reasonable cause to not believe, that the material disclosed was in one of the restricted categories of restricted material within ss 1–4, or that, where relevant, the disclosure would be damaging (see ss 1(5), 2(3), 3(4), 4(4), and (5)). Note that this is a true defence, in that the burden of proof of this state of mind lies (on the balance of probabilities) on the person charged. The question of whether such 'reverse' burdens of proof are compatible with the guarantee of the presumption of innocence in Art. 6(2) of the ECHR received extensive consideration by the House of Lords in *Sheldrake* v *DPP* [2004] UKHL 43, [2005] 1 All ER 237 (as discussed in chapter 2 (2.3.3.1)). The application of the principles set out in that case to the OSA 1989 was considered by the Court of Appeal in *R* v *Keogh* [2007] EWCA Crim 528, [2007] 3 All ER 789, which concerned the unauthorized disclosure by a civil servant to an MP's researcher of a memo recording a meeting between the Prime Minister and the President of the United States, discussing the Iraq War. As was suggested should be the case in the 8th edition of this book, the Court concluded that the prosecution should be required to prove the knowledge or belief of the defendant, in order to obtain a conviction. In other words, the imposition of a burden of proof on the defence as regards these matters was disproportionate and unnecessary. The section should be 'read down' as only applying an evidential burden on the defendant. (When the case came to trial, Keogh was nevertheless convicted—see 7.6.7.)

In relation to disclosures by the public or the press under s. 5 or s. 6, the proof of the relevant state of mind in any case remains with the prosecution (to be proved beyond reasonable doubt).

7.6.6.2 Lawful authority

All the offences under the Act so far considered require the prosecution to prove that the disclosure was made, as a matter of fact, 'without lawful authority'. In addition, s. 7(4) provides that there is a defence if the discloser proves:

> ...that at the time of the alleged offence he believed that he had lawful authority to make the disclosure in question and had no reasonable cause to believe otherwise.

The concept of 'lawful authority' is dealt with in s. 7(1), (2), and (3). The definition differs according to who is the discloser. Where the disclosure is by a Crown servant, or a person subject to a notification under s. 1(1) (see 7.6.3.1), it is only made 'with lawful authority' if it is made in accordance with the discloser's 'official duty'. This carries echoes of the *Ponting* case, where Clive Ponting tried to argue in relation to his disclosure, that it was his 'moral duty' in the public interest, to reveal what was going on in his department. The trial judge, however, ruled that the word 'duty' in s. 2 of the Official Secrets Act 1911 had to be interpreted as meaning a civil servant's official duty. The same approach is perpetuated by the definition in s. 7(1).

Where the disclosure is by government contractor, lawful authority means 'in accordance with an official authorisation', or:

> ...for the purposes of the function by virtue of which he is a government contractor and without contravening an official restriction.

'Official authorisation' and 'official restriction' are further defined in s. 7(5), as essentially meaning an authorization or restriction duly given or imposed by a Crown servant or government contractor.

Finally, where the disclosure is made by any person who is not a Crown servant or government contractor, a disclosure will only be made with lawful authority if it is made to a Crown servant, or in accordance with an official authorization (s. 7(3)). It was suggested by the House of Lords in *R v Shayler* [2002] UKHL 11, [2003] 1 AC 247, that the ability to obtain an 'authorisation' for disclosure is more powerful than might appear at first sight, in that the refusal of such an authorization would be susceptible to judicial review. This case is discussed fully in 7.6.6.3.

7.6.6.3 Public interest

The Act makes no provision for a defence of public interest in relation to any type of disclosure. The White Paper considered the possibility but rejected it for two main reasons. First, to introduce such a defence would inevitably reduce the clarity of the law, because its availability would be likely to lead to a broad range of arguments as to when it should be available. Second, the reforms were intended to limit the scope of the criminal law to disclosures which are damaging, and therefore contrary to the public interest. The White Paper continues (para. 60):

> It cannot be acceptable that a person can lawfully disclose information which he knows may, for example, lead to loss of life simply because he conceives that he has a general reason of a public character for doing so.

This is no doubt true, but it goes too far. Those who support a public interest defence do not argue that it should override the danger of loss of life; but as we have seen, 'damaging' disclosures can involve consequences considerably less serious than this, such as 'endangering the interests of the United Kingdom abroad' (s. 2(2)). In relation to consequences such as this it is hard to accept that there could be no circumstances in which a public interest in disclosure would outweigh the possible damage that might be caused.

The lack of any public interest defence also seems to be out of line with the approach of the ECtHR. In the *Spycatcher* case (see 7.7), the Court held that injunctions issued by the English courts against newspapers at the early stages of the action did not involve an infringement of Art. 10 of the ECHR partly on the basis that the domestic courts had recognized the conflicting public interests involved, and had given them careful consideration (*Observer and Guardian* v *United Kingdom*, para. 63). It was suggested in the third edition of this book that the lack of a public interest defence would make the Act vulnerable to challenge under the HRA 1998. Such a challenge was made in *R* v *Shayler*.

David Shayler was a member of the Security Service (MI5) from 1991 to 1996. After leaving the service he disclosed various secret documents to certain newspapers, which published articles based on some of them. Shayler also claimed that he was exposing improprieties which had taken place in the security and intelligence services, including an alleged plan to assassinate Colonel Gaddafi, the Head of State of Libya. When it appeared that he might be the subject of legal action, Shayler went to France. On his return to the UK in August 2000 he was arrested, and charged with offences under ss 1 and 4 of the OSA 1989.

At a preparatory hearing he raised possible defences of duress, necessity, and public interest. These matters were considered at a preliminary issue. The judge at the initial hearing ruled that a defence of duress was possible, but not made out on the facts, that a defence of necessity or 'duress of circumstances' was not available as a matter of law, and that there was no defence of 'public interest' under the Act. On appeal, the Court of Appeal held that the defence of necessity was potentially available, though there was no evidence in the case of circumstances which would give rise to it. In other respects it upheld the decision of the judge below. Shayler appealed to the House of Lords.

The House refused to become involved in consideration of the defence of necessity, which had formed much of the judgment in the Court of Appeal. It was not prepared to agree that the Court of Appeal's conclusion on the potential availability of this defence was correct, but nor did it specifically reject it. On the facts, however, it was clearly not available. The same was true of duress. The House, therefore, concentrated on the question of whether the OSA 1989 could be read so as to include a defence of public interest, and, if it could not, whether this meant that it was incompatible with the HRA 1998.

On this issue Lord Bingham, who gave the leading speech, considered the history of the OSA 1989, and noted in particular that the White Paper which preceded it had specifically rejected a 'public interest' defence. He then considered in detail the wording of the sections under which Shayler had been charged. His conclusion was as follows (para. 20):

> It is in my opinion plain, giving sections 1(1)(a) and 4(1) and (3)(a) their natural and ordinary meaning and reading them in the context of the OSA 1989 as a whole, that a defendant prosecuted under these sections is not entitled to be acquitted if he shows that it was or that he believed that it was in the public or national interest to make the disclosure in question or if the jury conclude that it may have been or that the defendant may have believed it to be in the public or national interest to make the disclosure in question. The sections impose no obligation on the prosecution to prove that the disclosure was not in the public interest and give the defendant no opportunity to show that the disclosure was in the public interest or that he thought it was. The sections leave no room for doubt, and if they did the 1988 White Paper quoted above, which is a legitimate aid to construction, makes the intention of Parliament clear beyond argument.

This left only the question of whether it was possible to find that the relevant provisions of the Act were compatible with Art. 10, or whether a declaration of incompatibility should be made. The answer to this was that although the OSA 1989 imposes a ban on disclosure of information or documents relating to security or intelligence by a former member of the service, it is not an absolute ban: it is a ban on disclosure without lawful authority (para. 27). Under s. 7(3)(a) Shayler, as a former member of the security services, could have made his concerns known to a relevant Crown servant. These would have included the 'staff counsellor' (established in response to the *Spycatcher* case), the Attorney-General, the Director of Public Prosecutions (DPP), or the Commissioner of the Metropolitan Police (re alleged illegal actions); or (if concerned about 'maladministration' or waste of resources) to a relevant Secretary of State, the Secretary to the Cabinet, or the Parliamentary Commissioner for the Administration. In relation to information falling within s. 4, concerns could be made known to the relevant Commissioners (for whom, see chapter 5 (5.3.2)).

These routes of communication would apply where the object was to express concerns about improper behaviour or procedures. Lord Bingham recognized, however, that 'there would remain facts which should in the public interest be revealed to a wider audience' (para. 29). In relation to these, the appropriate action would be to seek authorization for disclosure under s. 7(3)(b). A decision to refuse authorization would be subject to judicial review, and it was to be expected that the approach set out by Lord Steyn in *R (Daly)* v *Secretary of State for the Home Department* [2001] 2 AC 532 would be adopted, under which a more rigorous review was possible than under the *Wednesbury* approach. In particular, the court would be able to take account of the 'proportionality' of any decision to refuse publication, which would be very relevant to the question of compatibility with Art. 10. It was to be hoped and expected that, where judicial review was being sought, disclosure of relevant information to a lawyer would be allowed under s. 7(3)(b) in order that the person concerned could prepare their case properly, and in accordance with their rights under Art. 6.

Lord Bingham's conclusion was that while it was necessary to protect the disclosure of certain information by members or former members of the security services (para. 36):

> ...it is plain that a sweeping, blanket ban, permitting of no exceptions, would be inconsistent with the general right guaranteed by Article 10(1) and would not survive the rigorous and particular scrutiny required to give effect to Article 10(2). The crux of this case is whether the safeguards built into the OSA 1989 are sufficient to ensure that unlawfulness and irregularity can be reported to those with the power and duty to take effective action, that the power to withhold authorisation to publish is not abused and that proper disclosures are not stifled. In my opinion the procedures discussed above, properly applied, provide sufficient and effective safeguards.

Substantial speeches coming to the same conclusion as Lord Bingham were delivered by Lord Hope and Lord Hutton. Lord Hope recognized more explicitly, however, that Parliament had probably not taken as much account of Art. 10 as it should have done when enacting the OSA 1989 (para. 41). He also noted that there was strength in some of the concerns about the Act expressed by commentators on it, including those of the present writer in the third edition of this book (para. 44). Nevertheless, with Lord Bingham, and the other members of the House, he concluded that the procedures under s. 7 were sufficient to ensure the Act's compatibility with Art. 10.

The result of the decision is that it is no longer possible to argue that a public interest defence should be read into the OSA 1989. It has also had the effect of giving additional importance to the procedures under s. 7. It should be noted, however, that while these procedures are available to former members of the security services, they will not assist current members or other Crown servants. For these, s. 7(1) applies, which states that a disclosure is only lawful if made in accordance with the Crown servant's 'official duty'. The authorization provisions under s. 7(3) do not apply. There is still an argument to be made, therefore, that the Act, in imposing what appears to be a blanket ban on disclosures by Crown servants, gives insufficient weight to the issues of necessity and proportionality which Art. 10 requires to be taken into account before freedom of expression is restricted.

Following his unsuccessful appeal to the House of Lords on the 'public interest' issue, David Shayler's trial took place. He was convicted of various offences under s. 2 of the OSA 1989 and was sentenced to six months' imprisonment (see, e.g. *The Times*, 5 and 6 November 2002).

7.6.6.4 Defence of previous publication

This too was considered in the White Paper, but again rejected. It was pointed out that in some cases repetition of a story may in fact be more harmful, if for example it involved a senior official in a government department confirming what had previously been a rumour based on little evidence. Moreover, in certain circumstances the gathering together of information previously published in different places may create a much more damaging disclosure. The example used in the White Paper is of a list of addresses of persons in public life, which in its compiled form might be of considerable use to terrorist groups (para. 62).

The White Paper also claims that where it is necessary for a disclosure to be proved to be damaging, the fact of earlier disclosure of the same information will be a relevant factor. If no further harm is done by the second publication, it will not be damaging. This argument would be more convincing if it were not for the fact that it is difficult to see that the relevant provisions of the OSA 1989 will be interpreted in this way. Many of them refer to a damaging disclosure as covering the situation where the unauthorized disclosure would be 'likely' to have damaging consequences. This seems to leave it open to the courts to ignore any earlier publication, and the actual effects of publication, and simply to consider the hypothetical possibility of disclosure. Such an approach, however, might well run the risk of being regarded as 'unnecessary' or 'disproportionate' in relation to the objective of protecting national security, and therefore open to challenge under the HRA 1998. By virtue of s. 3 of the HRA 1998, the courts might, therefore, feel obliged to interpret the word 'likely' narrowly so as to relate it simply to the actual effects of the particular disclosure under consideration.

Finally, the Act itself does not follow the White Paper's line consistently. As can be seen in 7.6.5.2, in s. 6 it is recognized that in certain circumstances previous disclosure of material should prevent a subsequent disclosure from constituting an offence, even if that subsequent disclosure is itself damaging (s. 6(1)). It is difficult to see why this exception to the general approach should have been allowed here, and not in relation to any other similar circumstances.

7.6.7 **The Official Secrets Act 1989 in practice**

An example of a successful prosecution under the OSA 1989 is the conviction of two men (David Keogh and Leo O'Connor) in May 2007 for leaking a confidential memo of a meeting between George Bush and Tony Blair in 2004, relating to the Iraq War. It was leaked by a civil servant in the Ministry of Defence to a researcher working for a Labour MP. The MP notified the police, and the civil servant and the researcher were convicted of offences of making damaging disclosures under the OSA 1989. The civil servant was jailed for six months, and the researcher for three months (see, e.g. http://news.bbc.co.uk/1/hi/uk/6639947.stm).

By contrast, in January 2008 charges were dropped, after 20 months, in relation to a Foreign Office civil servant, Derek Pasquill, who had leaked documents dealing with the government's policy towards radical Islam. He had sent the material to a journalist, resulting in articles on the issue being published in *The Observer* and the *New Statesman*. It was suggested that the charges were dropped because internal Foreign Office documents cast doubt on whether the disclosure of the information could be said to be damaging (see http://news.bbc.co.uk/1/hi/uk/7179247.stm). It is also difficult to see which of the categories of information within the OSA 1989 this material would have fallen into. Mr Pasquill was subsequently dismissed from his post for 'gross misconduct'.

7.6.8 **Miscellaneous**

7.6.8.1 **Other offences**

Section 8 of the OSA 1989 creates various offences relating to the unauthorized retention or failure to take care of documents. These are not really of much relevance to freedom of expression. Section 8(4) and (5), however, are more directly applicable to press freedom. They apply where a person has under their possession or control a document or article which it would be an offence to disclose under s. 5 or s. 6, respectively. It is an offence to fail to return such a document or article, where there has been an official direction to do so. An official direction is one that has been issued by a Crown servant or government contractor (s. 8(9)). This means, presumably, that in a situation such as that which occurred in *Secretary of State for Defence* v *Guardian Newspapers* there would no longer be any need to rely on tortious remedies to recover the document. A direction for return could be issued to the newspaper, and if it failed to comply, an offence would be committed. It is to be hoped that the courts would, however, be prepared in appropriate circumstances to allow a newspaper to rely on s. 10 of the Contempt of Court Act 1981, which permits non-disclosure of sources. This was recognized, though not applied, in *Secretary of State for Defence* v *Guardian Newspapers*.

7.6.8.2 Search powers

Section 11(2) extends the search warrant powers under s. 9 of the Official Secrets Act 1911 to offences (other than those under s. 8) under the OSA 1989.

7.6.8.3 Prosecution

For all prosecutions, the consent of the Attorney-General or, in the case of s. 4(2), the DPP, is required.

7.6.8.4 Penalties

All offences, other than those under s. 8(1), (4) and (5), are triable either way. On indictment the maximum penalty is a fine, plus imprisonment for up to two years. On summary conviction the maximum is six months' imprisonment, or a fine not exceeding the statutory maximum, or both. This is the same level of penalties as applied to offences under s. 2 of the Official Secrets Act 1911.

Section 8 offences (other than s. 8(6)) are summary only, punishable by three months' imprisonment, or a fine not exceeding level 5 on the standard scale.

7.7 Breach of confidence

So far in this chapter we have been primarily concerned with the criminal law, that is, restrictions on freedom of expression which operate by punishing those who publish. The government, however, has also attempted at times to exercise controls in this area by means of the civil law, and the use of injunctions. This type of prior restriction on disclosure is not generally available under the criminal law. The courts take the view that if a publisher is not deterred by the threat of penalties imposed under the criminal law, the threat of imposing similar penalties for contempt of court as a result of non-compliance with an injunction is likely to be similarly ineffective. The injunction, however, is often used as part of the range of remedies under the civil law. The area of civil law which is of particular relevance to the issues discussed in this chapter is 'breach of confidence'.

7.7.1 **The background**

The action for breach of confidence has its origins mainly in the law relating to trade secrets, for example, *Morison v Moat* (1851) 9 Hare 241, though the case of *Prince Albert v Strange* (1848) 2 De G & Sm 652 shows it also being used in a quasi-copyright situation raising privacy issues. As Lord Keith pointed out in *Attorney-General v Guardian Newspapers Ltd (No. 2)* [1990] 1 AC 109, however, most of the cases on confidentiality have been concerned either with actual or threatened disclosures by 'an employee or ex-employee of the plaintiff, or where the information about the plaintiff's business affairs has been given in confidence to someone who has proceeded to exploit it for his own benefit'. The extension of the action into the more general 'privacy' area is discussed further in chapter 6. Here the focus is on the use of the action to protect politically sensitive information.

The starting point for discussion is the case of *Attorney-General v Jonathan Cape* [1976] QB 752. Richard Crossman was a Cabinet minister in the Labour governments under Harold Wilson in the 1960s and 1970s. He had a keen interest in the processes of government, and made no secret of the fact that he was keeping detailed diaries, with a view to eventual publication. After his death, his literary executors proposed to publish an edited version of these diaries, covering the period 1964–6. They were to contain details of discussions with fellow Ministers, both inside and outside Cabinet, and also of dealings with civil servants in Crossman's department. Crossman's own frank opinions of his colleagues, and his subordinates, were also included. The Attorney-General sought an injunction to restrain breach of confidence. He claimed *locus standi* as guardian of the public interest, in the same way as it is well established that the Attorney-General can intervene to prevent the disclosure of evidence in a trial if such disclosure would be contrary to the public interest (*Conway v Rimmer* [1968] AC 910). He also argued that the disclosures would constitute a 'breach of confidence', by analogy with *Argyll v Argyll* [1967] Ch 302 where it was established that disclosure of secrets arising from a marriage could be restrained on this basis. This principle could be extended to government information on the basis of conventions, such as the doctrine of the collective responsibility of the Cabinet, and the more general argument, that 'confidentiality is an inherent and essential part of the administrative machinery of government'.

Lord Widgery accepted that the Attorney-General had a role in protecting the public interest in this area. This was not enough in itself, however. To obtain an injunction the Attorney-General needed to show a breach of confidence. In relation to Cabinet discussions, Lord Widgery said these were clearly confidential; but the confidence was not owed to other members of the Cabinet, but to the Sovereign, as head of the Privy Council. There was no question, therefore, of other members of the Cabinet releasing Crossman from his obligation of confidence. In sum, what the Attorney-General had to show in order to obtain an injunction to stop a publication was:

(a) that such publication would be a breach of confidence;

(b) that the public interest requires that the publication be restrained; and

(c) that there are no other facets of the public interest contradictory and more compelling than that relied upon.

Even where restraint was justified on this basis, the court must be careful not to impose a restriction which goes beyond 'the strict requirement of public need'. This approach would seem to be broadly in line with the requirements of Art. 10(2) of the ECHR that restrictions on freedom of expression should be 'necessary' and 'proportionate' to the objective sought to be protected.

Applying this approach, Lord Widgery found that the delay of ten years between the events described in the diaries, and their publication, meant that there was no risk to the doctrine of collective responsibility, or of inhibition of discussion at the present time. Nor was there any need to restrict disclosure of Crossman's discussions with, or comments on, his civil servants. This was a matter of taste only, and did not affect the public interest. No injunction should be granted.

The Crossman case thus resulted in a victory for the publishers, but at the same time established the possibility of the Attorney-General using breach of confidence to restrain the publication of government secrets in an appropriate case. The later Australian case of *Commonwealth of Australia* v *John Fairfax & Sons Ltd* (1980) 147 CLR 39, which was concerned with the publication of information about the Australian government's dealing with other countries, confirmed that it was a question of balancing two public interests: the interest in 'keeping the community informed and in promoting discussion of public affairs', and the interest in secrecy where otherwise 'national security, relations with foreign countries or the ordinary business of government will be prejudiced'. As Mason J concluded, this will not always be an easy process:

> There will be cases in which conflicting considerations will be finely balanced, where it is difficult to decide whether the public's interest in knowing and in expressing its opinion, outweighs the need to protect confidentiality.

This, then, was the background to the most important case on the question of the use of breach of confidence by the government, which arose out of the attempt by Peter Wright to publish his book *Spycatcher*.

7.7.2 The *Spycatcher* saga

Peter Wright was a member of MI5 from 1955 to 1976. He then retired to Australia. He there wrote a book about his experience within MI5, entitled *Spycatcher*, which he proposed to publish in Australia. The book contained allegations, among other things, of a plot to assassinate President Nasser of Egypt at the time of the Suez crisis in the 1950s; various illegal burglaries and related activities carried out as part of surveillance operations; and a conspiracy within MI5 to 'destabilise' the Labour government of Harold Wilson in the 1970s. Publication of the book in the United Kingdom would undoubtedly have been an offence under the Official Secrets Act 1911. Since the initial publication was proposed for Australia, however, the Attorney-General started an action in the Australian courts, in New South Wales, seeking an injunction to restrain publication on the basis of breach of confidence. This action was started in 1985, though the trial did not begin until November 1986. In the meantime, undertakings were given by all concerned not to publish any relevant information from the book pending the trial.

In June 1986 *The Observer* and *The Guardian* published articles reporting on the forthcoming proceedings, and outlining some of Wright's allegations. The Attorney-General at once obtained interlocutory injunctions restraining the newspapers from disclosing any information obtained by Wright as an MI5 officer: see *Attorney-General* v *The Observer* (1986) 136 NLJ 799.

In March 1987 the New South Wales court dismissed the Attorney-General's action, but the undertakings not to publish or disclose were continued, pending an appeal.

In April 1987 *The Independent*, the *Evening Standard*, and the *London Daily News* published articles based on the book. These publications led to lengthy contempt proceedings, which are discussed in chapter 5 (5.4.7.7).

In July 1987, *The Sunday Times* obtained a copy of *Spycatcher* which was about to be published in the United States. On 12 July *The Sunday Times* published in its second edition, an extract from the book, as the first instalment of a serialization. The extract was not put into the first edition, because it was thought that this might have prompted legal proceedings to stop distribution of the paper. By leaving it to the second edition, the newspaper ensured that the paper was on sale on Sunday morning. The Attorney-General at once sought and obtained an interlocutory injunction preventing publication of any further extracts. By this stage *Spycatcher* was freely on sale in the United States, and the government made no serious attempt to prevent copies being imported into this country. Nevertheless, on 30 July 1987, the House of Lords confirmed all the interlocutory injunctions: *Attorney-General* v *Guardian Newspapers Ltd* [1987] 3 All ER 316.

In September 1987 the New South Wales Court of Appeal dismissed the Attorney-General's appeal, and refused to restrain publication pending a further appeal to the High Court of Australia. As a result *Spycatcher* was published in Australia in October 1987. At the same time, it was also published in Ireland. In June 1988, the High Court of Australia dismissed the Attorney-General's appeal, thus concluding the Australian proceedings.

Against this background the House of Lords came to consider, in October 1988, the appeals in relation to the breach of confidence actions against *The Observer*, *The Guardian*, and *The Sunday Times*. Their decision, which was concerned with whether the interlocutory injunctions should be made permanent, is reported as *Attorney-General* v *Guardian Newspapers Ltd (No. 2)* [1990] 1 AC 109.

A first issue which needed to be clarified in this case was the obligations, if any, of those, for example, newspaper reporters, who receive confidential material in a situation where they themselves have given no undertaking of confidence. As far as *The Observer* and *The Guardian* were concerned, their information came primarily from the legal proceedings in Australia. The House of Lords were clear that the recipient of information in this situation may well be subject to an obligation of confidence. As Lord Goff put it, as a broad general principle:

> ...a duty of confidence arises when confidential information comes to the knowledge of a person (the confidant) in circumstances where he has notice...that the information is confidential

Since the newspapers were quite aware of the background to the *Spycatcher* material they must be taken to have had notice of its confidentiality, and thus were themselves under an obligation of confidence. That did not determine, however, whether they could be restrained from disclosure. As Lord Keith pointed out, in relation to private confidences it may well be possible to take action without proof of damage, but as far as the government is concerned, some harm to the interests of the nation must be shown to follow, or to be likely to follow, from disclosure. Where the discloser was a Crown servant, such as Wright, then it would probably be relatively easy to show that it was contrary to the public interest that disclosure should occur. As regards the newspapers, however, there was a need to show that their disclosures were specifically damaging to the public interest.

The articles in *The Observer* and *The Guardian* in 1986 simply gave some account of the proceedings in Australia, and repeated some of the allegations contained in the book. The majority of the House of Lords, with Lord Griffiths dissenting, did not feel that this could be said to be contrary to the public interest.

In relation to *The Sunday Times* serialization, however, the House was unanimous that this was a breach of confidence which was actionable. The newspaper had been deliberately trying to 'steal a march' on the imminent American publication of the book, but the fact that that publication was about to take place provided no excuse. *The Sunday Times* had published detailed material which they knew had been communicated in breach of confidence. The fact that someone else was also about to breach the confidence did not give them any defence. The House viewed the likelihood of damage to the public interest differently here from *The Observer* and *The Guardian* publications, because of the information concerning the detailed working of the security service which was revealed, and because the newspaper went beyond simply reporting allegations, to publish substantial parts of the text of the book.

Was there any countervailing public interest which might justify publication? All the members of the House recognized that 'disclosure of iniquity' may be a valid defence to an action for breach of confidence. In other words, if the confidential information is revealed in order to expose the wrongdoing of others, this may outweigh any public interest in keeping it secret. This did not help *The Sunday Times*, however. To establish the defence, as Lord Keith pointed out, it was not enough simply to report that allegations of wrong-doing had been made: 'There must at least be a prima facie case that the allegations have substance'. The mere fact that the allegations emanated from a former member of MI5 was not enough to do this. Moreover, as Lord Goff and Lord Griffiths made clear, the disclosure of iniquity defence does not necessarily justify publication in the press. The first port of call for such disclosures should be those who may be in a position to investigate the alleged wrongdoing and, if necessary, take action against it. Only as a last resort, where no other avenue was likely to succeed, would publication in the national press be justified on this ground.

The unanimous conclusion, then, was that the 1987 *The Sunday Times* article was a breach of confidence, in relation to which the paper should be liable to make an account of profits to the Crown. The majority, however, with Lord Griffiths again dissenting, thought that the fact that *Spycatcher* had by the time of the hearing been widely published, and that this was through no fault of *The Sunday Times*, meant that there was no longer any harm in publication. *The Sunday Times* should now be free to publish a serialization of the book, if it so wished.

The newspapers concerned in this case were unhappy with the House of Lords' decision, and took their complaint to the ECtHR. The European Court found against the government, in part, and awarded the newspapers substantial costs. These proceedings are discussed fully at 7.8.

7.7.3 **After** *Spycatcher*

A further opportunity to consider issues relating to the disclosure of information by former members of the security services occurred in *Attorney-General* v *Blake* [2000] 4 All ER 385. George Blake was a member of the Secret Intelligence Service (SIS) from 1944 to 1961. For much of that time he acted as an agent for the Soviet Union. In 1961 he was convicted of offences under s. 1 of the Official Secrets Act 1911, and sentenced to 42 years' imprisonment. He escaped from prison in 1966, and has since lived in Moscow. In 1989 he wrote his biography, which was published by Jonathan Cape Ltd in 1990. The present action was brought by the Attorney-General in relation to this publication. The Attorney-General, however, to the surprise, it seems, of both the judge and the defence counsel, did not base his action on breach of confidence. Rather, he sought to argue that there was an independent fiduciary duty on Blake not to make a profit out of the disclosure of information acquired from his work for the SIS. He claimed, therefore, that the government was entitled to an account of profits, and that all royalties due to Blake in relation to the publication of his autobiography should be paid to the Crown. The reason for not basing the action on breach of confidence was that the information which related to the SIS was not, by 1989, any longer confidential. Scott J was not prepared to accept, however, that, in the absence of confidentiality, there was any basis for the Attorney-General's action: [1996] 3 All ER 903.

The case was appealed to the Court of Appeal and then to the House of Lords, with a variety of views being expressed as to the basis on which the Attorney-General might succeed. The House of Lords did not favour the Court of Appeal's view that it would be appropriate to allow, in exceptional circumstances, an injunction to restrain a criminal from gaining benefit from a criminal offence which had been already been committed. There were in existence various statutory provisions (such as Pt. VI of the Criminal Justice Act 1988—now the Proceeds of Crime Act 2002), under which orders for the property deemed to be the proceeds of crime could be forfeited. This case did not fall within these powers, and there was no power at common law 'to remedy any perceived deficiencies in this statutory code' ([2000] 4 All ER 385, p. 402, per Lord Nicholls). An attempt to develop one would offend against 'the established general principle of high constitutional importance, that there is no common law power to take or confiscate property without compensation' ([2000] 4 All ER 385, p. 402, per Lord Nicholls).

The view of the House on this issue was strictly obiter, since it in fact decided the case and dismissed the appeal, by using contractual principles. It heard full argument on this issue, as suggested by the Court of Appeal. Its conclusion was that although contract damages were generally compensatory, and the Attorney-General had suffered no financial loss, in certain circumstances an 'account of profits' was the appropriate remedy. Blake's undertaking of 'non-disclosure', given when he joined the service, was close to a 'fiduciary' obligation, though it did not actually fall into that category. Exceptionally, therefore, and taking account of the fact that 'most of the profits of the book derive indirectly from the extremely serious and damaging breaches of the same undertaking committed by Blake in the 1950s', it was appropriate to make an order requiring the publisher to pay to the Attorney-General the £90,000 (less expenses) which was due to Blake as royalties.

This decision has attracted some powerful criticism in the way in which it deals with the principles relating to contract damages. (For some particularly trenchant criticism of the House of Lords' reasoning, see S. Hedley, ' "Very Much the Wrong People": The House of Lords and Publication of Spy Memoirs', [2000] 4 Web JCLI.) The result of the decision is, however, that former members of the security services will find it difficult in future to make a profit out of writing their memoirs.

An encouraging feature of these cases, however, is that the courts have shown a willingness to consider for themselves the issue of 'the public interest', and not to rely too heavily on the government's view of what this entails. This approach is in marked contrast to the approach under the Official Secrets Act 1911, where the 'interests of the State' were regarded as being resolved by Ministerial fiat. It is an approach which it is hoped will also be applied in deciding the question of whether disclosures are 'damaging' under the OSA 1989. If it is, then this will lead to the possibility of freedom of expression interests carrying far more weight in this area than has previously been the case.

7.8 Breach of confidence and the Human Rights Act 1998

The main consideration of the English law in this area by the ECtHR arose out of the *Spycatcher* litigation, and this must provide the best guide to how the English courts should approach the relevant issues under the HRA 1998. It is important to note that in this area the law is the product of case law rather than statute. The courts thus have much greater freedom to develop the law than they do in relation to, for example, the areas covered directly by the Official Secrets Acts.

The three newspapers primarily affected by the government's breach of confidence actions in relation to *Spycatcher*, that is *The Sunday Times, The Observer*, and *The Guardian*, all challenged the decisions to grant injunctions against them as a breach of Art. 10 of the ECHR. The decision of the European Court is reported as *Observer and Guardian* v *United Kingdom* (1992) 14 EHRR 153, and *Sunday Times* v *United Kingdom* (1992) 14 EHRR 229. The Court came to the same conclusions in both the actions (see (1992) 14 EHRR 153, paras 66–70, and (1992) 14 EHRR 229, paras 52–6).

The Court started from the basis that the injunctions amounted to a restriction of freedom of expression under Art. 10(1). The question was then whether this restriction was justified under Art. 10(2). In answering this, the Court adopted the approach which it had developed in earlier cases on Art. 10, such as *Handyside* v *United Kingdom* (1976) 1 EHRR 737 (see chapter 8 (8.2)) and *Lingens* v *Austria* (1986) 8 EHRR 737. This involves considering as separate issues, first whether the interference was 'prescribed by law', then whether it has a legitimate aim under Art. 10(2), and finally whether it was 'necessary' in a democratic society.

7.8.1 'Prescribed by law'

The newspapers argued that although the injunctions were applied in accordance with English law, the principles upon which interlocutory injunctions were granted were unclear, and therefore neither adequately accessible, nor sufficiently foreseeable. The Court rejected this contention, considering that the guidelines laid down in *American Cyanamid v Ethicon* [1975] AC 396 as to the imposition of interlocutory injunctions were sufficiently settled that the newspapers must have been able reasonably to foresee a risk that such injunctions would be imposed.

7.8.2 'Legitimate aim'

This refers to the list of reasons contained in Art. 10(2) as possible justifications for interfering with freedom of expression. These are:

> ...national security, territorial integrity or public safety...the prevention of disorder or crime...the protection of health or morals...the protection of the reputation or rights of others...preventing the disclosure of information received in confidence...maintaining the authority and impartiality of the judiciary.

The first and last of these justifications were relevant in this case; that is, the Court had no doubt that one of the aims of the interlocutory injunctions was to preserve the Attorney-General's rights in relation to the alleged breach of confidence. If the confidential information were to be published pending trial of the full action, the whole point of the proceedings from the Attorney-General's point of view would be lost. This came within the scope of 'maintaining the authority...of the judiciary', since the Court had previously interpreted 'the judiciary' as meaning in effect the whole judicial process (see further on this chapter 9 (9.2.2)).

It was also accepted that one of the Attorney-General's aims was to protect national security interests. The Court commented, however, that 'the precise nature of the national security considerations involved varied over time' (para. 56).

On both these grounds, it was held that the restrictions were imposed in pursuit of legitimate aims within Art. 10(2).

7.8.3 'Necessary in a democratic society'

This is the most complex issue. The Court started by enunciating a number of general principles, drawing on its own previous decisions on Art. 10.

First, it was noted that 'freedom of expression constitutes one of the essential foundations of a democratic society'. Because of this, the freedom must extend to information and ideas which may offend, shock, or disgust. Exceptions to the freedom must be narrowly interpreted, and the necessity for restriction convincingly established.

Second, 'these principles are of particular importance as far as the Press is concerned'. The press has a vital role as 'public watchdog'. It is incumbent on it to deal with ideas and information related to matters of public interest. Moreover the public has a right to receive them.

Third, 'the adjective "necessary"...implies the existence of a "pressing social need"'. This was the test first stated in *Sunday Times* v *United Kingdom* (1979) 2

EHRR 245. Although the Contracting States have a certain discretion ('margin of appreciation') as to whether such a need exists, this is subject to an overall European supervision.

Finally, the Court's task is not to take the place of the national authorities, but to review their decisions. This does not mean simply asking whether the national authority exercised its discretion reasonably, carefully and in good faith. It must also be considered whether the interference was in all the circumstances 'proportionate to the legitimate aim pursued', and whether the reasons given to justify it were relevant and sufficient.

In addition to outlining the above principles, the Court pointed out that Art. 10 does not prohibit all forms of prior restraint on publication (such as the issue of an interlocutory injunction). Nevertheless, such restraints need to be carefully scrutinized, especially where the press is concerned. As the Court pointed out 'news is a perishable commodity, and to delay its publication, even for a short period, may well deprive it of all its value and interest' ((1992) 14 EHRR 153, para. 60).

Applying the above approach to the *Spycatcher* litigation, the Court divided the period of the operation of the injunctions into two. The first period was from the initial granting of the injunctions against *The Observer* and *The Guardian* on 11 July 1986, to the continuation of them by the House of Lords on 30 July 1987. The second period ran from 30 July 1987 to 13 October 1988, at which point the House of Lords discharged all the injunctions, including the one which had subsequently been obtained against *The Sunday Times*.

In relation to the first period the main question was whether the reasons for restraining publication noted above, that is protection of national security, and maintenance of the authority of the judiciary, were 'sufficient' to justify the restriction imposed. The Court considered that the national courts had not simply applied the *American Cyanamid* approach rigidly, but had recognized that there was a conflict between the public interests in preventing and allowing disclosure, and had weighed the relevant considerations carefully. In the light of this, and in particular the need to prevent potential prejudice to the Attorney-General's breach of confidence actions, the Court decided that the reasons for restriction were 'sufficient' ((1992) 14 EHRR 153, para. 63).

Were the actual restraints imposed 'proportionate' to the legitimate aims pursued? Again, the Court noted that the injunctions did not constitute a blanket prohibition. The newspapers were not restricted from pressing for reform of the security service, or from re-publishing information which had appeared elsewhere, relating to matters covered by *Spycatcher*, but emanating from other sources. The newspapers could, and did, seek variation or discharge of the injunctions. The Court concluded that, for this period, the restraint was proportionate.

Turning to the period from 30 July 1987 onwards, the Court took a different view. The significant change resulted from the publication of *Spycatcher* in the United States on 14 July 1987. This publication destroyed the confidential nature of the book's contents. Although the Attorney-General could argue that further publication in this country might still prejudice his actions against the newspapers, and this was a relevant reason for restraint, the Court did not think that in the circumstances it was 'sufficient'. As to the national security argument, the Court noted that this had shifted over time. At the outset, the argument was based on the secret character of the information contained in the book. Once the contents had been disclosed, however, the purpose of the injunctions had become confined to ((1992) 14 EHRR 153, para. 69):

> ...promotion of the efficiency and reputation of the Security Service...by: preserving confidence in that Service on the part of third parties; making it clear that the unauthorised publication of memoirs by its former members would not be countenanced, and deterring others who might be tempted to follow in Mr Wright's footsteps.

The Court was not prepared to regard these objectives as sufficient to justify the continuing restrictions. There was some doubt as to whether attacking the newspapers, as opposed to Peter Wright himself, would further these aims. In any case, and most importantly, the restrictions prevented the newspapers from carrying out their right and duty to inform the public about matters, already available elsewhere, which were clearly of legitimate public concern.

For these reasons the Court found that there was a violation of Art. 10 in relation to the period 30 July 1987 to 13 October 1988. They ordered the United Kingdom to make a substantial contribution to the newspapers' costs.

7.8.4 Conclusions

The decision of the ECtHR was hailed as a victory for the newspapers. It is important to note its limitations, however, since these may be very important to the way in which the English courts approach similar issues under the HRA 1998. The European Court did not dispute that the government's original objective in preventing the publication of *Spycatcher* was legitimate, and that this could equally extend to stopping newspapers publishing information drawn from the book. It was only when the book itself was published elsewhere that the position changed, since that removed the confidential nature of the material. While the end result was in the newspapers' favour, the government could draw some comfort from the fact that the Court's decision in no way precluded the taking of similar injunctive action in the future to protect government secrets. In the era of the internet, however, where exchange of information across borders is so difficult to control, the likelihood must be that many situations where the government might wish to intervene will run up against the problem that the information sought to be controlled will already be freely available to anyone with an internet connection. The defence of 'prior publication' may well prove to be the most effective way of circumventing a government's desire for secrecy.

7.9 Freedom of information

Despite the reforms of the OSA 1989, the general attitude towards official information in the United Kingdom has continued to be one of secrecy. Information is to be kept secret, unless there is a good reason for disclosing it. This attitude is reinforced by such extra-legal procedures as requiring civil servants to 'sign the Official Secrets Act'. This means signing a document containing provisions of the

Act together with a declaration that the signer understands the effect of these provisions, and that it will be an offence to act contrary to them. This ritual has no legal significance whatsoever. A person cannot be more or less liable under the Official Secrets Acts according to whether they have, or have not, signed such a document. The procedure has the effect, however, of making people nervous of disclosure, and encouraging an attitude of 'if in doubt, keep quiet'.

The same type of criticism might be made of the system of 'DA Notices', commonly known as 'D Notices'. Under this, the Defence Press and Broadcasting Advisory Committee, which is composed jointly of officials from government departments concerned with national security, and representatives of the press and broadcasting organizations, issues notices (there are currently five in force), indicating that certain categories of sensitive information should not be published. The current notices deal with such matters as nuclear and non-nuclear weaponry, ciphers, and the security and intelligence services. The system is entirely separate from the Official Secrets Acts. It smacks of collusion between the government and a compliant press, and the need for its continued existence has been doubted by those working within and outside the media. There is, at least, openness about the existence and membership of the committee and the nature of the notices, since all of this is available on the Committee's website at http://www.dnotice.org.uk. Nevertheless, the system may be regarded as symptomatic of an approach based on a presumption of secrecy.

Many other countries across the world have long adopted a different approach, operating an assumption that government information should be made available to the press and the public, unless there is a good reason for keeping it secret (see, e.g. N. Marsh, *Public Access to Government-Held Information* (London: Stevens, 1987)). Successive governments, however, both Labour and Conservative, consistently rejected such a reform. Two arguments against were generally used. First, such a system was said to be very expensive to operate, and second, there was no need for it, since our particular brand of Parliamentary democracy, which holds Ministers responsible for their departments, and directly accountable to Parliament, provides adequate safeguards.

Neither of these arguments could be regarded as conclusive. Clearly there is an expense involved in operating a system of freedom of information. In other jurisdictions, however, it is common for at least part of such costs to be passed on to those who obtain information. In any case, advocates of this freedom would argue that it is a price worth paying for the more general benefits to the democratic process which would follow. Following the introduction of freedom of information legislation in the 1980s in Australia, New Zealand, and Canada—countries operating Parliamentary democracies similar to the UK—reform eventually arrived.

The Labour government elected in 1997 committed itself to introducing freedom of information legislation. This took the form of the Freedom of Information Act 2000.

7.9.1 **The Freedom of Information Act 2000**

This Act, although passed in 2000, was introduced slowly, in order to give time for the relevant public authorities on whom it imposes obligations to adjust to its requirements. It came fully into force in 2005.

7.9.1.1 **Right to obtain information**

The Freedom of Information Act 2000 starts in s. 1(1) with the positive state-ment that a person, on making a written request for information to a 'public authority', is entitled to be told whether such information is held by the author-ity and, if it is, to have the information communicated. This statement of intent is encouraging, as is the very long list of 'public authorities' to which the obliga-tion in s. 1 applies (as set out in Sch. 1). They include, as well as central and local government, the police, the National Health Service, certain maintained schools, universities and further education colleges, and a long list (stretching over more than seven pages) of non-governmental organizations including, for example, the BBC (other than in relation to information held for purposes of journalism, art, or literature), the Equality and Human Rights Commission, the National Lottery Commission, the Post Office, the UK Sports Council, the Tate Gallery, and the Zoos Forum. A further 48 bodies were added in July 2003. Every pub-lic authority must produce a 'publication scheme', setting out the information which it intends to publish and how this will be done (including whether there will be a charge for the material).

The rest of Pt. I of the Act deals with the procedures for dealing with a request under s. 1(1). The authority may require more information from the applicant before responding, and is entitled to charge a fee (subject to regulations to be pro-duced by the Secretary of State) (s. 9). In general, the obligation under s. 1(1) must be complied with within 20 days of the receipt of the request (s. 10). Where a request is acceded to, the ways in which the information can be given are speci-fied in s. 11. It should be remembered that in this legislation, as with the Code of Practice, the obligation is to provide information, not documents. Section 11 allows the information to be given 'in permanent form'; for the applicant to be given a reasonable opportunity to inspect a record containing the information; or for the information to be given in the form of a 'digest or summary'.

Where an authority refuses a request because of an 'exemption' (see 7.9.1.2), there is an obligation to state the exemption relied on, and the reason why the exemption applies (unless this in itself would involve the disclosure of exempt information) (s. 17).

The operation of the provisions of the scheme set out in the Act is under the supervision of the 'Information Commissioner' and the 'Information Tribunal' (s. 18) (for which see 7.9.1.3).

7.9.1.2 **Exemptions**

The largely positive provisions of Pt. I of the Act are considerably reduced in impact by the lengthy list of exemptions. Part I itself contains exemptions based on the cost of providing the information (s. 12), and in relation to vexatious requests or repeated requests for the same information (s. 14). The main exemptions, however, are contained in Pt. II of the Act (ss 21–44). The list is lengthy, and what follows is not comprehensive. An exemption from disclosure will arise in relation to:

(a) Information which is reasonably accessible by other means (s. 21).

(b) Information which the public authority intends to publish in the future (s. 22).

Other exemptions apply based on the subject matter of the information, such as:

(a) Information emanating directly or indirectly from the security and intelligence services (s. 23).

(b) Information the disclosure of which would prejudice national security (s. 24).

(c) Defence information (s. 26).

(d) Information which if disclosed would be likely to prejudice international relations (s. 27).

(e) Information which if disclosed would be likely to prejudice relations between the administrations operating in different parts of the United Kingdom (i.e. England, Scotland, Wales, and Northern Ireland) (s. 28).

(f) Information which if disclosed would be likely to prejudice the economic or financial interest of the United Kingdom, or any part of it (s. 29).

(g) Information held for the purposes of a criminal investigation or prosecution (s. 30).

(h) Information related to law enforcement, disclosure of which might, for example, prejudice the prevention of crime, the apprehension of offenders, or the operation of immigration controls (s. 31).

There are also some exemptions relating to the operation of government. Thus, s. 35 exempts, among other things, information relating to 'the formulation or development of government policy'. Section 36 exempts information which, if disclosed, might prejudice the 'collective responsibility' of Ministers, or inhibit the 'free and frank' giving of advice, or might otherwise 'prejudice the effective conduct of public affairs'.

Finally, there are exemptions relating to court records (s. 32), Parliamentary privilege (s. 34), communications with Her Majesty (s. 37), 'health and safety' (s. 38), personal information (s. 40), legally privileged information (s. 42), and private or commercial confidences (ss 41 and 43).

It will be seen that the breadth and scope of the exemptions is very wide. Indeed, it could be argued that the majority of government information will be exempt under one heading or another. To that extent the Act is disappointing. Much of the positive tone of s. 1(1) appears to be dissipated by Pt. II. There is, however, an important further provision in s. 2 which requires information in many of the exempt categories to be disclosed, unless the public interest in maintaining the exemption outweighs the public interest in disclosing the information. Section 2 does not apply to certain of the more sensitive exemptions (such as security and intelligence, personal information, Parliamentary privilege, or court records). It does apply, however, to the 'national security' category and defence information. In all cases where s. 2 applies, the public authority, if asked to reveal exempt information, is obliged to consider whether the public interest in disclosure outweighs the public interest in maintaining the exemption. If the balance is in favour of disclosure, the public authority 'shall' make the relevant disclosure. It remains to be seen, of course, how far the public authorities concerned will be prepared to recognize the public interest in disclosure. Given the culture of secrecy which has traditionally pervaded government in the United Kingdom it would be surprising if this provision led to regular disclosure of exempt information. But, as will be seen below, refusals under s. 2 are subject to appeal, and it may be that in time the culture of openness which the current administration professes to be anxious to encourage, may start to develop.

7.9.1.3 Supervision and enforcement

Codes of Practice relating to the policies to be followed by public authorities as to the operation of the obligations under Pt. I of the Act, and as to the keeping of records by the Public Record Office, etc. have been issued under ss 45 and 46 respectively. They are available on the website of the Ministry of Justice at http://www.justice.gov.uk/information-access-rights/foi-guidance-for-practitioners/code-of-practice. The Code relating to public authorities' responsibilities was issued in November 2004; the one on managing records dates from 2009. A code on handling datasets was issued in July 2013 (see http://www.justice.gov.uk/downloads/information-access-rights/foi/code-of-practice-datasets.pdf). In general, supervision and enforcement powers are in the hands of the Information Commissioner (s. 18). The Commissioner has a duty to promote good practice (s. 47), including the making of recommendations to specific public authorities in relation to any shortcomings as regards compliance with the Codes of Practice (s. 48).

Enforcement powers are contained in Pt. IV of the Act. The Commissioner will receive complaints from individuals who feel that a request for information has not been dealt with in accordance with the requirements of Pt. I. The Commissioner has powers to obtain information from the public authority (by issuing an 'information notice' (s. 51)), and in certain circumstances can obtain a search warrant from a circuit judge authorizing entry on to the public authority's premises (Sch. 3).

The Commissioner will issue a 'decision notice' on the complaint (s. 50(3)). Either the complainant or the public authority may appeal to the 'Information Tribunal' (s. 57). From there, there is an appeal on a point of law to the High Court (s. 59). Even if the Commissioner decides that the information is not held by a public authority, the appeal should be to the Tribunal. That is the effect of the decision in *BBC v Sugar* [2009] UKHL 9, [2009] 4 All ER 111. An application had been made for an unpublished report on possible bias in the BBC's news coverage in relation to the Middle East. The Commissioner had decided that the report was held 'for the purposes of journalism'. Since Sch. 1 to the Act lists the BBC as a public authority in respect of information 'held for purposes other than those of journalism, art or literature', this meant that the BBC was not a public authority in relation to this information. In responding to the applicant, the Commissioner did not refer to the right of appeal to the Tribunal, but only to the possibility of judicial review. Nevertheless the applicant did appeal to the Tribunal, which held that it had jurisdiction, and that the information was not held for the purposes of journalism. The BBC appealed to the High Court which heard both that appeal and the conjoined judicial review of the Commissioner's initial decision. The High Court held that where the Commissioner found the information was not being held by a public authority, he was not entitled to issue a decision notice under s. 50(3), and that therefore the Tribunal did not have jurisdiction. This view was confirmed by the Court of Appeal, but overturned by the House of Lords. The House (by a majority of 3:2) took the view that the decision that the information was not being held by a public authority was nevertheless a decision under s. 50(3), so that the appropriate route of appeal was to the Tribunal. Subsequent proceedings confirmed that the information sought was held for journalistic purposes and was, therefore, exempt from disclosure ([2012] UKSC 4).

The Commissioner also has the power to issue an 'enforcement notice' where a public authority has failed in its obligations under Pt. I, specifying the action to be taken by the public authority. As with decision notices, the public authority has a right of appeal to the Tribunal against an enforcement notice.

Where a decision notice is served on a government department, the National Assembly for Wales, or any public authority designated for the purpose by an Order made by the Secretary of State, that it has not complied with its obligations under s. 1(1), and the alleged duty arises in relation to information which falls within any provision of Pt. II stating that the duty to confirm or deny does not arise, or 'exempt information', the duty to comply with the notice can be avoided if the 'accountable person' in relation to the authority certifies that 'he has on reasonable grounds formed the opinion' that the authority did not fail to comply with its obligations (s. 53(1)). The accountable person is defined in s. 53(4). For example, in relation to government departments it will be a Minister; in relation to most other authorities, the 'accountable person' will be specified in an Order made by the Secretary of State. In *R (Evans)* v *Attorney-General* [2013] EWHC 1960 (Admin), the Attorney-General had issued a certificate under s. 53 in relation to a request for the disclosure of correspondence between the Prince of Wales and various government departments. This was upheld by the Divisional Court, which found that the Attorney-General's decision had been based on 'reasonable grounds'.

Any other failure to comply with an information notice, decision notice, or enforcement notice can be treated as a contempt of court, and dealt with by the High Court as such (s. 54).

7.9.1.4 Conclusions

The Freedom of Information Act 2000 is another step forward towards the position which operates in many other Western democracies whereby citizens have a right to obtain information about the workings of their government. The legislation is, however, complex, and leaves considerable scope for the discretion of public authorities to be operated in favour of secrecy. It is by no means clear that the Information Commissioner will have sufficient resources to police the system effectively. The success of the legislation in improving access to information will therefore be likely to depend on the Codes of Practice, and how they are interpreted and applied by public authorities. The current Code encourages public authorities to provide assistance to an applicant in relation to the formulation of a request, and exhorts them to 'be flexible in offering advice and assistance most appropriate to the circumstances of the applicant' (para. 7). It remains to be seen how far this will be followed. It is likely that authorities will look to central government to give the lead. If it is seen that ministries are being prepared to disclose information, and are operating the 'public interest' provision in a liberal way, then it is likely that others will follow suit. If, on the other hand, the traditions of secrecy prevail, much will depend on whether the Information Commissioner is prepared to take a strong line in encouraging a different approach, and is given the resources to be able to do so.

QUESTIONS

1 Should freedom of expression have any greater protection than other freedoms? If so, why? Does it depend on the type of expression?

2 Is it satisfactory that the appropriate use of s. 1 of the Official Secrets Act 1911 depends on the discretion of the Attorney-General? Would it be possible to define the relevant offence more precisely?

3 Are the defences available under the OSA 1989 satisfactory? Is there a case for a broader defence of 'public interest'? If so, should this be available to Crown servants, or only to the press?

4 To what extent was the outcome of the *Spycatcher* litigation, both in the United Kingdom and at Strasbourg, a victory for the press?

5 Has the implementation of the Freedom of Information Act 2000 had a significant effect on the culture of 'official secrecy' which has been prevalent in the United Kingdom for many years?

FURTHER READING

Amos, M. (2002), 'Can We Speak Freely Now? Freedom of Expression under the Human Rights Act', [2002] EHRLR 750

Barendt, E. (2005), *Freedom of Speech*, 2nd edn, Oxford: Oxford University Press

Barendt, E. and Hitchens, L. (2000), *Media Law Cases and Materials*, Harlow: Longman

Best, K. (2001), 'The Control of Official Information: Implications of the Shayler Affair', (2001) 6 J Civil Liberty 18

Birkinshaw, P. (2001), *Freedom of Information—The Law, the Practice and the Ideal*, 3rd edn, London: Butterworths

Fish, S. (1994), *There's No Such Thing as Free Speech*, New York, NY: Oxford University Press

Franks, Lord (1972), 'Report and Evidence of the Committee on Section 2 of the Official Secrets Act 1911', Cmnd 5104, HMSO

Hedley, S. (2000), ' "Very Much the Wrong People": the House of Lords and Publication of Spy Memoirs', [2000] 4 Web JCLI

Marsh, N. (1987), *Public Access to Government-held Information*, London: Stevens

Mill, J. S. (1962) (first published 1859), 'On Liberty', in Warnock, M. (ed.), *Utilitarianism*, London: Fontana

Nicol, A. (1979), 'Official Secrets and Jury Vetting', [1979] Crim LR 284

Ponting, C. (1985), *The Right to Know*, London: Sphere Books

Stone, R. (1990), 'National Security versus Civil Liberty', in Patfield, F. and White, R. (eds), *The Changing Law*, Leicester: Leicester University Press

White Paper (1988), 'Reform of Section 2 of the Official Secrets Act 1911', Cm 408, HMSO

Williams, D. G. T. (1978), 'Official Secrecy and the Courts', in Glazebrook, P. (ed.), *Reshaping the Criminal Law*, London: Stevens

8

Freedom of Expression
(Article 10) II: Obscenity and Indecency

The English law relating to the control of obscenity and indecency is a mess. As long ago as 1979 the 'Report of the Committee on Obscenity and Film Censorship', Cmnd 7772, HMSO, chaired by Bernard Williams (the Williams Committee), commented that (para. 2.29):

> ... [t]he law is scattered among so many statutes, and these so often overlap with each other and with the various common law offences and powers which still exist in this field, that it is a complicated task even to piece together a statement of what the law is, let alone attempt to wrestle with or resolve the inconsistencies and anomalies to which it gives rise.

Over the past 35 years further legislation and decisions of the courts have only added to the confusion. This is also an area in which arguments about policy have a tendency to become high on emotion and low on coherence. It is, however, with the policy issues which we shall start, looking at the arguments for and against restriction, before moving on to examine in detail the current state of the legal controls.

8.1 Arguments for, and against, restriction

Explicit pictorial depictions of sex or violence, or both, in magazines, films, or on the internet, which are the most common point of attack for the obscenity laws, are often difficult to justify in terms of arguments for freedom of expression *per se*. Of the arguments outlined in chapter 7, the argument from democracy has little relevance. Free access to sex magazines does not make one better able to exercise the responsibilities of a voting citizen. Similarly, the argument for truth advocated by John Stuart Mill can provide little protection for material which carries no overt 'message', but is designed primarily for titillation and entertainment. Self-expression and personal autonomy are perhaps more credible arguments for freedom in relation to sexual material, though they tend to concentrate on the author rather than the reader, whereas the debate about pornography tends to be concerned not so much with what people may write, but what others may read. It is for this reason that in recent years much of the debate in this area has centred on the question of the effects of sexual and violent material. Another, more general, civil libertarian principle derived from John Stuart Mill's essay 'On Liberty', has often been brought into play in this context. This is the idea that, as summarized succinctly by the Williams Committee (para. 5.1), 'no conduct should be suppressed by law unless it can be shown to harm someone'. This approach rejects paternalism. As Mill himself put it ('On Liberty', ch. 1), a person 'cannot rightfully be compelled to do or forbear because it will be better for him to do so, because it will make him happier, because in the opinion of others, to do so would be wise, or even right'.

The Williams Committee dubbed this concept 'the harm condition', and that convenient shorthand is adopted in this chapter. The problem that it raises, of course, even if it is accepted as a guiding principle, is that its operation is dependent on the precise definition given to the word 'harm'. Does this mean simply physical harm, or are there other types of harm which should be included? It is clear that the supporters of the harm condition are in part drawing a distinction between law and morality, so that the fact that behaviour is immoral is not enough to justify restraint. It is not so clear that behaviour which might cause a general lowering of moral standards can equally be regarded as non-harmful. There is a range of possible harmful effects which might justify restrictions. For example, restrictions on pornography might be justified because its distribution caused:

1. an increase in sexual assaults or rape; or
2. an increase in non-violent criminal offences, such as indecent exposure; or
3. a widespread acceptance of lower moral standards in sexual matters; or
4. a reinforcement of undesirable attitudes towards one section of society, for example women.

This list is not exhaustive, but in each case a plausible argument can be made for saying that if pornography has this effect, then it is in some sense 'harmful'. The next problem is that it is notoriously difficult to obtain empirical evidence of the effects of pornography. Research has been done by both psychologists and sociologists, but is generally accepted as being inconclusive. The Williams Committee certainly found it so, and refused to accept that any harms had been shown as existing beyond reasonable doubt, other than harms involving the participants in the creation of pictorial pornography ('Report of the Committee on Obscenity and Film Censorship', ch. 10, in particular para. 10.8). A subsequent survey for the Home Office, by Howitt and Cumberbatch, concluded that: '[t]he research evidence is clearly inadequate, partial and incomplete', and thus provides no foundation for any firm conclusions (D. Howitt and G. Cumberbatch, 'Pornography: Impacts and Influences', Home Office, 1990, p. 93).

A rather different approach has been advocated by some feminist writers, such as Andrea Dworkin (see, e.g. *Pornography: Men Possessing Women* (London: Women's Press, 1981)), and Catherine MacKinnon. They attack pornography (defined as 'the graphic sexually explicit subordination of women through pictures or words' (C. Mackinnon, *Feminism Unmodified* (Cambridge, MA: Harvard University Press, 1987), p. 175)) not because it causes violence against women, but because it is in itself violence against women. It violates the rights of women as a group, and as individuals, and may be regarded as a form of discrimination on sexual grounds. A powerful collection of writing from this perspective is to be found in C. Itzin (ed.), *Pornography: Women, Violence and Civil Liberties* (Oxford: Oxford University Press, 1992). Itzin herself summarizes her argument in this way (p. 70):

> Pornography is propaganda against women. It is a practice which perpetuates sexism, sex discrimination and sexual violence. It is therefore one of the basic means of maintaining the sexual status quo. Sexual equality depends on the elimination of pornography as part of the elimination of sex discrimination. The two must go hand in hand. The elimination of pornography is an essential part of the creation of genuine equality for women—and for men.

Not all feminists subscribe to this analysis, however. See, e.g. A. Assiter and A. Carol (eds), *Bad Girls and Dirty Pictures* (London: Pluto Press, 1993). An almost direct contradiction of Itzin's argument can be found in Gayle Rubin's chapter in that collection, 'Misguided, Dangerous and Wrong' (p. 38):

> Anti-porn activity distracts attention and drains activism from more fundamental issues for women. Porn is a sexier topic than the more intractable problems of unequal pay, job discrimination, sexual violence and harassment, the unequal burdens of child-care and housework, increasing rightwing infringements on hard-won feminist gains, and several millennia of unrelenting male privilege vis-à-vis the labour, love, personal service and possession of women. Anti-porn campaigns are pitifully misdirected and ineffective. They cannot solve the problems they purport to address.

Dworkin and MacKinnon advocated the availability of civil remedies rather than the use of the criminal law to control pornography, but the Canadian Supreme Court in the early 1990s adopted an approach closely related to that put forward by these writers as the basis for criminal liability. In *R v Butler* (1992) 89 DLR (4th) 449, the view was taken that pornography which portrays explicit sex with violence would usually fall within the definition of obscenity as the 'undue exploitation of sex'. Furthermore, the portrayal of explicit sex without violence, but 'which subjects people to treatment that is degrading or dehumanizing', would also be obscene if it causes 'harm'. Harm is then taken to include offence to 'the fundamental values of our society' (p. 479). The particular problem of the way in which women are portrayed in pornography is recognized in the following passage from Sopinka J's judgment (p. 479):

> [I]f true equality between male and female persons is to be achieved, we cannot ignore the threat to equality resulting from the exposure of audiences to certain types of violent and degrading material. Materials portraying women as a class as objects for sexual exploitation and abuse have a negative impact on 'the individual's sense of self-worth and acceptance'.

'Harm' is thus being defined broadly. Catherine MacKinnon was reported as welcoming this decision as a recognition that 'what is obscene is what harms women, not what offends our values' (*New York Times*, 28 February 1992). It is not clear, however, that the Supreme Court's approach can lead to a satisfactory and workable form of control of obscene material.

A similar argument to that put forward by Dworkin and Mackinnon is often used in relation to the area in which the laws in this area are most frequently used in the UK at the moment—that of child pornography, and child pornography on the internet in particular. In other words, it is said that pictures of children which constitute such material are in themselves abusive of the children concerned. Although this is an emotive and difficult area, it is not clear that the argument has any logic. If the picture is of a child being abused, then clearly that child is a victim and whoever was responsible should be punished for what has happened to it. But does a person who simply looks at the picture also abuse the child? Those who support this line of argument will point out that the 'consumer' of pornography is in some ways the main culprit—if that person did not provide a market for such material, others would not produce it, and thereby abuse children. The position, however, becomes even more difficult in relation to pictures taken with the consent of the child which do not in themselves depict abuse, but which a paedophile would find sexually arousing. It is the problem of finding the right approach in this area which has led to some of the problems (see 8.5.2.4), where the taker of the photograph has acted for completely innocent motives, but others have found the pictures indecent.

Are there any positive arguments for allowing the production of pornography? The only one that has been put with any force in favour of work which has no pretensions to literary or artistic merit, is that it may have a 'psychotherapeutic' value. In other words, the availability of pornography may help people with sexual problems and may, by providing an outlet for the release of sexual tension, actually decrease the likelihood of sexual violence. There is as little in the way of scientific evidence for this beneficial effect, as there is for pornography's harmful effects. The English courts have rejected any possibility of a defence for publication of obscene material on these grounds (see *DPP* v *Jordan* [1976] 3 All ER 775; 8.5.1.3).

8.2 Obscenity and the Human Rights Act 1998

The provision of the European Convention on Human Rights (ECHR) which is most relevant to issues of obscenity and indecency is Art. 10, though there may be some situations where restrictions in this area might also be argued to impinge on the right to respect for a person's private life under Art. 8. In relation to both these articles, however, the list of legitimate grounds for restriction includes the 'protection of health or morals'. This is an area in which the European Court of Human Rights (ECtHR) has been prepared to allow an extensive 'margin of appreciation' to domestic jurisdictions. Its decisions may not be very helpful, therefore, to English courts trying to apply the Human Rights Act 1998 (HRA 1998) to this area. The approach taken by the Strasbourg Court is nevertheless a good starting point for consideration of these issues.

The main decision to consider is *Handyside* v *United Kingdom* (1976) 1 EHRR 737. Handyside had published in the UK a book entitled *The Little Red Schoolbook*. This had 208 pages, and was aimed at schoolchildren aged 12 and upwards. Alongside sections on education, teachers, pupils, and the system it had a 26 page section dealing with sexual matters. This included sections on such things as masturbation, orgasm, homosexuality, and methods of abortion. The book was seized under s. 3 of the Obscene Publications Act 1959, forfeited, and destroyed. Handyside brought proceedings under the ECHR alleging, among other things, a breach of Art. 10. The government relied on the restriction on the basis of protecting morals. To fall within this allowable restriction the control would have to be found by the court to be 'prescribed by law', to promote a legitimate objective, and to be 'necessary in a democratic society' for the achievement of that objective. The court had no difficulty in finding that the procedures which had been taken under the Obscene Publications Act 1959 were 'prescribed by law'. It was also of the view, despite Mr Handyside's claim that in reality the action against him was politically based, that the application of the restriction was carried out for the purpose of 'protecting morality' amongst the children towards whom the book was directed. As regards the 'necessity' of the action, Mr Handyside laid stress on the fact that the book had circulated freely (in translation) in many other States which were signatories to the ECHR. If these States had not thought it necessary to prevent the distribution of the book, how could the action taken in the UK be deemed to be 'necessary'? On this issue the Court relied on the 'margin of appreciation' or discretion which is allowed to Member States (p. 759):

> The Contracting States have each fashioned their approach in the light of the situation obtaining in their respective territories; they have had regard, *inter alia*, to the different views prevailing there about the demands of the protection of morals in a democratic society. The fact that most of them decided to allow the work to be distributed does not mean that the contrary decision of the Inner London Quarter Sessions was a breach of Article 10.

The conclusion was, therefore, that there was no breach of Art. 10 by the action taken against *The Little Red Schoolbook*. The decision also has the effect that there would seem very little point in challenging any of the laws looked at later in this chapter under the ECHR. Certainly in all of the situations where criminal offences are created it seems certain that the ECtHR would say that the restrictions fell within the allowable margin of appreciation. The decision of the Court in *Wingrove v United Kingdom* (1997) 24 EHRR 1 suggests that the same is true of the censorship system applying to films and videos. The case concerned a video entitled *Visions of Ecstasy* which depicted St Teresa of Avila in erotic scenes with the body of the crucified Christ. The British Board of Film Classification (BBFC) (see 8.6) had refused it a certificate on the basis that it was likely to be found to infringe the laws against blasphemy. The ECtHR upheld this decision as not involving a breach of Art. 10. The Court noted that the application of blasphemy laws was rare in the various European countries in which they still existed, and that the fact that the case involved prior restraint 'called for special scrutiny'. Nevertheless, it held that the concern of the BBFC that the public distribution might 'outrage and insult the feelings of believing Christians', and in particular that it might involve the commission of a criminal offence, meant that the interference could not be said to be 'arbitrary or excessive'.

Here, as with *Handyside*, the Court shows a reluctance to become involved with standard-setting in the area of sexual or religious morality. A case combining both sex and religion was probably particularly difficult in that respect.

The existence of this very broad margin of appreciation means that English courts have to set their own standards in applying the HRA 1998. It seems unlikely that they will be inclined to interfere with or challenge offences approved by Parliament. It would seem, therefore, that in this area there is less scope than in many other areas covered in this book for the use of the HRA 1998 to challenge existing law. This is confirmed by the Court of Appeal's approach in *R* v *Perrin* [2002] EWCA Crim 747, 22 March 2002. This case was concerned with the publication of images on a website, in relation to which the defendant had been convicted of an offence under s. 2 of the Obscene Publications Act 1959. The court rejected the defendant's arguments based on Art. 10 that the restrictions contained in the Act were not 'prescribed by law' because they were too uncertain. It took the same approach as in *Handyside* v *United Kingdom* and upheld the conviction.

8.3 Methods of control

There are various ways in which the distribution and availability of obscene or indecent material can be controlled. Three main devices are used in English law, i.e. pre-censorship, criminalization, and controlling outlets. The first two act as direct controls; the third is indirect.

8.3.1 Pre-censorship

By this is meant a system whereby any material which it is proposed should be published must be submitted to some person or organization for official approval before publication can take place. The censor may have strict guidelines laid down by law, or may operate with a broad degree of discretion. There may or may not be an appeal from the censor's decision.

This type of control is regarded by proponents of liberty as the most insidious, in that it refuses to allow material even to see the light of day, and generally puts the issue of what can and cannot be published into the hands of a small group of officials. It has produced some notable attacks, from Milton's *Areopagitica*, to Lord Chesterfield's speech in the debates on the Theatres Licensing Act 1737, to Blackstone's *Commentaries on the Laws of England* (Oxford: Clarendon Press, 1769), Book IV, pp. 151–2. In current English law such a system operates in relation to films and DVDs (see 8.6).

8.3.2 Criminalization

Control by means of criminal offences generally, but not always, operates after publication. This is regarded as more acceptable than pre-censorship, in that it allows a work to be put into circulation before it is controlled, and, perhaps more importantly, the decision as to control is in the hands of the courts. This means that controls must be imposed on the basis of legally defined categories or offences (rather than the often vague discretion of the censor), and that it is always possible to argue against restriction before a final decision is taken.

This is the most common form of control in English law. In particular, in relation to books, magazines, and electronic publications, a range of offences exists to control different types of objectionable publication (see 8.5).

8.3.3 **Controlling outlets**

The third method of control does not try to restrict publications themselves, but operates against the ways in which they may be made available to the public. It may take the form of requiring shops or other premises dealing in certain types of material to display warning notices, or to restrict their clientele (see, e.g. the Indecent Displays (Control) Act 1981, at 8.9.1.1). It may go further and require establishments dealing in certain types of activity to be licensed (e.g. the Local Government (Miscellaneous Provisions) Act 1982; see 8.9.1.2).

We can also put into this category attempts to control internet access to particular types or categories of website.

This approach may appear to be in many ways a more liberal system than either pre-censorship or criminalization, but, as we shall see, in some circumstances it can be just as restrictive.

8.4 **Problems of definition**

Any system of control needs to define the behaviour to be restricted to some extent. This is most necessary in relation to criminal offences, where it is not possible to rely on the discretion of a censor or a licensing authority to give content to a general set of guidelines. It is, however, very difficult to provide satisfactory, workable definitions in this area of the law. Indeed, one of the two main words used in English legislation, i.e. 'obscene', has two, mutually contradictory, legal definitions. The other, 'indecent', has no clear definition at all. The result is that there is a constant danger that controls will result from an approach based on the idea that 'I cannot define pornography, but I know it when I see it'. This is clearly unacceptable where people are being charged with criminal offences which may well carry sentences of imprisonment on conviction. What, then, are the current definitions?

8.4.1 **Obscenity**

8.4.1.1 **The 'deprave and corrupt' test**

The definition of 'obscenity' used in the Obscene Publications Act 1959 and the Theatres Act 1968 derives from the case of *R v Hicklin* (1868) LR 3 QB 360, where Lord Cockburn defined it as a tendency 'to deprave and corrupt those whose minds are open to such immoral influences, and into whose hands a publication of this sort may fall'. In its modern form it has been recast to remove the emphasis, which Lord Cockburn felt was important, on the dangers to the young who might possibly see such material, even if this was unlikely. The wording in s. 1 of the Obscene Publications Act 1959 states that an article is to be deemed obscene if:

> ... its effect or (where the article comprises two or more distinct items) the effect of any one of its items is, if taken as a whole, such as to tend to deprave and corrupt persons who are likely, having regard to all relevant circumstances, to read, see or hear the matter contained or embodied in it.

The rewording means that only 'likely' readers, as opposed to all possible readers, need to be considered. All likely readers must be taken into account, however, not simply the most likely readers: *DPP v Whyte* [1972] AC 649. In addition, the reference to taking the article 'as a whole' makes it impermissible to select a few pages out of a lengthy novel, and argue that they are obscene, without looking at their context. The central element of the definition is, however, still the tendency to deprave and corrupt. How have the courts interpreted this phrase?

First, it is well established that the tendency is to be looked at objectively, i.e. without reference to the intention of the author or publisher. This had been the position under the common law. In *R v Hicklin* it was said that innocent motives or objects would not justify an otherwise obscene publication. This was followed in the first reported case on the Obscene Publications Act 1959, *R v Penguin Books* [1961] Crim LR 176, which concerned the publication of D. H. Lawrence's *Lady Chatterley's Lover.* Byrne J ruled that it was not open to the defence to establish that there was no intention to deprave and corrupt (though in the end the publishers were acquitted). The Court of Appeal took the same view in *Shaw v DPP* [1962] AC 220, commenting (p. 227) that 'obscenity depends on the article and not upon the author'. This approach is clearly based on the concept that, as Blackburn J put it in *R v Hicklin* (p. 375), although the publisher may have had another object in view 'he must be taken to have intended that which is the natural consequence of [his] act'. Since the enactment of s. 8 of the Criminal Justice Act 1967, this method of establishing *mens rea* has been rejected generally within the criminal law, in preference for a requirement that it must be proved that the accused actually foresaw or intended the consequences of acting in a particular way. As far as obscene publications are concerned, however, there has been no serious challenge to the proposition that all that is needed is an intention to publish, and that awareness or intention as to the consequences of that publication are irrelevant.

The crucial question therefore remains that of what is meant by 'deprave and corrupt'. The decisions of the courts have provided a few guidelines, without coming up with a comprehensive definition. In *R v Calder and Boyars* [1969] 1 QB 151, for example, the Court of Appeal ruled that an article which shocked and horrified people, and thus turned them against the activities described or depicted, would not tend to deprave and corrupt them. In *Shaw v DPP*, it was held that it was wrong to have regard to what people might do after reading an article in deciding whether it was obscene. In other words, no particular acts were necessary in order to establish depravity and corruption. This point was especially relevant in *Shaw*, where the publication was a directory of prostitutes and their services, and the question was whether people were encouraged to visit the prostitutes as a result of reading the directory. The Court of Appeal held that this was irrelevant. The point was upheld in a more general way by the House of Lords in *DPP v Whyte*, where the view was taken that an effect on the mind was all that was required, and that there was no need for this to be established by any overt activity. The question of what precise effect on the mind is required is unfortunately not made clear in the cases, but is discussed further below.

The issue of the number of people who must be likely to be affected by an article in order for it to be considered obscene was considered in *R v Calder and Boyars*. The Court of Appeal stated that the question for the jury was 'whether the effect of the book was to tend to deprave and corrupt a *significant proportion* of those likely to read it' ([1969] 1 QB 151, p. 168, emphasis added). What is a 'significant' proportion is a matter for the jury, or magistrates, to decide, but it is clear that it means more than a negligible number, but may be much less than half (Lord Cross, in *DPP* v *Whyte*, at p. 870). The Court of Appeal has more recently ruled, however, in *R* v *Perrin* [2002] EWCA Crim 747, 22 March 2002, that it is not generally necessary for a judge to direct the jury on this issue at all. The Court, relying on statements by Lord Pearson in Whyte (pp. 864–5), concluded that (para. 30):

> ... [w]here, as in the present case, there is and can be no suggestion that publication is for the public good and the provisions of the 1964 Act are not in issue we see no reason why the task of the jury should be complicated by a direction that the effect of the article must be such as to tend to deprave and corrupt a significant proportion, or more than a negligible number of likely viewers.

The reference to the 1964 Act is to the provisions in the Obscene Publications Act 1964 relating to the question of what further publications may follow from an initial publication, where the charge is possessing for publication for gain. In a straightforward 'publication' charge, therefore, the jury should be left to the statutory wording without further guidance from the judge.

It is apparently possible to be corrupted more than once. In *DPP* v *Whyte* the magistrates had accepted an argument put by the defendants, who owned a bookshop, that their customers were almost entirely middle-aged men who were already corrupt. The House of Lords ruled that this was wrong. They confirmed the view expressed by the Court of Appeal in *DPP* v *Shaw* [1962] AC 220, p. 228, that such an argument is false in that 'it assumes that a man cannot be corrupted more than once and there is no warrant for this'. Moreover, the House of Lords in *Whyte* felt that the pornography 'addict' should be discouraged from feeding or increasing his addiction.

One other important point of interpretation is that the courts have made it clear that obscenity under the 'deprave and corrupt' definition is not limited to sexual material. In *John Calder Publications Ltd* v *Powell* [1965] 1 QB 509, it was held that a book dealing with drug-taking could be obscene in this sense. This was confirmed subsequently in *R* v *Skirving* [1985] QB 819. In *DPP* v *A & BC Chewing Gum Ltd* [1968] 1 QB 159 pictures, contained in packets of bubble-gum, depicting scenes of (non-sexual) violence, were also held to be covered. So far, however, there has been no extension of the scope of the definition beyond sex, drugs, and violence.

These rulings as to the scope of obscenity do not, however, get very far in helping to explain exactly what is meant by a tendency to deprave and corrupt. It must surely mean that the material has some sort of adverse effect on the reader, though not one which necessarily results in any undesirable conduct. It presumably also has something to do with moral perversion. Remembering that it must be assessed objectively, this suggests that the concept depends on there being some core of morality which is accepted by society as a whole. The existence of such a core is in itself an arguable proposition, and in any case difficult to identify. For example, in previous editions of this book engagement in sado-masochistic sexual practices has been used as an example of a departure from generally accepted moral standards. Following the success of the novel *Fifty Shades of Grey*, however, in which the main characters engage in bondage and spanking, it cannot be assumed that this characterization of such activities is accurate. However, assuming some general standard can be identified, 'deprave and corrupt' then comes to mean 'pervert from contemporary moral standards'. We now come to the question of what kind of article will have such an effect.

For an article to pervert someone from contemporary moral standards it must, either explicitly or implicitly, be persuasive in its effect. A book which expounded the theme that having unprotected sex with prostitutes is good for you would be explicitly persuasive. Implicit persuasion might arise from a publication which depicted a person who engaged extensively in such unprotected sex as a happy, fulfilled human being, who was more successful in life than those who did not act in this way. This might have the effect of encouraging others to partake in what society in general probably deems to be an undesirable activity. Support for this approach to defining obscenity comes from the summing-up of Stable J in *R v Martin Secker and Warburg* [1954] 1 WLR 1138, where he said (p. 1142):

> The theme of this book is the story of the rather attractive young man who is absolutely obsessed with his desire for women. It is not presented as an admirable thing, or a thing to be copied. It is not presented as a thing that brought him happiness or any sort of permanent satisfaction, and throughout the book you hear the note of impending disaster.

The clear implication is that the way in which the story was presented militated against the book being obscene. This analysis leads us to the conclusion, then, that an obscene article means one that presents deviation from contemporary moral standards in an attractive light. There are, however, three serious objections to such a conclusion.

First, there is the problem that in *Knuller (Publishing, Printing and Promotions) Ltd v DPP* [1973] AC 435, p. 456, Lord Reid stated that one may 'lead persons morally astray without depraving and corrupting them'. On this basis, perversion from contemporary moral standards is not enough, and there must be some additional factor which renders an article obscene. This connects with the second objection to defining 'deprave and corrupt' as 'pervert from contemporary moral standards', which is that this does not explain why obscenity is limited to sex, drugs, and violence. A book which explains how to pick pockets, or how to make bombs, or how to help people commit suicide, may be condemned as encouraging crime, but it is unlikely to be categorized as obscene. Yet such a book may well 'pervert from contemporary moral standards' as regards theft, for example, just as much as an explicit magazine perverts from such standards as regards sexual behaviour. Again, it seems that there must be some additional factor which explains the limitations of obscenity. The case law, however, provides no clue as to what it might be.

The third objection to the above analysis is that it does not match reality. The Obscene Publications Act 1959 is used in practice almost exclusively against explicit pictorial material dealing with what is generally regarded as deviant behaviour: in other words, non-consensual sexual violence, bestiality, paedophilia, etc (see, e.g. the DVDs described in *R v Snowden (John)* [2009] EWCA Crim 1200). It is hard to believe that faced with such material a jury or magistrate spends much time in deliberation on nice points relating to the precise effect that it will have on the moral standards of those likely to read it. One suspects that the decision is much more likely to be based simply on a feeling as to whether the material is within the limits of acceptable adult reading or viewing, which will in turn be based on an assumption as to the general standards applying within society. This is a decision based on the nature of the material itself, rather than its effects.

If this is right, then the conclusion must be that the definition of obscenity in terms of a tendency to deprave and corrupt is both incoherent in theory, and of little help in practice. The words 'deprave and corrupt' serve to emphasize the seriousness of the issue, but do not actually function as a definition.

8.4.1.2 The 'shock and disgust' test

The test of obscenity described in the last section, based on the tendency to deprave and corrupt, is only used in two statutes: the Obscene Publications Act 1959 and the Theatres Act 1968. A number of other statutes use the word 'obscene', but without defining it, and usually in association with the word 'indecent'. Examples include s. 85 of the Postal Services Act 2000 (discussed at 8.5.2.1), and s. 42 of the Customs Consolidation Act 1876 (discussed at 8.9.2). In *R* v *Anderson* [1972] 1 QB 304, in relation to a charge under the Post Office Act 1953 (the predecessor to the Postal Services Act 2000) it was argued that 'obscene' in s. 11 of the 1953 Act should be defined in the same way as in the Obscene Publications Act. The judge had directed the jury to consider whether the material under consideration was 'repulsive', 'filthy', 'loathsome', and 'lewd'. The Court of Appeal held that while this was a misdirection in relation to a charge under the Obscene Publications Act 1959, it was acceptable in relation to the Post Office Act offence. This was because here the word 'obscene' should be given its dictionary meaning, which includes things which are 'shocking, lewd, indecent and so on'. So, in direct contrast to the Obscene Publications Act test, material can be found to be obscene under these statutes if it shocks and disgusts the reader. As we have seen, if the 'deprave and corrupt' test applies, the fact that the likely effect of the material is to shock and disgust may well provide a defence. It is small wonder that juries can become confused, when the same word can have directly opposite meanings depending on which offence is being charged.

8.4.2 Indecency

The other word, apart from 'obscene', which is frequently used in this area is 'indecent'. In some statutes, as noted at 8.4.1.2, it is used in conjunction with 'obscene'. In *R* v *Stanley* [1965] 2 QB 327, Lord Parker tried to explain the difference (p. 333):

> The words 'indecent or obscene' convey one idea, namely, offending against the recognised standards of propriety, indecent being at the lower end of the scale and obscene at the upper end of the scale...

It would appear from this that 'indecent' means shocking and disgusting, but not as shocking and disgusting as 'obscene'. This is confirmed by the statement of Lord Reid in *Knuller* v *DPP* [1973] AC 435, p. 458, that it includes 'anything which an ordinary decent man or woman would find to be shocking, disgusting or revolting'. There has been little else in the way of judicial definition of the word. Indeed, during debates on the Indecent Displays (Control) Act 1981, some Members of Parliament (MPs) clearly thought it an advantage that the word was vague, in that this would allow magistrates to apply local standards in different districts (see, e.g. *Hansard*, HC, vol. 997, cols 1196 and 1207). Whether this is a proper basis for the formulation of a criminal offence is open to question.

Indecency is also used as the basis for some common law offences, such as presenting an indecent exhibition, keeping a disorderly house, or outraging public decency (see 8.5.5.2 and 8.7.2). In this context at least it is not limited to sexual indecency, as is shown by the case of *R v Gibson* [1991] 1 All ER 439. This concerned an item on display in an art gallery which consisted of a model of a head to which were attached earrings made out of freeze-dried human foetuses. The owner of the gallery and the artist were convicted of outraging public decency (see also 8.5.5.2).

This case, and the use of the word 'impropriety' by Lord Parker, point to the fact that essential elements of indecency seem to be offence, and inappropriateness. Pictures may be indecent if they depict behaviour which is quite acceptable in private (such as consensual sexual intercourse), but offensive and inappropriate if it takes place in public. A freeze-dried foetus is appropriate (though some might still feel offensive) in a medical laboratory, but may be felt to be inappropriate in an art gallery. The problem with this, as with the word indecent itself, is that both offence and appropriateness are largely subjective concepts, which do not therefore provide a firm basis for legal definition. What is clear, however, is that, just as the innocent motives of the creator of an obscene article cannot prevent its obscenity (see 8.4.1.1), so an improper motive cannot render a decent article indecent. This was confirmed in *R v Graham-Kerr* [1988] 1 WLR 1098, a case on the Protection of Children Act 1978 (see 8.5.2.4). The judge had allowed at trial evidence as to the accused's purpose and motive in photographing a seven-year-old boy at a naturists-only session at a swimming pool. The Court of Appeal held that this was irrelevant to the issue of the indecency of the photographs. On what constitutes indecency, however, the court only felt able to refer to Lord Parker's 'recognised standards of propriety'. In that case this 'objective' approach led to the quashing of the conviction, because the judge had allowed inadmissible evidence to be given. In *R v Smethurst* [2001] EWCA Crim 722, [2002] 1 Cr App R 6, the Court of Appeal applied the same approach to uphold a conviction under the Protection of Children Act 1978. The prosecution concerned photographs of young girls which the defendant had downloaded from the internet. Part of his defence was that he was a keen photographer, interested in the female form, and he denied that he looked at the pictures for sexual gratification. It was held that this was irrelevant. The jury simply had to consider whether the pictures were 'indecent', and this was to be decided objectively on the basis of the views of 'right-thinking' people, ignoring the motives or purposes of the person charged with the offence.

All this suggests that, although the word 'indecent' has caused less controversy, it is just as vague a term as 'obscene', and therefore its scope depends heavily on the subjective reaction of the jury or magistrates to the material under consideration. This would suggest that offences using 'indecency' as the test of criminality might be open to challenge under the HRA 1998 in that they are not sufficiently 'prescribed by law' as required by Art. 10 of the ECHR. In *R v Smethurst*, however, the Court of Appeal, without apparently much consideration of the issue, ruled that the offences under the Protection of Children Act 1978, based on the 'indecency' test, were sufficiently certain to meet the standards required by Art. 10. A similar view was taken by the Divisional Court in *Connolly* v *DPP* [2007] EWHC 237 (Admin), [2007] 2 All ER 1012, in relation to an offence under the Malicious Communications Act 1998. The Court held that the fact that material was produced for political or educational purposes did not prevent it from being indecent, and that the particular restriction on publication concerned in the case was compatible with Art. 10. This is not, perhaps, a surprising conclusion given that in *Handyside* v *United Kingdom* (1976) 1 EHRR 737 the ECtHR was, as can be seen at 8.2, prepared to accept that the equally vague test of obscenity under the Obscene Publications Act 1959 met the required standard.

8.5 Controls over books and magazines, etc.

The main targets for the criminal law in England and Wales as far as allegedly obscene or indecent materials are concerned, are books and magazines containing photographs, internet sites, DVDs, and videos. The specific controls over DVDs and videos are considered further at 8.6. In this section the offences and other procedures which apply to printed material and internet publications are considered.

The main statutes are the Obscene Publications Acts of 1959 and 1964, but various other more specific statutes, often enacted to deal with particular issues of concern at the time, are also relevant.

8.5.1 Obscene Publications Acts 1959 and 1964

The Obscene Publications Act 1959 was enacted in response to concerns that the common law offence of obscene libel was inadequate to deal with modern literature. This issue had been considered by a committee set up by the Society of Authors, and by a Parliamentary select committee. One point of criticism was that the law failed to take account of the literary or other merits of the work under consideration. Accordingly, the long title of the Obscene Publications Act 1959 states its aim as being 'to provide for the protection of literature; and to strengthen the law concerning pornography'. Two means of attack are used, namely criminal offences, and a forfeiture procedure.

8.5.1.1 The offences

The main offence enacted in the Obscene Publications Act 1959 is that of publishing an obscene article, under s. 2(1). The publication does not have to be for gain. All three elements of the offence are the subject of further definition within the Act. The meaning of 'obscene' is considered at 8.4.1.1, so here we need only look at 'publication' and 'article'.

The definition of publication is contained in s. 1(3) which states:

> For the purposes of this Act a person publishes an article who—
> (a) distributes, circulates, sells, lets on hire, gives, or lends it, or who offers it for sale or for letting on hire; or

> (b) in the case of an article containing or embodying matter to be looked at or a record, shows, plays or projects it, or, where the matter is data stored electronically, transmits that data.

This is a broad definition. An individual copy of a work which is simply handed by one person to another is 'published' for the purposes of the Act (confirmed by *R v Smith* [2012] EWCA Crim 398, where the publication took the form of an internet 'chat log' between the defendant and one other unidentified individual). On the other hand, 'offer for sale' has been interpreted as being limited by the contractual rules as to offer and acceptance. In *Mella v Monahan* [1961] Crim LR 175 there was a prosecution under s. 2 on the basis that a packet of photographs had been published by being offered for sale. The packet had been displayed in the window of a shop. The Divisional Court took the view that this was not an offer for sale, but an invitation to treat, and so the prosecution failed. The inclusion of electronically transmitted data means that communication of obscene material over a computer network, including over the internet, will amount to a publication. It is not clear, however, whether every person involved in the chain of such transmission will be a 'publisher'. The issue is important for internet service providers who may have limited control over the content of what is transmitted. Since the offence under s. 2(1) does not require any intention or even recklessness as regards the obscene nature of what is published, the likelihood is that such service providers could be charged with an offence under this section. This would seem to be confirmed by the approach taken to 'publication' in the defamation case of *Godfrey v Demon Internet Ltd* [1999] 4 All ER 342. The internet service provider would then have to rely on the defence of 'innocent publication' under s. 2(5), which puts the burden of proof on the defendant. It was in fact held by the Court of Appeal in *R v Fellows* [1997] 2 All ER 548 that electronically stored and transmitted images were capable of falling within the Obscene Publications Act 1959, even without the specific reference to such material which was added by the Criminal Justice and Public Order Act 1994 (CJPOA 1994). The Court took the view that the hard disk on which the data was stored was an 'article' for the purposes of the Act, and that the data itself was 'shown, played or projected' to a person who gained access to it. In the unreported case of *R v Waddon* (6 April 2000), the Court of Appeal held that publications on the internet could take place both where the material was transmitted and where it was downloaded. The fact that the defendant had put the relevant material on a website based in the US did not prevent him from being charged with publication in the UK.

The only other ruling on the meaning of publication in this section relates to the showing of a video in a cinema. This is discussed in the section dealing with DVDs and videos (see 8.6).

An 'article' is defined in s. 1(2) as:

> ...any description of article containing or embodying matter to be read or looked at or both, any sound record, and any film or other record of a picture or pictures.

This is again a wide definition. Its limits were, however, indicated in *Conegate* v *Commissioners of Customs and Excise* [1987] QB 254, where the 'articles' in question were rubber sex dolls, inflatable to life-size. It was accepted that these were not within the s. 1(2) definition, presumably because they were intended to be used, rather than looked at. (This case is discussed further at 8.10.) In other cases, however, the courts have been prepared to interpret the phrase to cover new technology, in the form of video-cassettes (as a 'record of pictures': *Attorney-General's Reference (No. 5 of 1980)* [1980] 3 All ER 816), and, as indicated by *R v Fellows*, to cover a computer disk containing obscene text or pictures. There is no doubt that similar electronic storage media, such as DVDs, memory sticks, or MP3 players, will fall within the definition of 'article' for these purposes.

What the prosecution has to prove for the publication offence under s. 2(1), then, is that an article was published to a person who was likely to be depraved or corrupted, or to a group of people, a significant proportion of whom were likely to be depraved and corrupted. In looking at the likely readers, the court need not only consider the initial publication. Section 2(6) makes it clear that any further publication that could be reasonably expected to follow can also be taken into account. So in the case of the distribution of a magazine by a publisher to a wholesaler, it might be difficult to establish that the wholesaler was someone who was likely to be depraved and corrupted. Section 2(6), however, allows the court to take account of the further likely publication to retailers, and thence to the general public.

In some situations, however, no further publication will be likely, and attention will then have to focus on the corruptibility of the initial recipient. This caused problems in *R v Clayton and Halsey* [1963] 1 QB 163. The publication took the form of the sale of a packet of photographs to two plain-clothes police officers. These officers admitted in evidence that they had seen thousands of photographs of the type purchased, and were totally unaffected by them. No further publication by the police officers was likely. On that basis, the Divisional Court felt bound to quash the defendants' convictions under s. 2 (though they were also convicted on a conspiracy charge). This decision clearly raised considerable problems for the police, and the result was the enactment in the Obscene Publications Act 1964 of an amendment to s. 2 of the Obscene Publications Act 1959 creating a further offence, that of 'having an obscene article for publication for gain'.

The differences between this offence and the original publication offence are two-fold. First, there is no need for any publication to be proved. Possession with a view to publication is enough (see s. 1(5) of the Obscene Publications Act 1964). Second, the proposed publication must be 'for gain'. The gain does not have to be that of the publisher, 'gain to another' is sufficient. 'Gain' is not defined. In practice it will normally be financial gain, but there is no reason why other types of benefit should not be considered. For example, a scheme for the exchange of pornography amongst enthusiasts might well come within its scope.

This offence not only deals with the difficulty raised by *R v Clayton and Halsey*, it also avoids the problems of *Mella v Monahan* as regards goods displayed in shop windows. As a result it is the offence most commonly used against those involved in the commercial production and distribution of pornography. As is the case with the original publication offence, the court is not limited to considering the effects of the initial publication which the possessor may reasonably be inferred to have had in mind, but can also take account of any further publication which could reasonably be expected to follow (s. 1(3) of the Obscene Publications Act 1964).

8.5.1.2 **The forfeiture provisions**

Many of the legal actions taken against pornographic books and magazines are not prosecutions under s. 2 but forfeiture proceedings under s. 3 of the Obscene Publications Act 1959.

Section 3 gives the police the power to obtain a search warrant to look for obscene articles. In order to be granted one, they will need to convince a magistrate that there are reasonable grounds for suspecting that obscene articles are being kept for gain on specified premises. Note that private possession is not enough; the prospect of 'gain' must be present. The procedures for obtaining and executing the warrant will of course be subject to the relevant provisions of the Police and Criminal Evidence Act 1984 (PACE) (see chapter 6 (6.4.4)). The warrant should specifically refer to 'obscene' articles. In *Darbo* v *DPP* [1992] Crim LR 56, the phrase used was 'material of a sexually explicit nature'. The Divisional Court held that this rendered the warrant invalid, because the category of material which was 'sexually explicit' was far wider than that which could be considered 'obscene'.

Once on the premises, the officers may search them, and seize any articles which they have reason to believe are obscene, and kept for publication for gain. In addition, if any such articles are taken, the police may also seize any documents relating to a trade or business carried on at the premises (s. 3(2)). The reason for giving the police this additional power was presumably to enable them to obtain evidence that the material was held for gain, though the wording of the section does not limit the police to seizing documents relating to the trade in obscene articles: the documents may concern any business carried out on the premises. The power to seize them also gives the possibility of providing information which might help to identify the chain of distribution of the articles seized.

Once items have been seized, the police will need to decide whether to bring a prosecution under s. 2, or go for forfeiture proceedings under s. 3. This may take some time. In *Roandale Ltd* v *Metropolitan Police Commissioner* [1979] Crim LR 254, the police had seized from a warehouse some 170,000 magazines, including 18,000 copies of one magazine which belonged to the plaintiff. The seizure took place on 22 November. On 11 December, the plaintiffs sought an injunction requiring the police to return their magazines. Their argument was that there was an obligation under s. 3(3) to bring the items before the magistrates, and that, although there was no specific requirement in the statute to this effect, this should be done within a reasonable time. The injunction was refused, and by the time the matter reached the Court of Appeal (on 26 January) the articles had been deposited with the magistrates. The Court of Appeal indicated, however, that the correct way to have challenged the police would have been by way of judicial review, rather than by seeking an injunction. (On this issue, however, see also the discussion in chapter 6 (6.8.3).) They agreed that the police had to act within a reasonable time, but regard had to be had to the quantity of material seized, and they were not prepared to say that the delay in this case was unreasonable.

Assuming that the police decide to proceed with forfeiture proceedings, the magistrates will issue a summons to the occupier of the premises from which the articles were seized, to appear to show cause why all or any of the articles should not be forfeited. Those who are simply wholesalers, or retailers, of the material may well not bother to challenge the forfeiture order, and simply regard the disappearance of their stock as a business loss; but s. 3(4) allows, in addition, any person involved with the production or distribution of the articles to appear to show cause (s. 3(4)). This gives the possibility of enabling the author or publisher of a serious work which has fallen into the possession of someone trading in pornography to come forward to argue their case. Since they are not required to be given notice of the proceedings, however, they may well be ignorant of what is going on.

The arguments that may be raised against forfeiture are that:

1. the articles are not obscene; or

2. that the publication of them would be for the public good (s. 4 (see 8.5.1.3)); or

3. that they were not kept for gain.

Section 3(3) requires the magistrates to decide in relation to each article whether or not it is obscene and kept for publication for gain. In practice, where large quantities of material are seized, shortcuts are taken. For example, in *R* v *Croydon Magistrates, ex p Rickman, The Times*, 8 March 1985, a stipendiary magistrate, faced with the long and distasteful job of examining many thousands of books, photographs, and films brought before him under s. 3, decided that he would reach a decision on the basis of a police officer's evidence, consisting of descriptions of the nature of the material. Both prosecution and defence objected. The Divisional Court agreed with the objection, considering this to amount to reliance on hearsay. They expressed approval, however, of a proposed sampling procedure, whereby the magistrate would take a decision on representative samples, agreed by prosecution and defence, of various categories of material. A similar scheme had been approved at the stage of appeal to the Crown Court in *R* v *Snaresbrook Crown Court, ex p Commissioner of the Metropolis* (1984) 79 Cr App R 184. This method of dealing with large-scale seizures is understandable, but it must be questionable whether it actually meets the letter of the requirements of s. 3. The wording of the section seems to require the decision as to 'obscenity' to be taken in relation to each article before the court. It is difficult to see that this is properly achieved by a process under which the magistrate decides that an article is obscene without looking at it, but simply by deciding that another article, which has been placed by someone else in the same category of seriousness, is obscene. The 'hearsay' element in the decision may be less direct than in relation to the process rejected in *Rickman*'s case, but it is nevertheless present. (See further on this, R. Stone, 'Obscene Publications: The Problems Persist', [1986] Crim LR 139.) It is possible that an HRA 1998 challenge might be made in relation to these procedures, relying on the First Protocol, Art. 1 of the ECHR, which provides that 'no one shall be deprived of his possessions except in the public interest and subject to the conditions provided for by law...'. Although the general power to forfeit obscene publications would undoubtedly be held to be legitimate 'in the public interest', it is arguable that the sampling procedures of the kind outlined above are not sufficiently 'provided for by law' to attract the protection of the public interest justification for forfeiture.

If the magistrates decide that all or any of the articles are not obscene they must be returned to the person from whom they were seized. Any that are found to be obscene will be ordered to be forfeited. Any person who appeared, or who was entitled to appear, before the magistrates, may appeal against this order to the

Crown Court, which will review the merits of the case. If the order for forfeiture stands, or is not appealed, then the articles will be destroyed. The same will be the fate of seized material which is found to be obscene in the course of proceedings for an offence under s. 2 of 'having for publication for gain' (s. 1(4) of the Obscene Publications Act 1964).

8.5.1.3 The defence of 'public good'

As noted at 8.5.1, one of the objectives of the Obscene Publications Act 1959 was to provide greater protection under the law for works of literature. One of the ways in which this was attempted was by the inclusion of a defence of public good, which is set out in s. 4. This states that there is to be no conviction under s. 2, or order for forfeiture under s. 3, if the defence proves:

> ...that publication of the article in question is justified as being for the public good on the ground that it is in the interests of science, literature, art or learning, or of other objects of general concern.

Note that, as with the test of obscenity, the emphasis here is not on the article itself, but on the publication of it. The court must look at the circumstances of publication and decide whether one of the interests mentioned outweighs any possible obscenity. It is also clear that the defence does not mean that the article is not obscene, but that it can be published despite the fact that it is obscene. The logic of this was accepted in *Olympia Press* v *Hollis* [1974] 1 All ER 108, where the magistrates refused to listen to arguments under s. 4 until they had decided whether or not the articles in question were obscene. The Divisional Court said that this approach, while unusual, was perfectly acceptable. This separation of the issues was approved by the majority of the House of Lords in *DPP* v *Jordan* [1976] 3 All ER 775.

The main arguments about this defence have centred on its scope. What interests are covered, in particular by the phrase 'other objects of general concern'? The matter came before the House of Lords in *DPP* v *Jordan*. The background to this case was that during the 1970s a number of prosecutions under the Obscene Publications Act 1959 took place in which the defence called doctors who were prepared to testify that the publications under consideration were 'for the public good' in that they helped people with sexual problems. More specifically it was argued that it was preferable that people should have access to sexual materials as aids to masturbation rather than that they should either act out their fantasies, or repress them, and therefore become neurotic or psychotic. This evidence was brought in as relating to 'other objects of general concern'. In *Jordan*, the trial judge had refused to allow evidence as to the 'psychotherapeutic' value of pornographic material. On appeal, the House of Lords agreed that it had rightly been excluded. There were two reasons for this. The first was that the evidence related to the effect that the material had on people. As such it was really more appropriate to the issue of 'obscenity' under s. 1 of the Obscene Publications Act 1959 (in relation to which, as we shall see, expert evidence is not usually allowed), than to that of 'public good'. Second, the defence, if allowed, would apply to virtually all pornographic material. Since the long title of the Act made it clear that one of Parliament's intentions in passing the Act was to control pornography, the s. 4 defence could not have been intended to operate in this way. For both these reasons, the evidence was rightly excluded. 'Other objects of general concern' does not therefore cover the alleged psychological benefits of the pornography, even if these could be established, nor is there any indication from the cases as to what else might be covered by this phrase. It is significant that when the equivalent public good defence was enacted in s. 3 of the Theatres Act 1968, 'other objects' were not included in the list of interests.

A further attempt to expand the scope of s. 4 was made in *Attorney-General's Reference (No. 3 of 1977)* [1978] 3 All ER 1166. Here the argument was that 'learning' should be taken to encompass 'teaching' and that this should cover sex education. Expert witnesses were prepared to give evidence that the sex magazines which had been seized could be used in relation to sex education, or in teaching people about sexual matters. The Court of Appeal refused to endorse this, ruling that 'learning' in s. 4 was a noun meaning 'the product of scholarship', or 'something whose inherent excellence is gained by the work of a scholar'.

In practice, then, it seems that an argument for 'public good' is unlikely to succeed unless based on the scientific, literary, or artistic merits of the publication.

8.5.1.4 The use of expert evidence

The main use of expert evidence under the Obscene Publications Acts is in relation to the public good defence. Section 4(2) specifically provides that 'the opinion of experts as to the literary, artistic, scientific or other merits of the article' may be admitted, for the defence, or the prosecution. In *R v Penguin Books* [1961] Crim LR 176, the Bishop of Woolwich was allowed to give evidence as to the 'ethical merits' of *Lady Chatterley's Lover*. The role of the expert is to speak to the qualities of the work, not directly to the issue of whether its publication is for the public good. This is a matter for the magistrates or jury, and they are perfectly entitled to ignore the expert evidence in reaching their decision: *Calder v Powell* [1965] 1 QB 509. In practice, however, it may be difficult to prevent witnesses from expressing an opinion as to whether or not the article should be published.

In general, expert evidence is not allowed on the issue of 'obscenity'. This is what the jury or magistrates have to decide, and the view is that they should normally be able to do this on the basis of their own judgment of the material, and its tendency to deprave and corrupt, without any external assistance. This was the line taken in *R v Calder and Boyars* [1969] 1 QB 151, and *R v Anderson* [1972] 1 QB 304. It was confirmed by the House of Lords in *DPP v Jordan* [1976] 3 All ER 775 (see 8.5.1.3). In two reported cases, however, expert evidence on obscenity has been allowed, and there are obiter dicta which suggest other circumstances where this might be possible. The first case to allow this type of evidence was *DPP v A & BC Chewing Gum Ltd* [1968] 1 QB 159. The case concerned cards depicting acts of violence which were distributed in packets of bubble-gum and were thus likely to fall into the hands of young children. The Divisional Court approved the admission of expert evidence for the prosecution as to the likely effect of the cards on such children. The justification for this was that the likely effect was something outside the range of experience of the ordinary jury member. Lord Wilberforce on two subsequent occasions suggested the extension of this principle to other areas. The first was in *DPP v Jordan*, where, having rejected the admissibility under s. 4 of evidence as to the 'psychotherapeutic' value of pornography, he suggested that if the material was published to a limited class of people, e.g. consisting entirely of sexual deviants, there might be room for expert evidence as to its effect on them: [1977] AC 699, p. 718. The second, similar suggestion came in *Gold Star Publications* v *DPP* [1981] 2 All ER 257, where the court was concerned with material destined solely for export. Lord Wilberforce again suggested (p. 259) that expert evidence might sometimes be admissible as to the effects of the material on its target audience. In both these cases the justification was that the ordinary jury member could not be expected to assess the effect of the material on a particular type of audience. The suggestions were both in the form of obiter dicta, however, and there are no reported examples of other judges adopting this approach. Indeed, until 1985, *DPP* v *A & BC Chewing Gum* remained the only case where expert evidence had been allowed on the s. 1 issue.

In *R* v *Skirving* [1985] 2 All ER 705 the Court of Appeal again approved the use of prosecution expert evidence in an obscenity trial. The publication in question was a pamphlet which apparently described various methods of ingesting cocaine, and compared the merits of one against another. As can be seen at 8.4.1.1, the Obscene Publications Acts are not limited in their scope to sexual material, but may also be used against publications concerned with drug-taking. In *Skirving* the judge allowed expert evidence to be given as to the effects of taking cocaine. The justification, which was accepted by the Court of Appeal, was superficially the same as in the *Chewing Gum* case, and in Lord Wilberforce's dicta; that is, that the effects of taking cocaine were outside the experience of the ordinary jury members, and therefore something on which it was permissible for them to have expert guidance. This misses the point, however, that what the jury had to decide on was the effect of reading the pamphlet ('would it deprave and corrupt'), not the effect of engaging in the activities described in it. It is not at all clear that they would have been incapable of deciding this issue from their own experience, without needing expert guidance. The analogy in the sexual area would be if evidence were allowed to show that indulging in sado-masochistic practices causes lasting physical or psychological problems, or that being homosexual increases the risks of contracting AIDS. Whether or not such evidence is true, it is irrelevant to the issue of the obscenity of a publication, where, as we have seen in *DPP* v *Whyte* (see 8.4.1.1) the emphasis is not on what people do after reading the publication, but the effect on their minds. (This point is argued at greater length in R. Stone, 'Obscene Publications: The Problems Persist'. For a contrary view, see D. Birch, [1985] Crim LR 318.)

8.5.1.5 **Other defences**

Apart from the arguments that the article is not obscene, or that its publication is for the public good, the Obscene Publications Acts allow one other defence, which is most likely to be of use to distributors. This is that the person charged was ignorant of the nature of what was published. Section 2(5) of the Obscene Publications Act 1959 makes it clear that the burden of proof is on the defendant. In relation to the publication offence, it must be proved that the defendant had not examined the article and 'had no reasonable cause to suspect that it was such that his publication of it would make him liable to be convicted of an offence' against s. 2. Section 1(3)(a) of the Obscene Publications Act 1964 provides an equivalent defence to the charge of having for publication for gain. The requirement of non-examination means that the only defendants likely to be able to make use of it are wholesale distributors, or retailers who have not at the relevant time removed the article from its packaging. It might also, however, in some circumstances provide protection for internet service providers who would be regarded as having published the material.

8.5.2 Protection of children

Child pornography, and in particular the availability of such material on the internet, has been one of the major concerns of recent years. As a result there have been several pieces of legislation aimed at the publication and possession of this type of material.

8.5.2.1 The Protection of Children Act 1978

This Act was passed in response to worries about a perceived growth in child pornography. Much of such material would, of course, fall foul of the Obscene Publications Act 1959, but there was thought to be a need to create a separate offence with respect to photographs and films. In terms of prosecutions the Protection of Children Act 1978 is now much more significant than the Obscene Publications Act 1959. A Consultation Paper produced by the Home Office in 2005 revealed that between 1994 and 2003 the number of Obscene Publications Act 1959 prosecutions had declined from 309 to 39 per year. In the same period the number of prosecutions under the Protection of Children Act 1978 had increased from 93 to 1,890 ('Consultation on the Possession of Extreme Pornographic Material', Home Office, 2005, para. 15 (Consultation)).

The Protection of Children Act 1978 is concerned with photographs or films (this will also be taken to cover video-cassettes and DVDs) which show children and are indecent. The definition of a 'child' was originally a person under the age of 16. This was changed by s. 45 of the Sexual Offences Act 2003 to a person under the age of 18. The change also necessitated the addition of provisions, set out in a new s. 1A, excluding from the scope of the Act the use of such photographs when in the possession of the husband, wife, or 'partner in an enduring family relationship' of the person depicted, and where there is no evidence of the involvement of or distribution to a third party. There was no clear rationale for this change in the White Paper which preceded the 2003 Act ('Protecting the Public', Cm 5668, 2002).

In *R* v *Fellows* [1997] 2 All ER 548, the Act was interpreted to cover electronically stored images. This type of material is now specifically covered by amendments contained in s. 84 of the CJPOA 1994. The child depicted does not necessarily have to be involved in any indecency, this element could be satisfied by something occurring elsewhere in the photograph or film. This interpretation was approved in *R* v *Owen* [1988] 1 WLR 134. In practice, however, the Act is used in relation to pictures where the indecency involves the children. Section 1 of the Act made it an offence to take such indecent photographs, to distribute or show them, or to possess them with a view to distribution or showing. There is no need for there to be any actual or intended gain (financial or otherwise) from the distribution or showing.

The meaning of 'indecency' is discussed at 8.4.2. Some guidance on the meaning of the word in the context of child pornography can be found in the Court of

Appeal's decision in *R v Oliver* [2002] EWCA Crim 766. In the context of sentencing it outlined five levels of seriousness in relation to pornographic images of children. These were (para. 10):

(1) images depicting erotic posing with no sexual activity;

(2) sexual activity between children, or solo masturbation by a child;

(3) non-penetrative sexual activity between adults and children;

(4) penetrative sexual activity between children and adults;

(5) sadism or bestiality.

This use of this scale (and not any other scale, such as the COPINE scale developed by the Combating Paedophile Networks in Europe Project) as a means of assessing child pornography has been recently approved by the Court of Appeal in *R v Dodd* [2013] EWCA Crim 660. As will be seen, the scale starts with 'erotic posing' as the least serious form of child pornography. It can be deduced from this that any photographs which depict naked or clothed children, but without any element of erotic posing is likely to fall outside the scope of the law. The decision as to indecency is, of course, in the hands of the finder of fact (magistrate or jury), but this gives a fairly clear indication of where the line should be drawn between indecent and non-indecent images of children.

There are three other cases on the Protection of Children Act 1978 which are relevant to this issue. In *R v Owen*, it was held that the age of the child was a relevant fact which the jury could take account of when assessing the alleged indecency of a photograph. The subject of the photograph was a girl aged 14, who was scantily clad and displaying her bare breasts. She had wanted to become a professional model. The defence submitted that the jury should judge the photograph simply as it stood, disregarding the girl's age. Presumably, it was thought that the girl might well appear to be older than her actual age, and that the type of photograph, if it had been of an 18-year-old, was not such that it would have been regarded as indecent. The judge ruled against the defence submission, and the Court of Appeal upheld this ruling. The jury could take into account the age of the girl as a relevant factor in deciding whether or not the photograph was indecent. If there is no evidence as to the age of the person depicted, then it seems that it is up to the jury to decide for itself whether he or she is a child. This was the view of the Court of Appeal in *R v Land* [1998] 1 All ER 403. It rejected an argument from the defence that expert evidence should be given on this topic. The burden of proof must, however, remain on the prosecution to establish that the person is actually a child, so that if the jury have any reasonable doubt on the issue, they should acquit. It has further been argued, following the decisions in *B v DPP* [2000] 2 AC 428 and *R v K* [2001] UKHL 41, [2001] 3 All ER 897 on the requirement of *mens rea* in relation to the age elements in other offences, that there should be implied here a requirement that the prosecution proves that the defendant knew, or was aware that, the person depicted was a child (see the commentary by Ormerod on *R v Smith* [2002] EWCA Crim 683 at [2002] Crim LR 659, p. 662). This suggestion was rejected in *R v Land* (which, of course, preceded the change of direction taken in *B v DPP* and *R v K*), where Judge LJ also suggested that it would always be possible to tell 'at a glance' whether a picture depicted someone who was, or might be, under the specified age ([1998] 1 All ER 403, p. 407). Whether it is in fact so easy to be sure of the age of, in particular, girls and young women between the ages of, say, 16 and 21, may be open to debate.

A slightly different approach was taken in *R v Graham-Kerr* [1988] 1 WLR 1098. Here the defendant had taken a photograph of a seven-year-old boy at a naturist swimming bath. The judge directed the jury that they could take into account the circumstances in which the photograph was taken, and the motivation of the defendant in taking it, when assessing the indecency issue. On this occasion the Court of Appeal ruled that evidence on these issues was not relevant to the question of whether or not the photograph was indecent, though it might have affected the issue of whether the photograph was taken intentionally or deliberately. Since the *mens rea* of the defendant was not disputed, the evidence was not relevant to any issue which was before the jury, and the judge should have directed them accordingly. To this extent the issue of indecency must be judged intrinsically on the basis of the photograph alone. The defendant's conviction was quashed. The same approach was adopted in *R v Smethurst* [2001] EWCA Crim 722, [2002] 1 Cr App R 6. In this case, the defendant had claimed that his motives in possessing the pictures was an interest in the female form, and not sexual gratification. The court held that this was irrelevant. Provided that the pictures were objectively 'indecent' then the defendant was properly convicted.

8.5.2.2 The Criminal Justice Act 1988

Continued concern about the availability of child pornography led to the creation in 1988 of an additional summary offence of possession of an indecent photograph. This is contained in s. 160 of the Criminal Justice Act 1988. Unlike the possession offence in the Protection of Children Act 1978, there is no need to show any intention to distribute or publish the photograph. Simple possession constitutes the offence. In all other respects, however, the new offence adopts the definitions and procedures of the Protection of Children Act 1978. It was held by the Divisional Court in *Atkins v DPP* [2000] 2 All ER 425 that 'possession' required knowledge. Thus, images which were automatically stored in a 'cache' on the hard disk of the defendant's computer were not in his possession, unless he was aware of their existence. It is in any case a defence under s. 160 for the defendant to prove that 'he had not himself sent the photograph and pseudo-photograph and did not know, nor had any cause to suspect, it to be indecent'. In *R v Collier* [2004] EWCA Crim 1411, [2005] 1 Cr App R 9 the Court of Appeal held that this defence would also be available if the defendant proved that he had not seen the item and had no reason to suspect it to be of a child (though he might have reason to suspect it to be an indecent photograph of an adult). The defendant had been found in possession of video-tapes and CD-Roms of adult homosexual pornography which included advertisements depicting child pornography. Other defences under s. 160 are that the defendant had a 'legitimate reason' for possession of the item, or that it was sent without any previous request and had not been kept for an unreasonable time.

8.5.2.3 'Pseudo-photographs'

There has been further extension of the scope of the Protection of Children Act 1978, and of s. 160 of the Criminal Justice Act 1988, by the provisions of Pt. VII of the CJPOA 1994. Section 84 introduced the concept of the 'pseudo-photograph', defined in that section as 'an image, whether made by computer-graphics or otherwise howsoever, which appears to be a photograph'. The concern is with the possibility, facilitated by new computer technology, that a photograph can be manipulated so that, for example, a child's face can be superimposed on an adult's body, or vice versa, or the appearance of physical characteristics can be altered. The resulting picture may be indistinguishable from a real photograph. Section 84 provides that such a composite image, or pseudo-photograph, shall be treated as being a photograph of a child, if the predominant impression conveyed by it is that one or more of the persons depicted in it is a child. If the image is also 'indecent', then an offence under the Protection of Children Act 1978, or s. 160 of the Criminal Justice Act 1988, may be committed in relation to it. Two decisions have clarified some points on this legislation. In *R v Bowden* [2000] 2 All ER 418 the Court of Appeal held that the offence of 'making' a photograph or pseudo-photograph could be committed simply by downloading an image onto a computer. This was followed by the Divisional Court in *Atkins v DPP*, subject to the limitation that automatic storage of an image in a 'cache' on the computer's hard disk would not amount to 'making'; the downloading had to be deliberate. Similarly, it was suggested, obiter, in *R v Smith* [2003] EWCA Crim 683, [2003] 1 Cr App R 13, that 'simply opening an unsolicited email message and opening the attachments to it in ignorance of their actual or likely contents' would not constitute an offence. The Divisional Court in *Atkins* also held that academic research could constitute a 'legitimate reason' for possession of indecent photographs of children; it is a question of fact in each case. Finally, it held that an item consisting of two parts of two different photographs fixed together with a sellotape 'hinge' did not constitute a photograph (or pseudo-photograph) for the purposes of the legislation.

8.5.2.4. Tracings

A further broadening of the scope of these offences was brought about by the Criminal Justice and Immigration Act 2008 which extended the definition of photograph to include 'tracings', whether produced freehand, or electronically. A new s. 7(4A) of the 1978 Act defines this as:

> (a) a tracing or other image, whether made by electronic or other means (of whatever nature)—
>   (i) which is not itself a photograph or pseudo-photograph, but
>   (ii) which is derived from the whole or part of a photograph or pseudo-photograph (or a combination of either or both); and
> (b) data stored on a computer disc or by other electronic means which is capable of conversion into a pseudo-photograph.

As with pseudo-photographs the requirement is simply that the impression is conveyed that the image is of a child, whether or not the original image was of a child.

8.5.2.5 Pornographic drawings or other images

The Coroners and Justice Act 2009 created a new child pornography offence of possession of a 'prohibited image' of a child. This is directed at images which are not photographs or pseudo-photographs (s. 65(3)). In other words its target is drawings, paintings, and computer-generated material (such as the images used in computer games, or some animated films). To be prohibited the image must be 'pornographic'. This means that it must reasonable be assumed to have been 'produced solely or principally for the purposes of sexual arousal' (s. 62(3)). Where the image is an image which forms part of a series, the pornographic nature, or otherwise, of it must be decided by its context (s. 62(4)). An image forming part of a narrative which is not found to be pornographic will not be treated as such, even if viewed in isolation it would appear to be produced for the purposes of sexual arousal (s. 62(5)).

In addition to being pornographic, the image must also have particular content. It must either focus solely or principally on a child's genital area or anus, or it must depict one of a number of specified sexual acts committed by, against, or in the presence of, a child. The acts are sexual intercourse, oral sex, masturbation, penetration of vagina or anus with a part of the body or an object, sexual intercourse or oral sex with an animal (alive, dead, or imaginary) (s. 62(6),(7)).

Films with a BBFC classification are excluded from the scope of this provision (s. 64). There is also a defence of possession for a legitimate reason, or innocent possession—i.e. where the person in possession had not seen the image and did not know, or have cause to suspect, that it was a prohibited image (s. 65). Unsolicited receipt of the image is also a defence, provided that the image has not been kept for an 'unreasonable' time. This presumably means that the person should delete it as soon as he or she is aware of its nature.

The maximum penalty for offences under these provisions, which are triable either way, is three years' imprisonment (s. 66).

8.5.2.6 Rationale for extension of control beyond photographs

The extension of the law to cover pseudo-photographs, tracings, and drawings is difficult to reconcile with the original policy of the 1978 Act which, as it name suggests, was directed at the protection of actual children. This was reflected by the decisions in *R* v *Owen* (i.e. it is the actual rather than the apparent age of the person depicted which is important—at least where the age is known (*R* v *Land*)), and *R* v *Graham-Kerr* (the motives of the person creating the image are irrelevant to indecency). A person may be convicted of creating or possessing an indecent pseudo-photograph or tracing where the actual person depicted is above the relevant age, or a pornographic drawing which is produced entirely from the drawer's own imagination. It seems to follow from this that protection of the 'child' who is depicted is no longer the main aim: the fact that a person has created for his or her own pleasure a picture which appears to be (though is not in fact) an indecent or pornographic picture of a child is sufficient to make him or her guilty of an offence. This seems to put the emphasis firmly on the motives and intention of the person creating or possessing the image. These changes are not simply technical amendments to deal with problems created by new technology, but constitute a significant extension and change of emphasis in relation to this area of law. (See further, R. Stone, 'Extending the Labyrinth: Part VII of the Criminal Justice and Public Order Act 1994', (1995) 58 MLR 389.)

8.5.2.7 Compatibility with Article 10

There is no doubt that the general policy of restriction in relation to child pornography would be found to be compatible with Art. 10. The only doubts which might be raised are, first, as to the whether the test of 'indecency' is sufficiently clear to be 'prescribed by law'. As noted at 8.4.2, the Court of Appeal has taken the view that it is: *R v Smethurst* [2001] EWCA Crim 722, [2002] 1 Cr App R 6. A second question which might be raised relates to the offences based on simple possession, without any intention to distribute, particularly where the relevant material has been created by the person in possession. The position under this legislation may be contrasted with the approach of the Canadian Supreme Court in *R v Sharpe* [2001] 1 SCR 45. While holding that controls over child pornography did not in general offend against the right to free expression guaranteed by the Canadian Charter of Rights and Freedoms, it also held that it was not necessary for these controls to extend to material created by the accused for his own private use. It is possible that a similar challenge could be made to certain of the 'possession' offences under English law.

These offences do not have any defence of 'artistic merit'. This meant that a display in a London gallery of photographs by the photographer Tierney Gearon of her own young children, in some of which they appeared naked, was potentially liable to prosecution. The police initiated action, but the Crown Prosecution Service decided that there was insufficient basis to proceed with a prosecution (see *The Times*, 13 and 16 March 2001). The need to rely to such an extent on the discretion of prosecutors to ensure that the law is not used inappropriately is not a desirable situation. The lack of an 'artistic merit' defence is another basis on which the legislation might be open to challenge under the HRA 1998.

8.5.3 Extreme pornographic material

In 2005 the Home Office began a consultation on the possibility of extending a possession offence similar to that which applies to child pornography to what it described as 'extreme pornographic material' (Consultation). The trigger for this seems to have been the increased availability of such material on the internet, together with concerns about a particular case (Consultation, Executive Summary):

> There has been increasing public concern about the availability of this extreme material, highlighted by the case of a young woman who was murdered by a man who had been accessing extreme pornographic websites. This document sets out options for creating a new offence of simple possession of extreme pornographic material which is graphic and sexually explicit and which contains actual scenes or realistic depictions of serious violence, bestiality or necrophilia.

Following the consultation, a possession offence of this type was included in the Criminal Justice and Immigration Act 2008. These provisions make it an offence to be in possession of an 'extreme pornographic image' (s. 63). Each of these words is further defined. 'Extreme' means that the image is of (s. 63(6), (7)):

- an act which threatens a person's life;
- an act which results in, or is likely to result in, serious injury to a person's anus, breasts, or genitals;
- an act which involves sexual interference with a human corpse;
- a person performing an act of intercourse or oral sex with an animal (whether dead or alive).

In each case the act, person, or animal must appear to be 'real'. In other words, cartoon depictions of such acts would not be covered, nor would obvious simulations.

'Pornographic' is defined in the same way as under s. 62 of the Coroners and Justice Act 2008, outlined at 8.5.2.5 (s. 63(3)–(5)). 'Image' means any still or moving image, however produced, or data from which such an image can be produced (s. 63(8)).

Films with a BBFC classification are excluded from the scope of this provision (s. 64). There is also a defence of possession for a legitimate reason, or innocent possession—i.e. where the person in possession had not seen the image and did not know, or have cause to suspect, that it was an extreme pornographic image (s. 65). Unsolicited receipt of the image is also a defence, provided that the image has not been kept for an 'unreasonable' time. This presumably means that the person should delete it as soon as he or she is aware of its nature.

The maximum penalty for offences under these provisions, which are triable either way, is three years' imprisonment (s. 67).

It will be seen that the scope of this offence is narrow. Much of the material it covers would be likely to fall within the definition of obscene under the Obscene Publications Acts. The difference is that those Acts only punish possession where it is possession for gain. The new offence will penalize simple possession, and thus provide a much easier route to successful prosecution. The reasons for creating it are understandable, but it does nothing to reduce the labyrinth of provisions in this area, or to increase the overall rationality of the laws governing sexual publications. A prosecution of a former aide to the Mayor of London failed in August 2012. The charges involved possession of explicit images depicting sexual activities such as fisting, urethral sounding (the insertion of surgical rods into the urethra), and BDSM. The jury acquitted after 90 minutes' deliberation (see, e.g. http://www.theguardian.com/uk/2012/aug/08/boris-johnson-aide-extreme-pornography-cleared). Taken with the acquittal by a jury in January 2012 of the distributor of similarly explicit DVDs who had been charged under the Obscene Publications Act 1959 (see, e.g. http://www.theguardian.com/law/2012/jan/07/obscene-publications-act-future-doubt) this case illustrates the difficulty of getting juries to convict in relation to material, however extreme, which depicts consensual sexual activity between adults.

8.5.4 Other statutory offences

In addition to the Obscene Publications Acts there are a number of other statutes which create specific offences which can be used against books or magazines, generally on the basis that they are indecent. Several of these were passed to deal with particular types of publication which were thought to be a problem at the time. The most important are noted here, in chronological order.

8.5.4.1 The Postal Services Act 2000

Section 85 of this Act makes it an offence to send a postal packet which encloses any indecent or obscene 'article'. The word 'obscene' here has its dictionary definition and does not mean having 'a tendency to deprave and corrupt' (see 8.4.1.1).

There is an additional offence where the outside of a packet contains material which is indecent or obscene (s. 85(4)).

8.5.4.2 **The Children and Young Persons (Harmful Publications) Act 1955**

This Act was passed to deal with a perceived problem in relation to 'horror comics'. The full story of the events which led up to the legislation is told in Martin Barker's *A Haunt of Fears* (London: Pluto Press, 1984). The Act is directed against books and magazines which are likely to fall into the hands of children, and consist wholly or mainly of stories told in pictures, though there may be some written content as well. To be within the scope of the Act the stories must portray: (a) the commission of crimes; or (b) acts of violence or cruelty; or (c) incidents of a repulsive or horrible nature. The effect of the publication must be to tend to corrupt a child or young person into whose hands it might fall (s. 1). The Act has in fact been little used. In many cases, the offences under the Obscene Publications Act 1959 could now be used in a situation where the 1955 Act might apply, particularly since the decision in the *A & BC Chewing Gum* (1968) case extended the Obscene Publications Act 1959 to publications dealing with non-sexual violence (see 8.4.1.1).

8.5.4.3 **The Unsolicited Goods and Services Act 1971**

The procedure known as 'inertia selling' was the main target of this Act. Unscrupulous publishers would send people books which they had not requested, and tell them that unless they returned them by a certain date they would have to pay for them. Although such an arrangement would not be enforceable in civil law (since silence cannot amount to acceptance of a contract: *Felthouse* v *Bindley* (1862) 11 CBNS 869), there was thought to be sufficient of a problem to require specific statutory intervention (which is now contained in reg. 24 of the Consumer Protection (Distance Selling) Regulations 2000 (SI 2000/2334)). At the same time, the opportunity was taken, in s. 4, to deal with a related issue, which is of more direct concern to the issues being looked at in this chapter. This was the sending of unsolicited explicit sexual material, or advertisements for such material. It is an offence under the Act to send, or cause to be sent, an unsolicited book, magazine, or leaflet which describes or illustrates human sexual techniques. It is also an offence to send unsolicited advertising material for such a publication. It was confirmed in *DPP* v *Beate Uhse (UK) Ltd* [1974] 1 All ER 753, that the advertising material does not itself have to describe or illustrate human sexual techniques. It will be seen that the offence is very limited in the type of material it covers. The justification is presumably that other types of sexual material would often be covered by the Postal Services Act 2000 offence (see 8.5.2.1), but that simply depicting consensual human sexual intercourse might well not be considered indecent, so that a special offence was needed.

8.5.5 **The common law**

Two common law offences need consideration, namely, conspiracy to corrupt public morals, and outraging public decency.

8.5.5.1 **Conspiracy to corrupt public morals**

It is generally agreed among academic commentators that in the case of *Shaw* v *DPP* [1962] AC 220, the House of Lords created a new offence, i.e. conspiracy to corrupt public morals. This piece of judicial law-making was the subject of much criticism, but the existence of the offence was confirmed by the House in *Knuller* v *DPP* [1973] AC 435, and by Parliament in s. 5 of the Criminal Law Act 1977. The *mens rea* of the offence is an intention to corrupt (*Knuller* v *DPP*). The *actus reus*, as with all conspiracies, is the agreement to carry out a particular course of conduct. The offence can thus be used against the dissemination of articles which fall within the scope of the Obscene Publications Act 1959, since the prohibition of the use of common law offences contained in s. 2(4) of that Act was held in *Shaw* only to apply where the *actus reus* of the common law offence consisted in publication of the material. At one time it was in practice mainly used where the Obscene Publications Act was not available, for example in relation to private film clubs, before these were brought within the scope of the Obscene Publications Act 1959. It has also been used against sex 'contact' magazines, particularly where these were concerned with paedophilia, or other deviant sexual activities. In this it returned to its origins, since *Shaw* was concerned with a 'Ladies Directory' (i.e. a directory of prostitutes) and *Knuller* with the publication of homosexual contact advertisements in a newspaper.

Despite fears that the offence might be used to circumvent the public good defence in the Obscene Publications Act 1959 (see 8.5.1.3), this has not proved to be the case. An assurance given by the Attorney-General in 1964 that the offence would not be used in this way has been honoured.

8.5.5.2 Outraging public decency

In *Knuller* the House of Lords recognized the existence of an offence of outraging public decency (and thus also an offence of conspiracy to outrage public decency). This has mainly been used, in its manifestations of 'presenting an indecent exhibition' or 'keeping a disorderly' house, against live performances of one kind or another (for which see 8.7.2). In *R* v *Gibson* it was used against the display of an article falling within the scope of the Obscene Publications Act 1959. This was a model head, to which were attached earrings made out of freeze-dried human foetuses of three or four months' gestation. It was displayed at a commercial art gallery. The Court of Appeal held that there was no need for the prosecution to prove an intention to outrage public decency; an intention to display the article was enough. Further, it was held that s. 2(4) of the Obscene Publications Act 1959 could not protect the defendant. This section states that:

> ...[a] person publishing an article shall not be proceeded against for an offence at common law consisting in the publication of any matter contained or embodied in the article where it is of the essence of the offence that the matter is obscene.

We have seen that in *Shaw* this section was regarded as inapplicable, because the *actus reus* of the conspiracy was the agreement, not the publication. In *Gibson* it was held that 'obscene' in s. 2(4) must be given the same meaning as elsewhere in the Act, i.e. having a tendency to deprave and corrupt. Since the essence of the common law offence charged here was not corruption, but shock or outrage, then s. 2(4) did not operate as a bar to the prosecution. The unfortunate result was that the defendant was unable to raise a defence of 'public good', which is not available to the common law charge, despite the fact that there were witnesses available who would have testified to the artistic merits of the display. This might be a basis for challenge under the HRA 1998 in respect of any future similar prosecution. The protection of freedom of expression under Art. 10 of the ECHR clearly covers artistic expression and it ought, therefore, to be possible to argue for the artistic merit of items which might otherwise be considered indecent.

The *Gibson* decision clearly opens the door to the wider use of the common law offence against public displays, such as posters, book or magazine covers, compact disc covers, etc. In most such cases, however, the more appropriate charge would probably be under the Indecent Displays (Control) Act 1981 (see 8.9.1.1). This was not available in *Gibson* because the offence under the 1981 Act does not apply to displays within art galleries (s. 1(4)(b)).

8.6 Controls over films, DVDs, and videos

Both films and video-cassettes are subject to many of the same controls as books and magazines. For example, the publisher of a film, DVD or video-cassette may be liable for an offence under the Obscene Publications Acts, or for conspiracy to corrupt public morals. In addition, however, all of these types of media are also subject to a system of censorship, in which the BBFC plays a leading role. The system operates slightly differently as regards cinema and video (including DVD) recordings, however, so they need to be considered separately.

8.6.1 Cinemas

The control of the public showing of films is in the hands of local authorities. They have the responsibility under the Licensing Act 2003 for licensing premises for the public showing of films. The original legislation (Cinematograph Act 1909) gave this power primarily in order to control safety, but it quickly became used as a means of imposing controls over the content of what was exhibited. The current Act recognizes this explicitly by imposing a duty on the local authority issuing a licence to impose conditions prohibiting the admission of children to film exhibitions deemed unsuitable for children (s. 20). It also gives a power to impose similar conditions as regards adults. In practice local authorities generally rely on the classifications of films issued by the BBFC, as is recognized by s. 20 of the 2003 Act. The BBFC is an independent body, originally established by the film trade itself. It now has a quasi-official status as the body designated by the Home Office for the purpose of censoring videos, and its existence is indirectly acknowledged in this respect by the s. 20(4) of the Licensing Act 2003. It puts into practice a form of censorship control, specifying the minimum age of children who may view particular films, and in some cases refusing a certificate altogether. The Board may ask for cuts or other alterations to be made before it will grant a certificate for a particular age group, or at all. In *Mills v LCC* [1925] 1 KB 213 it was held that a local authority could in effect delegate its censorship powers to the BBFC, by requiring a licensee to follow the classifications of that body, provided that the authority retained the final say. At times a local authority will exert this power, usually to ban a film which has been passed by the BBFC. In 1988, for example, a number of local authorities banned the film *The Last Temptation of Christ* despite the fact that it had been granted a certificate by the BBFC. In 1997 the same fate befell *Crash*, a film based on J. G. Ballard's novel exploring the connections between car crashes and sex. (For the scheme of classification used by the BBFC, see 8.6.2.)

The local authorities' censorship powers were fully considered by the Court of Appeal in *R* v *Greater London Council, ex p Blackburn* [1976] 1 WLR 550. The Greater London Council (GLC) had allowed the exhibition of a film which had been refused a certificate by the BBFC. The Court of Appeal re-affirmed the decision in *Mills* v *LCC* as to the relationship between the BBFC and the local authority, and that there is no compulsion to censor films for adults as opposed to children. If, however, the local authority does exercise censorship in relation to adults it must not do so in a way which might allow the exhibition of a film which would amount to an offence under the criminal law. At the time of the *Blackburn* case films were governed by the common law indecency offences rather than the Obscene Publications Acts, and so the GLC's use of a test based on the likelihood of a film 'depraving and corrupting' its audience was held to be *ultra vires*. By virtue of the Criminal Law Act 1977, films are now subject to the Obscene Publications Acts, so a test based on this wording would now be acceptable. In practice, however, as we have seen, local authorities are content to leave most decisions to the BBFC.

There are also special provisions covering 'sex cinemas' in the Local Government (Miscellaneous Provisions) Act 1982. These are dealt with at 8.9.1.2.

8.6.2 The Video Recordings Acts 1984 and 2010

In August 2009 an issue arose in relation to the validity of the 1984 Act. The Department for Culture, Media, and Sport announced that at the time of its passage through Parliament the Act, and in particular regulations made under it, had not been referred to the European Commission, as they should have been because of their potential affect on the free movement of goods within the European Community. The Act was said to be unenforceable, so that no prosecutions could be brought under it until it was re-enacted, which was expected to take three months. This was done through the Video Recordings Act 2010, which came into force on 21 January 2010. The government received legal advice that those who had been convicted in the previous 25 years of the Act's operation would not be able to challenge their convictions. The accuracy of this conclusion was disputed in *Interfact Ltd* v *Liverpool City Council* [2010] EWHC 1604 (Admin), [2011] QB 744. The Court of Appeal, however, rejected the appeal principally on the basis that no injustice had been done to those convicted during the period when the 1984 Act was presumed by everyone to be validly in force. The Supreme Court subsequently refused leave to appeal against this decision.

The boom in the sale and rental market for video-cassettes during the 1980s brought with it concerns over the content of some videos. Up until 1984, videos sold or rented for use in the home were simply subject to the Obscene Publications Acts and the other relevant statutory and common law offences noted at 8.5. All these offences still apply. In 1983, however, a campaign was started, led by various pressure groups and sections of the press, against so-called 'video-nasties'. These were videos of films such as *Driller Killer, I Spit on Your Grave*, and *Death Trap*. They were all films which contained scenes of extreme violence, sometimes combined with sex. Some were the subject of prosecutions under the Obscene Publications Acts, but juries were inconsistent in their verdicts on them. Research findings (the methodology of which was later shown to be very suspect) were then produced purporting to show that as many as 37 per cent of children aged under seven had seen one of these videos. The issue was taken up by Graham Bright, MP, who introduced a Private Members' Bill to deal with the problem. With government support, this eventually became the Video Recordings Act 1984. (For a full account of the events leading up to this see M. Barker (ed.), *The Video Nasties* (London: Pluto Press, 1984).)

It is no doubt true that there were some very distasteful films circulating on video at the time, and that the Obscene Publications Act was not providing a consistent response to them. The Video Recordings Act 1984, however, goes much further than the problem of video-nasties. It in effect introduced a comprehensive censorship system for all videos supplied to the public. The system also applies to DVDs. In what follows all references to 'videos' or 'video-cassettes' should be taken to include DVDs unless the context suggests otherwise.

There are only very narrow exceptions to the system, relating to education, sport, religion, or music (s. 2(1)). Even these categories lose their exemption if the video depicts 'to any significant extent' human sexual activity (or acts of force or restraint associated with such activity), gross violence towards humans or animals, or human genital organs, or urinary or excretory functions (s. 2(2)). This restriction of the exemption was extended by s. 89 of the CJPOA 1994 to cover videos which depict 'techniques likely to be useful in the commission of offences', or 'criminal activity which is likely to any significant extent to stimulate or encourage the commission of offences'. Videos which, for example, show how to make explosives or depict high-speed car chases would be caught by these provisions. All videos other than exempted videos must be submitted for approval to a body designated by the Home Secretary (currently the BBFC) prior to distribution. This body, in deciding whether to grant a certificate, and if so, what age restrictions to place on the video, is required to have 'special regard' to the likelihood of the video 'being viewed in the home' (s. 4). At first sight this focus on the home might seem to impose a general standard of what is suitable for 'family' viewing. In fact, as Robertson and Nicol have argued (G. Robertson and A. Nicol, *Media Law*, 5th edn (London: Penguin, 2008), p. 833), the reason for including the phrase was because of the existence of the facility on video recorders (and now on DVD players) to replay passages over and over again, and, on some machines, to slow them down or 'freeze' particular shots. A scene that is viewed once on the cinema screen may, it is argued, have a very different impact if treated in this fashion. For this reason, films which have been given a particular classification in the cinema may receive a more restrictive one, or only receive the same one after cutting, when released on video. This aspect of the Act, however, does seem to encourage the censor to take an unusual interest in what people do within their own homes. After all, passages in books can be re-read an infinite number of times, and photographs can be pored over at much greater length than is likely in relation to a video, yet no particular account has ever been taken of this factor. Indeed, when the removal of censorship on the theatre was being debated in Parliament during the passage of the Theatres Act 1968 (see 8.7.1), those who wished to retain the existing system argued that the theatre needed greater control than books, because what was done in the theatre was done in public, whereas books were generally read in the privacy of one's own home. Yet the theatrical experience is if anything more transitory than the cinema.

Further guidance as to how the BBFC should exercise its powers is given by s. 4A which was inserted by s. 90 of the CJPOA 1994. Section 4A(1) requires the censor to:

> ...have special regard...to any harm that may be caused to potential viewers or, through their behaviour, to society by the manner in which the work deals with—
>
> (a) criminal behaviour;
>
> (b) illegal drugs;
>
> (c) violent behaviour or incidents;
>
> (d) horrific behaviour or incidents; or
>
> (e) human sexual activity.

This places the focus of the censor's concern on the harm caused by the video in terms of its effect on viewers or their behaviour. Rather than concentrating on the type of material contained in the video itself (e.g. does it depict sexual violence?), or on whether it is obscene, or shocking and disgusting, the censor is to 'have special regard' to how a viewer would react after watching it. The approach is 'harm-based' rather than 'morality-based', but the definition used, incorporating the vague phrase 'harm...to society', is not at all precise. These criteria leave the BBFC with a very wide discretion in deciding how to use its powers to censor and classify.

The BBFC currently uses the following categories of classification for videos:

- U Universal: Suitable for all
- Uc Universal: Particularly suitable for pre-school children
- PG Parental guidance: Some scenes may be unsuitable for young children
- 12: Suitable only for persons of 12 years or over
- 15: Suitable only for persons of 15 years and over
- 18: Suitable only for persons of 18 years and over
- R18: Suitable only for restricted distribution through segregated premises to which no one under 18 is admitted.

In relation to films to be shown in the cinema, '12A' replaces the '12' category. No one under 12 years may see a film in this category in a cinema unless accompanied by an adult.

It is an offence under the 1984 Act to supply an unclassified video-cassette or DVD, or to supply a classified cassette or DVD to a person under the age for which it is deemed suitable. The penalties for these offences were originally purely financial (fines of up to £20,000 on summary conviction), but since 1994 include the possibility of imprisonment (up to two years on indictment) (s. 88 of the CJPOA 1994). The supply does not have to be for gain: lending an unclassified video to a friend will constitute the offence. On the other hand, certain supplies are exempt, for example gifts, or supply for the purposes of broadcasting (s. 3). As regards videos classified as 'R18', it was held in *Interfact Ltd* v *Liverpool City Council* [2005] EWHC 995 (Admin), [2005] 1 WLR 3118 that the supply must take place 'face to face'—i.e. in the premises authorized for the purpose (in this case a licensed sex shop—for which see 8.9.1.2). Telephone sales or mail order supplies were not permitted.

There is a right of appeal against a decision of the BBFC, by the person who submitted the video (who will usually be the distributor), but not by any other interested party such as an author or director: s. 4. The Video Appeals Committee (VAC) is independent in the sense that it does not comprise members of the BBFC, but it is selected by the BBFC. It allows legal representation, may sit in public, and gives reasoned judgments. In 2000 the BBFC and the VAC came into conflict over the licensing of videos containing detailed scenes of actual, rather than simulated, sexual intercourse. The Board thought that seven videos of this type should be denied a certificate, but the VAC ruled that they should be given R18 certification, allowing them to be sold in licensed sex shops. One member of the VAC was reported as describing them as '[v]iagra without the damage to the liver'. The BBFC sought judicial review of the VAC's decision. In *R* v *Video Appeals Committee of the BBFC, ex p BBFC, The Times*, 7 June 2000, the High Court held, however, that the VAC had properly taken account of all the relevant factors, including s. 4A and the risk that children might gain access to the videos. The decision was not one which no reasonable decision maker could have reached, nor was there any error in law. There was therefore no basis for intervention by the court, and the VAC's decision should stand. The immediate response from the Home Secretary was that the law would need to be tightened. No such action has, as yet, been taken, however.

The BBFC is in practice mainly concerned with sex and violence, or both. In some cases, however, it has strayed into other areas. In 1989, a video entitled *Visions of Ecstasy* concerning St Teresa was refused a certificate by the Board on the grounds that it was blasphemous, and this decision was upheld by a majority of the VAC. The committee felt that it could not allow a certificate to be granted to a film, the publication of which might constitute a criminal offence, but they were perhaps being rather cautious, given the infrequency with which the blasphemy laws have been used in recent times. Nevertheless the Board's view was, as we have seen (see 8.2) upheld by the ECtHR: *Wingrove* v *United Kingdom*. In 1990 the Board decided to refuse a certificate to *International Guerrillas*, which contained a clearly libellous portrayal of the author Salman Rushdie. The VAC on this occasion reversed the Board's decision, on the basis that it was unlikely that proceedings for criminal libel would be taken. Rushdie himself was in support of this decision.

The result of the 'video-nasty' scare, and the consequent Video Recordings Act 1984, is an intrusive and fussy system of censorship, and it is doubtful whether it has any significant beneficial effect on the moral health of the nation. Those who seek hard-core porn can no doubt still find what they want on the black market in unclassified DVDs, or on the internet. Aficionados of the films of Alfred Hitchcock, however, were at one time only allowed a bowdlerized version of *Psycho* to view at home, because of the intervention of the BBFC (G. Robertson and A. Nicol, *Media Law*, 3rd edn (London: Penguin, 1992), p. 592).

8.7 **Controls over live performances**

There are two sets of controls which are relevant to the content of live performances. One set is to be found in the Theatres Act 1968, the other in the common law offences of presenting an indecent exhibition, or keeping a disorderly house. Which is applicable will depend on the type of performance. If it is a 'play' or a 'ballet' then the Theatres Act 1968 will apply. If it is not, then the common law offences will apply.

8.7.1 **The Theatres Act 1968**

This piece of legislation was passed following the recommendations of a joint Parliamentary committee that the previous system of theatre censorship operated by the Lord Chamberlain should be abolished ('Joint Committee on Censorship of the Theatre', HMSO, 1967). At a time when the theatre was exploring its limits in the 1950s and 1960s through the work of playwrights such as John Osborne, Edward Bond, Joe Orton, and Harold Pinter, the restrictive pre-censorship of the Lord Chamberlain was seen as old-fashioned and stifling. Apart from anything else, the Chamberlain's insistence (as required by the Theatres Act 1843) on a script to approve, prevented any improvised work from being lawfully presented. The Committee recommended that instead the theatre should become subject to the control of the criminal law, in the same way as books and magazines.

As noted at 8.7 the Act applies to 'plays'. Section 18(1) defines a play as a dramatic piece where what is done by one or more persons actually present and performing 'involves the *playing of a role*' (emphasis added). It also includes 'any ballet', whether or not the performance involves the 'playing of a role'. The effect of this definition is that live performances in the form of singing, dancing (other than ballet), striptease, or monologue (as by a 'stand-up comedian') are all unlikely to fall within the scope of the Act. Although the definition is not without ambiguity (would it include a puppet show, for example?), and despite the fact that 'ballet' is not further defined, it does not seem to have caused problems in practice.

The main offence under the Act is to be found in s. 2, which prohibits the presentation of an obscene performance of a play. 'Obscenity' is defined in the same terms as under the Obscene Publications Act 1959, that is as a tendency to deprave and corrupt a likely audience. It is the performance rather than the script that must be considered. The offence is, however, committed by the presenter or director of the performance, rather than by the actors.

There is a defence of public good in s. 3, in similar terms to s. 4 of the Obscene Publications Act 1959, though the list of 'interests' is appropriately amended, and excludes the troublesome phrase 'other objects of general concern' which led to difficulties under the 1959 Act (see 8.5.1.3).

Use of the common law, including indecency and conspiracy offences, against 'plays' is excluded by s. 2(4).

Prosecutions under the Act are subject to the approval of the Attorney-General (s. 8). He has shown great reluctance to initiate prosecutions, despite having had a number of productions referred to him (e.g. *Oh! Calcutta!* (1971), *The Romans in*

Britain (1981)). In fact, there has only ever been one prosecution under the Act, in relation to a revue by Sebastian Kane entitled *Dee Jay,* and presented in Manchester (see *R v Brownson* [1971] Crim LR 551). It is not entirely clear why this production was singled out for prosecution, though the account later given by one of the performers (V. Nicholson and S. Smith, *Spend, Spend, Spend!* (London: Jonathan Cape, 1977), pp. 163–6) suggests that some of the other performers taking part in simulated sex and rape scenes were very young (though over 16).

The fact that the Act has been so little used means that the theatre is in practice probably the least legally controlled of all visual media. Extra-legal controls, however, such as the need not to alienate local audiences, and the need to retain the approval of funding bodies, probably operate as a curb on any tendency to excess amongst theatrical producers. It may also be significant that theatre-going is a relatively expensive and predominantly middle-class activity.

8.7.2 Common law offences

The two common law offences which are relevant in this area are both closely related to the offence of outraging public decency, dealt with at 8.5.5.2. They both use the common law test of 'indecency' rather than the 'deprave and corrupt' test.

8.7.2.1 Presenting an indecent exhibition

This derives from *R v Saunders* (1875) 1 QBD 15 in which two showmen were convicted of keeping a booth on Epsom Downs for the purpose of presenting an indecent exhibition to those who paid. It has also been used against non-sexual exhibitions, such as the display of a photograph of a man suffering from eruptive sores in a herbalist's window (*R v Grey* (1864) 4 F & F 72). An example of its use against a live sex show can be found in a case in 1975 which involved a striptease and lesbian act by three women culminating in their having sexual intercourse with three of the customers (*The Times,* 21 January 1975). (It was, of course, also this offence which was used in *R v Gibson,* discussed at 8.5.5.2.)

8.7.2.2 Keeping a disorderly house

This offence has been used in relation to performances by strippers and 'exotic dancers', both male and female (see, e.g. *R v Farmer and Griffin* (1974) 58 Cr App R 229 and *Moores v DPP* [1991] 4 All ER 521). The definition of the offence approved by the Court of Appeal in *R v Quinn and Bloom* [1962] 2 QB 245, seems to have achieved general acceptance. It was there defined as:

> ...a house conducted contrary to law and good order in that matters are performed or exhibited of such a character that their performance or exhibition in a place of common resort (a) amounts to an outrage of public decency or (b) tends to corrupt or deprave or (c) is otherwise calculated to injure the public interest so as to call for condemnation and punishment.

In practice the element of the offence most commonly relied on is (a). The word 'keeping' implies some element of persistence. This was confirmed in *Moores v DPP,* where evidence of a single indecent performance was held to be insufficient to constitute the offence. As with the Theatres Act, the offence is primarily directed against the presenter of the performance, rather than the performers themselves.

Few would argue that the restriction of shows of the kind under consideration in *Moores* v *DPP*, which involved a male 'exotic dancer' having his penis rubbed with oil by a female member of the audience, would be a significant blow to artistic freedom. To the extent, however, that these offences are used against shows put on for a willing audience, and which are not thought to be depraving and corrupting, there does not seem to be any clear public benefit involved sufficient to outweigh the restriction of personal freedom.

8.8 Controls over broadcasting

Section 162 of the Broadcasting Act 1990 made television and radio subject, for the first time, to the Obscene Publications Act 1959. This change, however, seems unlikely to be of great practical significance. It is hard to believe that a jury would convict any of the output of the mainstream terrestrial or satellite channels as having a tendency to deprave and corrupt. Surveys of audience concern regularly show that more offence is caused by bad language in television programmes than by sex or violence. It is much more possible that the range of programmes which have become available as a result of the increase in satellite broadcasting will include obscene material. The problem here will be that the publisher of the material will almost certainly be based outside the jurisdiction, and if the origin of the broadcasts is from within Europe, the scope for action will be limited by the 1989 EC Directive on Broadcasting. The issue was raised in 1992 by the broadcast from Denmark of an 'adult' television channel under the name 'Red Hot Dutch' (see F. Coleman and S. McMurtrie, 'Too Hot to Handle', (1993) 143 NLJ 10). Rather than acting directly against the broadcasters, the government made it an offence to deal in the decoding equipment necessary to receive the transmissions. An initial challenge to the legality of this under European law failed in the English courts, and any further action was precluded by the subsequent insolvency of the broadcasting company. It may well be that international conventions and co-operation will turn out to be more effective controls in these circumstances, as opposed to the English criminal law offences relating to obscenity and indecency. There is a power under s. 329 of the Communications Act 2003 for the Secretary of State to proscribe certain foreign broadcasts, at the instigation of the Office of Communications (Ofcom), but this does not apply to satellite broadcasts.

Of more practical significance to domestic broadcasting is the supervisory regime operated by Ofcom under the Communications Act 2003. Such a regime was initially operated under the Broadcasting Act 1990 by the Broadcasting Standards Council, and then under the Broadcasting Act 1996 by the Broadcasting Standards Commission. Section 319 of the Communications Act 2003 imposes a duty on Ofcom to issue codes setting standards for the content of programmes. These must take into account, among other things, the need to protect persons under the age of 18 and to protect members of the public generally from 'offensive and harmful material' (s. 319(2)). In setting the standards Ofcom should also take account of the likely size and composition of audiences for the programmes and the likely expectation of that audience as to the nature of the programmes' content (s. 319(4)). The possibility of a person being unintentionally exposed to the content must also be recognized. Ofcom must have a procedure for dealing with complaints which might arise from alleged non-observance of the standards set.

In relation to the previous regimes, the Broadcasting Standards Council considered a fair number of complaints, and issued its adjudications in monthly bulletins. It was criticized that in a number of cases it 'displayed both an ignorance of the nature of television, and an intention to damage it as a medium for providing education, information and entertainment' (G. Robertson and A. Nicol, *Media Law*, 3rd edn, p. 608). (See *Media Law*, 3rd edn, pp. 606–52 for a full account of the operation of the Broadcasting Standards Council, and the enforcement of its Codes of Practice.) The Commission seemed to attract less criticism than the Council. In the sexual area its Code was fairly permissive, simply requiring broadcasters to be sensitive to their different audiences and to the way in which issues are handled. The only matters which were specifically prohibited under the Code were broadcasts in fiction programmes of actual sexual intercourse, and any broadcast of explicit sexual conduct between humans and animals.

The current Code issued by Ofcom took effect in February 2011. Other than in relation to what should be broadcast before the 'watershed'—i.e. 9 p.m.—the Code is not very proscriptive. It lists sex and sexual violence among the types of material in relation to which care must be taken to ensure that any offence caused is 'justified by the context' (para. 2.3). 'Context' is stated to include:

- the editorial content of the programme, programmes or series;
- the service on which the material is broadcast;
- the time of broadcast;
- what other programmes are scheduled before and after the programme or programmes concerned;
- the degree of harm or offence likely to be caused by the inclusion of any particular sort of material in programmes generally or programmes of a particular description;
- the likely size and composition of the potential audience and likely expectation of the audience;
- the extent to which the nature of the content can be brought to the attention of the potential audience, for example by giving information; and
- the effect of the material on viewers or listeners who may come across it unawares.

In *R (ProLife Alliance)* v *The British Broadcasting Corporation* [2003] UKHL 23, [2003] 2 All ER 977, the statutory obligation on broadcasters to ensure that programmes did not offend against 'good taste or decency' (s. 6 Broadcasting Act 1990; see now the reference to protection from 'offensive and harmful' material, Communications Act 2003, s. 3(2)(e)) was considered in relation to a party election broadcast. The appellants had wanted to screen such a broadcast which would have included graphic images of abortions. The BBC and independent television broadcasters had refused to show it. The Court of Appeal ([2002] EWCA 297, [2002] 2 All ER

756) held that 'the freedom of political speech to be enjoyed by a credited party at a public election...could not be interfered with save on most pressing grounds, and such grounds will rarely be shown by appeal to considerations of taste or decency alone'. It would take an extreme case, probably involving 'gratuitous sensationalism or dishonesty' for a refusal to transmit the broadcast to be justified. This was not such a case, and the broadcast should have been transmitted. The House of Lords, however, disagreed with the Court of Appeal. It held (Lord Scott dissenting) that the issue of whether the content of party election broadcasts should be subject to the same test of offensiveness as other broadcasts was not before the court. Parliament had imposed a restriction on broadcasters and had chosen to apply the restriction as much to party broadcasts as to other programmes. The only question was therefore whether the broadcasters had applied the right standard in this case. In the view of the House of Lords there was nothing in the reasoning of the broadcasters or in their overall decision to suggest that they applied an inappropriate standard.

The House was not prepared to engage in the issue of whether it was appropriate, in the light of Art. 10 of the ECHR to impose the offensive restriction on party broadcasts. If that issue had been before the court it would have involved a consideration of the possibility of issuing a declaration of incompatibility and the relevant government minister would have needed to be given notice, probably being joined as a party to the proceedings.

This is a rather unsatisfactory decision, turning, as it seems, more on the way in which the case was presented to the court than on the substantive issue of what the controls should be over the content of party election broadcasts. The House of Lords refused to use Art. 10 to read into the legislation a different standard for such broadcasts. As a result it reached a decision which, while logical within its own terms, failed to take account of the broader issues raised by Art. 10 and the ECtHR case law on its application to political expression. It is arguable that the Court of Appeal's more imaginative approach is more in keeping with the spirit of the HRA 1998 and the associated jurisprudence on the ECHR.

8.9 General controls

This section looks at two types of general control which are not specifically linked to a particular type of publication or article. The first relates to the distribution of sexual material, and covers controls over premises. The second type of control considered here is that covering the import of materials, and exercised by HM Revenue and Customs (HMRC).

8.9.1 Control over premises

8.9.1.1 The Indecent Displays (Control) Act 1981

This Act resulted from a Private Members' Bill, which received government support, and which picked up one of the concerns about pornography which was emphasized by the Williams Committee, 'Report of the Committee on Obscenity and Film Censorship'. The Williams Committee had found that an issue which raised widespread objection was the display of pornographic magazines on the shelves of general newsagents, and in the windows of sex shops ('Report of the Committee on Obscenity and Film Censorship', para. 9.1). In other words, what might be termed the 'public nuisance' aspect of pornography. Accordingly, the Indecent Displays (Control) Act 1981 makes it an offence to display publicly 'any indecent matter'. The word indecent is not defined, and so the approach outlined at 8.4.2, based on the idea of what is found 'shocking', 'disgusting', or offensive, will be used. It was accepted in the debates on the Act that the vagueness of this approach might well result in magistrates in different parts of the country applying different standards. This was not thought to be a significant problem, either because it was right that local standards of decency should be applied, so that what was acceptable in London might be unacceptable in Manchester, or because the Act was only concerned with public displays, and would not restrict the availability of any material. The possibility of such diversity of standards might form the basis of a challenge under the HRA 1998 because the behaviour made criminal would not be sufficiently 'prescribed by law' as required by the ECHR (discussed at 8.4.2). Although it was suggested there that a degree of vagueness in the definition of offences in this area may be acceptable, given the approach taken by the ECtHR, if it were to be clearly established that courts in different areas were applying radically different standards, then the argument would become much stronger.

The Indecent Displays (Control) Act 1981 covers the display of any matter, other than the 'actual human body' (s. 1(5)). By this is meant the human body itself, rather than a portrayal of it. Live displays of the human body were thought to be adequately covered by the offences noted at 8.7. On the other hand, pictures, book and magazine covers, drawings, photographs, sex aids, and slogans will all be within the scope of the Act.

The display must be 'public', which means that it must be visible from a place to which the public have, or are permitted to have, access (whether on payment or otherwise) (s. 1(3)). This will include the inside of shops. There is no public good defence, but there are specific exemptions for museums and art galleries, cinemas, and matter included within either a television broadcast, or the performance of a 'play' within the meaning of s. 18 of the Theatres Act 1968 (see 8.7.1). In addition, there is no offence if members of the public can only see the display by paying an entrance fee specifically to do so, or if it is in a shop, or part of a shop which cannot be entered without passing a warning notice (s. 1(3)). These latter two exceptions only apply if people under the age of 18 are excluded from entry. The text of the warning notice which must be displayed to give protection to a shop is set out in s. 1(6), together with a requirement that it must be 'easily legible'.

Although the Indecent Displays (Control) Act 1981 was widely welcomed, it cannot be said that it has had any very significant practical effects. The range of sex magazines to be seen on the top shelf of most newsagents is just as wide, if not wider, as in 1981. It is true that sex shop window displays have ceased to be a problem, but this is more a consequence of the more general provisions controlling sex shops in the Local Government (Miscellaneous Provisions) Act 1982 (see 8.9.1.2), than of the Indecent Displays (Control) Act 1981. On the other hand, the Act has been used to prosecute, for example, the showing of a sex video on a coach travelling up a motorway, which was visible from other vehicles, and the wearers of T-shirts containing indecent words or pictures. It is unlikely that these are the kinds of behaviour which the sponsors of the Act had in mind as needing control.

8.9.1.2 The Local Government (Miscellaneous Provisions) Act 1982

At the start of the 1980s there were some 160 establishments in the Soho area of London which were engaged in one way or another in the commercial exploitation of sex. The Westminster City Council had shown that it was possible to use planning controls against some of these activities. Shops which had set up booths in which individuals could watch videos, for example, were found to have 'changed their use' under the planning laws from being a shop to being a 'cinema'. As a result, this type of activity was effectively outlawed. Sex shops, as such, however, were not in any separate planning category from other shops. A change from a clothing shop to a sex shop, therefore, was subject to no planning control. The proliferation of sex shops in the Soho area was thought to be threatening its whole character, as most other commercial enterprises were being driven out. Moreover, there was concern in other parts of the country that sex shops could be opened anywhere, even in close proximity to a school or a church, and there was nothing that could be done about it. The response of the government was not to amend the planning laws, but to legislate for a separate licensing scheme for 'sex establishments'.

Section 3 of the Local Government (Miscellaneous Provisions) Act 1982 (the 1982 Act) empowers a local authority (generally the district council) to set up a licensing scheme for sex establishments in its area. 'Sex establishment' means a sex cinema or sex shop. Cinemas have really ceased to be a problem since the enactment of the wider licensing provisions originally contained in the Cinemas Act 1985 and now in the Licensing Act 2003. The concentration will, therefore, be on 'sex shops' here. The detailed provisions of the licensing scheme are set out in Sch. 3 to the 1982 Act. Under these, a sex shop is defined as premises used for a business which consists 'to a significant degree' in dealing in 'sex articles' or 'other things intended for use in connection with, or for the purpose of stimulating or encouraging: (i) sexual activity; or (ii) acts of force or restraint which are associated with sexual activity' (para. 4(1)). 'Sex article' is itself the subject of a rather complicated definition in paras 4(3) and 4(4). These state that a sex article means:

(a) anything made for use in connection with, or for the purpose of stimulating or encouraging (i) sexual activity or (ii) acts of force or restraint associated with sexual activity; or

(b) any article containing or embodying matter to be read or looked at, or any recording of sound or vision, which is concerned primarily with the portrayal of, or primarily deals with or relates to, or is intended to stimulate or encourage, sexual activity or acts of force or restraint associated with sexual activity, or is concerned primarily with the portrayal of, or primarily deals with or relates to, genital organs, or urinary or excretory functions.

As this definition shows, the approach in the 1982 Act, unlike that of most of the other legal rules which have been considered in this chapter, is not to attempt to define on the basis of the effect of the material. It is irrelevant whether it depraves and corrupts, or shocks and disgusts. The approach is instead to try to describe the material in terms of its content, or what it is used for. As will be noted, the definition of 'sex article' is wide enough to cover books, magazines, photographs, films, videos, audio tapes, records, compact discs, sex aids (vibrators, dildos, etc.), bondage equipment, and probably many other things, for those with vivid enough imaginations! It is certainly wide enough to cover condoms or other birth control equipment, and a special exemption has had to be included (in para. 6(2)) to exclude trade in such items from the scope of the licensing scheme.

The definition of 'sex shop' under the Schedule fell to be considered in *Lambeth London Borough Council* v *Grewal* (1985) 82 Cr App R 301. The council had introduced a licensing scheme under the 1982 Act. The defendant owned a shop which sold 'newspapers, magazines, children's books and comics, greetings cards, toys, ice-creams, stationery, toiletries, tobacco, dairy produce and groceries'. Amongst the magazines were some which could clearly be regarded as 'sex articles'. The defendant was advised by council officials that if he intended to display more than five sex articles he should apply for a sex shop licence. He failed to do so, and on a number of occasions, 16–20 different sex magazines were found on display. He was charged with operating a sex shop without a licence. In the Divisional Court the argument turned on the phrase 'to a significant degree', in that the Schedule, as we have seen, defines a sex shop as one where the business consists 'to a significant degree' in dealing in sex articles. The Divisional Court rejected the prosecutor's argument that 'significant' here meant simply more than *de minimis*. The following approach was, rather diffidently, suggested by Mustill LJ (p. 307):

> The word 'significant' has more than one meaning. It is capable, in some contexts of meaning 'more than trifling'. It does not have this meaning in the present context. A higher standard is set: how much higher cannot be prescribed by any rule of thumb. The ratio between the sexual and other aspects of the business will always be material. So also will the absolute quantity of sales. Since the fundamental question is whether the establishment is a 'sex shop'..., the court will no doubt find it appropriate to consider the character of the remainder of the business. The nature of the display can be a relevant factor, and the nature of the articles themselves will also be material, since the definition...covers a wide spectrum of offensiveness. It would be wrong to say in law that any single factor is decisive.

Applying this approach to the facts, and bearing in mind that it was the proportion of the business that was devoted to sex articles that was important, the court found that, since the weekly turnover of about £45 in relation to sex articles amounted to less than 1.5 per cent of the shop's business, it could not be said that the Crown Court's view that this was not a sex shop was wrong.

The result of this case is that local councils cannot operate a strict rule that a certain number of articles on display turns a shop into a sex shop. The test will have to relate to the proportion of the shop's business that is devoted to this type of item.

Once a shop is classified as a sex shop, then a licence will be required. The local authority is entitled to refuse a licence on a wide range of grounds, set out in para. 12 of the Schedule. Some of the grounds are mandatory, for example if the applicant is under 18, or not resident in the United Kingdom (para. 12(1)). Others are discretionary, and may relate to such matters as the suitability of the applicant, the character of the locality, or the number of sex shops in that locality (para. 12(3)). The authority is specifically given the possibility of deciding that the appropriate number of sex shops in a particular locality is 'nil' (para. 12(4)).

If a licence is granted it may, and almost certainly will, be subject to conditions relating to such matters as the hours of opening, window displays (or lack of them!), and visibility of the interior to passers-by. There is the possibility of some overlap with the Indecent Displays (Control) Act 1981 here, but compliance with the terms of a licence will not provide a defence to a charge under that Act, nor will the holding of a licence provide any immunity against the Obscene Publications Acts. Licensed sex shops can be, and not infrequently are, the subject of police searches under s. 3 of the Obscene Publications Act 1959 (see 8.5.1.2).

There is no indication in the 1982 Act of the fee that may be charged for the issue of a licence. This has led some local authorities, including Westminster (in relation to Soho), to set fees of several thousand pounds a year. A licence may be withdrawn at any time on certain of the grounds which would have justified the refusal of a licence in the first place (though not those relating to the nature of the locality; para. 17). In any case, all licences must be renewed annually, allowing the local authority close control over sex shops.

This Act can be said to have been a considerable success in achieving its objectives. In Soho, for example, the number of sex establishments was reduced from 160 plus, to just six. In other parts of the country there has ceased to be concern at the proliferation, and location, of sex shops. Moreover, this form of control is less restrictive of freedom of expression than others considered in this chapter, in that it simply controls the outlets. People who wish to buy sex articles are still able to do so. They are simply put to the relatively minor inconvenience of perhaps having to travel a little further in order to find a licensed sex shop.

An HRA 1998 challenge to the licensing system under the equivalent legislation in Northern Ireland (i.e. the Local Government (Miscellaneous Provisions) (Northern Ireland) Order 1985 (SI 1985/1208)) was nevertheless attempted in *Belfast City Council* v *Miss Behavin' Ltd* [2007] UKHL 19, [2007] 1 WLR 1420. The Council had rejected the claimant's application for a licence to run a sex shop, on the basis that it had decided that there should be no sex shops in the locality proposed, and because of the identity of some of those involved with the company making the application. The House of Lords rejected the challenge that this decision had ignored the claimant's rights under Art. 10. It held that the question was whether the Council's action had actually interfered with the claimant's Art. 10 rights, not, as the Northern Ireland Court of Appeal had suggested, whether the Council had given proper consideration to those rights. On the substantive issue, the House noted that, as Lady Hale put it (para. 38):

> ... [t]here are far more important human rights in this world that the right to sell pornographic literature and images in the back streets of Belfast. Pornography comes well below celebrity gossip in the hierarchy of speech which deserves the protection of the law.

There were good reasons for the Council's decision to decide that 'nil' was the appropriate number of sex shops in this part of Belfast, because of the 'proximity of certain public buildings and shops of particular attraction to children, and of places of worship' (per Lord Neuberger, para. 95). Overall, the infringement of the applicant's Art. 10 rights was not disproportionate. The legitimate objective of the control was, presumably, protecting morals, as allowed for by Art. 10(2), and as suggested by Lord Rodger (para. 19) though the majority of the House preferred to talk in general terms of 'proportionality'.

8.9.2 Import controls

One of the fears which recurs in public debates about pornography, particularly amongst politicians, is that of the influx of highly obscene material from overseas, originating in countries with less restrictive laws than ours.

The current controls are contained in the Customs Consolidation Act 1876 and the Customs and Excise Management Act 1979. Section 42 of the Customs Consolidation Act 1876 prohibits the import of:

> ...[i]ndecent or obscene prints, paintings, photographs, books, cards, lithographic or other engravings, or any other indecent or obscene articles.

In *Derrick* v *Commissioners of Customs and Excise* [1972] 1 All ER 993, this definition was held to be wide enough to cover cinematograph film (as being *eiusdem generis* with photographs) and no doubt it would also be interpreted as covering video-cassettes. It has also been held to cover sex aids, such as inflatable sex dolls (*Conegate* v *Commissioners of Customs and Excise* [1987] QB 254, discussed at 8.10).

Powers of forfeiture, together with related offences, are contained in s. 49 of and Sch. 3 to the Customs and Excise Management Act 1979.

It will be noted that the test in s. 42 of the Customs Consolidation Act 1876 is 'obscene or indecent'. 'Obscene' here has its dictionary meaning, rather than that of 'deprave and corrupt' (see 8.4.1). This means that a stricter control is available as regards the importing of 'articles' covered by the Obscene Publications Acts, than in relation to their publication. This has given rise to some potential conflict with the concept of free movement of goods under EU law. This is considered further in the next section (8.10). Robertson and Nicol (*Media Law*, 5th edn, p. 245) state that as a result HMRC officers do not now seize articles, whatever their country of origin, unless they would appear to fall within the Obscene Publications Act 1959 'deprave and corrupt' test. This is, however, a matter of practice rather than law, at least in relation to goods coming from outside the European Union.

8.10 European law

As indicated, there have been several cases which have concerned the application of the free movement of goods provisions of European Law to the importation of pornography into the United Kingdom.

Article 34 (originally Art. 30) of the Treaty on the Functioning of the European Union states that '[q]uantitative restrictions on imports and all measures having equivalent effect shall...be prohibited'. In *R* v *Henn* [1981] AC 850 it was argued that this meant that the rules restricting the importing of pornography into the United Kingdom were unlawful. The defendant had been convicted, in relation to the same material, under both the customs legislation, and the Obscene Publications Act 1959, and was appealing against those convictions. The House of Lords referred the issue to the European Court of Justice (ECJ). That Court ruled that the import restrictions applying to pornography did constitute a quantitative restriction within Art. 34. However, Art. 36 of the Treaty provides that the provisions of Art. 34 'shall not preclude prohibitions or restrictions on imports...justified on grounds of public morality...'. The ECJ took the view that the United Kingdom's restrictions came within those permitted by Art. 36. The House of Lords, therefore, upheld Henn's conviction.

The subject matter of the prosecution in *Henn* was films and magazines, which are clearly articles falling within the scope of the Obscene Publications Act 1959. A slightly different issue arose in *Conegate* v *Commissioners of Customs and Excise* [1987] QB 254. The objects which were seized in this case were life-size inflatable rubber sex-dolls, complete with 'orifices, one with a vibrator...attached to the head...'. Some 'sexy vacuum flasks' were also seized. In this case, the ECJ, applying the same Articles as in *Henn* came to the conclusion that the seizure of these items was contrary to European law. This was because, while it could not be said in *Henn* that there was any lawful trade within the United Kingdom in the items seized because of the Obscene Publications Act, that Act did not apply to the type of articles under consideration in *Conegate*. There were thus no restrictions within the United Kingdom on the manufacture or sale of such items. This prevented the UK government in this case relying on Art. 36 to justify the seizure. As the ECJ put it (para. 20):

> ...a member State may not rely on grounds of public morality within the meaning of Art. 36 of the Treaty in order to prohibit the importation of certain goods on the grounds that they are indecent or obscene, where the same goods may be manufactured freely on its territory and marketed on its territory subject only to an absolute prohibition on their transmission by post, a restriction on their public display and, in certain regions, a system of licensing of premises for the sale of those goods to customers aged 18 or over.

It is for this reason that, as noted at 8.9.2, customs officers now only seize goods which appear to be subject to the Obscene Publications Act 1959.

A further attempt to use European law in this area was made in *R* v *Bow St Magistrates, ex p Noncyp* [1990] 1 QB 123. This concerned the seizure by Customs officers of books destined for a bookshop called *Gay's the Word* in London. They were of a homosexual nature, with titles such as *Men Loving Themselves* and *Below the Belt*. The defence argument in this case was that the Customs officers should have taken into account the possibility of a defence based on the defence of public good under s. 4 of the Obscene Publications Act 1959. The Court of Appeal did not feel the need in this case to refer the issue to the ECJ. Applying the principles from *Henn* and *Conegate* it took the view that, as long as there was a restriction on the trade in the United Kingdom as regards articles of the type seized (in this case books with a sexual content), then they could be forfeited provided that they were 'obscene' within the meaning of s. 42 of the Customs Consolidation Act 1876. There was no need, therefore, to consider the possible availability of a public good defence under s. 4 of the Obscene Publications Act 1959.

8.11 **Proposals for reform**

There have been many attempts over the years to suggest ways in which the laws in this area should be reformed. In practice, however, the changes in the law which have taken place have been reactions to particular perceived problems, and as a result piecemeal and lacking in coherence. It is disappointing that the most recent set of fully thought-through proposals for comprehensive reform should date from as long ago as 1979. These are the proposals of the Williams Committee. They are discussed here, not because there is any likelihood of those proposals being adopted, but as an example of one way in which the law could be redesigned, starting with a blank sheet, and arguing from basic principles.

The starting point for the Williams Committee was its acceptance of what it called 'the harm principle'. This is the idea, adapted from John Stuart Mill, that the law should only be used to prevent behaviour (in this case the publication of pornography) where it could be shown to cause harm to others. The Committee looked, therefore, at the available evidence of the harmful effects of pornography. It took, as another fundamental premise, that the presumption should be in favour of freedom, and the burden of proof in establishing harm should lie on those who wished to restrict expression. On this basis they concluded, as we have seen others have done (see 8.2), that the case was at best 'not proven'. The research evidence was equivocal, and it could not be said that any clear harm to individuals resulted from the reading of pornographic material, for example, encouraging criminal sexual activity. Nor was the Committee prepared to accept the alleged social or moral harms resulting from it, nor the idea of 'harm' caused to the consumer alone, as justifying prohibition. This meant that the only harm of which they were prepared to take account, was harm to the participants in the production of pornographic films or photographs. Two possible types of harm of this kind were identified, and were summarized in s. 19 of the Committee's summary of its proposals ('Report of the Committee on Obscenity and Film Censorship', p. 161), which stated that prohibited material should consist of photographs and films whose production appears:

> ...to have involved the exploitation for sexual purposes of any person where either
>
> (a) that person appears from the evidence as a whole to have been at the relevant time under the age of sixteen, or
>
> (b) the material gives reason to believe that actual physical harm was inflicted on that person.

There should be no restriction on the production or publication of any material falling outside these two categories. On the other hand, the Committee found a 'remarkable balance of opinion' in favour of controlling the availability and display of pornographic material. This led the Committee to accept that the availability of certain types of material should be 'restricted'. The test of restriction would be whether its unrestricted availability would offend a reasonable person. Three points must be noted about this test. First, the standard is that of the reasonable person at any particular time, and is thus, as the Committee recognized, liable to change with changing social mores. Second, it is the offensiveness resulting from the material's free availability, rather than its inherent character, that justifies restriction. Third, the offensiveness refers not only to what is actually visible when, for example, a magazine is displayed on a shelf, but also to the content of the material. So the fact that the cover of a magazine is less explicit than the material inside, as is usually the case, would not protect it from restriction. As we have seen, the Indecent Displays (Control) Act 1981, which attempted to achieve some of the same objectives as the Williams Committee's restriction controls, does not operate in this way, but concentrates solely on what is visible to the public. Under the Committee's proposals, restricted material would only be available in specialist shops, from which persons under 18 would be excluded, and which would be required to display warning notices.

The third area considered by the Committee was film censorship. Here many commentators felt that the Committee lost its nerve. Rather than simply applying the principles outlined above to films, the Committee, concerned about the willingness of some film makers to 'exploit a taste for torture and violence', advocated the retention of censorship, with, however, specific statutory guidelines as to how the powers should operate (proposals 35–56, 'Report of the Committee on Obscenity and Film Censorship', pp. 163–6).

It should be noted that none of the Committee's proposals would apply to written as opposed to pictorial material. The printed word, since it cannot involve either of the harms recognized by the Committee, and was not felt to be capable of being 'offensive' within the Committee's definition, would not be subject to prohibition or restriction. For this reason, among others, the Committee rejected any idea of a 'public good' defence, since it was in relation to printed matter that such a defence was likely, in the Committee's view, to have most justification.

The reaction to the Committee's report was mixed. Conservatives saw it as too liberal, whereas liberals thought that it did not go far enough. There would also be considerable problems in the practical operation of the test of 'offensiveness' (see R. Stone, 'Obscenity Law Reform: Some Practical Problems' (1980) 130 NLJ 872). As a result, the report was shelved by the Conservative government of the day, and there seems no prospect of its being revived.

QUESTIONS

1 How should 'obscenity' and 'indecency' be defined? Would a definition which was based on 'offensiveness' rather than 'harm' be more satisfactory?

2 Was the ECtHR correct in the *Handyside* case to suggest that standards of 'obscenity' may legitimately be different in different countries? How does this fit with the idea of a universal right to freedom of expression?

3 Does the development of the internet mean that all attempts to control publications with a sexual or violent content are doomed to failure?

4 Why should possession of certain types of sexual photograph or film be an offence, even if there is no intention to publish, and they are held purely for the gratification of the possessor?

5 Why should films and DVDs be the subject of tighter control (in the form of pre-publication censorship) than any other media?

FURTHER READING

Assiter, A. and Carol, A. (eds) (1993), *Bad Girls and Dirty Pictures*, London: Pluto Press

Barker, M. (1984), *A Haunt of Fears*, London: Pluto Press

Barker, M. (ed.) (1984), *The Video Nasties*, London: Pluto Press

Blackstone, Sir William (1769), *Commentaries on the Laws of England*, Oxford: Clarendon Press

Coleman, F. and McMurtrie, S. (1993), 'Too Hot to Handle', (1993) 143 NLJ 10

Dworkin, A. (1981), *Pornography: Men Possessing Women*, London: Women's Press

Easton, S. M. (ed.) (1994), *The Problem of Pornography*, London: Routledge

Gillespie, A. (2004), 'Tinkering with Child Pornography', [2004] Crim LR 361

Hofler, A. (2006), 'Are the Victims of Lust Expendable?', (2006) 158 Crim Law 3

Home Office (2005), 'Consultation on the Possession of Extreme Pornographic Material', Home Office

Howitt, D. and Cumberbatch, G. (1990), *Pornography: Impacts and Influences*, London: Home Office

Itzin, C. (ed.) (1992), *Pornography: Women, Violence and Civil Liberties*, Oxford: Oxford University Press

Kearns, P. (2000), 'Obscene and Blasphemous Libel: Misunderstanding Art', [2000] Crim LR 652

Lewis, T. (2004) 'Human Earrings, Human Rights and Public Decency', (2004) 1 ELSLJ 50

McGlynn, C. and Rackley, E. (2007), 'Striking a Balance: Arguments for the Criminal Regulation of Extreme Pornography', [2007] Crim LR 677

Mackinnon, C. (1987), *Feminism Unmodified*, Cambridge, MA: Harvard University Press

Manchester, C. (1986), *Sex Shops and the Law*, Aldershot: Gower Publishing

Mill, J. S. (1962) (first published 1859), 'On Liberty', in Warnock, M. (ed.), *Utilitarianism*, London: Fontana

Nicholson, V. and Smith, S. (1977), *Spend, Spend, Spend!*, London: Jonathan Cape

Robertson, G. (1979), *Obscenity*, London: Weidenfeld & Nicolson

Robertson, G. and Nicol, A. (1992), *Media Law*, 3rd edn, London: Penguin

Robertson, G. and Nicol, A. (2008), *Media Law*, 5th edn, London: Penguin

Rowbottom, J. (2006), 'Obscenity Laws and the Internet: Targeting the Supply and Demand', [2006] Crim LR 97

Stone, R. (1977), 'Indecent Performances: the Law Commission's Proposals', (1977) 127 NLJ 452

Stone, R. (1980), 'Obscenity Law Reform: Some Practical Problems', (1980) 130 NLJ 872

Stone, R. (1986), 'Obscene Publications: The Problems Persist', [1986] Crim LR 139

Stone, R. (1995), 'Extending the Labyrinth: Part VII of the Criminal Justice and Public Order Act 1994', (1995) 58 MLR 389

White Paper (2002), 'Protecting the Public', Cm 5668, TSO

Williams Committee (1979), 'Report of the Committee on Obscenity and Film Censorship', Cmnd 7772, HMSO

9

Freedom of Assembly and Public Order

9.1 Introduction

No one who observed the events which occurred in Eastern Europe during the early 1990s or the 'Arab Spring' of 2011 can have any doubts as to the power of the demonstration as a political weapon. In Eastern Europe, the Solidarity movement in Poland was the precursor of much that followed, as in country after country people took to the streets to indicate that they had had enough of the existing political regime and that it was time for change, thus contributing to collapse of the Soviet Union and its influence. Similarly, in the first part of 1997 daily peaceful protests on the streets of Belgrade eventually produced a change in the Serbian government's attitude to the recognition of local elections. In 2005 the 'Orange Revolution' in the Ukraine, which led to the rerun of the presidential election, was substantially assisted by mass street demonstrations. On the other hand, pro-democracy demonstrations in Burma during 2007, led by Buddhist monks, were brought to an end by police and military action by the ruling regime. In 2011, demonstrations in Tunisia and Egypt led to largely peaceful regime change (though in Egypt the resulting government was again replaced, following demonstrations, by the intervention of the military). In other countries (e.g. Bahrain) demonstrations were put down with force, whereas in Libya and Syria a civil war resulted (though eventually resulting in a relatively stable situation in Libya).

In the UK we had an example in the 1980s of mass demonstrations playing at least a part in forcing a government to change course. The reform of local taxation which introduced the Community Charge (more commonly known as the 'Poll Tax') led to meetings, processions, and other demonstrations around the country, and contributed to the opposition which forced the then Conservative government to change what had been put forward as a central policy; a change which furthermore played some part in the enforced resignation of the Prime Minister at the time, Margaret Thatcher.

The Poll Tax demonstrations, however, also illustrated the dangers inherent in mass meetings. At times considerable disorder resulted from these events, including violence against people and property, and, in some cases, looting. As well as being counterproductive in terms of the demonstrators' political objectives, such behaviour also indicates the justification for the existence of legal controls designed to draw the line between legitimate mass action and the breakdown of public order.

Similar problems have arisen in relation to protests about the export of live animals (see, e.g. *R v Chief Constable of Sussex, ex p ITF Ltd* [1999] 1 All ER 129), and against road developments. In these cases the action taken has had the dual purposes of trying to stop the activity in question (by blocking lorries, occupying trees which need to be felled, etc.) and drawing attention to the cause. There have been inevitable conflicts with the police, bailiffs, and private security staff. Often such encounters have passed off without serious incident, and sometimes even with good humour. There have been occurrences of violence, however, resulting in injury both to protesters, and those trying to control or stop the protest. On one occasion a protester was killed under the wheels of a lorry she was trying to halt. Such events emphasize the inherent risks in allowing mass protests. The only way to avoid such risks would be to prevent all protests. Given that this is not an acceptable answer (even if practicable) the question then becomes the one of the extent to which the law, and those empowered to enforce it, should be able to restrict the freedom of the demonstrators. A further example of the difficult borderline between acceptable and unacceptable protest has been seen in the form of the worldwide 'anti-capitalist' demonstrations in, which started in 1999 and have continued until the present. One such event, in London in May 2000, which was initially peaceful, ended in the destruction of a restaurant, and the defacing of various war memorials and other monuments. This in turn led to calls for more restrictions on demonstrations. By contrast, the way in which the police dealt with the demonstrations at the time of the G20 meeting in London in April 2009 caused concern about 'heavy-handed' policing, and calls for changes in the way in which such demonstrations are policed have followed.

Two further related issues need consideration as preliminary matters. First, the demonstration has particular importance in a situation where the majority of the population has no access to the most effective means of communicating a political message, that is, through the mass media. The control of broadcasting and the press is in the hands of a very small number of people. Moreover, national terrestrial television, which is the most powerful of the mass media, is under a legal duty to provide 'balanced' programming. This tends to leave little scope for the presentation of viewpoints which fall outside those held by the main political parties. If, however, a demonstration is held, and sufficient numbers of people participate, then the news media may feel obliged to cover the event, and therefore give publicity to the views of the demonstrators.

The second issue referred to above follows from this, and is that the freedom of assembly can in some senses be looked at as an aspect of freedom of expression. Many of the arguments which we look at in the chapters concerned with that topic will also be relevant here. This is particularly so where the demonstration is addressed by a speaker who may put forward views which only have minority support. To what extent should such a speaker be protected, on the basis of John Stuart Mill's argument from truth, or any of the other arguments for allowing freedom of expression (see chapter 7 (7.2.1))?

9.1.1 The Human Rights Act 1998 and Freedom of Assembly

A challenge under the Human Rights Act 1998 (HRA 1998) to the restrictions on demonstrations or meetings dealt with in this chapter might be based on one of two provisions of the European Convention on Human Rights (ECHR). Article 11 recognizes that 'everyone has the right to peaceful assembly...', which clearly covers the right to demonstrate and hold public meetings on controversial issues.

As regards what happens at such events, Art. 10 is relevant, protecting the freedom of expression of the speaker at a meeting, a person holding a placard, or a person chanting slogans. Indeed it may be that Art. 10 will prove to be the more significant. In *Steel and ors* v *United Kingdom* (1998) 28 EHRR 603 (discussed at 9.6), the European Court of Human Rights (ECtHR), having dealt with the cases before it under Art. 10 did not feel the need to go on to consider Art. 11, since the issues raised were identical. In the light of the stress placed on freedom of expression in the HRA 1998 it may well be that Art. 10 is used more than Art. 11 in domestic challenges to restrictions on demonstrations as well.

Both the Articles have qualifying second paragraphs in very similar terms. The provisions of Art. 10(2) have been noted elsewhere (see chapter 1 (1.6.3.4)). The second paragraph of Art. 11 is slightly narrower in scope, and reads (in part):

> No restrictions shall be placed on the exercise of these rights other than such as are prescribed by law and are necessary in a democratic society in the interests of national security or public safety, for the prevention of disorder or crime, for the protection of health or morals or for the protection of the rights and freedoms of others.

Most of the restrictive provisions dealt with later in this chapter would no doubt be held to be justified as being prescribed by law, and necessary for the prevention of disorder. The scope for challenges under the HRA 1998 are, therefore, probably limited, but one or two possible situations where such a challenge might be made are noted at the appropriate points.

9.1.2 **European Union law**

It also should not be overlooked that there is a potential in certain circumstances for the law of the European Union to have an impact in the area of control of demonstrations. This is particularly the case where the demonstration affects one of the freedoms protected by EU law, such as the free movement of goods. In *Commission* v *France* [1997] ECR I–6959 the European Court of Justice found that the French government's failure to take sufficient steps to control demonstrations by farmers against the import of agricultural products from other Member States involved a breach of Art. 28 of the European Treaty (now Art. 34 of the Treaty on the Functioning of the European Union (TFEU)). As far as the United Kingdom is concerned, the issue was raised in *R* v *Chief Constable of Sussex, ex p ITF Ltd* [1999] 1 All ER 129. This concerned demonstrations against the export of live animals, and the fact that the police were only willing, for reasons of availability of resources, to provide a police presence to allow the exporting company to carry on its business on a limited basis. The company challenged this by means of judicial review of the chief constable's decision under domestic law, and also as a breach of Art. 29 of the European Treaty (now Art. 35 of the TFEU). The House of Lords dismissed both claims. They were not prepared to find that the chief constable's decision was so unreasonable as to be challengeable by judicial review. As far as European law was concerned, the House took the view that, even if the chief constable's decision was an action which fell within the scope of Art. 29 (which it did not decide), it would be justified by Art. 30 (now Art. 36 of the TFEU) which allows controls over imports on the grounds of 'public policy'. Thus the law in this area is not fully developed, but there is clearly scope for this in the future, though courts will also need to take account of the fact that the European Union subscribes to the rights and freedoms guaranteed by the ECHR. Actions which allow for restrictions on demonstrations in order to protect the free movement of goods, therefore, may at the same time be in conflict with Art. 10 or Art. 11 of the ECHR. This was recognized explicitly by the European Court of Justice in *Eugen Schmidberger, Internationale Transporte und Planzüge v Austria* (Case C–112/00) [2003] CMLR 34. Here the Court held that the Austrian government, in allowing an environmental protest to block for 30 hours a motorway used for international trade, had in principle acted contrary to Art. 28 of the European Treaty. This had to be balanced, however, against the rights of freedom of expression and freedom of assembly guaranteed by Arts 10 and 11 of the ECHR, to which the Austrian government was also bound to show respect. Provided that a proportionate balance was struck between the conflicting rights, as the Court felt had been the case here, then there was no infringement of EU law. (For further discussion of the impact of EU law in this area, see E. Baker, 'Policing, Protest and Free Trade: Challenging Police Discretion under Community Law', [2000] Crim LR 95, and C. Barnard and I. Hare, 'Police Discretion and the Rule of Law', (2000) 63 MLR 581.)

With these considerations in mind we now turn to look at the traditional approach in English law to demonstrations and public order, and then at the background to the main piece of legislation which now governs this area: the Public Order Act 1986 (POA 1986).

9.1.3 The courts' approach

In *Hubbard v Pitt* [1976] QB 142 Lord Denning referred (p. 176) to the comment of the Court of Common Council in 1819 recognizing 'the undoubted right of Englishmen to assemble together for the purpose of deliberating upon public grievances', and continued (p. 176):

> Such is the right of assembly. So also is the right to meet together, to go in procession, to demonstrate, and to protest on matters of public concern. As long as all is done peaceably and in good order, without threats or incitement to violence or obstruction to traffic it is not prohibited.

Although Lord Denning starts with a clear assertion of 'rights', it becomes clear in the later part of this quotation that he is not in fact talking about a very strong right. In Hohfeldian terms (see chapter 1 (1.3.1)) it appears to be simply a 'privilege', that is a freedom to act in a particular way as long as no one else is affected by the behaviour. This approach has tended to be that generally adopted by the courts in relation to meetings and demonstrations. They are permissible, but if they constitute any type of interference with others' rights, even politically insignificant rights, such as the use of the highway, the courts will be quite prepared to intervene. A particular problem can arise where the cause of the problem is not the person who has organized the demonstration, but people who wish to oppose it. In *Beatty v Gilbanks* (1882) 15 Cox CC 138, a procession by the Salvation Army was being disrupted by an opposing group which styled itself the 'Skeleton Army'. Beatty, a Salvation Army captain leading the procession, was arrested when he failed to obey a police instruction to stop, and that the procession should cease. The Divisional Court held that the Salvation Army procession could not be regarded as an 'unlawful assembly' simply because others were trying to disrupt it in a way which might well lead to a breach of the peace. This decision is, however, perhaps one of the high points in the recognition of rights of assembly (though a similar approach was taken in *Redmond-Bate* v *DPP* [1999] Crim LR 998 (discussed at 9.6), without specifically recognizing any right to assembly). Later decisions, focusing more directly on the power of the police to deal with a breach of the peace, such as *Wise* v *Dunning* [1902] 1 KB 167 and *Duncan* v *Jones* [1936] 1 KB 218, have generally not accorded such rights any high status. Indeed in *Duncan v Jones* Lord Hewart CJ expressed the view that:

> English law does not recognize any special right of public meeting for political or other purposes. The right of assembly . . . is nothing more than a view taken by the Court of the individual liberty of the subject.

A slightly more robust approach to the right was taken in *Hirst v Chief Constable for West Yorkshire* (1986) 85 Cr App R 143. This concerned the offence of obstructing the highway contrary to the s. 137 of the Highways Act 1980. Some animal rights demonstrators were standing in a pedestrian precinct, outside a shop selling furs. The demonstrators were holding a banner, and distributing leaflets. They were convicted of obstruction, the magistrates taking the view that the only lawful use of the highway was to pass and repass about one's lawful business, and for any purposes incidental to that. This followed the views expressed in cases such as *Homer* v *Cadman* (1886) 16 Cox CC 51 and *Waite* v *Taylor* (1985) 149 JP 551. The Divisional Court in *Hirst* however, preferred the approach taken in *Nagy* v *Weston* [1965] 1 All ER 78 which simply stated that the use must be 'reasonable' to be lawful, which was a question of fact in each case. Applying this to the case, Otton J said that the magistrates had failed to consider this question. If they had done so the balance between the right to protest and demonstrate on the one hand, and the need for peace and good order on the other would have been properly struck, and 'the "freedom of protest on issues of public concern" would be given the recognition it deserves'. This recognizes the right to demonstrate as a relevant factor to be considered in assessing the reasonableness of a person's use of the highway. In *DPP v Jones* [1999] 2 All ER 257, however (discussed further at 9.3.4), the House of Lords, overturning by a majority of three to two the decision of the Divisional Court also gave some, though not conclusive, support to a right of assembly. Two of the majority (Lord Irvine and Lord Hutton) held that there is a right of peaceful assembly on the public highway provided that it does not obstruct the public's primary right of passage. The other member of the majority (Lord Clyde) did not recognize any right of assembly on the highway, but held that in the circumstances the defendant's use of the highway did not amount to a trespass. Since the two dissenting judges (Lord Slynn and Lord Hope) also held that there was no right of assembly, the outcome of the case is inconclusive on this issue. Subsequently, the Divisional Court has held in *Birch* v *DPP* [2000] Crim LR 301 that a person lying down in the road outside premises which were being targeted by a demonstration had no defence to a charge under s. 137. The defendant alleged that illegal activities were being carried out on the premises, and that his actions were, therefore, justifiable as being taken in 'prevention of crime', as permitted by s. 3 of the Criminal Law Act 1967. The court thought that in the circumstances the defence could not be used in relation to the charge under s. 137. The use of the highway was, therefore, not 'reasonable'. *Hirst* and *Nagy* were distinguishable. There was 'no right to demonstrate in a way which obstructs the highway'. This has not made the law any clearer, but does not add any support to the most liberal view taken in *Jones* (that is, that of Lord Irvine and Lord Hutton). In *City of London Corporation* v *Samede* [2012] EWCA Civ 160 a protest camp on the highway outside St Paul's Cathedral in London was held to clearly constitute an obstruction. Any interference with the demonstrators' rights under Art. 10 or Art. 11 was necessary and proportionate (see also *Mayor of London* v *Hall* [2010] EWCA Civ 817).

The traditional approach of the English courts can, therefore, only be said to have been ambivalent. On the one hand, the right to demonstrate and protest has sometimes been recognized; on the other, even where it has, obstruction to the traffic might well be enough to override it. It cannot be said that there has been any strong support given to the right.

9.1.4 Background to the Public Order Act 1986

The sequence of events which led to the passing of the POA 1986 can probably be traced back at least to 1974 and the demonstration against the National Front in Red Lion Square in London, which led to the death of one of the demonstrators. An inquiry was chaired by Lord Scarman, and its report ('Report on the Red Lion Square Disorders', Cmnd 5919, 1975) made a number of recommendations for reform of the law, which were not, however, acted on at the time. In 1981 there was rioting in Brixton (and in other parts of the country), which again led to Lord Scarman being asked to report. Again his recommendations ('Report on the Brixton Disorders, 10–12 April 1981', Cmnd 8427, 1981)) were not immediately acted on. Throughout the period there was also concern about football violence. In addition, a number of public order issues arose from industrial disputes, particularly the miners' strike of 1984–5. A feature of the Brixton disorders, and to some extent the miners' strike, was that, whereas in many situations of public disorder the conflict is between two groups of citizens (Salvation Army/Skeleton Army; fascists/communists (1930s); Mods/Rockers (1960s); National Front/anti-racists (1970s); football supporters/rival supporters (1980s)) with the police intervening as a third party, in these two cases the target for the demonstrations was largely the police itself. This was particularly the case in Brixton where the riots are thought to have been sparked off by a certain degree of insensitive and heavy-handed policing. This development in itself gave an additional impetus to the need for a fresh look at the public order laws. Moreover in 1983 the Law Commission had reviewed the existing public order offences, and proposed some significant amendments ('Criminal Law: Offences Relating to Public Order', Law Com No. 123, 1983). It was with this background that the government published in 1985 its White Paper, 'Review of Public Order Law' Cmnd 9510, 1985, which formed the basis of the POA 1986.

The POA 1986 was passed with very little controversy. Its effect was to put the law relating to public order almost entirely on a statutory basis, whereas before the relevant offences it had been found in a mixture of common law and statute (principally the Public Order Act 1936). The one continuing exception is the group of powers which the police have available to deal with actual or apprehended breaches of the peace. These powers are still defined by case law rather than statute. In 1994 the POA 1986 was amended and extended by the Criminal Justice and Public Order Act 1994 (CJPOA 1994).

The POA 1986 did two principal things. First, it provided a framework of controls which apply to processions and demonstrations. These are aimed at the events themselves, and if, when, and how, they should take place. Second, it enacted a range of offences to deal with disorderly conduct of various degrees of seriousness, from riot, to behaviour causing alarm or distress. For our purposes we can look on these as controls over behaviour once an event is taking place. They relate to what people can say or do while participating in a procession or other form of demonstration.

9.2 **Processions**

The most dramatic form of demonstration is probably the procession. The sight of many thousands of people marching down a street, carrying banners and chanting, is a powerful image, whether viewed in person or on a television screen. It is also one of the most disruptive forms of demonstration. A large-scale march will prevent all other traffic from using that route, and may bring normal activities in a town centre to a standstill. For this reason the tightest controls in the POA 1986 relate to processions.

9.2.1 **Definitions**

Perhaps surprisingly there is no attempt to define a procession in the Act. In most cases this is unlikely to cause a problem—though in one case there was a problem distinguishing between a procession and a static assembly: *DPP v Jones* [2002] EWHC 110 (Admin), discussed at 9.3.2. What, however, of the situation where processions have been banned for a period, because of, say, disturbances caused by anti-racist demonstrations against processions organized by a group opposed to immigration? If one member of the group marches through the town centre on a Saturday afternoon carrying a placard, is that a procession? If not, what if two or three members march together? The only case law on the issue is the statement by Lord Goddard in *Flockhart v Robinson* [1950] 2 KB 498, p. 502 that:

> ... [a] procession is not a mere body of persons: it is a body of persons moving along a route.

The reference to a 'body' of persons rules out the 'one-person' procession, but does not conclusively require any minimum number beyond this. It seems that a procession does not necessarily have to involve pedestrians. In *Kay v Commissioner of Police of the Metropolis* [2008] UKHL 69, [2009] 2 All ER 935, it was accepted by the House of Lords that a mass cycle ride could constitute a 'procession'. The same would presumably also be the case if the 'processors' were on horseback. It is not clear whether a column of motor vehicles would also be covered, but there seems no reason in principle why it should not, provided that such a column can be regarded as comprising a 'body of persons'.

The only processions covered by the provisions of Pt. II of the POA 1986 are public processions. These are defined in s. 16 as processions 'in a public place'. The section also defines 'public place' as:

(a) any highway…, and

(b) any place to which at the material time the public or any section of the public has access, on payment or otherwise, as of right or by virtue of express or implied permission.

The law is normally used in relation to processions taking place on highways. The definition of public place is wide enough, however, that it would cover a procession into a theatre or cinema, for example, to protest about the play or film being performed or shown. Nor is it necessarily limited to areas within such premises where the public have specific permission to be. In *Cawley v Frost* [1976] 3 All ER 743 an almost identical definition of 'public place' was held to be wide enough to cover the speedway track surrounding a football pitch. Spectators admitted to the stadium to watch a football match had no licence to be on the speedway track, but it was still regarded as a public place. If a group of fans decided to hold a procession around the track to protest about the manager's team selection, for example, this would therefore appear to be a public procession.

9.2.2 **Notice requirements**

A requirement to give the police notice of a public procession is imposed by s. 11 where the procession has one of three purposes. These are: to demonstrate support for or opposition to the views of any person or body of persons; to publicize a cause or campaign; or to mark or commemorate an event. A crocodile of schoolchildren being led from school to nearby playing fields is not therefore subject to the notice requirements. All processions which are in the nature of a 'demonstration' will, however, be covered. There are, however, also a number of exceptions even where the procession prima facie falls within one of the above purposes.

First, the notice requirement does not apply to a procession which is one that is commonly or customarily held in the police area (s. 11(2)). Two examples of processions of this type would be May Day processions, which are common in some parts of the country, and Good Friday processions which some churches hold. The exception only applies to established processions, however. A person wishing to initiate a procession of this type within a police area would have to give notice. The exception is, therefore, not there to exclude certain types of event because of their purpose, but simply to indicate that where a procession has regularly occurred in the past the police will be presumed to have notice of it for the future. It will presumably simply be a question of fact as to how often a procession has had to be held to fall within the exception. Will it be five years or 10 years or more? The issue arose for decision in *Kay v Commissioner of Police of the Metropolis*. The case concerned mass cycle rides taking place in central London, under the name 'Critical Mass', on the last Friday of each month. They began in 1994, and have continued ever since. There are no clear organizers of these events, and there is no fixed route, or indeed, apparently, any route planned before the event starts. The Divisional Court held that the event was now customary, so as not to require notice under s. 11. This view was upheld by the House of Lords. It did not matter that the route was not the same on each occasion—it could still be a customary procession. A 12-year period is clearly sufficient, therefore, for a procession to become customary. The decision does not help to clarify what shorter period, if any, might be sufficient to give a procession this status. Organizers of events other than those of very long standing will be well advised to give notice until such time as the police indicate that this is unnecessary, or until a period similar to that in *Kay* has elapsed.

Funeral processions organized by a funeral director in the normal course of business are also excluded from the notice requirements (s. 11(2)).

Finally, there is a more general exception to the notice requirement where it is not reasonably practicable to give any advance notice. This is intended to legitimate the instant reaction to a particular event. For example, people exiled from their home country might hear on the radio that the regime is now thought to be about to carry out summary executions of political prisoners. A procession organized for that evening to march to the country's embassy in London in protest would not be unlawful for failure to comply with the notice provisions. In *Kay* v *Commissioner of Police of the Metropolis* all members of the House of Lords expressed doubts as to whether it was reasonably practicable to give notice of a procession which had no pre-determined route—though the majority decided the case on the narrower ground noted above, that the procession was customary.

The length of notice required is normally six clear days before the date on which the procession is to be held. The 'clear days' will exclude the day on which the notice is received, and the day of the proposed procession. Notice of a procession to be held on a Saturday must therefore be given by the previous Saturday. Section 11(6), however, recognizes that in some situations it may not be practicable to give six days' notice. A procession may be organized on the Wednesday to take place on the following Friday. This might happen, for example, where a child is knocked down by a car outside a school on the Wednesday morning, and parents decide to hold a procession from the school to the council offices on the Friday, when a meeting of the council is to decide whether to install a pedestrian crossing outside the school.

The form of the notice is dealt with in s. 11(3)–(6). It is not specifically stated that it must be in writing, but this is implied by the fact that it is to be given either by post or delivery by hand. It must specify the date of the procession, the intended starting time, the proposed route, and the name and address of at least one person responsible for organizing it. There is no need to state the purpose of the procession. It is to be delivered, by hand or (if six clear days in advance) by post, to a police station in the police district in which it is proposed that the procession will start. There is no provision for the notice to be delivered by fax or email.

Failure to give the proper notice, or organizing a procession which does not correspond to details given in the notice, is a summary offence, punishable with a fine not exceeding level 3 on the standard scale.

This requirement of notice may look as though the permission of the police is being required before someone can hold a procession. This is not strictly the case, however. As the exception for traditional processions shows, the requirement is primarily one of 'notice', so that the police can organize any necessary resources to cope with the proposed procession. Once the notice has been given the organizer does not need to wait for any 'go-ahead' from the police. As will be seen, however, the police may in some cases wish to impose conditions, and can also initiate procedures which may lead to a ban. The notice requirements themselves are unlikely to be susceptible to an HRA 1998 challenge under Art. 10 or Art. 11 of the ECHR.

9.2.3 Conditions

The power to impose conditions applies to all public processions, not simply those organized for one of the purposes which gives rise to the requirement of notice. There must, however, presumably be at least some implied agreement between the people concerned for it to constitute a 'body of persons' and therefore a procession (see 9.2.1).

The power is given to the 'senior police officer' which means different things in different circumstances. Where conditions are being imposed before the event, the senior police officer means the chief officer of police (that is the chief constable, or the Commissioner; s. 12(2)(b)). In this case, the conditions should be given in writing (s. 12(3)), presumably to the organizers. If the procession is assembling, however, or is under way, the senior police officer simply means the most senior officer (in terms of rank) who is present (s. 12(2)(a)). If only a constable is present, then that constable is the senior police officer and has the power to impose conditions on the procession. The conditions do not have to be given in writing. They may be communicated verbally to those assembling, or taking part in the procession. Where the conditions are imposed under s. 12(2)(b), that is, before the event, there will be an obligation to give reasons, sufficient to enable the demonstrators to understand why they have been imposed, and for a court to assess whether they were based on reasonable grounds falling within the areas listed below (see 9.2.3.1). This is the implication of the decision in *R (Brehony)* v *Chief Constable of Greater Manchester Police* [2005] EWHC 640 (Admin), *The Times*, 15 April 2005, on the equivalent powers to impose conditions on assemblies under s. 14 of the Act. This case is discussed further at 9.3.2.

In *Austin* v *Commissioner of Police for the Metropolis* [2007] EWCA Civ 989 (the facts of which are given at 9.6) the Court of Appeal was inclined to disagree with a suggestion by the trial judge that the police might justify steps taken to control a crowd by reference to conditions imposed under s. 12 or s. 14, even though no explicit reference to these powers had been made at the time. Without finally deciding the issue the Court of Appeal took the view that there was force in the argument that the lack of reference to these powers at the time meant that they could not be relied on (para. 82). In any case, whatever the position as a strict matter of law, if the police decide to use their powers under these sections 'it is at least desirable to make it clear that they are doing so', particularly since a failure to comply with a condition can lead to a criminal sanction (para. 83). (This issue was not dealt with by the House of Lords in the further appeal in this case.)

9.2.3.1 Grounds for imposing conditions

The power to impose conditions only arises where the senior police officer reasonably believes either that certain undesirable consequences may flow from the procession, or that the procession is being organized for an illegitimate purpose (s. 12(1)). The undesirable consequences and illegitimate purpose which will have this effect are set out in s. 12(1). The consequences are that the procession may result in:

1. serious public disorder; or

2. serious damage to property; or

3. serious disruption to the life of the community.

The only one of these which can be regarded in any way as controversial is the last. What exactly is meant by serious disruption? If the traffic in a town centre is brought to a standstill is this sufficient? If so, it runs the risk of failing to take account of the fact that the whole point of a demonstration may be lost if nobody is inconvenienced in any way. A certain amount of disruption is inevitable from any large-scale procession, and the power to impose conditions on this basis will need to be used sensitively if it is not to operate oppressively. An oppressive use would be open to an HRA 1998 challenge under Art. 10 or Art. 11 of the ECHR as being a disproportionate response.

The illegitimate purpose which will justify the imposition of conditions is intimidation, with a view to compelling others either not to do an act which they have a right to do, or to do an act which they have a right not to do. The inclusion of this results directly from events which occurred during the miners' strike of 1984–5, where there were allegations that groups of striking miners processed outside the houses of those continuing to work, or accompanied them along the street on the way to work, with a view to intimidating them into joining the strike. It is difficult to see many situations where this ground for imposing conditions would apply outside the context of an industrial dispute (see also *Police* v *Reid* [1987] Crim LR 702, discussed at 9.3.2).

9.2.3.2 Conditions which can be imposed

A very broad discretion is given to the senior officer of police as to the type of conditions which can be imposed. Section 12(1) states that the officer may impose such conditions 'as appear to him necessary' to prevent the disorder, damage, disruption, or intimidation that is feared. This formulation does not require the officer's decision as to what is necessary to be based on reasonable grounds. There is no list of the types of condition which may be imposed, but it is specifically mentioned that they may include conditions as to the route to be followed, and may specify that the procession is not to enter a particular public place. The power to alter the route is perhaps inevitable, but has the potential for significantly reducing the effectiveness of the procession. If the purpose of the procession is to draw attention to activities going on in a particular factory, or in a particular country, the diversion of the procession away from the factory, or the relevant embassy, may deprive it of virtually all purpose. Once again there is a heavy burden on the police to ensure that the aim of maintaining an orderly society does not entirely emasculate the opportunities for protest. Once again, the HRA 1998 requires that the conditions imposed are 'proportionate' in response to the problems which they are supposed to avert.

Offences are committed by those who organize, or take part in a procession, and knowingly fail to comply with a condition (s. 12(4) and (5)). Incitement of others to commit such an offence is in itself a specific offence under the POA 1986 (s. 12(6)). There was previously a specific power of arrest in relation to these offences. This has been repealed, now that the general power of arrest under s. 24 of the Police and Criminal Evidence Act 1984 (PACE) (see chapter 3 (3.5.3.1)) extends to all offences. So, if a procession is under way, and the senior officer directs that it should change route, perhaps in order to avoid a confrontation with a rival demonstration, any person who does not follow the new route is liable to be arrested (cf. *Broadwith* v *Chief Constable of Thames Valley Police* [2000] Crim LR 924). In *Jukes* v *DPP* [2013] EWHC 195 (Admin) demonstrators participating in a procession in London about education cuts who crossed a police cordon in order to set up a different, anti-capitalism demonstration in Trafalgar Square, were held to be still part of the original procession, and to have breached the conditions as to its route imposed under s. 12.

9.2.4 The power to ban processions

The power to initiate the procedures leading to a ban is exclusively in the hands of the chief officer of police (s. 13(1), (4)). That officer must reasonably believe that because of particular circumstances existing in the police area, or part of it, the powers to impose conditions under s. 12 will not be sufficient to prevent serious public disorder. Note that the risk of damage to property, disruption to the community, or intimidation, is not enough to justify a ban. The procedure that must then be followed is different for London as opposed to the rest of the country.

In London, the Commissioner for the City of London, or the Commissioner for the Metropolis, makes the banning order with the consent of the Home Secretary. Outside London, the chief constable must apply to the district council, which has the power to issue the ban, subject to the approval (which may be given with modifications) of the Home Secretary. There is, then, an element of political control over the issue of bans. In practice it is unlikely, however, that either a district council or the Home Secretary are going to risk 'second-guessing' a chief of police who says that unless a ban is imposed serious public disorder will ensue. The political consequences of a refusal to ban being followed by rioting in the streets suggests that most councils and Home Secretaries will be prepared to listen to the advice of the professional police officer in such matters.

The nature of the ban is that it may apply to the holding of all, or a particular class of, public processions. There is no power to ban a specific public procession, other than by defining the 'class' so narrowly that only one procession is covered. This was deliberate. Lord Scarman in his Brixton report had come out in favour of a power to ban a particular procession in certain circumstances ('Report on the Brixton Disorders', paras 7.41–7.49), having changed his mind since his earlier 'Red Lion Square' report. The government did not follow his recommendation because it was felt that the targeting of a specific procession might appear to be based too obviously on political considerations. There is also the problem of sufficiently identifying a particular procession. If it were named by the organization under the auspices of which it is being held, it would be all too easy for virtually the same procession to take place ostensibly on behalf of a different, or even newly created, organization.

The ban can cover all or part of a police area, and last for up to three months (s. 13(1)). The order containing the ban should be put into writing (s. 13(6)), but there are no other formal requirements. There is no obligation on the person issuing the ban to give it any particular form of publicity.

The issue of a ban is susceptible to judicial review, as shown by *Kent* v *Metropolitan Police Commissioner, The Times*, 15 May 1981, which arose under the very similar power to ban given by the Public Order Act 1936. The Commissioner had issued a ban on all processions for 28 days from 25 April, except those traditionally held on May Day, and those of a religious character customarily held. The applicant was a leading member of the Campaign for Nuclear Disarmament which had planned to hold public processions during this period. The Court of Appeal, while accepting the application as the proper way to challenge a ban, refused to interfere with the Commissioner's decision. The definition of a 'class' could be achieved by excluding certain types of procession, as had been done here. Moreover, although at least one member of the court felt that the Commissioner's stated reasons for the ban were 'meagre', there was no evidence that the decision was capricious or unreasonable. It was taken in a context where there had been significant outbreaks of violence (that is, the 1981 Brixton disorders). The court was reluctant to interfere with the Commissioner's exercise of discretion, particularly since his actions had been approved by the Home Secretary. We see here, perhaps, the same reluctance to 'second-guess' the police that we have already seen is likely to arise at other stages of the banning process. In truth, although there is in form the possibility of supervision of this power by the local authorities, the Home Secretary, and the courts, in practice the chief constables and Commissioners have a power which they are largely free to operate at their own discretion, and to which there is unlikely to be any serious challenge. It is unlikely that the fact that judicial review will have in future to take account of the ECHR standards will make a significant difference to this situation. The only possibility might be where a ban was expressed in terms so wide that it could be said to be 'disproportionate' to the legitimate aim of preventing disorder, and therefore not 'necessary in a democratic society'. It is suggested that the ban in Kent would not be regarded as sufficiently wide to fall foul of this standard.

Organizing, or participating in, a banned procession are summary offences (s. 13(7), (8)) as is inciting such participation (s. 13(9)).

9.3 **Public assemblies**

Prior to 1986 there was no statutory control over the holding of public meetings as opposed to processions. The addition of such a power in the POA 1986 was a recognition that the static demonstration might raise as many public order problems as the mobile procession. It can also be seen as a response to the particular problems caused by mass picketing during the printers' dispute at Warrington, and the miners' strike of 1984–5. The long-term 'peace camp' at Greenham Common was also mentioned in the White Paper ('Review of Public Order Law', para. 5.1) as an event which gave rise to serious public order concerns. The scope of the power is not, however, limited to such situations, as will be seen from the definitions. The power to control was originally limited to the imposition of conditions. There was no power to ban public meetings. The White Paper commented that (para. 5.3):

> Meetings and assemblies are a more important means of exercising freedom of speech than are marches: a power to ban them, even as a last resort, would be potentially a major infringement of freedom of speech (especially at election time). It might also be difficult to enforce: and there was no strong request from the police for a power to ban.

For all these reasons, the power to impose conditions was thought to be sufficient. The CJPOA 1994 has, however, now given a power in certain circumstances to ban 'trespassory assemblies'.

9.3.1 Definitions

A 'public assembly' is defined in s. 16 of the POA 1986 as:

> ...an assembly of two or more persons in a public place which is wholly or partly open to the air.

A public place is defined in the same way as for processions (see 9.2.1).

The definition is very wide. It would appear to cover, for example, a crowd gathered to listen to the patter of a street trader, or to the performance of a brass band, as much as people attending a political meeting. The purposes of the assembly are entirely irrelevant to the power to impose conditions which is given by s. 14.

Unlike the position as regards processions, a minimum number of participants is stated, that is, two. This was reduced from the original figure of 20 by the Anti-social Behaviour Act 2003. The change significantly expands the scope of the powers for controlling public assemblies—if a gathering of two people can properly be regarded as an 'assembly'. It reduces the problems for the police and prosecution, however, as regards the need to establish that a particular number were present before the powers come into play, or before people can be prosecuted for breaking conditions (see 9.3.2).

The assembly must be in the open air, at least in part. This seems to be a consequence of a view endorsed by the White Paper ('Review of Public Order Law', para. 5.17), that it is in relation to open-air assemblies that disorder is most likely to result. The extension to assemblies which are only partly in the open air removes potential difficulties as regards stadiums which are partly covered. Problems of definition might arise, however, in relation to a meeting held within premises, with an 'overflow' (perhaps with closed circuit television coverage of the speeches) outside (see D. Bonner and R. Stone, 'The Public Order Act 1986: Steps in the Wrong Direction', [1987] PL 202, p. 223).

9.3.2 Conditions

The procedures for imposing conditions on public assemblies (s. 14) are virtually the same as for public processions (see 9.2.3). Conditions may be imposed by chief officers of police before the event, or by the most senior officer present in relation to an assembly which is taking place (s. 14(2)). As regards a future event, the Divisional Court in _DPP v Baillie_ [1995] Crim LR 426 held that the police must be able to identify the time and place at which it is to occur before they can validly impose conditions. The grounds for imposing conditions are listed in s. 14(1) and are identical to those in s. 12(1) which apply to processions, that is a reasonable belief that the assembly will result in serious public disorder, serious damage to property, or serious disruption to the life of the community, or that its purpose is intimidation. It is possible, however, that there is more scope here for intimidation. Much industrial picketing takes the form of a static assembly rather than a procession. It might also apply, for example, in situations where crowds assemble outside the place where an event is being held, and try to stop people entering. There must be an intention to force people to act differently, however, not just to make it less pleasant to carry on as they originally intended. In _Police_ v _Reid_ [1987] Crim LR 702, there was an anti-apartheid demonstration outside South Africa House, where a reception was being held, with much shouting at guests as they arrived. The stipendiary magistrate ruled that the chief inspector who had tried to impose conditions had acted _ultra vires_, in that he had interpreted 'intimidation' as including 'causing discomfort'. There would have had to be an intention to compel the guests not to go into the reception for the activities of the demonstrators to amount to intimidation. As with the imposition of conditions on processions, they will need to be 'proportionate' in order to survive a challenge under the HRA 1998. This was confirmed by Bean J in _R (Brehony)_ v _Chief Constable of Greater Manchester_ [2005] EWHC 640 (Admin), _The Times_, 15 April 2005. There had been a regular Saturday demonstration outside a branch of Marks & Spencer in the centre of Manchester, protesting about the firm's support for the government of Israel. For some months there had also been a counter-demonstration in support of Israel in the same location. In November 2004, the Chief Constable issued a notice under s. 14, requiring the demonstration to move to the Peace Gardens in Manchester, over the Christmas period, because of the serious disruption which would otherwise be likely during the Christmas shopping period (29 November to 3 January), when there was an expected trebling of the numbers of visitors to the city centre. The organizers of the demonstration sought judicial review of this decision. The judge refused the application, because in his view, the conditions were both reasonable, and proportionate to the Chief Constable's legitimate objectives of maintaining public order and preventing disruption to the life of the community. In relation to proportionality he applied the test set out by Dyson LJ in _R (Samaroo)_ v _Secretary of State for the Home Department_ [2001] EWCA Civ 1139, asking whether this objective could have been achieved by means which interfered less with the claimant's rights. The judge also held, however, that in imposing conditions before an event, though not once it has begun, there is an obligation on the Chief Constable to provide reasons. These should be 'sufficient to enable the demonstrators to understand why the directions are being given, and to enable a court... to assess, once the judge is presented with evidence as to the facts, whether the belief was reasonable or not' (para. 18). Once again, he found that on the facts sufficient reasons had been given.

The question of the type of condition that can be imposed under s. 14 was considered by the Divisional Court in _DPP_ v _Jones_ [2002] EWHC 110 (Admin). A demonstration was planned outside the premises of a firm involved in scientific experimentation involving animals. This demonstration would clearly be an 'assembly'. The police, however, in imposing conditions under s. 14, included some which dealt with the place where the demonstrators were to 'disembark' from the transport which had brought them to the demonstration, and the route which they were to take from that point to the actual site of the demonstration, and vice versa. It was held that these conditions, relating to the movement of the demonstrators were ultra vires, since they purported to be imposed under s. 14 which only applied to static assemblies. Nor would it have been appropriate to use s. 12 to impose the conditions, since that section related to 'public processions' as defined in s. 16 of the Act, and the court felt that moving people from a disembarkation point to a demonstration point and back again did not fall within the s. 16 definition (see [2002] EWHC 110 (Admin), para. 28). On the facts, the Court felt able to sever the offending conditions, leaving the rest intact, but the decision clearly raises problems about the exact distinction between a static assembly and a procession, and the conditions that can be imposed in each case.

It is a summary offence to organize or participate in an assembly and knowingly fail to comply with a condition (s. 14(4), (5)). Incitement to such participation is also an offence (s. 14(6)). A power of arrest is given to a constable in uniform by virtue of s. 14(7).

The offence under s. 14(5) was considered by the Divisional Court in *Broadwith* v *Chief Constable of Thames Valley Police* [2000] Crim LR 924. The police had imposed conditions on a proposed demonstration against the breeding of cats for scientific research. Under the conditions, the demonstration was to take the form of an assembly in one place, followed, at a specified time, by a procession to a second location where a further assembly would take place. The defendant tried to walk down the route to the second location before the specified time. He was arrested and charged with an offence under s. 14(5), and was convicted. On appeal he argued that the offence under s. 14(5) only applied to people taking part in assemblies. He was not participating in an assembly at the time of his arrest; indeed, he was on his own. This defence was rejected by the Divisional Court. There was evidence that he had been with a larger group of protesters immediately before being stopped. He was, therefore, a part of the larger assembly even though he was walking away from it. He was aware that access to the road on which he was arrested was not permitted at the relevant time, and he had been properly convicted of the s. 14(5) offence.

9.3.3 Demonstrations in the vicinity of Parliament

A further special control over public demonstrations was introduced by ss 132–8 of the Serious Organised Crime and Police Act 2005 (SOCPA 2005). The aim was to control demonstrations in the vicinity of Parliament which could disrupt its business—in particular where loudspeakers were used. The demonstrations did not have to involve large numbers to have this effect—indeed one of the prime motivations for introducing the provisions was the 'one-man' protest against the Iraq War which had been carrying on since 2001 in Parliament Square, by Mr Brian Haw. The provisions could be applied to any 'designated area'—the power of designation lying with the Secretary of State (s. 138)—but this had to lie within one kilometre of Parliament Square (s. 138(3)).

These provisions led to a significant amount of litigation, generally involving Mr Haw (see, e.g. *R (Haw)* v *Secretary of State for the Home Department* [2006] EWCA Civ 352; *DPP* v *Haw* [2007] EWHC 1931 (Admin); *Mayor of London* v *Haw* [2011] EWHC 585 (QB)), with some of the decisions turning on the recognition of Mr Haw's rights under Arts 10 and 11 of the ECHR. Mr Haw managed to maintain his demonstration until his death in June 2011. The remains of his camp were removed by the police at the end of August in the same year.

These provisions have now been repealed and replaced by ss 141–9 of the Police Reform and Social Responsibility Act 2011. These provisions relate solely to Parliament Square, and are designed to prevent the use of 'amplified noise equipment' (e.g. loudspeakers or loud hailers—s. 143(4)), or camping on Parliament Square. They empower the police and authorized local authority officers to issue directions that prohibited activities should cease, and create a criminal offence in relation to a failure to comply with such directions (s. 143(8)). There are also powers to seize property used in connection with the commission of an offence under s. 143 (s. 145). There is no direct or indirect reference in these provisions to the requirements of Arts 10 and 11 of the ECHR, but the ways in which the powers under them are used must be susceptible to review, on the basis that they would have to be proportionate to the legitimate need to preserve public order in the vicinity of Parliament. This was held to be the case in *R (Gallastegui)* v *Westminster City Council* [2013] EWCA Civ 28, which concerned an order (under s. 143) to remove tents being used by demonstrators. Although the protesters Convention rights were engaged, the powers were used in a way which was necessary and proportionate.

9.3.4 **Trespassory assemblies**

As noted at 9.3, the CJPOA 1994 added to the POA 1986 a power in certain circumstances to ban trespassory assemblies. These powers are contained in ss 14A–C of the POA 1986 and were added to by ss 70 and 71 of the CJPOA 1994.

The procedure for imposing a ban is similar to that which applies to the banning of processions (see 9.2.4), in that the initiative lies with the chief officer of police, subject to the approval of the Home Secretary, and, outside London, the local authority. The power applies to assemblies of 20 or more persons on land in the open air to which the public has no, or only a limited, right of access. The reference to a limited right of access means that the public's use of the land is restricted to use for a particular purpose (as in the case of a highway or road) (see s. 14A(9)). The assembly must be held without the permission of the occupier, or be likely to be conducted in a way which exceeds the occupier's permission. The grounds on which the chief officer can seek a ban of such an assembly are that there is reason to believe that it (s. 14A(1)(b)):

...may result—

(i) in serious disruption to the life of the community, or

(ii) where the land, or a building or monument on it, is of historical, architectural, archaeological or scientific importance, in significant damage to the land, building or monument.

It will be noted that these grounds are different from those which justify the banning of a procession. The risk of 'serious public disorder' is the only basis on which processions may be banned: this is not, however, a ground for banning a trespassory assembly. On the other hand, the two grounds which do allow a ban in relation to an assembly would not be sufficient for a ban on processions.

An order made under this section will prohibit the holding of all trespassory assemblies within a specified area, for a specific period (s. 14A(1)). The order may not last for more than four days (s. 14A(6)). It is thus much more limited in this respect than the equivalent order in relation to processions, which may last up to three months. Similarly, an order in relation to assemblies is likely to be more limited as regards area. Section 14A(6) provides that it may not exceed 'an area represented by a circle with a radius of five miles from a specified centre', whereas a ban on processions may cover the whole of a police area. Even so, if the centre of the circle is the middle of a town or city, the whole of the town or city is going to be covered by a circle ten miles in diameter.

Once a ban is in force it will be an offence knowingly to organize or participate in an assembly affected by it (s. 14B).

The operation of a ban under these provisions was considered in *DPP* v *Jones* [1999] 2 All ER 257. An order had been made covering an area of four miles around Stonehenge, for the period 29 May 1995 to 1 June 1995 inclusive. On 1 June a group of people gathered on a grass verge beside a road next to the perimeter fence of Stonehenge. They draped banners over the fence and played music. They were protesting about the lack of access to Stonehenge. The police decided that there were more than 20 people present (three officers apparently counted 21 people), and that this was therefore a trespassory assembly. They moved to disperse it, and some of those who refused were arrested, and charged with offences under s. 14B(2) of the POA 1986. They were convicted by the magistrates, but succeeded in an appeal to the Crown Court, on the basis that the group had not exceeded the public's limited right of access to the highway. The Director of Public Prosecutions (DPP) appealed by way of case stated. Two questions were stated for the Divisional Court:

(1) Where there is in force an Order under s. 14A(2) and on the public highway within the area and time covered by the Order there is a peaceful assembly of 20 or more persons which does not obstruct the highway, does such assembly exceed the public's right of access to the highway so as to constitute a trespassory assembly within the terms of s. 14A?

(2) In order to prove an offence under s. 14B(2) of the Public Order Act 1986, is it necessary for the prosecution to prove that each of the 20 or more persons present is exceeding the limits of the public's right of access or merely that 20 or more persons were present and that some of them were exceeding the limits of the public's right of access?

As regards the first question, the answer given by the Divisional Court was 'yes'. The only 'right' to use the highway which the court was prepared to recognize was to pass and repass, and matters incidental to this. The holding of a demonstration or vigil, however peaceable, had nothing to do with the right of passage, and the justices had therefore been right to convict. On appeal, however, a majority of the House of Lords took a different view, and decided that the decision of the Crown Court that the actions of the defendants did not constitute a trespassory assembly had been correct. Lord Irvine stated his view in this way ([1999] 2 All ER 257, p. 263):

> The question to which this appeal gives rise is whether the law today should recognize that the public highway is a public place, on which all manner of reasonable activities may go on…Provided these activities are reasonable, do not involve the commission of a public or private nuisance, and do not amount to an obstruction of the highway unreasonably impeding the general right of the general public to pass and repass, they should not constitute a trespass. Subject to these qualifications, therefore, there would be a right of peaceful assembly on the public highway.

Similarly Lord Hutton took the view that ([1999] 2 All ER 257, p. 292):

> …[t]he common law recognizes that there is a right for members of the public to assemble together to express views on matters of public concern and I consider that the common law should now recognize that this right, which is one of the fundamental rights of citizens in democracy, is unduly restricted unless it can be exercised in some circumstances on the public highway.

The third member of the majority (Lord Clyde) decided the case on the more restricted ground that the particular activity, a peaceful assembly which did not obstruct the highway, was not in the circumstances a trespassory assembly.

Lord Irvine and Lord Clyde make reference to the right of assembly under Art. 11 of the ECHR, but without using it as a major element in their decision. Lord Hutton, surprisingly, makes no mention of it at all. Under the HRA 1998, of course, courts will be obliged to take account of Art. 11 in dealing with this area. It is likely that the broad approach taken by Lord Irvine and Lord Clyde will be found to be most compatible with the requirements of Art. 11.

The second question raised in the case stated was answered in the negative by the Divisional Court, and this aspect of its decision was not challenged in the appeal. Provided that the assembly falls within the terms of the ban, then anyone participating in it, knowing it to be prohibited, is guilty of an offence. As McCowan LJ put it ([1997] 2 All ER 119, p. 124):

> In my judgment, the prosecution need prove no more than that the assembly consisted of 20 or more persons and that the particular person accused was taking part in that assembly knowing it to be prohibited by an order under s. 14A.

The decision in *Jones* indicates the type of situation where a ban on assemblies may be used. There has been concern for some years in relation to access to Stonehenge by groups wishing to hold religious, or quasi-religious, ceremonies there, and the damage that might be caused to the stones. Here, however, the ban affected not the holding of such a ceremony, but the right to protest about the restrictions being imposed.

A further power in relation to trespassory assemblies is given by s. 14C, and assists the police to prevent trespassory assemblies forming. This power is a statutory version of the common law breach of the peace power used in *Moss v McLachlan* [1985]

IRLR 77, and discussed at 9.6, to prevent people joining picket lines during the 1984 miners' strike. The power under s. 14C of the POA 1986 arises where a ban on trespassory assemblies has been imposed. It empowers a constable in uniform to stop any person reasonably believed to be on the way to such an assembly, and direct that person not to proceed in the direction of the assembly. The power may only be used within the area covered by the ban. Failure to comply with a direction constitutes an offence, for which the person can be arrested without warrant (s. 14C(3), (4)). This power is a significant restriction on the free movement of individuals. It is, nevertheless limited in scope, and is to that extent preferable to the much broader power existing under the common law in relation to actual or anticipated breaches of the peace. It is unlikely that the power itself would successfully be challenged under the HRA 1998. If it were used in a particular case in an excessive or oppressive manner, however, such a challenge might be possible, in that it might constitute a disproportionate restriction of the rights under Art. 11 or Art. 10 of the ECHR.

9.3.5 Raves

The final addition to the public order controls introduced by the CJPOA 1994 is the set of provisions to control 'raves'. These are large-scale outdoor musical events, held with the permission of the landowner (and therefore not 'trespassory assemblies'; see 9.3.4) but liable to cause disruption to the local community both in terms of noise and the large numbers of people attending. There was concern at the time when the CJPOA 1994 was being passed about the lack of controls over such events, and so ss 63–7 contain powers to prevent them taking place. A rave is defined in s. 63(1) as a gathering on open land of 20 or more people:

> ...at which amplified music is played during the night...and is such as, by reason of its loudness and duration and the time at which it is played, is likely to cause serious distress to the inhabitants of the locality

'Music' is defined in s. 63(1)(b) to include 'sounds wholly or predominantly characterised by the emission of a succession of repetitive beats'.

The Anti-social Behaviour Act 2003, as well as reducing the number required from 100 to 20, also extended the powers to trespassory gatherings of 20 or more not in the open air. This will cover events held in, for example, barns or disused warehouses, without the permission of the owner.

The power under the section is given to a police officer of at least the rank of superintendent, who may order people to leave land, with their vehicles and other property, on the basis of a reasonable belief that (s. 63(2)):

> (a) two or more persons are making preparations for the holding there of a gathering to which this section applies,
>
> (b) ten or more persons are waiting for such a gathering to begin there, or
>
> (c) ten or more persons are attending such a gathering which is in progress.

Failure to comply with such an order, or returning to the land within seven days, is a summary offence (s. 63(6)).

Supplementary powers include the right to enter land to seize vehicles and sound equipment (s. 64), and to forfeit such equipment following a conviction (s. 66).

Finally, s. 65 gives a power similar to that under s. 14C of the POA 1986 (see 9.3.4). Within five miles of a rave which is the subject of a direction under s. 63(2) a constable in uniform may stop any persons reasonably believed to be on their way to the event, and direct them not to proceed in the direction of the event. Failure to comply is a summary offence (s. 65(4)).

Research into the CJPOA 1994 in the late 1990s found that the powers to deal with raves had not been used extensively (T. Bucke and Z. James, 'Trespass and Protest: Policing Under the Criminal Justice and Public Order Act 1994', Home Office Research Study No. 190, 1998)). This was in part because (p. 21):

> ... [a] common theme in interviews with officers was that by the time the CJPOA provisions were available illegal raves had become a rare phenomenon compared with the late-1980s.

To the extent that the powers were used, the powers to direct people away were generally effective. Little use was made of the power to seize equipment. There were also few arrests or prosecutions. In 1995 there were no prosecutions, and in 1996 only seven (resulting in four convictions). It may well be that the changes introduced by the Anti-social Behaviour Act 2003 have led to more extensive use of these powers, but no statistics are available in relation to this.

9.4 Public order offences

In this section we are looking at the controls over behaviour which is to a greater or lesser extent 'disorderly'. The offences are in many ways simply ordinary criminal offences, raising no special civil liberties issues. Three aspects, however, make them of particular significance in a book on civil liberties. First, there is the possibility of the offences being used to restrict protest, rather than disorder itself. In other words, they are offences which may be particularly apposite for dealing with the consequences of demonstrations, or public meetings, where disputes have arisen between opposing groups, or between the demonstrators and the police. The dividing line between acceptable protest, and unacceptable disorder, is at times a fine one, and we need to consider whether the range of offences is, or has the potential to be, used in relation to behaviour which it might be argued falls on the acceptable side of the borderline.

Second, there is the problem of 'disorder' itself. To what extent is it acceptable for a society to insist on 'order', and to condemn 'disorderly' behaviour, unless that behaviour has resulted in some identifiable harm to others? As will be seen, a number of the offences are based on the potential of the behaviour for causing harm, rather than the fact that such harm has in fact resulted from it, and the range of harms recognized by the law is very broad.

Finally, the fact that the offences are sometimes directed at what people say, rather than what they do, clearly raises freedom of expression issues. These become particularly problematic in the context of 'incitement to racial or religious hatred' (see 9.7 and 9.8), where it may be the offensiveness of what is said that forms the basis for condemnation. Parallels can be drawn between this area, and the area of obscene publications, where again the criterion of offensiveness rather than harm is sometimes put forward as the basis for legal controls (see chapter 8 (8.4.2)).

The relevant offences are almost entirely contained in Pt. I of the POA 1986, which was largely based on the recommendations of the Law Commission ('Criminal Law: Offences Relating to Public Order'). These were in turn accepted in the White Paper ('Review of Public Order Law'). The Law Commission's principal task was to produce a coherent set of offences appropriate for dealing with different levels of disorder, and in this it was largely successful. The offences contained in the POA 1986 range from riot (the most serious) to disorderly behaviour. Before considering them in detail, however, it will be convenient first to deal with one recurring concept, that is, 'unlawful violence'.

9.4.1 Unlawful violence

One of the central concepts in the common law in relation to public order offences was that of the 'breach of the peace'. (For a definition of this, see chapter 3 (3.5.1).) The Law Commission, however, regarded the concept as too vague and uncertain to continue to be used in the reformed law ('Criminal Law: Offences Relating to Public Order', para. 5.14). In its place is put the concept of 'unlawful violence'. 'Violence' is defined in s. 8 as meaning 'any violent conduct', whether or not intended to cause injury or damage. It specifically includes violence towards property and throwing something capable of causing injury at another person (even if the missile does not hit its target).

9.4.2 Riot

The offence of riot is defined in s. 1 of the POA 1986. It is the most serious offence, and is designed to deal with large groups acting together, in a way which causes, or could cause, violence. The way in which it achieves this is to define a setting or context in which riot may occur, and then to specify that certain behaviour taking place within that context will constitute an offence.

The required setting is that 12 or more people use or threaten 'unlawful violence'. They must be acting together for a common purpose. A fight involving six people on each side presumably would not meet the definition. On the other hand there seems to be no requirement that the purpose is itself unlawful. It could cover, therefore, a picket aimed to persuade people not to enter a place of work, established as part of a legitimate trade dispute. The behaviour can take place in public or in private. If 12 or more people at a private party on domestic premises decide, for example, to attack others at the party, this has the potential to constitute a 'riot'. The conduct of the 12 must be such as would cause a 'person of reasonable firmness present at the scene to fear for his personal safety'.

This test of the effect on a 'person of reasonable firmness' is the standard of 'disorderliness' that appears at a number of points in the POA 1986 as the test of criminality. It looks at the likely effect of the behaviour on the average adult who might be present. It excludes the particularly timid, or the especially bold. No such person has actually to be present, however, or be likely to be present (s. 1(4)). The test is purely hypothetical. If, however, people who could be categorized as 'persons of reasonable firmness' were actually present, no doubt their evidence as to the effect of the behaviour on them would be very relevant. On the other hand, the fact that an elderly person, or child, was in fact frightened by the behaviour does not turn it into a riot, if a person of reasonable firmness would not have been so affected. The fear has to be for the person of reasonable firmness's own safety; fear as to what might happen to the participants, their victim (if any), or other persons present is not relevant. In theory, this seems a reasonable standard to apply. People should not be put in terror by the violent activities of others. In practice, however, it may be difficult to assess exactly what level of behaviour has such an effect, particularly where there were no 'reasonably firm' people present at the time.

All the above only constitutes the setting in which the offence of riot can take place. The offence itself is only committed by those amongst the group of 12 or more who actually use unlawful violence; threatening such violence is not sufficient for criminal liability. There is also a mental element, set out in s. 6(1). This is that a person is guilty of riot 'only if he intends to use violence or is aware that his conduct may be violent'. While it is right that an offence of the seriousness of riot should have a clearly defined mental element, in practice it seems that this is unlikely to cause difficulty for the prosecution. The mental element relates not to the consequences of the behaviour, but to its nature. In other words, the prosecution does not have to prove that the rioter realized that the behaviour might have the effect of causing fear in a person of reasonable firmness, but simply an awareness that the behaviour was, or might be violent. There is a certain unreality in asking whether a person who is proved to have used violence was aware of the nature of this conduct, unless there is evidence of automatism. One situation in which such a defence might commonly be raised, that is, where the rioter was intoxicated, is ruled out by s. 6(5). This states that, unless the intoxication was not self-induced or was the result of taking medically prescribed substances, people's awareness is to be judged on the basis of what they would have been aware of when sober. Finally, the prosecution only needs to prove the mental element in relation to a person actually charged with riot. It is not necessary to show that there were at least 11 others who were similarly aware of the nature of their behaviour (s. 6(7)).

The consent of the DPP is required for a prosecution for riot. This indicates the seriousness of the offence, and the fact that there was some feeling that, in relation to the 1984 miners' strike, there was over-enthusiastic charging of the common law offence of riot, which resulted in a number of prosecutions being abandoned (see, e.g. P. Scraton, ' "If You Want a Riot, Change the Law": The Implications of the 1985 White Paper on Public Order', (1985) 12 J of Law and Soc 385, p. 390). The seriousness of the offence is also reflected in the mode of trial and penalty. It is an indictable offence, punishable with up to 10 years' imprisonment (s. 1(6)).

9.4.3 **Violent disorder**

This offence, which did not exist at common law, was created by s. 2 of the POA 1986, and was to some extent a replacement for the common law offence of 'unlawful assembly'. The White Paper anticipated that it would be used as the most usual charge in relation to 'serious outbreaks of public disorder' ('Review of Public Order Law', para. 3.13).

The offence has some similarities with riot, but requires only a group of three people, rather than 12. Unlike the offence of riot, however, the three people do not have to be acting for any common purpose. The three must simply use or threaten unlawful violence, such that a person of reasonable firmness would 'fear for his personal safety'. Each person who uses or threatens unlawful violence will be guilty of the offence. The concept of the 'person of reasonable firmness' is exactly the same as in relation to riot (see 9.4.2), as are the following elements, which are not, therefore, discussed in detail again. The offence may be committed in public or in private (s. 2(4)). The mental element is intention or awareness that the behaviour is or may be violent, or may threaten violence (s. 6(2)). Lack of awareness resulting from self-induced intoxication is no defence (s. 6(5)).

This offence does not require the DPP's consent. It is triable either way, with a maximum penalty on indictment of five years' imprisonment (s. 2(5)).

An early example of the use of this offence may be found in *R* v *Hebron* [1989] Crim LR 839. The accused was present during a fight in a city centre on New Year's Eve. Bottles and other missiles had been thrown at the police. Hebron was simply proved to have shaken his fists and shouted 'kill the Bill' (referring to the police). He was convicted of violent disorder. The conviction makes clear the fact that this offence can be committed by threats, as well as by the use of violence. Moreover, Hebron's participation was seen as sufficiently serious to justify a custodial sentence.

The other case law on violent disorder has mainly been concerned with the requirement that there should be three people involved. In *R* v *Abdul Mahroof* (1988) 88 Cr App R 317, three people were named in the indictment as committing violent disorder. Two were acquitted, but the third was convicted. The Court of Appeal held that, since the jury had not been directed on the possibility that there were others involved not named on the indictment, and the issue had not been dealt with by the defence, the conviction must be quashed. This was followed in *R* v *Fleming* [1989] Crim LR 658, where of four people charged, one was acquitted, and on another the jury could not agree. The conviction of the remaining two for violent disorder was quashed, but the Court of Appeal noted, obiter, that in some circumstances a person may be convicted even though it is not possible to prove that two others were guilty, for example, where the others were in fact using threatening violence but lacked *mens rea* (see s. 6(7)) or have a defence of some kind. The same must be true where there is clear evidence that two or more others were using or threatening unlawful violence, but they are not before the court (perhaps because they evaded arrest). Problems may still arise, however, unless the judge puts the issue to the jury correctly. In *R* v *Worton* [1990] Crim LR 124, there was prosecution evidence of eight to ten people being involved in fighting. Only four were charged, however. Of these, one was acquitted, and in relation to another, the charge was simply left on the file. The two who were convicted appealed successfully because the judge had not specifically directed the jury that they could only convict if either they found three of the people before them guilty, or they were satisfied that others not charged had participated in the unlawful violence.

Great care needs to be taken, therefore, in directing a jury on this offence. These technical problems aside, however, the main concern with the offence must be that it is possible for people who have had a very low level of involvement in any unlawful violence to be convicted of a serious offence. One threat will be enough, if at least two others have done the same. No one needs to have actually used any violence, and if others have used violence, the issue of threats alone may, as we have seen, lead to a custodial sentence (*R v Hebron*).

9.4.4 **Affray**

Affray existed at common law, and was regularly used to deal with any unlawful fighting. The Law Commission and the White Paper anticipated that this would continue to be the case ('Criminal Law: Offences Relating to Public Order', para. 3.5; 'Review of Public Order Law', para. 3.15). As a result, the offence, although it follows in many ways the pattern established by the definitions of riot in s. 1, and violent disorder in s. 2, has certain limitations. Thus, as with violent disorder, a person commits affray by using or threatening unlawful violence so that a person of reasonable firmness would fear 'for his personal safety'. No minimum number of participants is required, but where two or more are involved, it is the effect of their joint behaviour which must be considered (s. 3(2)). Unlike riot, or violent disorder, however, the threats or violence must be directed towards another person. Violent conduct towards property is not sufficient for affray (s. 8). Moreover, a verbal threat is insufficient: it must be accompanied by some threatening actions (s. 3(3)). A shaking of the fist would, however, presumably be enough. In *I v DPP* [2001] UKHL 10, [2001] 2 All ER 583, the House of Lords held that a group seen carrying petrol bombs could properly be convicted of affray, even if there had been no threat to use them. Although mere possession of a weapon would not constitute a threat of violence, the visible carrying of petrol bombs by persons within a large gang that was obviously 'out for no good, was clearly capable of constituting a threat of violence'. There must, however, be a threat to someone 'present at the scene'. In this the House of Lords differed from the courts below which had held that a threat towards unknown persons or the public at large would be sufficient. In the case before it the evidence showed that the only other people present were police officers. There was clearly no threat to them because the gang dispersed as soon as the police appeared. The conviction for affray was, therefore, quashed.

One reported decision shows the offence being charged in a situation which was not really one of public disorder. In *R v Davison* [1992] Crim LR 31 the events took place in the accused's flat, highlighting the fact that affray, like the other offences so far considered, does not have to be committed in a public place. There had been a domestic incident, as a result of which the police had been called. One of the police officers was threatened by the accused, who was holding a kitchen knife. He waved the knife from side to side saying 'I'll have you'. He was arrested before any further assault took place. It was held that there was a case to answer on an affray charge, though it would have to be shown that the hypothetical person of reasonable firmness would have feared for their own safety, rather than that of the policeman. It might be thought, however, that a more appropriate charge would have been common assault. In *I v DPP*, Lord Hutton noted the increasing use of the offence of affray in the Metropolitan Police area (1,891 charges in the year 2000), and specifically discouraged its use where other offences might be more appropriate to the facts.

Affray is an offence triable either way, with a maximum penalty of three years on conviction on indictment.

9.4.5 Fear or provocation of violence

Whereas affray does not seem particularly appropriate for dealing with problems arising out of assemblies and demonstrations, the offence under s. 4, headed 'Fear or provocation of violence', has considerable potential in relation to such events. Its predecessor, that is s. 5 of the Public Order Act 1936, was certainly used in this way (e.g. *Jordan* v *Burgoyne* [1963] 2 All ER 225 and *Brutus* v *Cozens* [1972] 2 All ER 1297) though, like s. 4 of the POA 1986, it had a scope extending far beyond this.

The offence is committed by using threatening, abusive, or insulting words or behaviour, towards another person, or by distributing or displaying any 'writing, sign or other visible representation' which is threatening, abusive, or insulting. In what follows the phrase 'words or behaviour' is used to cover all the types of conduct which may give rise to the offence. Some of the language of the section is taken over from the Public Order Act 1936 and so we can safely assume that the case law on this will stand. The most important decision is that of the House of Lords in *Brutus* v *Cozens*, which arose out of an anti-apartheid demonstration during the Wimbledon tennis championships. It was held that the word 'insulting', and therefore presumably the words 'threatening' and 'abusive' as well, must be given its natural meaning. Whether any particular words or behaviour are capable of being 'threatening, abusive or insulting' should be regarded as a matter of fact, not law.

The phrase 'towards another person' did not appear in the Public Order Act 1936 offence. In *Atkin* v *DPP* (1989) 153 JP 383 it was held that the 'other person' towards whom the words or behaviour are directed must be present when the threats, etc. are made. The fact that they were reported to him shortly afterwards, causing him to be frightened for his safety, was not sufficient.

The use of such words or behaviour towards another person does not in itself constitute an offence. They must be intended, or be likely, to provoke, or to cause fear of, immediate unlawful violence. The requirement of immediacy was emphasized in *R* v *Horseferry Road Justices, ex p Siadatan* [1990] Crim LR 598, where there was an attempt to prosecute the publishers of a book which was alleged to constitute a blasphemy against the Islamic religion. Although the Divisional Court took the view that 'immediate' did not mean the same as 'instantaneous', there must be proximity in time and place. In *DPP* v *Ramos* [2000] Crim LR 768, the Divisional Court drew an analogy with the House of Lords' approach to the definition of an 'assault' in *R* v *Ireland* [1997] AC 148. The House held that the requirement of the offence of assault, that the victim should suffer an apprehension of immediate unlawful violence, could be satisfied by telephone calls, as long as the victim feared that the express or implied threats could be carried out in the very near future. Applying this approach the court in *Ramos* held that the offence under s. 4 could be committed by the sending of letters containing threats of violence (in this case in the form of a bombing campaign) (cf. also *R* v *Constanza* [1997] 2 Cr App R 492—threat sent by letter could constitute an assault).

The precise intentions or likely consequences which will constitute the offence are as follows: first, an intention: (a) to cause the person towards whom the words or behaviour were directed 'to believe that immediate unlawful violence will be used against him or any other person'; or (b) to provoke that person or another to use such violence; second, a likelihood (c) that that person will believe that such violence will be used; or (d) that such violence will be provoked.

As with the other offences under Pt. I of the POA 1986 there is a further mental element, over and above any intention to bring about either of the consequences in (a) or (b), which is that the person using the words or behaviour must intend it to be threatening, abusive, or insulting, or be aware that it may be so (s. 6(3)). As can be seen below, this *mens rea* requirement may have more significance in relation to this offence than the equivalent requirement in relation to riot, violent disorder, or affray.

The easiest version of the offence for the prosecution to prove, and therefore perhaps the most likely to be used (it was the version attempted in *ex p Siadatan*) is that based on consequence (d), that is, that it is likely that violence will be provoked. The question arises as to whether the likelihood has to be a reasonable one, or one that a reasonable person would foresee. There is no case law under the POA 1986, but the decision in *Jordan* v *Burgoyne* on a similar issue under s. 5 of the Public Order Act 1936 would suggest that the test is entirely a question of what was in fact likely to happen. In *Jordan* v *Burgoyne* the issue was the likely effect of a public speech which expressed support for Hitler, and condemned 'world Jewry', and in particular whether it would be likely to provoke a breach of the peace. The speaker knew that his audience contained representatives of Jewish organizations and left-wing groups who would be hostile to his view, but he argued that their violent reaction to his speech was unreasonable. It was held by the Divisional Court that once a speaker has used 'threatening, abusive or insulting' words or behaviour then, in Lord Parker's words:

> ...that person must take his audience as he finds them, and if those words to that audience are likely to provoke a breach of the peace, then the speaker is guilty of that offence.

There seems no reason why the word 'likely' as used in s. 4 of the POA 1986 should not be interpreted in the same way. It may be, however, that there would now be an escape route for a speaker like Jordan in that it might be possible to argue that there was no intention or awareness as regards the insulting nature of the words or behaviour. This would be particularly true where the speaker was not aware of the presence of the hostile group (though this was not the situation in *Jordan*). In addition, it might well be argued that the *Jordan* approach is susceptible to a challenge under the HRA 1998 as giving inadequate weight to freedom of expression under Art. 10 of the ECHR.

The offence under s. 4 may be committed in a public or a private place, except that it does not apply where the conduct takes place inside a 'dwelling' (as defined in s. 8), and the person to whom the conduct is directed is also inside that or another dwelling. This means that it is of more limited scope than riot, violent disorder, or affray but would still apply, for example, to threatening words or behaviour used at a private meeting being held on business premises, or in a hired room. It was held in *Rukwira* v *DPP* [1993] Crim LR 882, that communal landings in a block of flats do not come within the meaning of a 'dwelling' for the purposes of s. 4.

The s. 4 offence is summary only, punishable with up to six months' imprisonment (s. 4(4)). If, however, the offence is 'racially or religiously aggravated' it becomes, by virtue of s. 31 of the Crime and Disorder Act 1998, an offence triable either way, with a maximum penalty on indictment of two years' imprisonment. An offence is racially or religiously aggravated if (s. 28 of the Crime and Disorder Act 1998 as amended):

(a) at the time of committing the offence, or immediately before or after doing so, the offender demonstrates towards the victim of the offence hostility based on the victim's membership (or presumed membership) of a racial or religious group; or

(b) the offence is motivated (wholly or partly) by hostility towards members of a racial or religious group based on their membership of that group.

The references to religious aggravation were inserted by the Anti-terrorism, Crime, and Security Act 2001 (ACTSA 2001). The particular concern was about attacks on Muslims in the wake of the terrorist attacks in New York of 11 September 2001, but the scope is wider than that. The definition of religious group is 'a group of persons defined by religious belief or lack of religious belief' (s. 28(4) as added by the ATCSA 2001).

9.4.6 Harassment, alarm or distress

There are now two offences in the POA 1986 based on the causing of 'harassment, alarm or distress', contained in ss 4A and 5. Section 5 was included in the Act as originally passed; s. 4A was added by the CJPOA 1994. For this reason, and because s. 4A uses much of the same terminology as s. 5, they are dealt with here in reverse order, even though on the scale of seriousness, s. 4A ranks in between s. 4 and s. 5.

9.4.6.1 Public Order Act 1986, s. 5

There was considerable debate prior to the passing of the POA 1986 as to whether there was any need for a 'lower-level' offence than that under s. 4, to deal with 'disorderly behaviour' which might cause annoyance or disturbance, but is not likely to gives rise to fear or provocation of unlawful violence. In the end the government decided that there was, and the result is s. 5 of the POA 1986, which is labelled 'Harassment, alarm or distress'. The kind of behaviour which it was intended to deal with was set out in the White Paper ('Review of Public Order Law', para. 3.22):

(a) hooligans on housing estates causing disturbances in the common parts of blocks of flats, blockading entrances, throwing things down the stairs, banging on doors, peering in at windows, and knocking over dustbins;

(b) groups of youths persistently shouting abuse and obscenities or pestering people waiting to catch public transport or to enter a hall or cinema;

(c) someone turning out the lights in a crowded dance hall, in a way likely to cause panic; and

(d) rowdy behaviour in the streets late at night which alarms local residents.

The White Paper suggested that if the offence were introduced then it should only apply to behaviour that has actually caused substantial alarm, harassment, or distress, to someone, and not to behaviour that was simply likely to do so. As we shall see, the requirement of an actual victim has been weakened in s. 5, and the need for a substantial effect has been dropped.

There are two ways in which the offence under s. 5 can be committed. The first, as originally enacted, involved the use of 'threatening, abusive or insulting words or behaviour'. This phrase is, of course, exactly the same as that used in s. 4, and so must be interpreted in the same way (see 9.4.5). Following a consultation in 2012–13 the Home Office accepted that the inclusion of the word 'insulting' was unnecessary and too proscriptive (see 'Police Powers to Promote and Maintain Public Order', HMSO, January 2013). Section 57 of the Crime and Police Act 2013 removes the word from s. 5 (though at the time of writing, s. 57 had not been brought into force).

The second method of committing the offence under s. 5 is by engaging in 'disorderly behaviour'. This is undefined. Presumably the examples used in para. 3.22 of the White Paper (set out above) may be used as guidance as to the kind of behaviour that is intended to be covered. In practice, however, the question will be treated as one of fact to be decided by the magistrates who will, therefore, set the standard for 'orderliness'. It seems unlikely that simple participation in an organized demonstration (whether a procession or a meeting) could be regarded as disorderly. It is much more likely that individual participants who carry placards or shout things at passers-by, or people opposed to the demonstration who try to disrupt it (but do so without using or threatening violence), will be found to be disorderly.

The behaviour, to constitute the offence, must have taken place 'within the hearing or sight of a person likely to be caused harassment, alarm or distress thereby' (s. 5(1)). The POA 1986 thus abandons here the 'person of reasonable firmness' used in ss 1–3. The object of the offence is to protect the 'weak and vulnerable' ('Review of Public Order Law', para. 3.26), and so the person who acts in a disorderly way must take the chance that there is an unusually sensitive victim in the vicinity. This assumes that 'likely' is interpreted in the same way as in *Jordan* v *Burgoyne* (see 9.4.5), so as to mean likely in fact, rather than reasonably likely. The person does not have to be proved to have been harassed, alarmed, or distressed as long as this consequence is likely. It was held to be sufficient in *Lodge* v *Andrews*, *The Times*, 26 October 1988, that the unidentified driver of a car might have been alarmed by the sight of the accused walking down the middle of the road late at night. There is unlikely to be a conviction, however, if the only potential victim admits to not having been affected by the behaviour. If the only witness to the accused's behaviour is a police officer, this does not preclude a charge. A police officer is capable of being harassed, alarmed, or distressed for the purposes of the section. This was held to be the case by the Divisional Court in *DPP* v *Orum* [1988] 3 All ER 449, and was applied in *DPP* v *Clarke* [1992] Crim LR 60 (discussed below).

The offence may be committed in public or private, but will not occur where the behaviour or display takes place inside a dwelling, and the person potentially harassed, alarmed, or distressed is also inside that or another dwelling (s. 5(2)). So, abusive language which is heard through the dividing wall of two houses cannot constitute this offence. If it is heard on the street outside, however, the offence may have been committed.

There are three specific defences set out in s. 5(3). The burden of proof is on the accused. The defences are: (a) that the accused had no reason to believe that there was anyone able to see or hear the behaviour who might be harassed, alarmed, or distressed; or (b) that the accused was inside a dwelling, and had no reason to believe that the behaviour would be seen or heard by someone outside a dwelling; or (c) that the conduct was reasonable. It is difficult to imagine, however, that courts are going to be very receptive to pleas that it was reasonable to cause people harassment, alarm, or distress.

Section 5 was used in a situation involving a demonstration in *DPP* v *Clarke*. This case also illustrates the importance of the *mens rea* requirement under s. 6(4) by virtue of which the prosecution must prove either that the accused intended the conduct to be threatening or abusive (or insulting under the original version, prior to the coming into force of s. 57 of the Crime and Police Act 2013), or was aware that it might be; or that the accused intended the behaviour to be disorderly, or was aware that it might be. The prosecution arose out of a demonstration outside an abortion clinic. Anti-abortion demonstrators, including Clarke, were carrying pictures of an aborted foetus, which they displayed to officers on patrol and passers-by. The demonstrators refused to comply with police requests not to display the pictures. Clarke was charged under s. 5. The magistrates found that the pictures were abusive and insulting, and that their display caused alarm and distress to one of the police officers present. They also found, however, that, applying the *mens rea* test in s. 6, the demonstrators did not intend the pictures to be threatening, abusive, or insulting, nor were they aware that they might be. They therefore acquitted. The prosecutor appealed on the basis that the only reasonable conclusion open to the magistrates was that the demonstrators were aware that the continued display of the pictures might be abusive or insulting. The Divisional Court held that the magistrates had approached all the issues correctly. Their finding on the *mens rea* issue was simply an acceptance of the evidence put forward by the defence. It could not be said to be unreasonable, and the acquittal should stand. It was noted, however, that it would be difficult for the accused in this case to argue in a subsequent case that they were unaware that the pictures might be abusive or insulting.

In *DPP* v *Fidler* [1992] Crim LR 62, a case arising out of the same facts, the same court ruled that a prima facie case under s. 5 could be made by evidence that the accused was not only anti-abortion but a member of the group organizing the protest, without any need to prove any particular threatening, abusive, or insulting act. There are considerable risks, therefore, for those who wish to participate in demonstrations in favour of causes where an impact may be sought by the display of striking and disturbing pictures, for example of torture, or starvation, or cruelty to animals.

Recent examples of behaviour leading to successful prosecutions under s. 5 include shouting abuse at soldiers parading through Luton on their return from Afghanistan (*Abdul* v *DPP* [2011] EWHC 247 (Admin)), and burning poppies on Remembrance Sunday (see http://www.bbc.co.uk/news/uk-england-london-12664346). On the other hand, simply swearing at a police officer has been held not in itself to constitute an offence under s. 5 (*Harvey* v *DPP* [2011] EWHC 3992 (Admin).

The penalty for the offence under s. 5, which is a summary offence, is a fine not exceeding level 3 on the standard scale. If the offence is 'racially or religiously aggravated' (for which see 9.4.5), then by virtue of s. 31 of the Crime and Disorder Act 1998 the maximum fine is increased to level 4.

9.4.6.2 Public Order Act 1986, s. 4A

The reason for the inclusion of this offence was apparently concern about racially motivated abuse and harassment (M. Wasik and R. Taylor, *Blackstone's Guide to the Criminal Justice and Public Order Act 1994* (London: Blackstone Press, 1995), p. 98), but this forms no part of the definition. The *actus reus*, based on threatening, abusive, insulting, or disorderly behaviour is virtually identical to that required for s. 5, with the exception that, whereas under s. 5 the 'harassment, alarm or distress' must be likely to result from the person's behaviour, s. 4A requires that such 'harassment, alarm or distress' is actually caused to the person against whom the behaviour is directed, or some other person. The other main difference relates to the *mens rea*, since s. 4A requires the behaviour to take place with the intention of causing another person harassment, alarm, or distress. In the unreported case of *Rogers* v *DPP* (22 July 1999) the issue of the need to prove intention was considered by the Divisional Court. The case arose out of a demonstration at a farm used for breeding cats. The defendants were part of a crowd of about 250 confronting police who were trying to prevent people entering the farm. Missiles were thrown. The defendants appealed against their conviction under s. 4A in that they could not have intended to cause harassment, alarm, or distress to the farmer, since there was no evidence that they had known that he was present or could directly experience any of the alleged disorderly behaviour. The Divisional Court held, however, the relevant intention could be inferred from the activities of the defendants committed in the context of the large crowd, there to express disapproval of the farmer's activities, and in the context of the removal of fences and the confrontation with the police.

In other respects s. 4A is very similar to s. 5. Thus, the offence may be committed in public or private, but there is the same exception and defence regarding behaviour taking place inside a dwelling. The defence of 'no reason to believe that anyone might be harassed, etc.', is obviously unavailable, as is the defence of 'reasonable behaviour'. In *Dehal* v *DPP* [2005] EWHC 2154 (Admin) the court emphasized the need to make sure that s. 4A was only used where there was a clear threat to public order, particularly where the right to freedom of expression was engaged by the conduct in question. The defendant had entered a temple and put up a notice accusing the preacher of being a 'hypocrite'. He was charged and convicted under s. 4A. The High Court held that the conviction should be quashed. It was not a case in which it was clear that any threat to public order required the involvement of the criminal, rather than the civil, law. A recent example of a successful prosecution under s. 4A was the conviction in October 2012 of a man for wearing a T-shirt containing slogans taken to be mocking the recent murder of two women police officers (see http://www.bbc.co.uk/news/uk-england-manchester-19911943).

The penalty on summary conviction is a fine not exceeding level 5, or six months' imprisonment, or both. If, however, the offence is 'racially or religiously aggravated' it becomes, by virtue of s. 31 of the Crime and Disorder Act 1998, an offence triable either way, with a maximum penalty on indictment of two years' imprisonment. For the meaning of 'racially or religiously aggravated' see 9.4.5.

9.4.7 **Conclusion on Public Order Act 1986, Pt I offences**

For the most part the offences under Pt. I of the POA 1986 seem to provide a reasonable set of controls at appropriate levels of disorder. Some doubts may be raised as to whether behaviour which occurs entirely on private property should be covered, as for example in *R* v *Davison* (1992) (see 9.4.4). Does such behaviour really affect public order? A distinction should probably be more clearly drawn between private property on to which the public, or a section of the public, have been invited (which would be a 'public place' within the definition of s. 16 of the POA 1986), and purely private events. It is submitted that even the narrowing of scope in ss 4 and 5 to exclude dwellings does not really go far enough. It is hard to see that the State has a legitimate interest in what happens between private individuals behind closed doors, unless it results in some injury to persons or damage to property which would in any case be covered by ordinary criminal law offences.

9.4.8 **Other offences**

9.4.8.1 **The Protection from Harassment Act 1997**

This Act makes it an offence to pursue a course of conduct which amounts to harassment of another, where the harasser knows or ought to know that this will be its effect (ss 1 and 2). In addition, by virtue of s. 4 it is an offence to pursue a course of conduct which causes 'another to fear, on at least two occasions that violence will be used against him', provided that the perpetrator knows or ought to know that his course of conduct will cause the other person such fear on each occasion. Section 5 provides for a restraining order to be made as part of the sentencing of a person convicted of an offence. Section 3 provides a civil remedy for the victim of harassment in the form of damages or an injunction.

The primary target of this legislation was 'stalking', rather than public order situations. It has been used quite extensively, however (around 5,000 prosecutions in both 1998 and 1999: J. Harris, 'An Evaluation of the Use and Effectiveness of the Protection from Harassment Act', Home Office Research Study No. 203, 2000), and among the reported cases are some involving animal rights protesters: *Huntingdon Life Sciences* v *Curtin, The Times*, 11 December 1997 (research on animals); *DPP* v *Mosely, The Times*, 23 June 1999 (farming mink). The Act must, therefore, be regarded as part of the weaponry available to the police in dealing with disorder. A major limitation is, however, the requirement of a 'course of conduct' which means that a single 'harassing' event will fall outside the scope of the Act (see *Saihau* v *DPP, The Times*, 29 March 2000). Section 7 defines a course of conduct as involving conduct on at least two occasions. It is only where there are continuing demonstrations in the same location, or directed at the same person or persons, that the Act will be available.

The s. 2 offence carries a maximum penalty on summary conviction of six months. The s. 4 offence is triable either way, with a maximum penalty of five years. These penalties are increased if the offence is 'racially aggravated' (s. 32 of the Crime and Disorder Act 1998), that is that it demonstrates or is motivated by hostility to the victim's membership (or supposed membership) of a racial group (s. 28 of the Crime and Disorder Act 1998).

9.4.8.2 **Criminal Justice and Police Act 2001, s. 42**

This provision sets out a police power in relation to 'harassing' behaviour directed at a person in a 'dwelling'. It was passed primarily in response to the activities of animal rights demonstrators in targeting of individuals involved, sometimes fairly indirectly, with companies engaged in research involving the use of animals. The section empowers a police officer to issue a direction to a person who is outside or in the vicinity of another's home, where the constable has reasonable grounds to believe that the person is there to represent to someone on the premises '(i) that he should not do something that he is entitled or required to do; or (ii) that he should do something that he is not under any obligation to do'. In addition the constable must also reasonably believe that the presence of the person (together with any others who are there) amounts to or is likely to result in harassment to the resident, or is likely to cause alarm or distress to the resident.

The direction which may be issued is to do 'all such things as the constable may specify' in order prevent the harassment, alarm, or distress. It is an offence know-ingly to contravene a direction issued under this section, punishable on summary conviction with a level 4 fine, or three months' imprisonment, or both.

This is potentially a very powerful provision, giving a very broad discretion to the police officer on the spot. It will not have any application to demonstrations in public places, but might be used, for example in relation to 'vigilante' cam-paigns against suspected paedophiles. It has also been suggested that it could be used against the press, in relation to the 'doorstepping' of those in the news (L. Hickman, 'Press Freedom and New Legislation', (2001) 151 NLJ 716), in which case it could run into problems of compatibility with Art. 10 of the ECHR. This would depend on the particular use of the power, however.

9.4.8.3 **Criminal Justice Act 2001, s. 1**

Note also the powers to impose 'on the spot' penalty notices for certain offences related to public order introduced by this section, as discussed in chapter 3 (3.4.5).

9.4.8.4 **Prohibition of uniforms: Public Order Act 1936, s. 1**

This surviving section of the Public Order Act 1936 was originally enacted in response to the adoption of quasi-military uniforms by certain fascist organiza-tions in the 1930s (such as Oswald Mosley's British Union of Fascists who wore, and became known as, 'black shirts'). It makes it an offence to wear in any public place or at any public meeting a uniform signifying association with any political organization or with the promotion of any political object. There is a proviso by which the chief officer of police, with the consent of the Home Secretary, may permit the wearing of such uniforms on occasions when there is not likely to be a risk of public disorder. Any prosecution must be brought with the consent of the Attorney-General.

What exactly constitutes a uniform for these purposes? The Act contains no definition or guidance, but the issue was considered in *O'Moran v DPP* [1975] QB 864, where the alleged uniform consisted of black berets, dark glasses, and dark (though not identical) clothing. Lord Widgery thought that the 'wearing' of a uni-form required some article of clothing, so that a lapel badge, for instance, could not on its own constitute a uniform. Thus, the adoption by the Labour Party of the red rose would not fall foul of this section. Beyond this, however, it seems to be a question of looking at all the circumstances. Lord Widgery was of the view that the wearing of the beret could, in itself, constitute the wearing of a uniform. The link with a political group could be established either by evidence of previous association, or from the present circumstances.

The section could still be used against the adoption of uniforms by political factions. Its most likely target, however, would be members of quasi-military political organizations, such as those which have operated in Northern Ireland. Many of these have been proscribed in this country under the terrorism legislation. This legislation contains its own broader provision making it an offence, in a public place to wear any item of dress, or wear, carry, or display any article in such a way or in such circumstances as to arouse reasonable apprehension that the person is a member or supporter of a proscribed organization (s. 13 of the Terrorism Act 2000). The reference to 'carrying' an article would be broad enough to cover the carrying of a placard or banner indicating support for an organization, as well as the wearing of a badge or emblem.

9.4.8.5 Aggravated trespass

Section 68 of the CJPOA 1994 created the offence of 'aggravated trespass'. The main target for this offence was expected to be hunt saboteurs, though it is expressed in terms wide enough to cover any trespasser who disrupts a lawful activity taking place on land. Thus, disruption of any type of sporting event, for example, has the potential of falling within this section, including the activities of the normally harmless, but occasionally infuriating, 'streakers'.

The *actus reus* of the offence involves trespass on land. As originally drafted the activity had to take place in the open air, but that requirement was removed by the Anti-social Behaviour Act 2003. 'Land' in this section does not include roads or other highways, apart from bridleways, footpaths, byways, and certain cycle tracks (see s. 61(9)). To commit the offence the trespasser must then act with a particular intention in relation to a lawful activity taking place, or about to take place, on that land, or adjoining land. In *Bauer* v *DPP* [2013] EWHC 634, which involved the invasion of a department store by demonstrators against the tax avoidance activities of certain companies, the court held that the continuation of trespassory occupation, in the form of a 'demonstration', could constitute the further 'act' required for the commission of the offence. The intention required is that this further act by the trespasser(s) should have the effect (s. 68(1)):

(a) of intimidating [persons engaged in or about to be engaged in the lawful activity] or any of them, so as to deter them or any of them from engaging in that activity,

(b) of obstructing that activity, or

(c) of disrupting that activity.

The offence therefore has the effect of criminalizing certain types of protest, particularly those involving direct action against the activities of others. In addition to the examples given above, the offence would also be available for use against, for example, protesters against a new road who lay down in front of tractors, or tied themselves to trees, with the intention of obstructing or disrupting those trying to clear the land. One of the first reported uses of the offence, however, was indeed concerned with hunt saboteurs. In *Winder* v *DPP*, *The Times*, 14 August 1996, the Divisional Court held that running after a hunt with the intention of getting close enough to disrupt it constituted the offence, even though the running itself was not intended to, and did not, cause any disruption.

There was concern when the CJPOA 1994 was being considered in Parliament that this provision might criminalize the activities of the Ramblers' Association, or other walking clubs, who might accidentally disrupt, for example, farming activities. The requirement, however, of an intention to intimidate, obstruct, or disrupt means that this is unlikely. In any case, it has now been held that the offence can only be committed where there are other people present on the land whose activities are being affected. In *Tilly* v *DPP*, *The Times*, 27 November 2001, the Divisional Court considered an appeal from an environmental protester who had been convicted of an offence under s. 68 resulting from the destruction of genetically modified (GM) crops.

The court held that the section 'contemplated a situation in which people were intimidated or could not get on with what they were there to do'. Since this had not been the situation in the case under consideration, the appeal was allowed. The simple disruption of farming activities is, therefore, not enough in itself to constitute the *actus reus* of the offence. A slightly different situation arose in *DPP* v *Bayer* [2003] EWHC 2567 (Admin), [2004] Cr App R 38. Here the demonstrators had attached themselves to tractors sowing seed, so there was clearly a disruption of people going about their work (unlike the situation in *Tilly* v *DPP*). At trial, however, the district judge had acquitted on the basis that the defendants had a defence of 'defence of property'—i.e. based on the effect that GM seed or crops might have on neighbouring land. On a prosecutor's appeal, the Divisional Court held that this was no defence. The sowing of the seed was not unlawful and the defence of 'defence of property' was not available on the facts.

In *Ayliffe* v *DPP* [2005] EWHC 684 (Admin) the Divisional Court considered three appeals relating to the defendants' trespass on to military premises. Their objective in each case was to protest against the Iraq War, and to disrupt activities being undertaken in relation to that war. Part of their defence was that the war was illegal, and that therefore they were not disrupting a lawful activity. The Divisional Court held that the magistrates' courts which convicted the defendants of aggravated trespass had been right to hold that the legality of the war was not a justiciable issue (relying on the earlier Court of Appeal decision in *R* v *Jones* [2004] EWCA Crim 1981, [2004] 4 All ER 955). As regards the defendants' additional argument that the activities at the establishments constituted 'war crimes' under the International Criminal Court Act 2001, this was a justiciable issue, but the defendants had provided no foundation for their claim. The offences under s. 68 were made out. The court did, however, rule that it was not open to the prosecution to select a particular lawful activity and argue that this had been disrupted. If the defendant argued that it was his or her intention to disrupt a specific activity, and that activity was found to be unlawful, there would be no offence under s. 68, despite the fact that the prosecution might be able to point to other, lawful, activities which had also been disrupted by the defendant's actions.

The offence under the section is summary, and punishable with up to three months' imprisonment, or a fine not exceeding level 4 (s. 68(3)).

The s. 68 offence is backed up by a power under s. 69 whereby a police officer may direct trespassers who are reasonably believed to be committing, or to have committed, or to be intending to commit an offence under s. 68 to leave the land. The power may also be used where there is reason to believe that two or more people are trespassing with the common purpose of intimidation, obstruction, or disruption in relation to a lawful activity. The decision to use this power must be taken by the senior police officer present (no minimum rank is specified), but the direction may be communicated by any constable. A person who knows that a direction has been given commits an offence by either failing to leave the land as soon as practicable, or re-entering as a trespasser within a period of three months. It is a defence, however, for the accused to show that (s. 69(4)):

(a) he was not trespassing on the land, or

(b) he had a reasonable excuse for failing to leave the land as soon as practicable or, as the case may be, for again entering the land as a trespasser.

The penalty on summary conviction is up to three months' imprisonment, or a fine not exceeding level 4, or both.

9.4.8.6 Assemblies of 'travellers'

One type of assembly which has caused problems in recent years has arisen where groups of travelling people, living in caravans or other mobile homes, have camped out on private land, and there have been problems in moving them on. These are the so-called 'hippy convoys' or 'New Age travellers'. A particularly notorious case occurred at about the time the POA 1986 was under consideration in Parliament, and as a result a section was added to try to deal specifically with this problem (s. 39). This has now been repealed and replaced by the very similar s. 61 of the CJPOA 1994.

The section has the effect of making a certain type of trespass by a group (though it may be as few as two) into a criminal offence. It is subject to a number of limitations, however.

First, it does not apply to buildings, other than agricultural buildings or scheduled monuments. So the offence has no relevance to squatters in residential property, nor does it apply to land forming part of a highway. It does, however, apply to common land.

Second, no offence is committed until there has been a direction to leave, issued by a police officer. The power to issue a direction arises when the officer reasonably believes that certain other conditions are fulfilled. These are, first, that the officer reasonably believes that the occupier, or someone acting on behalf of the occupier, has taken reasonable steps to ask the trespassers to leave. It was held in *Krumpa and Anderson* v *DPP* [1989] Crim LR 295, a case on s. 39 of the POA 1986, that an indication that a request to leave will be made at some point in the future is not sufficient to satisfy this requirement. Moreover, the officer must reasonably believe either that one or more trespassers has caused damage to property on the land, or has used threatening, abusive, or insulting words or behaviour towards the occupier, or the occupier's family, employee, or agent, or that the trespassers have brought six or more vehicles on to the land.

Once the direction has been given (there is no indication of the form it should take), anyone knowing of it who fails to comply as soon as reasonably practicable, or tries to re-enter the land within three months, will commit an offence. There is, of course, a power of arrest in relation to this offence under s. 24 of PACE 1984 (see chapter 3 (3.5.3.1)). Thus, if a direction is given, and there is no attempt to comply, everyone on the land can be arrested. The 'assembly' will be broken up, and the land cleared. Supplementary powers of seizure are given by s. 62 in relation to 'vehicles' (broadly defined in s. 61(9)) which are left on the land following a direction.

The High Court considered the operation of s. 61 and its compatibility with the HRA 1998 in *R (on the Application of Fuller)* v *Chief Constable of Dorset* [2001] EWHC 1057 (Admin), [2002] 3 All ER 57, and made the following rulings:

- A direction to leave under the section can only be issued by the police following a failure to comply with an occupier's request to leave.
- The section only gives a power to direct trespassers to leave as soon as reasonably practicable after the issue of the direction; it does not permit the giving of a direction to leave at some future time.
- The section is compatible with Art. 6 of the ECHR—the possibility of challenging the exercise of the powers under the section before a court satisfies the requirements of this article.
- The section is not incompatible with Art. 1 of the First Protocol to the ECHR (peaceful enjoyment of possessions). Exercise of the powers under the section may engage Art. 8 of the ECHR (right to respect for private and family life) but may well be justified under Art. 8(2) (particularly where the establishment of an encampment is unlawful). (This issue is discussed further below.)
- While a local authority must pay attention to the relevant Convention rights in considering whether to enforce its rights to possession of land, the police in exercising their powers under s. 61 were entitled to assume that the local authority had carried out its responsibilities in this respect. A challenge to the police's action under the section could not be used as a means of challenging a local authority's decision.

There is also a power under s. 62A, introduced by the Anti-social Behaviour Act 2003, to remove trespassers on land with a vehicle with an intention of residing there.

The implications of Art. 8 of the ECHR on the rights of 'travellers' to remain on property have been considered in some cases. In *Leeds City Council* v *Price* [2006] UKHL 10, [2006] 2 WLR 570 the defendants were Gypsies who had moved their caravans on to a council recreation ground. The council took action to remove them, which the Gypsies resisted, relying on Art. 8 of the ECHR. They relied in part on a decision of the ECtHR in *Connors* v *United Kingdom* (2004) EHRR 189, where the court had found a violation of Art. 8 in connection with the eviction of a Gypsy family from a licensed site. The council in *Connors* had a right to terminate on notice, to which proprietary right there was no legal defence in English law. The ECtHR held that this lack of a means of challenging the eviction, for which judicial review was an inadequate remedy, constituted a breach of the claimants' rights under Art. 8. In *Leeds City Council* v *Price* the council argued that the position was governed in English law by the House of Lords decision in *Harrow London Borough Council* v *Qazi* [2003] UKHL 43, [2003] 4 All ER 461, where it was held by the majority that a valid possessory claim under domestic property law would automatically defeat an Art. 8 argument. In *Leeds City Council* v *Price* it was accepted by the House of Lords that the very strict line taken in *Qazi* could not stand alongside the judgment of the ECtHR in *Connors*. The Art. 8 right was engaged by the eviction, and there was a need to establish that the infringement of the right was properly justified as being 'necessary in a democratic society' under Art. 8(2). On the facts, however, and in particular the fact that the Gypsies had been on the site for a very short time before being evicted, it was held that there was no unjustifiable infringement of their Art. 8 right.

9.5 Civil orders

In two areas of relatively low-level public disorder, recourse has been had to civil, rather than criminal, procedures as a means of control. These are orders directed at anti-social behaviour and football banning orders.

9.5.1 Orders concerning anti-social behaviour

Anti-social behaviour orders (ASBOs) were introduced by s. 1 of the Crime and Disorder Act 1998. They are issued by a magistrates' court, but could be applied for by a range of authorities, including the police, local authorities, and social landlords. They were civil orders but backed up by criminal sanctions. This led the House of Lords in *McCann* v *Manchester Crown Court* [2002] UKHL 39, [2002] 4 All ER 593 to hold that the applicant for an order should be required to prove the case according to the criminal standard—i.e. beyond reasonable doubt.

The orders were used in a wide range of situations, with the kind of behaviour against which they were made being predictable, mainly involving verbal abuse, threats, and intimidation. There were some inventive uses as, for example, in relation to a number of orders made in relation to prostitution. One council has also successfully used ASBOs against corporations found to have been fly-posting in its area (see D. Whyte, 'Punishing Anti-social Business', (2004) 154 NLJ 1293).

Following a review of ASBOs in 2011, they are now to be replaced by provisions of the Anti-Social Behaviour and Policing Bill, which at the time of writing was concluding its consideration by Parliament. Its provisions are expected to be in force at some point during 2014. Under the new legislation, ASBOs will be replaced by Injunctions to Prevent Nuisance and Disorder (IPNA). These will be available in relation to behaviour which is 'capable of causing nuisance or annoyance to any person'. This a broader definition than in relation to ASBOs, which depended on proof of 'harassment, alarm or distress'. There will be no criminal offence for breaking an IPNA; a breach will be treated as a contempt of court in the same way as any other injunction. This removal of the criminal sanction means that it has been thought possible to require proof of the relevant behaviour on simply the civil standard—i.e. the balance of probabilities rather than beyond reasonable doubt. Another difference is that IPNAs may involve positive requirements as to behaviour, as well as restrictions. It remains to be seen whether these changes will result in an improved system for controlling anti-social behaviour.

9.5.2 **Football banning orders**

The provisions which relate to these orders originated in the POA 1986, but are now contained in ss 14–21 of the Football Spectators Act 1989, as amended by the Football (Disorder) Act 2000. There are two situations when a banning order can be made. The first (under s. 14A) is where a person is convicted of a 'relevant offence', as set out in Sch. 1 to the Act. It is basically concerned with offences of violence or drunkenness at, or near, a football match. The second situation is where an application for such an order is made to a magistrates' court by a chief constable (s. 14B). Such an application can be made where it appears to the chief constable that the person has 'at any time caused or contributed to any violence or disorder in the United Kingdom or elsewhere' (s. 14B(2)). The order will be designed to prevent the person attending certain football matches in England and Wales, or abroad. This may be achieved by requiring the person to attend a police station at the relevant time. In relation to a banning order applying to matches abroad, the person may be required to surrender their passport to the police. If made under s. 14A the order may last between three and 10 years; if made under s. 14B it will last between two and three years.

The operation of international banning orders, which were introduced by the Football (Disorder) Act 2000 following problems with England supporters at the European Championships in Italy in June 2000, was considered in *Gough* v *Chief Constable of Derbyshire* [2002] EWCA Civ 351, [2002] 2 All ER 985. The Court of Appeal confirmed their 'civil' nature, but stressed that, because of the serious restraint on freedom involved, a standard of proof close to the criminal standard should be applied. The provisions were, however, found to be compatible with the ECHR and the EU laws on 'free movement'.

9.5.3 **Dispersal orders**

Dispersal orders are of a slightly different type to ASBOs and football banning orders, in that they are issued by the police rather than a court, but can conveniently be dealt with here. They were introduced by Pt. 4, ss 30–6 of the Anti-social Behaviour Act 2003. For the relevant power to arise, a superintendent must have reasonable grounds for believing that members of the public have been intimidated, harassed, alarmed, or distressed by the behaviour of groups of two or more people, in public places in any locality in the superintendent's police area, and that anti-social behaviour is a significant problem in that locality. He or she will then have the power to issue an 'authorisation' under s. 30, which may last for up to six months. Section 31 requires that the authorization must be in writing, signed by the officer issuing it. It must specify the grounds on which it is given, the location it covers, and its duration. The approval of the relevant local authority must be given. Publicity must be given to it by a newspaper announcement, or notices conspicuously placed in the relevant area, or both.

Once a valid authorization has been issued it will allow any constable to take action when he or she has reasonable grounds to believe that the presence or behaviour of a group of two or more persons in the relevant locality has resulted, or is likely to result, in members of the public being intimidated, harassed, alarmed, or distressed. Note that 'presence' is sufficient—no intimidating, etc, behaviour is necessary—and that no one has to have been intimidated, etc. It is sufficient that such intimidation, etc, is 'likely'. The powers may also be used by Police Community Support Officers (s. 33).

There are two sets of powers which may be used by the constable. The first set, under s. 30(4), relates to the dispersal of the group. The constable may:

- require the group to disperse—immediately or within a specified time;
- require any members of the group who do not live in the locality to leave that locality;
- prohibit any members of the group who do not live in the locality from returning to it for a period of up to 24 hours.

This set of powers does not apply to those engaged in conduct which is part of a lawful trade dispute (under s. 220 of the Trade Union and Labour Relations Consolidation Act 1992), or to people taking part in a public procession falling within s. 11 of the POA 1986, for which the relevant notice (if required) has been given to the police.

The use of this set of powers as a means of controlling demonstrations was considered by the Court of Appeal in *R (Singh)* v *Chief Constable of West Midlands Police* [2006] EWCA Civ 118, [2007] 2 All ER 297. Two authorizations had been issued, overlapping in locality, in relation to Birmingham city centre. One related to problems with drunken behaviour, and the other to skateboarding. The areas included the site of Birmingham Repertory Theatre, which at the relevant time was presenting performances of a play, *Bezhti*, to which certain members of the local Sikh community objected. There were demonstrations outside the theatre, some of them peaceful, but at other times attempts were made to enter the theatre. On the relevant day a group of about 30 entered the theatre. There was evidence that some members of the audience, and others, were alarmed by what was going on. After some time the police decided to issue a dispersal notice under s. 30. The appellant was then found outside the theatre, and refused to leave the area. He was arrested for failing to comply with the dispersal order. He later challenged the validity of the dispersal order on the basis that s. 30 was not intended to apply to demonstrators; that the use of the power in this way was incompatible with the ECHR; and that an authorization issued for one purpose could not be used against a completely different kind of behaviour. The application was dismissed by the Divisional Court, and this decision was upheld by the Court of Appeal. On the first point, the Court of Appeal noted that the exclusion from the scope of s. 30 of trade disputes and processions falling within s. 11 of the POA 1986 would not have been necessary if the s. 30 power did not apply to any type of demonstration. It could be used to cover such situations. On the third point—the fact that the authorizations had been issued for different purposes than the one for which they were used in this case—the Court held that the wording of s. 30 did not require any link between the initial reason for the authorization and the constable's exercise of the dispersal power. Provided that the conditions for the exercise of the power were satisfied, its use was lawful. Finally, on the ECHR point, the court considered that the use of the power in these circumstances was proportionate. The police had considered various options for dealing with the situation and had decided that the use of s. 30 was the least intrusive. In those circumstances there was no incompatibility with convention rights under Art. 10 or Art. 11 (both of which are, of course, qualified rights).

This use of the first set of powers under s. 30 is surprising. On the special facts of the case, it is understandable that the court felt that its use was acceptable. It would be another matter, however, if the police started routinely to use this power to disperse demonstrations. Two factors militate against this. First, there is the requirement of local authority approval for the issue of an authorization. This is unlikely to be forthcoming in relation to an authorization designed primarily to limit the right to demonstrate. Second, the authorization can only be made where there has been intimidatory, etc., behaviour and the dispersal power can only be used where further such behaviour is occurring or likely to occur.

The second set of powers under s. 30 is rather different. It operates between 9 p.m. and 6 a.m. and empowers a constable in uniform to remove from the area a young person under the age of 16, who is not under the effective control of a parent or responsible person of 18 or over. The young person may be removed to his or her place of residence, unless the constable has reasonable grounds to believe that he or she would be likely to suffer significant harm there (s. 30(6)). In that case, it appears there is no power of removal, since no alternative destination is provided for in the section. Where the power under s. 30(6) is used, the relevant local authority must be informed (s. 32(4)).

This power was challenged in *R (W)* v *Metropolitan Police Commissioner* [2006] EWCA Civ 458, [2006] 3 All ER 458. The applicant, lived in the Richmond area, in which an authorization was in place. While out with a friend during the daytime he had been warned by a Community Support Officer. He then discovered the power of the police to take young people found out after 9 p.m. back to their homes. Not wishing to risk the embarrassment of this happening, he felt unable to go out in the evenings without his parents. He brought an action for judicial review, contending that the powers infringed his Convention rights. The Divisional Court interpreted the power under s. 30(6) as being purely permissive—that is, it simply gave the police the power to take home a young person who was willing to be removed from the area. On appeal, the Court of Appeal reversed this decision. It held that the police did have the power to use reasonable force to remove a young person and take him or her home. The power was not to be used arbitrarily, however, in relation to any young person found out at night. The purpose of the power, and the grounds on which it may be used were set out as follows (para. 35):

> The purpose for which the power was conferred is, in our view, clear and largely uncontentious. It is to protect children under the age of 16 within a designated dispersal area at night from the physical and social risks of anti-social behaviour by others. Another purpose is to prevent children from themselves participating in anti-social behaviour within a designated dispersal area at night. The subsection does not confer an arbitrary power to remove children who are not involved in, nor at risk from exposure to, actual

> or imminently anticipated anti-social behaviour. It does not confer a power to remove children simply because they are in a designated dispersal area at night. Children are, so far as this legislation goes, free to go there without fear of being removed, provided that they do not themselves participate in anti-social behaviour and provided that they avoid others who are behaving anti-socially.

Interpreted in this way, there was no conflict with Convention rights.

9.6 The common law: breach of the peace

The power that any constable has to take reasonable steps to stop an actual or imminent breach of the peace is clearly of considerable significance in relation to the policing of disorder. The definition of the concept and the power of arrest attaching to it are discussed in chapter 3 (3.5.1). Here its specific use in the context of the freedom of assembly is considered. The traditional approach to this area has been relatively unhelpful to those seeking to hold demonstrations. Recent case law, both domestic and from the ECtHR, has, however, suggested a more liberal attitude. The whole area has been the subject of a full reconsideration by the House of Lords in *R (Laporte)* v *Chief Constable of Gloucestershire Constabulary* [2007] UKHL 55, [2007] 2 All ER 529. This is now the leading authority on the extent of police powers to deal with a breach of the peace, and all the earlier case law must be reviewed in the light of it. Aspects of the power (primarily the use of the power to contain crowds, commonly known as 'kettling') were also considered by the House of Lords in *Austin* v *Commissioner of Police for the Metropolis* [2009] UKHL 5, and by the ECtHR in *Austin* v *United Kingdom*, App. No. 39692/09 (2012) 55 EHHR 14.

The traditional view, as exemplified by the cases of *Duncan* v *Jones*, *Piddington* v *Bates*, and *Moss* v *McLachlan* is outlined first, and then the effect of the more recent cases is considered.

The case of *Duncan* v *Jones* [1936] 1 KB 218 shows how the power might be used effectively to prevent a public meeting. The appellant had attempted to address a meeting of about 30 people protesting about the Incitement to Disaffection Bill. The meeting was taking place in the road, opposite the entrance to an unemployed training centre. There was some evidence that meetings previously held at the same location, and addressed by the appellant, had led to breaches of the peace. A police officer (the chief constable, in fact), told the appellant that the meeting could not be held where she wanted it, but could be held some 175 yards away. When she refused to move, she was arrested, and was charged with obstructing a police officer in the execution of his duty. She was convicted, and appealed, by way of case stated to the Divisional Court. The Court refused to recognize that the case had anything to do with the rights to hold public meetings, or whether an assembly could become unlawful simply because a breach of the peace might be caused by people opposed to it. They had no doubt that the police officer was acting within his powers in trying to prevent an apprehended breach of the peace; indeed it was his duty to do so. The conviction was upheld.

A similar result occurred in *Piddington* v *Bates* [1961] 1 WLR 162, which was concerned with an industrial dispute. There was a picket of 18 outside a printers' works where eight men were working. A police officer tried to limit the pickets to two at each entrance. The appellant resisted this limitation, and gently pushed past the police officer. He was arrested, and charged with obstructing a police office in the execution of his duty. Once again, the Divisional Court upheld the conviction. Provided that there were reasonable grounds for anticipating that a breach of the peace was a real possibility, then the police officer had acted lawfully. While not being prepared to express an opinion on the appropriate number of pickets to allow in such a situation, the court was also not prepared to interfere with the magistrate's decision of fact that the appropriate conditions for the exercise of the restriction existed. In *Laporte's* case Lord Bingham referred to *Piddington v Bates* as an 'aberrant decision', in that it did not recognize that the police have only the same powers as the private citizen in relation to breaches of the peace, it put the test for risk of a breach of the peace too low, and it stated, incorrectly, that a police officer could take 'such steps as on the evidence before him he thinks are proper' in order to preserve the peace (*Laporte* [2007] UKHL 55, para. 47).

The third case to be considered is also drawn from the context of industrial disputes, that is, the case of *Moss v McLachlan* [1985] IRLR 77. During the 1984 miners' strike the police regularly placed patrols near motorway exits on the M1, to try to prevent so-called 'flying pickets' from militant areas in Yorkshire, joining picket lines at more moderate pits in Nottinghamshire. On this occasion the police stopped a group of 25 cars containing 60–80 men. From badges and car stickers, the men were clearly identifiable as striking miners. Some of the men refused to obey an instruction from a police officer to turn back from the pits, and were arrested. They were convicted by the magistrates of obstructing a police officer in the execution of his duty. The Divisional Court held that the police had not simply a right, but a duty to prevent breaches of the peace occurring. In the words of Skinner J (p. 78):

> Provided [the police officers] honestly and reasonably form the opinion that there is a real risk of a breach of the peace in the sense that it is in close proximity both in place and time, then the conditions exist for reasonable preventive acting [*sic.*] including, if necessary, the measures taken in this case.

As to the proximity, the court thought that the police, if satisfied that 'there was a real possibility of the occupants [of the cars] causing a breach of the peace one-and-a-half miles away, a journey of less than five minutes by car', would be under a duty to prevent the convoy proceeding further. It is clear, then, that the breach of the peace does not have to be likely to occur 'immediately' in the normal sense of that word. A delay of five minutes still justifies police action. Presumably the delay would in practice have been longer, unless it was thought that a breach of the peace would have occurred as soon as the miners arrived at the pits. It is more likely that such a breach would in fact only have occurred at a point where working miners were trying to get into or out of the pit, which might have been some time later.

The approach outlined in the above three cases makes the breach of the peace powers a very effective weapon for the police in dealing with demonstrations and assemblies. It would appear to enable the police to take whatever action is appropriate to stop a breach of the peace, even in relation to people who are otherwise acting lawfully. The House of Lords, in *Laporte*'s case, however, has indicated that this view goes too far, as is discussed in detail below. The approach of the House in this case was foreshadowed by cases such as *Foulkes v Chief Constable of Merseyside* [1998] 3 All ER 705 and *Bibby v Chief Constable of Essex*, *The Times*, 24 April 2000, which held that the power to arrest for a breach of the peace should not be used in relation to a person who is otherwise acting lawfully, other than in the most exceptional circumstances, and where that person's behaviour was likely to involve a breach. This approach was applied in the context of a 'demonstration' in *Redmond-Bate v DPP* [1999] Crim LR 998. The appellant was one of three women preaching from the steps of Wakefield Cathedral. A hostile crowd of about 100 people had gathered. A police officer, fearing that a breach of the peace would occur, asked the women to stop preaching. When they refused, the constable arrested them. They were charged with obstructing an officer in the execution of his duty; that is to prevent a breach of the peace. The Divisional Court held that the arrest was unlawful. The women's conduct had been lawful, and no threat to the peace came from them. The Court pointed out that the right to freedom of speech, as protected by the ECHR, did not only apply to the inoffensive, but extended to the 'irritating, the contentious, the heretical, the unwelcome and the provocative provided it did not tend to provoke violence'. Accordingly, the constable was not acting in the course of his duty when he asked the women to stop preaching, and they were not obstructing him when they refused to do so.

The decision in the *Redmond-Bate* case cast doubt on whether *Duncan v Jones*, *Piddington v Bates*, and *Moss v McLachlan* were correctly decided. Significant clarification has now been provided by the House of Lords in *R (Laporte) v Chief Constable of Gloucestershire* [2007] UKHL 55, [2007] 2 AC 105. Coaches travelling from London to RAF Fairford in Gloucestershire were taking the applicant and others to an anti-war demonstration at the airbase. The police had received notice of the demonstration, and conditions and procedures were in place governing the route of a procession from Fairford village to the airbase, and in relation to the proposed demonstration outside the airbase. Many police had been deployed to deal with the situation. The police were also aware of the coaches travelling from London. There was some evidence that those on the coaches included members of an anarchist group known as the Wombles (White Overalls Movement Building Libertarian Effective Struggles), who had been known to be violent. Ms Laporte was not part of this group, nor were the majority of the coach passengers, though some of them were wearing white overalls, like the Wombles, as part of a peaceful group called the Gloucestershire Weapons Inspectors. While the coaches were en route, Chief Superintendent Lambert, who was in charge of the operation at Fairford noted in his log that the coaches were to be intercepted and searched. If weapons, etc, were found, the coaches were to be returned to London. He also noted however (*Laporte* [2007] UKHL 55, para. 10):

They are not to be arrested to prevent a breach of the peace at that particular time, if that is the only offence apparent, as I do not consider there to be an imminent breach of the peace.

In accordance with Mr Lambert's orders, the coaches were stopped some 5km (by road) from Fairford by the Gloucestershire police. The coaches were searched, and some items were seized, in other words (*Laporte* [2007] UKHL 55, para. 11):

> ...some dust and face masks, three crash helmets, hoods, five hard hats, overalls, scarves, a can of red spray paint, two pairs of scissors and a safety flare. In the luggage compartment of the first coach the police found five polycarbonate home-made shields.

Eight members of the Wombles were identified, and one arrest was made of a person suspected of violent involvement in an earlier incident at Fairford. The applicant and others were then detained for two-and-a-half hours, loaded back on to the coaches, and returned to London with a police escort. They were not allowed to leave the coaches during the journey back to London, despite their requests for 'comfort stops'. Ms Laporte subsequently sought judicial review of Mr Lambert's action. The Divisional Court and the Court of Appeal held that the action in preventing the applicant proceeding to the demonstration was justified by the breach of the peace powers, as interpreted in *Moss* v *McLachlan*, and was not in conflict with Art. 5 of the ECHR. However, neither the detention, nor the forcible return to London, could be justified on this basis. Such action was a disproportionate response to any risk of a breach of the peace. To that extent the police had acted unlawfully. On appeal to the House of Lords, the House went further, and held that the police were not justified in preventing the coaches proceeding, so that this action was also unlawful.

In coming to this conclusion, the House undertook a comprehensive review of the powers of the police (and private citizens) in relation to actual or anticipated breaches of the peace. All five members of the House gave judgment, and there is some variation in their reasoning, but the following points seem to emerge. First, there is no difference between the powers of a police officer and those of a private citizen in relation to breaches of the peace. Second, in relation to anticipated breaches of the peace there is no 'sliding scale' under which the more imminent the breach the more coercive the powers that can be used, and vice versa. Any suggestion in earlier cases to this effect, e.g. *Piddington* v *Bates* and *Moss* v *McLachlan*, was disapproved. There is one test for using any of the powers relating to an anticipated breach of the peace, and that is that the breach is 'imminent'. 'Imminence' in this context has the meaning of 'immediacy'—the breach must be 'about to happen' in the near future. The decision in *Moss* v *McLachlan* was not disapproved, but some members of the House regarded it as being at the limits of 'imminence' (e.g. Lord Bingham, para. 51 and Lord Brown, para. 118).

Applying this approach to the facts in *Laporte*'s case, the police's position was not assisted by the note in Mr Lambert's log, referred to above, that he did not regard a breach of the peace as imminent, so that in his view the power of arrest was not available. If the power of arrest was not available then, in the view of the House, no other power to deal with a breach of the peace was available either, since the test was the same for all of them. It was also relevant that there was no suggestion that the coach passengers as a whole were intent on violence, and that in any case there were very detailed procedures in place at Fairford, backed by a strong police presence, to ensure that the protest and demonstration took place without a breach of the peace occurring. On this basis the purported exercise by the police of a power to prevent the coaches proceeding on the basis of an anticipated breach of the peace was unlawful. The view was also expressed, obiter, by some members of the House of Lords, that even if the test of imminence is satisfied, then it is only in exceptional circumstances that steps to prevent a breach of the peace may be taken against those who are acting lawfully.

This analysis of the powers of the police in relation to a breach of the peace is welcome, and places clear limits on what was becoming a very broad discretionary power. The subsequent application of the *Laporte* decision by the House of Lords in *Austin* v *Commissioner of Police of the Metropolis* and by the ECtHR in *Austin* v *United Kingdom* (discussed below) is less encouraging. The approach in the *Laporte* case is, however, supported by the decision of the ECtHR in *Steel and ors* v *United Kingdom* (1998) 28 EHRR 603, to which the House of Lords made reference, with approval. In *Steel*, there were in fact three different situations considered by the Court. In the first, the applicant S took part in a protest against a grouse shoot. She attempted to obstruct and distract those taking part. At one point she intentionally walked in front of a member of the shoot as he was lifting his shotgun, thereby preventing him from firing. She was arrested and detained for a number of hours in order to prevent 'any further breach of the peace'. The second applicant, L took part in a protest against the building of an extension to a motorway. The group of which she was a part climbed trees and onto machinery. Eventually, while L was standing under the 'bucket' of a JCB digger, she was arrested for conduct 'likely to provoke a disturbance of the peace'. The third, fourth, and fifth applicants, N, P, and C, all participated in protest outside a conference centre in London where a conference concerning 'Fighter Helicopters' was taking place. Their protest took the form of handing out leaflets and holding up banners saying: 'Work for Peace and not War'. They too were arrested for conduct 'likely to provoke a disturbance of the peace'.

Various issues relating to Arts 5 and 6 of the ECHR were raised by all the applicants, but the only finding in their favour in this area was that the arrest and detention of N, P, and C involved a breach of Art. 5(1). This was because in their case, in contrast to the actions of S and L which might have provoked others to violence, the protest of N, P, and C had been entirely peaceful. The police were therefore not justified in fearing a breach of the peace, and the arrests were therefore not lawful under English law or under Art. 5(1) of the ECHR.

The Court also considered in some detail the applicants' claim that their right to freedom of expression under Art. 10 had been infringed. The Court regarded the actions of S and L as constituting 'expression' even though they took the form of disrupting the activities of others. The question was, therefore, whether the action taken against them, and thereby infringing their freedom of expression, was legitimate under Art. 10(2). The Court held that the action was 'prescribed by law'. The concept of 'breach of the peace' was sufficiently well defined by the case law to meet the standards required by the Convention, and as had been held in relation to Art. 5, the police had acted within those powers in arresting S and L. There was no doubt that the arrests were to achieve the legitimate aim under Art. 10(2) of preventing disorder and protecting the rights of others. The only question was therefore whether the action went beyond what was 'necessary in a democratic society'. Although both the applicants had been detained for some time, and had in fact both been imprisoned for refusing to be 'bound over to keep the peace', the Court held that risks of disorder and violence which had been raised by their behaviour meant that the action taken against them was not 'disproportionate'. In relation to S and L, therefore there was no breach of Art. 10.

As regards N, P, and C there was no dispute that their protest was a form of expression, and that their freedom of expression had been infringed by the actions of the police. The question was again, whether this could be justified under Art. 10(2). Here the Court held that the action was not justifiable. Although the action was ostensibly to achieve a legitimate aim, as with S and L, in this case it was not 'prescribed by law' because the police had exceeded their powers. Nor was the action proportionate to the aim; it was therefore not 'necessary in a democratic society' and the rights of N, P, and C under Art. 10 had been unjustifiably infringed.

Having reached these conclusions on Art. 10, the Court did not consider it necessary to deal with the Art. 11 right to assembly since it took the view that this raised the same issues as had already been considered in relation to Art. 10.

The conclusion to be drawn from *Steel and ors v United Kingdom* is that the powers to arrest, etc, on the basis of an apprehended breach of the peace do not necessarily involve any breach of Convention rights. As has now been held by the English courts, however, these powers should only be used where the behaviour of the persons concerned creates an imminent risk of provoking violence or disorder. Where the behaviour of those concerned is lawful and peaceful the mere fact that others may object to it is not enough to justify an arrest. It seems therefore that English law (as explained in the *Laporte* case) and Convention law (as set out in *Steel and ors v United Kingdom*) are very much in unison in this area.

One further decision must be considered, however. This is the decision in the post-*Laporte* case of *Austin* v *Commissioner of Police for the Metropolis* and the subsequent application to the ECtHR. This case arose out of an anti-globalization demonstration held in central London on 1 May 2001. A crowd of around 3,000 people had gathered in Oxford Circus, at around 2 p.m. The police had known that a demonstration was planned, but had no notification, or other specific information in relation to this gathering, or the route of any procession that might follow from it. The police took the decision that it was necessary to retain the crowd in Oxford Circus in order to prevent a breach of the peace—a process which has come to be known as 'kettling'. In the event the majority of the crowd were kept there until after 8 p.m. in the evening, at which point the police decided that it was safe to allow a controlled dispersal. During the afternoon about 400 of the crowd were released. Ms Austin, who was there to demonstrate, and had taken an active part in the demonstration, and Mr Saxby, who simply happened to be caught in the crowd, were among those detained for the whole afternoon, despite their requests to be able to leave (in Ms Austin's case to collect her 11-month-old child). They brought an action for false imprisonment, and under s. 7 of the HRA 1998 for breach of their Art. 5 right to liberty. The trial judge dismissed their claims, and this decision was confirmed by the Court of Appeal. Between the trial and the appeal the decision of the House of Lords in the *Laporte* case was delivered, and this formed the background to the Court of Appeal's decision. The court relied on the obiter statements in the *Laporte* case to the effect that, in exceptional circumstances, the powers to prevent a breach of the peace could be used against those who were otherwise acting lawfully, and held that in all the circumstances it had been justifiable to hold the crowd in Oxford Circus for the relevant time. The judge had found that the police were not dealing with a static crowd, but a group containing demonstrators some of whom at times resorted to violence, lighting fires, and breaking up paving slabs and throwing pieces at the police. As a result, despite the fact that the court accepted that (para. 67):

> ...the containment of the crowd for hours without any or any sufficient toilet facilities and in many cases without food or drink was intolerable, with consequent risk to the health and safety of innocent members of the public, and we can well understand that being in Oxford Circus for so long without any idea when one would be released would have been very unpleasant.

Nevertheless (para. 68) the Court concluded that:

> ...in this very exceptional case, on the basis of the judge's finding that what the police did in containing the crowd was necessary in order to avoid an imminent breach of the peace, the actions of the police were lawful at common law

The claims for false imprisonment thus failed. Perhaps more surprisingly, in considering the claim under Art. 5, the court concluded, contrary to the view of the trial judge, that the Article was not even engaged by the action taken in containing the crowd. The claimant appealed against this aspect of the Court of Appeal's decision, though not against its decision on the common law issues.

The House of Lords confirmed the decision of the Court of Appeal, finding that Art. 5 was not engaged. Lord Hope, with whom the rest of the court agreed, placed considerable weight on the question of the purpose for which the police were using their powers, and the intention behind them The fact that the police view was that the containment was necessary for public order and safety, and that the actions were, in the view of the court, reasonable and proportionate to that purpose, meant that the claimant's Art. 5 rights were not infringed—there was no deprivation of liberty. The overall approach of the court seems to be well summed up by the following passage from Lord Neuberger's judgment (para. 64):

> [I]t is worth bearing in mind that, at least as I see it, if the restraint in the present case did amount to detention within article 5, it would not be possible for the police to justify the detention under the exceptions in paras (b) or (c), not least because of the reasoning of the European Court in *Lawless v Ireland (No 3)* (1961) 1 EHRR 15. I consider that the fact that the restraint in the present case could not be justified under any of the exceptions in paras (a) to (f) supports the contention that the constraint did not amount to detention within article 5 at all. It would appear to me to be very odd if it was not be open to the police to act as they did in the instant circumstances, without infringing the article 5 rights of those who were constrained.

In other words, the House took the view that the police's actions were reasonable, and that Art. 5 needed to be interpreted to fit that conclusion.

In coming to this conclusion, the Court drew analogies with the control of football crowds, or motorists confined to a motorway following an accident, or keeping people away from a fire or a terrorist incident. Whether the detention for such a long period still failed to engage Art. 5 seems dubious, but the court was persuaded by the evidence that the police had considered release at various points during the afternoon, but had decided it was not safe to proceed. It seems bizarre to hold that a group of people, including bystanders who had no part in the demonstration, held in one place for six to seven hours, should be regarded as not being deprived of their liberty. Nevertheless, when the case was considered by the ECtHR it came to the same conclusion—i.e. that Art. 5 was not engaged by these facts. Its decision was very much based on the particular situation which had arisen, rather than being a general approval of kettling. It accepted the findings of the judge that the police had considered releasing people at various points during the afternoon, but that it had always seemed likely that a breach of the peace would follow. It was impossible, in that context, to identify a particular time when a lawful detention might have become a deprivation of liberty. The court stated (para. 67):

> In these circumstances, where the police kept the situation constantly under close review, but where substantially the same dangerous conditions which necessitated the imposition of the cordon at 2 p.m. continued to exist throughout the afternoon and early evening, the Court does not consider that those within the cordon can be said to have been deprived of their liberty within the meaning of Article 5 § 1

It concluded (para. 68):

> The Court emphasises that the above conclusion, that there was no deprivation of liberty, is based on the specific and exceptional facts of this case...It must be underlined that measures of crowd control should not be used by the national authorities directly or indirectly to stifle or discourage protest, given the fundamental importance of freedom of expression and assembly in all democratic societies. Had it not remained necessary for the police to impose and maintain the cordon in order to prevent serious injury or damage, the "type" of the measure would have been different, and its coercive and restrictive nature might have been sufficient to bring it within Article 5.

Despite the caveats set out in para. 68, this was a disappointing decision, and has been subject to much criticism (see, e.g. the views of Professor Ashworth, 'Human Rights: Article 5—Application to Measures of Crowd Control by Police' [2012] Crim LR 545). It should be noted that it does not give the police carte blanche to use kettling whenever there is an imminent breach of the peace. As para. 68 makes clear, it is only where there is a risk of 'serious injury or damage' that the power arises—a stricter standard than a simple breach of the peace (which might, e.g. simply involve two people having a fist fight, with no substantial risk of either being seriously injured).

One decision of an English court post-*Austin* has indicated that the power only relates to detention, and does not give any ancillary powers. In *Mengesha v Commissioner of Police for the Metropolis* [2013] EWHC 1695 the police had contained a crowd, but then had made it a condition of leaving that those doing so gave their personal details and were photographed. The court held that this was unlawful and the police could not make such procedures a condition of allowing people to be released from the containment.

The considerable scope for the use of the powers relating to breach of the peace in relation to demonstrations and assemblies is shown by the above cases. Using these powers, the police might in some cases avoid the need to use the power under the POA 1986 (see 9.2.3) to control the route of a procession. If the reason for the need for such control is the fact that rival groups might otherwise come into violent conflict, then the breach of the peace power may be an appropriate one to use. Similarly, when behaviour at a demonstration is becoming unruly, the breach of the peace power may allow those who are the cause of the disturbance to be arrested, even before they have reached the stage of committing any of the offences under Pt. I of the Act. This flexibility is a clear advantage for the police, but also raises concerns from the civil liberties point of view. To give the police so much discretion always raises the danger the powers will be misused, or overused (as in the case of N, P, and C in *Steel and ors* v *United Kingdom*). It is, therefore, unfortunate that the opportunity has not been taken in the POA 1986, or elsewhere, to put the powers relating to breach of the peace on a statutory footing. This would have enabled their scope to have been defined more precisely, and would have allowed the introduction of appropriate safeguards (perhaps along the lines of those which exist under PACE in relation to stop and search powers (see chapter 3 (3.4)) to guard against the problems of improper or over-enthusiastic use.

9.7 Incitement to racial hatred

This topic is difficult to place. It clearly has strong links with the issue of freedom from discrimination, and indeed, the offences in this area started life as part of the race relations legislation. There has always been the difficulty, however, with any suggestion that all racist statements should constitute a criminal offence. If, for example, a researcher purports to have found as a result of research, that a particular racial group is less intelligent than others, should it be an offence to publish this in an academic journal? To make it so would constitute a very serious encroachment on free speech. There has always been an understandable reluctance to restrict serious attempts to present asserted facts, or genuinely held opinions, however objectionable, provided they are put forward in a context which is not inflammatory. To impose controls on such speech would run counter to all the arguments against restriction outlined at the beginning of chapter 8. The compromise which the British government has made is to make it an offence to publish racist material only where it is presented in immoderate language, and in a context where it is intended or likely to stir up racial hatred. This has meant that the English law on this topic has more in common with the laws protecting public order than with those aimed at preventing discrimination. This was formally recognized in 1986, when the 'racial hatred' offences were re-enacted, and expanded, within the framework of the POA 1986. Part III of the Act contains the relevant provisions. That is the justification for dealing with the offences in this chapter, rather than chapter 13. As will be seen, the offences are apt to control racist speech at public assemblies, but in fact extend beyond that, and in particular cover written material, against which they have most commonly been used. This broader scope to the offences must be kept in mind in considering what follows.

9.7.1 **Meaning of racial hatred**

Racial hatred is defined in s. 17 of the POA 1986. It means 'hatred against any group of persons defined by reference to colour, race, nationality (including citizenship) or ethnic or national origins'. This definition is similar to the definition of 'racial group' in the Race Relations Act 1976, which is discussed in chapter 12 (12.3.3.1). The words 'in Great Britain' which previously appeared after 'persons' were repealed by s. 37 of the ACTSA 2001.

9.7.2 **The offences**

The Act contains a number of offences, all of which have common elements. First, the words or behaviour used must be 'threatening, abusive or insulting' (compare ss 4, 4A, and 5 of the POA 1986 at 9.4.5 and 9.4.6). This is the way in which moderately phrased debate on issues of race is kept out of the scope of the offences. Second, the actions of the person charged must either have been intended to stir up racial hatred, or be likely to do so. The issue of 'intention' in this context has a strange history. In the original version of the offence, in the Race Relations Act 1965, intention was required. It was argued, however, that this placed too heavy a burden on the prosecution and made conviction difficult (see, e.g. the comments of Lord Scarman in his 'Report on the Red Lion Square Disorders', para. 125). As a result, the offence was amended so that it was only necessary to prove that the consequence was likely. This was the form in which it appeared in s. 70 of the Race Relations Act 1976. It was then argued, however, that this was also too restrictive, in that it meant that there could be no conviction if the only publication of the offending words which could be shown was to people who would not be incited to racial hatred (such as, perhaps, MPs or clergymen), or who were perhaps sympathizers who could not be incited further. So in the POA 1986 version of the offences, both the 'intention' and the 'likelihood' version of the offences appear.

In all offences, if the person is not shown to have intended to stir up racial hatred, it will be a defence if there was no intention or awareness that the words or behaviour would or might be threatening, abusive, or insulting (e.g. s. 18(5)).

9.7.2.1 **The publication offences**

These are contained in ss 18–22. Section 18 is the section which deals with speeches at meetings or demonstrations. It makes it an offence to use words or behaviour, or display written material, which fulfils the elements outlined at 9.7.2. The offence may be committed in private, but not within a dwelling (unless seen or heard outside; s. 18(2)). There is a power of arrest without warrant in relation to anyone a constable reasonably suspects is committing this offence (s. 18(3)).

The other offences all deal with different types of publication. Thus, s. 19 covers publishing or distributing written material. It can be used against racist organizations which circulate pamphlets, newsletters, etc, intended or likely to stir up racial hatred. Section 20 deals with the performance of plays, s. 21 with the showing or playing of films, videos, or records, and s. 22 with broadcasting and cable services. It is unlikely that any of these will be used with any frequency. (For detailed discussion of these offences, see A. T. H. Smith, *Offences Against Public Order*, 2nd edn (London: Sweet & Maxwell, 1996), ch. 9.)

9.7.2.2 **The possession offence**

The POA 1986 for the first time made it an offence simply to possess racist material (s. 23). The offence covers both written and visual material (films, videos, tapes, etc). The material must be held with a view to its being published in some way.

Section 24 provides a power of entry and search under warrant where it is suspected that a person is in possession of material contrary to s. 23. This power will be subject to most of the standard procedures under PACE (see chapter 6 (6.4.4)), except that a warrant issued under s. 24 can be used to search for excluded or special procedure material, without the need to use Sch. 1 to PACE (see chapter 6 (6.7.2).

9.7.3 **Enforcement procedures**

No proceedings for any of the offences outlined may be brought without the consent of the Attorney-General. This indicates that this is an area where it is thought that prosecutions might be politically sensitive. It also means that a private individual who might take exception to, for example, a speech by an MP advocating a policy of ending immigration because of the danger that traditional British culture is being 'swamped', will be unable to use the POA 1986 offences against the MP.

The offences are all triable either way and punishable on indictment with up to seven years' imprisonment, or a fine, or both; or on summary conviction with six months' imprisonment, or a fine not exceeding the statutory maximum, or both (s. 27).

Finally, there is a power of forfeiture of relevant material where there has been a conviction under ss 18, 19, 21, or 23 (s. 25).

9.8 **Incitement to religious hatred**

The Racial and Religious Hatred Act 2006 added a Pt. 3A to the POA 1986, consisting of ss 29A–N. These provisions were enacted in the context of increasing concerns about 'religious hatred', in particular arising from the linking of terrorism with Islam. The concern was in relation to the Muslim population being the targets of religious hatred, as a result of this perceived link, and with certain Muslim clerics who were thought to be stirring up hatred against non-Muslims. 'Religious hatred' is thus defined in s. 29A as 'hatred against a group of persons defined by reference to religious belief or lack of religious belief'. There is no attempt to define what constitutes a 'religious belief'.

The offences largely follow the pattern of those considered in 9.7, dealing with the incitement to racial hatred. They cover speech, publications, plays, recordings, and broadcasts (ss 29B–F). There is an offence relating to the possession of inflammatory material (s. 29G). There are powers of entry, search, and seizure (s. 29H), and powers of forfeiture (s. 29I).

There are, however, significant differences in relation to the elements of the offences which the prosecution has to prove. These largely derived from amendments to the Act introduced against the wishes of the government during its passage through Parliament. First, the *actus reus* of the offences is limited to behaviour which is 'threatening', as compared with the 'racial hatred' offences where it is enough for it to be 'abusive' or 'insulting'. Second, whereas the 'racial hatred' offences can be committed when the consequences are 'likely' as well as when they are intended, for the 'religious hatred' offences the prosecution has to prove that the defendant 'intended to stir up religious hatred' by his or her behaviour. Both of these differences significantly limit the scope of the offences.

Because of concerns about the implications for freedom of expression of these new offences, there is a specific limitation provision in s. 29J. This states:

> Nothing in this Part shall be read or given effect in a way which prohibits or restricts discussion, criticism or expressions of antipathy, dislike, ridicule, insult or abuse of particular religions or the beliefs or practices of their adherents, or of any other belief system of the beliefs or practices of its adherents, or proselytising or urging adherents of a different religion or belief system to cease practising their religion or belief system.

This is a further significant limitation on the scope of the offences. It makes it clear that comedians who lampoon a particular religion have nothing to fear from these offences. It also has relevance to the events of February 2006, when a Danish newspaper published cartoons which depicted the prophet Mohammed, and caused great offence to Muslims around the world. There were protests in many cities, including London, and in some cases these were violent. Section 29J makes it clear that a publisher who reprinted the cartoons in England would be unlikely to commit an offence under Pt. 3A of the POA 1986.

Given these limitations, it is likely that there will be very few prosecutions under these offences. They exist as an indication that some restraint should be exercised in relation to attacks on others for their religious beliefs, but they may well be regarded more as 'window dressing' than providing effective criminal law controls.

9.9 Other offences relating to racial or religious hatred

9.9.1 Racially and religiously aggravated offences

The Crime and Disorder Act 1998 provided for increased penalties for certain offences if they are 'racially aggravated'. This was extended to cover religious aggravation by the ACTSA 2001. The particular concern was about attacks on Muslims in the wake of the terrorist attacks in New York of 11 September 2001, but the scope is wider than that. The definition of religious group is 'a group of persons defined by religious belief or lack of religious belief' (s. 28(4) as added by the ATCSA 2001). The effect in relation to offences under ss 4, 4A, and 5 of the POA 1986 is noted earlier in this chapter (see 9.4.5–9.4.6.2). Racially or religiously aggravated means that (s. 28 of the Crime and Disorder Act 1998 as amended):

> (a) at the time of committing the offence, or immediately before or after doing so, the offender demonstrates towards the victim of the offence hostility based on the victim's membership (or presumed membership) of a racial or religious group; or

> (b) the offence is motivated (wholly or partly) by hostility towards members of a racial or religious group based on their membership of that group.

The other offences to which this applies are assaults (ss 20 and 47 of the Offences Against the Person Act 1861 and common assault), criminal damage, and harassment (under the Protection from Harassment Act 1997, for which see 9.4.8.1).

'Racial aggravation' can also be taken into account in sentencing for other offences: s. 82 of the Crime and Disorder Act 1998.

9.9.2 **Racist chanting**

Section 3 of the Football (Offences) Act 1991 provides for an offence of 'indecent or racialist' chanting at a 'designated football match' (as specified by the Secretary of State—s. 1(1)). Racialist chanting means chanting (whether alone or with others) 'consisting of or including matter which is threatening, abusive or insulting to a person by reason of his colour, race, nationality...or ethnic or national origins'.

The offence is punishable on summary conviction with a level 3 fine. In *DPP* v *Stoke-on-Trent Magistrates' Court* [2003] EWHC 1593 (Admin), [2003] 3 All ER 1086, the magistrates had held that the use of the word 'Paki' in a chant of 'you're just a town full of Pakis' was 'mere doggerel' and was no more 'racialist' than terms such as 'Pom', 'Brit', 'Aussie', or 'Kiwi'. Such words were not in themselves insulting (as opposed to, e.g. 'Frog' or 'Kraut'). The Divisional Court disagreed. It held that the common understanding of the word was that it was slang that was racially offensive (as indicated by the *Shorter Oxford English Dictionary*, 5th edn (Oxford: Oxford University Press, 2002)) and often used as a prelude to violence. The behaviour of the defendant in engaging in the chant fell squarely within the mischief at which the statute was directed, and the prosecution's appeal was allowed.

QUESTIONS

1 To what extent should direct protests, for example demonstrations and meetings, which disrupt the lives of other citizens, be seen as involving rights under Art. 10 of the ECHR?

2 Does English law recognize a 'right to protest'?

3 Do the 'notice' requirements under the POA 1986 mean that processions require the permission of the police?

4 Since there is no power to ban public assemblies (other than trespassory assemblies), is it justifiable for there to be a power to ban processions?

5 Is the fact that certain behaviour is 'disorderly' sufficient justification for making it a criminal offence?

6 Do you think that the application in *Austin*'s case of the principles drawn from *Laporte*'s case is in line with the House of Lords' decision?

FURTHER READING

Ashworth, A. (2004), 'Social Control and "Anti-Social Behaviour": the Subversion of Human Rights', (2004) 120 LQR 263

Baker, E. (2000), 'Policing, Protest and Free Trade: Challenging Police Discretion under Community Law', [2000] Crim LR 95

Barnard, C. and Hare, I. (2000), 'Police Discretion and the Rule of Law', (2000) 63 MLR 581

Bonner, D. and Stone, R. (1987), 'The Public Order Act 1986: Steps in the Wrong Direction', [1987] PL 202

Bucke, T. and James, Z. (1998), 'Trespass and Protest: Policing Under the Criminal Justice and Public Order Act 1994', Home Office Research Study No. 190, Home Office

Campbell, S. (2002), 'A Review of Anti-Social Behaviour Orders', Home Office Research Study No. 236, Home Office

Card, R. (2000), *Public Order Law*, Bristol: Jordan Publishing Limited

Fenwick, H. (2009) 'Marginalising Human Rights: Breach of the Peace, "Kettling", the Human Rights Act and Public Protest', [2009] PL 737

Fenwick, H. and Phillipson, P. (2000), 'Public Protest, the Human Rights Act, and Judicial Responses to Political Expression', [2000] PL 627

Geddis, A. (2004), 'Free Speech Martyrs or Unreasonable Threats to Social Peace?—"Insulting" Expression and Section 5 of the Public Order Act 1986', [2004] PL 853

Harris, J. (2000), 'An Evaluation of the Use and Effectiveness of the Protection from Harassment Act', Home Office Research Study No. 203, Home Office

Hickman, L. (2001), 'Press Freedom and New Legislation', (2001) 151 NLJ 716

Mead, D. (2009), 'Of Kettles, Cordon and Crowd Control—Austin, Commissioner of Police for the Metropolis and the Meaning of "Deprivation of Liberty"', [2009] EHRLR 376

Mead, D. (2010), *The New Law of Peaceful Protest*, Oxford: Hart Publishing

O'Donnell, T. and McGoldrick, D. (1998), 'Hate-speech Laws: Consistency with National and International Human Rights Law', (1998) 18 LS 453

Padfield, N. (2004) 'The Anti-Social Behaviour Act 2003: The Ultimate Nanny-State Act', [2004] Crim LR 712

Rumney, P. (2003), 'The British Experience of Racist Hate Speech Regulation: A Lesson for First Amendment Absolutists?', (2003) 32 CLWR 117

Scarman, Lord (1975), 'Report on the Red Lion Square Disorders', Cmnd 5919, HMSO

Scarman, Lord (1981), 'Report on the Brixton Disorders, 10–12 April 1981', Cmnd 8427, HMSO

Scraton, P. (1985), ' "If You Want a Riot, Change the Law": The Implications of the 1985 White Paper on Public Order', (1985) 12 J of Law and Soc 385

Smith, A. T. H. (1996), *Offences Against Public Order*, 2nd edn, London: Sweet & Maxwell

Stone, R. (2001), 'Breach of the Peace: the Case for Abolition', [2001] 2 Web JCLI

Stone, R. (2003), 'From Unlawful Assembly to Aggravated Trespass: The Control of Protest in the 1880s and 1990s', in Stevenson, K. and Rowbotham, J. (eds), *Behaving Badly: Social Panic and Moral Outrage, Victorian and Modern Parallels*, Burlington, VT: Ashgate

Thornton, P. (1987), *Public Order Law*, London: Financial Training

Turns, D. (2000), 'Racism and Xenophobia in English Law', (2000) 22 Liverpool LR 47

Wasik, M. and Taylor, R. (1995), *Blackstone's Guide to the Criminal Justice and Public Order Act 1994*, London: Blackstone Press

White Paper (1985), 'Review of Public Order Law', Cmnd 9510, HMSO

Whyte, D. (2004), 'Punishing Anti-social Business', (2004) 154 NLJ 1293

Williams, D. G. T. (1967), *Keeping the Peace*, London: Hutchinson

10

Terrorism and Human Rights

10.1 Introduction

One of the major challenges for modern democracies is posed by terrorism. The threats raised by terrorist activity are very real, but also very difficult to deal with in a proportionate manner. The temptation for governments, wishing to reassure their population that steps are being taken to minimize the threat from an enemy that uses unpredictable means to strike directly at civilian targets, is to take measures which significantly restrict civil liberties and human rights. This is often expressed in terms of 'balance'. We must balance our freedoms against the need for security. The analogy is unhelpful. It suggests that governments are entitled simply to reduce human rights if it will lead to a more secure society. Freedom and security are regarded as being of equal value, with one being able to be traded off against the other. This is not acceptable in a society which aspires to democracy, and the human rights principles which underpin that concept. Rather than 'balance', the concept that should be used is one of necessity. The question that should be asked is, given the nature of the threats, what are the minimum steps which are necessary to respond to them. Individual freedom should only be restricted when there is a real and pressing need to do so, not simply when it might be regarded as helpful to the police and security services. Lord Hoffmann in *A v Secretary of State for the Home Department* [2004] UKHL 56, [2005] 3 All ER 169, considering the exceptional powers of detention without trial which were being challenged in that case, expressed the view that (para. 97):

> [t]he real threat to the life of the nation, in the sense of a people living in accordance with its traditional laws and political values, comes not from terrorism but from laws such as these. That is the true measure of what terrorism may achieve. It is for Parliament to decide whether to give the terrorists such a victory.

After the London bombings of July 2005, the Prime Minister queried whether Lord Hoffmann would still put forward this view. There is no reason why he should not do so. At the particular level, the restrictions which were found to be incompatible with our Convention obligations in *A v Secretary of State for the Home Department* did not prevent the July 2005 attacks; indeed the main perpetrators were UK citizens, and so would not have been caught by the indefinite detention powers under the Anti-terrorism, Crime, and Security Act 2001 (ATCSA 2001) (see 10.6). More generally, the argument which Lord Hoffmann was putting forward is a matter of principle, and principles are not destroyed by an individual circumstance which may appear to provide a challenge to them. Maintaining freedom in a stable and unchallenged society is easy; no government deserves congratulations for achieving this. What is more difficult is to maintain respect for freedoms when a society is facing serious challenges, and to ensure that any restriction of those freedoms is at the minimum level necessary for the situation.

It should not be forgotten that 'terrorism' is not a new phenomenon in the United Kingdom. From the late 1960s until the late 1990s there were very real threats on the mainland of the United Kingdom from Irish terrorism, as well as the very significant problems in Northern Ireland itself. Our modern terrorism legislation has its origins in legislation passed in the 1970s to deal with this area. Although the attack on the World Trade Center of September 2001 (9/11) heightened the concern, and confirmed that we need to guard against international terrorism, and the particular threat of the suicide bomber, we should not forget the lessons that our experience with more domestic terrorism have taught us. One of these is that detention without trial is likely to be counter-productive. The use of internment in Northern Ireland was a failure, and is widely thought to have assisted recruitment for the Irish Republican Army (IRA). A second lesson is that innocent people are not necessarily protected by the legal system. The cases of the Birmingham Six, the Guildford Four, and the Maguire Seven are three high-profile examples of miscarriages of justice which led to people serving long prison sentences for offences which they did not commit. These cases should make us wary of simply increasing the powers of the police and other authorities, without considering the potential risks to liberty that they involve, and ensuring that safeguards are in place so that exceptional powers, when needed, are not misused.

The approach in the rest of this chapter is to consider first the definition of 'terrorism', and then to look at the laws which the UK government has put in place to attempt to deal with this area, including proscription of organizations, modification of police powers, and various forms of restrictions on movement, including 'control orders' and their successors—Terrorism Prevention and Investigation Measures (TPIMs).

10.1.1 **Definition of 'terrorism'**

Defining 'terrorism' is not easy. Most terrorist acts involve the commission of a criminal offence—criminal damage, assault, murder, and causing explosions. How should the law go about distinguishing the terrorist act from the merely criminal? The way which is most commonly used is to focus on the motives of the actor. The European Union's 2002 Council Framework Decision on combating terrorism (2002/475/JHA), for example, lists various offences which have the capability of being 'terrorist offences'—such as attacks upon a person's life, attacks on a person's physical integrity, kidnapping, hijacking of planes or ships, causing extensive destruction to a government or public facility, manufacturing weapons or explosives. These offences become terrorist offences if committed with the aim of:

— seriously intimidating a population, or

— unduly compelling a Government or international organisation to perform or abstain from performing any act, or

— seriously destabilising or destroying the fundamental political, constitutional, economic or social structures of a country or an international organisation.

As far as English law is concerned terrorism was defined in s. 20 of the Prevention of Terrorism (Temporary Provisions) Act 1989 as meaning 'the use of violence for political ends'. It also included 'any use of violence for the purpose of putting the public, or any section of the public in fear'. This definition, and in particular the first part of it, was very wide. Should members of a left-wing organization, who use force to break up a fascist rally, be regarded as terrorists? What about pickets on strike against the policies of the government, who forcibly prevent workers from entering their work place, or intimidate them by gathering outside their houses and chanting? Their behaviour may well be unlawful, but should it be treated as terrorism?

Section 1 of the Terrorism Act 2000 (TA 2000) uses a definition which is much more similar to that used in the European Framework document, namely:

(1) ...the use or threat of action where—

   (a) the action falls within subsection (2),

   (b) the use or threat is designed to influence the government or an international governmental organisation or to intimidate the public or a section of the public, and

   (c) the use or threat is made for the purpose of advancing a political, religious, racial, or ideological cause.

(2) Action falls within this subsection if it—

   (a) involves serious violence against a person,

   (b) involves serious damage to property,

   (c) endangers a person's life, other than that of the person committing the action,

   (d) creates a serious risk to the health or safety of the public or a section of the public, or

   (e) is designed seriously to interfere with or seriously to disrupt an electronic system.

If firearms or explosives are used, then the requirement in s. 1(1)(b) does not need to be satisfied (s. 1(3)).

The reference to 'serious violence' and the other provisions in s. 1(2) give a slightly narrower scope to the concept than under the Prevention of Terrorism (Temporary Provisions) Act 1989 definition—though the offences are defined more broadly than in the European Framework document. On the other hand, the inclusion of religious, racial, or ideological causes extends it beyond the area covered by the Prevention of Terrorism (Temporary Provisions) Act 1989. Moreover, the TA 2000's definition of terrorism no longer contains the exclusion which existed under the 1989 and previous Acts for terrorism in mainland Britain which is not concerned with Northern Ireland or international terrorism. Activities anywhere within the UK which are directed purely at 'domestic' targets and have no Irish or international connection can now be treated as 'terrorism'.

There is thus still clearly a danger that actions taken in connection with a broad range of political protests could come within the definition, though at the time the Act was passed the government was at pains to insist that it would not catch 'lawfully organised industrial action in connection with a legitimate trade dispute' (Lord Bassam, *Hansard*, HL Debates, vol. 614, col. 1449). The problem is that demonstrations which might begin peacefully may at times lead to damage to property, and injury to individuals. Should they thereby fall within the scope of the TA 2000? There is also the question of how s. 1(2)(d) is interpreted. The phrase 'a serious risk to the health or safety of the public or a section of the public' could be taken to cover quite a wide range of behaviour. It is to be hoped that it will be interpreted within the context of the prime targets of the Act and, therefore, not lead to inappropriate use of the extended terrorist powers. The inclusion of s. 1(1)(e) should also be noted. This is designed to cover interference with computer systems. It would not, presumably, generally cover the hacking of a system owned by a private company, because such action would not be intended to 'influence government or to intimidate the public or a section of the public'. It would be otherwise if, for example, the home page of a widely used internet service provider was 'taken over' and used to distribute threats of bomb attacks, or other violent action. Where government computer systems are the target, however, much less serious behaviour might be caught. An animal welfare group which hacked into the Department for Environment and Rural Affairs (DEFRA) website to replace the Department's material with messages protesting about the treatment of farm animals and government policy in this area, might well fall within the definition. It would be 'designed to influence the government' and it might well be regarded as seriously disrupting an 'electronic system'. There is no doubt that such behaviour ought to be a criminal offence, but the Computer Misuse Act 1990 would surely provide a more appropriate approach than the TA 2000.

A further problem with the above definitions is that they do not provide any basis for distinguishing between the 'terrorist' and the 'freedom fighter'. Some might argue that there is no distinction. Others apply what is sometimes called the 'Mandela test'—that is, would the definition label the activities of Nelson Mandela, when working for the African National Congress (ANC) against the apartheid regime in South Africa as terrorism? If so, it is argued, it is too broad in its scope. A further test that may be put forward is to ask whether those using or proposing violent means to overthrow a government have any access to the democratic process. Where the ballot box is available, it is suggested, there is no justification for resort to the bullet. If, however, a significant proportion, perhaps even a majority (as in apartheid South Africa), of the population of a country are denied proper political rights, and the means to express their political views, then perhaps violent means become more justifiable, even if in other contexts the behaviour would be categorized as terrorism.

No resolution of these difficult issues is suggested here. The main point is that the legal definitions do not provide any basis for making distinctions of the kind suggested. Even the actions of the oppressed, if falling within the definition, are liable to be treated as terrorism. This was confirmed by the Court of Appeal in *R v F* [2007] EWCA Crim 243, [2007] 2 All ER 193, which held that the definition of 'government' in s. 1 was not limited to those governments which are based on democracy. In its judgment (para. 32):

> The terrorism legislation applies to countries which are governed by tyrants and dictators. There is no exemption for criminal liability for terrorist activities which are motivated by, or said to be morally justified by, the alleged nobility of the terrorist cause.

In essence, the Court of Appeal was happy to give the wording of the statute its literal meaning, and not to seek to interpret it in the context of any broader human rights arguments. This approach has now been confirmed by the Supreme Court in *R v Gul* [2013] UKSC 64. The offence for which the appellant was convicted was the distribution of a 'terrorist publication' in the form of videos uploaded on to websites, contrary to s. 2 of the Terrorism Act 2006 (see 10.5.2). The videos showed, for example, attacks by Al-Qa'ida, the Taliban, and other groups on military targets in Chechnya and on the Coalition forces in Iraq and Afghanistan, and excerpts from 'martyrdom videos'. These were accompanied by commentaries praising the bravery, and martyrdom of those carrying out the attacks, and encouraging others to emulate them. The question certified for the Supreme Court by the Court of Appeal (which had upheld the convictions) was (para. 8):

> Does the definition of terrorism in section 1 of the Terrorism Act 2000 operate so as to include within its scope any or all military attacks by a non-state armed group against any or all state or intergovernmental organisation armed forces in the context of a non-international armed conflict?

The appellant's argument was that the definition should take account of the UK's international treaty obligations, and that the concept of terrorism in international law does not cover the type of attacks listed in the question for the Supreme Court. In other words, that it should not extend to military action undertaken in a civil war. The Supreme Court rejected this argument, and held that the answer to the question posed by the Court of Appeal was 'yes'. It noted that there is no internationally agreed definition of terrorism. Although there was support at the international level for the idea that 'terrorism' should not extend to the acts of insurgents or 'freedom fighters' in non-international armed conflicts, there was not a sufficient consensus to enable the Court to use it as a guide to statutory interpretation (paras 44 and 45). In that context, the Supreme Court felt bound to accept the definition contained in s. 1 of the Terrorism Act 2000 without any 'reading down'. Its wording was clearly wide enough to cover the situations raised by the case, and the appeal, therefore, failed. However, in coming to that conclusion, the Supreme Court was clearly not entirely happy with the breadth of the definition, and the fact that it depended on prosecutorial discretion to ensure that it was not used in inappropriate situations (para. 36). The fact that police officers and immigration officers are given extensive and intrusive powers based on the basis of the definition was also of concern (para. 63). It suggested that (para. 62):

> Any legislative narrowing of the definition of "terrorism", with its concomitant reduction in the need for the exercise of [prosecutorial] discretion under section 117 of the 2000 Act, is to be welcomed, provided that it is consistent with the public protection to which the legislation is directed.

Given this decision of the Supreme Court, confirming the breadth of the current definition, it seems that the only possibility for pursuing the argument that 'noble cause' terrorism should be treated differently will be at the European Court of Human Rights (ECtHR). Lord Carlile, the government's independent reviewer of terrorism legislation, considered the issue in a 2007 report on the definition of terrorism ('The Definition of Terrorism', Cm 7052, Home Office, March 2007). He had some sympathy with the idea of 'terrorism in a good cause' being treated differently, but concluded that the 'zero tolerance' approach adopted in international conventions on terrorism meant that the UK government would have difficulty introducing a defence on these lines (para. 80) and remaining within its international obligations.

10.2 **Proscription**

One of the ways in which the UK government has attempted to deal with terrorism is by 'proscribing' certain organizations. This makes it an offence to belong to the specified organization or to support it actively. The relevant provisions are contained in the TA 2000, as amended by the Terrorism Act 2006 (TA 2006).

10.2.1 **The process of proscription**

The power to proscribe an organization lies with the Secretary of State. The list of such organizations is contained in Sch. 2 to the TA 2000. Some organizations, principally those concerned with Irish terrorism, were included in the original version of Sch. 2. The Secretary of State has the power under s. 3 of the TA 2000 to add an organization to, or remove an organization from, this list, by order. The grounds for adding an organization are that the Secretary of State believes that it is 'concerned with terrorism'. The section does not require the belief to be based on reasonable grounds, but it may well be that a court would read in such a requirement. 'Concerned in terrorism' is further defined by s. 3(5) as:

(a) commits or participates in acts of terrorism;

(b) prepares for terrorism;

(c) promotes or encourages terrorism;

(d) is otherwise concerned in terrorism.

The TA 2006 provides that (c) should also cover 'the unlawful glorification' of terrorism. The concept of 'glorification' is discussed further at 10.5.1.

The current list in Sch. 2 runs to over 60 organizations. As well as Irish organizations such as the IRA and the Ulster Freedom Fighters, it includes a large number of Islamic groups, including Al-Qa'ida, Hamas–Izz al-Din al-Qassem Brigades, and the Islamic Jihad Union. The Basque separatist group, ETA, the Tamil Tigers, and the Kurdistan Workers Party (PKK) are also included. The most recent additions (July 2013) were the group commonly known as Boko Haram and Minbar Ansar Deen (Ansar Al Sharia UK). The listing is therefore truly international in its coverage. In *R* v *Z* [2005] UKHL 35, [2005] 3 All ER 95, an issue arose about the scope of the names listed in the Schedule. The appellant had been convicted under s. 11 of the TA 2000 of the offence of belonging to a proscribed organization, namely the Real IRA. He argued that the Real IRA was not listed in the Schedule—it simply referred to 'The Irish Republican Army'. The House of Lords rejected the appeal.

The majority did so on the basis that the phrase 'Irish Republican Army' was intended to be an 'an umbrella term, capable of describing all manifestations or splinter groups' (para. 51, per Lord Carswell). It covered, therefore, the Provisional IRA and the Real IRA, both of which were to be regarded as part of the proscribed organization, the IRA (see para. 67, per Lord Brown).

An organization which thinks that it has been incorrectly proscribed can apply to the Secretary of State for 'de-proscription' (s. 4 of the TA 2000). The procedure for this is set out in regulations (SI 2001/107). The application is to be in writing, and is to be determined by the Secretary of State within 90 days. There is the possibility of a further appeal to the Proscribed Organisations Appeal Commission (s. 5 of the TA 2000), appointed by the Lord Chancellor (Sch. 3 to the TA 2000). The Commission may exclude people, including representatives, from its proceedings, and may withhold evidence (Sch. 3, para. 5(3)). It is to take its decision on the same basis as for judicial review (s. 5(3) of the TA 2000). There is then a further appeal on a point of law to the Court of Appeal (s. 6 of the TA 2000).

10.2.2 Consequences of proscription

Where an organization is proscribed, it becomes an offence to be a member of it or to profess to be a member (s. 11 of the TA 2000). Section 11(2) states that it is a defence for the person to prove that the organization was not proscribed when he or she became a member or professed to be a member, and that he or she has not taken part in the activities of the organization at any time when it was proscribed. The House of Lords has held in *Sheldrake v DPP* [2004] UKHL 43, [2005] 1 All ER 237 that, in order to comply with Art. 6 of the European Convention on Human Rights (ECHR), this should be interpreted, under s. 3 of the Human Rights Act 1998 (HRA 1998), as imposing only an evidential burden on the defendant. The case is discussed more fully in chapter 2 (2.3.3.1).

The Act also makes it an offence to provide support to a proscribed organization, in various ways. The offences are set out in s. 12 of the TA 2000, and include inviting support; arranging or running meetings to support or further the activities of the organization (including being addressed by a member of the organization); and addressing a meeting with the purpose of encouraging support for the organization. A 'meeting' may be a small gathering—three people are sufficient (s. 12(5) of the TA 2000). There is a defence, however, for the organizer of a private meeting, addressed by a member of a proscribed organization, that the organizer had no reasonable cause to believe that the address would support or further the activities of the organization (s. 12(4)). It would seem likely that the courts would interpret this defence in the same way as the one discussed in *Sheldrake*.

All the above offences carry the potential of a substantial penalty—up to 10 years' imprisonment.

Finally, it is an offence for a person in a public place to wear an item of clothing or to wear, carry, or display an article, so as to arouse reasonable suspicion that the person is a member of or supporter of a proscribed organization (s. 13 of the TA 2000). This is a summary offence only, with a maximum penalty of 6 months' imprisonment.

10.3 **Financial support for terrorism**

Pt. III of the TA 2000 deals with terrorist property. It creates offences in relation to fund raising for terrorist purposes (s. 15), using money or other property for terrorist purposes (s. 16), making funds available for terrorism (s. 17), and money laundering (s. 18). There are also duties of disclosure placed on anyone who, as a result of information arising in the course of his or her trade, profession, business, or employment, suspects that offences under ss 15–18 may have been committed (ss 19–21B). Special provisions were added by the ATCSA 2001 to deal with the procedures in the financial services industry (as defined in Sch. 3A). Disclosure should be made either to a person designated for this purpose by the discloser's employer, or to the police. Extensive powers of this kind are also given to HM Treasury under Sch. 7 to the Counter-Terrorism Act 2008.

10.3.1 **Forfeiture powers**

There is a procedure for forfeiture of terrorist property following a conviction which has some similarities to the general confiscation powers under the Proceeds of Crime Act 2002. Where a person has been convicted of certain offences under ss 15–18 of the TA 2000, a power to order forfeiture is given by s. 23. The power applies to money or other property which the person intends, or has reasonable cause to suspect, would or might be used for the purpose of terrorism.

The detailed procedures in relation to forfeiture orders are set out in Sch. 4 to the TA 2000, and are very similar to those applying to confiscation orders. As with such orders there is a power to apply to the High Court to obtain a 'restraint order' preventing property from being dealt with pending consideration of the making of a forfeiture order.

The purpose of these provisions is not to prevent people from benefiting from crime but to make the operation of terrorist groups and organizations more difficult by forfeiting assets which might be used to support their activities. The fact that they are concerned with terrorism will no doubt be regarded as justification for the wide powers which they give to the courts.

10.4 **Modification of police powers**

One of the standard responses to a terrorist outrage is to say that the police should have greater powers. In a number of areas, English law modifies police powers when the offences under investigation relate to terrorism.

10.4.1 **Stop and search**

In relation to stop and search, there is a power under s. 43 of the TA 2000 to stop and search on reasonable suspicion that the person concerned is a terrorist. The purpose of the search will be to discover whether the person has in his or her possession anything which may constitute evidence of that fact. This is a fairly standard power, in that it is based on 'reasonable suspicion', and should operate in the same way as the other stop and search powers discussed in chapter 3 (3.4.2). The procedures in the Police and Criminal Evidence Act 1984 (PACE), and Code A of the PACE Codes of Practice, will apply to this power.

A broader power, not based on reasonable suspicion was, until recently, provided in ss 44–7 of the TA 2000. The powers under these sections were originally added to the previous terrorism legislation by the Criminal Justice and Public Order Act 1994 (CJPOA 1994). They were similar to the power under s. 60 of the CJPOA 1994, discussed in chapter 3 (3.4.6.2), in that they permitted random and routine searching for limited periods, and within a specified area. The powers covered the stop and search of vehicles and their occupants; and the stop and search of pedestrians and anything carried by them. Provided a relevant authorization by a senior officer was in place then any police officer could use the power under s. 44 to stop and search people and vehicles without the need to show any reasonable suspicion. These powers are widely used, particularly in London. Figures produced by the Home Office show that between April 2008 and March 2009 there were 119,811 stops and searches under s. 44, of which 86,719 took place in the Metropolitan Police District.

The powers under these provisions were, however, found to be incompatible with Art. 8 of the ECHR in *Gillan v United Kingdom* (2010) 50 EHRR 45.The facts of *Gillan* were that one applicant (Gillan) had been stopped and searched while on the way to attend a demonstration outside an international 'arms fair' being held in East London. The second applicant (Quinton) had been a journalist on her way to take photographs of the demonstration, and was also stopped and searched under the terrorism powers. They both sought judicial review of this use of the power, which did not seem to be directly linked to terrorism. The Court of Appeal expressed concerns at the lack of evidence that the police had been properly briefed on the use of terrorism powers, and that they should only be used in relation to terrorism ([2004] EWCA Civ 1067, paras 52–56). But all the English courts, up to and including the House of Lords, found no breach of any Convention rights in the case of either Mr Gillan or Miss Quinton. They then took their case to Strasbourg.

The Strasbourg Court considered whether the power under s. 44 engaged Art. 5, as involving a deprivation of liberty. It reached no final conclusion on this issue, but commented that (para. 57):

> [A]lthough the length of time during which each applicant was stopped and search did not in either case exceed 30 minutes, during this period the applicants were entirely deprived of any freedom of movement. They were obliged to remain where they were and submit to the search and if they had refused they would have been liable to arrest, detention at a police station and criminal charges. This element of coercion is indicative of a deprivation of liberty within the meaning of art.5(1).

The suggestion is, therefore, that any stop and search may engage Art. 5. No final conclusion was reached on this, however, because the Court decided the case under Art. 8. There was no doubt in the Court's view that a stop and search power engages Art. 8, in that it involves an infringement of the individual's privacy (para. 63):

> Irrespective of whether in any particular case correspondence or diaries or other private documents are discovered and read or other intimate items are revealed in the search, the Court considers that the use of the coercive powers conferred by the legislation to require an individual to submit to a detailed search of his person, his clothing and his personal belongings amounts to a clear interference with the right to respect for private life.

Given that Art. 8 was engaged, did the powers fall within the permitted exceptions in Art. 8(2)—that is that were they 'in accordance with law', for a legitimate purpose, and no more than is necessary for that purpose (i.e. was the interference proportionate to that purpose)? The Court held that s. 44 of the TA 2000 fell at the first hurdle—in other words the restrictions were not 'in accordance with law'. The Court noted first that the power to issue an 'authorisation', triggering the availability of the stop and search power, was based on what the authorizing officer considered 'expedient'. There was no obligation to consider whether the authorization was 'necessary' or proportionate to its objective (para. 80). It noted also that the authorization could cover the whole of a police area, and that, although it initially could only last 28 days, it could be renewed, so that, an authorization for the Metropolitan Police District had been continuously renewed in a 'rolling programme' since the powers were first granted (para 81). The breadth of discretion available to the individual officer was also of concern. It was possible for a decision to stop and search to be based exclusively on the 'hunch' or 'professional intuition' of the officer concerned. Not only is it unnecessary for the officer to demonstrate the existence of any reasonable suspicion; the officer was not even required subjectively to suspect anything about the person stopped and searched (para. 83). It was 'likely to be difficult if not impossible to prove that the power was improperly exercised' (para. 86). For all these reasons, the Court held that neither the authorization nor the power to stop and search was 'in accordance with law'.

Following this decision, the coalition government announced that the powers under s. 44 would no longer be used. Using the powers under s. 10 of the HRA 1998 (chapter 2 (2.3.3.4)) it enacted a more limited form of stop and search by means of the Terrorism Act 2000 (Remedial) Order 2011 (SI 2011/631). This has now been replaced by new provisions (enacted by the Protection of Freedoms Act 2012) contained in s. 47A and ss. 47AA–AE of, and Sch. 6B to, the Terrorism Act 2000.

The changes introduced by these provisions relate mainly to the issue of authorizations and to the provision for a Code of Practice relating to stop and search under the TA 2000. The authorization must still be given by an officer of the rank of Assistant Chief Constable, or Commander (in the Metropolitan Police District), but must now be based on 'reasonable suspicion that an act of terrorism will take place' (s. 47A(1)(a)). In addition the officer must consider that 'the authorisation is necessary to prevent such an act'; that 'the specified area or place is no greater than is necessary to prevent such an act'; and that 'the duration of the authorisation is no longer than is necessary to prevent such an act' (s. 47A(1)(b)). The maximum period for an authorization is reduced from 28 days to 14 days, but a further order may be issued on its expiry (Sch. 6B, paras 5 and 11).

Once the authorization is in place, the power of the constable remains that of stopping and searching pedestrians and vehicles for evidence of terrorist activity (s. 47A(2) and (3)). But it is still not necessary for the constable to have any reasonable suspicion before carrying out such a stop and search (s. 47A(5)). Anything discovered which is reasonably suspected to be evidence of terrorism may be seized (s. 47A(6)).

Schedule 6B provides for the issue of a Code of Practice covering the powers of stop and search under both s. 43 and s. 47A and this is now available on the Home Office website at https://www.gov.uk/government/uploads/system/uploads/attachment_data/file/97944/stop-search-code-of-practice.pdf.

Do these changes meet the concerns of the ECtHR? As regards the authorization, the fact that the powers are much more specifically directed towards particular acts of terrorism, and that they must be based on reasonable suspicion, is an improvement. The Parliamentary Joint Committee on Human Rights (JCHR) has suggested that the factors that the authorizing officer must 'consider' to be present should be 'reasonably considered' to be present ('The Report of 2011–12', HL paper 192, HC 1483, para. 23).

10.4.2 Arrest

Since 1974, when the Prevention of Terrorism (Temporary Provisions) Act 1974 was enacted in response to the problems of Irish terrorism as it affected the British mainland, English law has contained special arrest powers to deal with terrorism. The latest manifestation of these powers is to be found in the TA 2000.

By virtue of s. 41(1) 'a constable may arrest without a warrant a person whom he reasonably suspects to be a terrorist'. Although this appears to create one arrest power, in effect it contains two, if the definition of 'terrorist' contained in s. 40 is taken into account. This defines a terrorist as a person who either: (a) has committed an offence under certain sections of the Act; or (b) 'has been concerned in the commission, preparation or instigation of acts of terrorism'. To the extent that arrest is based on reasonable suspicion of having committed an offence this is a standard form of arrest power. Where the suspicion relates to behaviour falling within (b), however, the position is rather different. Although acts of 'terrorism' (the definition of which is discussed at 10.1.1) will almost certainly involve the commission of an offence, what is unusual here is that the police need have no particular offence in mind; nor need they worry overmuch about the level of involvement of the person arrested. The person does not need to be a principal, an accessory, a conspirator, or an attemptor. 'Being concerned in' is certainly wider than any of these. In particular, it allows police to arrest on the basis of intelligence information that a person has links with terrorist organizations, or with other individuals who are themselves suspected of being involved in terrorism. It is also important to remember that this may be the first stage of up to 14 days' detention without charge (see 10.4.3.2) during which time the police may question the person arrested with a view to obtaining valuable information about terrorist activities, and activists, rather than acquiring the evidence necessary for a charge to be brought. That this is the way the power is used seems to be confirmed by figures showing that over 80 per cent of those detained under this power, or one of its predecessors, between 1980 and 1990 in connection with Northern Ireland terrorism, were released without charge. In more recent years, the percentage of detentions which result in further action has been even smaller. During the years 1991–5, 560 people were detained, but only 49 (8.75 per cent) were charged, and another 19 (3.4 per cent) excluded or deported (Home Office Statistical Bulletin, 2/96). The IRA ceasefire of 1994–6 led to a significant reduction in the use of the power, however. In 1993 a total of 152 people were detained, but in 1994 this fell to 61, and in 1995 to 34. The ending of the ceasefire in 1996 led to an increase to 84 detentions in 1996. The figures for 1997 and 1998 were, however, 43 and 45 respectively, reflecting the new moves towards a settlement in Northern Ireland. In 1999 the figure was 99, but this included 79 people detained in connection with an occupation of the Greek Embassy in London. Only 12 people were detained in connection with Northern Ireland terrorism, and only one of these was subsequently charged with an offence. In 2000 this reduced to only seven people who were arrested in connection with Irish terrorism, of whom only one was charged with an offence. Thirty-nine people were arrested in connection with international terrorism, of whom 25 were charged with offences (but only eight with offences under the terrorism legislation) (Home Office, 'Statistics on the Operation of Prevention of Terrorism Legislation', Home Office Paper 16/01, 2001)). These figures confirm that the main use of the terrorism powers has moved from Irish to international terrorism. More recent figures published by the Home Office do not distinguish between Irish and international terrorism. They show, however, a significant increase in the use of such powers since 2001—no doubt explicable by the aftermath of the terrorist attacks in New York on 11 September 2001. The average number of terrorist related arrests (not all under s. 41) per year since 2002–03 has been 210, though there is significant variation between years—in 2005–06 the figure was 285 (including 273 under s. 41), whereas in 2010–11 it was 125 (including 50 under s. 41). There was a steady decline after 2005–06, with the figures for 2008–09 being 191, 2009–10 being 178, and 2010–11 being 125. It has now started to increase again, with the figure for 2012–13 being 249 (though only 23 per cent were under s. 41) (Home Office, 'Operation of Police Powers under the Terrorism Act 2000 and Subsequent Legislation', 12 September 2013, available from the Home Office website at https://www.gov.uk/government/uploads/system/uploads/attachment_data/file/116756/hosb1112.pdf). Of the 249 arrests in 2012–13, 105 (42 per cent) resulted in a charge, with 37 (35 per cent of those charged) being charged with terrorism-related offences.

Consideration of whether the exceptional power of arrest under s. 41 is justifiable will depend to some extent on its scope, and the problems against which it is directed. Once again, it will be up to the police and prosecutors to ensure that only behaviour which really merits the use of the special powers provided by the TA 2000 is brought within its scope. The power of arrest under s. 41 is an exceptional one, which, as Lord Jellicoe stated in his 1983 'Review of the Operation of the Prevention of Terrorism (Temporary Provisions) Act 1976', Cmnd 8803, HMSO, 'should be exercised only where the use of no other power is appropriate to the end sought' (p. 23).

Apart from the grounds for its exercise, the power of arrest under s. 41 is like any other arrest power. The procedures to be followed at the time it is used (see chapter 3 (3.5) and subsequently (see 3.5.4) are the same.

What of the possibility of an HRA 1998 challenge to the powers under s. 41 of the TA 2000? In *Lawless* v *Ireland* (1961) 1 EHRR 1, it was emphasized that the *purpose* of arrest under Art. 5(1)(c) of the ECHR must be to bring the arrested person before a competent judicial authority. This was confirmed in *Brogan* v *United Kingdom* (1989) 11 EHRR 117, which was concerned with the equivalent of s. 41 of the TA 2000 under the Prevention of Terrorism (Temporary Provisions) Act 1984. In *Brogan*, however, the ECtHR stated that the fact that those arrested are not charged, nor brought before a court, does not necessarily mean that the purpose of the arrest was out of line with Art. 5(1)(c). There was no need for the police to have, at the time of the arrest, sufficient evidence to bring charges (para. 53). As the European Court then commented:

> There is no reason to believe that the police investigation in this case was not in good faith or that the detention of the applicants was not intended to further that investigation by way of confirming, or dispelling, the concrete suspicions which, as the Court has found, grounded their arrest.

This approach by the Court makes it harder for a person arrested under s. 41 of the TA 2000 to argue that the arrest falls outside the scope of what is permitted under Art. 5(1) because it is being used to gather intelligence. As has been suggested above, the figures indicate that this is the common way in which this particular power is used.

10.4.3 Detention and questioning

10.4.3.1 Detention of those concealing information

Generally speaking, powers of arrest and detention are used against people who are suspected of direct involvement in criminal activity. Witnesses to criminal events cannot normally be arrested or detained for questioning, nor can those who are thought to have information relevant to an offence. In some situations involving terrorism, however, it may be an *offence* to fail to give information. As has been noted above (see 10.3), under s. 19 of the TA 2000 it is an offence in certain circumstances not to provide information about a belief or suspicion that an offence under ss 15–18 of the Act (mainly concerned with the funding of terrorism) has been committed. A more general provision of this kind, covering information likely to be of assistance in preventing acts of terrorism, or in apprehending offenders, was added to the TA 2000 by s. 117 of the ATCSA 2001, and now appears as s. 38B of the TA 2000. In these limited circumstances, therefore, it is possible for the police to detain and question someone who is not directly involved in the commission of an offence, but may have relevant information.

10.4.3.2 Extended detention under the terrorism provisions

The standard periods for which detention is permissible in relation to those being detained in connection with criminal offences is dealt with in chapter 4 (4.3.2).

The maximum period of detention without charge is 96 hours. Where a person is held in relation to terrorism different procedures apply and longer periods of detention are possible.

The detention of people arrested under s. 41 of the TA 2000 (see 10.4.2) is governed by the provisions of that section and Sch. 8 to the Act, rather than by PACE. There is now a separate Code of Practice, Code H, dealing with detention under these powers, though much of it duplicates what is in Code C (as discussed in chapter 4). Section 41(3) allows an initial period of up to 48 hours from the time of arrest on the authority of the police. By virtue of s. 41(7) and Sch. 8, as amended by the TA 2006, a further period of detention, up to 14 days from the time of arrest, may be granted by an appropriate judge. The period was originally seven days; this was extended to 14 days by the Criminal Justice Act 2003. Following the bombings in London of 7 July 2005, the police advised the government that a longer period of detention would be desirable. The government sought to extend the period to 90 days, but was defeated in the Commons—with the period of 28 days being approved. This extended period was in practice very seldom used, and in January 2011 the coalition government decided not to renew the extension to 28 days. As a result the period reverted to 14 days. This still leaves a significant difference in the position between the most serious non-terrorist offences, where four days remains the maximum, and terrorism offences, where a person can be held for two weeks.

Under the pre-2000 terrorism legislation the power to permit extended periods of detention was given to the Home Secretary. This led to problems with compliance with Art. 5 of the ECHR, which are discussed below. A further addition to the powers to detain is that s. 41(5) and (6) provide that the detention can be continued after the end of the 48-hour period while an application for extended detention is made (which must be done within six hours (Sch. 8, para. 31(1)), or while such an application is being considered.

Throughout the period of detention, regular reviews, generally at not more than 12-hour intervals, should be carried out to assess whether continued detention is necessary (Sch. 8, para. 21). During the first 24 hours the 'review officer' (who, as under PACE, should be unconnected with the investigation) must be of at least the rank of inspector; beyond that time a superintendent must act as the review officer (para. 24).

The first review should take place as soon as practicable after the beginning of the detention (para. 21(2)). This review is, therefore, comparable to the custody officer's initial decision in relation to ordinary criminal proceedings as to whether there are grounds to justify detention (see 4.2.3). Subsequent reviews must take place at intervals of not more that 12 hours (para. 21(3)) though there are powers of postponement equivalent to those applying under PACE (see 4.3.2.1) (para. 22). Once a warrant for extended detention has been issued, however, no further reviews need take place (para. 21(4)).

The grounds for authorizing continued detention are that the review officer is satisfied (note that there is no requirement of 'reasonable grounds') that it is necessary in order to preserve or obtain evidence which relates to an offence under the sections of the Act mentioned in s. 40(1)(a), or which indicates that the detained person is, or has, been concerned with the commission, preparation, or instigation of acts of terrorism (i.e. the person falls within s. 40(1)(b)) (para. 23(1)). The obtaining of evidence may be by questioning or otherwise. This ground appeared in the

Prevention of Terrorism (Temporary Provisions) Act 1989. In addition, the TA 2000 provides that continued detention may be authorized where the review officer is satisfied that it is necessary pending a decision whether to make an application for a deportation notice; or pending the making of such an application; or pending the consideration of such an application by the Secretary of State; or pending a decision whether the person should be charged with an offence (para. 23(1)). In all cases the review officer must be satisfied that the relevant investigation or decision-making process is being conducted diligently and expeditiously (para. 23(3)).

Before reaching a decision the review officer must give the detainee (unless unfit to do so), and the detainee's solicitor (if available), the opportunity to make representations (para. 26).

The review officer has a duty to record the outcome of each review, in the presence of the detainee (para. 28). If detention is being continued, the detainee should be told the grounds (which should also be recorded).

From the above, it will be seen that, within the first 48 hours, the position of the detainee is very comparable to that of a person detained under the PACE provisions. The big change comes at the end of the 48 hour period. At that point, the decision about continued detention passes to a judge. Under the Prevention of Terrorism (Temporary Provisions) Act 1989, the power to extend detention rested with the Home Secretary, and appeared to be entirely at his or her discretion. The lack of any judicial review of this extended period brought the UK government into conflict with the ECtHR, in the case of *Brogan* v *United Kingdom* (1989) 11 EHRR 117. There were four applicants who had been detained, on the authorization of the Home Secretary, for periods of between four days and six hours, to six days and 16½ hours.

The ECtHR recognized the particular problems presented by terrorist offences. It also acknowledged that these difficulties might have the effect of prolonging the period during which a person suspected of terrorist offences may, without violating Art. 5(3), be kept in custody before being brought before a judge. They might also result in special procedures in relation to judicial control (para. 61). Presumably the Court was referring here to possibilities such as the court sitting *in camera*, or dealing with the matter 'without notice' (that is, hearing the police case for detention but not giving the detainee an opportunity to rebut it at that stage).

In the end, however, it had to be recognized that Art. 5(3) called for 'promptness' in bringing the detainee before a judge. This meant that the scope for flexibility was very limited. It was the view of the Court, by a vote of 12:7, that even the shortest period of detention under consideration, that is four days and six hours, was too long to fit with the notion of promptness. All four applicants had therefore been unlawfully detained, in breach of Art. 5(3), and should have had an enforceable right to compensation under Art. 5(5).

The UK government's initial response to this was to use the power under Art. 15 to derogate from the provisions of Art. 5(3) on the grounds of the public emergency in Northern Ireland. The legitimacy of this was confirmed by the European Court in *Brannigan and McBride* v *United Kingdom* (1993) 17 EHRR 539, and the derogation was continued by the HRA 1998 (s. 14 and Sch. 3). The TA 2000, however, while continuing to provide for extended detention of up to seven days, provided for judicial approval for any detention over 48 hours. This met the requirements of

Art. 5(3), so that once the new provisions were in force, there was no need for the derogation to continue. It was, therefore, lifted on 19 February 2001. The current position, following the amendments contained in the Criminal Justice Act 2003 and the TA 2006, is that an extension up to 14 days from arrest can be approved by a district judge. The extension should be for no more than seven days at a time. Although the period of detention is now potentially very long, it seems likely that the ECtHR would not find any breach of Art. 5, because of the requirement for regular judicial approval of the extensions.

10.4.3.3 The right to have someone informed and the right to legal advice

The powers of the police to delay exercise of the right to have someone informed, and the right to legal advice, in relation to ordinary criminal offences are dealt with in chapter 4 (4.4.1 and 4.4.2). The powers are slightly different where the detainee is held under the terrorism provisions. Section 65 defines these to mean s. 41 of the TA 2000 and any provision of Sch. 7 to that Act which confers a power of arrest or detention. The rights themselves are set out in paras 6 and 7 of Sch. 8 to the TA 2000, rather than in ss 56 and 58 of PACE. Note that the right is to legal advice, not necessarily to advice from the solicitor of the detainee's choice. In *R (Malik)* v *Chief Constable for Greater Manchester* [2007] EWHC 2396 (Fam), for example, the police refused to allow a particular solicitor to represent M, because it was likely that the solicitor would be a witness in any subsequent trial. This decision was upheld by the High Court. M was allowed access to the duty solicitor.

The differences in the way in which the rights to have someone informed and to legal advice operate under the TA 2000 are set out in Sch. 8. In relation to the grounds for delay, these must be based on a reasonable belief that one of the following consequences will follow from the exercise of the right:

(a) interference with or harm to evidence of a serious offence,

(b) interference with or physical injury to any person,

(c) the alerting of persons who are suspected of having committed a serious offence but who have not been arrested for it,

(d) the hindering of the recovery of property obtained as a result of a serious offence or in respect of which a forfeiture order could be made under s. 23,

(e) interference with the gathering of information about the commission, preparation, or instigation of acts of terrorism,

(f) the alerting of a person and thereby making it more difficult to prevent an act of terrorism, and

(g) the alerting of a person and thereby making it more difficult to secure a person's apprehension, prosecution, or conviction in connection with the commission, preparation, or instigation of an act of terrorism.

'Serious offence' here means an indictable offence. These are broader consequences than those relating to people held for ordinary criminal offences. The decision to delay must be taken by an officer of at least the rank of superintendent, rather than an inspector, but it will be difficult to challenge an officer's stated belief that there were reasonable grounds to fear one of these consequences. The prohibition on authorizing delay on the basis that the legal advice will be to refuse to answer questions applies equally to those held under the terrorism provisions (para. 4 of Annex B of Code H).

The maximum period for delay in relation to both rights is extended from 36 hours to 48 hours in relation to people held under the terrorism provisions (Sch. 8, para. 8(2)). This is also the maximum period for which a person may be held under these provisions on the authority of the police. As we have seen above, after 48 hours continued detention must be approved by a judge.

Finally, whilst the right to legal advice under para. 7 is specifically stated to be a right to consult 'privately', para. 9 provides an exception to this. An officer of at least the rank of commander or assistant chief constable may in certain circumstances give a direction that the detainee may only consult a solicitor in the sight and hearing of a uniformed officer of at least the rank of inspector. This officer should not, in the opinion of the authorizing officer, have any connection with the case. The circumstances which will justify such a direction are that the authorizing officer has reasonable grounds to believe that without this supervision one of the consequences justifying denial of access to legal advice for someone held under the terrorism provisions will follow (Sch. 8, para. 9). In other words, this allows for access to legal advice to be allowed under supervision, in circumstances which would otherwise justify refusal of access altogether. It must be very doubtful, however, that this provision would survive a challenge under the HRA 1998, given the ECtHR decision in *Brennan* v *United Kingdom* (2002) 34 EHRR 18. The applicant had been arrested in Northern Ireland on suspicion of involvement in terrorism. He was initially refused access to legal advice, but was eventually allowed to consult a solicitor. During the first consultation, a policeman was present, a decision to require this having been taken under the Northern Ireland provisions equivalent to those outlined above under the TA 2000. The policeman was close enough to the applicant and his solicitor to be able to listen in to their conversation. The officer told the solicitor in the presence of the applicant that no names were to be discussed or information passed which could assist other suspects; the interview was to involve simply legal advice. The Court, while not ruling that the lack of confidentiality in the circumstances in which legal advice was given would always amount to a breach of Art. 6, found that there was such a breach in this case. It noted that the supervision here was not as extensive as it had been in *S* v *Switzerland*, 28 November 1991, where the Court had previously emphasized the need for confidentiality. But it also noted that there was no evidence here to suggest that the solicitor would, for example, have assisted with the passing of coded messages to associates of the applicant. Moreover, this was the first occasion since his arrest at which the applicant was able to seek advice from his lawyer. The applicant had already made incriminating admissions and was in considerable need of legal advice. Although there was no specific evidence that the discussions had been inhibited by the supervision, the Court concluded (para. 62):

> ...that the presence of the police officer would have inevitably prevented the applicant from speaking frankly to his solicitor and given him reason to hesitate before broaching questions of potential significance to the case against him. Both the applicant and the solicitor had been warned that no names should be mentioned and that the interview would be stopped if anything was said which was perceived as hindering

> the investigation. It is immaterial that it is not shown that there were particular matters which the applicant and his solicitor were thereby stopped from discussing.

There was, therefore, an infringement of the applicant's right to an effective exercise of his defence rights. This constituted a violation of Art. 6(3)(c) read in conjunction with Art. 6(1) of the ECHR. It seems, therefore, that it is only where there is clear evidence that discussions between the solicitor and client may lead to prejudicial consequences that the exercise of the power to supervise a consultation would be justified.

The power to defer access to legal advice has been used more frequently in terrorism cases than in relation to ordinary criminal offences. Nevertheless, the government stated in 1998 that it was not aware of any formal denial of access in terrorism cases in the past two years in the UK ('Consultation Paper on Terrorism', Home Office, 1998)). The reason for what may well be a decline in the use of the power is likely to be attributable largely to the views expressed by the ECtHR in a number of Northern Ireland cases. The first of these was *Murray (John)* v *United Kingdom* (1996) 22 EHRR 29, in which the Court considered the operation of the Northern Ireland provisions allowing the drawing of inferences from silence on a similar basis to the position now applying in England and Wales under ss 34–7 of the CJPOA 1994 (see chapter 4 (4.5.1). The applicant had refused to answer questions or to explain his presence at a particular house where the IRA had been holding a suspected informer. He had then challenged the legitimacy of the inferences which the court at his trial had drawn from this silence under questioning. The Court did not accept this part of his claim (see chapter 4 (4.5.1.2). His application succeeded, however, on the ground that he had been denied access to a lawyer for the first 48 hours of his detention. The Court felt that, particularly in a situation where the decision whether or not to answer questions could itself have serious implications for the suspect, it was incompatible with Art. 6 to deny access for this length of time. It is, of course, only under the terrorism provisions that this length of delay is permitted; the maximum period for other offences being 36 hours. Even this amount of delay may be felt to be too great, however, in the light of the provisions as to the effect of silence introduced by the CJPOA 1994. This point is probably confirmed by the decision of the Court in *Averill* v *United Kingdom* (2000) 31 EHRR 839, where the same approach as that taken in *Murray* was applied. The applicant had again been arrested under the terrorism provisions. On this occasion he was only denied access to a lawyer for 24 hours, during which time he maintained silence, though subsequently he produced an alibi and an innocent explanation for forensic evidence linking him with the offence. At trial adverse inferences were drawn from his initial silence and failure to mention his subsequent explanations. The Court stated that although the drawing of such inferences did not infringe Art. 6, the delay in access to a lawyer did. Although this was for a shorter period than in *Murray*, the rules relating to adverse inferences meant that a suspect was presented with a dilemma as to whether to maintain silence or to give an explanation, which required that legal advice should be available—'under such conditions the concept of fairness in Art. 6 requires that the accused has the benefit of the assistance of a lawyer already at the initial stages of police interrogation' ((2001) 31 EHRR 839, para. 57). Thus, where there is the possibility of adverse inferences being drawn from the suspect's behaviour at the time of questioning, any delay in access to a lawyer is likely to infringe Art. 6. *Magee* v *United Kingdom* (2000) EHRR 822, another terrorism case, dealt with the slightly different situation where the accused made incriminating statements during the 48 hours when he was denied access to legal advice. The Court again held that there was an infringement of Art. 6. It found that (para. 43):

> ... [t]he austerity of the conditions of his detention and his exclusion from outside contact were intended to be psychologically coercive and conducive to breaking down any resolve he may have manifested at the beginning of his detention to remain silent. Having regard to these considerations, the Court is of the opinion that the applicant... should have been given access to a solicitor at the initial stages of the interrogation as a counterweight to the intimidating atmosphere specifically devised to sap his will and make him confide in his interrogators.

These decisions suggest that any delay in access to legal advice is always going to result in a breach of Art. 6. The most recent decision, however, *Brennan* v *United Kingdom*, indicates that this is not necessarily the case. The applicant had again been arrested under the terrorism provisions. He was denied access to a solicitor for 24 hours, but his solicitor did not in fact see him until the day after the expiry of this period. In the period between the expiry of the 24 hours and being seen by his solicitor, he confessed his involvement in a murder and signed a statement to this effect. The European Court noted that, in this case, no adverse inferences were drawn at trial from the applicant's initial silence, and that the confession was made at a time when he was no longer being denied access to legal advice (even though such advice had not been received). In all the circumstances, there was no breach of Art. 6. It seems, then, that denial of access to legal advice will only infringe Art. 6 where incriminating statements have been made, or adverse inferences have been drawn from silence, the statements or the silence occurring when the denial of access was still operative. This approach seems to ignore the point made in *Averill* v *United Kingdom* that the decision which a suspect has to make when being questioned in a situation where there is the *possibility* of adverse inferences being drawn means that legal advice should be available from the start of any questioning. Whereas in the previous cases the Court appeared to be moving towards a position that any refusal of legal advice would of itself involve a breach of Art. 6, the decision in *Brennan* involves a slight retreat from such a position. Nevertheless, it is clearly the case that it is now very difficult, if not impossible, to rely on incriminating statements, or to draw adverse inferences from silence, where access to a lawyer was being denied at the relevant time.

The response of the UK government to the *Murray* decision was to introduce an amendment to the relevant provisions of the CJPOA 1994, by virtue of s. 58 of the Youth Justice and Criminal Evidence Act 1999. This prevents an inference from silence being drawn unless the accused has had an opportunity to consult a solicitor before being questioned. This provision was brought into effect on 1 April 2003 to coincide with the revised provisions as to cautions contained in new Codes of Practice, which took account of the fact that in some circumstances silence in the absence of legal advice should not lead to adverse inferences (see chapter 4 (4.5.1.1)). As with the normal criminal powers, where an interview takes place in the absence of legal advice, for 'safety' reasons, adverse inferences from silence may not be drawn. Evidence of statements made during such safety interviews may, however, be used in evidence subject to the overall issue of 'fairness' as set out in s. 78 of PACE (discussed in chapter 4 (4.6.4)): *R* v *Ibrahim* [2008] EWCA Crim 880, [2008] 4 All ER 208.

10.4.3.4 **Interviews after charge**

Normally, once a person has been charged with an offence, no further interviews by the police are allowed. Part 2 of the Counter-Terrorism Act 2008 provides for post-charge questioning of terrorist suspects under the authorization of a Crown Court judge. This power is intended to compensate for the failure to enact an extended period of detention before charge. It was brought into force in July 2012. The authorizing judge will have to be satisfied of the following (s. 22(6)):

(a) that further questioning of the person is necessary in the interests of justice,

(b) that the investigation for the purposes of which the further questioning is proposed is being conducted diligently and expeditiously, and

(c) that what is authorised will not interfere unduly with the preparation of the person's defence to the charge in question or any other criminal charge.

The maximum period of any authorization under s. 22 is 48 hours.

10.4.4 **Entry, search, and seizure**

10.4.4.1 **Power to search in cordoned areas—Terrorism Act 2000, Sch. 5, para. 3**

This power was originally added to the Prevention of Terrorism (Temporary Provisions) Act 1989 by the CJPOA 1994. It is now contained in the TA 2000. Sections 33–6 of this Act allow police officers of at least the rank of superintendent to establish in certain circumstances a police cordon around an area in connection with a terrorism investigation. Where such a cordon is in place, para. 3 of Sch. 5 gives a power of search. It can be exercised on the written authority of an officer of at least the rank of superintendent, who must have reasonable grounds for believing that material which would be of substantial value to the investigation is on specified premises within the cordon. The material must not be excluded, special procedure, or legally privileged material. The constable exercising the power will have the right to enter, search the premises, and seize items (other than those protected by legal privilege) which the constable has reasonable grounds to believe will be of substantial value to the investigation.

10.4.4.2 **Production orders**

The production order procedure first enacted in Sch. 1 to PACE (see chapter 6 (6.7)) has been adopted for other purposes in various other statutes. It was included in Sch. 7 to the Prevention of Terrorism (Temporary Provisions) Act 1989 in relation to excluded or special procedure material sought in the course of a 'terrorist investigation'. Equivalent powers are now contained in Sch. 5 to the TA 2000. A 'terrorist investigation' basically means an investigation into terrorist activities, or the resources of a proscribed organization. Paragraph 1 of Sch. 5 gives a power to obtain a search warrant in relation to material, not being legally privileged, or excluded or special procedure material, which would be of substantial value to the investigation. It does not have to be relevant evidence. If the material is excluded or special procedure material, however, an order for production can be obtained from a circuit judge (para. 5). The application must be made with the authority of an officer of at least the rank of superintendent (PACE, para. 3.4 of Code B). It will be without notice, rather than the 'with-notice' procedure under PACE, presumably because of the nature of the investigation, and the risk of material being destroyed. This was the view taken in *R v Crown Court at Middlesex Guild Hall, ex p Salinger* [1993] 2 All ER 310, p. 317, where Stuart-Smith LJ set out certain guidelines for such applications. The application should be accompanied by a written statement of the evidence which is relied on but need not disclose the source of information if this is sensitive. The *nature* of the information should be disclosed, unless 'there are grounds for thinking that it is too secret', and the constable making the application should be available to give oral evidence if necessary. If an order is made the judge should decide what information is given to the person to whom it is directed as to the evidence on which the order has been granted: 'The information should be as full as possible without compromising security'. On an application for the variation or discharge of an order (which should preferably be before the judge who made the order) oral evidence from the police should be available to supplement the information already given to the applicant, if necessary, but the judge should not permit questions 'as to the nature or identity of the source of information'.

Before making an order, the judge must be satisfied that a terrorism investigation is being carried out, that there are reasonable grounds for believing that the material sought is likely to be of substantial value to the investigation, and that it is in the public interest (on the same basis as under the first set of access conditions under PACE; see chapter 6 (6.7.2.1)) that access should be granted (Sch. 5, para. 6). There is no need for other means of obtaining access to the material to have been tried, or to be shown to be likely to fail. Otherwise the procedure is very similar to that under PACE except that if the order relates to material which is not in the possession of the person to whom it is addressed, that person may be required to state where the material is believed to be (para. 5(3)). Moreover, if the material is expected to come into existence within 28 days the order can require a person to notify a constable as soon as it comes into his possession (para. 7(2)). As under PACE, a search warrant may be obtained where an order for production or access has not been complied with, or where communication with the relevant people is impracticable, or where the purposes of the investigation might be seriously prejudiced unless a constable is able to obtain immediate access (para. 11).

If material is produced in response to an order, or seized under a search warrant, a circuit judge may order a person to provide an explanation of it unless this would involve disclosing information protected by legal professional privilege (para. 13). This exception to the right of silence and the privilege against self-incrimination is limited by the fact that any statements made cannot be used in any criminal proceedings against the person, other than where the person is prosecuted for giving false information in the statement (under Sch. 5, para. 14).

A refusal to produce material in response to an order will amount to a contempt of court to which it is no defence to plead that disclosure would prejudice confidential sources even if there may be a grave risk of personal injury or death: *DPP* v *Channel Four Television* [1993] 2 All ER 517.

In a situation which a police officer of at least the rank of superintendent has reasonable grounds to believe is one of 'great emergency', and that immediate action is necessary, the officer may authorize a search by a constable by means of a written order (para. 15). The Home Secretary must be notified 'as soon as may be' when this power has been used.

Although the provisions under Sch. 5 are more intrusive than those under Sch. 1 to PACE, the search warrant powers are subject to the provisions in paras 6.14–6.15 of Code B (noted at chapter 6 (6.4.3.2)) as to the conduct of any search. In addition, the fact that there is full judicial supervision of the powers, other than in cases of 'great emergency' means that it is likely that they would meet the standards set by the ECtHR as regards Art. 8(2) of the ECHR. The prospects for challenging these powers successfully under the HRA 1998 are, therefore, probably not very high.

10.5 Preparatory offences

Some offences relating to acts done in preparation for terrorism were included in the TA 2000. There has also been concern since 9/11 about the fact that prospective terrorists may have been receiving encouragement, support, advice, and training in the United Kingdom. The TA 2006 enacts various offences designed to deal with this area.

10.5.1 The Terrorism Act 2000

The relevant offences in the TA 2000 are to be found in ss 57–9. Section 57 makes it an offence to possess an article in circumstances which give rise to reasonable suspicion that the possession is for a purpose connected with the commission, preparation, or instigation of acts of terrorism. This clearly covers the possession of weapons, or material that might be used to create explosives. In *R v Zafar* [2008] EWCA Crim 184 the court considered the application of the section to documents, compact discs or hard drives containing material including ideological propaganda. The court held that there must a very direct connection between the object possessed and the act of terrorism. In this case the prosecution had alleged that the defendant and others had planned to travel to Pakistan, be trained there, and then to fight for the Taliban in Afghanistan. The court considered that only the last of these was an act of terrorism. The prosecution needed to prove that the documents had been used to encourage others to fight in Afghanistan. Since the trial judge had not directed the jury on these lines, the conviction was quashed. The court noted that a more appropriate charge might have been under s. 58 or s. 59 which are discussed below.

Section 58 provides that a person commits an offence if he collects or makes a record of information, or possesses a document or record containing information, of a kind likely to be useful to a person committing or preparing to commit an act of terrorism. There is a defence of 'reasonable excuse'. The case law on this section has focused on the defence, with the leading case being *R v G* [2009] UKHL 13. This case considered whether, if a person raised a possible 'non-terrorist' reason for possession of a document, the prosecution then had to prove that he had a terrorist purpose, or simply that his reason for possession was not a 'reasonable excuse'. The House of Lords held that the latter was the case—otherwise a person who was in possession of documents relating to the making of explosives might avoid conviction if his 'reasonable excuse' was that he was planning a bank robbery, unconnected with terrorism. On the facts of the case the defendant, who was in prison at the relevant time, claimed that he collected the material simply in order to 'wind-up' the prison officers. This was held not to be a 'reasonable excuse'.

Section 58A makes it an offence to publish information of a kind likely to be useful to a terrorist about:

- a member of the armed forces;
- a police officer;
- a member of the intelligence services.

Again there is defence of reasonable excuse.

Section 59 deals with the incitement of terrorist offences overseas. The relevant offences are:

- murder;
- s. 18 of the Offences Against the Person Act 1861 (wounding or causing grievous bodily harm);
- poisoning (s. 23 or s. 24 of the Offences Against the Person Act 1861);
- criminal damage endangering life (s. 1(2) of the Criminal Damage Act 1971).

An example of the use of this offence is to be found in *Attorney-General's Reference (Nos. 85, 86, and 87 of 2007)* [2007] EWCA Crim 3300, where the defendants had been involved in the operation of websites and internet chat forums, which included incitement of murder, particularly in Iraq. Graphic jihadist material could be downloaded, included the beheading of civilians. The defendants were convicted of conspiring to incite offences under s. 59.

10.5.2 **Encouragement of terrorism**

Section 1 of the TA 2006 makes it an offence to publish (or cause another to publish) a statement that is likely to be understood 'as a direct or indirect encouragement or other inducement... to the commission, preparation or instigation of acts of terrorism'. The statement must be published with the intention that members of the public should be so encouraged or induced, or recklessly as to whether that would be its effect. Where recklessness is relied on by the prosecutor, then there is a defence of, in effect, 'innocent publication', by virtue of s. 1(6).

The meaning of 'encouraging' is further expanded by s. 1(3), which was one of the most controversial provisions of this legislation. It involves the concept of 'glorification', which the House of Lords tried very hard to have removed. As enacted it states that encouragement includes:

...every statement which (a) glorifies the commission or preparation (whether in the past, in the future or generally) of such acts or offences; and (b) is a statement from

> which those members of the public [to whom it is published] could reasonably be expected to infer that what is being glorified is being glorified as conduct that should be emulated by them in existing circumstances.

No further elucidation of what is meant by 'glorification' is provided.

Section 2 of the TA 2006 extends the offence to dissemination of publications of the same kind, and s. 3 deals with publications on the internet. In relation to the internet, there is a procedure for a constable to give a person responsible for a publication, such as an internet service provider, a notice that a particular statement, article, or record is unlawfully terrorist-related, and requiring that it should no longer be made available to the public. Failure to comply within two working days will be treated as an endorsement of the statement, and therefore render the provider liable to the offence under s. 3.

There has been considerable concern that these offences do not pass the 'Mandela test' (see 10.1), to the extent that they refer to past acts. Could an historical evaluation of the actions of those fighting against oppression, which concludes that their actions were justified, fall within the scope of the section? The government would no doubt argue that, first, an historical evaluation is not 'glorification' and, second, that the requirement of 'emulation' means that it would fall outside the offence. There is clearly a danger, however, of this offence having at least a chilling effect on legitimate freedom of expression. People may be afraid to address sensitive areas for fear of falling foul of these provisions. It is likely that at some point, if prosecutions are brought, a defence based on proportionality under Art. 10 of the ECHR will be attempted. As noted at 10.1.1 the Supreme Court in *R v Gul* [2013] UKSC 64, dealing with an appeal against conviction under s. 2 of the 2006 Act has rejected any limitation of the scope of the current broad definition of 'terrorism'.

A power of entry, search, and seizure under warrant, in relation to suspected terrorist publications, is provided in s. 28, together with a power of forfeiture.

10.5.2 **Preparation and training for terrorism**

Section 5 of the TA 2006 makes it an offence to engage in any preparation for the commission of acts of terrorism, or assisting another to commit such acts. This is a very broad offence, particularly as the preparation does not have to be in relation to any particular act of terrorism. It is similar in scope to the offence under s. 7 of the Official Secrets Act 1920, and discussed in chapter 7 (7.5.2). As with that offence, the act can be very remote from the intended consequences. For example, accessing a website to find out about explosives could be an offence, provided that the prosecution can prove that the action was done with the intention, at the time, of engaging in or assisting terrorist acts. It can be argued, therefore, that it is really an offence which penalizes unlawful thoughts (i.e. the intention to commit or assist terrorism) rather than dangerous actions. Given that the maximum penalty is life imprisonment, so that it is presumably only intended to deal with seriously dangerous behaviour, it will be up to the discretion of prosecutors to ensure that it is not used disproportionately.

Section 6 of the TA 2006 deals with training for terrorism. It is an offence to pro-vide training, knowing that the person trained intends to use the skills acquired for terrorist purposes, in:

(a) the making, handling, or use of a noxious substance, or of substances of a descrip-tion of such substances;

(b) the use of any method or technique for doing anything else that is capable of being done for the purposes of terrorism, in connection with the commission or prepar-ation of an act of terrorism…or in connection with assisting the commission or preparation by another of such an act…; and

(c) the design or adaptation for the purposes of terrorism, or in connection with the commission or preparation of an act of terrorism…of any method or technique for doing anything.

It is also an offence to receive such training (s. 6(2)). As with the s. 5 offence, the actions do not need to be related to any particular act of terrorism.

This is another very broad offence, which will depend on prosecutorial discre-tion for its appropriate use. The maximum penalty in this case is 10 years' impris-onment. A power of forfeiture of anything related to the offence is given by s. 7; this power arises following a conviction under s. 6.

Attendance at a place used for terrorist training, or where terrorist training is available, is an offence under s. 8 of the TA 2006. The training must fall within s. 6 of the TA 2006 or s. 54 of the TA 2000 (weapons training). The defendant must be proved to have known that the place was being used for terrorist training, or it must be proved that a person attending could not reasonably have failed to understand that it was being so used (s. 7(2)). The latter part of this test provides, therefore, an objective mental element—it is not necessary to prove that the particular defend-ant understood what was going on, provided that a reasonable person would have done so. Moreover, it is not necessary for the defendant to have actually received any training for the offence to be committed (s. 7(3)). The maximum penalty is 10 years' imprisonment.

These 'preparatory' offences significantly increase the scope of the law, and make it much easier for the police and security services to intervene at an early stage in terrorism-related activity. To that extent they have a legitimate purpose; it is clearly better to be able to intervene to prevent terrorist acts, than to rely on prosecuting after the event—particularly when the direct perpetrators may well have killed themselves in the course of their actions. There are dangers, however, in defining offences quite so broadly as is done in ss 5–7 of the TA 2006, and it will be up to those responsible for their implementation to ensure that they are not used oppressively or inappropriately.

10.6 Control orders and terrorism prevention and investigation measures

10.6.1 The background

The background to the introduction of 'control orders' in the Prevention of Terrorism Act 2005 (PTA 2005) is to be found in the powers of detention contained in the ATCSA 2001, and the challenge to them by the House of Lords' decision in *A v Secretary of State for the Home Department* [2004] UKHL 56, [2005] 3 All ER 169. The ATCSA 2001 introduced a power of indefinite detention without charge or trial for certain suspected terrorists. Its enactment was justified by the government as necessary in response to the heightened dangers of international terrorism in the wake of the attacks in New York on 11 September 2001. The problem that it sought to address arises where a person whose presence in this country the Home Secretary thinks is contrary to the interests of national security cannot be deported because there is no 'safe' country to which they can be sent. In other words, if they were returned to the only country, or countries, which would take them they would be at risk of death, torture, or other mistreatment; to return them would thus put the United Kingdom in breach of its obligations under Art. 2 or Art. 3 of the ECtHR. This was the situation, for example, in *Chahal v United Kingdom* (1997) 23 EHRR 413 (discussed in chapter 11 (11.1.1). The response was to make provision for indefinite detention without trial (though subject to periodic review) and at the same time make a derogation from Art. 5 (with which the detention power is clearly incompatible). The power was contained in ss 21–35 of the ATCSA 2001.

The mechanism for achieving the objective was started by the Secretary of State issuing a certificate in relation to a person indicating that they were a suspected international terrorist. Section 21(1) provided that there were two basic requirements for the issue of such a certificate. The Secretary of State must, reasonably, first have believed that the person's presence in the United Kingdom was a risk to national security and, second, have suspected that the person was a terrorist involved in some way with international terrorism. Once a certificate was issued reasonable steps had be taken to notify the person concerned, and a copy had to be sent to the Special Immigration Appeals Commission (SIAC) (see chapter 11 (11.3.3.4)). A person concerning whom a certificate had been issued was, for the purposes of the Act, a 'suspected international terrorist'.

More importantly, however, s. 23 provided that such a person could be detained under para. 16 of Sch. 2 to the Immigration Act 1971 (see chapter 11 (11.3.4.1)) or para. 2 of Sch. 3 to that Act (detention pending deportation). Bail was possible, but subject to the supervision of the SIAC (s. 24). If the person was detained then no time limit was placed on the detention, other than in connection with the provisions for review under s. 26, discussed below.

The only means of challenge to the issue of a certificate was by appeal to the SIAC, under s. 25.

As discussed, the powers of detention provided by these provisions were incompatible with Art. 5 of the ECHR. The government, therefore, issued a derogation from Art. 5, as provided for by Art. 15. The derogation was contained in a statutory instrument (SI 2001/3644) which came into force on 13 November 2001. Article 15 of the ECHR allows for derogation 'in time of war or other public emergency...to the extent strictly required by the exigencies of the situation'. The government's basis for the derogation from Art. 5 was the 'public emergency' arising from the heightened threats of international terrorism in the wake of the terrorist attacks of 9/11.

A relatively small number of people (14) were detained under the ATCSA 2001. A challenge was brought in *A v Secretary of State for the Home Department*. The SIAC found that the powers were discriminatory, and therefore infringed Art. 14 of the ECHR, in that they did not apply to UK citizens, even if such citizens posed a similar terrorist threat to those subject to the detention power. The Court of Appeal reversed this decision and held that, taking account of the derogation from Art. 5, the power did not infringe against Convention rights. The appeal was heard by a nine-member panel of the House of Lords. Its decision is very important, not only as an evaluation of the powers under consideration, but also as an indication of the limits of deference to the executive by the judiciary, even in the very sensitive area of terrorism. The trenchant views of Lord Hoffmann are quoted at 10.1. The rest of their Lordships did not go quite so far, but eight of the nine found that the powers contained in the ATCSA 2001 were incompatible with the Convention rights. All but Lord Hoffmann were prepared to accept that there was an emergency threatening the life of the nation of a kind which justified derogation. They also held, however, that the provisions acted in a discriminatory way, because they did not apply to UK nationals. Since such nationals might well be people who were involved with Al-Qa'ida or other terrorist groups, it was irrational to impose controls simply on non-nationals. The discriminatory nature of s. 23 of the ATCSA 2001 meant that it could not be strictly justified by Art. 15, and was therefore disproportionate. As a result the derogation order was quashed (under the HRA 1998), and s. 23 was held to be incompatible with Art. 5 of the ECHR, taken together with Art. 14. A declaration of incompatibility was issued under s. 4 of the HRA 1998.

The response of the government was to introduce a system of 'control orders' in the PTA 2005, though these have now been replaced by a less restrictive type of control (see 10.6.2.4).

10.6.2 The control order system under the Prevention of Terrorism Act 2005

The PTA 2005 made provision for two types of 'control order'—derogating and non-derogating. Only the latter type of power was ever used. The system gave rise to a number of cases testing the extent of the powers. For example, in *Secretary of State for the Home Department* v *GG* [2009] EWCA Civ 786 the Court of Appeal held that a power contained in a control order which made the subject of it liable to personal searches, including intimate searches, whenever requested by the police went beyond what was permitted by s. 1(3) of the PTA 2005.

In *Secretary of State for the Home Department* v *JJ* [2007] UKHL 45, [2007] 3 WLR 642 the court was concerned with appeals by six people who had been made subject to non-derogating control orders. The effect of the orders followed what was apparently a standard pattern as to the restrictions imposed. They provided as follows (para. 20):

Each respondent is required to remain within his 'residence' at all times, save for a period of six hours between 10 a.m. and 4 p.m. In the case of GG the specified residence is a one-bedroom flat provided by the local authority in which he lived before his detention. In the case of the other five respondents the specified residences are one-bedroom flats provided by the National Asylum Support Service. During the curfew period the respondents are confined in their small flats and are not even allowed into the common parts of the buildings in which these flats are situated. Visitors must be authorised by the Home Office, to which name, address, date of birth and photographic identity must be supplied. The residences are subject to spot searches by the police. During the six hours when they are permitted to leave their residences, the respondents are confined to restricted urban areas, the largest of which is 72 square kilometres. These deliberately do not extend, save in the case of GG, to any area in which they lived before. Each area contains a mosque, a hospital, primary health care facilities, shops and entertainment and sporting facilities. The respondents are prohibited from meeting anyone by pre-arrangement who has not been given the same Home Office clearance as a visitor to the residence.

The House concluded (by a 3:2 majority) that the level of restrictions in these orders meant that the respondents were being deprived of their liberty, as guaranteed by Art. 5 of the ECHR, and that the deprivation did not fall within any of the exceptions contained in that Article. They were, therefore, quashed. The curfew period was too long. This decision was distinguished in a judgment handed down by the House of Lords on the same day: *Secretary of State for the Home Department* v *E* [2007] UKHL 47, [2007] 3 WLR 720. The curfew was only of 12 hours' duration and the other restrictions were less onerous. As a result of these differences it was held that there was no infringement of Art. 5 in this case, and the trial judge had been wrong to quash the order.

A further House of Lords' decision was the most problematic for the government. In *Secretary of State for the Home Department* v *AF* [2009] UKHL 28, the House ruled that it was incompatible with the right to a fair hearing under Art. 6 that the individual and his legal team were unable to hear some of the evidence on the basis of which the order was requested. Instead, a procedure involving the use of security-accredited special advocates was used with those advocates representing the individual's interests in closed hearings. In coming to this decision the House was strongly influenced by the decision of the Strasbourg Court in *A* v *United Kingdom* (2009) 49 EHRR 29, which was the Strasbourg decision on the cases of indefinite detention under the ATCSA 2001, discussed at 10.6.1. Although the Strasbourg Court recognized that it might be permissible on national security grounds for some evidence to be given in secret, it was necessary that the individual and his, or her, legal team should have access to sufficient material on which to make their case. The conclusions of the Court on this issue appear at paras 220–1 of its judgment:

220 … While this question must be decided on a case-by-case basis, the Court observes generally that, where the evidence was to a large extent disclosed and the open material played the predominant role in the determination, it could not be said that the applicant was denied an opportunity effectively to challenge the reasonableness of the Secretary of State's belief and suspicions about him. In other cases, even where all or most of the underlying evidence remained undisclosed, if the allegations contained in the open material were sufficiently specific, it should have been possible for the applicant to provide his representatives and the special advocate with information with which to refute them, if such information existed, without his having to know the detail or sources of the evidence which formed the basis of the allegations. An example would be the allegation made against several of the applicants that they had attended a terrorist training camp at a stated location between stated dates; given the precise nature of the allegation, it would have been possible for the applicant to provide the special advocate with exonerating evidence, for example of an alibi or of an alternative explanation for his presence there, sufficient to permit the advocate effectively to challenge the allegation.

> 221. Where, however, the open material consisted purely of general assertions and SIAC's decision to uphold the certification and maintain the detention was based solely or to a decisive degree on closed material, the procedural requirements of art.5(4) would not be satisfied.

The House of Lords felt that exactly the same approach had to be applied to hearings in relation to control orders and, therefore, the cases had to be reconsidered on an individual basis to see if the open material provided sufficient basis for the making of the control orders.

10.6.2.3 Conclusions on control orders

The use of control orders clearly involved less of an infringement on human rights than did the power of indefinite detention. They nevertheless placed very real constraints over an individual's freedom of movement, association, and general involvement in the life of society. The coalition government elected in May 2010 committed itself to abolishing control orders but found it difficult to do so quickly. The control order regime was renewed in March 2011, but then replaced by the Terrorism Prevention and Investigation Measures Act 2011.

10.6.2.4 The Terrorism Prevention and Investigation Measures Act 2011

This Act abolished control orders (s. 1) and replaced them with TPIM notices. These allow for the imposition of similar restrictions to those used in relation to control orders, but only in more limited situations, and normally only after permission has been obtained from a court.

The initiative for the issue of a TPIM notice still lies with Home Secretary. Before a notice can be issued, however, he or she must be satisfied that five conditions are met, labelled A to E by s. 3 of the Act (s. 2(1)). These conditions are:

- A: the Secretary of State reasonably believes that the individual concerned is, or has been, involved in terrorism related activity (as defined by s. 4);
- B: some or all of the activity is 'new'. This means 'new' since the most recent TPIM notice issued against the individual. If no such notice has been issued any activity will be 'new' (s. 3(6)). This may include an activity which had previously formed the basis of a control order: *Secretary of State for the Home Department* v *AM* [2012] EWHC 1854 (Admin);
- C: the Secretary of State reasonably considers that the TPIM notice is necessary to protect the public from terrorism;
- D: the Secretary of State reasonably considers that the imposition of the particular restrictions contained in the notice are necessary to prevent the individual's involvement in terrorism;
- E: either a court has approved the TPIM notice, or the situation is one which the Secretary of State reasonably considers to be of such urgency that it requires the imposition of the restrictions without the court's prior permission. In the latter situation s. 7 and Sch. 2 provide that application must be made to the court immediately after the notice has been served.

'Involvement in terrorism-related activity' is broadly defined by s. 4. It includes not only the commission, preparation, or instigation of acts of terrorism but also facilitating or encouraging such behaviour, or giving support or assistance to others who are involved in such behaviour.

In considering a TPIM the court must refuse or quash the notice if any of the conditions A–C are not met (s. 6(7), Sch. 2, para. 4(1)). As regards condition D, the court has the power to direct the Home Secretary to amend the particular restrictions imposed (s. 6(9), Sch. 2, para. 4(2)). If the Home Secretary has dealt with the case as one of urgency, but the court disagrees, it must issue a declaration to that effect (Sch. 2, para. 4(4)). In exercising its powers the court is to use the principles applicable to judicial review proceedings. The court can hear the case without the individual being present, or having been given notice, or having had an opportunity to make representations. However, at the application hearing, the court must give directions for a hearing at which the individual concerned can be present and represented to take place within seven days (s. 8). The main purpose of this hearing is to give directions for a full 'review' hearing which is to take place 'as soon as reasonably practicable' (s. 8(6)). At the review hearing the court has the power to confirm, quash, or revise the TPIM (s. 9).

The restrictions that can be imposed under a TPIM are specified in detail in Sch. 1 to the Act. They are too lengthy to set out in detail here, but the following list of headings within the Schedule will indicate the range of controls that can be imposed:

- *Overnight residence*: the individual may be required to live at a particular residence (with which the individual should generally have some connection) and to remain there overnight, and also to provide the names of others living there.

- *Travel:* the individual may be restricted to remaining in a particular area, specified in the order.

- *Exclusion:* the individual may be forbidden from entering a specified place or area.

- *Movement directions:* power may be given for any constable to give directions as to the individual's movements. Any such direction cannot last for more than 24 hours.

- *Financial services:* controls may be imposed over the bank accounts (or equivalent) that the individual may hold.

- *Property:* transfer of property to or by the individual may be restricted (e.g. transfer out of the United Kingdom may be forbidden).

- *Electronic communication:* controls may be imposed on access to and use of computers, telephones, fax machines, and any similar devices.

- *Association:* the individual may be forbidden to associate or communicate with specified people, without the permission of the Secretary of State.

- *Work or studies*: these may be restricted. The permission of the Secretary of State may be required before undertaking work or study.

- *Reporting*: the individual may be required to report to a police station at specified times.

- *Photographs*: the individual may be required to allow himself, or herself, to be photographed at such locations and at such times as the Secretary of State may require.

- *Monitoring*: the individual may be required to co-operate with procedures for monitoring the individual's movements, communications, etc. This might included electronic tagging.

These types of control are very similar to those which have been applied in control orders. As regards the requirement to remain in a residence, the general requirement of a connection with the individual, where the residence is not the individual's home, means that the person cannot be sent to a part of the country with which he or she has no association, and where he or she may have no friends or family (as could happen with control orders). Moreover, the requirement is expressed in terms of 'overnight' residence, so the long periods of daytime 'house arrest' imposed in some control orders would again no longer be appropriate.

A further distinction from the control order regime is the time limit. Section 5 provides that a TPIM notice will initially last for one year. It may be extended for a further year, but only on one occasion. The maximum period for any person to be restricted by a TPIM is, therefore, two years. As noted above, condition A means that any subsequent TPIM notice must be based on new evidence of terrorism-related activity (s. 3).

The TPIM notice system is an improvement on the control order system, but only a limited improvement. A relatively small number of TPIMs have been issued. In both August 2012 and August 2013 the Home Office reported that 9 were in place, in all but one case involving a British citizen. There have been a number of cases in which TPIMs have been challenged. The challenges have tended to relate to the conditions imposed as part of the TPIM rather than to the TPIM itself. For example, in *CF* v *Secretary of State for the Home Department* [2013] a curfew of 9 p.m. to 7 a.m. was approved as were restrictions on the use of electronic devices, including an iPod, and the requirement to report daily to a police station. The only variation which the court required related to restrictions on the applicant, who was a university student, associating with fellow students. The TPIM said this must be for study purposes only. The court found this unrealistic and too restrictive, and required it to be varied. As in this case the courts have generally upheld all, or most, of the restrictions imposed by the TPIMs.

The small number of TPIMs issued means that they do not constitute a major area of concern. Nevertheless, for the individuals concerned they constitute a significant restriction on their freedom. It is important that those imposing the TPIMs (i.e. the Home Secretary), and the courts in reviewing them, make sure that the controls are necessary and proportionate to the risks posed by the person concerned.

QUESTIONS

1 What is 'terrorism'? Is it possible to produce a satisfactory definition which distinguishes the 'freedom fighter' from the 'terrorist'?

2 Does the proscription of an organization run the risk that it will make membership *more* attractive to certain members of society?

3 Are the powers to stop and search under s. 47A of the TA 2000 sufficiently limited so as to meet the concerns of the ECtHR in Gillan v UK?

4 Is there any justification for having extended periods of detention without charge for terrorism offences? Are the investigations likely to be any more complex than in relation to a complex international fraud?

5 What is meant by the 'glorification' of terrorism? Should it be a criminal offence?

6 Is the TPIM notice system a significant improvement on the control order system? Is it legitimate to impose severe limitations on an individual's freedom when he or she has not been convicted of any offence?

FURTHER READING

Brandon, B. (2004), 'Terrorism, Human Rights and the Rule of Law: 120 Years of the UK's Legal Response to Terrorism', [2004] Crim LR 981

Carlile, Lord (2007), 'The Definition of Terrorism', Cm 7052, Home Office, March 2007

Dickson, B. (2005), 'Law versus Terrorism: Can Law Win?', [2005] EHRLR 11

Ewing, K. (2004), 'The Futility of the Human Rights Act', [2004] PL 829

Feldman, D. (2006), 'Human Rights, Terrorism and Risk: the Roles of Politicians and Judges', [2006] PL 364

Fenwick, H. (2002), 'The Anti-terrorism Crime and Security Act 2001; a Proportionate Response to 11 September?', (2002) 65 MLR 724

Home Office (2001), 'Statistics on the Operation of Prevention of Terrorism Legislation', Home Office Paper 16/01, Home Office

Home Office (2009), 'Operation of Police Powers under the Terrorism Act 2000 and Subsequent Legislation', Home Office Statistical Bulletin 18/09,, 26 November 2009, Home Office

Jellicoe, Lord (1983), 'Review of the Operation of the Prevention of Terrorism (Temporary Provisions) Act 1976', Cmnd 8803, HMSO

Joint Committee on Human Rights (2005), 'Counter-Terrorism Policy and Human Rights: Terrorism Bill and Related Matters', 3rd Report of Session 2005–06, HL Paper 75–1, HC 561–1, TSO

Walker, C. (2004), 'Terrorism and Criminal Justice: Past, Present and Future', [2004] Crim LR 311

Walker, C. (2009), *The Anti-Terrorism Legislation*, 2nd edn, Oxford: Oxford University Press

11

Extradition, Deportation, and Asylum

11.1 Introduction

The right that is under consideration in this chapter is the right of residence in the United Kingdom. It is concerned with rights that are often discussed under the more general heading of 'freedom of movement'. The primary focus here is not, however, the freedom to come and go, but rather the right to remain; in other words, the freedom from being forced, against one's will, to leave the country, or some part of the country. As a result, the details of immigration procedures are not discussed, despite the fact that they may raise human rights issues. For reasons of space, the emphasis is on those who are lawfully here and wish to stay, rather than on those who are seeking entry. The law surrounding immigration control cannot be ignored entirely, however, because, at least in relation to deportation, it helps to define who may be subject to these powers. In addition, the issue of 'asylum seekers', which has been the subject of debate, and specific legislation, in recent years is considered in a separate section.

The order of treatment is to move from the most generally applicable of the powers (extradition) to the more limited (deportation).

Note that throughout this chapter, where powers are exercisable by 'the Secretary of State', in practice this will normally mean the Home Secretary.

11.1.1 The right of residence and the Human Rights Act 1998

The European Convention on Human Rights (ECHR) contains no provision guaranteeing freedom of movement or providing a right of entry. Article 2 of the Fourth Protocol guarantees freedom of movement within a State, and Art. 1 of the Seventh Protocol deals with the rights of aliens not to be expelled, but the United Kingdom is not yet a party to these, and so they are not included in the Schedules to the Human Rights Act 1998 (HRA 1998). Even if they were, both Articles contain exceptions related, amongst other things, to national security and public order, which might well be held to justify the use of powers to remove or expel people from the jurisdiction.

In so far as the main Articles of the ECHR are concerned, the ones which might most obviously be relevant to the powers considered in this chapter are Arts 3, 5, 6, and 8. In *Chahal* v *United Kingdom* (1997) 23 EHRR 413, for example, an order to deport on the grounds of national security was held to involve breaches of Arts 3 and 5(4) of the ECHR. The applicant was a Sikh activist whom the Home Secretary had ordered to be deported to India. The European Court of Human Rights (ECtHR) accepted evidence from Amnesty International and the US State Department that at least some of the Punjabi police did not respect the human rights of Sikh militants. The risk that the applicant if returned would suffer torture, or inhuman or degrading treatment, meant that his deportation to India would involve a breach of Art. 3. Moreover, the lack of any judicial involvement in the decision to deport on national security grounds meant that there was in this respect a breach of Art. 5(4) (which requires that everyone who is deprived of his or her liberty by arrest or detention shall be entitled to challenge the lawfulness of his or her detention in a court). *Chahal* confirms, therefore that, to the extent that decisions to remove or expel a person from the United Kingdom depend on purely administrative procedures and informal reviews, they offend against Art. 5(4). The particular procedure which was found to be lacking in *Chahal*'s case was, however, amended by the Special Immigration Appeals Commission Act 1997, discussed at 11.3.3.4. Article 3 can be invoked even where the problem is not that the applicant is likely to be positively mistreated by the authorities in the receiving State. In *D* v *United Kingdom* (1997) 24 EHRR 423 it was held that it would be 'inhuman treatment' to deport a person suffering from a terminal illness to a country which did not have adequate medical facilities to deal with his condition. This decision must now be viewed as exceptional in the light of *N* v *United Kingdom*, App. No. 26565/05, in which the ECtHR upheld the House of Lords' decision in *N* v *Secretary of State for the Home Department* so that Art. 3 would usually only be applied to intentional acts or omissions of a State or non-State body. (See also *Soering* v *United Kingdom* (1989) 11 EHRR 439—breach of Art. 3 in extradition to United States where there was a likelihood of spending years on 'death row'.) In *Y and Z (Sri Lanka)* v *Secretary of State for the Home Department* [2009] EWCA Civ 362 the appellants, who had failed in their asylum application, claimed that they would be at risk of committing suicide if returned to Sri Lanka. Sedley LJ reasoned that return would constitute a breach of Art. 3. The appellants had a genuine, overwhelming fear of return which resulted from the torture they had previously experienced at the hands of the Sri Lankan authorities. In the Court's view the risk of suicide derived from the actions of the Sri Lankan authorities rather than a particular illness.

In *Saadi* v *Italy*, App. No. 37201/06 the State argued that it should be able to balance the risk of exposing the deportee to torture on return with the security threat posed by allowing him to remain. The European Court unanimously rejected this contention, emphasizing the absolute nature of Art. 3. The fact that the ill-treatment would occur abroad did not deprive the State of its obligations.

The fear of ill-treatment does not necessarily need to relate to the activities of government authorities. In *A* v *Secretary of State for the Home Department* [2003] EWCA Civ 175, 147 SJLB 114 the Court of Appeal held that fear of mistreatment by drug gangs in the applicant's home country (Jamaica) could bring the case within the scope of Art. 3. (But note that Jamaica is now listed as a country from which any asylum application will be presumed to be clearly unfounded—see 11.3.3.3.) A breach will only be established if the State has failed to provide protection (*R* v *SSHD, ex p Bagdanavicius* [2005] UKHL 38). The ECtHR has confirmed that the threshold of Art. 3 can be reached in circumstances of civil war where the fear of persecution arises from a general threat experienced by sections of the population (*Sufi and Elmi* v *United Kingdom* [2011] ECHR 1045.

The 'extra-territorial' effect of Art. 3, whereby deportation can be restricted because of fear of torture or other inhumane treatment in another country, can also be applied to qualified rights. The House of Lords in *R v Special Adjudicator, ex p Ullah; Do v Secretary of State for the Home Department* [2004] UKHL 26 took a different view from the Court of Appeal and held that, in appropriate circumstances, it would be possible to challenge a decision to deport on the basis that the applicant's rights under Art. 9 would be infringed on return to the country to which it was proposed to send him or her. The threshold is high, the feared breach would need to be flagrant, or in the case of a qualified right, amount to a fundamental denial of that right. On the particular facts before the court the appeals were dismissed. Nevertheless, the case provides very important confirmation of the extra-territorial scope of the HRA 1998. The requirement of a flagrant breach was examined in the context of the applicant's fair trial rights in the ECtHR's judgment in *Othman (Abu Qatada) v United Kingdom* [2012] ECHR 56. The Court ruled that (paras 260–1):

> ...it is for the applicant to adduce evidence capable of proving that there are substantial grounds for believing that, if he is removed from a Contracting State, he would be exposed to a real risk of being subject to a flagrant denial of justice.

It can also be argued that certain uses of the powers discussed in this chapter will infringe Art. 8, which gives a right to respect for private and family life. To the extent that extradition or deportation involves splitting families, or disrupting domestic arrangements, it can be argued that it infringes this right. This will be particularly likely where the person concerned has been resident in the country for a long time—as in *Moustaquim v Belgium* (1991) 13 EHRR 802—or is heavily dependent on the support of the family—as in *Nasri v France* (1995) 21 EHRR 458 (the applicant was deaf and dumb). Unlike the rights under Arts 3 and 6, however, the right under Art. 8 is qualified where the interference is:

> ...in accordance with law and...necessary in a democratic society in the interests of national security, public safety or the economic well-being of the country, for the prevention of disorder or crime, for the protection of health or morals, or for the protection of the rights and freedoms of others.

It is possible, therefore, for the government to argue that the powers discussed below are justified on one or more of these grounds. In many cases such an argument is likely to be successful. This was the case in *R (Samaroo) v Secretary of State for the Home Department* [2001] EWCA Civ 1139, [2001] UKHRR 1150. The applicant had been convicted of importing cocaine, and was ordered to be deported to Guyana. He argued that this would infringe his Art. 8 rights as, since living in the United Kingdom, he had married and had a son. Neither his wife nor his son had any connection with Guyana and it would be unreasonable to expect them to accompany him there. The Court of Appeal ruled that, although his Art. 8 rights were infringed, this was justifiable within Art. 8(2) on the basis of the applicant's involvement with Class A drugs. The courts' approach to the balancing act inherent in Art. 8 has been controversial. In *Samaroo*, Dyson LJ applied a 'significant margin of discretion to the decision of the Secretary of State' (para. 36). The Court of Appeal applied this approach in *Edore v Secretary of State for the*

Home Department [2003] EWCA Civ 716, [2003] INLR 361. In the Court of Appeal's decision in *Huang and Kasmiri* v *Secretary of State for the Home Department* [2007] UKHL 11, LJ Laws examined the standard to be applied in Art. 8 appeals and developed the 'exceptionality test' whereby a tribunal would only overturn the ruling of the Secretary of State on the basis of Art. 8 rights in exceptional cases (para. 59). However, this approach was rejected on appeal to the House of Lords (*Huang and Kasmiri* v *Secretary of State for the Home Department* [2007] UKHL 11). The tribunal must now be prepared to examine all the circumstances before making its own assessment of proportionality. Nevertheless, in *R (Razgar)* v *Secretary of State for the Home Department* [2004] UKHL 27, [2004] 2 AC 368 Lord Bingham anticipated that such appeals will only be successful in a 'very small minority' of cases (para. 20).

In *Razgar*, Baroness Hale made a distinction between 'domestic' and 'foreign' cases under Art. 8. In domestic cases, the State must always act compatibly with Convention rights whereas in foreign cases there is an additional threshold test 'indicating the enormity of the violation to which the person is likely to be exposed if returned'. The State will only be responsible if that threshold is crossed. In *EM (Lebanon)* v *Secretary of State for the Home Department* [2008] UKHL 64 the appellant feared that on removal to Lebanon she would automatically lose custody of her son to her abusive husband. The threshold of 'flagrant breach' was applied successfully such that removal would constitute a violation of Art. 8.

The quality of family life that may be disrupted following removal is very significant to the proportionality assessment. In *Khan* v *United Kingdom* [2011] ECHR 2533 the ECtHR held that a father's deportation would not contravene Art. 8 as he had not seen his children for at least ten years.

Recent changes in the immigration rules make it difficult to successfully deploy Art. 8 in an argument against deportation following the commission of a serious criminal offence. In *JO (Uganda)* v *Secretary of State for the Home Department* [2001] EWCA Civ 10, Richards LJ reasoned that even when it would be unreasonable to disrupt family life, the commission of a serious offence may nevertheless justify deportation. Much will depend on the nature of the offence and the persistence of the offender (para. 398 of the Immigration Rules, HC 395. The qualifications inherent in Art. 8 do not apply to the right to marry under Art. 12. In *R (on the Application of Baiai and ors)* v *Secretary of State for the Home Department* [2008] UKHL 53, the House of Lords ruled that a marriage fee of £295 required for marriage certificates when one or more party has limited leave to remain was incompatible with the right to marry. The certificates were subsequently deemed to contravene Art. 12 by the ECtHR in *O'Donoghue and ors* v *United Kingdom*, App. No. 34848/07.

An attempt to use Art. 10 to challenge the operation of immigration control failed in *R (Farrakhan)* v *Secretary of State for the Home Department* [2002] EWCA Civ 606, [2002] 4 All ER 289. The Court of Appeal held that, although the refusal to grant entry to a person who wished to address meetings of followers of a political/religious movement of which he was the leader involved a restriction of freedom of expression under Art. 10, it was justified under Art. 10(2) because of the risks to public order. A similar conclusion was reached in *Naik* v *Secretary of State for the Home Department* [2011] EWCA Civ 1546, though here the Art. 10 rights involved were held to be those of the potential audience for the applicant, rather than his own Art. 10 right. These decisions also reflect the difficulty in asserting the qualified Convention rights when the applicant has no right of entry.

11.2 **Extradition**

The law of extradition is primarily concerned with the situation where a person is alleged to have committed a criminal offence in country A, but is currently residing in country B. It also applies where the person has been convicted of an offence in country A, but has escaped or evaded custody there, and is again to be found in country B. It seems reasonable at first sight that the suspect or convict should be returned to stand trial, or to serve the appropriate sentence. Complications arise, however, where there may be suspicions that the requesting State has improper motives. In particular, it may be alleged that the return is being requested in order to try the person for a 'political' offence, or for some offence other than that to which the request relates, or in order to persecute the person for religious or political beliefs. For that reason English law has always required a degree of formality before extradition will be allowed. The procedure is recognized to be entirely a creature of statute: extradition is not possible under common law powers.

It is a very significant power in that, as we shall see, it is the only way in which a UK citizen can be forcibly removed from the United Kingdom. In relation to non-citizens executive deportation powers may be available, and in some cases it has been alleged that these have been used as a form of 'disguised extradition' (see 11.3.3.2).

The law on extradition underwent a fundamental revision a few years ago in the form of the Extradition Act 2003, which repealed all previous legislation dealing with the area. This revision was mainly undertaken in response to agreements within the European Union as to the desirability of speeding up procedures for extradition between Member States, particularly in the light of concerns about international crime and international terrorism in particular. One aspect of this was the adoption of the concept of the 'European Arrest Warrant' by the Council of the European Union in June 2002. This was designed to simplify and speed up extradition between Member States.

Under the previous law there were various safeguards against extradition. These included:

- the principle of 'double criminality'—that is, that the offence for which extradition was sought must be an offence in the United Kingdom as well as in the requesting State;
- the principle of 'specialty'—that is, that the requesting State would be required to undertake that the person extradited would not be proceeded against for offences other than the one for which extradition was sought;
- the concept of the 'political offence'. Traditionally, English courts have refused to extradite where the offence was deemed to be 'political', and this concept was recognized, for example, by s. 6 of the Extradition Act 1989. Its importance was considerably reduced, however, by the provisions of the Suppression of Terrorism Act 1978, giving effect to the European Convention on the Suppression of Terrorism. This prevented a range of offences from being treated as political offences; and
- the principle of 'double jeopardy'—i.e. that a person should not be tried more than once for the same offence (or for a different offence based on the same conduct).

Under the Extradition Act 2003, as we shall see, the principles of 'specialty' (though referred to in the Act as 'speciality') and 'double jeopardy' are retained. The 'political offence' exception, however, has disappeared entirely, and the requirement of 'double criminality' has been significantly weakened in a number of situations.

The previous law also involved both a judicial and a political decision, in that once a judge had approved a request for extradition, this had to be confirmed by the Secretary of State. The Extradition Act 2003 removed the involvement of the Secretary of State in certain cases.

The scheme of the Act is to divide countries into 'categories' and to enact slightly different procedures for each category. Category 1 countries are those to which extradition is easiest. This was the United Kingdom's response to the implementation of the 2002 'European Framework Decision on the European Arrest Warrant', 2002/584/JHA. Accordingly, Category 1 is limited to the members of the European Union (see SI 2003/3333, SI 2004/1898, SI 2005/365, SI 2005/2036, SI 2006/3451, and SI 2007/2238). No country may be included within Category 1 if it retains the death penalty as part of its general criminal law (s. 1(3) of the Extradition Act 2003). All other countries with which the United Kingdom has extradition agreements fall into Category 2, and these are currently listed in the Extradition Act 2003 (Designation of Part 2 Territories) Order 2003 (SI 2003/3334). This category needs to be subdivided, however, in that there are certain countries within Category 2 in relation to which the requirements as to the information which must be produced to support an extradition request, and the grounds on which it can be refused, are significantly reduced. Within the following discussion, countries falling into this group will be labelled 'Designated Category 2' countries and countries falling outside it 'Non-designated Category 2' countries. It must be noted, however, that this labelling is not adopted in the Extradition Act 2003 itself. Section 194 of the Act provides for special arrangements for extradition to be made in particular cases, where there is no extradition treaty in place. The existence of such arrangements must be certified by the Secretary of State. The extradition will then be dealt with as a Non-designated Category 2 case.

The approach adopted here is to deal with the categories in reverse order, that is Non-designated Category 2, then Designated Category 2, then Category 1. In other words, we shall start with the category where the procedures most closely resemble those under the previous law, and then move to those in relation to which extradition becomes progressively easier.

There have been two recent reviews of UK extradition law. One was by the Joint Committee on Human Rights (JCHR), and is entitled 'The Human Rights Implications of UK Extradition Policy, Fifteenth Report of Session 2010–12', HL Paper 156, HC 767, June 2011 (JCHR Report). The second was a review set up by the Home Office, which reported in September 2011: Scott Baker, 'A Review of the United Kingdom's Extradition Arrangements', Home Office, 2011) (Baker Review). The comments and proposals from these two reviews will be noted at the appropriate points in the rest of this chapter.

11.2.1 Non-designated Category 2 countries

The relevant procedure is set out in Pt. 2 of the Extradition Act 2003. It starts with a State sending a request for extradition to the Secretary of State (the Home Secretary). Provided that the request comes from the appropriate authority

(s. 70(5)–(7)) and indicates that the person concerned is accused of a criminal offence, or is unlawfully at large following conviction, the Secretary of State must issue a certificate. This is sent with appropriate supporting documents to an 'appropriate judge'. This will be a District Judge (Magistrates' Courts) designated for the purpose by the Lord Chancellor (s. 139). Extradition requests have generally been dealt with by the District Judge at the Bow Street Magistrates' Court.

11.2.1.1 Proceedings before the judge

The judge receiving the request from the Secretary of State may then issue a warrant for the arrest of the person, provided that the offence specified is an extradition offence, and there is evidence of a kind which would justify issuing a warrant for arrest if the offence had been committed in England or Wales (s. 71). The meaning of 'extradition offence' is discussed further below.

There is also provision for a provisional warrant for arrest to be issued by a Justice of the Peace, on the basis of a sworn information, supported by evidence of the same kind as is needed to support the issue of an arrest warrant by the District Judge (s. 73).

In either case, the arrested person is brought before the District Judge. Where the person has been arrested under a provisional warrant, the documentation needed to support a certificate from the Secretary of State must generally be brought before the court within 45 days, or the person must be discharged. There are some States where a longer period is allowed, as specified in SI 2003/3334. For example, the period is currently either 65 days (e.g. United States) or 95 days (e.g. Liberia). The power to extend the period is available in cases where the extradition is based on a special arrangement in relation to the particular case, rather than an extradition treaty: *Brown* v *Governor of Belmarsh Prison* [2007] EWHC 498 (Admin), [2007] 2 All ER 633.

Once the judge has the relevant documentation, a decision must be taken as to whether extradition should be ordered. The judge must be satisfied, on the balance of probabilities, that the person before him or her is the right person. He or she must also be satisfied that the documentation has been served on the person, and that the offence is an 'extradition offence' (s. 78(4)). The meaning of 'extradition offence' for the purposes of Category 2 countries is to be found in s. 137. The basic definition continues the requirement of 'double criminality'. That is, the conduct must not only amount to an offence in the requesting State, but must also amount to an offence in the United Kingdom, and in both cases be punishable by a sentence of at least 12 months' imprisonment. The test is not whether there is an exact match between offences in the requesting State and the United Kingdom, but whether conduct of the kind alleged is criminal in the United Kingdom. This was the view of the House of Lords in *Norris* v *Government of the United States of America* [2008] UKHL 16. In that case, price-fixing, the alleged criminal conduct, was not a crime in the United Kingdom and so there could be no extradition on this basis; the accused was also alleged to have interfered with an investigation by the US authorities. Since it would have been an offence to interfere with an investigation by the relevant UK authorities, the double criminality rule was satisfied in relation to this conduct, and extradition could be ordered in relation to this offence.

There are also provisions which mean that in certain circumstances conduct which was committed outside the territory of the requesting State can be an extradition offence (s. 137(3)–(6)). This includes in particular offences such as genocide, crimes against humanity, and war crimes. These provisions apply in an adapted form where the request relates to someone who has been sentenced for an offence (s. 138).

If the above conditions are met, then the judge must proceed to consider whether any of the four bars to extradition specified in s. 79 apply. These are:

- the rule against double jeopardy (s. 80);
- extraneous considerations (s. 81);
- the passage of time (s. 82); and
- hostage-taking considerations (s. 83).

As regards double jeopardy, if it appears that the person, if charged with the offence in this country, would be entitled to be discharged because of a previous conviction or acquittal, the extradition proceedings must be discharged.

The concept of 'extraneous considerations' has to some extent replaced the idea of the 'political offence'. Section 81 provides that a person's extradition should be barred if the request:

> …is in fact made for the purpose of prosecuting or punishing him on account of his race, religion, nationality, gender, sexual orientation or political opinions; or, if extradited he might be prejudiced at his trial or punished, detained or restricted in his personal liberty by reason of his race, religion, nationality, gender, sexual orientation or political opinions.

It will, of course, be up to the person whose extradition is sought to bring evidence before the judge to support such concerns.

'Passage of time' will operate as a bar where it appears that the lapse of time since the alleged offence (or since the person became unlawfully at large) means that it would be 'unjust or oppressive' to proceed. In *Kociukow v District Court of Bialystok III Penal Division* [2006] EWHC 56 (Admin), a Category 1 case, the Divisional Court held that a delay of six years from the date on which the alleged offence was committed meant that it would be unjust to extradite the applicant. This decision was distinguished in *McKinnon v USA* [2007] EWHC 762 (Admin), *The Times*, 19 April 2007, where a delay of five years in relation to a complex case involving computer hacking was held to be justifiable. If the delay is the result of the accused having fled from the jurisdiction where his or her trial was pending, then generally passage of time will not in itself prevent extradition: *Gomes v Government of Trinidad and Tobago* [2009] UKHL 21 (affirming the pre-Extradition Act 2003 House of Lords' decision in *Kakis v Cyprus* [1978] 2 All ER 364).

The final bar relates to 'hostage-taking' offences (s. 83). If:

- the requesting State is a party to the Hostage Taking Convention 1979; and
- the person might be prejudiced at trial through not being able to communicate with authorities entitled to exercise rights of protection in relation to him or her; and
- the conduct alleged would also constitute an offence under the Taking of Hostages Act 1982 (thus enabling the person to be tried in this country),

then the extradition will be barred.

If none of these bars applies then the judge must proceed, in relation to a person not yet convicted, to consider whether there is sufficient evidence against the person to mean that he or she would have a case to answer at a summary trial in this country (s. 84). Certain documentary evidence, which might not be admissible at a trial, can be taken into account (s. 84(2)–(3)). There was some case law on admissibility of evidence under the Extradition Act 1989 which may well also be relevant under the Extradition Act 2003. It was held by the House of Lords in *R v Levin* [1997] AC 741 that the judge has a discretion to refuse to hear evidence on the basis of s. 78 of the Police and Criminal Evidence Act 1984 (PACE) (see chapter 4 (4.6.4.3)). In *Re Proulx* [2001] 1 All ER 57 it was emphasized that the test of admissibility may be less strict than in an English context, in that the issue for the magistrate is simply whether there is a prima facie case. The question of the admissibility of evidence will finally fall to be determined at the full trial of the case following extradition. The court referred to Lord Hoffmann's comment in *R v Levin* that exclusion of evidence under s. 78 in extradition proceedings was likely to be 'very rare' and only occur where it had been obtained in a way that 'outrages civilised values'. The case also confirmed that exclusion under s. 76 of PACE (see chapter 4 (4.6.4.1)) was possible, though again it did not apply on the facts. The same approach to s. 78 was applied by the Divisional Court in *Re Saifi* [2001] 4 All ER 168. Here, however, although the magistrate had been entitled not to exercise his discretion to exclude under s. 78, he had failed to take full account of all the circumstances of the retraction of a confession by an alleged accomplice of the applicant. The evidence of the accomplice was worthless and should have been ignored on the grounds of 'insufficiency'.

If the judge thinks that there is sufficient evidence to support the request, then he or she must proceed to consider whether the person's extradition would be compatible with the HRA 1998 (s. 87). The Baker Review found that this had been working satisfactorily (Baker Review, paras 5.29–5.89). The JCHR, however, felt that the courts had generally been setting the bar too high in the relation to this issue, in particular by assuming that signatories to the ECHR would also comply with the obligations contained in it (JCHR Report, para. 71). It expressed approval, however, for the approach taken in *R (Targosinski) v Judicial Authority of Poland* [2011] EWHC 312 (Admin). Here the judge held that if the ECtHR had found consistent evidence of relevant human rights abuses in a Member State (in this case in relation to prison conditions), and there was no evidence that these deficiencies had been resolved, then this would provide a basis to challenge the assumption that members of the Council of Europe would comply with their human rights obligations. On the facts, however, while the ECtHR had found the Polish government to be in breach of its obligations as regards prison conditions, there was evidence that these had improved, and the applicant's HRA challenge to extradition to Poland was rejected. For further examples of 'human rights' challenges, see *Ahman v United States* [2006] EWHC 2927 (Admin), [2007] HRLR 8, and *R (on the Application of Wellington) v Secretary of State for the Home Department* [2009] UKHL 72, discussed at 11.2.2.

If the HRA question is answered in the affirmative, i.e. the extradition would be compatible with the Convention, then the case must be sent to the Secretary of State for a final decision (as discussed at 11.2.1.2). Otherwise the person must be discharged.

In cases where the person is unlawfully at large, having been convicted of an offence in the requesting State, the judge needs to consider simply whether the person was present at the trial. If the person was present, or was intentionally absent, the judge can proceed directly to the HRA 1998 issue, as above. If the person was tried in his or her non-deliberate absence, then the judge must consider whether the person would be entitled to a retrial in the requesting State. If not, then the person must be discharged. If so, then the judge must consider whether there would be sufficient evidence to support a case to answer, as in relation to a person not yet convicted (s. 86). If so, the HRA 1998 issue must be considered, as above, following which the person will be discharged, or the case sent to the Secretary of State.

There is one final way in which the person may avoid the case being sent to the Secretary of State. By virtue of s. 91, if the judge at any stage is satisfied that the physical or mental condition of the person is such that it would be oppressive to extradite him or her, the person may either be discharged, or the hearing suspended until the person recovers. An example of the application of s. 91 is to be found in *Government of the United States* v *Tollman* [2008] EWHC 184 (Admin).

11.2.1.2 **The Secretary of State's decision**

The final stage in the extradition process for Category 2(b) countries is the decision of the Secretary of State. Under the Extradition Act 2003, however, very little discretion is given. There are three specified grounds on which extradition must be refused (s. 93). The first is where the person would be at risk of the death penalty if returned (s. 94). This is in line with the United Kingdom's rejection of the death penalty by acceptance of Protocol 13 to the ECHR, and with the decision of the ECtHR in *Soering* v *United Kingdom* (1989) 11 EHRR 439. It held that to return the accused to the United States, where a sentence of death would be followed by a very long period on death row, would be a breach of Art. 3. More recently the ECtHR has held that imposing the death penalty may in itself constitute a breach of Art. 3: *Al Saadoon* v *United Kingdom* (2010) 51 EHRR 9. The second ground compelling refusal is the requirement of 'specialty'. This means that there must be arrangements in place with the requesting State under which a person extradited will not be dealt with other than for the extradition offence (or another extradition offence disclosed by the same facts, or for which the Secretary of State has given consent to the person being dealt with) without first being given an opportunity to leave that State (s. 95). The third ground for refusal is where the person has been extradited to the United Kingdom from another country, and that country's permission is required for further extradition from the United Kingdom and has not been given (s. 96).

The Secretary of State may receive representations in relation to these matters, but these must be made within six weeks of the case being referred to the Secretary of State. If the Secretary of State finds that none of the above three bars applies, then the wording of the Act suggests that extradition *must be* ordered. There appears to be no residual discretion. However, in the case of Gary McKinnon (see the earlier proceedings in *R (Mackinnon)* v *Secretary of State for Home Affairs* [2009] EWHC 2021), a man with Asperger's syndrome accused of hacking into US defence computer systems, the Home Secretary refused to authorize his extradition, on the grounds that to do so would infringe his human rights (because of the risk of suicide) (see, e.g. http://www.bbc.co.uk/news/uk-19957138). It seems, then, that the Home Secretary's obligation as a 'public authority' under the HRA 1998 to act compatibly with Convention rights overrides the strict wording of the statute. The position thus seems to be similar to that under the previous law as applied in, for example, the *Pinochet* case (see 11.2.5) where the ill health of the accused was used by the Secretary of State as the basis for a refusal to extradite.

11.2.1.3 **Appeals**

There is a right of appeal to the High Court, on law or fact, against the decision of a judge to refer the case to the Secretary of State, or of the Secretary of State to order extradition. A further appeal to the Supreme Court may be made if the High Court certifies a point of law of general public importance (s. 114). Appeals may similarly be made against the discharge of the person by either a judge or the Secretary of State.

Under the previous law, the writ of *habeas corpus* was specifically recognized as a means of challenging extradition decisions. It was accepted by the Divisional Court in the Category 1 case of *Nikonovs* v *The Governor of Brixton Prison* [2005] EWHC 2405 (Admin), [2006] 1 All ER 927, however, following consideration of the Parliamentary debates on the issue, that the Extradition Act 2003 does not preclude the use of *habeas corpus* or judicial review. The approach taken in *Nikonovs* was approved by the House of Lords in another Category 1 case, *Re Hilali* [2008] UKHL 3, though on the facts before the House, it held that *habeas corpus* had been inappropriately used by the lower court, since it had been based on a detailed consideration of evidence, which, as noted at 11.2.3, should not be undertaken in a Category 1 case. Although these cases were concerned with Category 1 extraditions, there is no reason to doubt that the approach as to the availability of *habeas corpus* should apply to the Extradition Act 2003 as a whole.

11.2.2 **Designated Category 2 countries**

Much of the above procedure applies to Designated Category 2 countries as well as to Non-designated Category 2 countries, with the relevant provisions appearing in Pt. 2 of the Extradition Act 2003. The main differences relate to the information that has to be supplied to support an extradition request and the basis on which the judge will take the decision to refer the case to the Secretary of State.

As regards the initial stage, where the decision is being taken as to whether to issue a warrant, the Extradition Act 2003 replaces the word 'evidence' with 'information' in ss 71 and 73. This implies that a lesser standard is to be applied to what is put forward and that material which would not be admissible evidence can be used to support the issue of a warrant.

The biggest difference, however, applies at the stage where the judge is taking the decision as to whether to refer the case to the Secretary of State. The judge will consider whether the documentation is correct, and whether any of the statutory bars to extradition apply (s. 79). He or she may also take account of the health of the person under s. 91. But the judge is precluded from considering the evidence under ss 84 and 85. There is to be no review of the evidence in order to decide whether there is a case to answer. Instead, in relation to Designated Category 2 countries, the judge must proceed directly to considering the HRA 1998 issue under s. 87. This obviously makes matters much easier for the requesting State, will speed up proceedings, and makes it far more likely that extradition will in the end be granted. In *R (Norris)* v *Secretary of State for the Home Department* [2006] EWHC 280 (Admin), [2006] 3 All ER 1011, the claimant tried to argue that the United States was improperly included as a Designated Category 2 country, because the United States had not ratified a 2003 Extradition Treaty. As a result, it was argued that the position was governed by an earlier treaty, under which the United States was required to provide evidence of the alleged offences. The High Court rejected this argument. The procedure for designating the United States under Category 2 had been correctly followed, and the procedure set out in the Extradition Act 2003 was correctly applied to the case. The United States has in any case now ratified the 2003 Treaty.

Three other cases involving the United States should be noted. The first, *R (Bermingham)* v *Director of the Serious Fraud Office* [2006] EWHC 200 (Admin), [2006] 3 All ER 239, involved the so-called 'NatWest Three'—senior executives of the National Westminster Bank who were implicated in the accounting scandal involving the collapse of Enron, a US company. Part of their challenge to their extradition was that the case should have been investigated by the Serious Fraud Office in the United Kingdom, and dealt with here. It was held that the Director of the Serious Fraud Office had not acted unreasonably (in the *Wednesbury* sense) in not taking action. Second, the question was raised as to whether under s. 137(2)(a) all the conduct had to have taken place in the Category 2 territory. The court held, following the interpretation of an equivalent provision relating to Category 1 territories by the House of Lords in *Office of the King's Prosecutor, Brussels* v *Cando Armas* [2005] UKHL 67, [2006] 2 AC 1, that it was sufficient if some of the conduct took place in that territory. The defendants' behaviour had a sufficient connection with the United States for it not to be an abuse of process for them to be tried there. The fact that the US prosecutor had refused to disclose material forming the basis for the extradition was not evidence of bad faith, since in relation to a Designated Category 2 territory s. 84 of the Extradition Act 2003 precludes a review of the evidence by the judge considering the extradition request. There was no need for a prima facie case to be established. Finally, the defendants' human rights under Art. 8 were not disproportionately infringed by their extradition.

In *Ahman* v *United States* [2006] EWHC 2927 (Admin), [2007] HRLR 8, the appellant was suspected of involvement in terrorism, and extradition was sought by the United States. The appellant challenged this on the basis that he would risk being subjected to the procedures introduced in the wake of the terrorist attacks in New York on 11 September 2001, for example, detention at Guantanamo Bay, and trial by military tribunal, rather than the ordinary courts. He alleged that this would infringe his human rights. The Court found that the United States had given assurances, in the form of Diplomatic Notes, that the appellant would be tried before the ordinary federal courts, and would not be treated as an 'enemy combatant' subject to detention at Guantanamo Bay. The Court accepted these assurances as sufficient to answer the appellant's human rights concerns, and his appeal was dismissed. Similarly, in *R (on the Application of Wellington)* v *Secretary of State for the Home Department* [2009] UKHL 72 the accused was facing extradition on a murder charge to Missouri. If convicted, the mandatory sentence was life imprisonment without the possibility of parole. The accused argued that such a sentence would infringe his right under Art. 3 of the ECHR not to be subject to inhuman or degrading punishment. The House of Lords held that while an irreducible life sentence might raise an Art. 3 issue, in *Wellington*'s case the irreducible nature of the sentence was challengeable by appeal to the State Governor, who had the power to commute it to, so as to allow for parole. On that basis, the accused's Art. 3 right was not engaged. In coming to this conclusion the majority of the House also expressed the view, strictly obiter, that Art. 3 might apply less stringently in the context of extradition than it would in a domestic context. It is unlikely that such an analysis would be approved by the Strasbourg Court, which has taken a strict line on the absolute character of the rights contained in Art. 3.

The United Kingdom's extradition arrangements with the United States were considered by the JCHR and the Baker Review. Concerns had been expressed that the relationship between the United Kingdom and the United States was imbalanced, in that in order for the United Kingdom to extradite a person from the United States, it has to be shown by the United Kingdom that it has 'probable cause'—i.e. 'such information as would provide a reasonable basis to believe that the person sought committed the offense for which extradition is requested' (JCHR Report, para. 187). There is no such obligation on the United States when seeking extradition from the United Kingdom (whereas under previous arrangements the United States would have had to show a prima facie case). The JCHR found that this imbalance was unsatisfactory, and recommended that the United Kingdom 'should increase the proof required for the extradition of British citizens to the US so as to require sufficient evidence to establish probable cause'. The Baker Review, by contrast, took the view that the requirement under s. 71 to provide to a judge information (as opposed to evidence) sufficient to establish reasonable suspicion that the person has committed the extraditable offence, was sufficiently similar to the 'probable cause' test to mean that there is no significant imbalance. It recommended no change in this area (Baker Review, paras 11.58–11.62).

The procedure, once the case has been referred to the Secretary of State, is the same as for Non-designated Category 2 countries.

11.2.3 Category 1 Countries—European Arrest Warrant

The procedures in relation to Category 1 countries are set out separately, in Pt. 1 of the Extradition Act 2003. The broad format is similar to that applying to Category 2, but with some significant differences. These are to ensure that the procedures are in line with the 'European Framework Decision on the European Arrest Warrant of 2002', which were intended to simplify extradition arrangements between Member States of the European Union, based on the expectation of mutual respect for the legal systems of such States.

The first difference is that the process is started by the issue of a warrant of arrest by the requesting State—relating to arrest for the purpose of prosecution for offence, or arrest of a person unlawfully at large following conviction. This is known in the Extradition Act 2003 as a 'Part 1 warrant', but is more commonly known as a European Arrest Warrant (EAW). It must contain the information required by s. 2 of the Act, including the identity of the person sought, details of the offence alleged (including the circumstances in which it occurred) or the conviction, and of the possible or actual sentence.

The EAW is presented to the 'designated authority' in this country, which is the National Crime Agency (s. 2(2), SI 2003/3109). That authority, if satisfied that the warrant was issued by the appropriate judicial authority in the requesting State, and is otherwise in order, may issue a certificate under s. 2 of the Extradition Act 2003. The effect of this certificate is that the warrant can be executed in the United Kingdom by any constable or customs official (s. 3). There is also a power of 'provisional arrest' without warrant, where a constable has reasonable grounds to believe that a Part 1 warrant (i.e. an EAW) has been or will be issued by the appropriate authority in a Category 1 country (s. 5). In *Dabas* v *Spain* [2007] UKHL 6, [2007] 2 All ER 641 the House of Lords held that the certificate did not need to be a separate document from the warrant itself. The basis for this decision was that to be too specific in requiring compliance with additional procedures which were not included within the Framework Agreement would run counter to the objective of the reform. As Lord Hope put it (para. 44):

> The European arrest warrant that was issued in this case contains all the information that was needed for it to be a Part 1 warrant. Its authentication by the issuing judicial officer was sufficient for it to satisfy the formality expected of a certificate that vouches the information contained in it. It follows that the district judge was entitled to hold that the appellant's alleged conduct constituted an extradition offence in relation to Spain within the meaning of section 64(2).

Once a person is arrested under a Part 1 warrant or a provisional warrant, the next stage in the procedure is similar to that applying to Category 2 countries. The person must be brought before the 'appropriate judge', which will again be a designated District Judge (Magistrates' Court), who will decide if the person should be remanded to an extradition hearing. Where the arrest was under a provisional warrant the person, together with the Part 1 warrant and certificate, must be brought before the judge within 48 hours. Where the arrest was under the Part 1 warrant itself, the person must be brought before the judge 'as soon as practicable' (s. 4(3)). The decision whether to remand or not is taken solely on the basis of whether the person before the court is the person specified in the warrant, which is to be decided on the balance of probabilities (s. 7(2), (3)).

The date fixed for the extradition hearing should be not more than 21 days from the person's arrest—though there is power for extensions to be granted to either party to the proceedings 'in the interests of justice' (s. 7(5)).

At the hearing the judge will decide whether or not to order extradition, exercising the same powers as a magistrates' court at a summary trial (s. 9(1)). The first issue to decide is whether the offence is an 'extradition offence'. The definition is different from that which applies to Category 2 countries. It may be satisfied by fulfilling the 'double criminality' test, in the same way as for Category 2 (see 11.2.1.1) (s. 64). In such a case, the judge may, if necessary, amend the warrant to cover only behaviour occurring at a time when the alleged offence existed in the United Kingdom (*Dabas* v *Spain*), or to excise countries in which the behaviour was alleged to have taken place (*Osunta* v *Germany* [2007] EWHC 1562 (Admin), [2007] 4 All ER 1038). The test of whether the offence alleged is an 'extradition offence' may also be satisfied, however, by the issue of a certificate from the appropriate authority of the Category 1 country showing that the conduct falls within the 'European framework list' and is punishable in the requesting country with at least three years' imprisonment. The 'European framework list' is set out in Sch. 2 to the Extradition Act 2003, and is derived from the European Framework Directive on Extradition of June 2002. The list consists of 32 categories of offence. Some are specific (e.g., 'murder', 'rape') but others are expressed in much more general terms ('participation in a criminal organisation', 'corruption', 'racism and xenophobia', 'swindling'). There is no need for an offence falling within one of these categories to have an exact parallel in this country. As long as the behaviour, falling within one of the 'framework' areas, constitutes a specific offence in the Category 1 country, attracting the appropriate penalty, then it will be held to be an 'extradition offence'. As emphasized by the House of Lords in *Re Hilali* [2008] UKHL 3, in a Category 1 case the judge should not get involved in considering the detail of the offence or the evidence on which the charges may be based. Whether the evidence supporting the application would be admissible at trial is a matter for the courts of the requesting State, not the judge considering the application for extradition. The vagueness of some of the offences in the list of 32 categories led the JCHR to recommend that this should be reviewed—while recognizing that this would require a renegotiation of the Framework Agreement (JCHR Report, para. 165). The Baker Review recommended that the European framework list should be amended to include a 'proportionality' test—to avoid EAWs being used for trivial or inappropriate offences (Baker Review, paras 5.12–5.155).

Once the judge has decided that the offence is an extradition offence, then it must be decided whether any of the bars to extradition apply (s. 11). These are mainly the same as operate in relation to Category 2 countries, that is, double jeopardy, extraneous considerations, passage of time, hostage-taking considerations. In addition, however, the judge must consider two issues which under Category 2 fall to the Secretary of State, that is, the 'specialty' requirement, and the situation where there has been an earlier extradition to the United Kingdom. Finally, there is an additional bar which does not apply in relation to Category 2. This relates to the age of the person to be extradited, and is dealt with by s. 15. If the person would be conclusively presumed not to be able to commit the extradition offence under English law (assuming that the conduct constituted an offence under that law), then their extradition will be barred. Currently English law imposes such a presumption where a person is under the age of ten, by virtue of s. 50 of the Children and Young Persons' Act 1933. To this extent only, the requirement of double criminality is applied to Category 1 countries. In relation to Category 2 countries, of course, the issue of age is dealt with by the more general requirement of double criminality.

If none of the bars applies, but the extradition relates to a person unlawfully at large following conviction, the judge must consider the issue of whether the person was tried in his or her absence, in the same way as for Category 2 countries.

If this issue is resolved in favour of the requesting State, and in any case where the person is sought for prosecution for the extradition offence (rather than following conviction), the judge must then move directly to considering the issue of compatibility with the HRA 1998 (s. 21), which applies in the same way as for Category 2. There is no need in relation to a person sought under a Part 1 warrant for the judge to give any consideration to the evidence against the person, or the information which has been supplied to support the warrant. In other words, there is no need for a prima facie case, or a case to answer, to be established. Provided the warrant itself has been validly issued, then the judge, assuming that none of the bars apply, and that the HRA 1998 issue is determined in favour of the requesting State, must order the extradition.

The only other basis on which extradition under a Part 1 warrant may be refused relates to the health of the person sought. As with Category 2 countries, if at any stage the judge is of the view that the person's physical or mental condition is such that it would be unjust or oppressive to extradite, then the judge may discharge the person, or adjourn the hearing pending his or her recovery (s. 25).

Following the judge's decision, there are routes of appeal, on fact or law, to the High Court, and from there, on a point of law of general public importance, to the House of Lords. The appeal rights operate in much the same way as for Category 2 countries (ss. 26–34).

11.2.4 Conclusions on the Extradition Act 2003

The procedures introduced under the Extradition Act 2003 were intended to streamline the process. This is most notable in relation to Category 1, where much of the judge's discretion has been removed, and there is no role for the Secretary of State. Whether this system is seen to operate satisfactorily will largely depend on the confidence which exists in the legal processes of the requesting country. It is perhaps encouraging that the current list of Category 1 countries was initially so short. This may be taken to indicate that the government was taking seriously the need for confidence in the system if it is not to be discredited. The situation of a UK citizen being arrested in this country under a 'foreign' warrant, and then being extradited to stand trial for an offence which does not exist under English law, is one which is fraught with danger—not least in terms of adverse media publicity.

Even in relation to Category 2, the system is intended to operate more speedily than under the previous regime, with the judge's discretion being reduced. This is particularly the case in relation to Designated Category 2 countries, where the information supporting an extradition request does not need to reach the level of a 'case to answer'. Again, the system supposes confidence in the requesting State's procedures.

The trend of decisions on the Extradition Act 2003 has been in favour of allowing extradition. The courts have been prepared to be flexible in relation to procedures, and not been willing to become involved in detailed examination of issues, such as the precise provisions of the foreign law which the suspect is alleged to have broken. Human rights arguments have not generally been successful. They have tended to be based on Art. 8, which of course can be readily overridden where allegations of criminal behaviour are involved.

One final point to note is that throughout the Extradition Act 2003 reference is made to extradition by consent, with various provisions requiring that the person sought to be extradited is made aware of this possibility. The object is presumably to reduce the number of cases where an extradition hearing is actually needed, and thereby also to speed up the process of return.

11.2.5 **Extradition and heads of state: the *Pinochet* case**

This issue is not directly dealt with by the Extradition Act 2003. It is assumed, therefore, that the approach taken by the House of Lords in *R v Bow Street Metropolitan Magistrate, ex p Pinochet Ugarte (No. 3)* [1999] 2 All ER 97, remains good law.

This case concerned the former President of Chile, Senator (formerly 'General') Pinochet. He was in power between 1973 and 1990, during which period there were many allegations of human rights abuses committed by officials of his regime, including torture, murder, and unexplained disappearance of individuals. It was accepted by the House of Lords that there was no real dispute that 'appalling acts of barbarism' had occurred ([1999] 2 All ER 97, p. 1010). In 1998 Senator Pinochet came to the United Kingdom on a private visit, to receive medical treatment. While he was here, the government of Spain sought to extradite him to stand trial for conspiracy to murder, conspiracy to torture, and hostage taking. The Senator, while not accepting the validity of any of the charges, raised the defence of 'State immunity', under which the Head of State of a country is immune from prosecution by another country. This is the same principle by which ambassadors and other diplomatic representatives have immunity from legal action in the country in which they are serving.

The issue was heard twice by the House of Lords. The first ruling, which went against Senator Pinochet, was set aside because one of the members of the appeal committee, Lord Hoffmann, was found to have connections with Amnesty International, which was represented as a party to the case (see *R v Bow Street Metropolitan Stipendiary Magistrate, ex p Pinochet Ugarte* [1998] 4 All ER 897, and *R v Bow Street Metropolitan Stipendiary Magistrate, ex p Pinochet Ugarte (No. 2)* [1999] 1 All ER 577). An entirely different appeal committee of seven Law Lords heard the appeal for the second time.

The House, with Lord Goff dissenting, held that it was possible for Senator Pinochet to be extradited for certain offences.

The central issue was that of State immunity. The House of Lords confirmed that the general principle is that a Head of State has complete immunity for all actions (public and private) while in office ('immunity *ratione personae*'). After leaving office immunity is lost in relation to private acts, but retained in relation to matters carried out in an official capacity while in office ('immunity *ratione materiae*'). This immunity would extend to 'ordinary' criminal offences such as murder or conspiracy to murder. The position was different, however, in relation to crimes recognized by international law as 'crimes against humanity', either punishable by an international tribunal, or subject to 'universal' jurisdiction (that is, triable by *any* State, no matter where the behaviour took place). In relation to such crimes State immunity would make no sense, since the main target was the officials of States acting in their official capacity. Torture had become such an international crime by virtue of the 1984 Convention against Torture and other Cruel, Inhuman or Degrading Treatment or Punishment (the Torture Convention). It was made criminal under English law by virtue of s. 134 of the Criminal Justice Act 1988, which came into effect on 29 September 1988. In relation to actions before that date, however, even though they amounted to torture, extradition was not possible. This was because of the 'double criminality' rule noted at 11.2.1.1, which requires that the conduct in question should have been criminal in the United

Kingdom at the time it took place. 'Torture', in its form of an international crime, was not a criminal offence in the United Kingdom prior to 29 September 1998. The Convention itself was ratified by the United Kingdom on 8 December 1998. This was the point at which Senator Pinochet lost his State immunity. In relation to actions involving torture, or conspiracy to torture, alleged to have taken place after 8 December 1998, the House of Lords held that Senator Pinochet had no immunity, and could be extradited.

There were also some complex arguments, set out in the speech of Lord Hope, as to the circumstances and times at which conspiracy to murder, or conspiracy to commit offences which might be involved in torture, such as assault or causing grievous bodily harm, where both the conspiracy and its intended result took place outside the United Kingdom, might be extraditable (see [1999] 2 All ER 97, pp. 135–43). He came to the conclusion that offences of this kind might be extraditable if they took place in countries to which the Suppression of Terrorism Act 1978 applies, after the date on which that Act came into force. In fact, however, the relevant conspiracies were all said to have taken place in the mid-1970s, before the 1978 Act came into force, and so were not extraditable. These points are, of course, strictly obiter, since these conspiracies would in any case have been protected by State immunity, since they did not constitute international crimes against humanity.

The conclusion of the House of Lords was, therefore, that Senator Pinochet could claim State immunity in relation to all the offences alleged against him, other than torture. In relation to torture, he was protected by State immunity prior to 8 December 1998 (the point at which the United Kingdom ratified the Torture Convention). Offences covered by the Convention which were alleged to have taken place after that date were ones on which he could be extradited to Spain.

The final outcome of the case was that, Senator Pinochet's health having deteriorated, the Home Secretary decided that he was not fit to stand trial. He therefore returned to Chile, escaping extradition.

11.3 Deportation

Deportation is very different from extradition. It has no necessary connection with the commission of criminal offences and it involves no judicial process comparable with the proceedings which operate in relation to extradition. The decision to deport was traditionally a matter of executive discretion (though, of course, operating within a framework of legal rules, which may make the decision susceptible to judicial review). The other important distinction from extradition is that deportation is not available in respect of British citizens. However, the Nationality, Immigration and Asylum Act 2002 (NIAA 2002) provides that a person with dual nationality may be deprived of their British citizenship if the Secretary of State reasons that their presence is not conducive to the public good (for further details see *Abu Hamza* v *Secretary of State for the Home Department*, Appeal No. SC/23/2003, 2010). The Immigration, Asylum and Nationality Act 2006 extends these powers so that a person can be deprived of citizenship and right of abode if their presence is not conducive to the public good. It is, therefore, necessary to look at the rules relating to citizenship, before moving on to consider in detail the grounds for deportation.

11.3.1 The concept of citizenship

At one time everyone who held a British passport had a right to enter and settle in the United Kingdom, even if their only connection with this country was that they were a citizen of a Commonwealth country or colony. Immigration controls only applied to those who did not hold a British passport, and were categorized as 'aliens'. It was thought necessary, however, in the 1960s and 1970s, because of the numbers who wished to enter the United Kingdom, and the increasing racial tensions which were developing in this country, to impose restrictions on immigration to the United Kingdom even in relation to certain categories of people from Commonwealth countries who held British passports. The Commonwealth Immigrants Act 1962 for the first time imposed significant limitations on the rights of those from the Commonwealth and colonies to enter and settle in the United Kingdom. Over the last 30 years the trend has continued to be increasingly restrictive. The position is now largely governed by the Immigration Act 1971, as amended by the British Nationality Act 1981 (BNA 1981). The Immigration Act 1971 introduced the two concepts of the 'right of abode' and 'patriality'. The latter concept has now disappeared, but the 'right of abode' survives as the test of whether a person has a right to settle and work in the United Kingdom, without being subject to immigration controls (s. 1(1) of the Immigration Act 1971). A person is defined by s. 2(1) of the Immigration Act 1971 as having a right of abode if:

(a) he is a British citizen; or

(b) he is a Commonwealth citizen who—

    (i) immediately before the commencement of the British Nationality Act 1981 was a Commonwealth citizen having the right of abode in the United Kingdom by virtue of s. 2(1)(d) or s. 2(2) of this Act as then in force; and

    (ii) has not ceased to be a Commonwealth citizen in the meanwhile.

It will be noted that the category in s. 2(1)(b) depends on rights existing under previous legislation. It is a complex business to work out exactly who is included in it, but since it is a limited category, in that no new members of it can now arise, it is not discussed further here. (For a full discussion see I. A. Macdonald and N. Blake, *Immigration Law and Practice in the United Kingdom*, 4th edn (London: Butterworths, 1995) ch. 6.) The definition of who is a 'British citizen' is to be found in Pt. I of the BNA 1981. All those citizens of the United Kingdom and colonies who had a 'right of abode' prior to the BNA 1981 are included. Since the BNA 1981 came into force in 1983, however, it has only been possible to obtain British citizenship in five ways, namely, place of birth, adoption by a British citizen, descent, registration, and naturalization. Of these, only place of birth and descent need further explanation here.

As regards place of birth, it is not enough simply to be born in the United Kingdom. In addition, one of the child's parents must either be a British citizen or be lawfully settled in the United Kingdom (s. 1(1) of the BNA 1981). As regards 'descent', a child born outside the United Kingdom will obtain British citizenship if one of the child's parents is a British citizen *other than by descent* (s. 2 of the BNA 1981). British citizenship can thus in general only be passed to one generation by descent alone (as opposed to birth in the United Kingdom combined with descent).

Turning now to the power of deportation, s. 3(5) of the Immigration Act 1971 provides that 'a person who is not a British citizen shall be liable to deportation from the United Kingdom' in certain circumstances. Note that Commonwealth citizens falling within s. 2(1)(b) of the 1971 Act, are to be treated as British citizens for this purpose (s. 2(2) of the 1971 Act).

A further complication arises in relation to citizens of other Member States of the European Economic Area (EEA). This consists of the 28 Member States of the European Union plus certain members of the former European Free Trade Area (currently Iceland, Switzerland, Norway, and Liechtenstein). EEA citizens are not British citizens, and thus under s. 3(5) of the Immigration Act 1971 are liable to deportation. However, traditionally EU law provides that EEA nationals have rights of free movement between Member States for certain economic purposes (such as working or establishing a business). Furthermore, Arts 20 and 21 of the Treaty on the Functioning of the European Union (TFEU) have established a right for EU citizens to move and reside in Member States in the absence of specific economic activity (as indicated in *Grzelczyk* v *Centre Public D'Aide Sociale D'Ottignies-Louvain-La-Neuve* (Case C–184/99) [2002] 1 CMLR 19, para. 31). The power to deport is governed by Art. 45 of the TFEU and Art. 27 of Council Directive 2004/38, and is limited to 'public policy, public security and public health'. This must be regarded as limiting the powers contained in s. 3 of the Immigration Act 1971 and Pt. 13 of the Immigration Rules as of July 2011). As a result, the grounds for deporting EEA nationals are considered separately at 11.3.2.

11.3.2 **Grounds for deportation**

11.3.2.1 **Non-EEA nationals**

Section 32 of the UK Borders Act 2007 makes it mandatory for the Secretary of State to make a deportation order against a non-British citizen who is convicted either:

(i) of any offence where they are sentenced to a term of imprisonment of 12 months, or

(ii) of certain specified offences which result in a term of imprisonment of any length. These are generally serious offences, including terrorist offences, murder, manslaughter, and sexual offences but also include some minor offence such as theft and criminal damage. They are specified in an order by the Secretary of State for the Home Department under s. 72(4)a of the Nationality Immigration and Asylum Act 2002.

Section 32 permits no appeal against automatic deportation orders. However, a person may appeal on the basis that removal would breach their rights under the ECHR or the 1951 Refugee Convention. In the case of the latter, a successful asylum claimant may still be removed if sentenced to more than two years' imprisonment.

The three grounds for deportation set out in s. 3(5) and (6) of the Immigration Act 1971 as amended by the Immigration and Asylum Act 1999 (IAA 1999) are retained. These are where:

(a) the Secretary of State deems the deportation of a person to be 'conducive to the public good' (s. 3(5)(a)): this ground is considered further below; or

(b) someone in the person's family (as defined in s. 5(4)) is or has been ordered to be deported (s. 3(5)(b)); or

(c) a person over the age of 17 has been convicted of an imprisonable offence, and the court recommends deportation.

Under s. 3(5) as it applied prior to the IAA 1999, people in breach of conditions of entry, or who 'overstayed' after the permission expired, were also liable to deportation. Under s. 10 of the IAA 1999, however, such people are now subject to removal by 'directions' given by an immigration officer. This is an administrative procedure which is no longer treated as 'deportation' (though it is hard to see the difference in practice). The main effect is to reduce the scope for appeals in relation to such people. These issues are discussed below.

The automatic deportation of serious offenders under the UK Borders Act 2007 reduces the discretion exercised by the Secretary of State. Where discretion is retained it is difficult to challenge the assessment that deportation is conducive to the public good under s. 3(5)(a). In *N (Kenya)* v *Secretary of State for the Home Department* [2004] EWCA Civ 1094 the court held that in any proportionality assessment, significant weight should be attached to the Home Secretary's policy of deporting those with serious criminal records. Furthermore, para. 398 of the Immigration Rules 1994 states that only in exceptional cases will the public interest in deportation be outweighed.

There are several circumstances where the Secretary of State retains discretion. The 'public good' ground may still be used where a person has been convicted of a less serious offence but no recommendation for deportation has been made by the court. It is accepted that the courts general discretion in this respect has been significantly reduced and that where it continues to exist, discretion should generally be exercised by the Secretary of State rather than the courts (*R* v *Kluxen* [2010] EWCA Crim 1081). In determining the public interest, the court in *OH (Serbia)* [2009] INLR 109 identified three factors for consideration: the risk of re-offending; the need to deter foreign nationals from committing serious crimes; and the role of deportation as an expression of society's revulsion over serious crimes coupled with the need to build public confidence in the criminal justice system.

Second, the fact that some sort of deception has been practised in order to obtain settlement in the United Kingdom may justify deportation on the 'public good' ground: *Patel* v *IAT* [1988] 2 All ER 378. This has also been accepted as an appropriate ground where the applicant is alleged to have entered into a 'marriage of convenience': *R* v *IAT, ex p Khan* [1983] QB 790.

Third, the public good ground has been used on occasion to deport people engaging in the promotion of political views which are regarded as dangerous (e.g. in 1970 Rudi Dutschke, a 'student' activist, was deported on this basis), or unduly offensive to certain sections of the community (e.g. members of the Ku Klux Klan could be deported on this ground). Adherents to particular religious sects may also come under this heading, as was the case in relation to members of the Church of Scientology during the 1980s.

Finally, concerns that the continued presence of the person will be detrimental to 'national security' will certainly be relevant, though this is in itself a nebulous concept. An example of its use is to be found in the case of *R v Secretary of State for the Home Department, ex p Hosenball* [1977] 3 All ER 452. Mark Hosenball was a US citizen who had been living on and off in the United Kingdom for over seven years. He originally came when he was 18, as a school pupil, but by 1976 was working as a general news reporter for the *Evening Standard*. He had previously worked as a journalist on the magazine *Time Out*. During all this time he had permission to remain. In November 1976, he received a letter from the Home Office stating that the Secretary of State had decided to deport him. The reasons were given as follows ([1977] 3 All ER 452, p. 455):

> The Secretary of State has considered information that Mr Hosenball has, while resident in the United Kingdom, in consort with others, sought to obtain and has obtained for publication, information harmful to the security of the United Kingdom and that this information has included information prejudicial to the safety and servants of the Crown.

As a result, the Secretary of State had decided that his departure from the United Kingdom would be conducive to the public good, as being in the interests of national security. This in effect tells us that collecting, and proposing to publish, information about the security services is regarded as being contrary to national security (see Lord Denning [1977] 3 All ER 452, p. 456). No further detail, however, of the allegations against Mr Hosenball, or their source, was forthcoming, and the courts were not prepared to look behind the statement contained in the letter (see 11.3.3.2). In *R v Secretary of State for the Home Department, ex p Chahal* [1995] 1 All ER 658, the Court of Appeal held that the Home Secretary, in exercising his discretion to deport on national security grounds, had to balance these considerations against the requirements of the 1951 Refugee Convention. On the facts, he had done this by seeking assurances from the Indian government as to the manner in which the applicant would be treated if deported to that country. This decision was, however, subsequently found to be in breach of the ECHR (see 11.1.1).

The case of Abu Qatada is perhaps the most well-known example where human rights arguments (specifically Art. 6) were advanced to prevent deportation on national security grounds (see 12.1.1). There seems little doubt that Mr Qatada's presence in the UK constituted a threat to national security and he was wanted in connection with terrorism charges in Jordan. The House of Lords had ruled that even if evidence used against him in a Jordanian court was obtained by torture there would not be a flagrant breach of Art. 6 (*RB (Algeria) v Secretary of State for the Home Department; OO (Jordan) v Secretary of State for the Home Department* [2009] UKHL 10). The ECtHR disagreed with their Lordships' assessment and found that there would be a flagrant breach of Art. 6 if Mr Qatada was returned to Jordan. In July 2013 Mr Qatada was eventually returned following an eight-year legal battle after the UK government succeeded in securing assurances of a fair trial from the Jordanian authorities.

The national security ground was also used in 1991, at the time of the first Gulf War, in relation to Iraqis and Palestinians against some of whom there was apparently information that they had links with an organization prepared to take terrorist action in support of the Iraqi regime: *R v Secretary of State for the Home Department, ex p Cheblak* [1991] 2 All ER 319 (see 11.3.3.1).

Finally, in *Secretary of State for the Home Department v Rehman* [2001] UKHL 47, [2002] 1 All ER 122 the House of Lords held that 'national security' considerations could include someone at risk of engaging in international terrorism which would have no direct effect in the United Kingdom. It accepted the Secretary of State's submission that (para. 17, p. 130):

> ...the reciprocal co-operation between the United Kingdom and other states in combating international terrorism is capable of promoting the United Kingdom's national security, and that such co-operation itself is capable of fostering such security 'by, *inter alia*, the United Kingdom taking action against supporters within the United Kingdom of terrorism directed against other states'.

Moreover, the House agreed with the Court of Appeal that it was not necessary that particular acts of terrorism should be proved on the balance of probabilities against the individual. Taking a global approach a person could be regarded as constituting a danger to national security, even though it could not be proved that the person had committed any individual act which would justify that conclusion. In essence the Secretary of State was entitled to make a conclusion about future risk on the basis of evidence which may or may not have been disclosed to the appellant.

Section 7 of the Immigration, Asylum and Nationality Act 2006 inserts a new s. 97A into the NIAA 2002 so that an appeal against deportation on national security grounds can only be made from outside the United Kingdom. If the appeal also raises human rights issues these will be heard prior to removal, unless the Secretary of State certifies that removal will not breach the ECHR.

The automatic expulsion provisions in the UK Borders Act 2007 can be applied to offences committed before the provisions came into force (1 August 2008). There are several exceptions to the mandatory nature of the provisions but they do not necessarily prevent the Secretary of State from using existing powers under s. 3(5)(a) of the Immigration Act 1971, namely:

(i) Where removal would be contrary to the ECHR or the Geneva Convention on the Status of Refugees 1951 (s. 33(2)).

(ii) Where the Secretary of State thinks the foreign criminal was under 18 on the date of conviction (s. 33(3)).

(iii) Where removal would be contrary to EU law (s. 33(4)).

(iv) Where a person is subject to extradition proceedings (s. 33(5)).

(v) Where certain provisions of the Mental Health Act 1983 apply (s. 33(6)).

(vi) Where the deportation would be contrary to the council of Europe Convention Against Trafficking in Human Beings.

Part 10 of the Criminal Justice and Immigration Act 2008 removes status from people who cannot be deported for legal reasons, for example due to the potential for human rights violations. As a result they will be unable to work or receive benefits in the United Kingdom.

11.3.2.2 **EEA nationals**

Nationals of other Member States of the EEA (see 11.3.1) are not British citizens, and therefore are in general subject to the deportation powers in s. 3(5) of the Immigration Act 1971. However EEA nationals do not require leave to enter or remain when exercising their treaty rights (s. 7(1) of the Immigration Act 1988). Articles 20 and 21 of the TFEU, which provide for citizenship of the Union coupled with specific provisions enabling the right to work (Arts 45–8 of the TFEU); to establish or join a business (Arts 49–55 of the TFEU); and to provide or receive services (Arts 56–62 of the TFEU) enable freedom of movement for Union citizens and their family members between EEA states. According to Directive 2004/38 (implemented by the Immigration (EEA) Regulation 2006 (SI 2006/1033)) the only grounds on which deportation may take place are public policy, public security, and public health. Thus, by virtue of Art. 27(1) of the Directive, previous commission of a criminal offence will not in itself provide justification for exclusion. There must be a real possibility of re-offending, or the offence must have been sufficiently serious to arouse public revulsion, for the public policy justification to come into play: *Bonsignore* v *Ober-stadtdirektor of the City of Cologne* [1975] ECR 297 and *R* v *Bouchereau* [1977] ECR 1999. The question of exclusion on grounds of public policy because of membership of a particular organization was considered in *Van Duyn* v *Home Office* [1974] 1 WLR 1107, [1974] ECR 1337. Miss Van Duyn was a member of the Church of Scientology. She was a Dutch national, but wished to enter the United Kingdom to work as a secretary at the Church's headquarters in East Grinstead. She was refused leave to enter because of her membership of the Church, whose activities the United Kingdom considered to be not conducive to the public good. The European Court took the view that, although in general a person's past associations should not restrict freedom of movement, where there was present membership of, and participation in the activities of an organization, this could be regarded as 'personal conduct' falling within Art. 27(1). Moreover, public policy 'may vary from one country to another' and national authorities therefore had an 'area of discretion within the limits imposed by the Treaty'. It followed that, if the activities of an organization are considered socially harmful, and administrative measures have been taken to counteract them, there was no need for them to be made unlawful before the public policy ground could be relied on. As regards the fact that no similar restrictions were placed on UK nationals, it was a principle of international law that a State cannot refuse entry or residence to its own nationals, but the whole point of Art. 45 (previously Art. 39) was that, while granting freedom of movement to nationals of other Member States, for certain purposes, that freedom was subject to restrictions.

It follows that a Member State, for reasons of public policy, can, where it deems necessary, refuse a national of another Member State the benefit of the principle of freedom of movement for workers in a case where such a national proposes to take up a particular offer of employment, even though the Member State does not place a similar restriction on its own nationals.

Article 27(3) of the Directive incorporates the principles established in *R* v *Bouchereau* and *Rutili* v *French Minister of the Interior* [1975] ECR 1219, namely that reliance on public policy presupposes the existence of 'a genuine and sufficiently serious threat to the requirements of public policy affecting one of the fundamental interests of society'. The Court in *Rutili* had also expressed the view that the action taken must be justified as being 'necessary...in a democratic society' for the protection of the public interests concerned. The breadth of the *Van Duyn* decision was further restricted by *Adoui and Cournaille v Belgian State* [1982] ECR 1665, where it was held that it would be difficult to regard conduct as being sufficiently serious to justify deportation or exclusion on public policy grounds unless some action was taken against the nationals of the Member State who engaged in such conduct:

> ...a Member State may not...expel a national of another Member State from its territory or refuse him access to its territory by reason of conduct which, when attributable to the former State's own nationals, does not give rise to repressive measures or other genuine and effective measures intended to combat such conduct.

It may well be, therefore, that if the *Van Duyn* case recurred, the United Kingdom would need to show that some restrictive measures (not necessarily involving the criminal law) were taken against members of the Church of Scientology who were British citizens in order to justify the deportation or exclusion of nationals of other Member States on the grounds of membership of the Church.

Article 28 of Directive 2004/38 requires that prior to taking an expulsion decision on security or policy grounds, Member States should consider factors such as how long the individual has resided in the country, his/her age, state of health, family, and economic situation, social and cultural integration into the host Member State and the extent of his/her links with the country of origin. Furthermore, if the EU citizen has achieved permanent residence status they can only be removed on 'serious grounds of public policy or security' (Art. 28(2)). The case of *HR (Portugal) v Secretary of State for the Home Department* [2009] EWCA Civ 371 determined that time spent in prison would not count as time in the UK for the purpose of calculating permanent residence.

11.3.3 Methods of challenge

There are four possible methods of challenge to a decision to deport, though some of them are likely to be of limited practical use, and others are only available in relation to certain categories of decision. In so far as the challenge may involve the court issuing an order, albeit a temporary one, restraining the removal of the applicant from the jurisdiction, this will bind even the Secretary of State. In *M v Home Office* [1993] 3 All ER 537, the applicant had been seeking asylum. A judge in chambers received an undertaking that the applicant would not be deported pending a further hearing. Nevertheless, the deportation of the applicant went ahead. The judge then ordered the Secretary of State to return the applicant to this country, but this order was not complied with. The House of Lords confirmed that this rendered the Secretary of State (in his official capacity) in contempt of court. Thus, although many of the powers in this area are exercised on the basis of Ministerial discretion, there is not unlimited power in the executive. The exercise of powers may be controlled by orders from the courts, with contempt as the sanction.

11.3.3.1 *Habeas corpus*

This is the ancient writ by which the legality of detention (on any ground) can be challenged. It is sought by means of an *ex parte* application to the High Court which takes precedence over all other business. If the court thinks that there is a case for the writ to issue, it will normally (unless there is a need to act with urgency) adjourn proceedings to enable an *inter partes* hearing to take place. The issue of the writ will have the effect of ordering the person to whom it is directed to release the applicant from detention immediately.

The High Court does not, however, act as a court of appeal in considering applications. It is concerned purely with procedural issues, and not with the merits. For this reason, although it is in theory available to a person detained pending deportation, in practice it is likely to be of limited use. Since the *habeas corpus* action is concerned entirely with the issue of jurisdiction, it will only be where the Secretary of State has clearly acted *ultra vires* that the writ will issue. This might be the case, for example, if the stated ground for deportation was a recommendation of a court following conviction for an offence, where it was shown that the person concerned was below the age of 17 at the relevant time (see s. 3(6) of the Immigration Act 1971). In general, however, the broad discretion given to the Secretary of State will make it unlikely that such a challenge can be mounted. In *R v Secretary of State, ex p Cheblak* [1991] 2 All ER 319 (see 11.3.2.1) the Court of Appeal held that the Secretary of State did not need to give reasons for a decision to deport on grounds of national security. A notice stating simply that the applicant's deportation was deemed to be for the public good 'for reasons of national security' was perfectly valid. The applicant's detention on the basis of the notice was therefore lawful, and could not be challenged by *habeas corpus*. (See also *R v Governor of Brixton Prison, ex p Soblen* [1963] 2 QB 243, discussed at 11.3.3.2.) In *R v Secretary of State for the Home Department, ex p Rahman* [1997] 1 All ER 796 the appellant argued that a court, in assessing the legitimacy of the Home Secretary's decision, should only take account of evidence that would normally be admissible in a court of law. Thus, in this case the Home Secretary had relied in part on evidence obtained from villagers in Bangladesh that the appellant was not who he claimed to be. It had led to the appellant being detained pending deportation. The evidence was clearly 'hearsay', however, and therefore generally inadmissible as evidence in legal proceedings. The Court of Appeal in considering an appeal against a refusal of *habeas corpus* held that the court could take into account all the material which the Home Secretary had legitimately used in reaching his decision, and was not limited to evidence which was in the strict sense 'admissible'. The weight given to such evidence might, however, be affected by the fact that it was hearsay. On the facts, the majority of the court upheld the decision of the Home Secretary that the appellant had gained his certificate of entitlement by deception, and was therefore liable to deportation.

The Court of Appeal in *Rahman* clearly took the view that the same principle as regards evidence admissibility should apply, irrespective of the type of proceedings.

If the basis for challenge is not that the order is *ultra vires*, but that a discretion has been exercised improperly, then *habeas corpus* will not be available, and judicial review proceedings should be used. The effect of s. 140(1) of the Immigration and Asylum Act 1999 which permits detention where there is reasonable grounds for believing that removal directions will be issued, means that the scope of *habeas corpus* is considerably narrowed today.

11.3.3.2 Judicial review

The decision to deport, and the procedures that have led to it, are clearly administrative acts that are susceptible to judicial review. This was the method of challenge used in *R v Secretary of State for the Home Department, ex p Hosenball* [1977] 3 All ER 452, and was an additional argument in *R v Secretary of State for the Home Department, ex p Cheblak* [1991] 2 All ER 319. The wording of the statutory powers means, however, that traditionally the applicant had to establish bad faith, or *Wednesbury* unreasonableness, to have any chance of success. Moreover, where the basis for the decision to deport is stated by the Secretary of State to relate to matters of national security, the courts would not look behind that assertion: *Hosenball*. As Lord Denning put it (p. 461):

> There is a conflict here between the interests of national security on the one hand and the freedom of the individual on the other. The balance between these two is not for a court of law. It is for the Home Secretary. He is the person entrusted by Parliament with the task.

Lord Denning then went on to express perhaps surprising confidence that the Secretary of State would never use the powers improperly, asserting that successive Ministers, in using such powers, 'have never interfered with the liberty of the freedom of movement of any individual except where it is absolutely necessary for the safety of the State'. Even if the power were misused, the Minister would be answerable to Parliament, rather than the courts. The impact of the HRA 1998 enables an alternative argument of proportionality to be advanced in judicial review proceedings (see further 11.3.5). Further, in cases where there is a prima facie breach of an absolute right (such as Art. 3) the state will not be given an opportunity to justify their actions (*R (on the Application of Adam, Limbuela, Tesema) v Secretary of State for the Home Department* [2005] UKHL 66).

It has been suggested that it may be possible to challenge a deportation order if 'the object of the exercise was simply to achieve extradition by the back door': Lord Lane in *R v Bow Street Magistrates, ex p Mackeson* (1982) 7 Cr App R 24. There is no reported case, however, in which an order has been overturned on this ground. In *R v Governor of Brixton Prison, ex p Soblen* [1963] 2 QB 243 (which in fact was an application for *habeas corpus* rather than judicial review) the applicant was sought by the United States in relation to espionage offences of which he had been convicted. Extradition was not at the time available for such offences, but the Home Secretary ordered Soblen's deportation to the United States. Soblen had asked to be sent to Czechoslovakia, which was prepared to accept him. He challenged the deportation order on the basis that, *inter alia*, it was being used for 'disguised extradition'. The Court of Appeal rejected this argument, because no bad faith on the part of the Home Secretary had been proved. In other words, it had not been shown that the request from the United States was the sole reason for the deportation order. Even in the absence of this request, the Home Secretary might well have ordered Soblen to be deported to the United States, on the public good ground. The order was thus upheld, but Soblen in fact committed suicide before he could be returned.

In *R v Mullen* [1999] 2 Cr App R 143 the Court of Appeal was faced with the converse situation—i.e. a deportation from another country (Zimbabwe) to the United Kingdom. There was evidence that the deportation had taken place as a result of unlawful actions by both the UK and Zimbabwean authorities, as a means of avoiding using extradition procedures. At the defendant's subsequent trial in England he was convicted of conspiracy to cause explosions. The Court of Appeal, however, allowed his appeal on the basis that the abuse of process in the pre-trial procedures rendered his conviction unsafe.

The relaxation and simplification of the procedures for extradition (see 11.2) may well mean that there will be less temptation in the future to use deportation as a substitute.

Judicial review may also be used in relation to claims for political asylum. This area is, however, dealt with separately at 11.3.4.

11.3.3.3 Appeal under the Nationality, Immigration and Asylum Act 2002

The system of immigration appeals has been regularly revised with a view to reducing the scope for appeal and speeding up the process. The current system is to be found in Pt. 5 of the NIAA 2002, as amended by the Asylum and Immigration (Treatment of Claimants, etc.) Act 2004 and the Immigration, Asylum, and Nationality Act 2006. The Act is supplemented by the Immigration and Asylum Appeals (Procedure) Rules 2005 (SI 2005/230).

The Immigration and Asylum Tribunal (IAT) consists of two chambers. The first tier Tribunal (Immigration and Asylum Chamber) deals with appeals against decisions of immigration officers. The Upper Chamber will hear appeals from the first tier on points of law but appeals are dependent on leave from either chamber. A further appeal on a point of law can be made to the Court of Appeal providing the Upper Chamber has given permission. The members of the Tribunal will generally have a seven year legal qualification as a solicitor or barrister (though there is provision to appoint others whose legal or other experience makes them suitable for appointment). The president of the AIT must hold, or have held, 'high judicial office' (that is, a High Court judge, or above).

An appeal against a decision to deport (as well as a range of other decisions relating to immigration, as set out in s. 82) will go initially to the first tier. The possible grounds of appeal are set out in an exclusive list, contained in s. 84. They include the fact that the decision is not in accordance with immigration rules, or that a discretion under those rules should have been exercised differently; that it is unlawful under s. 19B of the Race Relations Act 1976 or s. 6 of the HRA 1998; that it is in breach of the rights of an EEA national under European law; that deportation would breach the United Kingdom's obligations under the Refugee Convention; or that it is otherwise unlawful.

The NIAA 2002 continues the restrictions contained in previous legislation designed to limit the situations in which a person may remain in the United Kingdom (i.e. suspensive appeals). These are set out in s. 92, and have the effect that in general appeals from within the United Kingdom may only take place where the person has previously been lawfully present here (e.g. where a grant of leave to remain is withdrawn), including where an order for deportation has been made under s. 5(1) of the Immigration Act 1971. A person may also remain to appeal where the appeal is based on an asylum claim, or a breach of the HRA 1998.

This is subject to a further limitation, however, in that under s. 94 the Secretary of State may issue a certificate that the asylum or human rights claim is clearly unfounded. The Secretary of State will normally issue such a certificate where the person is entitled to residence in one of the States listed in s. 94(4), unless satisfied that the claim is clearly not unfounded. The 26 listed States include certain eastern European countries (e.g. Albania and Serbia) as well as Jamaica, South Africa, India, and some countries in South America (Bolivia and Brazil). Pursuant to s. 94(5A) eight of the listed states have been designated as safe for men only (including Sierra Leone, Nigeria, and Ghana).

More generally, under s. 94(7) such a certificate may be issued to the effect that there is no reason to believe that a person's rights under the ECHR would be infringed in the country to which it is proposed to remove him or her. This means that the certified country is deemed to be one where (s. 94(8)):

> ...a person's life and liberty is not threatened by reason of his race, religion, nationality, membership of a social group, or political opinion, and
> ...from which a person will not be sent to another country otherwise than in accordance with the Refugee Convention.

No route of appeal against the issue of a certificate is provided in the Act, but it could be subject to challenge by judicial review. The approach established in *R (Thangarasa) v Secretary of State for the Home Department* [2002] UKHL 36, [2002] 4 All ER 800 made such a challenge particularly difficult, placing the onus on the applicant to demonstrate substantial grounds for believing in a real risk of inhuman or degrading treatment contrary to Art. 3 of the ECHR if they were to be removed.

However, successful judicial review actions have since resulted on the basis that the particular certification satisfies the high threshold required for irrationality. As a consequence of these decisions both Pakistan and Bangladesh have been removed from the list of safe countries (*R v Secretary of State for the Home Department, ex p Javed and Ali* [2001] Imm AR 529 and *R (on the Application of Zahir Husan) v Secretary of State for the Home Department* [2005] EWHC 189 (Admin)).

The rules provide a very short time limit for appeals. If the person is in detention under the immigration legislation notice of the appeal must be given within five days of the notification of the decision being appealed; otherwise, the time limit is ten days. This period is reduced to two days, by virtue of the Immigration and Asylum Appeals (Fast Track Procedure) Rules 2005 (SI 2005/560), where the person is detained at either the Harmondsworth or Yarlswood detention centres. The fast-track procedure is applied by the UK Borders Agency in cases which appear to be uncomplicated. Several categories of people should not be detained under this procedure including persons who have experienced torture, persons with serious mental health problems or disabilities, and minors.

The normal appeal process does not apply to a decision to deport on the basis that this would be in the interests of national security, or the interests of relations between the United Kingdom and any other country (s. 97). In these cases the deportee must use the special appeal procedure outlined at 11.3.3.4.

An amendment to s. 82 of the NIAA 2002 enables an appeal against the automatic deportation in s. 32 of the UK Borders Act 2007 but it cannot be brought from within the United Kingdom unless on human rights, asylum, or EEA grounds. Furthermore, if the asylum or human rights claim is certified as clearly unfounded under s. 94 of the NIAA 2002 the only challenge will be by way of judicial review.

11.3.3.4 The Special Immigration Appeals Commission

Under the Immigration Act 1971, there was no appeal against deportation on the basis that it was conducive to the public good on grounds of national security, the interests of relations between the United Kingdom and any other country, or 'other reasons of a political nature'. Instead the deportee was allowed to make representations to three advisers appointed by the Home Secretary. They reported to the Home Secretary who took the final decision. These procedures were subject to criticism by the ECtHR in *Chahal* v *United Kingdom* (1997) 23 EHRR 413. As a result the Special Immigration Appeals Commission Act 1997 (SIACA 1997) set up a more judicial procedure. Cases which formerly went to the advisers may now be the subject of an appeal to the Special Immigration Appeals Commission (SIAC). The SIAC consists of three members, one of whom must have held high judicial office (e.g. a High Court judge), and one of whom must have experience as a chief immigration adjudicator or as a member of the Immigration Appeal Tribunal.

Rules for the operation of the SIAC have been issued (SI 2003/1034). As required by the SIACA 1997 they provide for the appellant to be legally represented (s. 5(2) of the SIACA 1997). They also provide that some material relied on by the Secretary of State may be withheld from the appellant and his legal adviser, and that where it is in the public interest they may be excluded from some parts of the SIAC's proceedings. In that case, the appellant will be represented by a 'special advocate' appointed for this purpose by the Attorney-General, at the request of the Secretary of State. The standard of proof as regards allegations of past actions is the balance of probabilities, notwithstanding the serious consequences for the unsuccessful applicant.

The SIAC is empowered to allow the appeal if it considers (s. 4(1)(a) of the SIACA 1997):

(i) that the decision or action against which the appeal is brought was not in accordance with the law or with any immigration rules applicable to the case, or

(ii) where the decision or action involved the exercise of a discretion by the Secretary of State or an office, that the discretion should have been exercised differently.

Note, however, the limitation of the scope of an appeal to the SIAC by an asylum seeker, discussed at 11.3.4.

An appeal on a point of law from a decision of the SIAC may be taken to the Court of Appeal, subject to leave being given by the SIAC or the court (s. 7 of the SIACA 1997). In *Secretary of State for the Home Department* v *Rehman* [2001] UKHL 47, [2002] 1 All ER 122 noted at 11.3.2.1, the Court of Appeal and House of Lords took a broader view than the SIAC as to what could be included within the concept of 'national security'. In 2007 the Court of Appeal heard an appeal from SIAC concerning an Algerian man who had been acquitted of involvement in the alleged Ricin plot (*MT (Algeria)* v *Secretary of State for the Home Department* [2007] EWCA Civ 808). In reversing the decision of SIAC the Court of Appeal held that the tribunal should reconsider the case, in particular the evidence and assertions of the Secretary of State that Algeria could be considered safe.

It is evident that this procedure introduces a clear independent judicial element which was lacking from the old advisory procedure. However the use of closed evidence remains a serious barrier to the protection of the applicant's human rights. In *A* v *UK* (2009) 49 EHRR 29 the ECtHR ruled that Art. 5(4) should be interpreted as conferring the same rights as Art. 6 in respect of applicants who were suspected of involvement in international terrorism. This decision was subsequently followed by their Lordships in *Secretary of State for the Home Department* v *AF* [2009] UKHL 28 in the context of control orders based on closed evidence. Closed evidence was used in *Othman* v *Secretary of State for the Home Department* [2012] UKSIAC 15/2005 2 where the SIAC upheld the ruling of the ECtHR and rejected the Home Secretary's continued arguments for Abu Qatada's removal.

11.3.4 Asylum seekers

There have been increasing concerns over the past few years about the number of entrants to the United Kingdom claiming asylum. The number rose from 40,000 in 1995 to a peak of 103,100 applicants in 2002. This has been followed by a steady decline to 26,430 applicants in 2011 (Eurostat Data in Focus, 2012). The expansion of the European Union may have contributed to this decline, but it also reflects the impact of the UK government's increasingly tight immigration controls. The issue of asylum remains a matter of concern but the problems faced by the United Kingdom must be looked at part of a general move in western countries, and particularly those of western Europe, to tighten their immigration controls, including claims for asylum (see, e.g. the 'Schengen Agreement' on border controls signed up to by a number of Member States of the European Union and the Dublin Regulation which aims to prevent all secondary movement within the EU). Special rules for asylum seekers were first introduced in the Asylum and Immigration Appeals Act 1993 (AIAA 1993) and modified by subsequent legislation. The IAA 1999 introduced a range of procedures intended to discourage illegal entry (e.g. a fixed penalty of £2,000 per person on haulage companies on whose lorries immigrants have gained entry) to speed up procedures for dealing with claims for asylum, and to deal more effectively with people while their claims are being considered. All the changes have been the subject of criticism. The procedures for penalties on haulage companies were found to be incompatible with Art. 6 of the ECHR by the Court of Appeal in *International Transport Roth GmbH* v *Secretary of State for the Home Department* [2002] EWCA Civ 158, [2003] QB 728. The focus here is simply on the legal procedures by which claims for asylum by those facing deportation, or 'administrative removal' under s. 10 of the IAA 1999, are considered and disposed of.

Since 2000 it has become impossible to decouple UK asylum policy from the development of the European Common Asylum System. Pursuant to Art. 78 of the TFEU the recent phase of directives has moved from minimum standards towards common standards in the fields of refugee recognition, asylum procedures, reception conditions, and returns (see H. O'Nions, *A Right Denied* (Aldershot: Ashgate, 2013)). Whilst the UK has opted out of some of these recast provisions it must nevertheless ensure compliance with the obligations in the ECHR and the EU Charter of Fundamental Rights. The latter specifically includes a right to asylum, the prohibition on refoulement, and the right to an effective remedy.

There is no 'right of asylum' under English law, as Lord Mustill pointed out in *T v Secretary of State for the Home Department* [1996] 2 All ER 865, p. 868. It is a matter of executive discretion, although a discretion which is restricted by statutory provision in relation to the destination to which a person refused asylum may be sent. A claim of asylum is based on a claim that removal would involve the United Kingdom in a breach of its obligations under the 1951 Refugee Convention (s. 1 of the AIAA 1993). The asylum seeker must be a 'refugee' within the meaning of that Convention, which (in Art. 1(A)) defines this as any person who:

> ...owing to a well-founded fear of being persecuted for reasons of race, religion, nationality, membership of a particular social group or political opinion, is outside his country of nationality and is unable or, owing to such fear, is unwilling to avail himself of the protection of that country; or who, not having a nationality and being outside the country of his former habitual residence as a result of such events, is unable or, owing to such fear, is unwilling to return to it.

Central to the status of refugee, therefore, is the fear of *persecution* in the country of the refugee's nationality or habitual residence. This is a strong word, meaning more than simply harassment (*R v Secretary of State for the Home Department, ex p Yurekli* [1990] Imm AR 334) or discrimination (*Ahmad v Secretary of State for the Home Department* [1990] Imm AR 61). The persecution must relate to one of the areas mentioned. It was held by the House of Lords in *Islam v Secretary of State for the Home Department* [1999] 2 All ER 545 that this could include a woman's fear that if she returned to Pakistan she would be accused of adultery by her husband, and become liable to being flogged or stoned to death under Sharia law. Pakistan's women were capable of constituting a 'social group' under the Convention because of the existence of State-sanctioned discrimination against them. In 2010, the Supreme Court rejected the Home Office's argument that gay men could avoid persecution by concealing their sexuality and ruled that gay, lesbian, and transsexual people could fall within the definition of 'social group' depending on the particular facts (*HJ (Iran) and HT (Cameroon) v Secretary of State for the Home Department* [2010] UKSC 31).

The persecution can come from 'non-State' agents, if the State fails to provide protection from such persecution: *Adan v Secretary of State for the Home Department* [1999] 1 AC 293 confirmed in *R v Secretary of State for the Home Department ex p Adan* [2001] 1 All ER 593. This has now been specifically recognized in the EU Qualification Directive (2011/95/EU). The fear of persecution, whatever the source, must, however, be well-founded. This part of the test was considered in *R v Secretary of State for the Home Department, ex p Sivakumaran* [1988] 1 All ER 193. In deciding whether it is satisfied the burden of proof is on the claimant on the balance of probabilities. The Home Secretary is, however, entitled to take into account all relevant information, even if this is not known to the claimant. The test is then whether there is a 'reasonable chance' or a 'real likelihood' of persecution occurring. The difficulties inherent in such a decision are shown by the fact that after the House of Lords had upheld the Home Secretary's decision in this case to refuse asylum, and return the six Tamil claimants to Sri Lanka, an immigration adjudicator upheld an appeal on the facts, and granted them asylum status. The procedure for appeals has, however, now been changed, as is explained below. Before considering these provisions, however, it should be noted that a person who has committed a serious, non-political crime, falling within the scope of Art. 1F of the 1951 Convention, will not be entitled to protection as a refugee. It was held by the House of Lords in *T* v *Secretary of State for the Home Department* that, in relation to the violent activities of a group which was intending to overthrow a government, there must be a 'sufficiently close and direct link between the crime and the alleged political purpose' in order for it to be regarded as 'political'. It will be relevant whether the target is civilian as opposed to military or governmental and 'whether it was likely to involve the indiscriminate killing or injuring of members of the public'. On the facts of the case, T had been involved in attempting to overthrow an undemocratic government, but the means used—an explosion at an airport—was likely to (and did) kill members of the public. There was therefore not sufficient proximity between the crime and the purpose to render it 'political'.

The EU Qualification Directive (2011/95/EU) has broadened the scope of protection for asylum seekers so that a claim can now be based on 'serious harm' which may fall short of the narrow interpretation typically given to persecutory treatment. Article 15 defines 'serious harm' as: the death penalty or execution; or torture or inhuman or degrading treatment or punishment of an applicant in the country of origin; or serious and individual threat to a civilian's life or person by reason of indiscriminate violence in situations of international or internal armed conflict. Although the UK has not opted in to the amended Directive it will continue to be bound by the provisions in the 2004 Qualification Directive (2004/83/EC) which are substantially the same on this point.

What, then, is the position of a person against whom a deportation order has been made, or directions for removal have been issued (under s. 10 of the IAA 1999) who wants to claim asylum? As we have seen, this is one of the bases for an appeal to the Tribunal under s. 84(1) of the NIAA 2002 (see 11.3.3.3). The fact that a claim is made on false or fraudulent grounds does not in itself automatically preclude a finding that the claimant is entitled to the protection of the Convention. In *KH* v *Secretary of State for the Home Department* [2006] EWCA Civ 1037 the Court of Appeal cautioned against reliance on an 'inherent probability' test as 'much of the evidence will be referable to societies with customs and circumstances which are very different from those of which the members of the fact-finding tribunal have any (even second-hand) experience' (para. 29). In *HH (Somalia)* v *Secretary of State for the Home Department* [2010] EWCA Civ 426 the court emphasized that even where a testimony appears unreliable the applicant must still be protected from refoulement. The determining authority must consider credibility under s. 8 of the Asylum (Treatment of Claimants) Act 2004 which establishes a list of factors that 'shall' be regarded as designed to conceal or mislead. Nevertheless, the Court of Appeal in *JT (Cameroon)* v *Secretary of State for the Home Department* EWCA Civ 878 ruled that despite the serious damage done to the applicant's credibility by his use of false documentation, this should not be determinative of his claim to have a well-founded fear.

Section 77 of the NIAA 2002 provides that a person who has claimed asylum shall not be removed from the United Kingdom until that claim has been determined (although this does not prevent the issuing of removal directions). This is subject to massive exceptions, however, by virtue of Sch. 3 to the Asylum and

Immigration (Treatment of Claimants, etc.) Act 2004. This lists certain countries (mainly those in the EEA) as 'safe' (Sch. 3, Pt. 2), and allows the Secretary of State to designate other countries as falling within this category (see 11.3.3.3). 'Safe' means that it is a place where a person's life and liberty are 'not threatened by reason of his race, religion, nationality, membership of a particular social group or political opinion'; from which he or she will not be sent to another State in breach of his or her rights under the ECHR (where applicable); and from which he or she will not be sent to another State otherwise than in accordance with the Refugee Convention.

In the many asylum cases, therefore, the claimant will not be entitled to remain in the United Kingdom while the claim is decided. The decision of the ECtHR in *Abdolkhani and Karimnia* v *Turkey*, App. No. 30471/08, suggests that the absence of a suspensive right of appeal in such cases may deny the applicant an effective remedy contrary to Art. 13.

The presumption that all EEA States can be deemed 'safe' is arguably a flawed presumption. The inclusion of Germany and France in this category was initially a cause for concern as the House of Lords in *ex p Adan*, had concluded that neither country applied the Refugee Convention correctly in that they did not recognize that 'persecution' could arise from the actions of non-State agents. Such an argument could now only be run as a claim that the asylum seeker's rights under the HRA 1998 were being infringed by the decision. Schedule 3 also contains, however, restrictions on HRA 1998 appeals.

Furthermore, the return of asylum seekers to Greece, which had been deemed lawful by the House of Lords in *Nasseri* v *Secretary of State for the Home Department* [2009] UKHL 23, must now be viewed sceptically in light of the ECtHR ruling in *MSS* v *Belgium and Greece*, App. No. 30696/09. The ECtHR held that the Belgian and Greek authorities were responsible for violations of Arts 13 and 3 of the Convention in the case of an Afghan asylum applicant who had been removed to Greece and mistreated on arrival. The CJEU has recently confirmed this approach in *NS* v *Secretary of State for the Home Department*, C411/10, in connection with transfers to Greece under the Dublin Regulation. Concerns have also been expressed in national courts relating to proposed Dublin transfers to other Member States including Hungary and Italy.

An asylum seeker's appeal against deportation will, of course, go to the SIAC (see 11.3.3.4) if the basis for the removal is on grounds of national security, the interests of relations between the United Kingdom and another country, or 'other reasons of a political nature'. In other cases the appeal will be heard by the first tier. Section 55 of the Immigration, Asylum and Nationality Act 2006 imposes a limitation on an asylum appeal where the Secretary of State certifies that the appellant is not entitled to the protection of Art. 33(1) of the 1951 Convention. This is because either Art. 1(F) or Art. 33(2) applies, and the removal of the appellant will be conducive to the public good. Article 1(F) applies where there are serious reasons for considering that the appellant has committed a war crime, a crime against humanity, or is guilty of acts contrary to the principles and purposes of the United Nations. Article 33(2) applies to remove the prohibition against expulsion or return to a country where the refugee would be threatened on account of race, religion, etc., where there are reasonable grounds for regarding the appellant as a danger to the security of the State in which asylum is sought. If a certificate is issued, then the Commission or Tribunal 'must begin its substantive deliberations on the asylum appeal by considering the statements in the Secretary of State's certificate' (s. 55(3)). If it agrees with those statements, it must dismiss the claim for asylum before considering any other aspects of the case (s. 55(4)). It is submitted that this may be incompatible with the UNHCR's guidelines which require a consideration of the asylum points before the exclusion is examined. The EU Qualification Directive is also significant here as Art. 12 appears to warrant a similar approach; see G. Clayton, *Textbook on Immigration and Asylum Law* (Oxford: Oxford University Press, 2011) p. 519. It has been held that s. 54 of the Immigration, Asylum and Nationality Act 2006, which allows reference to s. 1 of the Terrorism Act 2000 when determining whether the acts are contrary to the purposes and principles of the United Nations, should be given a narrow interpretation so that it complies with the EU Qualification Directive (*Al-Sirri* v *Secretary of State for the Home Department* [2009] EWCA Civ 222). These decisions must also be scrutinized to ensure that they do not contravene the absolute prohibition of refoulement contrary to Art. 3 of the ECHR.

11.3.4.1 Detention of asylum seekers

Powers to detain intending entrants or those who are to be deported are contained in Sch. 2 to the Immigration Act 1971. These may be needed in order, for example, to examine the person applying for admission, or to make sure that they do not abscond when a decision to deport has been taken. Government policy had been to use detention only as a last resort, preferring to grant temporary admission subject to conditions. Detention would only be used where there was a risk of absconding or non-compliance with conditions. In March 2000, however, a change was introduced in relation to asylum applications. Where it was thought that an application could be dealt with quickly then the applicants would be detained at a special centre (Oakington Removal Centre, which closed in November 2010) for about seven days with a view to resolving their status. This new category of detention was challenged in *R (Saadi)* v *Secretary of State for the Home Department* [2002] UKHL 41, [2002] 4 All ER 785.

The challenge was based on two grounds. First, that the detention was unlawful under the Immigration Act 1971. Second, that it offended against the right to liberty guaranteed by Art. 5 of the ECHR. On the first ground, Collins J held that the power to detain fell within para. 16(1) of Sch. 2 to the Immigration Act 1971 which allows a person to be detained on the authority of an immigration officer 'pending his examination or pending a decision to give or refuse him leave to enter'. The statutory provision does not put limits on the circumstances in which the power should be used—it does not, for example, limit it to cases where the individual was likely to abscond. Provided that detention was reasonably used for a purpose stated in the statute it was for the Secretary of State to decide on the particular circumstances in which it should be used ([2001] EWHC 670 (Admin), para. 22, [2001] 4 All ER 961, p. 974). Detention at Oakington under the new policy for asylum seekers was, therefore, lawful under domestic law.

As regards Art. 5 of the ECHR, the right there guaranteed can be restricted in certain situations. In particular, Art. 5(1)(f) allows:

...the lawful arrest or detention of a person to prevent his effecting an unauthorised entry into the country or of a person against whom action is being taken with a view to deportation or extradition.

Collins J took the view that the language of this Article made it clear that it could not be used to justify detention 'on the ground that it may speed up the process of determination of applications generally and so may assist other applicants' (para. 30; p. 977). Indeed, the detentions at Oakington could not be justified under either part of the Article. As regards the first part, once someone who is in the country (however they arrived) has made an application for asylum, and is unlikely to abscond, it was 'impossible to see how it could reasonably be said that he needs to be detained to prevent his making an unauthorised entry' (para. 30, p. 977). On the contrary, the person is endeavouring to achieve an authorized entry. Similarly, the second part of Art. 5(1)(f) was also inapplicable, because the relevant investigation was not 'with a view to deportation' but with a view to seeing whether permission to enter should be granted. Collins J, therefore, concluded that the detentions at Oakington were in breach of the obligations under Art. 5 of the ECHR.

Collins J's decision caused something of a political storm as it was seen as undermining an important part of the government's policy of 'fast-tracking' certain asylum applications. It was a matter of some relief to the government, therefore, that the Court of Appeal took a different view. It agreed that the powers to detain were lawful under domestic law. As regards Art. 5 it felt that the interpretation by Collins J would put an obligation on the Secretary of State to grant temporary admission whenever a claim for asylum was made (absent the likelihood of absconding or other misbehaviour). The court did not think that this could be right. It did not accept that Art. 5 of the ECHR could have been intended effectively to overturn the well-established position in international law that a State has the right to control the entry of non-nationals into its territory. This right had been recognized by the ECtHR in *Abdulaziz* v *United Kingdom* (1985) 7 EHRR 471, p. 497. Moreover, in *Chahal* v *United Kingdom* (1997) 23 EHRR 413 the ECtHR had noted that Art. 5(1)(f) did not require that detention should be necessary to prevent a person committing an offence or fleeing:

> Indeed, all that is required under this provision is that 'action is being taken with a view to deportation'. It is therefore immaterial, for the purposes of Art. 5(1)(f), whether the underlying decision to expel can be justified under national or convention law. (para. 112)

The only constraint imposed by the ECtHR in *Chahal* was that the deportation proceedings should be prosecuted 'with due diligence'. Even here, this did not mean that detention could only be for a short period. The ECtHR had found that Chahal's detention for a period of five years was not in itself a breach of Art. 5. As to the argument that a person whose case was being considered with a view to granting asylum, was therefore not being considered with a view to deportation, the Court of Appeal could find no support for this in the ECHR cases.

In conclusion, it held that the detentions under the 'Oakington' procedure were proportionate in achieving the objectives legitimated by Art. 5(1)(f). The only test was whether ([2001] EWHC 670 (Admin), para. 66, [2001] 4 All ER 961, p. 996):

> ...the process of considering an asylum application has gone on too long to justify the detention of the person concerned having regard to the conditions in which the person is detained and any special circumstances affecting him or her.

On this basis, the Secretary of State's policies probably went beyond what was required in terms of compliance with Art. 5. The detentions which were the subject of the application before the court were, therefore, all lawful. The Court of Appeal's decision was confirmed by the House of Lords. Although the detention engaged Art. 5, it had a legitimate objective under Art. 5(1)(f) (detention to prevent unauthorized entry) and the procedures used were not disproportionate to the achievement of that objective. The only difference between the Court of Appeal and the House of Lords was that while the Court of Appeal based its decision on the reference in Art. 5 to the action being taken with a view to deportation, the House of Lords relied on the reference in Art. 5(1)(f) to preventing unauthorized entry.

The ECtHR in *Saadi* v *United Kingdom* [2008] App. 13229/03 upheld the view of the House of Lords that there was no breach of Art. 5(1)(f) as the detention was not disproportionate to the aim of preventing unauthorized entry. Furthermore, the ECtHR expressly and controversially dismissed any suggestion that immigration detention should be necessary as is required for the other exceptions to Art. 5. The decision has now been confirmed by the Grand Chamber of the ECtHR.

In *R (on the Application of A)* v *Secretary of State for the Home Department* [2007] EWCA Civ 804 the Court of Appeal reversed the decision of the High Court which held that the detention of a Somalian man awaiting deportation was unlawful because of its length (18 months), the impossibility of removal, and misleading statements from decision makers (per Calvert-Smith J, para. 49). The Court recognized that for removal to be 'pending' under Sch. 3, para. 2(2) of the Immigration Act 1971 the detention must be exercised only for the purpose for which the power exists, and second, that it must be exercised only for such period as is reasonably necessary for that purpose. However, they held that the detention was lawful as the appellant had the opportunity to leave the United Kingdom voluntarily and his continued detention could be justified due to the likelihood of the respondent absconding and the high risk of him re-offending.

In 2011 the Supreme Court, reversing the Court of Appeal ruling, held that an action in false imprisonment could lie against the Home Office when it had secretly reversed a policy concerned with the release of foreign national prisoners (*WL (Congo) and KL (Jamaica)* v *Secretary of State for the Home Department* [2011] UKSC 12). In *S, C and D* v *Secretary of State for the Home Department* [2007] EWHC 1654 (Admin) a breach of Arts 5 and 8 was found when a mother and her two young children were detained for four months in the absence of evidence that they would abscond. Furthermore, Williams J reasoned that the United Kingdom's reservation to the United Nations Convention on the Rights of the Child in immigration cases, should not apply in cases involving detention of children (para. 49). This reservation has since been removed.

Despite assurances from the Liberal Democrat Coalition partners, children continue to be detained under immigration powers. It has also been established that, contrary to UNHCR guidelines and the Home Office's own rules, torture victims continue to be held in detention facilities. In *R (on the Application of EO, RA, CE, OE, and RAN)* v *Secretary of State for the Home Department* [2013] EWHC 1236) Burnett J ruled that four torture victims were entitled to compensation for unlawful detention after their case history had been largely ignored by the immigration authorities. It is anticipated that many more actions for wrongful detention will follow this decision and in some cases it seems probable that the threshold of Art. 3 will be met.

11.3.4.2 **Inhuman and degrading treatment: the denial of welfare support**

Section 55 of the NIAA 2002 was enacted to restrict welfare benefits to those asylum seekers who claimed asylum immediately on arrival in the United Kingdom. The initiative was introduced as a response to the concern that the asylum process was being abused by 'economic migrants' who were engaging in a process of 'asylum shopping' in order to take advantage of particular States that provide generous welfare packages. In the United Kingdom this generous package amounts to 70 per cent of the minimum level of subsistence provided as income support. No evidence was adduced to support the contention that late applicants are more likely to be 'bogus'; indeed evidence suggests that there is no correlation.

In *R* v *Secretary of State for the Home Department, ex p Adam, Limbuela and Tesema (conjoined appeals)* [2005] UKHL 66, the House of Lords was required to review the effects of s. 55(1) and s. 55(5)a in the light of Art. 3. The House of Lords emphasized that Art. 3 involves a positive obligation on the State to avoid treatment which is inhuman and degrading. In all three cases the respondents had claimed asylum on the first day of arrival in the United Kingdom and had subsequently been deprived of support. As a direct result they had been forced to sleep rough indefinitely and had experienced significant deterioration in their health. The House unanimously upheld the decision of the Court of Appeal and found that the treatment had reached the minimum level of severity needed to constitute a breach of Art. 3.

Reflecting on the reasons for the introduction of s. 55 it is perhaps worth mentioning that two of the three respondents were eventually acknowledged as presenting credible cases of persecution and were afforded refugee status.

11.3.5 **Challenging deportation under the Human Rights Act 1998**

Decisions to deport will always be taken by a 'public authority'—e.g. an immigration adjudicator, or the Secretary of State—and therefore will be potentially open to challenge under the HRA 1998. It is noted at the beginning of the chapter (see 11.1.1) that the most likely Articles to provide a basis for challenge are Arts 3 and 8.

Although it is, of course, possible to challenge a decision directly under s. 7 of the HRA 1998, the procedure by which the HRA 1998 issue is brought before a court may well be as part of judicial review proceedings. As noted at 11.3.3.2, the courts have not shown any great willingness in the past to look behind the decisions of the Secretary of State, particularly when the 'not conducive to the public good' grounds are being relied upon. It is to be hoped, however, that when HRA 1998 issues are raised such an approach will not continue to be taken. The need to take account of Convention rights and principles should encourage a greater willingness to regard the public interest as put forward by the Secretary of State as not being conclusive in itself, but only one factor to be weighed against the rights of the individual. This is clearly evidenced by the Abu Qatada saga which suggests that the courts may be adopting a more proactive role in national security cases. Certainly where Art. 3 is concerned, since this is not subject to qualification in the same way as Art. 8, once there is a finding that to deport would involve inhuman or degrading treatment then that should be conclusive of the issue. This was the view of the ECtHR in *Chahal* v *United Kingdom* (1997) 23 EHRR 413 (see 11.1.1). The English courts should, therefore, be expected to adopt the same approach.

The key case on the definition of family life in the immigration context is *Beoku-Betts* v *Secretary of State for the Home Department* [2008] UKHL 39. The appellant had failed in his asylum claim but the particularly close relationship with his family, most of whom resided in the United Kingdom, prevented his removal on human rights grounds. The House of Lords held that the interests of the whole family, not just the applicant, must be considered. To decide otherwise would be: 'missing the central point about family life, which is that the whole is greater than the sum of the individual parts' (para. 4, per Baroness Hale). This approach was applied in *ZB (Pakistan)* v *Secretary of State for the Home Department* [2009] EWCA Civ 834. In *Chikwamba (FC)* v *Secretary of State for the Home Department* [2008] UKHL 40 the Home Secretary attempted to remove a married Zimbabwean mother who had failed in her asylum application. It was argued that Home Office policy required her to be removed but that she could then use family life arguments to ground a fresh application for entry clearance. Lord Scott reasoned that this rigid approach elevated policy to dogma and their Lordships ruled that it would be disproportionate to require her to leave the UK in such circumstances (para. 6). In many ways the judiciary has frustrated the wishes of the home Office by continuing to apply Art. 8 considerations in removal cases, notwithstanding rule 398 (see, for example, MF (Nigeria) v SSHD [2013] EWCA Civ 1192). In 2012 the Home Office introduced new rules in family cases including the extension of the probationary period for non-EEA spouses and partners who wish to acquire settlement from two to five years.

When the applicant contends that his or her Art. 8 rights will be violated following removal, the House of Lords established in *EM (Lebanon)* v *Secretary of State for the Home Department* [2008] UKHL 64 that the test will be whether treatment abroad would constitute a flagrant breach so as to destroy the essence of the right. This is the same approach as the courts have applied in cases concerning potential breaches of Arts 5 and 6 abroad.

The situation is complicated by the provisions of the IAA 1999 which, as noted in the previous section, attempt to place certain restrictions on the way in which appeals under the HRA 1998 can be pursued. It would, of course, be open to the courts to hold that such restrictions were in themselves in breach of the right under Art. 6 to a fair hearing in relation to the determination of the applicant's civil rights and obligations. The ECtHR had indicated that Art. 6 is unlikely to apply to the rights of aliens subject to expulsion proceedings (*Maaouia* v *France* (2001) 33 EHRR 42. However, the Administrative Court recently ruled that a fast track removal scheme introduced in January 2010, which set the minimum notice period for removal at 72 hours, was unlawful as it did not provide sufficient access to the courts as required by Art. 6 (*R (On Application of Medical Justice)* v *SSHD* [2010] EWHC 1925 (Admin). Overall, then, where it is possible to introduce an HRA 1998 element to a challenge to a decision to deport, this will add significant weight to the appeal, and may well have the effect of counterbalancing some of the more restrictive aspects of the immigration legislation.

11.3.6 **Conclusions on deportation**

It is no doubt necessary that in certain circumstances the executive should have the power to deport, and that there may be situations where it is appropriate that this should be done without any judicial process being involved. This is perhaps most obviously the case with those who are in the country with knowledge that they are in breach of immigration regulations. It is less clear that the power is needed in other situations, or that, if it is, it is justifiable that there is in effect no independent review of its exercise in many cases. The use of the magic words 'national security' will emasculate the already rather weak (in this context) remedy of judicial review, and we are therefore left to trust in the good faith of the Home Secretary only to use the power where it is really necessary. Even those who are not entirely cynical about the way in which government ministers carry out their public duties may feel that a less optimistic attitude than that taken by the courts in the *Hosenball* and *Cheblak* cases is justified.

In addition, the restrictions now placed on those seeking to claim asylum run the risk that genuine cases are going to be turned down as a result of procedures intended to deal with spurious claims. It has been argued that the right to seek asylum which is provided by Art. 14 of the Universal Declaration on Human Rights has been undermined by efforts to deter asylum seekers from accessing the West. These measures include carriers' liability provisions, safe-country lists, increased use of administrative detention, and restrictions on welfare provision. There has been a gradual rise in the number of successful appeals against initial asylum decisions (28 per cent in the first quarter of 2011: Home Office, Control of immigration: quarterly statistical summary first quarter 2011). This reflects concerns over the quality of initial decision-making and illustrates the importance of a thorough and effective appeals process. While the NIAA 2002 specifically recognizes the right to challenge decisions on HRA 1998 grounds, these rights are also hedged about with controls based on the Secretary of State's discretion. As noted above, there must be doubts as to whether the power of the executive to issue a certificate that such a claim is 'clearly unfounded' is compatible with the right under Art. 6 to a fair trial of a person's 'civil rights'—even if such a decision is susceptible to judicial review. It is to be hoped that the English courts will be robust in this area in holding that the HRA 1998 rights must be given full weight, and not curtailed by the political considerations which have led to the introduction of strict controls over claims for asylum. It remains to be seen whether recent developments on the reliance of closed evidence in control order cases will soon be applied more generally to national security cases. The power of interpretation given by s. 3 of the HRA 1998 has been used in many immigration and asylum decisions to ensure that the broad range of powers given by the legislature are used appropriately, and that the claims of those who have genuine fears for their safety if removed from the United Kingdom are given appropriate weight.

QUESTIONS

1 Does the EAW, and the way in which it has been applied in the United Kingdom, provide sufficient protection for British citizens being sought for trial in other jurisdictions?

2 Has the Extradition Act 2003 been a success? Are there areas in which reform is needed?

3 What protection does the ECHR provide to those who are facing deportation or extradition from the United Kingdom? Are Arts 3 and 8 interpreted in ways which are helpful to such people?

4 Should the courts be prepared to accept an assertion from a Secretary of State that a person's deportation would be 'conducive to the public good'? Should they demand evidence, and if so, of what sort?

5 What is an 'asylum seeker', and how does he or she differ from an 'economic migrant'? If such a distinction is possible, how does English law distinguish between the two? Are the protections for those claiming asylum sufficient?

FURTHER READING

Alegre, S. and Leaf, M. (2004), 'Mutual Recognition in European Judicial Co-operation: A Step Too Far Too Soon?', (2004) 10 *European Law Journal* 200

Braza, N. (2011), 'The Relationship Between the UK Courts and Strasbourg' (2011) 5 EHRLR 505

Baker, S., Perry, D., and Doobay, A. (2011), 'A Review of the United Kingdom's Extradition Arrangements', Home Office

Chakrabati, S. (2005), 'Rights and Rhetoric: The Politics of Asylum and Human Rights Culture in the United Kingdom', (2005) 32 *Journal of Law & Society* 131

Clayton, G. (2012), *Textbook on Immigration and Asylum Law*, 5th edn Oxford: Oxford University Press

Conway, G. (2005) 'Judicial Interpretation and the Third Pillar', (2005) 13 Eur J Crim L Cr J 255

Craig, P. and de Búrca, G. (2011), *EU Law: Text, Cases, and Materials*, 5th edn, Oxford: Oxford University Press

Forde, M. (1995), *The Law of Extradition in the United Kingdom*, Ilford: The Round Hall Press

Gilbert, G. (1991), *Aspects of Extradition Law*, Dordrecht: Martinus Nijhoff

Gilbert, G. (1998), *Transnational Fugitive Offenders in International Law*, Dordrecht: Martinus Nijhoff

Goodwin-Gill and McAdam (2007), *The Refugee in International Law*, Oxford: Oxford University Press

Guild, E. (2001), *Immigration Law in the European Community*, The Hague: Kluwer Law International

Guild, E. and Minderhoud, P. (eds) (2001), *Security of Residence and Expulsion*, The Hague: Kluwer Law International

Hailbronner, K. (2000), *Immigration and Asylum Law and Policy of the European Union*, The Hague: Kluwer Law International

Joint Committee on Human Rights (2011), 'The Human Rights Implications of UK Extradition Policy, Fifteenth Report of Session 2010–12', HL Paper 156, HC 767, HMSO

Jones, A. (2001), *Jones on Extradition and Mutual Assistance*, London: Sweet & Maxwell

Juss, S. S. (1993), *Immigration, Nationality and Citizenship*, London: Mansell Publishing

Juss, S. S. (1997), *Discretion and Deviation in the Administration of Immigration Control*, London: Sweet & Maxwell

Lynshey, O. (2006), 'Complementing and Completing the Common European Asylum System: A Legal Analysis of the Emerging Extra Territorial Elements of EU Refugee Protection Policy', (2006) 31 EL Rev 230

Macdonald, I. A. and Blake, N. (1995), *Immigration Law and Practice in the United Kingdom*, 4th edn, London: Butterworths

O'Nions, H. (2006), 'The Erosion of the Right to Seek Asylum', (2006) 2 Web JCLI

O'Nions, H. (2008), 'No Right to Liberty: The Detention of Asylum Seekers for Administrative Convenience', (2008) 2 *European Journal of Migration and Law* 149

O'Nions, H (2013) *Asylum. A Right Denied* Aldershot: Ashgate

Phelan, M. and Gillespie, J. (2013), *Immigration Law Handbook*, 8th edn, Oxford: Oxford University Press

Rogers, N. (2003), 'Immigration and the European Convention on Human Rights: Are New Principles Emerging?', [2003] EHRLR 53

Stevens, D. (2004), *UK Asylum Law and Policy*, London: Sweet & Maxwell

Supperstone, M. and Cavanagh, J. (1988), *Immigration: the Law and Practice*, 2nd edn, London: Longman

Symes, M. and Jorro, P. (2010), *Asylum Law and Practice*, 2nd edn, Haywards Heath: Bloomsbury Professional

Thomas, R. (2003), 'The Impact of Judicial Review on Asylum', [2003] PL 479

Vaughan, A. (2007), 'The Tribunal's New Role in Article 8 Statutory Appeals', (2007) 21(2) JINL 129

Woodhouse, D. (ed.) (2000), *The Pinochet Case—A Legal and Constitutional Analysis*, Oxford: Hart Publishing

Wouters, J. and Naert, F. (2004) 'Of Arrest Warrants, Terrorist Offences and Extradition Deals: An Appraisal of the EU's Main Criminal Law Measures Against Terrorism after "11 September"', (2004) 41 CMLRev 909

12

Freedom from Discrimination (Article 14)

12.1 General issues

12.1.1 The meaning of discrimination

The word 'discrimination' is not in itself a 'dirty word'. To say of a person that she is discriminating in her choice of boyfriends would probably be taken as a compliment. In this sense, to show discrimination is a virtue, not a vice. Similarly, to discriminate against blind people in relation to the issue of driving licences, against unqualified people in appointing doctors, or against rich people in imposing taxes, is not seen as being something which should be criticized. Discrimination only becomes objectionable where it is arbitrary, or where the basis of the discrimination has no connection with the decision being taken. In other words, it is only *unjustifiable* discrimination that is thought to be wrong. Even here there are different levels of discrimination which will provoke different responses. To refuse to sell your house because the prospective purchaser has dyed hair, or blue eyes, might be seen as strange, but not particularly heinous. On the other hand, for an employer to decide as between a number of female applicants for a job to employ the one who wears the shortest skirts, would be seen as objectionable (though probably not unlawful), particularly if the employer is male.

English law has intervened to control unjustifiable discrimination in only a limited way. It only applies to certain types of discrimination, and only in relation to discrimination for certain purposes. The types of discrimination originally covered were discrimination on the basis of race or sex. To these have now been added disability and, most recently, gender reassignment, sexual orientation, religion or belief, and age. These developments have been strongly influenced by European law and many of the new developments were intended to put into effect European Directives. This is discussed further at 12.2. The areas of activity covered by these laws include employment, education, housing, the provision of goods and services, and the actions or decisions of public authorities.

12.1.2 Discrimination and the Human Rights Act 1998

The European Convention on Human Rights (ECHR) deals with discrimination in Art. 14. This states that:

> ...[t]he enjoyment of the rights and freedoms set forth in this Convention shall be secured without discrimination on any ground such as sex, race, colour, language, religion, political or other opinion, national or social origin, association with a national minority, property, birth, or other status.

The scope of this Article is in one way rather narrow, but in another way quite broad, and this, of course, affects the way in which it can be used under the Human Rights Act 1998 (HRA 1998). The broad aspect is in the list of illegitimate grounds for discrimination, which goes beyond the categories recognized by English law, and is even then (as indicated by the use of the phrase 'such as') not exclusive. It covers, for example, discrimination on the ground of political opinions, which is not generally protected by English law. The narrow aspect is that the principle of non-discrimination is stated not as a general right, but as existing only in relation to the other rights and freedoms set out in the ECHR (including, however, those contained in the Protocols). It is thus parasitic on these other rights. If, therefore, the ECHR has nothing to say on a particular issue, such as the right to a job, or a house, then Art. 14 will be of no relevance or use to an individual who has suffered from discrimination in this context. The European Court of Human Rights has, however, interpreted Art. 14 as providing a remedy as long as the discrimination occurs within a general area covered by the ECHR, even if it relates to a right which is not specifically spelt out. In the *Belgian Linguistic* case (1968) 1 EHRR 252, the Court gave two examples of how this might operate. First, although Art. 2 of the First Protocol (see chapter 1 (1.6.3)) does not provide a right to the establishment of a particular type of school, nevertheless 'a State which had set up such an establishment could not, in laying down entrance requirements, take discriminatory measures within the meaning of Article 14' (para. 9). Second, Art. 6, which deals with the right to a fair trial, does not compel states to institute a system of appeal courts. If such a system is put in place, however, it would infringe Art. 14 to discriminate on illegitimate grounds in allowing access to the system (para. 9). The Council of Europe has put forward a Protocol to the ECHR (Protocol 12) which goes further than Art. 14, and does provide for a self-standing right to freedom from discrimination. This provides that as far as any legal right is concerned it should be:

> ...secured without discrimination on any ground such as sex, race, colour, language, religion, political or other opinion, national or social origin, association with a national minority, property, birth or other status.

Moreover, no public authority may discriminate on any of the above grounds in any of its activities. This goes much further than Art. 14 or any of the provisions of domestic law in the United Kingdom, and so far the United Kingdom has indicated that it does not intend to ratify this Protocol. For the time being, in terms of obligations under the ECHR or under the HRA 1998, Art. 14 is the only relevant provision as far as anyone wishing to take action in the United Kingdom is concerned.

The freedom as stated in Art. 14 is unqualified, unlike, for example, freedom of expression under Art. 10. There is here no list of grounds on which discrimination will be regarded as permissible. Nevertheless, the Court held in the *Belgian Linguistic* case that the Article did not imply a right to complete equality of treatment in every situation. Drawing on the common approach to be found in many democratic States, the Court stated that the principle of equality of treatment is violated if a distinction is drawn which has 'no objective and reasonable justification'. Such a justification will require, first, that the differential treatment has a legitimate aim, and, second, that there is a reasonable relationship of 'proportionality' between the means employed, and the aim being pursued (para. 10). Thus, in a subsequent case concerning United Kingdom immigration procedures (*Abdulaziz, Cabales, and Balkandali v United Kingdom* (1985) 7 EHRR 471), the Court held that a procedure for the admission of spouses of those with a right of abode in the United Kingdom, which operated more harshly in relation to husbands than wives, was pursuing a legitimate aim, that is the protection of the labour market. It also held, however, that it was not reasonable to pursue this aim by means of such a sexually discriminatory policy. In reaching this conclusion the Court pointed out that (para. 78):

> . . . the advancement of the equality of the sexes is . . . a major goal in the Member States of the Council of Europe. This means that very weighty reasons would have to be advanced before a difference of treatment on the ground of sex could be regarded as compatible with the Convention.

The avoidance of sex discrimination is thus given a particularly high status, and the margin of appreciation allowed to States to formulate laws appropriate to local circumstances is likely to be much narrower in relation to this than to other types of discrimination. It is surprising that freedom from racial discrimination has not been given a similar status. This is particularly so given that in *East African Asians v United Kingdom* (1981) 3 EHRR 76 the Commission held that racially discriminatory immigration procedures could amount to degrading treatment contrary to Art. 3 of the ECHR. The case was not referred to the Court, and by the time it was considered by the Committee of Ministers, all the applicants had been admitted to the United Kingdom, so that there was no final ruling on this issue.

Article 14, then, has the potential to provide the basis for an HRA 1998 challenge in areas not currently covered by English law, and to that extent to develop the law on discrimination.

It should be noted in addition that other Articles can be, and have been, used to deal with situations of discrimination. Discriminatory treatment in relation to private or family life may fall foul of Art. 8 (as in some of the cases on sexual orientation—see 12.3.3.2). As regards religion, the guarantee of freedom of religious practice in Art. 9, though subject to limitations 'prescribed by law' and 'necessary in a democratic society in the interests of public safety, for the protection of public order, health or morals, or for the protection of the rights and freedoms of others', means that discrimination on religious grounds will be open to challenge. There is also potential for using Art. 8 in a religious context as is shown by *Hoffmann v Austria* (1994) 17 EHRR 293 (refusal of parental rights on religious grounds, the mother being a Jehovah's Witness).

In various ways, therefore, the HRA 1998 has broadened the scope for arguments that a person's rights have been infringed by unlawful discrimination.

The structure of this chapter, however, is to consider discrimination primarily in the context of the existing statutory framework, with the possibilities of expansion of the law being noted at appropriate points. The European law context will be discussed first, and then the general principles on which English discrimination law is based. The chapter concludes with a consideration of the means of enforcing the law, by organizations and individuals.

12.2 **European Union law**

The starting point for the influence of European law on English discrimination law is what is now Art. 157 of the Treaty on the Functioning of the European Union (previously Art. 141 of the European Treaty), which sets out the general principle of 'equal pay for male and female workers for equal work or work of equal value'. The European Court of Justice (ECJ) has held that this applies to indirect discrimination as well as direct discrimination: *Bilka-Kaufhaus GmbH* v *Weber von Harz* (Case 170/84) [1986] 5 ECR 1607. The Article was supplemented by Directive 75/117, which specifically included within the concept of 'equal pay', the absence of discrimination on grounds of sex in respect of work of 'equal value'. Freedom from discrimination was extended beyond the area of 'pay' by the 'equal treatment' Directive (76/207), and this was subsequently been applied by other Directives to matters such as social security (79/7), pension schemes (86/378), and self-employment (86/613). All of these Directives, apart from 79/7 have now been replaced by Directive 2006/54 which has consolidated much of European law relating to equal treatment between the sexes. For further detail, see e.g. N. Foster, *Foster on EU Law*, 3rd edn (Oxford: Oxford University Press, 2011), ch. 11.

Article 157 (or its predecessors) has been held to have (in the terminology of EU law) both 'vertical' and 'horizontal' direct effect in the law of Member States: *Defrenne* v *SABENA (No. 2)* (Case 43/75) [1976] ECR 455. This means that it can be relied on in domestic courts for claims against the State (that is, vertical direct effect) and also in claims between individuals (horizontal direct effect) without any need to rely on municipal law. In other words, EU law itself provides the basis for a legal action in the courts of each Member State. In the United Kingdom, the Equality Act 2010 provides relevant rights and remedies, but it is still possible for an individual to base a claim on the Article itself, if it is thought that English law does not provide the protection required under EU law.

The directives, however, can have only *vertical* direct effect: *Marshall* v *Southampton & South West Hampshire Area Health Authority (Teaching)* (Case 152/84) [1986] 2 All ER 584. So an individual cannot bring an action against another individual, or a private organization, in the English courts, as a result of an alleged breach of one of the directives. Organs of the State can, however, be made the subject of an action. Thus, the British Gas Corporation, prior to privatization, was held to be an organ of the State, and bound by the Equal Treatment Directive: *Foster* v *British Gas* [1990] IRLR 353 (ECJ), [1991] IRLR 268 (HL). The scope for such actions is likely to be reduced by the United Kingdom's increasing use of privatization, and the reduction in the role of the State. The government, of course, may be liable under EU law if it fails to give effect to a directive and enact appropriate remedies in English law. See, e.g. *EC Commission* v *United Kingdom* (Case 61/81) [1982] ECR 2061, concerning the inadequacy of the Equal Pay Act 1970 (as originally drafted) in situations where no job evaluation scheme was in operation. This led to amendment of the legislation (Equal Pay Act (Amendment) Regulations 1983 (SI 1983/1794)).

It will be clear from the above that any consideration of the operation of the Equality Act 2010 must take account of the impact of EU law. Although it may be that in some situations the domestic legislation goes further in protecting against discrimination than is required by Art. 157, or the directives, these EU documents, as interpreted by the ECJ or (now) the CJEU, provide a minimum standard below which English law must not fall. They may, therefore, provide not only a valuable point of reference, but also a basis for action, for individuals who consider that their rights have been infringed in this context.

More recent developments have extended the scope of European law beyond the area of sex discrimination. Directive 2000/43/EC, adopted in June 2000, deals with racial discrimination. It imposes an obligation on States to ensure that 'there shall be no direct or indirect discrimination based on racial or ethnic origin' (Art. 1). This is to cover not only the area of employment, but also such areas as education, housing, and 'access to and supply of goods and services' (Art. 3). English law has been in advance of the rest of Europe in this area, with the Race Relations Act 1976 (RRA 1976) already providing the kind of general protection required by the Directive.

A broader provision is contained in Directive 2000/78/EC, adopted in November 2000. This focuses purely on the area of employment, but in that context outlaws discrimination, either direct or indirect, on the grounds of 'religion or belief, disability, age or sexual orientation'. This has meant that English law has had to change to ensure its compliance with this Directive. It indicates the broadening scope of anti-discrimination provisions in European law. The culmination of this is, perhaps, Art. 21 of the Charter of Fundamental Rights of the European Union (2000/C 364/01), which states that:

> ... [a]ny discrimination based on any ground such as sex, race, colour, ethnic or social origin, genetic features, language, religion or belief, political or any other opinion, membership of a national minority, property, birth, disability, age or sexual orientation shall be prohibited.

The Charter has now become part of European law with the ratification in November 2009 of the Lisbon Treaty. As far as the United Kingdom is concerned, however, the government has negotiated an 'opt out' in relation to the Charter, so that it will not be directly applicable in the United Kingdom.

As will be seen, the Charter contains the broadest anti-discrimination provision of any so far considered, both in relation to the types of discrimination covered, and the fact that it applies to all areas of activity, and not just employment.

There is, therefore, potential for further development in this area, under the influence of European law. We now turn, however, to look at the current position under English law.

12.3 English law

12.3.1 The problems of race and sex

Why did English law traditionally focus on race and sex as areas of unacceptable discrimination which require a legislative response? It is not simply that these are features of a person over which the individual has virtually no control. It is not unlawful to discriminate against people on the basis of the size of their feet or their height. It is the social context which is important. In terms of race, it was the immigration of the 1950s and 1960s which brought the problem of discrimination to the surface. Although it is discussed in terms of race, in practice it is colour of skin which has been the basis for most discrimination on racial grounds. Immigrants from the West Indies, from Kenya, and from India and Pakistan, were clearly identifiable from their skin colour, and therefore easy targets for those who felt that they were responsible for taking jobs from the indigenous workforce, or for bringing about increases in crime, or the lowering of social standards. By the mid-1960s the problem was sufficiently widespread to require a legislative response, which came initially in the Race Relations Acts of 1965 and 1968, and which is discussed further at 12.3.2. Although this legislation has contributed to considerable progress towards racial harmony, there are still significant problems as evidenced by the concern often expressed about 'institutional racism' in the police and other organizations (see, e.g. W. Macpherson, 'The Stephen Lawrence Inquiry: Report on an Inquiry by Sir William Macpherson of Cluny', Cm 4262, 1999, referred to at 3.4.2.1). More recently, concerns similar to those expressed about earlier immigrants have been raised in relation to the influx of people from eastern Europe, resulting from the expansion of the European Union. In this case, it is not colour, but nationality or ethnicity which provides the basis for discrimination.

As regards sex, it was again in the 1960s that the women's movement began to develop, first in the United States, and then here. Many would point to the growth in use of the contraceptive pill, and the consequent freedom that this gave to women to decide whether to become pregnant, and so to control their own lives, as one of the most significant developments. Whatever the reason, it came to be recognized that women were being disadvantaged in many areas of life and that there was little chance of any significant improvement without government intervention. The problem here was not that of an oppressed and easily targeted minority, as in the case of racial discrimination; rather the problem lay in long-established societal attitudes as to the proper role of women within an essentially patriarchal society. These attitudes were too firmly entrenched to expect them to change without some direction from the government and the legal system. It was in this context, and with the added influence of European law, discussed at 12.2, that the Equal Pay Act 1970 and the Sex Discrimination Act 1975 (SDA 1975) came to be passed (both now repealed and replaced by the Equality Act 2010).

As noted at 121.1, other areas where there have come to be perceived to be social problems have now been added to the list of grounds on which discrimination may be unlawful. Disability discrimination was the first to be added, then gender reassignment, followed most recently (in 2003) by sexual orientation, religion or belief, and age.

12.3.2 The legislative response

The English common law could provide no remedy against unjustifiable discrimination, except as an incident of a legal action based on some other grounds (as, e.g. in *Constantine* v *Imperial Hotels Ltd* [1944] KB 693: refusal of innkeeper to serve a *bona fide* customer). If racial or sexual discrimination was to be tackled, therefore, legislation was inevitable. The first, rather limited, attempt in relation to race was the Race Relations Act 1965. This dealt with discrimination in the provision of certain types of services to the public, for example in public houses, and also created an offence of 'incitement to racial hatred'. It was followed in 1968 by the wider Race Relations Act 1968, which extended the scope of the law into the areas of employment and housing. As far as sex discrimination was concerned, the first step was the Equal Pay Act 1970. This did not come into force, however, until 1975, at the same time as the more broadly based SDA 1975, which established the current legislative framework. This model was then followed in the RRA 1976.

The approach in the SDA 1975 and the RRA 1976, which has been followed in subsequent legislation, is to use not the criminal law but civil remedies. Unlawful discrimination becomes a kind of statutory tort, giving a right to damages and injunctions. The civil nature of the action means that the onus is put on the private citizen who has suffered from discrimination to bring an action. The unlawful act is thus categorized as a dispute between individuals, rather than a conflict between the wrongdoer and the State. Some support for the citizen was provided, however, by the creation of three statutory bodies, the Equal Opportunities Commission (EOC), the Commission for Racial Equality (CRE), and in the disability area, the Disability Rights Commission (DRC) (all three are now merged into the Equality and Human Rights Commission (EHRC)), with the responsibility of furthering the aims of the legislation, conducting investigations, and in some circumstances, providing support for the individual complainant. The success of the legislation in achieving its objectives nevertheless depends to a large extent on the willingness of the victim of unlawful discrimination to take advantage of its provisions.

The relevant law is now to be found in the Equality Act 2010, which has repealed and replaced the earlier legislation, and consolidated all anti-discrimination legislation. In the rest of this chapter all references are to this Act, unless otherwise stated. The Act defines four basic types of discrimination: direct discrimination (s. 13), indirect discrimination (s. 19), harassment (s. 26), and victimization (s. 27). In what follows, race and sex will be used as the primary examples of discrimination. The law in this area is complex. The approach here is to outline the broad principles which apply, and their relation to issues of human rights, rather than to give a detailed account of all the provisions.

The Act lists, in s. 4, the 'protected characteristics' in relation to which discrimination may be unlawful. These are:

- age;
- disability;
- gender reassignment;
- marriage and civil partnership;
- pregnancy and maternity;
- race;
- religion or belief;
- sex;
- sexual orientation.

With these characteristics in mind, the concepts of direct discrimination, indirect discrimination, harassment, and victimization are considered.

12.3.3 **Direct discrimination**

Direct discrimination occurs when a person is treated less favourably than someone else would have been in the same situation, and the reason for the difference is because of one of the protected characteristics (s. 13). To deny a person a job because of their race, or to refuse promotion on the grounds of sex, is clearly direct discrimination. The motive is irrelevant. It would not be a justification to prefer a female to a male employee because it was thought that male employees were more likely to drink alcohol at lunchtime, and so perform their work less competently. It would have to be shown that this fear applied to the particular individual concerned (compare *Hurley* v *Mustoe* [1981] ICR 490: where all married women with small children were thought to be unreliable). Even if the motive is protective towards the individual, as e.g. in *Greig* v *Community Industry* [1979] ICR 356, where a girl was refused a place on a training scheme because of fears of the way in which she would be treated by her all-male fellow trainees, the action is still discriminatory. It follows that it is not necessary to show an intention to discriminate on one of the unlawful grounds, if that is the effect of a decision. The test is a 'but for' one. That is, would the treatment have been different but for the person's race, sex, sexual orientation, or religion or belief? As Lord Goff stated in *James* v *Eastleigh Borough Council* [1990] 2 AC 751:

> ...cases of direct discrimination...can be considered by asking the simple question: would the complainant have received the same treatment from the defendant but for his or her sex?

As Lord Goff went on to point out, this simple test:

> ...avoids, in most cases at least, complicated questions relating to concepts such as intention, motive, reason, or purpose, and the danger of confusion resulting from the misuse of these elusive terms.

The case concerned the free admission to public swimming baths of people of retirement age. Since at the moment (though the position is in the process of changing) the statutory retirement age (i.e. the age at which a person qualifies for the State pension) is different for men and women, any distinction using this as a criterion is potentially discriminatory. The House of Lords, in using the 'but for' test, followed its earlier decision in *Equal Opportunities Commission* v *Birmingham City Council* [1989] 1 All ER 769, which was concerned with differing admissions procedures as between boys and girls seeking entry to grammar schools, applied because there were fewer places available to girls.

As regards racial discrimination, there are two further aspects of direct discrimination which need to be noted. First, s. 13(5) of the Equality Act 2010 states that segregation on racial grounds is to be regarded as less favourable treatment. Thus, even if facilities provided to two racial groups are exactly equal in quality, there will still be discrimination. Second, discrimination does not necessarily have to be on the basis of the *victim's* race, as long as it is based on racial grounds. Thus, in *Zarcynska* v *Levy* [1979] 1 All ER 814, a white barmaid was dismissed after she had refused to obey an instruction not to serve black customers. It was held that she had been discriminated against on racial grounds. The same view was taken in *Showboat Entertainment Centre* v *Owens* [1984] 1 WLR 384. These decisions were distinguished in *Redfearn* v *Serco* [2006] EWCA Civ 659, [2006] ICR 1367. The applicant was employed as a bus driver and escort for people with disabilities. He was elected as a local councillor, representing the British National Party, which is known to have hostile views towards immigration, and is alleged to be racist towards non-white citizens of the United Kingdom. Many of those whom the applicant provided services for were of Asian origin, as were a significant number of his co-workers. Following pressure from a trade union, the applicant was dismissed, and claimed that this was 'on racial grounds', relying on the decisions noted above. The Court of Appeal rejected his claim. An employer who was not pursuing a policy of race discrimination would not normally be liable for direct discrimination. Although 'racial considerations' may have entered into the decision, the applicant 'was no more dismissed "on racial grounds" than an employee who is dismissed for racially abusing his employer, a fellow employee or a valued customer' (para. 46). In coming to this decision, the Court of Appeal noted that this was *not* a claim for unfair dismissal (the applicant did not have sufficient service for such a claim), and that the discrimination was, in effect, on political grounds, which is not unlawful.

Previously the issues discussed in these cases did not arise in relation to sex discrimination, since the wording of s. 1(1)(a) of the SDA 1975 specifically referred to a person being less favourably treated 'on the ground of *her* sex'. Under the Equality Act 2010, however, the general definition of direct discrimination in s. 13(1) (noted at 12.3.3) means that the approach taken in relation to race cases will now apply more generally.

12.3.3.1 Race

'Race' as a ground for discrimination is further defined in s. 9, which states that it includes: 'colour, nationality or ethnic or national origins'. It is made clear by s. 9(4) that a racial group can itself be made up of other racial groups. It follows that a person can be a member of several racial groups at the same time. A Sikh, for example, will be in at least three racial groups on the basis of colour of skin, nationality (e.g. British or Indian), and ethnic origins (see *Mandla* v *Dowell Lee* [1983] 2 AC 548, discussed in full at 12.3.4.2).

The problem of deciding what is covered by the concept of 'ethnic origins' has been considered in a number of cases. The starting point is *Mandla* v *Dowell Lee*, where the House of Lords had to decide whether Sikhs constituted a racial group. Lord Fraser set out what he considered to be seven relevant criteria for identifying a group on the basis of ethnic origins. The first two he considered to be essential, namely:

1. a long shared history, of which the group is conscious as distinguishing it from other groups, and the memory of which it keeps alive; and

2. a cultural tradition of its own, including family and social customs and manners, often but not necessarily associated with religious observance.

The other five criteria were, in his view, relevant, but not essential. They were:

3. either a common geographical origin, or descent from a small number of common ancestors;

4. a common language, not necessarily peculiar to the group;

5. a common literature peculiar to the group;

6. a common religion different from that of neighbouring groups or from the general community surrounding it; and

7. being a minority or being an oppressed or dominant group within a larger community.

Lord Templeman, while agreeing with Lord Fraser's conclusion that Sikhs did constitute a racial group, put the emphasis simply on the fact that a racial group must have some of the characteristics of a race, namely 'group descent, a group of geographical origin and a group history'.

As well as bringing Sikhs within the scope of a racial group defined by ethnic origins, the case confirmed that Jews similarly constitute a racial group. In *Commission for Racial Equality* v *Dutton* [1989] 1 All ER 306, the Court of Appeal applied the same approach discussing the status of 'gypsies'. In the narrow sense of this word, meaning those originally descended from a people who originated in the Punjab and migrated to Europe via Persia (Iran) in medieval times, the court found that in the light of their shared customs, distinctive dress and furnishings, particular dialect, and repertoire of folktales and music passed on from one generation to another, they did constitute a racial group. To the extent, however, that the word 'gypsies' is applied to all travelling people who move around the country in caravans, this wider group did not constitute a racial group.

On the other hand, the Employment Appeal Tribunal (EAT) has refused to recognize Rastafarians as a racial group, primarily because it was felt that a group that has existed for only 60 years cannot be said to have a 'long shared history': *Crown Suppliers (PSA)* v *Dawkins* [1991] IRLR 327 (approved by the Court of Appeal [1993] IRLR 284).

Muslims have also been denied the status of a racial group. This emphasizes the fact that the RRA 1976 did not cover discrimination on religious grounds. A religious movement, such as Sikhism, would not be protected under the prohibition of racial discrimination unless its adherents also satisfy the other criteria laid down in *Mandla*. Islam is too broadly based as a worldwide religion for it to be able to claim to do so, any more than could Christianity. Thus, the protection given to Jews does not relate primarily to the religion of Judaism, but to the shared cultural traditions of those of Jewish descent. The anomalies consequent on these distinctions have now been addressed by the inclusion of religion and belief in the 'protected characteristics' within the Equality Act 2010.

12.3.3.2 Marital status and sexual orientation

For the most part 'sex' in the SDA 1975 was taken to mean simply whether a person is male or female. The Act was not regarded as protecting against prejudice based on sexual orientation or sexual practices. The homosexual, the transvestite, and the transsexual received no protection under this legislation. This limitation was held not to be inconsistent with European Community law in *Grant* v *South West Trains Ltd* [1998] All ER (EC) 193. The issue concerned whether the partner of a lesbian employee was entitled to the same travel concessions as would have been available under the employee's contract of employment to a partner of the opposite sex. Treating a male homosexual differently from a female homosexual may, however, amount to unlawful discrimination. This was not the case in *Grant*, where all homosexual relationships were treated the same. But in *Smith* v *Gardner Merchant* [1998] 3 All ER 852 the Court of Appeal held that homophobic harassment against a male employee could constitute sex discrimination if it could be shown that a homosexual female employee would not have been treated in the same way.

The ECHR has on several occasions found that actions based on sexual orientation infringe Convention rights (though the cases have been dealt with primarily on the basis of interference with private life under Art. 8, rather than Art. 14). Examples include *Dudgeon* v *United Kingdom* (1981) 4 EHRR 149 (criminalization of homosexual activity), *Smith and Grady* v *United Kingdom* (1999) 29 EHRR 493, and *Lustig-Prean and Beckett* v *United Kingdom* (1999) 29 EHRR 548 (both the latter cases dealing with the exclusion of homosexuals from the armed forces). The House of Lords (*Advocate-General for Scotland* v *Macdonald* [2003] UKHL 34, [2004] 1 All ER 339) firmly rejected any argument for the expansion of the SDA 1975 to cover sexual orientation. 'Sex' in the SDA 1975 meant 'gender' and not 'sexual orientation'. The situation has been overtaken by legislation since, under the Equality Act 2010, sexual orientation (defined in s. 12) is a protected characteristic.

Two recent decisions illustrate direct discrimination on the grounds of sexual orientation—*Hall* v *Bull* [2012] EWCA Civ 83 and *Black* v *Wilkinson* [2013] EWCA Civ 820. Both cases involved the refusal to let a room to a male homosexual couple on the grounds of religious belief. In *Hall* v *Bull*, the defendants were Christian hoteliers who did not let rooms to unmarried couples. In *Black* v *Wilkinson* the defendants ran a bed and breakfast in their own home. Again they refused to let rooms to homosexual couples because of their Christian beliefs. In both cases the Court of Appeal held that there was unlawful discrimination. There was a conflict between two rights recognized in the Convention, i.e. the right to be discriminated against in terms of one's private life (Art. 8, supported by Art. 14) and the right to manifestation of religious belief under Art. 9. In both cases the court held that the restriction on the defendants' Art. 9 rights was justifiable and proportionate. The decision in Hall v Bull has been confirmed by the Supreme Court: [2013] UKSC 73.

12.3.4 **Indirect discrimination**

Some of the most insidious types of discrimination, and therefore the most difficult to tackle, arise not through the direct imposition of discriminatory conditions, such as 'only whites need apply', but through the imposition of requirements that appear on their face to be neutral, but which have the effect of prejudicing members of a particular racial group or sex. For example, a club which has only white members might require all new members to be proposed by an existing member, which may well make it more difficult for non-whites to join; or an employer might require all applicants to have attended school in this country, or to have been baptized into the Church of England. Again, these conditions will have an indirectly discriminatory effect.

Section 19 defines indirect discrimination in the following way. It states that a person (A) 'discriminates against another person (B) when A applies to B a provision, criterion or practice which is discriminatory in relation to a relevant protected characteristic of B's'. A provision, criterion or practice is discriminatory if (s. 19(2)):

(a) A applies, or would apply, it to persons with whom B does not share the characteristic,

(b) it puts, or would put, persons with whom B shares the characteristic at a particular disadvantage when compared with persons with whom B does not share it,

(c) it puts, or would put, B at that disadvantage, and

(d) A cannot show it to be a proportionate means of achieving a legitimate aim.

The objective is to deal with the situation where a person's actions place a person in one of the protected categories at a disproportionate disadvantage as opposed to those not in the protected category. There are four basic elements:

1. the application of a 'hurdle' in the form of, for example, the imposition of a condition or the operation of a practice;

2. the disproportionate effect of the hurdle;

3. the detriment or disadvantage to the victim; and

4. the lack of justification for the action.

These will be considered in turn. Most of the case law inevitably relates to the definitions as they originally appeared in the RRA 1976 and the SDA 1975.

12.3.4.1 The application of the 'hurdle'

The original definition in the SDA 1975 and RRA 1976 referred to a 'requirement or condition', which was taken to mean that what is imposed must be something which *has* to be complied with: *Perera* v *Civil Service Commission (No. 2)* [1983] ICR 428. A statement that applicants without children are 'preferred', which would probably disproportionately affect married people, would not fall within the definition. Similarly, factors which are simply to be taken into account (as in *Perera*: command of English and experience in the United Kingdom), but are not in themselves conclusive, are not requirements or conditions. This approach considerably limited the scope of the concept of indirect discrimination, and later courts followed the Court of Appeal's ruling in *Perera* with some reluctance (see, e.g. *Meer* v *London Borough of Tower Hamlets* [1988] IRLR 399). The point was, however, again confirmed by the EAT in *Bhudi* v *IMI Refiners Ltd* [1994] IRLR 204. The new definition, as set out in the Equality Act 2010 reduces these problems. The reference to a 'provision, criterion or practice' means that any factors that formed part of the decision can be looked at, even if they only add weight to it, rather than being an essential element. For example, 'desirable' elements in a specification attached to a job advertisement could be taken into account, as well as those that are indicated as 'essential'.

12.3.4.2 The disproportionate effect of the 'hurdle'

Under the original definition the number of people falling into the victim's group who can comply with the requirement or condition had to be 'considerably smaller' than those not of that group who can do so. This proved difficult to interpret and has now been abandoned. The current definition does not use the same terminology, but refers simply to the victim being 'at a particular disadvantage' compared to others. This does not focus on numbers as being the central issue, but it may well be that in interpreting what constitutes a 'particular' disadvantage a very similar approach will have to be adopted.

The next issue is to decide on the groups between which the comparison is to be made. This is relatively easy in relation to sex and marital status, in that the other group will be people of the opposite sex, or who are unmarried. Even here, however, the provision of s. 23 must be noted. This states that where a comparison of cases is made, 'there must be no material difference between the circumstances relating to each case'. Thus, if the complainant is a university lecturer who is claiming that a requirement of 10 years' continuous service before promotion to senior lecturer is indirectly discriminatory against women, the comparison is to take 'university lecturers' as the overall 'pool' and then see whether the 10 years' service requirement is particularly disadvantageous to women within that pool. In *Shamoon* v *Chief Constable of the RUC* [2003] UKHL 11, [2003] 2 All ER 26 the House of Lords stressed the need, when selecting comparators (real or hypothetical), to ensure that the requirement of no material difference in the circumstances was met. In this case a female Chief Inspector had been removed from appraisal duties following complaints from some of the constables concerned. She used two male Chief Inspectors as her comparators, and the tribunal held in her favour. The House of Lords, however, confirming the view of the Court of Appeal, overturned the tribunal's decision, because it had failed to take account of the fact that there was no evidence that a male Chief Inspector against whom complaints had been made would not have been treated in the same way as the applicant.

In relation to discrimination on the grounds of race, comparison between groups is further complicated in this context by the fact that every person belongs to at least two racial groupings (colour and nationality) and, as we have seen, may well belong to more. It seems that it is up to the complainant to decide which racial group is the significant one in relation to a claim. The comparison is then with similar people not of that racial group. The court or tribunal will decide exactly what are the appropriate 'groups' for comparison, and the complainant may well be expected to provide statistics to back up the claim of particular disadvantage on the basis of these 'groups'. In *Perera* v *Civil Service Commission (No. 2)* [1983] ICR 428, for example, the relevant overall pool was those who had passed the English bar or solicitors' examinations. Within that pool, the comparison was to be made between people of Sri Lankan nationality, as compared with people not of that nationality. If the court takes an unexpected view as to the relevant groups, this may cause difficulties to the complainant in providing the evidence necessary.

In *Coker* v *Lord Chancellor* [2001] EWCA Civ 1756, [2002] IRLR 80 the Court of Appeal considered the application of indirect discrimination where the condition or requirement being applied excludes almost all of the pool. The case concerned the appointment by the Lord Chancellor of a 'Special Adviser'. The condition applied was that the candidate must be personally known to the Lord Chancellor. In fact the Lord Chancellor did not advertise the post, and only gave serious consideration to one person, a white man, who was appointed. Two women objected to the procedure adopted, and brought actions alleging indirect discrimination on the grounds of sex and race. The Employment Tribunal considered that the procedure was indirectly discriminatory. The Court of Appeal disagreed, however. The pool in this case was those who met certain (fairly stiff) qualifications. The tribunal had found that the Lord Chancellor's condition that the person appointed be personally known to him would have screened out more women or those from ethnic minorities than white men. The Court of Appeal held, however, that this reasoning was fundamentally flawed (para. 38):

> The test of indirect discrimination focuses on the effect that the requirement objected to has on the pool of potential candidates. It can only have a discriminatory effect…if a significant proportion of the pool are able to satisfy the requirement. Only in that situation will it be possible for the requirement to have a disproportionate effect on the men and the women, or the racial groups, which form the pool. Where the requirement excludes almost the entirety of the pool it cannot constitute indirect discrimination

Since that was the effect of the Lord Chancellor's condition in this case (only one person from within the pool met the requirement of personal acquaintanceship) then there was no indirect discrimination. The same would be true of appointments made from within a small circle of family or friends. Such appointing methods, while they might be objectionable on equal opportunities grounds, are unlikely to be unlawful on the basis of sex or race discrimination.

The final issue to consider in relation to proportionality is the meaning of the phrase 'can comply'. This only applies to the original definition. It was considered by the House of Lords in *Mandla* v *Dowell Lee*, where the alleged indirect discrimination arose out of the refusal to admit a Sikh boy to a school, on the grounds that since his religious obligations involved the wearing of a turban, he would not be able to comply with the school uniform requirements which involved the wearing of a cap. It was clear that a Sikh could *physically* have complied with the uniform requirements by removing his turban and having his hair cut. The House of Lords, however, interpreted the phrase 'can comply' in s. 1(1)(b) of the RRA 1976 as meaning 'can in practice' or 'can consistently with the customs and cultural traditions of the racial group'. The proportion of Sikhs who could, in that sense, comply with the uniform requirement, was clearly considerably smaller than the proportion of non-Sikhs, and this element of the test of indirect discrimination was therefore made out.

12.3.4.3 **The requirement of detriment or disadvantage**

The complainant must be able to show detriment or disadvantage resulting from the actions of the alleged discrimination. Under the original definition the wording appeared to require that detriment was solely attributable to the imposition of the requirement or condition. If, for example, there was an unjustifiable language provision attached to a job, but the reason that the complainant was rejected was failure to meet some other, justifiable condition, then it would seem that there had been no detriment. The complainant would be unable to bring an action for indirect discrimination, but the EHRC might be able to investigate the possibility that the employer is engaging in a discriminatory practice (see 12.5.2.2). The revised wording in the new definition seems to be intended to avoid this. As long as the person is at a disadvantage, the fact that there might be other reasons for their failure to be appointed to a job, for example, would not be relevant. Whether the wording will in fact have this effect will depend on the view taken by the courts. It is certainly arguable that a causal link is still needed.

'Detriment' has been interpreted broadly under both the SDA 1975 (*Ministry of Defence* v *Jeremiah* [1980] ICR 13, p. 26) and the RRA 1976 (*BL Cars Ltd* v *Brown* [1983] ICR 143, p. 146) as meaning simply 'put under a disadvantage'. It is not necessary for any material loss to have been suffered. It seems, therefore, that the use of 'disadvantage' rather than 'detriment' in the new definition will not be likely to have any significant effect in practice.

12.3.4.4 Lack of independent justification

In relation to all the tests of indirect discrimination, the alleged discriminator has the possibility of justifying his or her actions. In the original test this was expressed in terms of the action being 'justifiable' irrespective of the sex, etc., of the person to whom it is applied. In the new definition the test is whether the action can be shown to be 'a proportionate means of achieving a legitimate aim'. This has clear echoes of the approach taken to assessing compliance with ECHR rights (see chapter 2 (2.4.1)). The burden of proof shifts, so that whereas in relation to the alleged discriminatory factor and the particular disadvantage issue, it lies on the complainant, it is up to the alleged discriminator to try to show that there was a justification for what was done irrespective of sex or race. For example, a require-ment that applicants for a university place to study law have a pass in English Language at GCSE grade C, or its equivalent, almost certainly disproportionately disadvantages people not of British nationality. It is nevertheless justifiable, in that people studying the course, for which the teaching, and probably all the reading material, will be in English, will need a certain level of proficiency in order to be able to cope. It would also be likely to be regarded as a proportionate means of achieving a legitimate aim. The same requirement, however, applied to people applying for work in a non-skilled job which does not require contact with the general public, would almost certainly be unjustifiable.

12.3.5 Harassment

This is dealt with by s. 26 of the Equality Act 2010. It provides that:

> (1) A person (A) harasses another (B) if—
>
>   (a) A engages in unwanted conduct related to a relevant protected characteris-tic, and
>
>   (b) the conduct has the purpose or effect of—
>
>   (i) violating B's dignity, or
>
>   (ii) creating an intimidating, hostile, degrading, humiliating or offensive envir-onment for B.

This category of discrimination is different from those considered so far, in that it does not require the complainant to show that they have been treated differ-ently, compared to others not sharing the relevant characteristic. The man-ager who teases an employee in relation to the fact that she is a lesbian may be guilty of harassment, even if he also teases all his other employees in relation to non-protected characteristics.

The protected characteristics for harassment do not include marriage, civil partnership, pregnancy, or maternity.

Harassment can also be committed by unwanted conduct of a sexual nature. There are two ways in which this can be harassment. First, if the behaviour has the purpose or effect set out in s. 26(1)(b) (above); second, if such behaviour (whether committed by the harasser or another) results in a person being treated less favourably because he or she has either submitted to or rejected the unwanted conduct.

In all cases, in deciding whether the requirements of s. 26(1)(b) have been met each of the following must be taken into account:

(a) the perception of B;

(b) the other circumstances of the case;

(c) whether it is reasonable for the conduct to have that effect.

12.3.6 **Victimization**

In relation to all types of discrimination there is always going to be a fear on the part of victims that if they make trouble by complaining, or taking legal action, they will simply end up suffering worse discrimination. Section 27 of the Equality Act 2010 goes some way to meeting this fear by treating 'victimization' itself as a form of discrimination. It will amount to such where a person is treated less favourably because that person has done one of four things, or is believed to have done or be going to do one of them. The four things are:

(a) bringing proceedings against the discriminator under the relevant Act; or

(b) giving evidence or information in connection with proceedings brought by any person under the relevant Act; or

(c) otherwise doing anything under or by reference to the relevant Act in relation to the discriminator or any other person; or

(d) alleging that the discriminator or any other person has committed an act which (whether the allegation so states or not) would amount to a contravention of the relevant Act.

The victimization provisions do not seem to have been greatly used, though perhaps this is because their existence operates as a deterrent to such behaviour. Two cases, however, illustrate a difficulty with trying to use the provisions. In *Cornelius v University College of Swansea* [1987] IRLR 147, the complainant alleged victimization when she was refused a job transfer on the grounds that this might prejudge proceedings based on sexual harassment which she was bringing. In *Aziz v Trinity Street Taxis Ltd* [1988] IRLR 204 a taxi driver was expelled from a company after making secret tape-recordings of conversations with other employees in connection with a prospective action for racial discrimination. In both cases the Court of Appeal found that there had been 'less favourable' treatment, but that it was not related to an act protected by the statutes. In *Cornelius* the same refusal of transfer would have occurred whatever the nature of the legal proceedings; it was irrelevant for this purpose that they were proceedings under the SDA 1975. Similarly, in *Aziz*, it was held that it was the breach of trust involved in the secret recordings which led to the expulsion, and that the same action would have been taken whatever the purpose of the recordings. Once again, the fact that they were made with a view to an action under the RRA 1976 was irrelevant. The same conclusion was reached in *Walters* v *Commissioner of Police for the Metropolis* [1995] IRLR 531, where the applicant had complained about an off-duty sexual assault by a fellow constable. It was held that, since the assault did not occur in the course of the assaulting constable's employment, it did not constitute a breach of the SDA 1975. The claim for victimization, therefore, also failed.

These decisions opened a large loophole in the victimization provisions. Provided that the alleged victimizer can convincingly argue that the same action would be taken against any person behaving in a similar way, and that the fact that their behaviour happens to be concerned with allegations of discrimination is irrelevant, it seems that the victimization will fall outside the scope of the Act.

This loophole appeared, however, to have been closed to some extent by two subsequent decisions—*Nagarajan* v *London Regional Transport* (also reported as *Swiggs* v *Nagarajan*) [1999] 4 All ER 65, and *TNT Express Worldwide (UK) Ltd* v *Brown* [2001] ICR 182. In *Nagarajan* it was held that there was no need for victimization to be the result of conscious motivation. This was not needed for direct discrimination under s. 1(1)(a) of the SDA 1975 or the RRA 1976, and a parallel interpretation should be given to victimization. Any suggestion to the contrary in *Aziz* v *Trinity Street Taxis Ltd* could not stand. The employment tribunal dealing with a victimization case should simply ask 'Did the defendant treat the employee less favourably because of his knowledge of a protected act?' Similarly, the Court of Appeal in *TNT* v *Brown* held that, in considering whether the claim of victimization was made out, it was not a sufficient defence for there to have been other reasons which might have justified the action taken. If the real reason was the fact that the claimant had previously brought a claim of discrimination, then victimization would be made out. So the tribunal is entitled to look behind the stated reasons and to decide what were the real reasons, and does not need the claimant to prove that the employer was deliberately acting in response to an earlier claim of discrimination.

The law as to which approach to adopt was not, however, clarified by the House of Lords' decision in *Khan* v *Chief Constable of West Yorkshire* [2001] UKHL 48, [2001] 4 All ER 834. This concerned a police officer who was refused a reference because he had a race discrimination case pending against his chief constable. Lord Nicholls, with whom the rest of the House agreed, emphasized that the test was not one of legal causation, but of subjective motivation, whether conscious or unconscious. In applying this to the case, however, he went back to *Cornelius* v *University College of Swansea* which he clearly regarded as being correctly decided. On that basis there was no victimization in the present case, because any police officer who had a legal action outstanding against the chief constable, whatever the reason, would have been treated the same way. The employer had acted honestly and reasonably in refusing the reference. None of the other decisions were specifically approved or disapproved, though inevitably *Nagarajan* had to be accepted, since it was a House of Lords decision, and indeed one in which Lord Nicholls was also involved.

The approach taken in *Khan* (though not the result) was disapproved by the House of Lords in *St Helens MBC* v *Derbyshire* [2007] UKHL 16, [2007] 3 All ER 81. The House in this case held that the focus should be on whether the actions of the employer caused 'detriment' to the other party, and might be reasonably expected to cause such detriment. In other words, the situation should be looked at from the point of view of the 'victim' rather than the employer, and the victim's reasonable reaction to what the employer did.

Both the *Khan* and *Derbyshire* approaches suggest that it will depend very much on the facts of each case. As Lord Nicholls comments in *Khan* (para. 29, p. 841) 'the reason why a person acted as he did is a question of fact'. Similarly in *Derbyshire* (para. 27) Lord Hope noted that 'one can do no more than resort to generalities on such a fact-sensitive issue'. Such an approach makes it difficult, however, for those who are the defendants in discrimination actions to know what they can or cannot do in relation to an applicant where there is a continuing relationship between them.

12.4 Positive discrimination

Both the RRA 1976 and the SDA 1975 attacked discrimination regardless of the motive of the discriminator, or the target for the discrimination. Thus the legislation could be, and was, used by white against black, and by men against women. The need for legislation of this kind, noted at 12.1.2, stems from a background of prejudice and inequality in relation to a particular section of the community. The legislation itself, however, is almost exclusively based on the premise of equal treatment as of now, without paying attention to past inequalities. Some may see this as a serious defect (see, for example, the comments of Lord Scarman in his 'Report on the Brixton Disorders, 10–12 April 1981', Cmnd 8427, 1981, para. 6.32). There may well be scope for what is sometimes called 'positive discrimination', or 'affirmative action', to favour a particular group or groups, and provide much more direct help, much more quickly, than can be achieved by a strict policy of equal treatment. The danger, however, is that such an approach may be counterproductive in terms of changing attitudes. The white worker who sees a job going to a person from an ethnic minority under an affirmative action programme is unlikely to become less prejudiced as a result. Moreover, the members of the favoured group may themselves find such programmes patronizing. Fears of this kind led to the original legislation containing only very limited provision for positive discrimination, as was recognized by the Court of Appeal in *Lambeth Borough Council* v *Commission for Racial Equality* [1990] IRLR 231. The council had advertised two jobs within the housing benefits department as open to Afro-Caribbean or Asian applicants only. The Court of Appeal said that it was not possible to justify this action by categorizing it as positive discrimination. As Balcombe LJ commented (p. 234):

> I am wholly unpersuaded that one of the two main purposes of the Act is to promote positive action to benefit racial groups...It is true that ss. 35, 37 and 38 do allow for limited acts of positive discrimination which would otherwise be unlawful, but that does not constrain us to give s. 5(2)(d) a meaning which its words do not naturally bear.

Both the RRA 1976 and the SDA 1975 contained limited provision for positive discrimination in specific situations. More general provisions allowing for 'positive action' are now to be found in ss 158 and 159 of the Equality Act 2010.

12.4.1 Positive action: general

Section 1 allows a person to take what would otherwise be discriminatory action if it is a proportionate means of redressing one of three situations which the person reasonably thinks exists. The situations are:

(a) persons who share a protected characteristic suffer a disadvantage connected to the characteristic,

(b) persons who share a protected characteristic have needs that are different from the needs of persons who do not share it, or

(c) participation in an activity by persons who share a protected characteristic is disproportionately low.

Situation (a) might arise where it was perceived that a high proportion of those of a particular ethnic group in an area had poor English skills, and so were disadvantaged in applying for jobs. The provision of English tuition open only to members of that ethnic group could constitute legitimate positive action. Situation (b) could arise if a particular religious group forbade men and women from swimming together. The provision of single-sex swimming sessions for members of the religious group could be legitimate positive action. Situation (c) could arise if an employer were to find that men were underrepresented in his workforce. The running of a 'men-only' open day designed to attract more applicants from males could be permissible under s. 158, as could the provision of pre-employment training aimed at men.

12.4.2 Recruitment and promotion

Section 159 relates to recruitment and promotion. Like s. 158 it is based on reasonable belief—in this case the person must reasonably think that:

(a) persons who share a protected characteristic suffer a disadvantage connected to the characteristic, or

(b) participation in an activity by persons who share a protected characteristic is disproportionately low.

The person may then, with the aim of rectifying either of these problems, select between two equally qualified candidates the one with the relevant characteristic, in preference to the one without. The selection might be in relation to either initial recruitment or subsequent promotion. It must not, however, be part of a general policy of treating people with the characteristic more favourably, and it must be a proportionate means of remedying a perceived problem.

12.5 Enforcement and remedies

This is dealt with in Chapter 3 of the Equality Act 2010.

12.5.1 **Right of individual action**

The primary means of enforcement of the rights to equal treatment contained in the legislation is through individual legal action taken by the victim of discrimination.

Claims in relation to employment must be brought before an employment tribunal. Non-employment claims are treated as a statutory tort, and will generally be dealt with in the county court. The legal aid position for discrimination cases is the same as for most other types of action, that is, that it may be available in relation to county court proceedings, but not those before an employment tribunal.

In order to assist a potential claimant, the legislation provides for a form of 'questionnaire' to be produced by the Secretary of State, by which the claimant can seek answers from the respondent 'on his reasons for doing any relevant act, or on any other matter which is or may be relevant' (s. 138 of the Equality Act 2010). Any answers provided will generally be admissible in evidence, and a failure to answer may lead to the court or tribunal drawing an inference, including an inference that the respondent has committed an unlawful act.

A full range of remedies is available in the employment tribunal or the county court, corresponding to those that would be available in any other action brought in those fora. Most claimants will be seeking damages. It is specifically provided that damages may be awarded for injury to feelings (s. 119(4) of the Equality Act 2010). In *Bradford City Metropolitan Council* v *Arora* [1991] 2 WLR 1377, the Court of Appeal accepted that exemplary damages might be available in discrimination cases. In *AB* v *South West Water Services Ltd* [1993] 1 All ER 609, however, a different Court of Appeal ruled that the House of Lords' decision in *Cassell* v *Broome* [1972] AC 1027 had restricted the availability of exemplary damages to those torts which were in existence in 1964, at the time of the earlier House of Lords' decision in *Rookes* v *Barnard* [1964] AC 1129. In *Kuddus* v *Chief Constable of Leicestershire* [2001] UKHL 29, [2001] 3 All ER 193, the House of Lords revisited this issue in a case concerned with the tort of misfeasance in a public office. A claim for exemplary damages had been struck out on the basis of the *AB* v *South West Water Services Ltd* ruling. The House of Lords held, however, that *AB* v *South West Water Services Ltd* was wrongly decided and should be overruled. There was no limit on the availability of exemplary damages other than that the case must fall within one of the two categories set out in *Rookes* v *Barnard*—that is, oppressive, arbitrary, or unconstitutional action by servants of the government, or cases where the defendant's conduct has been calculated by him to make a profit which may well exceed any compensation payable. In *Kuddus* the claim potentially fell into the first category, and so should not have been struck out. It seems, therefore, that in appropriate cases exemplary damages will be available for breaches of the Equality Act 2010.

Where the claim is for indirect discrimination, and the court or tribunal is satisfied that the requirement or condition was not applied with the intention of treating the claimant unfavourably, damages may be awarded, but only after other means of redress have been considered (ss 119(5), (6) and 124(4) and (5)).

12.5.2 **Role of the Equality and Human Rights Commission**

In 2007 the EHRC, created by the EA 2006, took over the roles of the Commission for Racial Equality, the Equal Opportunities Commission, and the Disability Rights

Commission. The Commission is an independent statutory body. Its members are appointed by the Secretary of State, but they are not part of the Civil Service. The duties of the Commission (s. 8 of the EA 2006) are to:

(a) promote understanding of the importance of equality and diversity;

(b) encourage good practice in relation to equality and diversity;

(c) promote equality of opportunity;

(d) promote awareness and understanding of rights under the Equality Act 2010;

(e) enforce the Equality Act 2010;

(f) work towards the elimination of unlawful discrimination; and

(g) work towards the elimination of unlawful harassment.

These duties are similar to those placed on the Commissions which the EHRC replaced. As will be seen, the activities of the Commission are wide-ranging. The concentration here will be on their powers in relation to enforcement in relation to the Equality Act 2010.

The available powers take the form of assisting individual claimants; taking action against certain breaches of the legislation where the Commission has exclusive rights to act; and carrying out formal investigations. There is case law on the exercise of the equivalent of these powers as operated by the CRE and EOC, and it is assumed that this will continue to be relevant in relation to the EHRC.

12.5.2.1 Assisting individual claimants

The power of the Commission to assist individual claimants is specifically recognized in s. 28. The previous legislation contained some limitations on the circumstances when assistance could be provided. The EA 2006 gives a very broad power to assist wherever the proceedings relate to the Equality Act 2010 and the individual claims to be a victim of behaviour contrary to that Act. There is, however, no obligation on the Commission to assist.

The type of help which can be given is set out in s. 28(4). It may include giving advice, negotiating a settlement, arranging legal advice or representation, or 'any other form of assistance'. The Commission thus has a broad discretion as to what assistance should be given. It may recover its expenses from any costs awarded to the claimant in an action, or under a settlement (s. 29 of the EA 2006).

The provision of legal assistance by the CRE and EOC had been falling in recent years. In 2004, the CRE received 556 applications for assistance. In 2002 the figure was 1,300 and in 2003, 903. Representation was granted in just four cases (Commission for Racial Equality, 'Annual Report for 2004'). This reflected a new policy of targeting resources, and was a massive reduction of support of this kind. In 2002, for example, 209 cases were granted representation. The EOC's number of cases was generally much smaller than for the CRE. In 2000, for example, 232 applications were received, with legal assistance being given in 50 (Equal Opportunities Commission, 'Annual Report for 2000/2001'). Statistics are not available for later years.

The EHRC has not produced the equivalent figures about its activities. Its website notes that:

> ...the Commission is well equipped to take legal action on behalf of individuals, especially where there are strategic opportunities to push the boundaries of the law. Where there are chances to create legal precedents or to clarify and improve the law, the Commission will seek to do so.

This suggests that where opportunities arise to take 'test cases' the Commission will be prepared to do so. In its report issued in April 2010 it indicated that between its inception in 2007 and March 2010 the Commission had taken formal action in 80 cases, of which by far the largest number (59) involved intervention in legal proceedings (see 'Legal Enforcement Update', available at http://www.equality-humanrights.com/legal-and-policy/enforcement/ (at the time of writing no more recent figures were available)). In June 2012 the figure for the total number of interventions since 2008 in proceedings in the United Kingdom (as opposed to at Strasbourg) was 70 (see 'Summary of the Commission's domestic interventions', available at http://www.equalityhumanrights.com/legal-and-policy/enforcement/ under the link 'a list of the cases the Commission has intervened in').

12.5.2.2 **Formal inquiries and investigations**

The powers of the Commission to conduct inquiries and investigations are contained in ss 16 and 20 of, and Sch. 2 to, the EA 2006. They were a very important part of the previous Commissions' powers, enabling them to investigate people, organizations, or general areas of activity, in the pursuit of their overall duties under the legislation. The decision in *Home Office* v *Commission for Racial Equality* [1982] QB 385 indicated that the general duties of the Commissions to promote equality of opportunity, or, in the CRE's case, good relations between racial groups, might entitle a Commission to investigate an activity which would not involve unlawful discrimination under the Act. This type of investigation is now called an 'inquiry' (s. 16). Where the EHRC believes that an individual may have committed an unlawful act under the equality enactments then it will hold an 'investigation' under s. 20.

The powers to inquire or investigate are strong in that they can involve the Commission in *requiring* information or documentary evidence to be given, with the possibility of court orders being used to back this up: Sch. 2 to the EA 2006. It is this aspect of the previous Commissions' powers which led the House of Lords in *R* v *Commission for Racial Equality, ex p London Borough of Hillingdon* [1982] AC 779, and *Re Prestige Group plc, Commission for Racial Equality* v *Prestige Group plc* [1984] 1 WLR 335 to distinguish between general investigations, and 'named-person' investigations. Under the new Act, the distinction is between an 'inquiry' (s. 16) and an 'investigation' (s. 20).

An inquiry might look at a broad area of activity, rather than what is being done by a particular organization or individual. Patterns of ethnic employment in the hosiery industry in Leicester might be investigated, for example. There is no need for there to be any suspicion or belief that unlawful discrimination is taking place.

The Commission must draw up terms of reference for an inquiry, and publish these in a way that is likely to come to the attention of those interested. Any person or organization named in the terms of reference should be also be given notice (Sch. 2, para. 3 to the EA 2006).

It was more common for the previous Commissions to carry out 'named-person' investigations, now simply called 'investigations', which are used when unlawful activity is suspected. As Lord Diplock pointed out in the *Prestige* case (p. 345), to be made the subject of such an investigation is not a trivial matter. An announcement of such an investigation by the CRE, for example, was:

> ...likely to be understood by many of those to whose attention it may come as pointing the finger of suspicion of racial bias at the persons who are named in it, and by doing so, it may well damage or put at risk harmonious race relations that presently exist in the employer's undertakings.

Moreover, the actual conduct of the investigation is likely to involve those subject to it in considerable 'inconvenience, expense and dislocation', which may extend over a number of years (more than four years in the *Prestige* case). Before embarking on an investigation the EHRC must prepare terms of reference and give the person to be investigated a chance to comment. As Lord Diplock put it in the *Hillingdon* case (p. 787):

> ...before deciding to embark on a full investigation the Commission should hear what any person whom it suspects of unlawful discriminatory acts has got to say as to why and to what extent the Commission's suspicions are unjustified.

Lord Diplock went on to rule that the right to be heard also implies that the terms of reference must be reasonably specific as to the acts which are to be investigated. These must be related to the particular belief which the Commission has as to the person's unlawful behaviour. Once any representations have been considered, the terms of reference must be published.

In relation to both inquiries and investigations the EHRC must provide opportunities for those concerned to make representations, which may, at the EHRC's discretion, be oral (Sch. 2, paras 6–8 to the EA 2006). The object of this right to be heard is to fulfil the natural justice requirement of *audi alteram partem*.

Once an inquiry or an investigation is under way, the EHRC has the power to serve a notice requiring a person to supply written information, or attend an oral hearing, at which documents may be required to be produced. This will not apply to information or documents which are subject to a statutory restriction on disclosure, or could not be required to be given in evidence or produced in civil proceedings. A requirement to attend in person means that travel expenses must be offered (Sch. 2, paras 9–11 to the EA 2006). Failure to comply with the notice can be backed up by court orders, and may in some circumstances amount to a criminal offence.

An inquiry or investigation will result in a report. The report of an inquiry must not, however, suggest that any identifiable individual has committed an unlawful act. As regards an investigation, any person who is found by the EHRC to have committed an unlawful act must have an opportunity to comment on the draft report before it is published (s. 20 of the EA 2006).

If, as a result of an investigation, the EHRC is satisfied that a person is committing, or has committed, an unlawful discriminatory act, it may issue an 'unlawful act notice' (previously a 'non-discrimination notice'). There is a right of appeal against this to the appropriate court or tribunal.

An unlawful act notice may require a person to prepare an 'action plan' to avoid the repetition or continuation of the unlawful act (s. 21(4) of the EA 2006). Court orders can be obtained to require the production of a plan or compliance with it. Failure to comply will constitute a criminal offence.

In addition to the above powers, the EHRC also has the power to carry out a formal 'assessment' as to whether a public body is complying with its obligations under the equality enactments (s. 31 of the EA 2006), and where appropriate to issue a compliance notice (s. 32 of the EA 2006). Similar provisions in relation to terms of reference, evidence, etc, apply to assessments as to inquiries and investigations (Sch. 2 to the EA 2006).

As will be seen from this outline, formal investigations are one of the most powerful ways in which the development of equal treatment can be promoted. As of October 2013 it appears that the EHRC has only carried out three such investigations including one which was concluded in 2009, relating to sexual harassment of employees at the Royal Mail (see http://www.equalityhumanrights.com/hafan/cyfraith-a-pholisi/enforcement/legal-enforcement-case-studies/).

12.6 Conclusions

The English law relating to discrimination is complex, but overall now provides protection in a broad range of areas, and for all the main grounds on which unjustified discrimination is likely to occur. There is scope for the development of enforcement procedures which put less emphasis on the individual complainant, and more on the attempt to change institutional procedures and cultures. The linking of discrimination with more general human rights considerations, through the creation of the Equality and Human Rights Commission is probably beneficial. The consolidation of the various pieces of legislation into one Equality Act will also help to make the area more manageable. The UK has 30 years' experience of anti-discrimination legislation, and for much of that period has been at the forefront of developments within Europe. More recently, domestic law has been having to catch up with what has been coming from Brussels. There is a need to ensure that the UK continues to develop its laws and legal processes so that it remains well placed to deal with the challenges of the twenty-first century in this area.

QUESTIONS

1   Why are only certain types of unjustifiable discrimination unlawful? Should there be further extension of the law's scope to cover, for example, discrimination on political grounds?

2   What is likely to be the impact of the Charter of Fundamental Rights on the development of anti-discrimination law in the United Kingdom?

3 Why is the concept of indirect discrimination so complicated? Would it be possible to construct a simpler definition?

4 What are the arguments for and against 'positive' discrimination? Should English law allow more scope for discrimination of this kind?

5 What should the role of the EHRC be? Is it successfully fulfilling that role?

FURTHER READING

Bamforth, N. (2000), 'Sexual Discrimination after *Grant* v *South West Trains*', (2000) 63 MLR 694

Collins, H. (2003), 'Discrimination, Equality and Social Inclusion', (2003) 66 MLR 16

Connolly, M. (2005), 'Discrimination on Grounds of Sexual Orientation Outside the Workplace—is it Actionable?', [2005] Web JCLI 2

Foster, N. (2011), *Foster on European Law*, 3rd edn, Oxford: Oxford University Press

Klug, F. and O'Brien, C. (2004), '"Fairness for All"? An Analysis of Human Rights Powers in the White Paper on the Proposed Commission for Equality and Human Rights', [2004] PL 712

Macpherson, W. (1999), 'The Stephen Lawrence Inquiry: Report on an Inquiry by Sir William Macpherson of Cluny', Cm 4262, TSO

Majumdar, S. (2000), 'Guilty Knowledge', (2000) 150 NLJ 497

Millns, S. (2005), 'Gender Auditing the Human Rights Act 1998', (2005) 8 *International Journal of Discrimination and the Law* 75

O'Connell, R. (2009), 'Cinderella Comes to the Ball: Art 14 and the Right to Non-discrimination in the ECHR', (2009) 29 Legal Studies 211

Scarman, Lord (1981), 'Report on the Brixton Disorders, 10–12 April 1981', Cmnd 8427, HMSO

Wintemute, R. (1997), 'Recognising New Kinds of Direct Sex Discrimination: Transsexualism, Sexual Orientation and Dress Codes', (1997) 60 MLR 334

Wintemute, R. (2000), 'Lesbian and Gay Inequality 2000: The Potential of the Human Rights Act 1998 and the Need for an Equality Act 2002', [2000] EHRLR 603

INDEX